SO-ARK-142

The four "bottom line" practices that managers and companies must deliver to their customers

Quality

Customers' expectation of a product or service must be met and exceeded. Managers must ensure attractiveness, lack of defects, reliability, and dependability in everything the organization produces.

Cost

Goods and services must be valuable and at prices the customer is willing to pay. To accomplish this goal, managers must keep costs under control to allow the company to set fair prices that cover costs and achieve profit.

Innovation

Managers should constantly strive to quickly create new competitive goods and services that customers value. This practice is the key to staying ahead of competitors.

Speed

Organizations must respond to market needs quickly by introducing new products first; quickly delivering customer orders; and responding quickly to customer requests.

MANAGEMENT

Building Competitive Advantage

MANAGEMENT
Building Competitive Advantage

Third Edition

Thomas S. Bateman
The University of North Carolina

Scott A. Snell
Pennsylvania State University

IRWIN

Chicago • Bogotá • Boston • Buenos Aires • Caracas
London • Madrid • Mexico City • Sydney • Toronto

About the Cover

We wanted the cover image to reflect the richness of the interior—in terms of both content and design. The four running themes of the book—cost, quality, speed, and innovation—are depicted symbolically. Each item, from the compact discs to the stopwatch to the greenery, represents a part of the unique story told in the third edition of *Management: Building Competitive Advantage*.

© Richard D. Irwin, a Times Mirror Higher Education Group, Inc. company, 1990, 1993, and 1996

All rights reserved. No part of this publication may be reproduced, stored in a retrieval system, or transmitted, in any form or by any means, electronic, mechanical, photocopying, recording, or otherwise, without the prior written permission of the publisher.

Sponsoring editor: John E. Biernat
Senior developmental editor: Libby Rubenstein
Senior marketing manager: Kurt Messersmith
Project editor: Mary Conzachi
Production supervisor: Bob Lange
Assistant manager, desktop services: Jon Christopher
Cover Designer: Keith McPherson
Interior Designer: Stuart Paterson
Assistant manager, graphics: Charlene R. Perez
Coordinator, graphics & desktop services: Keri Kunst
Compositor: PC&F, Inc.
Typeface: 10/12 Times Roman
Printer: Von Hoffmann Press, Inc.

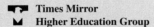 **Times Mirror**
Higher Education Group

Library of Congress Cataloging-in-Publication Data

Bateman, Thomas S.
    Management: building competitive advantage/Thomas S. Bateman,
  Scott A. Snell.—3rd ed.
      p. cm.
    Includes index.
    ISBN 0-256-14053-7
    1. Management. I. Snell, Scott. 1958- . II. Title.
HD31.B369485 1996
658.4—dc20   95–36620

Printed in the United States of America
1 2 3 4 5 6 7 8 9 0 VH 2 1 0 9 8 7 6 5

For my parents, Tom and Jeanine Bateman,
and Mary Jo, Lauren, T. J., and Jamie
and
My parents, John and Clara Snell,
and Marybeth, Sara, Jack, and Emily

About the Authors

THOMAS S. BATEMAN completed his doctoral program in business administration in 1980 at Indiana University. Prior to receiving his doctorate, Dr. Bateman received his B.A. from Miami University. Dr. Bateman is now chair of the management area and a chaired professor of management at the Kenan-Flagler Business School where he teaches courses in organizational behavior to undergraduates, M.B.A. students, Ph.D. students, and practicing managers.

Before accepting his current position, Dr. Bateman taught organizational behavior at Texas A&M University and Tulane University, where he received teaching honors. While at Texas A&M, he also taught and served as course coordinator for Principles of Management, a course that involved over 1,000 students per year. Dr. Bateman also conducted a six-week course in Europe, where he taught classes and visited with the managers of companies such as Porsche, Löwenbräu, Caterpillar, and the Scotland office of Hewlett-Packard.

Dr. Bateman is the coauthor (with Dennis Organ) of the book *Organizational Behavior,* and the coeditor (with Gerald Ferris) of a book of readings, *Method and Analysis in Organizational Research.* He is a business consultant, has served on the editorial boards of academic journals, and has presented numerous papers at professional meetings on topics including managerial decision making, job stress, negotiation, employee commitment and motivation, group decision making, and job satisfaction. These articles appeared in professional journals such as the *Academy of Management Journal, Journal of Applied Psychology, Strategic Management Journal, Business Horizons, Organizational Behavior and Human Decision Processes,* and *Decision Sciences.*

Dr. Bateman's current consulting and research centers around entrepreneurship in the United States, Central Europe, and Southeast Asia. He's currently working closely with companies including Arthur Andersen, Kaiser Permanente, and Dusit Thani Hotel in Thailand.

SCOTT A. SNELL is associate professor of business administration at Pennsylvania State University. He holds a B.A. in psychology from Miami University, as well as an M.B.A. and Ph.D. in business administration from Michigan State University. During his career, Dr. Snell has taught courses in human resources management, principles of management, and strategic management to undergraduates, graduates, and executives. He is actively involved in executive education and serves as faculty director for Penn State's Strategic Leadership Program, as well as faculty leader for programs in human resources, developing managerial effectiveness, the engineer/scientist as manager, and managing the global enterprise. In addition to his teaching duties, Dr. Snell also serves as director of research for Penn State's Institute for the Study of Organizational Effectiveness.

As an industry consultant, Professor Snell has worked with companies such as Arthur Andersen, AT&T, General Electric, and Shell Chemical to redesign human resources systems to cope with changes in the competitive environment. His specialization is the realignment of staffing, training, and reward systems to complement technology, quality, and other strategic activities. Recently, his work has centered on the development of transnational teams in global network organizations.

Dr. Snell's research has been published in the *Academy of Management Journal, Human Resource Management Review, Industrial Relations, Journal of Business Research, Journal of Management, Journal of Managerial Issues, Personnel Administrator, Strategic Management Journal,* and *Working Woman.* In addition, Dr. Snell is on the editorial boards of *Journal of Managerial Issues, Digest of Management Research,* and *Journal of Quality Management.* He is author of two additional books: *Managing Human Resources* with Arthur Sherman and George Bohlander, and *Strategic Human Resource Management* with Patrick Wright.

Preface

*O*ur mission with this book is threefold: to inform, instruct, and inspire. We hope to *inform* by providing descriptions of the important concepts and practices of modern management. We hope to *instruct* by describing how you can take action on the ideas discussed. In other words, you will learn practical applications that will make you more effective in ways that benefit both you and your organization.

We hope to *inspire* not only by writing in a positive, interesting, optimistic way, but also by providing a real sense of the unlimited opportunities ahead of you. Whether your goal is starting your own company, leading a team to greatness, building a strong organization, delighting your customers, or generally forging a positive future, we want to inspire you to take positive actions.

We hope to inspire you to be both a thinker and a doer. We want you to think about the issues, think about how to become a better manager, think about the impact of your actions, think before you act. But being a good thinker is not enough; you also must be a doer. Management is a world of action. It is a world that requires timely and appropriate action. It is a world not for the passive, but for those who commit to positive accomplishments.

We also hope to inspire you to keep learning. Keep applying the ideas you learn in this course, read about management in sources outside of this course, and certainly keep learning about management after you leave school and continue your career. Make no mistake about it, learning about management is a personal voyage that will last years, an entire career, your entire lifetime.

Competitive Advantage

Today's world is competitive. Never before has the world of work been so challenging. Never before has it been so imperative to your career that you learn the skills of management. Never before have people had so many vast opportunities with so many potential rewards.

You will compete with other people for jobs, resources, and promotions. Your organization will compete with other firms for contracts, clients, and customers. To survive the competition, and to thrive, you must perform in ways that give you an edge over your competitors, that make the other party want to hire you, buy from you, and do repeat business with you. You will want them to choose you, not your competitor.

To survive and thrive, today's managers have to think and act strategically. Today's customers are well educated, aware of their options, and demanding of excellence. For this reason, managers today must think constantly about how to build a capable workforce and manage in a way that delivers the goods and services that provide the best possible value to the customer.

By this standard, managers and organizations must perform. The four types of performance, on which the organization beats, equals, or loses to the competition, are *cost, quality, speed,* and *innovation*. These four performance dimensions, when done well, deliver value to the customer and competitive advantage to you and your organization. We will elaborate on all of these topics throughout the book, but here is a brief overview.

Cost competitiveness means the company delivers valuable products (goods and services) priced at levels the customer is willing to pay. Good management requires managing so that costs are kept under control and the company can sell its products at fair prices that cover costs and achieve a profit.

Quality refers to the all-around excellence of your goods and services. It includes such things as attractiveness, lack of defects, reliability, and long-term dependability. Quality means doing the job right and meeting or surpassing customer expectations.

Speed means the organization can respond to market needs quickly. It includes introducing new products to the market before competitors do, delivering fast on customer orders, and responding quickly to customer services requests. You are at a competitive advantage if you do these things faster and better than your competitors, and at a competitive *dis*advantage if *they* are faster and better.

Innovation is the ability to create new goods and new services that customers value. Moreover, effective innovation occurs quickly and results in products that are competitive on the basis of cost and quality. Innovative management practices often are the key to staying abreast or ahead of competitors who are constantly trying to outdo you in all four of these arenas of competitive advantage.

Good managers find ways to make their organizations successful. The ways to do this are to build competitive advantage in the forms of cost competitiveness, quality, speed, and innovation. Because of the importance of the four sources of competitive advantage—which really are goals that every manager should constantly try to achieve and improve upon—we refer to them frequently throughout the book. The idea is to keep you focused on a type of "bottom line," to make sure you think continually about "delivering the goods" that make both the manager (you) and the organization a competitive success.

▮▼ RESULTS ORIENTATION

An important theme of this book, then, is how to manage in ways that deliver *results*—results that customers want. When you deliver high-quality, innovative products, quickly, and at a competitive price, you are achieving the results that can give you the competitive edge. And keep in mind, these are the same results that your competitors strive for as they try to gain an edge over you.

This approach makes this book unique among management texts. Rather than offering only concepts and processes, which nonetheless are integral parts of this text, we have a clear results orientation that is essential to success. The concepts and processes are means to an end, or the ways by which you can achieve the results you need.

It goes without saying that this textbook, in its third edition, remains on the cutting edge of topical coverage, as updated via both current business examples and recent management research. Chapters are thoroughly updated and students are exposed to a wide variety of important current topics, including:

New overseas markets	Transnational organizations
Product and process innovation	Customer service
Core competencies	Crisis management
Learning organizations	Empowerment
European unification	Codetermination
Privatization	Strategic HRM
NAFTA	Post-heroic leadership
Technology leadership	Cross-functional teams
Reengineering	Network organizations
Total quality management	Sexual harassment
Rightsizing	Mass customization
Future economic scenarios	Sustainable growth

Benchmarking

Corporate political activities

Strategic alliances

Competitor analysis

The MBA Enterprise Corps., working to bring the free market to Eastern Europe and Southeast Asia

This list, of course, is just a sampler of the comprehensive coverage offered by this text. We have done our very best to draw from a wide variety of subject matter, sources, and personal experiences.

FORGING THE FUTURE

By highlighting the sources of competitive advantage and using a clear results orientation, we continue our efforts to create a new generation of management texts. Our previous edition was more integrative than other texts and was the first to devote chapters to the vital management topics of managing in our natural environment and managing workforce diversity. And, we have broken the traditional mold by encouraging students to "forge the future."

Still, in this edition we retain the traditional functional organization. Even though the world has changed, it is not chaos. A functional approach still is useful in that it provides students and instructors with a framework within which to tackle dynamic issues. Moreover, we of course give full coverage to all the topics other texts tout as their primary emphases: globalization, total quality, change, ethics, teams, and so on.

As this textbook forges the future for management texts, we want to influence students to forge *their* futures. Throughout the text, a proactive rather than passive approach to management is encouraged. For example, Chapter 9, New Ventures, doesn't merely describe small business management; it inspires readers to create new ideas and new businesses. And Chapter 21, Becoming World Class, speaks to the importance of creating a world-class future, not just being ready for the future and adapting to it.

With your help, we want to influence business in the future. Through our mission of informing, instructing, and inspiring, we hope you will apply these ideas to create your own organizations and/or make the organizations in which you work more successful and outstanding.

A TEAM EFFORT

We wrote this book believing that we would form a team with the course instructor and with students. The entire team is responsible for the learning process.

Our goal, and that of the instructor, is to create a positive learning environment in which you can excel. But in the end, the raw material of this course is just words. It is up to you to use them as a basis for further thinking, deep learning, and constructive action.

What you do with the things you learn from this course, and with the opportunities the future holds, *counts*. As a manager, you can make a dramatic difference for yourself, and for other people. What managers do matters, tremendously.

OUTSTANDING PEDAGOGY

Management: Building Competitive Advantage is pedagogically stimulating and is intended to maximize student learning. With this in mind, we used a wide array of pedagogical features—some tried and true, others new and novel:

- Learning Objectives, which open each chapter, identify what students will learn by reading and studying the chapter.
- Opening quotes provide a thought-provoking preview of chapter material. The quotes are from people like Peter Drucker (on the external environment), Jack Welch (on strategic management), Henry David Thoreau (on ethics), Margaret Meade (on the natural environment), and Julius Caesar (on leadership).

- Setting the Stage describes an actual organizational situation and provides a rich introductory example of the chapter topic. Setting the Stage is placed before the text material as a practical application.
- Logos representing the four running themes of the book—cost, quality, speed, and innovation—are placed at appropriate points in the text to indicate an extended example, best practice, or issue for discussion. The logos continually reinforce and enhance the learning of these important themes.

End-of-Chapter Elements

- Key Terms, which are page-referenced to the text and are part of the vocabulary-building emphasis. These terms are defined in the glossary at the end of the book.
- A Summary of Learning Objectives provides clear, concise responses to the learning objectives, giving students a quick reference for reviewing the important concepts in the chapter.
- Discussion Questions, which follow the Summary of Learning Objectives, are thought-provoking questions that test the student's mastery of concepts covered in the chapter.
- Concluding Cases, which provide focus for class discussion.
- A Video Case or Video Exercise appears at the end of the chapter. These cases/exercises reinforce the concepts presented in the videos for each chapter.
- Two Experiential Exercises are included. Most of them are group-based, and many involve outside research.

End-of-Part Elements

- An Integrating Case and two Case Incidents appear at the end of each of the five parts of the book. The short Case Incidents focus on managerial problems that include issues from multiple chapters in each part and are a stimulating arena for discussion.
- The Company Directory appears at the end of the text. It lists over 400 existing companies discussed in the text and gives the following information about each: company name, subsidiary data when applicable, address, phone number, yearly sales figures, and number of employees. Students will find this directory useful for employment and case research purposes.

COMPREHENSIVE SUPPLEMENTS

FOR THE STUDENT

- Study Guide, prepared by Sue Stewart-Belle, Illinois State University, contains chapter previews, a listing and definition of key terms, and over 100 true/false, multiple choice, matching, short answer, and essay questions, and exercises per chapter.

FOR THE INSTRUCTOR

- Instructor's Manual, prepared by William Matthews, William Patterson College, contains chapter outlines, suggested discussion questions and answers for Setting the Stage, two lecturettes for each chapter, suggested answers to end-of-chapter Discussion Questions, suggested answers to the Concluding Case discussion questions, objectives and teaching tips for the experiential exercises, and discussion questions and suggested answers for Case Incidents and Integrating Cases.
- Test Bank, prepared by Jane Pettinger, North Dakota State University, contains approximately 100 questions for each chapter and consists of true/false, multiple choice, fill-in, matching, and essay questions.

- Powerpoint Presentation software contains tables and figures from the text plus additional graphic material. A self-contained viewer is packaged with each disk so that those who do not have the Powerpoint software can easily view the presentation.

- Color acetates consisting of figures and tables from the book are also available.

- Videos are available for each chapter and are accompanied by a videoguide that ties the videos closely to the chapter.

- Irwin's Computerized Testing Service enables you to pick and choose questions and develop tests and quizzes quickly and easily on the computer.

- Teletest enables you to phone an exam request directly to Irwin. Just tell the Irwin representative what you want, and within a few days you will receive your exam.

ACKNOWLEDGMENTS

This book could not have been written and published without the valuable contributions of many individuals. Special thanks to Scott Bateman of Cox Enterprise for help with the cases and vignettes about the "information superhighway," to Carol Smolinski for help with the experiential exercises and the glossary, and to Courtney Hunt, Mark Youndt, and David Lepak for their help with research.

Our reviewers over the last two editions contributed time, expertise, and terrific ideas that signficantly enhanced the quality of the text. The reviewers of the third edition are:

Robert W. Allen
California State Polytechnic University

Falih M. Alsaaty
University of the District of Columbia

Deborah A. Arvanites
Villanova University

Harold C. Babson
Columbus State Community College

Charles A. Beasley
State University at New York–Buffalo

Judith Bulin
Monroe Community College

Carmen M. Caruana
St. John's University

Gary Coombs
Ohio University–Athens

Charles Franz
University of Missouri

William Jedlicka
Harper College

John F. Keeling
Old Dominion University

Esther Long
University of West Florida

William Matthews
Wm. Patterson College

Jana Minife
Southwest Texas State

Ali Mir
University of Massachusetts–Amherst

Joseph B. Mosca
Monmouth College

Raghavan Parthasarthy
Seton Hall University South

Jim Swenson
Moorehead State University

Alice M. Warner
Marietta College

Leslie Wiletzky
Hawaii Pacific University

James M. Wilson
University of Texas–Pan American

Many individuals contributed directly to our development as textbook authors. Dennis Organ provided one of the authors with an initial opportunity and guidance in textbook writing. John Weimeister has been a friend and advisor from the very beginning. John Wood was a crucial early sponsor for the project. The entire Richard D. Irwin team demonstrated continued and generous support for this book. John Biernat was a great champion for the project, and is a talented editor and good friend. Kurt Strand is, too! What a team!

Mary Conzachi provided guidance and support throughout this process. And Libby Rubenstein was the hub around which everything revolved. Libby gave tireless attention to all phases of the creative process, leading to a final product in which we all take great pride.

Finally, we thank our families. Our parents, Jeanine and Thomas Bateman and Clara and John Snell, provided us with the foundation on which we have built our careers. They continue to be a source of great support and encouragement. Our wives, Mary Jo and Marybeth, demonstrated great patience, insight, and understanding throughout the entire process. Our children, Lauren, T. J., and Jamie Bateman and Sara, Jack, and Emily Snell, are an inspiration for everything we do.

Thomas S. Bateman

Scott A. Snell

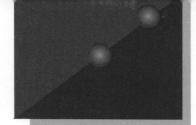

CONTENTS IN BRIEF

CONTENTS

PART IV

PART V

CONTROL AND CHANGE 460

CHAPTER 18

MANAGERIAL CONTROL 462

CHAPTER 19

OPERATIONS MANAGEMENT 490

CHAPTER 20

MANAGING TECHNOLOGY AND INNOVATION 516

CHAPTER 21

BECOMING WORLD CLASS 542

MANAGEMENT

Building Competitive Advantage

FOUNDATIONS OF MANAGEMENT

FOUNDATIONS OF MANAGEMENT

Managers and Organizations
The Evolution of Management
The External Environment
Managerial Decision Making

PLANNING AND STRATEGY

Planning and Strategic Management
Ethics and Corporate Responsibility
Managing in our Natural Environment
International Management
New Ventures

STRATEGY IMPLEMENTATION

ORGANIZING AND STAFFING

Organization Structure
The Responsive Organization
Human Resources Management
Managing the Diverse Workforce

LEADING

Leadership
Motivating for Performance
Managing Teams
Communicating

CONTROL AND CHANGE

Managerial Control
Operations Management
Managing Technology and Innovation
Becoming World Class

The four chapters in Part I describe the foundations of management. Chapter 1 introduces key functions, skills, and competitive goals of effective managers. Chapter 2 provides an overview of the history of management thought, emphasizing the important ideas that inform modern management. Chapter 3 describes the external environment in which managers and their organizations operate. Finally, Chapter 4 discusses the most pervasive managerial activity—decision making. Sound decision-making skills are essential for effective managerial performance.

1

MANAGERS AND ORGANIZATIONS

It takes something other than wages to hold good employees; and it
takes something other than low prices to hold a good customer.

Imperial Metal & Chemical Company

After studying Chapter 1, you will know:

1. The functions of management.

2. The nature of management at different organizational levels.

3. How you can benefit from studying management.

4. The nature of organization.

5. The keys to gaining advantage over your organization's competitors.

6. The skills you need to be an effective manager.

7. What outstanding managers do.

8. What to strive for as you manage your career.

A FEW GOOD MANAGERS

*I*n June 1991, Cathleen Black took over leadership of the Newspaper Association of America, the newspaper industry's major trade group, which represents 1,500 newspapers. No stranger to the difficult task of heading a large and diverse organization, Black was hired as president of the fledgling *USA Today* in 1983. One year later, she was promoted to publisher, and helped turn *USA Today* into the largest general-interest newspaper in the country. Black believes the greatest threat to her industry comes from members who "continue to do things the way they have always done them." She argues that she is "certainly a person who has embraced change and taken a number of risks." This approach should be important as Black's industry attempts to "reinvent the newspaper" in the face of growing competition from other consumer information sources.

Pat Riley coached the Los Angeles Lakers to four NBA championships before becoming head coach of the New York Knicks, a job he resigned in June 1995. His recent book *The Winner Within* includes the following quotes: "If there's one thing on which I'm an authority, it's how to blend the talents and strengths of individuals into a force that becomes greater than the sum of its parts" (p. 15). "The complex inner rhythms of teamwork are the keys to making dreams come true" (pp. 16–17). "The highest levels of competition have taught me that there are common chal-

■ _____

By taking risks and embracing change, Cathleen Black transformed *USA Today* into the country's best-selling general interest newspaper.

(Courtesy Newspaper Association of America)

lenges that every team, and every team player, must conquer on their road to significant achievement" (pp. 16–17). Pat Riley is a consummate manager.

John Zimmerman became president of Steiner/Bressler Advertising at age 38. The first thing he worked on was the money mess. He negotiated down and then liquidated the company's debt, and overhauled a system that had not recorded cost projections or profit breakdowns. Zimmerman also went to work improving employee morale. "What did I always want as an employee?" he asked himself. "Openness, honesty, and an ability to affect my future." Accordingly, he gave everyone quarterly financial reports and created a company-wide bonus pool; *everyone* at Steiner/Bressler began working harder to keep costs down. He also had groups of employees work together to design the ideal ad agency. A consensus formed around the idea that the agency should exist to serve the client in whatever ways the client wishes. Expenses dropped 25 percent, and billings almost doubled in little more than a year. The keys to success, says Zimmerman, are teamwork, mutual support, and common goals.

Sources: "Departing *USA Today* Exec Taking On Another Big Role," *The Chapel Hill Newspaper,* June 9, 1991, pp. C1, C15; P. Riley, *The Winner Within* (New York: G. P. Putnam's Sons, 1993); P. Sellers, "When Tragedy Forces Change," *Fortune,* January 10, 1994, p. 116.

Intel CEO Andy Grove is a model of effectiveness *and* efficiency. Working out of a 175-square-foot-cubicle, Grove produces an average annual return to Intel investors of 28.7 percent.
(Christopher Irion)

*S*etting the Stage portrays a fascinating and diverse group of managers: a top newspaper executive, a basketball coach, and an advertising executive. You might be hard put to decide what they have in common. As you can see, however, they are all very successful managers in their chosen careers. Throughout this textbook you will read about many other managers who have attained significant achievements in their organizations and industries. The purpose of this book, then, is to provide you with a variety of ideas and tools that will help you become a successful manager, too.

MANAGEMENT AND ITS FUNCTIONS

Management is the process of working with people and resources to accomplish organizational goals. *Good* managers do those things both effectively and efficiently. To be *effective* is to achieve organizational goals. To be *efficient* is to achieve goals with minimum waste of resources, that is, to make the best possible use of money, time, materials, and people. Some managers fail on both criteria, or focus on one at the expense of another. The best managers maintain a clear focus on both effectiveness *and* efficiency.

THE FUNCTIONS OF MANAGEMENT

What can managers do to be effective and efficient? The management process, properly executed, involves a wide variety of activities including planning, organizing, leading, and controlling. These activities, described below and discussed throughout the book, are the traditional **functions of management.**

Planning
Planning is specifying the goals to be achieved and deciding in advance the appropriate actions taken to achieve those goals. Planning activities include analyzing current situations, anticipating the future, determining objectives, deciding what types of activities the company will engage in, choosing corporate and business strategies, and determining the resources needed to achieve the organization's goals.

A few years ago a business person announced his plans to create a new national television network out of a small collection of stations. People laughed at first, but CBS, ABC, and NBC are not laughing at the Fox network now.[1] BMW developed a clear long-term strategy to change from a high-cost German company into a true global car company, and then acted decisively by building a plant in South Carolina and purchasing Rover from British Aerospace.[2] Small firms, too, such as those owned by CPAs and plumbers, can benefit greatly from comprehensive planning.[3] Plans set the stage for action and for major achievements.

Plans are developed for entire organizations, for specific work units, and for individuals. These plans may cover long periods of time (five years or more) or a short time horizon (days or weeks). They may be very general (e.g., to improve profits through new product development) or very specific (e.g., to reduce product defects by 10 percent over the next month through an incentive system). In each case, however, managers are responsible for gathering and analyzing the information on which plans are based, setting the goals to be achieved, and deciding what needs to be done.

Part II of this book focuses on planning, and covers topics such as strategy, ethics, new ventures, and the global environment.

Organizing

Organizing is assembling and coordinating the human, financial, physical, informational, and other resources needed to achieve goals. Activities include attracting people to the organization, specifying job responsibilities, grouping jobs into work units, marshalling and allocating resources, and creating conditions so that people and things work together to achieve maximum success. The chapters in Part III discuss organizing.

For example, when Dorothy Terrel of Digital Equipment Corporation was asked to manage the computer company's high-density interconnect and multichip module operation, her organizing and staffing skills proved essential. Her challenge was to transform a high-tech, nonmanufacturing operation into a high-volume producer of endurance technology for high-end office products. Terrell was chosen for the job because she had a thorough knowledge of the company, had an extensive network of business and community contacts in the Boston area, and could, in her words, "put technical minds together." In three years Terrell built the staff and plant management team from 200 to 1,200, was producing quality products at a competitive cost, and controlled a budget of more than $300 million at the new facility.[4]

Leading

Leading is stimulating people to be high performers. It is directing, motivating, and communicating with employees, individually and in groups. Leading involves close day-to-day contact with people, helping to guide and inspire them toward achieving team and organizational goals. Leading takes place in teams, departments, divisions, and at the tops of entire organizations.

Livio DeSimone is chief executive officer of 3M, one of the great corporations of the world. The main tenets of his leadership philosophy include creating a cooperative work environment, maintaining constant communications, giving people some freedom to pursue their ideas, being honest at all times (with bad news as well as good), assigning people tasks that allow them to learn and grow, and publicly praising and rewarding people who do their jobs well.[5] Of course, Mr. DeSimone's leadership style is far more complex than this brief description; Part IV will elaborate on the best approaches to leading, motivating, communicating, and forging teamwork.

Controlling

Comprehensive plans, solid organization, and outstanding leaders do not guarantee success. The fourth function, controlling, monitors progress and implements necessary changes.

When managers implement their plans, they often find that things are not working out as planned. The **controlling** function makes sure that goals are met. It asks and answers the question, "Are our actual outcomes consistent with our goals?" It makes adjustments as needed.

Specific controlling activities are to set performance standards that indicate progress toward long-term goals; to monitor performance of people and units by collecting performance data; to provide people with feedback or information about their progress; to identify performance problems by comparing performance data against standards; and to take actions to correct problems. Budgeting, information systems, cost cutting, and disciplinary action are just a few of the tools of control.

These MBA Enterprise Corps members are meeting in Slovakia with political and business leaders to learn about the current economic and political situation.
(Courtesy MBA Enterprise Corps)

Successful organizations, large and small, pay close attention to how well they are doing. They take fast action when problems arise, and are able to change as needed. Part V covers control-related topics, including organizational control processes, operations management, innovation, and change.

PERFORMING ALL FOUR MANAGEMENT FUNCTIONS

Some managers are particularly interested in, devoted to, or skilled in a couple of these four functions but not in the others. The manager who does not devote adequate attention and resources to *all four* functions will fail. You can be a skilled planner and controller, but if you organize your people improperly or fail to inspire them to perform at high levels, you will not be an effective manager. Likewise, it does no good to be the kind of manager who loves to organize and lead, but who doesn't really understand where to go or how to determine whether you are on the right track. Good managers don't neglect *any* of the four management functions. Knowing what they are, you can periodically ask yourself if you are devoting adequate attention to *all* of them.

In the following example, recent MBAs describe their work experiences in central Europe. Virtually everything in their messages pertains to the functions performed by managers the world over.

THE MBA ENTERPRISE CORPS: SPREADING MANAGEMENT SKILLS

S elected graduates of the top U.S. business schools took their first jobs not making big paychecks with a Fortune 500 corporation but earning about $150 per month in Hungary, Poland, and the Czech Republic. They are members of the MBA Enterprise Corps, a new organization based in Chapel Hill, North Carolina, and modeled after the Peace Corps. The MBAEC's mission is to help former communist countries successfully manage the transition to a free-market society of private rather than government-run enterprises.

The corps members engage in all four management functions: planning, organizing, leading, and controlling. Following are some excerpts (a few paraphrased) from letters corps members wrote back to the United States while overseas:

On the management challenges:

- I'm engineering a new organizational structure to optimize the utilization of our scarce resources. The division has little managerial experience as we know it, but our director is determined that, with my advice, we can create a fully functioning, modern, competitive company.

- My role is to help in creating a general business strategy. The biggest problem is the enormous bureaucracy of the firm.

- The most fundamental of business skills—such as how to conduct business meetings—are not well developed. Overcoming resistance to change will be difficult.

- At times the place feels like it has the potential to be the next McKinsey of Poland, and at others it seems that it could explode and disintegrate at any moment.

On planning and decision making:

- I'm here to help implement needed changes. The problem is that there is absolutely no means of predicting the future. I've been attempting to persuade people to prepare a strategy under each possible scenario, but the people's general reaction to uncertainty is: It's safer to continue what we're doing now and wait to see what happens.

- I have spent a lot of my time developing three-month marketing plans. I had wanted to develop six-month plans, but there are too many changes occurring in the market and economy for us to effectively plan that far in advance.

- Decisions are based more on basic common sense, gut feelings, and trust than on what the numbers say.

- The village elders are hoping we could come up with a use for a deserted Soviet tank base in western Hungary. It's located in a swamp, is run down, and probably has a great deal of damage. If you have any ideas, let me know.

On the rewards:

- There is a world of opportunity here. It's a very rewarding experience. When I make a suggestion, their eyes light up as if I have just made a revelation. It's really fun.

- I am constantly required to apply the things I've learned in a new and different manner. In many ways, I believe I've learned as much from my Polish counterparts as I have taught to them.

- The most critical traits for corps members are curiosity, a wide range of interests, and large doses of courage and humility. This has been the most interesting, intellectually challenging adventure I have ever undertaken. ●

MANAGEMENT LEVELS

Different managers emphasize different activities or exhibit different management styles. Recall the three successful managers described in "Setting the Stage." These individuals do not manage using identical techniques.

There are many reasons for these differences, including the managers' training, personalities, and backgrounds. However, you will find that the organizational level at which the manager operates often influences the *mixture of important functions and skills.* Organizations (particularly large organizations) have many levels. In this section, you will learn about three types of managers found at three different levels in virtually all large organizations: strategic managers, tactical managers, and operational managers. Figure 1.1 shows the levels these managers occupy within the large organization.

STRATEGIC MANAGERS

Strategic managers are the senior executives of an organization and are responsible for its overall management. Major activities include developing the company's goals and plans. Typically strategic managers focus on long-term issues and emphasize the survival, growth, and overall effectiveness of the organization.

These managers have titles such as chair of the board, president, chief executive officer, and vice president. These top managers are concerned primarily with the interaction between the organization and its external environment. This interaction often requires managers to work extensively with outside individuals and organizations.

FIGURE 1.1

Management levels

Strategic managers

Tactical managers

Operational managers

The chief executive officer (CEO) is one type of strategic manager found in large corporations. This individual is the primary strategic manager of the firm. To some people, the CEO seems all-powerful. But it is an exceedingly demanding position that, like all other positions, can be managed well or poorly.

CEO DISEASE: HOW *NOT* TO LEAD

*T*he CEO job can easily go to one's head. A recent article in *Fortune* described the "CEO Disease"—the belief of some CEOs that they are omnipotent, with the result being poor leadership. Most CEOs don't have the disease. Those who do have it exhibit the following symptoms. They

- Believe they can do no wrong and refuse to admit any mistakes.
- Surround themselves with people who say yes to their every whim.
- See themselves as the individual genius on whom success depends.
- Use degradation and humiliation to control people.
- Blame others for the CEO's own mistakes.
- Don't interact with "underlings."
- Want to make every decision, even if others know more of the relevant facts.
- Are overly preoccupied with being ahead of other CEOs in salary and perks.
- Are overly concerned with sitting in the "power position" in meetings and whether people rise when they enter the room.
- Relish media attention, not so much for the company but for personal fame and gain.

CEO Disease does not enhance the CEO's power. Instead, it leads to his or her demise. It hurts the company, in part by harming employee motivation and creating a we-versus-them atmosphere. By learning the material in this text, you will know the keys to avoiding the disease: a humble awareness of the complexities of management, an understanding of how to make decisions, a knowledge of what kinds of people to hire, an understanding of how to generate employee involvement instead of cynicism, and other things that make for good leadership and effective management.

Sources: J. Byrne, W. Symonds, and J. Siler, "CEO Disease," *Fortune,* April 1, 1991, pp. 52–60; D. J. Cornwall, "The Demise of the Imperial CEO," *Fortune,* February 8, 1993, p. 38; M. Cox and J. L. Roberts, "How the Despotic Boss of Simon & Schuster Found Himself Jobless," *The Wall Street Journal,* July 6, 1994, pp. A1, A8. ●

TACTICAL MANAGERS

Tactical managers are responsible for translating the general goals and plans developed by strategic managers into more specific objectives and activities. These decisions, or *tactics,* involve both a shorter time horizon and the coordination of resources. Tactical managers are often called **middle managers,** because in large organizations they are located between the strategic and operational managers.

Today's best middle managers have been called "working leaders."[6] They focus on relationships with other people *and* on achieving results. They are hands-on, working managers. They don't just make decisions, give orders, wait for others to produce, and then evaluate results. They get dirty, do hard work themselves, solve problems, and produce value.

OPERATIONAL MANAGERS

Operational managers are lower-level managers who supervise the operations of the organization. These managers often have titles such as supervisor or sales manager. They are directly involved with nonmanagement employees, implementing the specific plans developed with tactical managers. This role is critical in the organization, because operational managers are the link between management and nonmanagement personnel. Your first management position probably will fit into this category.

THE COMPLETE MANAGER

You may have noted that several times we have qualified our descriptions of strategic, tactical, and operational managers by referring to large organizations. These descriptions represent the traditional model for large organizations. But the trend today is toward less hierarchy, more teamwork, and smaller organizations. Small companies have become more common and important as large corporations lay off people, those people and other entrepreneurs start their own firms, and these smaller firms prove themselves capable of beating the giants with specialized products and strategies and the ability to adapt quickly to change.

In these small firms—and in those large companies that have adapted to the times—managers have strategic, tactical, *and* operational responsibilities. They are *complete* business people; they have knowledge of all business functions, are accountable for results, and focus on serving customers both inside and outside their firms. All this requires the ability to think strategically, translate strategies into specific objectives, coordinate resources, and get "down and dirty" with operative-level workers. In short, the best managers can do it all; they are the working leaders described above.

WHY STUDY MANAGEMENT?

Sometime during this term, a member of your class (who did not study this chapter) will make a statement similar to one of the following:

"Why should I study management? I'm going to be an accountant."

"Why should I study management? It's all common sense."

"Why should I study management? Experience is the best teacher."

On the surface, these statements seem to have merit. Let's consider each argument carefully.

MANAGERS ARE UNIVERSAL

Managers work in all types of organizations, at all levels, and in all functional areas. Large and small businesses, hospitals, schools, governments, and churches benefit from efficient and effective management. The leaders of these organizations may be called executives, administrators, principals, or pastors, but they are all managers and are responsible for the success or failure of the organization. This success or failure is reflected in a manager's career. For example, when a CEO saves a failing corporation, the board rewards this success with bonuses and stock options. When a professional football team starts losing, the owner fires the coach, not the team.

Even the military is not exempt from the need for good management. In his book *The Straw Giant*, Arthur Hadley describes a long list of U.S. military disasters and fiascoes from World War II through the operations in Iran, Lebanon, and Grenada.[7] He cites a variety of reasons for these problems, most of which were management related: inadequate and mismanaged human resources, overcontrol from Washington, lack of coordination among the different branches of the military, and poorly allocated resources. Conversely, many of these basic management activities were executed much more effectively in the successful campaign against Iraq in 1991. No matter where you intend to work, effective managers are a necessity.

Managers are also found in each functional area of an organization. Accountants are promoted to accounting department heads, sales representatives become sales managers, writers become editors, and nurses become nursing administrators. Management skills are important to anyone who intends to pursue a career. Beginning to prepare now for a career in management will yield benefits sooner than you may think.

MANAGEMENT BY COMMON SENSE

Many of the basic ideas you will learn in this course do not sound revolutionary or earth shattering: Managers should plan for the future; organizations should adapt to their environments; and managers should identify things their employees value and offer them as rewards for high performance. Most of this sounds like common sense.

Although some of the management concepts discussed in this text may seem obvious, developing them on your own or putting them into practice in the proper way, at the right time, and under appropriate conditions is difficult. If management was all common sense there would not be so many failing companies, and so many people who complain about their incompetent bosses. Our natural ability to make the right decision or take the proper action—our common sense—can be improved greatly through systematic study.

MANAGEMENT BY EXPERIENCE

One successful entrepreneur often makes statements like "Management can be learned only from the school of hard knocks." This person never took a business course; instead, he learned everything on his own. Although he was fired from two jobs and failed in three previous business attempts, he is now the owner of a thriving firm with sales of $100 million. This person believes a textbook and a college course cannot replace the experience he gained from his years in business.

Although this book cannot replace the knowledge and skills you will develop through experience, a management course can offer valuable preparation and supplement your experience. Many of the concepts covered in this text will help you make sense out of your experiences more quickly. These concepts will provide you with a head start in your management career. Furthermore, this text is an organized summary of the experiences of many managers. The management research reported here is another form of experience. Through this course, you can learn from the experiences of others and perhaps avoid being fired twice or failing the first three times you start a business.

ORGANIZATIONS

Managers operate in organizations. Exactly what is an organization? An **organization** is a managed system designed and operated to achieve a specific set of objectives.

As Figure 1.2 shows, a **system** is a set of interdependent parts that processes inputs (such as raw materials) into outputs (products). Business inputs typically are called *resources*. Most businesses use a variety of human, financial, physical, and informational resources. Managers function to transform these resources into the outputs of the business. Goods and services are the outputs of the business. Some of the major components of the external environment include customers, competitors, suppliers, and investors.

An organization is not a random group of people who come together by chance. It is consciously and formally established to accomplish certain goals that its members would be unable to reach by themselves. A manager's job is to achieve high performance relative to the organization's objectives. For example, a business organization has objectives to (1) make a profit for its owners; (2) furnish its customers with goods and services; (3) provide an income for its employees; and (4) increase the level of satisfaction for everyone involved.

FIGURE 1.2

Major parts of an
organizational
system

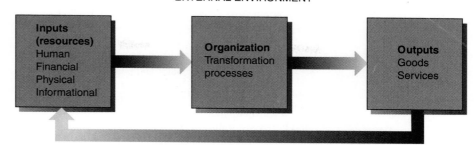

A hospital delivers health care services. A professional sports team is organized to win games and make money. A charitable organization attempts to raise funds to alleviate some social problem. The managers of these organizations are responsible for achieving those objectives. What are the goals of the organizations to which you belong (your university, your fraternity or sorority, your employer, your church, or your team)?

Because this course is about managers and organizations, you may be interested in the results of a survey that *Fortune* magazine conducts each year. The survey asks executives, board members, and financial analysts to rate the 10 largest companies in their industries on the following eight key attributes of reputation:

1. Quality of management.
2. Quality of products or services.
3. Innovativeness.
4. Long-term investment value.
5. Financial soundness.
6. Ability to attract, develop, and keep talented people.
7. Community and environmental responsibility.
8. Use of corporate assets.

As you can see in Table 1.1, Rubbermaid was the most admired corporation for two years in a row.[8] Why do you think certain firms are consistently admired? The following description of Rubbermaid may give you some answers to this question.

TABLE 1.1

Fortune's
"most admired"
corporations

1993	1994
1. Rubbermaid (rubber and plastic products)	1. Rubbermaid (rubber and plastic products)
2. Home Depot (specialist retailers)	2. Microsoft (computer and data services)
3. Coca-Cola (beverages)	3. Coca-Cola (beverages)
3. Microsoft (computer and data services)	4. Motorola (electronics, electrical equipment)
5. 3M (scientific and photographic equipment)	5. Home Depot (specialist retailers)
6. Walt Disney (entertainment)	6. Intel (electronics, electrical equipment)
6. Motorola (electronics, electrical equipment)	7. Procter & Gamble (soaps, cosmetics)
8. J. P. Morgan (commercial banking)	8. 3M (scientific and photographic equipment)
8. Procter & Gamble (soaps, cosmetics)	9. United Parcel Service (trucking)
10. United Parcel Service (trucking)	10. Hewlett-Packard (computers and office equipment)

Note: Same number denotes ties.
Source: T. Welsh, "Best and Worst Corporate Reputations," *Fortune,* February 7, 1994, p. 59.

Source: R. Jacob, "Corporate Reputations," *Fortune,* March 6, 1995, p. 54.

ADMIRATION FOR RUBBERMAID

Fortune magazine calls Rubbermaid a "master of the mundane and a champion innovator." Under CEO Stanley Gault and now Wolfgang Schmitt, Rubbermaid has for years been one of the most successful and admired companies in the United States. In 1993 the company set records for sales ($1.8 billion) and earnings ($184.2 million). How do they do it? What are their great strengths?

One of Rubbermaid's great strengths is that it does not depend on any single product or on any single person. What the company *does* rely on is 5,000 products that it continually improves. And to improve continuously, Rubbermaid relies on its people. Its managers care about the company and its products, and they know that teamwork is a wellspring of new ideas. Teams of five to seven people from different functional areas (marketing, manufacturing, finance, and so on) focus their productive efforts on particular product lines. Rubbermaid executives believe that organizing by teams is the key to their success.

The products themselves are not very fancy—they include mail boxes, mops, dust mitts, spatulas, drink coasters, and ice cube trays. And in addition to improving these constantly, Rubbermaid introduces *new* products at a rate of one per day—and 9 out of 10 succeed. With this in mind, CEO Schmitt sets special goals for his company, among them: (1) entering a new product category every 12 to 18 months; (2) getting 33 percent of sales from products introduced in the past five years; and (3) getting 25 percent of revenues from non–U.S. markets by the year 2000.

The details that people at other companies don't take seriously are studied carefully by dedicated Rubbermaid employees. As *Fortune* put it, "Engineers pour over blueprints of beverage coolers and sandwich keepers with the same intensity General Dynamics might bring to an F-111." Rubbermaid's laundry baskets are ergonomically engineered to fit comfortably against the waists; its mailboxes have flags that pop up automatically to show they have mail.

Most innovations at Rubbermaid come from teams of people who all think and talk about their own product lines. They get their ideas from everywhere—a recent trip to the British Museum and its Egyptian antiquities led a team to 11 new product ideas. The ancient Egyptians had a lot of well-designed kitchen utensils. Why not learn from them?

Source: A. Farnham, "America's Most Admired Company," *Fortune,* February 7, 1994, pp. 50–54. ●

Innovation, attention to detail, challenging goals, continuous improvement, good leadership, motivated people, awareness of what customers value, constant desire to learn . . . these and other things you will learn about in this course typify the great companies, and the great managers.

MANAGING FOR COMPETITIVE ADVANTAGE

Management is about helping your firm survive and win in competition with other companies. If your firm is well managed, it is more likely to be a success and a leader in the highly competitive business world.

To survive and win, you have to gain advantage over your competitors. You need to be better than your competitors at doing valuable things for your customers. You gain competitive advantage by adopting management approaches that satisfy people (both inside and outside your firm) through cost competitiveness, high-quality products, speed, and innovation.[9]

COST COMPETITIVENESS

Cost competitiveness means that your product (good or service) can be priced at a level that is attractive to consumers. Needless to say, if you can offer a desirable product at a low price, it is more likely to sell. Southwest Airlines is a good example of a company that has a big cost advantage over its rivals, in that it can reduce prices and survive fare wars.[10]

You can offer low prices by managing your costs and keeping them down. This means being efficient: accomplishing your goals by using your resources wisely and minimizing waste. If your cost structure is competitive (as low or lower than your competitors'), your success is not guaranteed. But you cannot be successful without a competitive cost structure.[11]

Costs include money spent on inputs, transformation processes, and delivering outputs to the market. Raw materials, equipment, capital, manufacturing, marketing, delivery, and labor are just some of the costs that need to be managed carefully.

The Denver International Airport became an international embarrassment when it came in more than $1 billion over budget and carriers were asked to pay per-passenger operating costs that were three times those charged at the existing Stapleton Airport.[12] Major league baseball owners did a poor job of keeping their labor costs down, although they were able to keep raising ticket prices for years. But when they claimed they were in financial trouble, and tried to halt rising salaries, the players struck. Many businesses and people were hurt financially by the owners' and players' inability to agree on a fair way to control costs.[13]

People are a central topic of this course. One obvious, simplistic way to reduce costs is to cut back the labor force, or to provide low wages and benefits. But a better way to achieve favorable costs is to pay people fairly and then make sure they add more value to your products than your competitors' employees add to theirs.[14]

QUALITY

A CPA in Michigan says, "People are more aware than ever that you are judged by the quality of your product above all."[15] Larry Harmon, a highly successful plumber in California, wants to start franchising: "I think the nation is ready for a national franchised plumbing company—as long as it is high quality."[16] Brio America, a division of the Swedish maker of high-quality toys, distributes through small specialty toy stores rather than the huge toy merchants. Why? The specialty stores "sell toys based on what is in the package rather than what is on the package."[17] In other words, they focus on quality products that provide the value customers want.

Quality is the excellence of your product, including its attractiveness, lack of defects, reliability, and long-term dependability. The importance of quality, and standards for acceptable quality, have increased dramatically in recent years. Firms cannot get by offering poor-quality products as they could a few years ago. Customers now demand high quality and value, and will accept nothing less.

Quality is very much under the control of the company and its management. Just as your people's behavior affects costs, so it determines quality. Throughout the course you will be learning about quality and how to provide it.

SPEED

Speed often separates the winners from the losers in the world of competition. How fast can you develop and get a new product to market? How quickly can you respond to customer requests? You are far better off if you are faster than the competition—or if you can respond quickly to the competition.

One of the biggest problems in the fashion industry—called by some the dirtiest secret in the fashion industry—is the speed with which expensive designer originals are turned into low-priced knockoffs or "interpretations."[18] Photographs taken at fashion shows are faxed overnight across the world, factories turn out samples a few hours later, and the samples can be shipped anywhere by the next day. Retail stores sell them in their private-label collections at the same time they offer the original designs in their pricier departments. Competitors' sheer speed is driving fashion designers crazy—and eroding their profits.

INNOVATION

Two Stanford business professors recently completed a study of 18 great companies. Impressed with all the companies, the authors still were able to choose one above them all that they believed would be the most successful over time. That company was 3M, and the reason is its extraordinary ability to innovate.[19]

Innovation is the introduction of new goods and services. Your firm must adapt to changes in consumer demands and to new sources of competition. Products don't sell forever; in fact, they don't sell for nearly as long as they used to, because so many competitors are introducing so many new products all the time. Your firm must innovate, or it will die. Like the other sources of competitive advantage, innovation comes from people; it must be a goal; and it must be managed. You will learn how 3M and other companies innovate in later chapters.

Remember three key points about these sources of competitive advantage. First, they represent the crucial results that your firm, and you, must achieve. Second, each is directly affected by your decisions and actions and by the decisions and actions of others with whom you work. Third, it is *how you manage* that determines how well you and your people achieve competitive advantage and deliver the valued results. Because of the importance of focusing on the sources of competitive advantage, and because managers can easily and often lose sight of them, we will highlight them throughout the book.

MANAGEMENT SKILLS

Performing management functions and achieving competitive advantage are the cornerstones of a manager's job. However, recognizing and understanding this does not ensure success. Managers need a variety of skills to do these things successfully. Skills are specific abilities that result from knowledge, information, practice, and aptitude. Although managers require many individual skills, which you will learn about throughout the text, we will group them into three general categories: technical skills, interpersonal and communication skills, and conceptual and decision skills.[20] As you can see in Figure 1.3, when the key management functions are performed by managers who have these critical management skills, the result is a high-performance work environment.

TECHNICAL SKILLS

A **technical skill** is the ability to perform a specialized task that involves a certain method or process. Most people develop a set of technical skills to complete the activities that are part of their daily work lives. When you leave school, you will have a set of technical skills that will provide you with the opportunity to get an entry-level position. Accounting majors will develop many of the basic skills needed to conduct an audit.

FIGURE 1.3

Management functions and skills

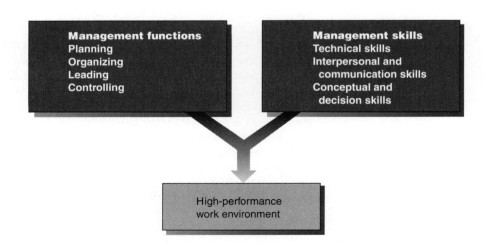

Information systems majors will have the skills necessary to construct a computerized management information system. Marketing majors may know pricing, market research, and sales.

The technical skills you learn in school will also help you as a manager. For example, your basic accounting and finance courses will develop the technical skills you need to understand and manage the financial resources of an organization. Managers may rely less on their basic technical skills as they rise through an organization, but these skills give them the background for their new responsibilities, as well as an appreciation of the activities of others in the firm.

INTERPERSONAL AND COMMUNICATION SKILLS

Interpersonal and communication skills influence the manager's ability to work well with people. These skills are often called the *human* or *people skills.* Senior executives spend well over half their time interacting with people.[21] Because managers must deal with others, they must develop their abilities to lead, motivate, and communicate effectively with those around them. The ability to get along with many diverse types of people and exchange information with them is vital for a successful management career. These skills are essential at all levels and in all parts of an organization.

A recent *Fortune* article decried the lack of communication and other "people" skills among recent MBAs launching their management careers.[22] It is vital to realize the importance of these skills in getting a job, keeping it, and performing well in it. As one expert commented, "In many, many companies, the reason a manager fails is not because he doesn't have the technical skills. It's because he doesn't have the people skills."[23]

While there are still plenty of traditional managers around, concentrating on being the boss, giving orders, and carefully monitoring employees, many believe that the manager of today and of the future must focus more on interpersonal skills such as being a team player, sharing information with others, and teaching and helping people learn. Table 1.2 asks you to consider whether you are (or will be) a traditional manager, or the contemporary manager needed now and in the future.

CONCEPTUAL AND DECISION SKILLS

Conceptual and decision skills involve the manager's ability to recognize complex and dynamic issues, to examine the numerous and conflicting factors that influence these issues or problems, and to resolve the problems for the benefit of the organization and everyone concerned. As you acquire greater responsibility you must exercise your conceptual and decision skills with increasing frequency. You will confront issues that involve all

TABLE 1.2

Which kind are you?

Traditional Manager	Contemporary Manager
Thinks of self as a manager, team leader, or boss.	Thinks of self as a sponsor, or internal consultant.
Follows the chain of command.	Deals with anyone necessary to get the job done.
Makes more decisions alone.	Invites others to join in decision making.
Hoards information.	Shares information.
Tries to master one major discipline, such as marketing or finance.	Tries to master a broad array of managerial disciplines.
Demands long hours.	Demands results.

Source: B. Dumaine, "The New Non-Manager Managers," *Fortune,* February 22, 1993, p. 81.

aspects of the organization, and must consider a larger and more interrelated set of decision factors. Such decisions have profound effects on the organization.

Senior executives use these skills when they consider the overall objectives and strategy of the firm, the interactions among different parts of the organization, and the role of the business in its external environment. A major portion of this text is devoted to enhancing your conceptual and decision skills, but remember that experience plays an important part in their development.

EXCELLENCE IN MANAGEMENT

Now that you know the basic functions and skills of management, let's discuss further what it takes to be a truly outstanding manager. Consider the three portraits that opened this chapter. These three people appear to possess similar characteristics related to their successes as managers. Each is committed to doing a great job. Each focuses on the organization's employees and how to motivate them. Each plans for the future and knows the competition. Each emphasizes achieving the objectives of the organization.

Although individual managers may have other specific characteristics, those just described are keys to becoming an outstanding manager. Great managers are active leaders who create a positive work environment in which the organization and its people have the opportunity and the incentive to achieve high performance (see Figure 1.4).

MANAGERS AS ACTIVE LEADERS

The best managers are leaders who are *active* participants in the departments or organizations for which they are responsible. They cannot be passive or detached observers, sitting in an office without regular contact with employees and operations. Managers must be intimately involved in key decisions and activities and have a broad and deep understanding of the tasks they delegate to others.

The best managers are leaders who can set an appropriate strategic direction and align employees behind the strategy so they can carry it out. To make intelligent decisions in these areas, managers must know their business. They also should have a *passion* for their

FIGURE 1.4

Key components of effective management

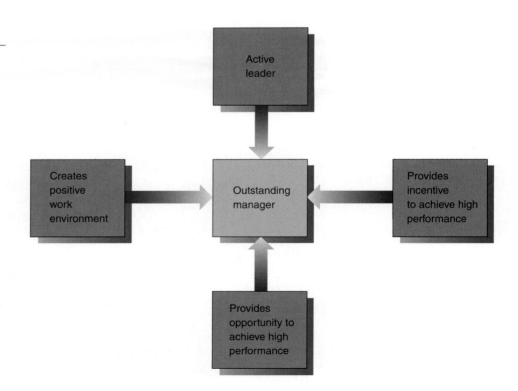

business to be able to make inspired decisions and to inspire others. Warren Buffett, a highly successful and sought-after chief executive, says, "The best CEOs love operating their companies."[24] His point is that they are there, *leading,* instead of playing golf at Augusta National or traveling to other companies' board meetings.

A POSITIVE WORK ENVIRONMENT

When you ask people to describe the job of a manager, they often respond, "Managers tell employees what to do" or "Managers give orders." Although managers give their employees direction, managers who spend all their time giving orders are not doing their job well. Instead, a great manager *creates a positive work environment.*

A positive work environment exists when the manager has done everything possible to establish the conditions that encourage success and to remove the causes of failure. In one sense, the best managers structure their work units so that employees have no alternative but high performance. This type of manager concentrates on placing employees in such a position that they are able and willing to achieve success through their own efforts. Pat Riley, former coach of the New York Knicks of the NBA, has said that he is interested in "creating an environment in which the talent can flourish," to put the people "in position to win."

A positive work environment provides the organization and its employees with the *opportunity to achieve high performance.* It also provides the organization and its employees with *incentive to achieve high performance.* Let's examine each of these characteristics more closely.

The Opportunity to Achieve High Performance

For the organization and its employees to have the opportunity to achieve high performance, people must understand their jobs thoroughly, in terms of both what they want to accomplish and how they are supposed to do it. Not only should they understand the organization's current status; people also should have a sense of the future of their job, work unit, and organization.

Another way managers provide the opportunity to achieve high performance is to ensure that people have all the resources they need to complete their tasks successfully. These resources should be available to people in proper quantity and quality and when and where they need them. Similarly, one of the most important jobs of any manager is to remove the impediments to an employee's effective performance. This may mean getting the employee a new piece of equipment, eliminating an unnecessary demand on the employee's time, or working out a difficult interpersonal relationship.

The Incentive to Achieve High Performance

For the organization and its employees to have the incentive to achieve high performance, managers must identify the factors that motivate people and build those factors into the work environment. The incentives may be part of the work process itself, such as an interesting, challenging job or good relationships with co-workers, or they may be the rewards that come from high performance, such as pay raises, promotions, and good assignments. Perhaps the ultimate incentive is the chance to be a full contributor to an organization that does great things.

To achieve high performance, managers usually need to link the factors that motivate people to clear goals. They need to identify, pursue, and monitor progress toward the goals of their work units, their employees, and their organization. Many successful individuals are goal-oriented people or bottom-line managers; that is, they identify the important objectives they need to achieve, and they focus everyone's efforts toward the achievement of those objectives. Whether publishing newspapers, achieving a specific level of sales, or earning a high return on investment, managers design the work environment so that organizational and individual goals are reached.

When incentives and goals are consistent, the manager's message is very simple: Everyone wins—the employee, the manager, and the organization. Establishing those incentives and objectives usually leads to the teamwork characteristic of well-managed and successful organizations. Familiar examples include Rubbermaid, Mary Kay Cosmetics, and Johnson & Johnson.

YOUR CAREER IN MANAGEMENT

What can you do to help ensure a successful management career for yourself in these challenging times? It will help if you can become both a specialist and a generalist.[25] Seek to become a *specialist:* you must be an expert in something. This will give you specific skills that help you provide concrete, identifiable value to your firm and to customers. And over time, you should learn to be a *generalist,* in that you know enough about a variety of business or technical disciplines so that you can understand and work with different perspectives.

It is also important to be both self-reliant and connected with other people.[26] To be *self-reliant* means to take full responsibility for yourself, your actions, and your career. You cannot count on your boss or your company to take care of you. A useful metaphor is to think of yourself as a business, with you as president and sole employee. Table 1.3 gives some specific advice about what this means in practice.

Being *connected* means having many good working relationships, and being a team player with strong interpersonal skills. For example, those who want to become partners in professional service organizations like accounting, advertising, and consulting firms strive constantly to build a network of contacts. Their goal is to work not only with lots of clients but also with a half-dozen or more senior partners, including several from outside their home offices and some from outside their country. Few would argue against the usefulness of having such a strong network of allies.

Look at this another way: all business is a function of human relationships.[27] Building competitive advantage for your firm depends not only on you but on other people. Management is personal. Commercial dealings are personal. Purchase decisions, repurchase decisions, and contracts all hinge on relationships. Even the biggest business deals—takeovers—are intensely personal and emotional. Without good work relationships, you are an outsider, not a good manager and leader.

TABLE 1.3

Keys to career management

Vicky Farrow of Sun Microsystems gives the following advice to help people assume responsibility for their own careers:

1. Think of yourself as a business.

2. Define your product: what is your area of expertise?

3. Know your target market: to whom are you going to sell this?

4. Be clear on why your customer buys from you. What is your "value proposition"—what are you offering that causes him to use you?

5. As in any business, strive for quality and customer satisfaction, even if your customer is just someone else in your organization—like your boss.

6. Know your profession or field and what's going on there.

7. Invest in your own growth and development, the way a company invests in research and development. What new products or services will you be able to provide?

8. Be willing to consider changing your career.

Source: W. Kiechel III, "A Manager's Career in the New Economy," *Fortune,* April 4, 1994, pp. 68–72.

KEY TERMS

conceptual and decision skills, p. 17
controlling, p. 7
cost competitiveness, p. 14
functions of management, p. 6
interpersonal and communication skills, p. 17
leading, p. 7
management, p. 6
middle managers, p. 10
operational managers, p. 11

organization, p. 12
organizing, p. 7
planning, p. 6
quality, p. 15
strategic managers, p. 9
system, p. 12
tactical managers, p. 10
technical skills, p. 16

SUMMARY OF LEARNING OBJECTIVES

Now that you have studied Chapter 1, you should know:

The functions of management.

Managers work with people and resources to achieve organizational goals. The primary functions of management are planning, organizing, leading, and controlling. Planning is analyzing a situation, determining the goals that will be pursued, and deciding in advance the actions needed to pursue these goals. Organizing is assembling the resources needed to complete the job and grouping and coordinating employees and tasks for maximum success. Leading is motivating people and stimulating high performance. Controlling is monitoring the progress of the organization or the work unit toward goals and then taking corrective action if necessary.

The nature of management at different organizational levels.

Strategic managers are the senior executives and are responsible for the organization's overall management. Tactical managers translate the general goals and plans developed by strategic managers into more specific objectives and activities. Operational managers are lower-level managers who supervise the operations of the organization.

How you can benefit from studying management.

This text will examine each management function and give you a solid foundation of knowledge and action ideas for your career. The ideas presented should supplement your common sense and experience, and help you avoid mistakes and create positive results.

The nature of organization.

An organization is a managed system designed and operated to achieve a specific set of objectives. This system processes human, financial, physical, and informational resources into outputs. These outputs are the goods and services demanded by the external environment. Meeting these demands allows an organization to achieve its goals.

The keys to gaining advantage over your organization's competitors.

Because management is a competitive arena, you need to deliver value to customers in ways that are superior to your competitors'. The four pillars of competitive advantage are low cost, quality products, speed, and innovation.

The skills you need to be an effective manager.

To execute management functions successfully, managers need technical skills, interpersonal and communication skills, and conceptual and decision skills. A technical skill is the ability to perform a specialized task involving a certain method or process. Interpersonal and communication skills enable the manager to interact and work well with people. Conceptual and decision skills help the manager recognize complex and dynamic issues, analyze the factors that influence those issues or problems, and make appropriate decisions.

What outstanding managers do.

An outstanding manager is an active leader who creates a positive work environment in which the organization and its people have the opportunity and incentive to achieve high performance. Managers should be leaders who take the initiative and participate fully in the activities of their operations. Successful managers encourage high performance by removing the causes of failure. Such managers ensure that people understand their jobs and have the resources necessary to do them well. The best managers create interesting jobs and motivate people with appropriate incentives.

What to strive for as you manage your career.

Keeping in mind four goals will help you succeed in your career: be expert in something valuable; know about all the business functions; take full responsibility for yourself and your career; and strive for good working relationships with other people.

DISCUSSION QUESTIONS

1. Identify and describe a great manager. What makes him or her stand out from the crowd?
2. Have you ever seen or worked for an ineffective manager? Describe the causes and the consequences of the ineffectiveness.
3. Describe an effective and ineffective organization.
4. Which companies are in *Fortune's* most recent "Most Admired" list? Why did they make the list?
5. Give examples you have seen of firms that are outstanding and weak on each of the four pillars of competitive advantage.
6. Discuss the importance of technical, interpersonal, and decision skills at school and in jobs you have held.

7. Review Table 1.2. Which type of manager are you or will you be? Give examples of both types you have seen or worked for. Which do you prefer to work for, and why?
8. What are your strengths and weaknesses as you contemplate your career? How do they correlate to the skills and activities identified in the chapter? How would you go about improving your managerial skills?
9. Use Table 1.3 to devise a plan for developing yourself and making yourself attractive to potential employers.

CONCLUDING CASE

IS PROCTER & GAMBLE BIG ENOUGH FOR BOTH OF THEM?

John Pepper and Durk Jager were supposed to lead Procter & Gamble into the 21st century. But the two men wouldn't talk to each other. Pepper believed in a teamwork approach to management, while Jager was aggressive with an eye toward quick results. Each was highly critical of the other.

Edwin Artzt, chairman and chief executive, was soon to retire. The board of directors hoped to keep both Pepper and Jager—but the two just didn't get along. Who should the board promote?

One option was to split the top job and name one of them chairman and the other chief executive—but the board didn't want to do that because the two men wouldn't work together. Another possibility was to name Mr. Pepper, the current president, to the top job and Mr. Jager to be president, with the promise that he would eventually succeed Pepper.

Jager was a native of the Netherlands who had worked overseas until 1990. Some believed he needed more experience in the United States. But he spoke six languages, had turned around P&G's business in Japan, had run P&G's domestic business for several years, and made some highly successful strategic decisions.

Under Mr. Artzt, P&G closed 30 plants and eliminated 13,000 jobs, or 12 percent of the workforce. His harsh decisions ruffled a

■

Who should Procter & Gamble promote—John Pepper or Durk Jager? Or can the top job be split between these two very different men?

(Mitchell Funk/The Image Bank)

lot of feathers, and Mr. Pepper was known for soothing those upset by Artzt's style. Pepper was known more for his popular personal style and broad experience than for any major successes. He received standing ovations at meetings, performed small acts of generosity, was free with compliments, and did not need to use fear and toughness to lead.

But his critics said Pepper was indecisive and slow to act. He constantly consulted employees and tried to reach agreement among all concerned, but was said to be persuaded by the last person to talk with him. For example, some customers and executives said he took too long to reshape P&G's sales force while he was trying to achieve total unanimity in how to do it.

P&G faced several important strategic decisions, including the development of an overall plan, and whether to stick to its basic businesses, such as detergents and toothpaste, or to pursue opportunities in cosmetics and pharmaceuticals. If Pepper became chairman, he was expected to preserve most of P&G's businesses and perhaps add new jobs. Jager was seen as more likely to demand results, get rid of weak businesses, cut costs, and eliminate jobs. For example, he believed Duncan Hines, Crisco, and Folgers were not strong brands for the long term because people don't bake as much as in years past, and they drink less coffee, or are switching to gourmet coffee.

On March 14, 1995, Mr. Pepper was named CEO and Mr. Jager was named president and chief operating officer. All P&G units would report to Jager, and he would report to Pepper.

QUESTIONS

1. Which executive—Mr. Pepper or Mr. Jager—would you rather work for?

2. Which one is more likely to lead a strong company into the 21st century?

3. Did the board do the right thing?

4. Can the two men be an effective team? How?

5. Is it possible for one person to manage with the strengths of each of these executives, and to minimize the weaknesses of each? How?

6. What is the current situation at P&G?

Sources: G. Stern, "Two Mismatched Men Compete for One Big Job," *The Wall Street Journal,* July 15, 1994, pp. B1, B7; N. Nohria and J. D. Berkley, "Whatever Happened to the Take-Charge Manager?" *Harvard Business Review,* Jan.–Feb. 1994, pp. 128–37. B. Horovitz and D. Enrico; "Artzt Departs, Brand New Age Starts," *USA Today,* March 15, 1995, B1, B2.

VIDEO EXERCISE

MANAGERS AND ORGANIZATIONS: A SKILL-DEVELOPMENT JOURNAL

The principles of effective management are nearly universal; that is, they apply to almost any type of organization. Whether it is a large or small business, nonprofit organization, or a hospital, they all benefit from efficient and effective management. The leaders of these organizations go by various titles, but they are all responsible for carrying out the goals of the organization. In trying to reach these goals, managers are most effective when they understand the four key functions of management: planning, organizing and staffing, leading, and controlling.

Purpose:

Each of the four critical areas of management requires special knowledge and a set of skills that can be developed in part through training, but also must be integrated with your life experiences. This textbook will provide you with a lot of information about effective management, and your personal management experiences will provide equally important training. This exercise is designed to help you integrate your formal training with your life experiences in the four important areas of management.

Materials:

A notebook dedicated to your development as a manager, and the respective sections you'll divide it into, will serve as your journal for significant information and life experiences in each of the four important areas of management. In the notebook, you'll provide yourself with an ongoing account that will help you develop your management effectiveness throughout this semester and beyond.

Procedure:

1. Divide your notebook into four approximately equal sections. If you have them, use divider tabs to mark the beginning of each section. The divider tabs should be labeled as follows: "Planning," "Organizing and Staffing," "Leadership," and "Control."

2. Divide the first few pages in each section into two equal columns by drawing a line down the middle of the page. As you fill your notebook over the coming weeks of the semester, do the same for new pages as you get them.

3. On the top of the left-hand column write "Formal Training" and on the top of the right-hand column write "Experience."

4. As you move through the chapters of the book, watch additional videotapes, and listen to your instructor and classmates, record significant ideas, techniques, and tools in the "Formal Training" side of your journal in the appropriate section. Make sure you date each entry, and leave plenty of room beneath each to add additional material.

5. As your managerial experience grows through your work, participation in student groups, or other outside activities, record your experiences in the right-hand column of your journal. Try to place records of your life experiences next to corresponding records of your formal training.

6. Use your journal to note discrepancies between your formal training and your life experiences. You should discuss discrepancies in class, and get feedback and ideas from your instructor and classmates. What tools and techniques have been effective for you? Which ones ineffective?

7. If you're going to continue business education and aspire to higher levels of management, you may want to continue or even expand your journal-keeping activities. Almost any management skills can be developed more quickly if you take an active approach to integrating your formal training and life experiences.

EXPERIENTIAL EXERCISES

1.1 Effective Managers

Objectives

1. To better understand what behaviors contribute to effective management.
2. To conceive a ranking of critical behaviors that you personally believe reflects their importance in your being a successful manager.

Instructions

1. Below is a partial list of behaviors in which managers may engage. Rank these items in terms of their importance for effective performance as a manager. Put a 1 next to the item that you think is most important, 2 for the next most important, down to 10 for the least important.
2. Bring your rankings to class. Be prepared to justify your results and rationale. If you can add any behaviors to this list which might lead to success or greater management effectiveness, write them in.

EFFECTIVE MANAGERS WORKSHEET

_____ Communicates and interprets policy so that it is understood by the members of the organization.

_____ Makes prompt and clear decisions.

_____ Assigns subordinates to the jobs for which they are best suited.

_____ Encourages associates to submit ideas and plans.

_____ Stimulates subordinates by means of competition among employees.

_____ Seeks means of improving management capabilities and competence.

_____ Fully supports and carries out company policies.

_____ Participates in community activities as opportunities arise.

_____ Is neat in appearance.

_____ Is honest in all matters pertaining to company property or funds.

Source: Excerpted from Lawrence R. Jaych, Arthur G. Bedeian, Sally A. Coltrin, and William F. Glueck, *The Managerial Experience: Cases, Exercises, and Readings,* 4th ed. Copyright © 1986 by The Drydon Press. Reprinted by permission of the publisher.

1.2 Career Planning

Objectives

1. To explore your career thinking.
2. To visualize your ideal job in as concrete terms as possible.
3. To summarize the state of your career planning, and to become conscious of the main questions you have about it at this point.

Instructions

Read the instructions for each activity, reflect on it, and then write your response. Be as brief or extensive as you like.

CAREER PLANNING WORKSHEET

1. Describe your ideal occupation in terms of responsibilities, skills, and how you
   would know if you were successful.

   _____

   _____

   _____

   _____

   _____

   _____

   _____

   _____

2. Identify ten statements you can make today about your current career planning.
   Identify ten questions you need answered for career planning.

Ten Statements   **Ten Questions**

1. _____   1. _____

   _____   _____

   _____   _____

2. _____   2. _____

   _____   _____

   _____   _____

3. _____   3. _____

   _____   _____

   _____   _____

4. _____   4. _____

   _____   _____

   _____   _____

5. _____   5. _____

   _____   _____

   _____   _____

6. _____   6. _____

   _____   _____

   _____   _____

7. _____   7. _____

   _____   _____

   _____   _____

Ten Statements

8. _____

_____

_____

9. _____

_____

_____

10. _____

_____

_____

Ten Questions

8. _____

_____

_____

9. _____

_____

_____

10. _____

_____

_____

Source: Pamela Shockley-Zalabak, *Fundamentals of Organizational Communication.* Copyright © 1995, 1991, and 1988 by Longman Publishers. Reprinted with permission.

THE EVOLUTION OF MANAGEMENT

It is a time for a new generation of leadership to cope with new problems and new opportunities. For there is a new world to be won.

John F. Kennedy

LEARNING OBJECTIVES

After studying Chapter 2, you will know:

1. The important classical approaches to management and their strengths and weaknesses.

2. The important contemporary approaches to management and their strengths and weaknesses.

3. The current forces that are shaping management practice and your future career.

AMERICA'S INDUSTRIAL REVOLUTION

"With a stride that astonished statisticians, the conquering hosts of business enterprise swept over the continent; 25 years after the death of Lincoln, America had become . . . [the foremost] manufacturing nation of the world. What England had accomplished in a hundred years, the United States had achieved in half the time." So wrote historians Charles and Mary Beard in the 1920s about America's amazing industrialization.

Change came at a dizzying pace. Steel production, which provided the structural underpinnings for industrial growth, soared from 19,000 tons in 1867 to 11.4 million tons in 1900. By the 1880s, the steel produced for nails alone amounted to twice the total steel output of the 1870s. Only 36,000 patents had been issued in the United States prior to 1860; from 1860 to 1890, 440,000 were granted. New inventions included the telephone, the light bulb, the typewriter, the phonograph, barbed wire, the adding machine, and the cash register.

Modern manufacturing was ushered in with the appearance of factories belching out the smoke of the Industrial Revolution.
(Courtesy The Bettman Archive)

As railroads crisscrossed the country, national markets tying remote rural areas to seaports and to the world economy emerged. In addition, the railroads, the first large corporations, demonstrated the usefulness of managerial skills and bureaucratic organizations. For instance, to meet their needs for efficiency and predictability the railroads set up time zones, which the government soon adopted.

Yet America's industrial "revolution" was not without its victims. The familial atmosphere of craftspeople's shops slipped away as emerging corporations drove smaller businesses into bankruptcy. Workers had little bargaining power as industrialists increasingly exploited the 25 million immigrants who poured into America's burgeoning cities between 1865 and 1915. Young children often worked 12-hour days 6 days a week. Moreover, America's accident rate was higher than that of any other industrialized nation. In 1913, 25,000 factory workers died because of hazards in the workplace, and 700,000 were injured so severely that they required at least four weeks' disability. Attempts by states to regulate child labor, hazardous work conditions, and business practices were blocked by the Supreme Court, Congress, and a federal system devoted to laissez-faire economics.

Scholars appropriately refer to the changes wrought by rapid industrialization as a "revolution." Patterns and traditions in everyday life were affected by the massive outpouring of goods. Labor relations were altered. Large businesses became the norm rather than the exception. Along with these trends, the need for more and better-skilled management became apparent to everyone.

Sources: Robert L. Heilbroner, *The Economic Transformation of America* (San Diego: Harcourt Brace Jovanovich, 1984); George B. Tindall, *America: A Narrative History,* Vol. II (New York: W. W. Norton, 1988); Robert H. Wiebe, *The Search for Order* (Westport, Conn.: Greenwood Press, 1967).

*F*or thousands of years, managers have wrestled with the same issues and problems confronting executives today. Around 1100 B.C., the Chinese practiced the four management functions—planning, organizing and staffing, leading, and controlling—discussed in Chapter 1. Between 350 and 400 B.C., the Greeks recognized management as a separate art and advocated a scientific approach to work. The Romans decentralized the management of their vast empire before the birth of Christ. During medieval times, the Venetians standardized production through the use of an assembly line, building warehouses and using an inventory system to monitor the contents.[1]

But throughout history most managers operated strictly on a trial-and-error basis. The challenges of the industrial revolution changed that. Management emerged as a formal discipline at the turn of the century. The first university programs to offer management and business education, the Wharton School at the University of Pennsylvania and the Amos Tuck School at Dartmouth, were founded in the late 19th century. However, by 1914 only 25 business schools existed.[2]

Thus, the management profession as we know it today is relatively new. This chapter explores the roots of modern management theory. Understanding the origins of management thought will help you grasp the underlying contexts of the ideas and concepts presented in the chapters ahead.

Although this chapter is titled "The Evolution of Management," it might be more appropriately called "The Revolutions of Management," because it documents the wide swings in management approaches over the last 100 years. Out of the great variety of ideas about how to improve management, parts of each approach have survived and been incorporated into modern perspectives on management. Thus, the legacy of past efforts, triumphs, and failures has become our guide to future management practice.

EARLY MANAGEMENT CONCEPTS AND INFLUENCES

Communication and transportation constraints hindered the growth of earlier businesses. Therefore, improvements in management techniques did not substantially improve performance. However, the industrial revolution changed that. As companies grew and became more complex, minor improvements in management tactics produced overwhelming increases in production quantity and quality.[3]

The emergence of **economies of scale**—reductions in the average cost of a unit of production as the total volume produced increases—drove managers to strive for further growth. The opportunities for mass production created by the industrial revolution spawned intense and systematic thought about management problems and issues—particularly efficiency, production processes, and cost savings.[4]

Production costs dropped as mass manufacturing lowered unit costs. Thus economies of scale was born, a concept that is alive and well in the modern manufacturing era.
(Martin Rogers/Tony Stone Images)

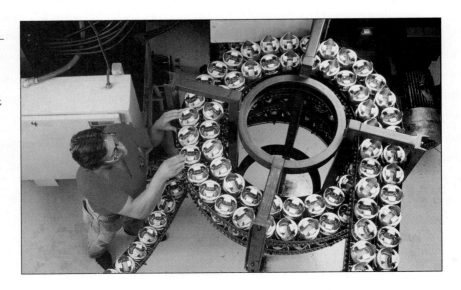

Figure 2.1 provides a timeline depicting the evolution of management thought through the decades. This historical perspective is divided into two major sections: classical approaches and contemporary approaches. Many of these approaches developed simultaneously, and they often had a significant impact on one another. Some approaches were a direct reaction to the perceived deficiencies of previous approaches. Others developed as the needs and issues confronting managers changed over the years. All the approaches attempted to explain the real issues facing managers and provide them with tools to solve future problems.

Refer to Figure 2.1 as you read the descriptions of each approach. It will reinforce your understanding of the key relationships among the approaches and place each perspective in its historical context.

CLASSICAL APPROACHES

The classical period extended from the mid-19th century through the early 1950s. The major approaches that emerged during this period were systematic management, scientific management, administrative management, human relations, and bureaucracy.

SYSTEMATIC MANAGEMENT

During the 19th century, growth in U.S. business centered on manufacturing.[5] Early writers such as Adam Smith believed the management of these firms was chaotic, and their ideas helped to systematize it. Most organizational tasks were subdivided and performed by specialized labor. However, poor coordination among subordinates and different levels of management caused frequent problems and breakdowns of the manufacturing process.

The **systematic management** approach attempted to build specific procedures and processes into operations to ensure coordination of effort. Systematic management emphasized economical operations, adequate staffing, maintenance of inventories to meet consumer demand, and organizational control. These goals were achieved through

- Careful definition of duties and responsibilities.
- Standardized techniques for performing these duties.
- Specific means of gathering, handling, transmitting, and analyzing information.
- Cost accounting, wage, and production control systems to facilitate internal coordination and communications.

FIGURE 2.1   The evolution of management thought

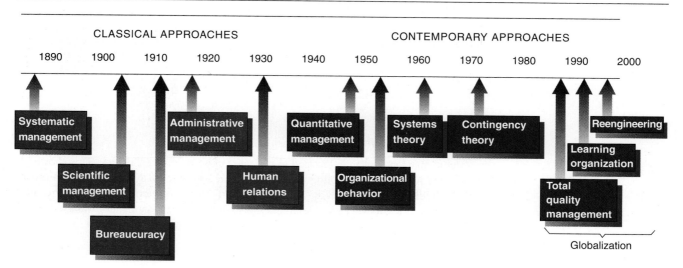

Systematic management emphasized internal operations because managers were concerned primarily with meeting the explosive growth in demand brought about by the Industrial Revolution. In addition, managers were free to focus on internal issues of efficiency, in part because the government did not constrain business practices significantly. Finally, labor was poorly organized. As a result, many managers were oriented more toward things than toward people.

The influence of the systematic management approach is clear in the following description of one organization's attempt to control its workers.

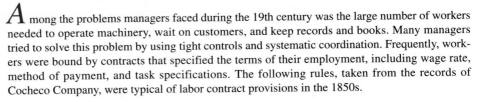

AN EARLY LABOR CONTRACT

A mong the problems managers faced during the 19th century was the large number of workers needed to operate machinery, wait on customers, and keep records and books. Many managers tried to solve this problem by using tight controls and systematic coordination. Frequently, workers were bound by contracts that specified the terms of their employment, including wage rate, method of payment, and task specifications. The following rules, taken from the records of Cocheco Company, were typical of labor contract provisions in the 1850s.

1. The hours of work shall be from sunrise to sunset, from the 21st of March to the 20th of September inclusively; and from sunrise until eight o'clock, P.M., during the remainder of the year. One hour shall be allowed for dinner, and half an hour for breakfast during the first mentioned six months; and one hour for dinner during the other half of the year; on Saturdays, the mill shall be stopped one hour before sunset, for the purpose of cleaning the machinery.

2. Every hand coming to work a quarter of an hour after the mill has been started shall be docked a quarter of a day; and every hand absenting him or herself, without absolute necessity, shall be docked in a sum double the amount of the wages such hand shall have earned during the time of such absence. No more than one hand is allowed to leave any one of the rooms at the same time—a quarter of a day shall be deducted for every breach of this rule.

3. No smoking or spiritous liquors shall be allowed in the factory under any pretense whatsoever. It is also forbidden to carry into the factory, nuts, fruits, etc., books, or papers during the hours of work . . .

Source: W. Sullivan, "The Industrial Revolution and the Factory Operative in Pennsylvania," *The Pennsylvania Magazine of History and Biography* 78 (1954), pp. 478–79. ●

Table 2.1 lists some of the key concepts, contributions, and limitations of systematic management. Although systematic management did not address all the issues 19th-century managers faced, it tried to raise managers' awareness about the most pressing concerns of their job.

SCIENTIFIC MANAGEMENT

Systematic management failed to lead to widespread production efficiency. This shortcoming became apparent to a young engineer named Frederick Taylor who was hired by Midvale Steel Company in 1878. Taylor discovered that production and pay were poor, inefficiency and waste were prevalent, and most companies had tremendous unused potential. He concluded that management decisions were unsystematic and no research to determine the best means of production existed.

TABLE 2.1

Systematic
management

Key concepts
Systematized manufacturing organizations.
Coordination of procedures and processes built into internal operations.
Emphasis on economical operations, inventory management, and cost control.
Contributions
Beginning of formal management in the United States.
Promotion of efficient, uninterrupted production.
Limitations
Ignored relationship between an organization and its environment.
Ignored differences in managers' and workers' views.

In response, Taylor introduced a second approach to management, known as **scientific management**.[6] This approach advocated the application of scientific methods to analyze work and to determine how to complete production tasks efficiently. For example, U.S. Steel's contract with the United Steel Workers of America specified that sand shovelers should move 12.5 shovelfuls per minute; shovelfuls should average 15 pounds of river sand composed of 5.5 percent moisture.[7]

Taylor identified four principles of scientific management:

1. Management should develop a precise, scientific approach for each element of an individual's work to replace general guidelines.
2. Management should scientifically select, train, teach, and develop each worker so that the right person has the right job.
3. Management should cooperate with workers to ensure that the job matches plans and principles.
4. Management should ensure an equal division of work and responsibility between managers and workers.

To implement this approach, Taylor used techniques such as time-and-motion studies. With this technique, a task was divided into its basic movements, and different motions were timed to determine the most efficient way to complete the task.

After the "one best way" to perform the job was identified, Taylor stressed the importance of hiring and training the proper worker to do that job. Taylor advocated the standardization of tools, the use of instruction cards to help workers, and breaks to eliminate fatigue.

Another key element of Taylor's approach was the use of the differential piecerate system. Taylor assumed workers were motivated by receiving money. Therefore, he implemented a pay system in which workers were paid additional wages when they exceeded a standard level of output for each job. Taylor concluded that both workers and management would benefit from such an approach.

Scientific management principles were widely embraced. Other proponents, including Henry Gantt and Frank and Lillian Gilbreth, introduced many refinements and techniques for applying scientific management on the factory floor. One of the most famous examples of the application of scientific management is the factory Henry Ford built to produce the Model-T.

Frederick Taylor (left) and Dr. Lillian Gilbreth (right) were early experts in management efficiency.
(Stock Montage, Inc.)

SCIENTIFIC MANAGEMENT AND THE MODEL-T

*A*t the turn of the century, automobiles were a luxury that only the wealthy could afford. They were assembled by craftspeople who put an entire car together at one spot on the factory floor. These workers were not specialized, and Henry Ford believed they wasted time and energy bringing the needed parts to the car. Ford took a revolutionary approach to automobile manufacturing by using scientific management principles.

After much study, machines and workers in Ford's new factory were placed in sequence so that an automobile could be assembled without interruption along a moving production line. Mechanical energy and a conveyor belt were used to take the work to the workers.

The manufacture of parts likewise was revolutionized. For example, formerly it had taken one worker 20 minutes to assemble a flywheel magneto. By splitting the job into 29 different operations, putting the product on a mechanical conveyor, and changing the height of the conveyor, Ford cut production time to 5 minutes.

By 1914 chassis assembly time had been trimmed from almost 13 hours to $1\frac{1}{2}$ hours. The new methods of production required complete standardization, new machines, and an adaptable labor force. Costs dropped significantly, the Model-T became the first car accessible to the majority of Americans, and Ford dominated the industry for many years.

Source: H. Kroos and C. Gilbert, *The Principles of Scientific Management* (New York: Harper & Row, 1911). ●

The legacy of Taylor's scientific management approach is broad and pervasive. Most important, productivity and efficiency in manufacturing improved dramatically. The concepts of scientific methods and research were introduced to manufacturing. The piecerate system gained wide acceptance because it more closely aligned effort and reward. Taylor also emphasized the need for cooperation between management and workers. Finally, the concept of a management specialist gained prominence.

Despite these gains, not everyone was convinced that scientific management was the best solution to all business problems. First, critics claimed that Taylor ignored many job-related social and psychological factors by emphasizing only money as a worker incentive. Second, production tasks were reduced to a set of routine, machinelike procedures that led to boredom, apathy, and quality control problems. Third, unions strongly opposed scien-

TABLE 2.2

Scientific
management

Key concepts

Analyzed work using scientific methods to determine the "one best way" to complete production tasks.

Emphasized study of tasks, selection and training of workers, and cooperation between workers and management.

Contributions

Improved factory productivity and efficiency.

Introduced scientific analysis to the workplace.

Piecerate system equated worker rewards and performance.

Instilled cooperation between management and workers.

Limitations

Simplistic motivational assumptions.

Workers viewed as parts of a machine.

Potential for exploitation of labor.

Excluded senior management tasks.

Ignored relationship between the organization and its environment.

tific management techniques because they believed management might abuse their power to set the standards and the piecerates, thus exploiting workers and diminishing their importance. Finally, although scientific management resulted in intense scrutiny of the internal efficiency of organizations, it did not help managers deal with broader external issues such as competitors and government regulations, especially at the senior management level. Table 2.2 summarizes some of the key concepts, contributions, and limitations of scientific management.

ADMINISTRATIVE MANAGEMENT

The **administrative management** approach emphasized the perspective of senior managers within the organization, and argued that management was a profession and could be taught.

An explicit and broad framework for administrative management emerged in 1916, when Henri Fayol, a French mining engineer and executive, published a book summarizing his management experiences. Fayol identified five functions and 14 principles of management. The five functions, which are very similar to the four functions discussed in Chapter 1, include planning, organizing, commanding, coordinating, and controlling. Table 2.3 lists and defines the 14 principles. Although some critics claim Fayol treated the principles as universal truths for management, he actually wanted them applied flexibly.[8]

A host of other executives contributed to the administrative management literature. These writers discussed a broad spectrum of management topics, including the social responsibilities of management, the philosophy of management, clarification of business terms and concepts, and organizational principles. Chester Barnard's and Mary Parker Follet's contributions have become classic works in this area.[9]

Barnard, former president of New Jersey Bell Telephone Company, published his landmark book *The Functions of the Executive* in 1938. He outlined the role of the senior executive: formulating the purpose of the organization, hiring key individuals, and

TABLE 2.3

Fayol's 14
principles of
management

1. *Division of work*—divide work into specialized tasks and assign responsibilities to specific individuals.
2. *Authority*—delegate authority along with responsibility.
3. *Discipline*—make expectations clear and punish violations.
4. *Unity of command*—each employee should be assigned to only one supervisor.
5. *Unity of direction*—employees' efforts focused on achieving organizational objectives.
6. *Subordination of individual interest to the general interest*—the general interest must predominate.
7. *Remuneration*—systematically reward efforts that support the organization's direction.
8. *Centralization*—determine the relative importance of superior and subordinate roles.
9. *Scalar chain*—keep communications within the chain of command.
10. *Order*—order jobs and material so they support the organization's direction.
11. *Equity*—fair discipline and order enhance employee commitment.
12. *Stability and tenure of personnel*—promote employee loyalty and longevity.
13. *Initiative*—encourage employees to act on their own in support of the organization's direction.
14. *Esprit de corps*—promote a unity of interests between employees and management.

maintaining organizational communications.[10] Mary Parker Follet's 1942 book *Dynamic Organization* extended Barnard's work by emphasizing the continually changing situations that managers face.[11] Two of her key contributions—the notion that managers desire flexibility and the differences between motivating groups and individuals—laid the groundwork for the modern contingency approach discussed later in the chapter.

All the writings in the administrative management area emphasize management as a profession along with fields such as law and medicine. In addition, these authors offered many recommendations based on their personal experiences, which often included managing large corporations. Although these perspectives and recommendations were considered sound, critics noted that they may not work in all settings. Different types of personnel, industry conditions, and technologies may affect the appropriateness of these principles.

Table 2.4 summarizes the administrative management approach.

HUMAN RELATIONS

A fourth approach to management, **human relations**, developed during the early 1930s. This approach aimed at understanding how psychological and social processes interact with the work situation to influence performance. Human relations was the first major approach to emphasize informal work relationships and worker satisfaction.

This approach owes much to other major schools of thought. For example, many of the ideas of the Gilbreths (scientific management) and Barnard and Follet (administrative management) influenced the development of human relations from 1930 to 1955. In fact, human relations emerged from a research project that began as a scientific management study.

The Hawthorne Studies

Western Electric Company, a manufacturer of communications equipment, hired a team of Harvard researchers led by Elton Mayo and Fritz Roethlisberger. They were to investigate the influence of physical working conditions on workers' productivity and efficiency in one of the company's factories outside Chicago. This research project, known as the

Table 2.4

Administrative
management

> **Key concepts**
>
> Fayol's five functions and 14 principles of management.
>
> Executives formulate the organization's purpose, secure employees, and maintain communications.
>
> Managers must respond to changing developments.
>
> **Contributions**
>
> Viewed management as a profession that can be trained and developed.
>
> Emphasized the broad policy aspects of top-level managers.
>
> Offered universal managerial prescriptions.
>
> **Limitation**
>
> Universal prescriptions need qualifications for environmental, technological, and personnel factors.

Hawthorne Studies, provided some of the most interesting and controversial results in the history of management.[12]

The Hawthorne Studies were a series of experiments conducted from 1924 to 1932. During the first stage of the project (the Illumination Experiments), various working conditions, particularly the lighting in the factory, were altered to determine the effects of these changes on productivity. The researchers found no systematic relationship between the factory lighting and production levels. In some cases, productivity continued to increase even when the illumination was reduced to the level of moonlight. The researchers concluded that the workers performed and reacted differently because the researchers were observing them. This reaction is known as the **Hawthorne Effect**.

This conclusion led the researchers to believe productivity may be affected more by psychological and social factors than by physical or objective influences. With this thought in mind, they initiated the other four stages of the project. During these stages, the researchers performed various work group experiments and had extensive interviews with employees. Mayo and his team eventually concluded that productivity and employee behavior were influenced by the informal work group.

The Human Relations Viewpoint

Human relations proponents argued that managers should stress primarily employee welfare, motivation, and communication. They believed social needs had precedence over economic needs. Therefore, management must gain the cooperation of the group and promote job satisfaction and group norms consistent with the goals of the organization.

Another noted contributor to the field of human relations was Abraham Maslow.[13] In 1943, Maslow suggested that humans have five levels of needs. The most basic needs are the physical needs for food, water, and shelter; the most advanced need is for self-actualization, or personal fulfillment. Maslow argued that people try to satisfy their lower-level needs and then progress upward to the higher-level needs. Managers can facilitate this process and achieve organizational goals by removing obstacles and encouraging behaviors that satisfy people's needs and organizational goals simultaneously.

Although the human relations approach generated research into leadership, job attitudes, and group dynamics, it drew heavy criticism.[14] Critics believed the philosophy of human relations—a happy worker was a productive worker—was too simplistic.

While scientific management overemphasized the economic and formal aspects of the workplace, human relations ignored the more rational side of the worker and the important characteristics of the formal organization. However, human relations was a significant step in the development of management thought, because it prompted managers and researchers to consider the psychological and social factors that influence performance.

Table 2.5 summarizes the human relations approach.

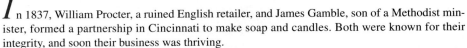

A Human Relations Pioneer

*I*n 1837, William Procter, a ruined English retailer, and James Gamble, son of a Methodist minister, formed a partnership in Cincinnati to make soap and candles. Both were known for their integrity, and soon their business was thriving.

By 1883, the business had grown substantially. When William Cooper Procter, grandson of the founder, left Princeton University to work for the firm, he wanted to learn the business from the ground up. He started working on the factory floor. "He did every menial job from shoveling rosin and soap to pouring fatty mixtures into crutchers. He brought his lunch in a paper bag . . . and sat on the floor [with the other workers] and ate with them, learning their feelings about work."

By 1884, Cooper Procter believed, from his own experience, that increasing workers' psychological commitment to the company would lead to higher productivity. His passion to increase employee commitment to the firm led him to propose a scandalous plan: share profits with workers to increase their sense of responsibility and job satisfaction. The surprise was audible on the first "Dividend Day," when workers held checks equivalent to seven weeks' pay.

Still, the plan was not complete. Workers saw the profit sharing as extra pay rather than as an incentive to improve. In addition, Cooper Procter recognized that a fundamental issue for the workers, some of whom continued to be his good friends, was the insecurity of old age. Public incorporation in 1890 gave Procter a new idea. After trying several versions, by 1903 he had discovered a way to meet all his goals for labor: a stock purchase plan. For every dollar a worker invested in P&G stock, the company would contribute four dollars' worth of stock.

Finally, Cooper Procter had resolved some key issues for labor that paid off in worker loyalty, improved productivity, and an increasing corporate reputation for caring and integrity. He went on to become CEO of the firm, and P&G today remains one of the most admired corporations in the United States.

Sources: O. Schisgall, *Eyes on Tomorrow* (Chicago: J. G. Ferguson, 1981); T. Welsh, "Best and Worst Corporate Reputations," *Fortune,* February 7, 1994, pp. 58–66. ●

TABLE 2.5

Human relations

Key concepts

Productivity and employee behavior are influenced by the informal work group.

Cohesion, status, and group norms determine output.

Managers should stress employee welfare, motivation, and communication.

Social needs have precedence over economic needs.

Contributions

Psychological and social processes influence performance.

Maslow's hierarchy of needs.

Limitations

Ignored workers' rational side and the formal organization's contribution to productivity.

Research findings later overturned the simplistic prescription that happy workers are always more productive.

BUREAUCRACY

Max Weber, a German sociologist, lawyer, and social historian, showed how management itself could be more efficient and consistent in his book *The Theory of Social and Economic Organizations*.[15] The ideal model for management, according to Weber, is the **bureaucracy** approach.

Weber believed bureaucratic structures can eliminate the variability that results when managers in the same organization have different skills, experiences, and goals. Weber advocated that the jobs themselves be standardized so that personnel changes would not disrupt the organization. He emphasized a structured, formal network of relationships among specialized positions in an organization. Rules and regulations standardize behavior, and authority resides in positions rather than in individuals. As a result, the organization need not rely on a particular individual, but will realize efficiency and success by following the rules in a routine and unbiased manner.

According to Weber, bureaucracies are especially important because they allow large organizations to perform the many routine activities necessary for their survival. Also, bureaucratic positions foster specialized skills, eliminating many subjective judgments by managers. In addition, if the rules and controls are established properly, bureaucracies should be unbiased in their treatment of people, both customers and employees.

Many organizations today are bureaucratic. Bureaucracy can be efficient and productive. However, bureaucracy is not the appropriate model for every organization. Organizations or departments that need rapid decision making and flexibility may suffer under a bureaucratic approach. Some people may not perform their best with excessive bureaucratic rules and procedures.

Other shortcomings stem from a faulty execution of bureaucratic principles rather than from the approach itself. Too much authority may be vested in too few people; the procedures may become the ends rather than the means; or managers may ignore appropriate rules and regulations. Finally, one advantage of a bureaucracy—its permanence—can also be a problem. Once a bureaucracy is established, dismantling it is very difficult.

Table 2.6 summarizes the key concepts, contributions, and limitations of bureaucracy.

TABLE 2.6

Bureaucracy

Key concepts

Structured, formal network of relationships among specialized positions in an organization.

Rules and regulations standardize behavior.

Jobs staffed by trained specialists who follow rules.

Hierarchy defines the relationship among jobs.

Contributions

Promotes efficient performance of routine organizational activities.

Eliminates subjective judgment by employees and management.

Emphasizes position rather than the person.

Limitations

Limited organizational flexibility and slow decision making.

Ignores the importance of people and interpersonal relationships.

Accumulation of power can lead to authoritarian management.

Rules may become ends in themselves.

Difficult to dismantle once established.

CONTEMPORARY APPROACHES

The contemporary approaches to management include quantitative management, organizational behavior, systems theory, and the contingency perspective. The contemporary approaches have developed at various times since World War II, and they continue to represent the cornerstones of modern management thought.

QUANTITATIVE MANAGEMENT

Although Taylor introduced the use of science as a management tool early in the 20th century, most organizations did not adopt the use of quantitative techniques for management problems until the 1940s and 1950s.[16] During World War II, military planners began to apply mathematical techniques to defense and logistic problems. After the war, private corporations began assembling teams of quantitative experts to tackle many of the complex issues confronting large organizations. This approach, referred to as **quantitative management,** emphasizes the application of quantitative analysis to management decisions and problems.

Quantitative management helps a manager make a decision by developing formal mathematical models of the problem. Computers have facilitated the development of specific quantitative methods. These include such techniques as statistical decision theory, linear programming, queuing theory, simulation, forecasting, inventory modeling, network modeling, and break-even analysis. Organizations apply these techniques in many areas, including production, quality control, marketing, human resources, finance, distribution, planning, and research and development.

Despite the promise quantitative management holds, managers do not rely on these methods as the primary approach to decision making. Typically they use these techniques as a supplement or tool in the decision process. Many managers will use results that are consistent with their experience, intuition, and judgment, but they will reject results that contradict their beliefs. Also, managers may use the process to compare alternatives and eliminate weaker options.

Several explanations account for the limited use of quantitative management. Many managers have not been trained in using these techniques. Also, many aspects of a management decision cannot be expressed through mathematical symbols and formulas. Finally, many of the decisions managers face are nonroutine and unpredictable.

Table 2.7 summarizes the quantitative management approach.

ORGANIZATIONAL BEHAVIOR

During the 1950s, a transition took place in the human relations approach. Scholars began to recognize that worker productivity and organizational success are based on

TABLE 2.7

Quantitative management

Key concept
Application of quantitative analysis to management decisions.
Contributions
Developed specific mathematical methods of problem analysis.
Helped managers select the best alternative among a set.
Limitations
Models neglect nonquantifiable factors.
Managers not trained in these techniques and may not trust or understand the techniques' outcomes.
Not suited for nonroutine or unpredictable management decisions.

more than the satisfaction of economic or social needs. The revised perspective, known as **organizational behavior**, studies and identifies management activities that promote employee effectiveness through an understanding of the complex nature of individual, group, and organizational processes. Organizational behavior draws from a variety of disciplines, including psychology and sociology, to explain the behavior of people on the job.

During the 1960s, organizational behaviorists heavily influenced the field of management. Douglas McGregor's Theory X and Theory Y marked the transition from human relations.[17] According to McGregor, Theory X managers assume workers are lazy and irresponsible and require constant supervision and external motivation to achieve organizational goals. Theory Y managers assume employees *want* to work and can direct and control themselves. McGregor advocated a Theory Y perspective, suggesting that managers who encourage participation and allow opportunities for individual challenge and initiative would achieve superior performance.

Other major organizational behaviorists include Chris Argyris, who recommended greater autonomy and better jobs for workers,[18] and Rensis Likert, who stressed the value of participative management.[19] Through the years, organizational behavior has consistently emphasized development of the organization's human resources to achieve individual and organizational goals. Like other approaches it has been criticized for its limited perspective, although more recent contributions have a broader and more situational viewpoint. In the past few years, many of the primary issues addressed by organizational behavior have experienced a rebirth with a greater interest in leadership, worker participation and incentives, and productivity.

Table 2.8 summarizes the key concepts, contributions, and limitations of organizational behavior.

SYSTEMS THEORY

The classical approaches as a whole were criticized because they (1) ignored the relationship between the organization and its external environment and (2) usually stressed one aspect of the organization or its employees at the expense of other considerations. In response to these criticisms, management scholars during the 1950s stepped back from the details of the organization to attempt to understand it as a whole system. These efforts were based on a

TABLE 2.8

Organizational behavior

Key concepts

Promotes employee effectiveness through understanding of individual, group, and organizational processes.

Stresses relationships among employees, managers, and the work they perform for the organization.

Assumes employees want to work and can control themselves (Theory Y).

Contributions

Increased participation, greater autonomy, individual challenge and initiative, and enriched jobs may increase performance.

Recognized the importance of developing human resources.

Limitation

Some approaches ignored situational factors, such as the environment and the organization's technology.

FIGURE 2.2

general scientific approach called **systems theory**.[20] As you recall from Chapter 1, systems theory provides a way to interpret organizations. Systems theory takes a holistic view of the entire organizational system and stresses processes. Important concepts from systems theory include open versus closed systems, efficiency and effectiveness, subsystems, equifinality, and synergy.

Open versus Closed Systems

A *closed system* does not interact with the outside environment. Although few systems actually take this form, some of the classical approaches treated organizations as closed systems. The assumption was that if managers improve internal processes, the organization will succeed. Clearly, however, all organizations are *open systems,* dependent on inputs from the outside world, such as raw materials, human resources, and capital, and outputs to the outside world that meet the market's needs for goods and services.

Figure 2.2 illustrates the open-system perspective. The organizational system requires inputs, which the organization transforms into outputs, which are received by the external environment. The environment reacts to these outputs through a feedback loop, which then becomes an input for the next cycle of the system. The process continues to repeat itself for the life of the system.

Efficiency and Effectiveness

The closed-system focus of the classical theorists emphasized the internal efficiency of the organization; that is, these perspectives addressed only improvements to the transformation process. **Efficiency** is the ratio of outputs to inputs. Systems theory highlights another important dimension for managers: effectiveness. **Effectiveness** is the degree to which the organization's outputs correspond to the needs and wants of the external environment. The external environment includes groups such as customers, suppliers, competitors, and regulatory agencies. Even a firm that has mastered Taylor's scientific management techniques and become extremely efficient is vulnerable if it does not consider the effectiveness of its outputs.[21]

Subsystems

Systems theory also emphasizes that an organization is one level in a series of **subsystems**. For instance, USAir is a subsystem of the airline industry and the flight crews are a subsystem of USAir. Again, systems theory points out that each subsystem is a component of the whole and is interdependent with other subsystems.

Equifinality

The concept of **equifinality** states that there are many avenues to the same outcome. Unlike scientific management proponents' "one best way," systems theory suggests that many different combinations of subsystems, ideas, and methods can lead to the same goal. The validity of this principle is clear in many businesses today. For instance, Domino's Pizza has been very successful with a low-cost, high-volume strategy, while Pizza Hut has been equally successful with a more full-service strategy.

TABLE 2.9

Systems theory

Key concepts

Organization is viewed as an open system.

Management must interact with the environment to gather inputs and return the outputs of its production.

Organizational objectives must encompass both efficiency and effectiveness.

Organizations contain a series of subsystems.

There are many avenues to the same outcome.

Synergies exist where the whole is greater than the sum of the parts.

Contribution

Recognized the importance of the organization's relationship with the external environment.

Limitation

Does not provide specific guidance on the functions and duties of managers.

Synergy

Systems theory also popularized the concept of **synergy**, which states that the whole is greater than the sum of its parts. For example, 3M has applied its core technology of adhesives to many products, from industrial sealers to Post-it™ notes. 3M has not had to start from scratch with each product; its adhesives expertise provides synergies across products.

Table 2.9 summarizes systems theory.

See how many of the elements of systems theory you can identify in the following example.

MANAGING AIRLINE DELAYS

Speed

A number of airlines are trying to cut turnaround times on targeted flights. It often takes 45 minutes from the time a plane lands to the time it is ready to depart again, but the speediest airlines accomplish the turnaround in 20 minutes. Once a plane arrives at the gate, the crew has 20 minutes to prepare it for the next takeoff.

Imagine the arrival of a Boeing 737. On board are 130 passengers, 4,000 pounds of luggage, and 2,000 pounds of freight. All must be removed and then replaced by an equivalent number of people and poundage of cargo. The following procedures occur: (1) As passengers disembark, the pilot loads flight plan information into the aircraft computer; (2) workers clean the cabin; (3) caterers replenish food, drinks, and snacks; (4) a fuel truck loads 5,300 gallons of fuel into the wings; (5) baggage crews unload luggage and freight; (6) new people board, and luggage and freight are loaded; and (7) ramp agents "push" the plane away from the gate.

A number of tactics are used to speed up the turnaround times. Six or seven baggage employees are used instead of three or four. Flight attendants inventory leftovers and tell the pilots, who call ahead so caterers know exactly what is needed. Cleaners do a less-than-perfect job, tidying up on an as-needed basis. Passengers face stricter rules regarding arrival times and carry-on luggage. (Southwest Airlines saves even more boarding time by not assigning seats.) And the crew really has to hustle.

Some crew members complain about the time pressure, and passengers lose some amenities. But business travelers now are a little more likely to be able to complete their business in one day.

Airlines that significantly reduce turnaround times can get more flights daily out of their planes, and can sell thousands more tickets per day.

Source: C. Quintanilla, "New Airline Fad: Faster Airport Turnarounds," *The Wall Street Journal*, August 4, 1994, pp. B1, B2. ●

TABLE 2.10

Contingency
perspective

Key concepts

Situational contingencies influence the strategies, structures, and processes that result in high performance.

There is more than one way to reach a goal.

Managers may adapt their organizations to the situation.

Contributions

Identified major contingencies.

Argued against universal principles of management.

Limitations

Not all critical contingencies have been identified.

Theory may not be applicable to all managerial issues.

CONTINGENCY PERSPECTIVE

Building on systems theory ideas, the **contingency perspective** refutes universal principles of management by stating that a variety of factors, both internal and external to the firm, may affect the organization's performance.[22] Thus, there is no "one best way" to manage and organize, because circumstances vary. For example, a universal strategy of offering low-cost products would not succeed in a market that is not cost conscious.

Situational characteristics are called **contingencies.** Understanding contingencies helps a manager know which sets of circumstances dictate which management actions. You will learn the recommendations for the major contingencies throughout this text. The contingencies include

1. The rate of change and degree of complexity in the organization's external environment.
2. The internal strengths and weaknesses of the organization.
3. The values, goals, skills, and attitudes of managers and workers in the organization.
4. The types of tasks, resources, and technologies the organization uses.

With an eye to these contingencies, a manager may categorize the situation and then choose the proper competitive strategy, organization structure, or management process for the circumstances.

Researchers continue to identify key contingency variables and their effects on management issues. As you read the topics covered in each chapter, you will notice similarities and differences among management situations and the appropriate responses. This perspective should represent a cornerstone of your own approach to management. Keep it in mind.

Table 2.10 summarizes the contingency perspective.

CHANGE AND THE FUTURE OF MANAGEMENT

Times pass, and things change. This may sound obvious, but it isn't to those managers who sit by idly while their firms fail to adapt to changing times. Competitors from other countries seem to come from nowhere and snatch market share. New technologies change how we work, how we produce, and what we can produce. Change continually creates both new opportunities and new demands for lowering costs and for achieving greater innovation, quality, and speed.

The essential facts about change are these: First, change is happening more rapidly and dramatically than at any other time in history. Second, if you don't anticipate change and adapt to it, you and your firm will not survive in a competitive business world.

Here is a brief introduction to just a few of the major trends currently having profound effects on the practice of management. We will revisit these topics in later chapters.

GLOBALIZATION

For U.S. and non–U.S. managers alike, isolationism is a thing of the past.[23] This must be so for organizations to survive worldwide competition in a global marketplace. U.S. companies are no longer the unrivaled stars of the business world. The great companies of the world now include Sony, Honda, Bayer, and BMW. After complete dominance of the banking world by U.S. banks just a few years ago, many of the world's 10 largest banks now are Japanese.

Multinational enterprises have sales offices and production facilities in countries all over the world. Corporations such as Reuters, Bertelsmann, Citicorp, ASEA Brown Boveri, and Nestlé are "stateless": They operate worldwide without reference to national borders.[24] Even small firms that do not operate on a global scale must make important strategic decisions based on international considerations. Many small companies export their goods. Many domestic firms assemble their products in other countries. And *every* organization is under pressure to improve its products in the face of intense competition from high-quality foreign producers. Firms today must ask themselves, "How can we be the best in the world?"

TOTAL QUALITY

Everyone connected with the business world in the past decade has heard a great deal about quality, and total quality management, or TQM. You read about the importance of high-quality products in Chapter 1, as one of the four pillars of competitive advantage. **Total quality management** refers broadly to an integrative management approach to customer satisfaction through a wide variety of tools and techniques meant to achieve high-quality goods and services.[25]

In earlier years, the traditional approach to quality was to check work after it was completed and then eliminate defects, using inspection and statistical data to determine whether products were up to standards. But then W. Edwards Deming, J. M. Juran, and other quality gurus convinced managers to take a more complete approach to achieving *total* quality. TQM includes *preventing defects* before they occur, achieving *zero defects* in manufacturing, *designing* products for quality, and providing quality services as well as goods. The goal is to solve and then eradicate at the front-end all quality-related problems.

TQM is still evolving.[26] A myriad of techniques, and many ideas you will read about in later chapters, fall under the huge TQM umbrella. Some of the general principles are:[27]

1. Do it right the first time to eliminate costly rework.
2. Listen to and learn from customers and employees.
3. Build teamwork, trust, and mutual respect.
4. Make continuous improvement an everyday matter.

The TQM philosophy of *continuous improvement* inspires people throughout the company to constantly upgrade and do better everything the company does. This can entail improving anything from the company's products to its methods of production to its ways of managing its people. Many of the ideas you read about in this book can be implemented in the spirit of continuous improvement.

Germany's superb Mittelstand (mid-sized companies) have a passion for continuous improvement, and they abhor the status quo.[28] They work to stay ahead of the competition, but they don't do this by focusing on the competition. This is because they themselves are the market pacesetters. They set the pace because they focus constantly on outdoing themselves.

THE LEARNING ORGANIZATION

As the old rules for doing business become obsolete, firms must be flexible and adaptable to rapidly changing times. Firms, like people, must continually learn new things and avoid obsolescence. Rather than merely reacting to change, they must *anticipate* change and stay ahead of it.

In the **learning organization**, employees are given the opportunity to know what's going on, think constructively about important issues, look for opportunities to learn new things, and seek creative solutions to problems.[29] Learning organizations are committed to openness to new ideas, to generating new knowledge, and to spreading information and knowledge. Learning organizations seek high levels of collaboration among people from different business disciplines. Obviously, learning organizations are more successful at continuous improvement.

Companies like McKinsey, 3M, Sony, Johnson & Johnson, Corning, Mitsubishi, and General Electric are learning organizations. The best management practices you will learn about in this book are found at companies that are doing better than the competition because they are willing to learn new things.

REENGINEERING

Sometimes firms need to do more than merely change, improve, and learn; they need to reinvent themselves to achieve quantum leaps in performance. Rather than improving things by merely fixing them, **business reengineering** is the process of starting all over from scratch, rebuilding the company and overhauling its ways of doing business. Reengineering, according to its proponents, is to the next revolution in business what Adam Smith's specialization of labor was to the Industrial Revolution.

Two of the best-known business reengineering consultants are Michael Hammer and James Champy. They see reengineering as the fundamental rethinking and redesign of all business processes, with the goal of achieving dramatic improvement in the critical performance measures of cost, quality, innovation, and speed.[30]

Reeingineering takes a systems perspective by improving the quality of raw materials and other key resource inputs, making sure each transformational process adds value to the product, and monitoring satisfaction in the marketplace. Hundreds of companies including Kodak, Hallmark, Bell Atlantic, Taco Bell, and Ford, as well as many small companies, have undergone reengineering in the past several years.[31] IBM Credit, which provides financing for customers who purchase IBM products, now processes in four hours financing requests that previously took six days. IBM Credit now handles 100 times as many deals as before.

TABLE 2.11

Values, old and new

Traditional values	Reengineered values
My boss pays my salary; I must keep my boss happy.	Customers pay all our salaries; I must do what it takes to please them.
I'm just a cog in the wheel; my best strategy is to keep my head down and not make waves.	Every job is essential and important; I get paid for the value I create.
If something goes wrong, I dump the problem onto someone else; why be identified with trouble?	The buck stops here; I must accept ownership of the problems and get them solved.
The more direct reports I have, the more important I am; the one with the biggest empire wins.	I belong to a team; we fail or succeed together, and if we fail, nobody's empire is a winner.
Tomorrow will be just like today; it always has been, so the company's past tells me all I need to know.	Nobody knows what tomorrow holds; constant learning is part of my job.

Source: M. Hammer and J. Champy, "The Promise of Reengineering," *Fortune*, May 3, 1993, pp. 94-97.

Reengineering requires a perspective quite different from traditional management practice. It requires an entirely new set of values, as summarized in Table 2.11. Consider carefully the values in the right-hand column, and use them as a touchstone for thinking about the issues discussed throughout this book.

AN EYE ON THE FUTURE

What are the other major trends that will reshape work for the year 2000? Among other things, it is predicted that (1) the average company will be much smaller than the huge corporations of the past; (2) highly educated, technically oriented "knowledge workers" will replace manufacturing employees as the "worker elite"; (3) the goal of business will be less making a physical product and more providing a service; (4) work will become less routine and predictable and require constant learning and complex thinking; and (5) employees will have more independence than workers of the past, and be expected to know more about the overall business, take on greater responsibility, take risks, and be accountable for business results.[32]

Such a list of predictions is merely an introduction to the forces of change affecting management. Throughout this book, you will learn about how to deal with the evolving issues of workforce diversity, self-managed work teams, new forms of organizations, the natural environment, ethics, and world-class excellence. The theme of change—what is happening now, what lies ahead, how it affects management, and how you can deal with it—permeates this entire book.

What are the implications of these changes for you and your career? How can you best be ready to meet the challenges? You must ask questions about the future, anticipate changes, know your new responsibilities, and be prepared to meet them head-on. We hope you study the remaining chapters with these goals in mind.

KEY TERMS

administrative management, p. 35
bureaucracy, p. 39
business reengineering, p. 46
contingencies, p. 44
contingency perspective, p. 44
economies of scale, p. 30
effectiveness, p. 42
efficiency, p. 42
equifinality, p. 42
Hawthorne Effect, p. 37

human relations, p. 36
learning organization, p. 46
organizational behavior, p. 41
quantitative management, p. 40
scientific management, p. 33
subsystems, p. 42
synergy, p. 43
systematic management, p. 31
systems theory, p. 42
total quality management, p. 45

SUMMARY OF LEARNING OBJECTIVES

Now that you have studied Chapter 2, you should know:

The important classical approaches to management and their strengths and weaknesses.

From the mid-19th century through the early 1950s, the classical approaches to management emerged as managers tried to cope with the growth of American industry. Systematic management represented the beginning of formal management thought in the United States, emphasizing economical operations, adequate staffing, inventory management, and other means of organizational

control. It emphasized the internal operations of manufacturing firms, because most management problems were focused there.

Around the turn of the century, Frederick Taylor introduced scientific management. This approach applied scientific methods to analyzing work in order to determine the "one best way" to complete production tasks. Scientific management made important contributions, achieving higher productivity and efficiency. But it was criticized for being too simplistic and ignoring too many important aspects of management, such as the relationships with the external environment, and the higher levels of the organization.

At about the same time, the administrative management school emerged, with the perspective that management was a profession that could be taught. This approach tried to identify major, overarching principles, adherence to which could achieve superior organizational performance. However, the goal of developing and applying universal prescriptions without qualification ignored the fact that different situations require different management approaches.

In the 1930s, the human relations approach evolved from the Hawthorne Studies. The human relations school highlighted the importance of the psychological and human elements of the organization. Despite its contributions, it made some simplistic prescriptions for improving worker efficiency and ignored economic factors and the formal structure of the organization.

By focusing on formal structure, Max Weber attempted to establish an overall management system based on bureaucracy. Bureaucracy allows efficient performance of many routine activities, but it hinders flexibility and tends to ignore the importance of people and interpersonal relationships.

The important contemporary approaches to management and their strengths and weaknesses.

The contemporary approaches, developed since World War II, have attempted to overcome the limitations of the classical approaches and to propose valid ideas for modern management. The quantitative management approach, with the aid of modern computers, allows managers to consider many variables as they search for optimal solutions to problems. The organizational behaviorists extended the human relations approach to adopt a broader viewpoint that took into consideration the complexities of behavior in organizational processes and introduced ideas of worker participation and self-management that recently have experienced a revival of interest.

Systems theory, which originated in the 1950s, considers organizations as open to their environments rather than as closed systems; stresses the importance of multiple goals, including effectiveness and efficiency at once; recognizes the existence of varying subsystems and methods within the organizations, leading to the concept of equifinality (there is no "one best way" to reach a given goal); and applies the notion of synergy (the whole is greater than the sum of its parts).

Recently, the contingency perspective has dominated the study of management. From the contingency perspective, situational characteristics, or contingencies, dictate the management strategies, structures, and processes that will be most effective. This approach argues that universal principles should not be applied. Rather, managers need to analyze the specific situation, and then, on the basis of their analysis of key contingencies, make decisions regarding the most appropriate approach, or mix of approaches.

The current forces that are shaping management practice and your future career.

Management thought and practice continue to evolve. Current events and trends are shaping the future of business and of managerial work. Among the major forces and ideas now revolutionizing work—and for which you need to be prepared—are globalization, total quality, continuous improvement, the learning organization, and reengineering.

DISCUSSION QUESTIONS

1. Reread this chapter's Setting the Stage, "America's Industrial Revolution." How does today's world compare with the age of the industrial revolution? What is different about today, and what is not so different?

2. What is scientific management? How might today's organization's use it?

3. Table 2.3 lists Fayol's 14 principles of management, first published in 1916. Are they as useful today as they were then? Why or why not?

4. What are the advantages and disadvantages of a bureaucratic organization?

5. In what situations are quantitative management concepts and tools applicable?

6. Describe an open system. Using an example, explain the major elements of systems theory.

7. Why did the contingency perspective become such an important approach to management? Generate a list of contingencies that might affect the decisions you should make as a manager.

8. For each of the management approaches discussed in the chapter, give examples you have seen. How effective or ineffective were they?

9. Consider the future of management. Describe examples of the trends discussed in the chapter. What are the implications for you as you prepare for your career?

10. Of the traditional and reengineered values described in Table 2.11, which ones are most common today? Which ones best describe *you?* Which ones will serve you best in your career? If you need to change, how will you do it?

CONCLUDING CASE

SURVIVAL OF THE FITTEST

IBM, General Motors, and Sears Roebuck were three great, dominant corporations for much of the 20th century. All three were among the top 6 companies in total market value in 1972. Twenty years later, none of them was in the top 20. Sears had absolutely ruled retailing, but now was 81st on the list. What happened?

By the 1990s, the three companies were being called dinosaurs, although they were hardly extinct. They were, however, characterized in *Fortune* as "painfully and wheezingly gasping for breath." Their industries had grown and prospered, but these former leaders had failed to keep up. Their successes and huge size had led to rigid bureaucracy and supreme overconfidence. Sears had a bewildering array of formal bulletins for dealing with every conceivable problem. According to a senior executive, "God forbid there should be a problem that comes up for which there isn't a bulletin. That means the problem's *new*." GM and IBM similarly were unable to act quickly and innovatively; a business partner of IBM's said that working with its bureaucracy was like swimming through peanut butter.

Market changes and new sources of competition rocked all three companies. Customer preferences changed as Kmart and then Wal-Mart offered low-priced alternatives to Sears. But Sears arrogantly looked down on the new stores as inferior and their customers as low-class. Rather than focusing on understanding and satisfying customers, Sears focused on itself and its storied past, and assumed its former greatness would reappear.

GM's story was much the same. It loved the profits it made on large cars, refused to believe consumers would want smaller ones, and presumed the Japanese were incapable of making any car that would sell. Eventually, GM started producing small cars to com-

With the closing of many of its stores, Sears Roebuck faced near extinction. After making major managerial changes, this former giant is gradually regaining prominence.

(Mark Richards/DOT)

pete with the Japanese, but it was far too late. IBM's late move from mainframes to smaller machines followed a similar storyline.

Since 1992, the heads of all three corporations have been replaced. Now Arthur C. Marinez, formerly of Saks Fifth Avenue, heads Sears. John Smith is CEO of GM. Louis Gerstner moved from RJR to the IBM chairmanship.

All three men are working hard to restore their companies to their former eminence. They do not sit by complacently, relishing old images and remembering happier times. They have conducted reality checks: looked at their companies' real strengths and weaknesses, current trends in the business environment, and possibilities for the years ahead. They are taking action to prepare and position their companies for a difficult future.

It can be done. Xerox spent years being arrogant, offering poor-quality products, and losing to superior Japanese competition. But David Kearns helped turn Xerox around. He did it by focusing intensely on improving quality. Can IBM, Sears, and GM also find a way? No doubt, the companies will survive—but will they return to greatness?

QUESTIONS

1. What themes from Chapter 2 are reflected in the troubles of IBM, GM, and Sears?

2. To what extent are the struggles of these three companies the fault of management? To what extent are corporate failures within management's control?

3. Can a company be successful without eventually encountering or developing the problems of these companies?

4. How are IBM, Sears, and GM doing today?

Source: C. J. Loomis, "Dinosaurs?" *Fortune,* May 3, 1993, pp. 36–42.

VIDEO CASE

THE EVOLUTION OF MANAGEMENT

The management profession, as we know it today, is relatively new, even though the issues and problems that confront managers have existed for thousands of years. Management emerged as a formal discipline at the turn of the century, when rapid industrialization called for better-skilled management of natural resources, capital, and labor. The various management approaches that have been developed can be divided into two major groups: classical and contemporary approaches.

The classical approaches, which extended from the mid-19th century through the early 1950s, emerged as managers tried to cope with the growth of American industry. These approaches were systematic management, scientific management, administrative management, human relations, and bureaucracy.

Systematic management represented the beginning of formal management thought in the United States. It emphasized the way in which manufacturing firms operated because most management problems were focused on manufacturing.

Scientific management was introduced around the turn of the century by Frederick Taylor, an engineer who applied scientific methods to analyze work and determine the best way to complete production tasks. Taylor stressed the importance of hiring and training the proper workers to do those tasks. One of the most famous examples of the application of scientific management is that the factory Henry Ford built to produce the Model T. Ford's used scientific management principles to yield higher productivity and efficiency. For example, by 1914, chassis assembly time had been trimmed from almost 13 hours to 1.5 hours.

Administrative management emerged at about the same time and emphasized the perspective of senior managers within the organization. It viewed management as a profession that could be taught.

The human relations approach to management evolved from the Hawthorne studies conducted from 1924 to 1932 at the Western Electric Company outside Chicago. Various working conditions, particularly lighting, were altered to determine the effects of these changes on productivity. But researchers, led by Harvard professor Elton Mayo, were ultimately unable to determine any relationship between factory lighting and productivity levels. This led the researchers to believe the productivity was affected more by psychological and social factors. This approach highlighted the importance of the human element in the organization. However, critics believed the human relations philosophy of "the happy worker as a productive worker" was too simplistic.

The bureaucracy approach to management was developed by Max Weber, a German sociologist and social historian. He attempted to establish an overall management system by focusing on a structured, formal network of relationships among specialized positions in an organization. Bureaucracy allowed efficient performance of many routine activities.

The contemporary approaches to management, which have been developed since World War II, attempted to overcome the limitations of the classical approaches. The contemporary approaches include quantitative management, organizational behavior, systems theory, and the contingency perspective.

Quantitative management was aided by the development of modern computers. It emphasizes the application of a formal, mathematical model to management decisions and problems.

The organizational behavior approach to management promotes employee effectiveness through an understanding of the complex nature of individual, group, and organizational processes.

The systems theory of management, which originated in the 1950s, was a major effort to overcome the limitations of the earlier approaches by attempting to view, the organization as a whole system. Systems theory introduced the concept of equifinality—that there is no "one best way" to reach a goal. And it stresses the notion of synergy—that the whole is greater than the sum of its parts.

The contingency perspective has most recently dominated the study of management. It asserts that situational characteristics, or contingencies, determine the management strategies that will be most effective. This approach argues that no universal principle should *always* be applied. Rather, managers, like those at Trek Bicycle, analyze situations and then, based on their analysis of key contingencies, make decisions regarding the most appropriate ways to manage. Trek, based in rural Wisconsin, has a very open-minded approach to managing, and meeting customer needs.

But the evolution of management doesn't end there. Management thought and practice continues to evolve. Current events and trends are shaping the future of business and management. Among the major forces now revolutionizing management are: globalization, learning organization, total quality management, and reengineering.

Globalization refers to the rise of multinational enterprises in the ever-expanding global marketplace. Even small firms that don't operate on a global scale must make important strategic decisions based on international considerations.

The learning organization is committed to openness, new ideas, generating new knowledge, and spreading information and knowledge to others. Continuing dialogue and open-mindedness with an eye toward achieving the organization's goals are the foremost concern. Tellabs, a Chicago-area manufacturer of telecommunications products and services, is a learning organization that has emphasized innovation, teams, and mentoring. It seems to be working. Tellabs' stock has increased by more than 1,600 percent over the last five years, outperforming every other publicly traded stock in the nation.

Total quality management refers to an approach to management that produces customer satisfaction by providing high quality goods and services. Its goal is to solve and then eliminate all quality-related problems. First National Bank of Chicago has an aggressive quality program that includes weekly performance review meetings. In the meetings, managers analyze dozens of charts that are designed to monitor the quality of their performance.

First National's Rich Gilgan said, "You can't manage what you don't understand. An you don't understand what you don't measure."

Finally, business reengineering is the process of starting all over to rebuild the company and overhaul its ways of doing business. The goal of reengineering is to achieve dramatic improvements in critical performance measures including cost, quality innovation, and speed. Reengineering requires a way of thinking that's quite different from traditional management practices.

From the classical approaches, through the contemporary approaches, and into the forces now revolutionizing management, the history of past efforts, triumphs, and failures has become the guide to future management practice. Since the mid-19th century, change has been the constant in the evolution of management. The marketplace keeps changing, the technology keeps changing, and the workforce keeps changing. Today's manager must learn how to deal with the forces of change affecting management. Only by understanding the implications of change and the challenges it presents will you be prepared to meet them head-on.

CRITICAL THINKING QUESTIONS

1. In general, how do contemporary approaches to management differ from classical approaches?

2. What are some modern organizational problems that are a result of classical approaches to managing?

3. The Hawthorne studies are frequently cited as a turning point in management thought. What is the significance of this research?

EXPERIENTAL EXERCISES

2.1 Approaches to Management

Objectives

1. To help you conceive a wide variety of management approaches.
2. To clarify the appropriateness of different management approaches in different situations.

Instructions

Your instructor will divide your class randomly into groups of four to six people each. Acting as a team, with everyone offering ideas and one person serving as official recorder, each group will be responsible for writing a one-page memo to your present class. Subject matter of your group's memo will be "My advice for managing people today is . . . " The fun part of this exercise (and its creative element) involves writing the memo from the viewpoint of the person assigned to your group by your instructor.

Among the memo viewpoints your instructor may assign are:

- An ancient Egyptian slave master (building the great pyramids).
- Henri Fayol (refer to The Classical Era in this chapter).
- Frederick Taylor (refer to The Classical Era).
- Mary Parker Follett (refer to The Behavioral Era).
- Douglas McGregor (refer to The Modern Era).

- A contingency management theorist (The Modern Era).
- A Japanese auto company executive.
- The chief executive officer of IBM in the year 2030.
- Commander of the Starship Enterprise II in the year 3001.
- Others, as assigned by your instructor.

Use your imagination, make sure everyone participates, and try to be true to any historical facts you've encountered. Attempt to be as specific and realistic as possible. Remember, the idea is to provide advice about managing people from another point in time (or from a particular point of view at the present time).

Make sure you manage your 20-minute time limit carefully. A recommended approach is to spend 2 to 3 minutes putting the exercise into proper perspective. Next, take about 10 to 12 minutes brainstorming ideas for your memo, with your recorder jotting down key ideas and phrases. Have your recorder use the remaining time to write your group's one-page memo, with constructive comments and help from the others. Pick a spokesperson to read your group's memo to the class.

Source: R. Krietner and A. Kinichi, *Organization Behavior,* 3d ed. (Burr Ridge, Ill.: Richard D. Irwin, 1994), pp. 30–31.

2.2 The University Grading System Analysis

Objectives

1. To learn to identify the components of a complex system.
2. To better understand organizations as systems.
3. To visualize how a change in policy affects the functioning of an organization system.

Instructions

1. Assume that your university has decided to institute a pass–fail system of grading instead of the letter-grade system it presently has. Apply the systems perspective learned from this chapter to understanding this decision.

2. Answer the questions on the Grading System Analysis Worksheet individually, or in small groups, as directed by your instructor.

Discussion Questions

Share your own or your group's responses with the entire class. Then answer the following questions.

1. Did you diagram the system in the same way?
2. Did you identify the same system components?
3. Which subsystems will be affected by the change?
4. How do you explain differences in your responses?

GRADING SYSTEM ANALYSIS WORKSHEET

Description

1. What subsystems compose the system (the university)? Diagram the system.

   _____

   _____

   _____

   _____

   _____

   _____

2. Identify in this system: inputs, outputs, transformations, feedback, system boundaries.

   _____

   _____

   _____

   _____

   _____

   _____

Diagnosis

3. Which of the subsystems will be affected by the change; that is, what changes are likely to occur throughout the system as a result of the policy change?

   _____

   _____

   _____

   _____

   _____

   _____

   _____

Source: J. Gordon, *A Diagnostic Approach to Organizational Behavior* (Englewood Cliffs, N.J.: Prentice-Hall, 1983), p. 38. Reprinted with permission of Prentice-Hall, Inc., Englewood Cliffs, N.J.

3

THE EXTERNAL ENVIRONMENT

The essence of a business is outside itself.

Peter Drucker

After studying Chapter 3, you will know:

1. How environmental forces influence organizations, as well as how organizations can influence their environments.

2. How to make a distinction between the macroenvironment and the competitive environment.

3. Why organizations should attend to economic and social developments in the international environment.

4. How to analyze the competitive environment in order to formulate strategy.

5. How environmental management strategies can be used to shape external forces.

MERCK HAS A BITTER PILL TO SWALLOW

For seven years running, Merck was the most admired company in *Fortune*'s annual survey of U.S. corporate reputations, and the undisputed champion in America's most profitable major industry—prescription drugs. Merck was "king of the hill," with an enviable view of its dominion. Then suddenly the hill started to shake and crumble, and Merck began to stumble. Because it did not respond quickly enough to sweeping environmental change, Merck found itself in a downward spiral. The same thing has happened to leaders in other industries, such as IBM, Sears, and General Motors. Their stories sound remarkably similar.

In an era of health care reform, the pharmaceutical industry is becoming increasingly turbulent, and the long-term impact of external pressures is still not clear. About 60 million Americans are now covered by managed care groups, such as health maintenance organizations (HMOs). Estimates are that within a decade more than 90 percent of Americans will have their drug costs included in some kind of managed health care plan. This trend represents a fundamental shift in the balance of power between buyers and sellers of prescription drugs. Instead of individual doctors making purchasing decisions, plan managers—many of whom are MBA types—are negotiating contracts with a fierce determination to lower costs. Because HMOs and other managed care plans buy drugs in bulk, they demand big discounts. As a consequence, even the mightiest drugmakers are learning they must bargain to secure a sale. For the first time ever, Merck has had to cut prices on its most profitable drugs.

In this era of health care reform, Merck has had to cut prices on its most profitable prescription drugs for the first time ever.
(Garry Gay/The Image Bank)

Beyond cutting prices, environmental changes have led even the major players to rethinking every aspect of how they do business. In the past, Merck thrived as the technological leader in high-priced medicines, many of which were safeguarded by patent protection. Of the 30 biggest-selling drugs in the United States, 14 will be off patent by the end of 1996. This leaves about $10 billion in annual sales vulnerable to copying by generic-drug houses. And while Merck's product line is still the envy of the industry (with some 16 drugs each having yearly revenues over $100,000), there has been a slowdown in advances in traditional chemistry-based research. The new breakthroughs are in biotechnology. Merck's reluctance to embrace new research methods in biotech has significantly hurt its prospects for the future.

To compete, Merck and several other drugmakers have not only cut prices but opened their own generic units that appeal to HMOs and third-party payers such as insurance companies and corporate benefit plans. To cut costs internally, Merck set aside $775 million for restructuring charges in 1993 and paid 2,100 of its employees to take early retirement. Since 1991, Merck has cut its direct sales force to about 2,500 (an 8 percent reduction). Industrywide, pharmaceutical firms have sliced more than 40,000 jobs, saving millions of dollars.

In addition, Merck has made a bold and controversial move acquiring Medco Containment Services, the fast-growing mail-order distributor of pharmaceuticals. The $6 billion purchase of Medco by Merck is a venture into uncharted waters. Medco has been growing at 35 percent a year by riding the very waves that have threatened to capsize Merck. Medco contracts with big medical plan sponsors—companies, unions, and HMOs—that seek to lower the cost of prescription drugs. Merck's then CEO, P. Roy Vagelos, argued that to enhance flexibility and adapt to rapid changes in the pharmaceutical industry, he wanted to create a "new kind of zebra," a dramatically different organization from what existed in either company at the time.

However, on taking over as Merck's new CEO, Raymond Gilmartin discovered that the acquisition of Medco had strained relationships with both independent and organized community pharmacists. These pharmacists, which distribute Merck's drugs, felt betrayed by Merck's partnering with the mail-order outfit. They see the mail-order business directly hurting their business, and they may be right.

Most observers believe these struggles are unavoidable in Merck's response to environmental forces affecting the industry. For now, the people at Merck have stopped the free-fall, and may indeed have positioned the company well for the future. Profits in 1994 were up 11 percent to $784.8 million, but it will take some time to see how it all settles out.

Sources: Joseph Weber and Sunita Wadekare Bhargava, "Drugmakers Get a Taste of Their Own Medicine," *Business Week,* April 26, 1993, pp. 104–5; Joseph Weber and Stephanie Anderson, "Withdrawal Symptoms: Drugmakers Are Waking Up to a Nightmare," *Business Week,* August 2, 1993, pp. 20–21; Joseph Weber and John Carey, "Merck Is Showing Its Age," *Business Week,* August 23, 1993, pp. 72–74; John Lindstrom, "Merck Taps Young Marketer as President," *Business Marketing,* January 1993, p. 22; Brian O'Reilly, "Why Merck Married the Enemy," *Fortune,* September 20, 1993, pp. 60–64; Michael F. Conlan, "Drug Industry in Turmoil: What's It Mean for Pharmacy?" *Drug Topics,* September 6, 1993, pp. 46–50; and Steve Sakson, "Drug Firms Earning More as Drug Prices Remain Stable," *Centre Daily Times* (State College, Penn.), October 24, 1994.

*M*erck, like other organizations, is struggling in an environment characterized by intense competition, economic difficulties, technological change, uncertainties about government policies, and other factors that threaten its future. In this chapter we will discuss these and other forces outside the firm that form the external context in which managers and their organizations operate.

As you learned in the first two chapters, organizations are open systems that are affected by, and in turn affect, their external environments. By **external environment,** we mean all relevant forces outside the firm's boundaries. By *relevant,* we mean factors to which managers must pay attention to help their organizations compete effectively and survive.

Many of these factors are uncontrollable. Companies large and small are victimized or buffeted about by recession, government interference, competitors' actions, and so forth. But their being uncontrollable does not mean that managers can ignore such forces, use them as excuses for poor performance, and try to just get by. Managers must stay abreast of and deal constantly with external developments. Moreover, as we will discuss later in the chapter, it sometimes *is* possible to influence components of the external environment. We will examine ways in which organizations can do just that.

Figure 3.1 shows the external environment of a firm. The firm exists in its **competitive environment**, which is composed of the firm and competitors, suppliers, customers, new entrants, and substitutes. At the more general level is **macroenvironment,** which includes the political environment, economic conditions, and other fundamental factors that generally affect all organizations.

A LOOK AHEAD

In this chapter, we discuss the basic characteristics of an organization's environment and the importance of that environment for strategic management. Later chapters will elaborate on many of the basic environmental forces introduced here. For example, technology will be discussed again in Chapter 20. The global environment gets a thorough treatment in Chapter 8, which is devoted entirely to international management. Other chapters focus on ethics, social responsibility, and the natural environment. Chapter 21 reiterates the theme that recurs throughout this text: Organizations must continually change because environments continually change.

FIGURE 3.1

The external
environment of
the firm

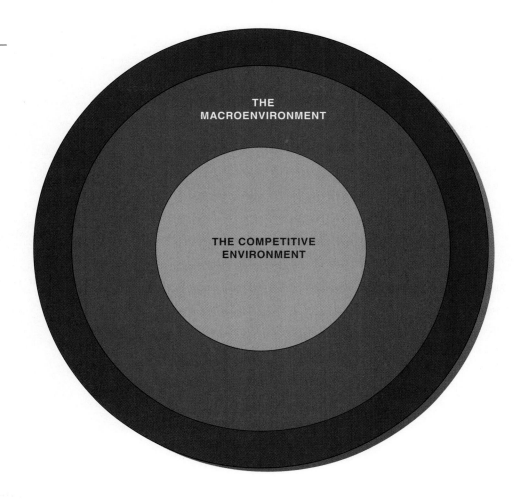

THE MACRO-ENVIRONMENT

All organizations operate in a macroenvironment, which is defined by the most general elements in the external environment that can potentially influence strategic decisions. Although a top executive team may have unique internal strengths and ideas about its goals, it still must consider external factors before taking action.

As Figure 3.2 illustrates, the general macroenvironment includes international, legal, political, economic, technological, demographic, and social/natural components.

THE INTERNATIONAL ENVIRONMENT

As mentioned in Chapter 2, it has become critical to keep abreast of developments abroad. Key recent developments include European unification, the downfall of communism, the rise of the Pacific Rim, NAFTA, and the fall of the peso.

European Unification
Europe is integrating economically to form the biggest market in the world. In concept, the European Union (EU) will allow goods, services, capital, and human resources to flow freely across national borders. Originally, the EU was composed of the following 12 nations:

- Belgium
- Denmark
- France
- Germany
- Greece
- Ireland
- Italy
- Luxembourg
- Netherlands
- Portugal
- Spain
- United Kingdom

FIGURE 3.2

The
Macroenvironment

Recently, these countries voted to add Sweden, Finland, and Austria to their ranks, and soon they will admit Norway. Their goal is to be the third economic superpower, right behind the United States and Japan. As a single entity, the EU has a population of 320 million and a gross national product of over $4 trillion.

GE's Jack Welch says, "The new Europe will make our experience with Japan seem like a cakewalk."[1] The impact is hard to predict, but there are many possibilities.[2] U.S. exports to Europe could be replaced by the goods of European producers; European exports could replace U.S. products in other markets; U.S. capital could flow into Europe to the detriment of capital formation and productivity growth in the United States. Another possibility is a "Fortress Europe" that restricts trade with countries outside EU walls.

Unification will create a more competitive Europe. The EU's share of the world's top 100 industrial firms is rising. The community is pursuing an active industrial police to enhance its competitiveness in information technology. It is making fast gains in semiconductors and is restructuring in defense and aerospace. These and other developments could adversely affect U.S. exports and employment.[3]

The year 1992 was the official date for the dropping of trade barriers among member countries. However, the pace of unification has been slower than anticipated. In part this has been due to a global recession, but there are other structural issues within Europe that need to be corrected for the EU to function effectively. In particular, Western Europeans on average work fewer hours, earn more pay, take longer vacations, and enjoy far more social entitlements than their counterparts in North America and Asia. To be competitive in a global economy, Europeans must increase their level of productivity. In the past, powerful trade unions have fiercely defended social benefits, and local governments have regulated the labor markets. Both these actions have encouraged companies such as Siemens

This balloon depicts the flags of the 12 nations that comprise the European Union. (*Courtesy European Commission Delegation, Washington, DC*)

and ABB Asea Brown Boveri Ltd. to move operations abroad. Now it appears that labor markets are being deregulated and there are more incentives to create jobs.[4]

The consensus among U.S. observers is that the United States must remain vigilant to ensure that a Fortress Europe does not close itself to U.S. goods and services. Management and labor must work cooperatively to achieve high levels of quality that will make U.S. products and services attractive to consumers in Europe and other markets across the world. The United States needs not only managers who will stay on top of worldwide developments and manage high-quality, efficient organizations but a well-educated, well-trained, and continually *retrained* labor force to remain competitive with the Europeans, the Japanese, and other formidable competitors.[5]

The Downfall of Communism

The Soviet Union has disbanded. This has created major changes not only in the military balance of power but in the global business environment. Similarly, the Berlin Wall has fallen and (the former) East Germany and Eastern and Central European countries have denounced communism. Now these countries are making major strides toward capitalism. **Privatization,** or the sale of government-run enterprises to private owners, is occurring all over the globe at an unprecedented rate. Market economies are taking root.

These events are providing new markets for goods and services, new sources of labor and raw materials, and the potential for new competitors. Already the airline industries in Eastern Europe and the former USSR are being privatized, and carriers in these countries are partnering with foreign investors to expand into more lucrative international markets.[6] Organizations worldwide are eyeing the region for new business and investment opportunities. And Poland, Hungary, and the Czech Republic are pressing for membership in the European Union.

The Pacific Rim

Among the Pacific Rim countries, Japan dominated world attention during the 1980s. Japan's aggressiveness and success have shaken U.S. confidence and competitiveness. But Japan is hardly the only important global player from the Pacific region.

Taiwan is booming, thanks to its supply of cheap labor and capital for small, entrepreneurial start-ups. China is developing and becoming more prosperous. Even Japan is concerned about the countries known as the "four tigers" or the "four dragons": South Korea, Taiwan, Singapore, and Hong Kong. Korea is foremost among them; its immediate goal is to become one of the world's 10 most technologically advanced nations by the year 2000. Already the four dragons, along with other Asian growth nations like Thailand, Malaysia, and the Philippines, account for more trade with the United States than Japan does.[7]

For the past several years, the 18 member countries of the Asia-Pacific Economic Cooperation (APEC) have been working to reduce trade barriers, and establish general rules for investment and policies that encourage international commerce. Although the U.S. has been trading with member countries such as Australia, Singapore, Malaysia, Japan, Indonesia, China, and South Korea, APEC holds much the same promise as NAFTA and the EU in facilitating and strengthening international business relationships. Member countries represent 40 percent of the world's population and 50 percent of the world's economic output.[8]

North America

The **North American Free Trade Agreement (NAFTA)** combined the economies of the United States, Canada, and Mexico into the world's largest trading bloc with more than 370 million customers and approximately $6.5 trillion in total GNP. Within the next 10 years, virtually all U.S. industrial exports into Mexico and Canada will be duty free. Although the United States has had a longer-standing agreement with Canada, Mexico has quickly emerged as the United States' third-largest trading partner as a result

This prospective buyer is looking at a General Electric Hotpoint refrigerator in a Mexico City chain store. In the wake of NAFTA's passage, such customers will help keep American exports growing. *(Sergio Dorantes)*

of NAFTA. U.S. industries that have benefited in the short run include capital-goods suppliers, manufacturers of consumer durables, grain producers and distributors, construction equipment manufacturers, the auto industry, as well as the financial industry, which now has privileged access into a previously protected market.

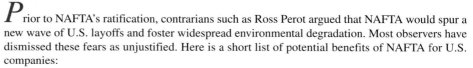

WHY NAFTA MAKES GOOD SENSE

*P*rior to NAFTA's ratification, contrarians such as Ross Perot argued that NAFTA would spur a new wave of U.S. layoffs and foster widespread environmental degradation. Most observers have dismissed these fears as unjustified. Here is a short list of potential benefits of NAFTA for U.S. companies:

NAFTA will create more jobs than it destroys. Some have claimed that NAFTA will cost "millions" of U.S. jobs. In truth, there will be some job losses in low-wage, labor-intensive businesses that have survived thanks to governmental protection. The pain of these losses will be eased by phasing out tariffs over time and by establishing a new federal program to retrain displaced workers. However, by tearing down restrictions on imports, any job losses caused by NAFTA will be more than offset by boosting exports to Mexico and Canada, thereby increasing demand for jobs in high-skill, high-wage American industries such as telecommunications, computers, automobiles, finance, and the like. Estimates are that NAFTA will provide modest job growth of up to 200,000 U.S. jobs in the first three to four years.

Low Mexican wages will not prompt an exodus of U.S. manufacturers. NAFTA critics tended to highlight the 7-to-1 ratio between U.S. and Mexican wages. However, if we consider that Mexican workers are only one-eighth as productive—and require enormous expense for training—the true labor bill is no bargain south of the Rio Grande. For example, estimates suggest that a car that costs $8,770 to build in the United States would cost $9,180 to build in Mexico and ship back. In fact, some companies such as GM, AT&T, and Xerox have taken advantage of open borders to shift Mexican production back to more efficient plants in the United States. Other companies such as Mercedes Benz and BMW have announced plans to build automotive plants, not in Mexico, but in South Carolina and Alabama.

U.S. exports to Mexico will continue to rise. Since Mexico opened its economy to foreign trade and investment in 1987, U.S. exports have increased over 300 percent. In 1990, the United States had a $2.1 billion trade deficit with Mexico, but by 1992 that number had switched to a $5.3 billion surplus. Over this same period, Mexico's economy grew at about twice the rate of the United States economy. If this growth continues, exports to Mexico should continue to grow also since Mexican families will be able to afford more consumer products such as televisions, refrigerators, washing machines, and automobiles.

Source: Ann Reilly Dowd, "Let's Just Say Yes to NAFTA," *Fortune*, November 29, 1993, pp. 108–9. ●

Despite the potential benefits of NAFTA, Mexico will need to bolster its infrastructure and take care of troubling environmental issues in order to support its economic growth. Mexico has recently established a comprehensive statute for environmental regulation to address issues such as air pollution, hazardous waste, water pollution, and noise pollution. Surprisingly, Mexico has very strict laws protecting natural resources, many of which were fashioned after U.S. laws. However, there has not been sufficient enforcement of those laws. Mexico has some way to go in developing a strong environmental services industry to handle environmental protection and cleanup. Both the U.S. and Mexico are committing up to $8 billion for environmental protection.[9]

The Rest of the World

We can't begin to fully discuss all the important developments, markets, and competitors shaping the global environment. But we can convey the immense potential for other major developments and new competitive threats and opportunities.

For example, globalization so far has left out three huge, high-potential regions of the world: the Middle East, Africa, and Latin America.[10] Together these regions comprise a major share of the world's natural resources and are among the fastest-growing economies. Their potential has not begun to be realized.

Also, consider the opportunities in individual countries. Few North Americans can point out Mauritius on a map. Mauritius is a 730-square-mile island in the middle of the Indian Ocean. The Esquel group, a Hong Kong–based multinational, has six knitting factories, a woolen spinning and dyeing mill, and a fully computerized package dyeing mill for cotton on the island. Exports grew by 30 percent per year in the 1980s, and the United States was a particularly good customer. Other African pioneers undergoing major economic reforms are Ghana, Malawi, Tanzania, and Zambia.

THE LEGAL/POLITICAL ENVIRONMENT

U.S. government policies both impose strategic constraints and provide opportunities. The government can affect business opportunities through tax laws, economic policies, and international trade rulings. One example of restraint on business action is the U.S. government's standards regarding bribery. In some countries, bribes and kickbacks are common and expected ways of doing business. But for U.S. firms, these are illegal practices. Indeed, some U.S. businesses have been fined for using bribery when competing internationally.

Regulators are specific government organizations in a firm's more immediate task environment. Regulatory agencies such as the Occupational Safety and Health Administration (OSHA), the Interstate Commerce Commission (ICC), the Federal Aviation Administration (FAA), the Equal Employment Opportunity Commission (EEOC), the National Labor Relations Board (NLRB), and the Environmental Protection Agency (EPA) have the power to investigate company practices and take legal action to ensure compliance with the laws.

For example, the Securities and Exchange Commission (SEC) regulates U.S. financial markets; since the insider-trading scandals, the SEC has dramatically changed investment houses' policies and practices. And the Food and Drug Administration (FDA) can prevent a company from selling an unsafe or ineffective product to the public. In the late 1980s, the FDA allowed the first biotechnology products to be marketed, creating the first profits in what will be a hugely profitable industry.

In a world economy, an important governmental influence on business is trade legislation. The United States has an enormous and persistent trade deficit (it imports more than it exports). Traditionally, Republican administrations prefer free trade, without legislation that restricts imports, provides subsidies (e.g., for agricultural products), or otherwise helps U.S. business interests. Democrats, in contrast, often believe the government needs to play an active, protective role in improving U.S. international competitiveness.[11]

The government can offer strategic opportunities. For example, the government has awarded billions of dollars to Rockwell International, General Electric, Boeing Aircraft

Aerospace Division, and McDonnell Douglas to work on the first staffed space station. And when a probusiness administration enters office, antitrust vigilance may be relaxed or deregulation may occur. With deregulation, companies are monitored loosely by the government and are allowed to compete more freely with whatever strategies they prefer.

THE ECONOMY

The international environment is an important contributor to another crucial component of the macroenvironment: the economy. Although most Americans are used to thinking in terms of the U.S. economy, the economic environment is created by complex interconnections among economies of different countries. Wall Street investment analysts begin their workday thinking not just about what the Dow Jones did yesterday but also about how the London and Tokyo exchanges did overnight. Growth and recessions occur worldwide as well as domestically.

The economic environment dramatically affects companies' ability to function effectively and influences their strategic choices. Interest and inflation rates affect the availability and cost of capital, the ability to expand, prices, costs, and consumer demand for products. Unemployment rates affect labor availability and the wages the firm must pay, as well as product demand.

The overriding concern for the U.S. economy in the 1990s is the size of the federal deficit. Because Congress has not been required to balance the budget each year, the federal government may spend more than it takes in. The overspending is covered by loans, in the form of bonds, that the government issues to be paid back in the future. In 1990 alone, the government racked up a debt of $220 billion.[12]

Economic conditions change over time and are difficult to predict. Bull and bear markets come and go. Periods of dramatic growth may be followed by a recession. Every trend undoubtedly will end—but when? Even when times seem good, budget deficits or other considerations create concern about the future.

TECHNOLOGY

Today a company cannot succeed without incorporating into its strategy the astonishing technologies that exist and continue to evolve. Technological advances create new products, production techniques, and ways of managing and communicating.

As technology evolves, new industries, markets, and competitive niches develop. The advent of computers created a huge industry. Early entrants in biotechnology are trying to establish dominant positions, while later entrants work on technological advances that will give them a competitive niche.

New technologies also provide new production techniques. In manufacturing, sophisticated robots perform jobs without suffering fatigue, requiring vacations or weekends off, or demanding wage increases. Until the U.S. steel industry began modernizing its plants, its productivity lagged far behind that of the technologically superior Japanese plants.

New technologies also provide new ways to manage and communicate. Computerized management information systems (MISs) make information available when needed. Computers monitor productivity and note performance deficiencies. Telecommunications allow conferences to take place without requiring people to travel to the same location.

Consider the following discussion of what is happening in the field of telecommunications. As you can see, technological advances create innovations in business. Strategies developed around the cutting edge of technological advances create a competitive advantage; strategies that ignore or lag behind competitors in considering technology lead to obsolescence and extinction. This issue will be addressed in Chapter 20.

TECHNOLOGY CHANGES TELECOMMUNICATIONS

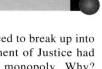

Over a decade ago, American Telephone & Telegraph (AT&T) was forced to break up into smaller companies because Judge Harold Greene and the U.S. Department of Justice had decided that long-distance calling no longer qualified as a natural monopoly. Why? Microwave technology had helped long-distance telephony take to the air—go wireless like the radio before it—and this had opened up some very new possibilities about who could provide long-distance service.

Technology changed the nature of competition in the mid-1980s, and has been changing the telecommunications industry ever since. When everyone moved to microwave technology, the telephone industry experienced excess capacity, so everyone has moved back to more traditional land-lined technologies such as fiber optics—again changing the structure of competition.

Technology has also changed the local telephone market. When spin-off Bell carriers such as Ameritech and Bell Atlantic wanted to change their copper lines to fiber, they found competition from cable television companies, which had already installed coaxial cable. This brought in a whole new set of potential competitors. Add to this fact that cellular technology is taking an ever-increasing share of local calling, and the picture gets even fuzzier. To gain a foothold in cellular technology, AT&T recently acquired McCaw. Meanwhile, MCI put together a consortium of companies to offer "personal communications services" over bands of the radio spectrum recently liberated by the Federal Communications Commission (FCC).

Although it is hard to see the future clearly, it appears that technologies such as fiber optics, digital radio, and cellular communications are merging, thereby putting computers, television, and telecommunications in a position to either compete or cooperate. For example, AT&T and its subsidiary NCR have been exploring plans to build a network of computer servers around the country that would store digitized movies and television shows and distribute them over AT&T's nationwide long-distance network, through connections with cable TV companies and local phone systems. If this "hosting" concept takes off, AT&T will act as navigator of virtual oceans of digitized data. The idea is so compelling that Viacom (owner of MTV) as well as Tele-Communications Inc. (TCI) and Time Warner have partnered with AT&T to pilot test interactive video. Microsoft has talked with cable-TV operators about forming a joint venture called CableSoft that would develop interactive software for TV. These are just a sample of the cooperative arrangements arising from technological innovations in telecommunications. The possibilities seem endless, and the number of "on-ramps" to the information superhighway appears to be growing.

Sources: Bruce W. Radford, "TechnoEconomics: The Life and Death of Unnatural Monopolies," *Public Utilities Fortnightly,* September 15, 1993, p. 45; Charles F. Mason and Richard Karpinski, "Sculpting a New Industry Structure," *Telephony,* April 10, 1993, pp. 88–97; and Bart Ziegler, "American Telephone & Multimedia?" *Business Week,* September 6, 1993, pp. 78–79. ●

DEMOGRAPHICS

Demographics are measures of various characteristics of the people composing groups or other social units. Work groups, organizations, countries, markets, or societies can be described statistically by referring to their members' age, gender, family size, income, education, occupation, and so forth.

Companies must consider workforce demographics in formulating their human resources strategies. Population growth influences the size and composition of the labor force. By 2005, the U.S. civilian labor force, growing at a rate of 1.3 percent annually, is expected to reach approximately 151 million. Fluctuations in the birthrate influence population trends somewhat. In past years, the number of younger workers (16 to 24 years of age) has declined, but now that children of the baby-boom generation are entering the workforce, this age group is expected to grow 13.2 percent by 2005. At the same time, baby boomers themselves are reaching retirement age, so the number of older workers (55 and above) will also rise to about 15 percent of the labor force. Eventually, declining participation in work of older persons will largely offset the increase in the number of persons in this population group.

Immigration is also a factor that significantly influences the U.S. population and labor force. Between 1980 and 1990, immigrants accounted for 39 percent of the increase in U.S. population growth, a trend that has an important impact on the labor force. Immigrants are frequently of working age but have different educational and occupational backgrounds from the rest of the labor force. By 2005, the labor force will be even more diverse than it is today. White males will constitute approximately 38 percent of the labor force, African-Americans 13 percent, Hispanics 16 percent, and Asians and others nearly 6 percent. Together these groups are expected to account for nearly 65 percent of the growth in the labor force by 2005.

Women continue to join the U.S. labor force in record numbers. In 1970, women made up only about one-third of the labor force. By 2005 women are expected to account for over 47 percent, a trend that provides companies with more talent from which to choose.

A more diverse workforce has its advantages, but managers have to make certain they provide equality for women and minorities with respect to employment, advancement opportunities, and compensation. Strategic plans must be made for recruiting, retaining, training, motivating, and effectively utilizing people of diverse demographical backgrounds with the skills needed to achieve the company's mission. Large numbers of single-parent and two-income families with children led to the creation and success of KinderCare and other day care facilities. These demographic trends also led to policies such as parental leaves, part-time employment, flexible work schedules, job sharing, telecommuting, and child care assistance.

The Social and Natural Environments

Social trends in how people think and behave have major implications for management of the labor force, corporate social actions, and strategic decisions about products and markets.

In the late 1970s, it was unfashionable for women pursuing careers to have children; instead, they dedicated themselves to their work, postponing or deciding against having children. In the 1980s, having children became popular again. Today, companies that want to create or maintain a competitive advantage—or that merely hope to stay competitive— are introducing more supportive policies regarding maternal leave (and even paternal leave), flexible working hours, and child care.

A prominent issue in the late 1980s was the involvement of U.S. businesses (and universities) in the apartheid regime in South Africa. Eaton, Bell & Howell, General Electric, Coca-Cola, Procter & Gamble, General Motors, IBM, Honeywell, and Warner Communications were among the first to end their business involvement with South

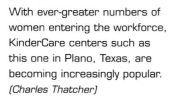

With ever-greater numbers of women entering the workforce, KinderCare centers such as this one in Plano, Texas, are becoming increasingly popular. *(Charles Thatcher)*

Africa.[13] Now with the new government of Nelson Mandela in place there, the trend is toward reinvestment in South Africa by some of these same companies. In the 1990s, protecting our natural environment is a predominant concern. This topic is so important in managerial decision making that we devote an entire chapter to it (Chapter 7).

THE COMPETITIVE ENVIRONMENT

All organizations are affected by the general components of the macroenvironment we have just discussed. Each organization also functions in a closer, more immediate competitive environment. The competitive environment comprises the specific organizations with which the organization interacts. As shown in Figure 3.3, Porter's model of the competitive environment includes current competitors, threat of new entrants, threat of substitutes, suppliers, and customers. Management means more than reacting to and adapting to environments; it can also mean *changing* or shaping the organization's environment. In strategic decision making, Porter's model is an excellent method for analyzing the competitive environment in order to adapt to or shape the nature of competition.

Michael Porter is a professor of corporate strategy at Harvard. As a strategist, prolific writer, and successful consultant, he has influenced thinking and practice in strategic decision making in the past decade. Porter believes the essence of strategy formulation is coping with competition.

COMPETITORS

Of the various components of the competitive environment, competitors within the industry must first deal with one another. When organizations compete for the same customers and try to win market share at the others' expense, all must react to and anticipate their competitors' actions.

The first question to consider is: Who is the competition? Sometimes answers are obvious. Coca-Cola and PepsiCo are competitors, as are the Big Six accounting firms. But sometimes organizations focus too exclusively on old rivalries. Historically, Sears, Roebuck competed with J.C. Penney. However, Sears' real competitors are Kmart and Wal-Mart at the low end; Mervyn's in the middle; Nordstrom at the high end; and a variety of catalogers, such as Spiegel. Xerox Corporation was obsessed with Eastman Kodak's copiers in the 1970s but ignored the smaller Savin, Canon, and other models until it lost half its market share.[14]

FIGURE 3.3

The Porter model of the competitive environment

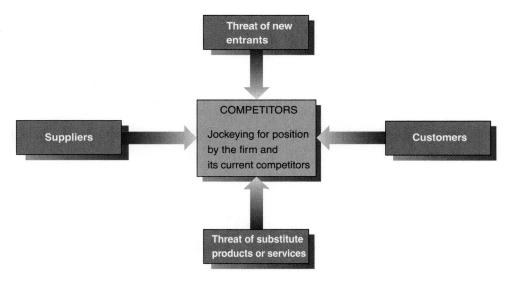

Source: Modified and reprinted by permission of the *Harvard Business Review.* An adaptation of an exhibit from "How Competitive Forces Shape Strategy" by Michael E. Porter (March–April 1979). Copyright © 1979 by the President and Fellows of Harvard College; all rights reserved.

Thus, organizations must identify their competitors, including (1) overseas firms, especially their first, unobtrusive entry into small niches (a traditional Japanese tactic); (2) small domestic firms, especially their entry into tiny, premium markets; (3) big, new domestic companies exploring new markets; (4) strong regional competitors; and (5) unusual entries such as TV home shopping and the explosion of retail catalogers.[15]

Once competitors have been identified, the next step is to analyze how they compete. Competitors use tactics like price reductions, new-product introductions, and advertising campaigns to gain advantage over their rivals. It's essential to understand what competitors are doing when honing your own strategy.

Competition is most intense when there are many direct competitors (including foreign contenders), when industry growth is slow, and when the product or service cannot be differentiated in some way. New, high-growth industries offer enormous opportunities for profits. When an industry matures and growth slows, profits drop. Then, intense competition causes an industry *shakeout:* Weaker companies are eliminated, and the strong companies survive.

THREAT OF NEW ENTRANTS

New entrants into an industry compete with established companies. If many factors prevent new companies from entering the industry, the threat to established firms is less serious. If there are few such **barriers to entry,** the threat of new entrants is more serious. Some major barriers to entry are government policy, capital requirements, brand identification, cost disadvantages, and distribution channels.

The *government* can limit or prevent entry, as when the FDA forbids a new drug entrant. Some industries, such as trucking and liquor retailing, are regulated; more subtle government controls operate in fields such as mining and ski area development. Patents are also entry barriers. When a patent expires (like Polaroid's basic patents on instant photography), other companies (e.g., Kodak) can then enter the market.

Other barriers are less formal but can have the same effect. *Capital requirements* may be so high that companies won't risk or try to raise such large amounts of money. *Brand identification* forces new entrants to spend heavily to overcome customer loyalty. The *cost advantages* established companies hold—due to large size, favorable locations, existing assets, and so forth—also can be formidable entry barriers.

Finally, existing competitors may have such tight *distribution channels* that new entrants have difficulty getting their products or services to customers. For example, established food products already have supermarket shelf space. New entrants must displace existing products with promotions, price breaks, intensive selling, and other tactics.

THREAT OF SUBSTITUTES

Technological advances lead to the development of substitutes for existing products. Sugar producers must cope with NutraSweet™. Fiberglass insulation faces competition from a number of substitutes, including cellulose, styrofoam, and rock wool. Substitute products or services limit an industry's potential. The industry could suffer in earnings and growth unless it improves the quality of its product or launches effective, aggressive marketing campaigns.

SUPPLIERS

Organizations must acquire resources from their environment and convert those resources into products or services to sell. Suppliers provide these resources. Every business must acquire people (supplied by trade schools and universities), raw materials (supplied by producers, wholesalers, and distributors), and capital (supplied by banks and other sources). But suppliers are important to an organization for reasons beyond the resources they provide. Suppliers can raise their prices or provide poor quality goods and services. Labor unions can go on strike, or demand higher wages. Workers may produce defective work. Powerful suppliers, then, can reduce an organization's profits, particularly if the organization cannot pass on price increases to its customers.

Although unionization in the United States has dropped to about 12 percent of the private labor force, labor unions are still a particularly powerful supplier of human resources in some industries, such as steel and autos. Labor unions recruit members, collect dues, and represent and protect employees. Unions ensure that employees are treated fairly with respect to wages, working conditions, job security, and due process appeals.

Traditionally, manufacturing jobs often were unionized. Today clerical workers, teachers, nurses, and other professionals may join unions as well. In fact, a large company with many kinds of jobs may deal with several unions representing different segments of its workforce.

Historically, the relationship between management and labor unions has been adversarial. Troubled labor relations can create higher costs and productivity declines. But declining productivity and high-quality overseas competition can create layoffs. To increase productivity and competitiveness, management and labor are increasingly working together in friendlier relationships. Adolph Coors and J. P. Stevens improved their relationships with the unions. Companies like GM and Ford allowed more labor involvement in decision making, marking a spirit of cooperation that bodes well for the long-term health of the auto industry.[16] Similar efforts took place between the United Steel Workers of America (USWA) and some of the major steel firms, and between AT&T and the Communications Workers.

The organization is at a disadvantage if it is overly dependent on powerful suppliers. A supplier is powerful if the buyer has few other sources of supply or if the supplier has many other buyers. It also is powerful if it has built up switching costs. **Switching costs** are fixed costs buyers face if they change suppliers. For example, once a buyer learns how to operate a supplier's equipment, such as computer software, the buyer faces both economic and psychological costs in changing to a new supplier.

Choosing the right supplier is an important strategic decision. Suppliers can affect manufacturing time, product quality, and inventory levels. The relationship between suppliers and the organization is changing in some companies. Instead of many suppliers and a competitive, distrustful atmosphere, Levi Strauss has limited its heavyweight-denim suppliers to four or five. With these few suppliers, Levi has made long-term commitments to cooperative relationships in which trusted suppliers provide high-quality materials.[17] The close supplier relationship has become a new model for many organizations, such as Ford Motor, that are using a just-in-time manufacturing approach (discussed in Chapter 19).

FORD ELIMINATES SUPPLIER SURPRISE

*E*xecutives at Ford understand very well how good supplier relationships can enhance a company's competitive capability. In an industry moving toward more frequent model changes, shorter product life cycles, and smaller production runs, coordination with suppliers is critical for raising quality and lowering costs. To improve coordination with its network of 1,500 suppliers, Ford has undertaken a number of important initiatives.

To ensure consistently high quality, Ford gives its Q1 quality award to suppliers whose quality has been so dependable that Ford no longer has to inspect their incoming shipments. Suppliers trying to win the Q1 award go through a process of correcting manufacturing inefficiencies and then inviting Ford teams in to visit them to see their progress. The program has been very successful, and Q1 has become the quality standard to which virtually all suppliers aspire. In the steel industry, Q1 awards have been given to Bethlehem Steel, Inland Steel, LTV, and USS.

In addition to setting quality standards for its suppliers, Ford has put in place a program called Direct Data Link (DDL) that provides suppliers with direct access to Ford's inventory control system. With DDL, suppliers have up-to-the minute data on supply requirements in each of Ford's 20 North American assembly plants, 61 manufacturing locations, and 10 parts and supply sites. In the past, Ford employed a staff of about 100 people in Detroit to identify material shortages and notify suppliers of any problems. Now, thanks to DDL, each supplier is responsible for taking care of stock levels and shipments on its own. With DDL, suppliers even have the capability (using a security code) to update Ford's database when they send shipments.

Because suppliers have better and more current information about Ford's needs, there are fewer surprises and emergencies. DDL enables suppliers to run their production schedules in parallel with Ford's, and in some cases suppliers such as Dana Corporation and O'Sullivan Corporation have even used DDL to design their own software systems that extract data and plan production cycles.

These efforts have helped reduce costs and upgrade quality for both Ford and its network of suppliers. In an environment where speed and quality are critical success factors, Ford has made great strides in creating a seamless buyer–supplier relationship.

Sources: Wayne Erickson, "Ford Profits by Letting Suppliers Tap into Systems," *Network World,* July 1, 1991, pp. 1, 49; Joanne Cummings, "Another Bright Idea," *Network World,* November 23, 1993, pp. 31, 34, 36, 37; Brian S. Moskal, "Rx for Success in the Year 2000," *Industry Week,* September 16, 1991, pp. 58–60; "Eliminating Redundant Quality Audits," *Quality,* January 1993, p. 16; Bryan Berry, "For Steelmakers, Quality Is Job Won," *Iron Age,* July 1992, pp. 24–27; and Gary S. Vasilash, "Car Talk: What Every Auto Supplier Ought to Hear," *Production,* October 1992, pp. 34–37. ●

CUSTOMERS

Customers purchase the products or services the organization offers. Without customers, a company won't survive. You are a **final consumer** when you buy a McDonald's hamburger or a pair of jeans from a retailer at the mall. **Intermediate consumers** buy raw materials or wholesale products and then sell to final consumers. Intermediate customers actually make more purchases than individual final consumers do. Examples of intermediate customers include retailers, who buy clothes from wholesalers and manufacturers' representatives before selling them to their customers, and industrial buyers, who buy raw materials (such as chemicals) before converting them into final products.

Like suppliers, customers are important to organizations for reasons other than the money they provide for goods and services. Customers can demand lower prices, higher quality, or more service. They can also play competitors against one another, such as when a car customer (or a purchasing agent) collects different offers and negotiates for the best price.

Customer service means giving customers what they want or need, the way they want it, the first time. This usually depends on the speed and dependability with which an organization can deliver its products or services. Actions and attitudes that mean excellent customer service include:

- Speed of filling and delivering normal orders.
- Willingness to meet emergency needs.
- Merchandise delivered in good condition.
- Readiness to take back defective goods and resupply quickly.
- Availability of installation and repair services and parts.
- Service charges (that is, whether services are "free" or priced separately).[18]

In *all* businesses—services as well as manufacturing—strategies that emphasize good customer service provide a critical competitive advantage.

The organization is at a disadvantage if it depends too heavily on powerful customers. Customers are powerful if they make large purchases or if they can easily find alternative places to buy. If you are the largest customer of a firm, and there are other firms from which you can buy, you have power over that firm, and you are likely to be able to negotiate with it successfully. Your firm's biggest customers—especially if they can buy from other sources—will have the greatest negotiating power over you.

ENVIRONMENTAL ANALYSIS: OPPORTUNITY AND THREATS

Analyzing these five environmental factors—current competitors, threat of new entrants, threat of substitutes, suppliers, and customers—enables a company to identify opportunities and threats in the external environment. Top management can ask:

- Who are our current competitors?
- Are there few or many entry barriers to our industry?
- What substitutes exist for our product or service?
- Is the company too dependent on powerful suppliers?
- Is the company too dependent on powerful customers?

Managers can also try to anticipate future changes in these factors and then decide how best to manage in the competitive environment they have identified.

Porter's competitive analysis can guide many types of strategic decisions, for example, acquisition and divestment decisions. The model helps evaluate the potential of different businesses by assessing their competitive environments. Table 3.1 describes two extreme environments: an attractive environment, which gives a firm a competitive advantage, and an unattractive environment, which puts a firm at a competitive disadvantage.

RESPONDING TO THE ENVIRONMENT

Organizations have options other than merely reacting to environmental forces. They can meet their needs by developing proactive strategies aimed at changing the environment in which the organization operates. Examples include acquiring a company in a new market, lobbying state or national government for changes in the laws, actively managing the company's image and public relations, and taking legal actions against competitors.[19]

The three general types of proactive responses are strategic maneuvering, independent strategies, and cooperative strategies.[20]

STRATEGIC MANEUVERING

Strategic maneuvering is the firm's conscious effort to change the boundaries of its competitive environment.[21] Table 3.2 defines and gives examples of several of these strategies, including domain selection, diversification, merger and acquisition, and divestiture.

Some companies, called **prospectors,** are more likely than others to engage in strategic maneuvering.[22] Aggressive companies continuously change the boundaries of their competitive environments by seeking new products and markets, diversifying, and merging or acquiring new enterprises. In these and other ways, corporations put their competitors on the defensive and force them to react.[23] **Defenders,** on the other hand, stay within a more limited, stable product domain.

TABLE 3.1

Attractive and unattractive environments

Factor	Unattractive	Attractive
Competitors	Many; low industry growth; equal size; commodity	Few; high industry growth; unequal size; differentiated
Threat of entry	High threat; few entry barriers	Low threat; many barriers
Substitutes	Many	Few
Suppliers	Few; high bargaining power	Many; low bargaining power
Customers	Few; high bargaining power	Many; low bargaining power

TABLE 3.2

Strategic
maneuvering

Strategy	Definition	Examples
Domain selection	Entering industries or markets with limited competition or regulation and ample suppliers and customers; entering high-growth markets.	IBM's entry into the personal computer market; Miller's entry into the light-beer market.
Diversification	Investing in different types of businesses; manufacturing different types of products; or geographic expansion to reduce dependence on single market or technology.	General Electric's purchase of RCA and NBC.
Merger and acquisition	Combining two or more firms into a single enterprise; gaining possession of an ongoing enterprise.	RJR and Nabisco; Sperry and Burroughs (now Unisys); Chrysler and AMC.
Divestiture	Selling one or more businesses.	Kodak and Eastman Chemical.

Source: Reprinted from *Journal of Marketing*, published by the American Marketing Association. C. Zeithaml and V. Zeithaml, "Environmental Management: Revising the Marketing Perspective," Spring 1984.

INDEPENDENT STRATEGIES

Organizations engage in strategic maneuvering when they move into different environments. However, they also can change their current environments to suit their needs. A company uses **independent strategies** when it acts on its own to change some aspect of its current environment.[24]

Table 3.3 shows several examples of these strategies. When the recording industry introduced the music videos played on MTV and in nightclubs, it made its environment more aggressively competitive. Kellogg Company has promoted the cereal industry as a whole, an example of pacifying its competitors. Pennzoil sued Texaco, Inc., and won billions of dollars; Weyerhaeuser Company advertised its reforestation efforts (public relations); and First Boston canceled its Christmas party and donated $50,000 to the poor (voluntary action).

SHOULD COMPANIES APOLOGIZE?

*P*ublic relations is an important form of independent strategy aimed at changing outsider perceptions of the firm. Most organizations are concerned about their public image. This concern usually means a company publicizes complimentary information while keeping negative information hidden. Until recently most companies refused to admit their mistakes. To apologize for any shortcomings drew attention to a negative and created bad PR. What company would want to publicize its errors? *Several* companies, recently. Consider a few examples:

- When two Chrysler Corporation executives were indicted in connection with disengaged odometers, Lee Iacocca apologized at a news conference.

- When a unit of Toshiba Corporation sold military technology to the Soviet Union, two top Toshiba executives resigned. Such an apology is ritual in Japan. But then Toshiba America also apologized, with full-page newspaper ads in the United States.

TABLE 3.3

Independent
strategies

Strategy	Definition	Examples
Competitive aggression	Exploiting a distinctive competence or improving internal efficiency for competitive advantage.	Aggressive pricing; comparative advertising (Advil).
Competitive pacification	Independent action to improve relations with competitors.	Helping competitors find raw materials.
Public relations	Establishing and maintaining favorable images in the minds of those making up the environment.	Corporate advertising campaigns (Exxon; Manville).
Voluntary action	Voluntary commitment to various interest groups, causes, and social problems.	Ronald McDonald Houses; contributions to AIDS research.
Legal action	Company engages in private legal battle with competitor on antitrust, deceptive advertising, or other grounds.	Blue Mountain Arts, Inc.'s lawsuit against Hallmark for allegedly copying its cards.
Political action	Efforts to influence elected representatives to create a more favorable business environment or limit competition.	ARCO's corporate constituency programs; issue advertising; lobbying at state and national levels.

Source: Reprinted from *Journal of Marketing,* published by the American Marketing Association. C. Zeithaml and V. Zeithaml, "Environmental Management: Revising the Marketing Perspective," Spring 1984.

- After it became public that American Express spread lies about a former business partner and Swiss banker, Edmond Safra, Amex formally apologized for its defamation attempts.

- When Ashland Oil spilled 4 million gallons of diesel fuel in Pittsburgh in 1988, CEO John Hall quickly apologized for "the inconvenience we have caused you." In addition, Ashland actually encouraged the filing of legitimate claims from individuals, businesses, and government agencies. Ashland Oil received great praise for its candid and cooperative behavior.

Other companies are reluctant to apologize. Lawyers advise against it, because an apology could be used against a company in court. In contrast to Ashland Oil, Exxon was slow to acknowledge any wrongdoing when 11 million gallons of crude oil were spilled in the *Valdez* disaster. Lawrence Rawl, Exxon CEO, was not visible for the first week of the disaster and at one point said, "It's not really clear to me why everyone is so angry."

Union Carbide never considered an advertised public apology for the poison gas leak that killed thousands of people in Bhopal, India. It considered an apology to be cosmetic and instead created a $1 million relief fund for the victims. "It's one thing to apologize for poor service," said Union Carbide spokesperson Earl Slack. "When you have something the magnitude of Bhopal, you address it with concerns and actions."

Sources: "In Ten Years You'll See 'Nothing,'" *Fortune,* May 8, 1989, pp. 50–54; C. Bruck, "The World of Business: Undoing the Eighties," *The New Yorker,* July 23, 1990, pp. 56–73; J. Nelson-Horchler, "We Were Wrong," *Industry Week,* April 16, 1990, pp. 20–26; and C. Ansberry, "Forgive or Forget: Firms Face Decision Whether to Apologize for Their Mistakes," *The Wall Street Journal,* November 24, 1987, p. 31. ●

COOPERATIVE STRATEGIES

In some situations, two or more organizations work together using **cooperative strategies.**[25] Companies cooperate in their attempts to change their environments when (1) taking joint action will reduce their costs and risks and (2) cooperation will increase their power (that is, their ability to successfully accomplish the changes they desire).

Table 3.4 shows several examples of cooperative strategies. When a supplier and customer, or management and labor, sign long-term contracts, they are cooperating to make their future relationship predictable. Coalitions arise when local businesses band together to curb the rise of employee health care costs and when organizations in the same industry form industry associations and special-interest groups. You may have seen cooperative advertising strategies, such as when companies jointly produce television commercials.

CHOOSING A RESPONSE APPROACH

Three general considerations help guide management's response to the environment. First, organizations should attempt to *change appropriate elements of the environment.* Environmental responses are most useful when aimed at elements of the environment that (1) cause the company problems; (2) provide it with opportunities; and (3) allow the company to change successfully. Thus, automobile companies faced with intense competition from Japanese automakers successfully lobbied (along with labor) for government-imposed ceilings on Japanese imports. And one charcoal producer, hoping to increase consumers' opportunities to use its product, launched a campaign to increase daylight saving time.

Second, organizations should *choose responses that focus on pertinent elements of the environment.* If a company wants to better manage its competitive environment, competitive aggression and pacification are viable options. Political action influences the legal environment, and contracting helps manage customers and suppliers.

Third, companies should *choose responses that offer the most benefit at the lowest cost.* Return-on-investment calculations should incorporate short-term financial considerations as well as long-term impact. Strategic managers who carefully consider these factors will more effectively guide their organizations to competitive advantage.

TABLE 3.4

Cooperative
strategies

Strategy	Definition	Examples
Contracting	Negotiation of an agreement between the organization and another group to exchange goods, services, information, patents, etc.	Contractual marketing systems.
Cooptation	Absorbing new elements into the organization's leadership structure to avert threats to its stability or existence.	Consumer and labor representatives and bankers on boards of directors.
Coalition	Two or more groups coalesce and act jointly with respect to some set of issues for some period of time.	Industry associations; political initiatives of the Business Roundtable and the U.S. Chamber of Commerce.

Source: Reprinted from *Journal of Marketing,* published by the American Marketing Association. C. Zeithaml and V. Zeithaml, "Environmental Management: Revising the Marketing Perspective," Spring 1984.

KEY TERMS

barriers to entry, p. 66
competitive environment, p. 56
cooperative strategies, p. 72
customer service, p. 68
defenders, p. 69
demographics, p. 63
external environment, p. 56
final consumer, p. 68

independent strategies, p. 70
intermediate consumer, p. 68
macroenvironment, p. 56
North American Free Trade Agreement (NAFTA), p. 59
privatization, p. 59
prospectors, p. 69
strategic maneuvering, p. 69
switching costs, p. 67

SUMMARY OF LEARNING OBJECTIVES

Now that you have studied Chapter 3, you should know:

How environmental forces influence organizations, as well as how organizations can influence their environments.

Organizations are open systems that are affected by, and in turn affect, their external environments. Organizations receive financial, human, material and information resources from the environment, transform these resources into finished goods and services, and then send these outputs back into the environment.

How to make a distinction between the macroenvironment and the competitive environment.

The macroenvironment is composed of international, legal/political, economic, technological, and social forces that influence strategic decisions. The competitive environment is composed of forces closer to the organization, such as current competitors, threat of new entrants, threat of substitutes, suppliers, and customers. Perhaps the simplest distinction between the macroenvironment and the competitive environment is in the amount of control that a firm can exert on external forces. Macroenvironmental forces such as the economy or social trends are much less controllable than forces in the competitive environment such as suppliers and customers.

Why organizations should attend to economic and social developments in the international environment.

Developments in other countries have a profound effect on the way U.S. companies compete. European unification, for example, is creating a formidable buying and selling bloc. The North American Free Trade Agreement opened up trade between the United States, Canada, and Mexico. Managed well, the EU and NAFTA represent opportunities for market growth, joint ventures,

and the like. Managed poorly, these free trade agreements may give advantage to more competitive firms and nations.

How to analyze the competitive environment in order to formulate strategy.

Environments can range from favorable to unfavorable. To determine how favorable a competitive environment is, managers should consider the nature of the competitors, potential new entrants, threat of substitutes, suppliers, and customers. Analyzing how these five forces influence the organization provides an indication of potential threats and opportunities. Attractive environments tend to be those that have high industry growth, few competitors, products that can be differentiated, few potential entrants, many barriers to entry, few substitutes, many suppliers (none with much power), and many customers. After identifying and analyzing competitive forces, managers must formulate a strategy that minimizes the power that external forces have over the organization (a topic to be discussed more fully in Chapter 5).

How environmental management strategies can be used to shape external forces.

Responding effectively to the environment often involves devising proactive strategies to change the environment. Strategic maneuvering, for example, involves changing the boundaries of the competitive environment through domain selection, diversification, mergers, and the like. Independent strategies, on the other hand, do not require moving into a new environment, but rather changing some aspect of the current environment through competitive aggression, public relations, legal action, and so on. Finally, cooperative strategies, such as contracting, cooptation, and coalition building, involve the working together of two or more organizations.

DISCUSSION QUESTIONS

1. This chapter's opening quote by Peter Drucker said, "The essence of a business is outside itself." What do you think this means? Do you agree?
2. What are the most important forces in the macroenvironment facing companies today?
3. Go back to the Merck example in Setting the Stage. What other organizations have faced or are facing similar circumstances in their external environments?
4. What are the main differences between the macroenvironment and the competitive environment?

5. Do you think European unification will help or hurt U.S. businesses? What are your views on NAFTA, APEC, and other types of trade agreements? How do they change the favorability/unfavorability of the business environment?
6. We outlined several proactive responses organizations can make to the environment. What examples have you seen recently of an organization's responding effectively to its environment? Did the effectiveness of the response depend on whether the organization was facing a threat or an opportunity?

CONCLUDING CASE

GREYHOUND IS LOOKING LIKE A DOG

In the 1934 movie *It Happened One Night,* Clark Gable romanced Claudette Colbert on a Greyhound bus, and moviegoers flocked to become passengers to share the glamour. Nowadays, Greyhound is more likely to be featured in a horror movie. Since the mid-1980s, the Dallas-based company has been fighting several monsters at once—fierce regional competition, substitutes in the airline and rental car businesses, labor strikes, economic downturns, a fickle customer base, a leveraged buyout, and at least one cliff-hanger in bankruptcy court.

In the modern era bus companies face stiff competition from substitute forms of transportation. In particular, the airlines have reduced their cost structures to a point where they are stealing a big chunk of Greyhound's business. Southwest Airlines, for example, charges $31 for a one-way ticket from Phoenix to San Diego. Greyhound charges $34—that's $3 more to travel by bus. Unless you especially like the view in Death Valley, you would probably take the plane.

Even those travelers who do decide to go by bus are more frequently taking a local or regional carrier rather than traveling with Greyhound. Peter Pan, for example, is a small enterprise that has been successful serving small towns in the Northeast that are ignored by major bus companies and air carriers. The company started off "connecting the dots" between Springfield, Boston, and western Massachusetts, but in 1986 bought the rights to Trailways' routes from New England to New York City. Now Peter Pan has gained a strong foothold in the lower-income, ethnic customer base of inner city travel. This has

Critics say Greyhound management lacks the know-how to keep the buses running on time.
(Tim Rasmussen/SYGMA)

been a mainstay of Greyhound's business, and Peter Pan is cutting into its market share.

In addition to problems with competitors and substitutes, Greyhound has had labor difficulties. In 1990, the Amalgamated Transit Union, which represented more than 6,000 drivers and 3,000 mechanics, struck Greyhound. To keep operations going, Greyhound took a hard line against the union, and hired 2,000 strike replacements. After a bitter and sometimes violent three-year work stoppage, the union finally allowed its members to return to work. Meanwhile, Greyhound had filed for chapter 11 bankruptcy protection. After emerging from bankruptcy in 1991, Greyhound embarked on a restructuring program designed to reduce operating expenses. CEO Frank Schmieder cut Greyhound's fleet by 50 percent to just under 2,000 buses and trimmed the workforce by about 20 percent.

But as management cut expenses, services on many routes were reduced. Overworked and unmotivated employees frequently allowed telephones to go unanswered during peak business hours, alienating would-be customers. To rectify the problem and streamline operations, Greyhound borrowed an idea from the airline industry and rolled out its first national computer reservation system in 1993. The system, known as *Trips,* had a toll-free telephone number that customers could use to make reservations nationwide. The computer system was a flop, requiring 45 seconds to respond to each key stroke, and taking up to seven minutes to print out a ticket. Unhappy customers either had to jump out of line or miss the bus—literally. To stop the exodus of passengers, Greyhound began shutting down the system and slashing fares, operating far below cost in some regions. The company hired Bradley Harslem, former guru of American Airlines' Sabre reservation system, to revamp the system, and response time was cut from 45 seconds to just 2 seconds. *Trips* now handles more than 70 percent of Greyhound's traffic, connecting over 250 cities, and providing the kind of information that will help the company identify which routes (Greyhound serves 2,600 destinations) are most profitable.

Other efforts by Schmieder to resuscitate Greyhound included a $184 million investment in new buses, bringing the average age of the fleet down from 11.5 years to 6.5 years. Greyhound tried an image-boosting promotion with the theme "I go simple, I go easy, I go Greyhound." But it may be a case of too little, too late. With strong competition and excellent substitutes, Greyhound's utilized capacity dropped way off historical levels of 80 percent to less than 50 percent. On-time performance slipped below 60 percent. It's hard to make money running a half-empty bus that arrives late.

In August 1994, Frank Schmieder was forced to resign as CEO and was replaced by Craig Lentzsch, a former Greyhound executive. Several other top executives have also been forced out, including Michael Doyle, Greyhound's chief financial officer. Greyhound's stock price has fallen by 90 percent since May 1993, and the company is once again on the brink of bankruptcy.

QUESTIONS

1. What factors in Porter's model of the competitive environment are operating in this example? How attractive is this industry?
2. What mistakes have Greyhound's executives made? What have they done right?
3. Imagine you were running Greyhound. What response(s) would you suggest given the company's environmental situation?
4. Do you see any similarities between Greyhound's situation and the situation facing Merck in Setting the Stage?

Sources: "Greyhound Lines: Bused Again?" *Economist,* November 12, 1994, pp. 81–82; Wendy Zeller, "Greyhound Is Limping Badly," *Business Week,* August 22, 1994, p. 32; Gregory E. David, "Greyhound Lines: Goodbye, Dog Days?" *Financial World,* July 5, 1994, p. 16; Alex Saunders, "Greyhound Utilizes Dynatech CPX Equipment to Integrate Protocols over Frame Relay," *Telecommunications,* September 1994, p. 68; Peter Fuhrman, "The Little Bus Company That Could," *Forbes,* August 25, 1986, p. 74; and Michael H. Cimini and Susan L. Behrmann, "Dispute Ends at Greyhound," *Monthly Labor Review,* July 1993, p. 56.

VIDEO CASE

THE ENVIRONMENT OF BUSINESS

Today more than ever, American businesses are feeling the heat from foreign competition. The combination of high tariffs at home, and cheaper labor costs in other countries, has made it increasingly difficult for American companies to beat the foreign competition's prices. The competition is fierce, but American businesses can meet the challenges both at home and abroad by emphasizing the quality of American products and services. And the key to developing a successful quality strategy is management. Managers must include quality in every aspect of their business. This requires a huge shift in most managing styles. But it's got to be done. If quality is not made top priority in American businesses, you bet the foreign competition will leave them in the dust.

One company that knows the realities of the global market is Trek. Trek was founded in 1976 by a small group of biking enthusiasts who wanted to combine American manufacturing technology with precision hand craftsmanship to build the highest quality bicycles in the world. At first, everything ran smoothly. But by the mid-80s, Trek began to run into trouble. Joyce Keehn, Sales Manager of International Accounts, said, "In the 80s, we sort of hit a brick wall, so to speak, in that we had high inventory, sales were down, we didn't have as many dealers as we should

have had so we were sitting here with a lot of inventory and we were nearly bankrupt. And we had to relook at the situation while we were still running the business from a management standpoint as well as quality and getting our orders in and how we were dealing with the marketplace."

Trek had to develop a new game plan. The company decided to capitalize on its reputation as a leader in technology and quality craftsmanship. Keehn said, "When we look at our quality back in the 80s it wasn't what our U.S. dealers expected our quality to be, so we realized that if we wanted to increase our business domestically we had to increase our quality. And we began doing that for the U.S. market but an interesting thing that we found is that when we began to get into other markets like Germany and Japan their standards were much higher than what we were experiencing here in the states."

Trek's international response was phenomenal and growth was rapid. Today, Trek sells its bicycles in 55 countries with international sales accounting for 40 percent of its business. International competition strengthened Trek in domestic markets as well. As a result, Trek has grown 700 percent since 1988, making it the largest manufacturer of quality bicycles in the United States. In fact, in 1992, when bicycle sales in the United States were down 6 percent, Trek's sales were up 17 percent. The key to Trek's amazing comeback was the increased emphasis on technology and quality in every aspect of the company.

Trek empowered its employees with decision making authority in several areas. It became a Trek policy that any employee can and should stop the assembly line if they detect the slightest problem with the product. Trek also organized employee group management teams. The focus of those teams has been to try to plan processes, work, and products as early as possible into the cycle. And by doing this planning, incorporate ideas into the quality system.

Trek management also opened up internal and external communication. Internally, every Trek employee knows the president's door is always open if they have questions and concerns. Externally, an open communication policy with employees, dealers, and customers affects Trek's design and marketing decisions. Dealer advice meetings allow dealers the opportunity to provide feedback, and see the results of previous suggestions. Field quality audits are set up to field questions from Trek's sales representatives.

Trek also realized that producing the highest quality bicycle in the world would require more than a shift in management function. The manufacturing process itself would have to be completely re-geared toward quality. At Trek this meant using the most innovative materials and technology available. Brad Wagner, engineer manager, said, "It's manufacturing's job to make sure that the product team's design is buildable. We have 10 of these manufacturing engineers. These guys design the fixtures and the processes. That's how each Trek gets the attention to detail, the flawless welds, and the detailed inspection that result in a great riding bike."

Trek engineers have become pioneers in the field of bicycle technology. They revolutionized the process in which bike frames are built, using stronger and lighter carbon fiber frames. Their most recent development is the carbon composite lug, which is used in the joints of the bicycle frame for increased, lightweight strength. Trek has also borrowed plasma welding techniques used in the aerospace industry to create a higher quality bike.

To discover and correct problems before they occur, Trek conducts extensive testing on every model. Every frame is inspected to ensure quality standards before it is allowed out of the factory. One such test is called the high fatigue test, which was developed using a Japanese industrial standard. In the test, weights are placed on a bike frame to simulate the weight of the rider. The frame is then put through a rigorous set of tests to check its durability.

Trek's emphasis on quality as a competitive strategy for success in the global market has not only helped it to survive but prosper. They are proof positive that quality must be integrated into every management process for American businesses to survive in a global market.

CRITICAL THINKING QUESTIONS

1. Why was Trek unable to compete with foreign bicycle manufacturing based on price?

2. Trek employees can stop the assembly line if they spot a defect. What are the advantages and disadvantages of this policy?

3. What is the importance of Trek's "dealer advice meetings"?

EXPERIENTIAL EXERCISES

3.1 Demography and the Future

Background Information and Objectives

What happened to Gerber Products? Why did it add new products beyond its baby food line? American Hospital Supply Company has grown at a phenomenal rate lately. Why? Part of the answer to these questions is that the baby boom became a baby bust. After a steady decline in the U.S. birthrate from the 1800s to 1940, a 20-year period of increased birthrate occurred in which the population grew from about two to four children per woman. This was followed by a decline in the 1960s and 1970s. The birthrate (among other variables) has an impact on total population size and affects age range proportions, which, in turn, affect basic demand patterns for certain goods and services.

Another significant feature of birthrate data is the number of families without children. Due to overall lifestyle, a two-paycheck family with no children results in different housing patterns, disposable income, and unique consumption patterns. A nation where the average family has two children will have a higher per capita income than a nation where the average family has three children. Disposable income would increase and be used for travel, entertainment, or a house at the beach. Although people would not eat more, they might eat more convenience foods or gourmet foods, or go to restaurants more often.

The workforce, meanwhile, also begins to take on a different composition. The post–World War II baby boom means more people competing for middle management positions in the 1980s. With fewer full-time students, thousands of teachers are also competing for jobs. A smaller group of young people, those growing up after the baby-boom generation, may see a perpetual barrier to success and prosperity. However, the scarcity of young people may place them in demand for jobs requiring youthful energy and fresh training. Demand for specialists may also change. For example, while there may be an oversupply of physicians, there may be less need for obstetricians and more need for specialists in geriatric care.

What some have come to call the "graying of America" could have significant impact on demand patterns for products and services, as well as both threats and opportunities for various segments of the economy in the future. Birthrate data and the population's age composition can give significant clues to the patterns that could emerge in the future, patterns that would affect businesses and their managers in predictable ways. This exercise seeks to stimulate your thinking about these patterns and their implications for you.

Instructions

1. Gather basic data on the population. Your library should have census data collected by the government. *The Statistical Abstract of the United States* provides convenient reference data.
2. Draw a series of bar charts showing trends for each decade from 1900 through 1990 (every ten years) for the following:
   a. Total population.
   b. Number of men and women.
   c. Children born per woman (births, rates, fertility).
   d. Percent of population by the following age categories: 1–13; 14–21; 22–35; 36–65; over 65.
3. For each of the categories of economic activity in the Demography and the Future Worksheet, indicate what your data suggest. (Check whether the segment will be hurt or helped, and provide a brief explanation indicating which of your charts leads you to your conclusions.)
4. Comment on how these data are likely to affect you as a manager.
5. Bring your findings to class to discuss and compare.

DEMOGRAPHY AND THE FUTURE WORKSHEET

Economic Segment	Helped	Hurt	Why? What chart supports it?
Advertising			
Autos			
Broadcasting			
Clothing			
Health care			
Housing			
Jewelry and watches			
Life insurance			
Liquor			
Movie theaters			
Restaurants			
Sports and recreation			
Tobacco			
Travel			

Source: Excerpted from Lawrence R. Jauch, Arthur G. Bedeian, Sally A. Coltrin, and William F. Glueck, *The Managerial Experience: Cases, Exercises, and Readings,* 4th Ed. Copyright © 1986 by the Dryden Press. Reprinted by permission.

3.2 Environmental Factors

Objective

To establish an Environmental Threat and Opportunity Profile (ETOP) for a company by utilizing environmental scanning.

Instructions

1. Select a company in the industry of your choice.
2. Under each of the environmental categories in the Environmental Threat and Opportunity Worksheet, list each relevant factor and include a brief description of how it will impact the company.

3. Calculate the environmental threat and opportunity by doing the following:
   a. Indicate the *impact* of each factor (from a + 5 "strongly positive" to 0 "neutral" to −5 "strongly negative").
   b. Rank the *importance* of each factor (from 0 "unimportant" to 10 "very important").
   c. Multiply the impact by the importance and place the score in the third column.
   d. Next to that score, indicate whether it is a potential opportunity or threat by placing either a + or − sign in front of the score.
   e. Total the scores to establish the Environmental Threat and Opportunity Profile.

ENVIRONMENTAL THREAT AND OPPORTUNITY WORKSHEET

Economic Factors
(e.g., inflationary trends, consumption, employment, investment, monetary and fiscal policies)

_____

_____

_____

_____

Political Factors
(e.g., political power, different ideologies, interest groups, social stability, legislation, and regulation)

_____

_____

_____

_____

Social Factors
(e.g., age distribution, geographic distribution, income distribution, mobility, education, family values, work and business attitudes)

_____

_____

_____

_____

Technological Factors
(e.g., rate of technological change, future raw material availability, raw material cost, technological developments in related areas)

_____

_____

_____

_____

Competitive Factors
(e.g., entry and exit of major competitors, major strategic changes by competitors)

_____

_____

_____

_____

ENVIRONMENTAL THREAT AND OPPORTUNITY PROFILE (ETOP)

Factors	Impact of Factor*	Importance of Factor‡	Potential Opportunity (+) or Threat (−)
Economic	_____	_____	_____
Political	_____	_____	_____
Social	_____	_____	_____
Technological	_____	_____	_____
Competitive	_____	_____	_____

*Impact: from +5 (strongly positive) to 0 (neutral) to −5 (strongly negative).
‡Importance of factor ranked from 0 (unimportant) to 10 (very important).

Source: Alan J. Rowe, Richard O. Mason, and Karl E. Dickel, *Strategic Management: A Methodical Approach,* 2nd ed., pp. 101–4. Reprinted by permission of Addison-Wesley Publishing Company, Inc.

4

MANAGERIAL DECISION MAKING

The business executive is by profession a decision maker.

Uncertainty is his opponent. Overcoming it is his mission.

John McDonald

After studying Chapter 4, you will know:

1. The kinds of decisions you will face as a manager.

2. How to make "rational" decisions.

3. The pitfalls you should avoid when making decisions.

4. The pros and cons of using a group to make decisions.

5. The procedures to use in leading a decision-making team.

6. How to encourage creative decisions.

7. How to make decisions in a crisis.

GUTSY DECISIONS

*I*n 1994, *Industry Week* nominated the following decisions as some of the gutsiest made by U.S. business leaders in the previous year:

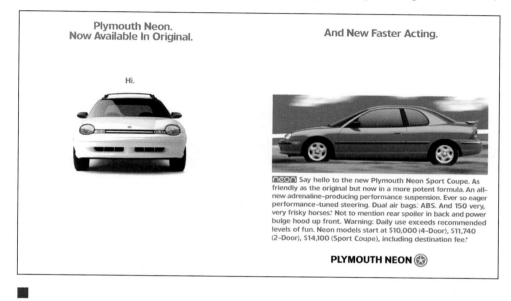

Plymouth Neon.
Now Available In Original.

Hi.

And New Faster Acting.

neon Say hello to the new Plymouth Neon Sport Coupe. As friendly as the original but now in a more potent formula. An all-new adrenaline-producing performance suspension. Ever so eager performance-tuned steering. Dual air bags. ABS. And 150 very, very frisky horses. Not to mention rear spoiler in back and power bulge hood up front. Warning: Daily use exceeds recommended levels of fun. Neon models start at $10,000 (4-Door), $11,740 (2-Door), $14,100 (Sport Coupe), including destination fee.

PLYMOUTH NEON ⊕

Chrysler dared to compete with the Japanese by giving the green light to Neon.
(Courtesy Bozell Worldwide, Inc., for Chrysler Corporation)

- Chrysler decided to go head to head with Japanese automakers by producing the Neon, a subcompact sourced and built in the U.S. and priced under $10,000. No other U.S. automaker has dared to try this.
- Jack Smith of General Motors infuriated Wall Street by not taking a tougher line in negotiations with labor. Whereas investors wanted lower labor costs, Smith wanted a labor force that was with the company rather than against it.
- John Sculley left Apple Computer to head a smaller, newer entrepreneurial firm, Spectrum Technologies. Apple is a household name, and Sculley is synonymous with it, whereas Sculley's new company was mired in legal actions and had never turned a profit in 10 years.
- TCI and Bell Atlantic announced they will merge the two companies, representing two industries, into the first interactive communications giant. The merger will help construct a nationwide information infrastructure. The question was, could they pull it off?
- With the Mississippi River rising, John Craig halted production in his furnace-making plant in St. Louis, putting his job on the line because others saw the move as unnecessary or premature. They didn't think a flood would hit the city, but he did. He and his people launched a save-the-plant operation, and spent $3.5 million to prepare it for flood.

Source: M. A. Verespej, "Gutsy Decisions of 1993," *Industry Week,* February 7, 1994, pp. 26–40.

*T*he decisions described in Setting the Stage are similar to other important business decisions. Risks are high, doubts persist, and often there is no rational way to arrive at "correct" answers. In the case of the St. Louis furnace-making plant, John Craig's decision proved to be the right one: the Mississippi floodwaters hit one week after shutting down, and the precautions saved the business. But the TCI/Bell Atlantic merger did not come off, and John Sculley left Spectrum within months.

 At CNN, president Tom Johnson makes critical decisions every minute or two, all day long, while standing eye-to-eye with reporters, editors, and others. Executive producers may make a hundred decisions during a live one-hour show. And these instantaneous decisions have lasting impact. It is no task for the indecisive or squeamish. As CNN's vice chairman says, "Nobody is going to tell you what to do. It's up to you to figure out what to do, then do it. Always take the proactive path. Ask for advice, sure, but don't sit on your hands waiting for an order."[1]

Decisions. If you can't make them, you won't be an effective manager. This chapter discusses the kinds of decisions managers face, how they are made, and how they *should* be made.

CHARACTERISTICS OF MANAGERIAL DECISIONS

Managers face problems constantly. Some problems that require a decision are relatively simple; others seem overwhelming. Some demand immediate action, while others take months or even years to unfold.

Actually, managers often ignore problems. For several reasons, they avoid taking action.[2] First, managers can't be sure how much time, energy, or trouble lies ahead once they start working on a problem. Second, getting involved is risky; tackling a problem but failing to solve it successfully can hurt the manager's track record. Third, because problems can be so perplexing, it is easier to procrastinate or to get busy with less demanding activities.

It is important to understand why decision making can be so challenging. Figure 4.1 illustrates several characteristics of managerial decisions that contribute to their difficulty and pressure. Most managerial decisions lack structure and entail risk, uncertainty, and conflict.

LACK OF STRUCTURE

Lack of structure is the usual state of affairs in managerial decision making.[3] Although some decisions are routine and clear-cut, for most there is no automatic procedure to follow. Problems are novel and unstructured, leaving the decision maker uncertain about how to proceed.

FIGURE 4.1

Characteristics of managerial decisions

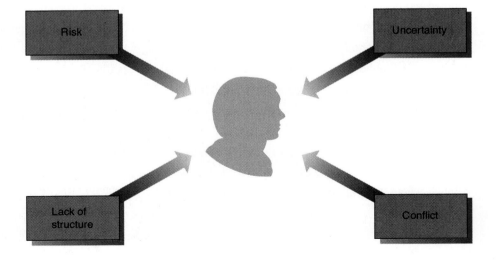

A well-known distinction illustrating this point is between programmed and nonprogrammed decisions. **Programmed decisions** have been encountered and made before. They have objectively correct answers, and can be solved by using simple rules, policies, or numerical computations. If you face a programmed decision, there exists a clear procedure or structure for arriving at the right decision. For example, if you are a small-business owner and must decide the amounts for your employees' paychecks, you can use a calculator—and if the amounts are wrong, your employees will prove it to you. Table 4.1 gives some other examples.

If most important decisions were programmed, managerial life would be much easier. But managers typically face **nonprogrammed decisions:** new, novel, complex decisions having no certain outcomes. There are a variety of possible solutions, all of which have merits and drawbacks. The decision maker must create or impose a method for making the decision; there is no predetermined structure to rely on. As Table 4.1 suggests, important, difficult decisions tend to be nonprogrammed, and they demand creative approaches.

UNCERTAINTY AND RISK

If you have all the information you need, and can predict precisely the consequences of your actions, you are operating under a condition of **certainty.**[4] But perfect certainty is rare. For important, nonprogrammed managerial decisions, uncertainty is the rule.

Uncertainty means the manager has insufficient information to know the consequences of different actions. Decision makers may have strong opinions—they may feel sure of themselves—but they are still operating under conditions of uncertainty if they lack pertinent information and cannot estimate the likelihood of different results of their actions.

When you can estimate the likelihood of various consequences, but still do not know with certainty what will happen, you are facing **risk.** Risk exists when the probability of an action being successful is less than 100 percent. If the decision is the wrong one, you may lose money, time, reputation, or other important assets.

TABLE 4.1

Types of decisions

	Programmed Decisions	Nonprogrammed Decisions
Type of problem	Frequent, repetitive, routine, much certainty regarding cause and effect relationships.	Novel, unstructured, much uncertainty regarding cause and effect relationships.
Procedure	Dependence on policies, rules, and definite procedures.	Necessity for creativity, intuition, tolerance for ambiguity, creative problem solving.
Examples	Business firm: Periodic reorders of inventory.	Business firm: Diversification into new products and markets.
	University: Necessary grade-point average for good academic standing.	University: Construction of new classroom facilities.
	Health care: Procedure for admitting patients.	Health care: Purchase of experimental equipment.
	Government: Merit system for promotion of state employees.	Government: Reorganization of state government agencies.

Source: J. Gibson, J. Ivancevich, and J. Donnelly, Jr., *Organizations,* 5th ed. (Plano, Tex.: BPI, 1985).

CONFLICT

Important decisions are even more difficult because of the conflict managers face. **Conflict,** which exists when the manager must consider opposing pressures from different sources, exists at two levels.

First, individual decision makers experience psychological conflict when *several* options are attractive, or when *none* of the options is attractive. For instance, a manager may have to decide whom to lay off, when she doesn't want to lay off anyone. Or she may have three promising job applicants for one position—but choosing one means she has to reject the other two.

Second, conflict arises between individuals or groups. The chief financial officer argues in favor of increasing long-term debt to finance an acquisition. The chief executive officer, however, prefers to minimize such debt and find the funds elsewhere. The marketing department wants more product lines to sell to its customers, and engineers want higher-quality products. But production people want to lower costs by having longer production runs of fewer products with no changes. Management wants to enforce some rigid work rules, while labor seeks looser rule enforcement. As you can see, few decisions are unanimous or uncompromised.

THE STAGES OF DECISION MAKING

Faced with these challenges, how are good decisions made? The ideal decision-making process moves through six stages. As Figure 4.2 illustrates, decision makers should (1) identify and diagnose the problem, (2) generate alternative solutions, (3) evaluate alternatives, (4) make the choice, (5) implement the decision, and (6) evaluate the decision.

IDENTIFYING AND DIAGNOSING THE PROBLEM

The first stage in the decision-making process is to recognize that a problem exists and must be solved. Typically, a manager realizes some discrepancy between the current state (the way things are) and a desired state (the way things ought to be). Such discrepancies—say, in organizational or departmental performance—may be detected by comparing current performance against (1) *past* performance, (2) the *current* performance of other organizations or departments, or (3) *future* expected performance as determined by plans and forecasts.[5]

Recognizing that a problem exists is only the beginning of this stage. The decision maker also must want to do something about it and must believe that the resources and abilities necessary for solving the problem exist.[6] Then the decision maker must dig in deeper and attempt to *diagnose* the true cause of the problem symptoms that surfaced.

For example, a sales manager knows that sales have dropped drastically. If he is leaving the company soon or believes the decreased sales volume is due to the economy (which he can't do anything about), he won't take further action. But if he does try to solve the problem, he should not automatically reprimand his sales staff, add new people, or increase the advertising budget. He must analyze *why* sales are down and then develop a solution appropriate to his analysis. Asking why, of yourself and others, is essential to understanding the real problem.

GENERATING ALTERNATIVE SOLUTIONS

In the second stage, problem diagnosis is linked to the development of alternative courses of action aimed at solving the problem. Managers generate at least some alternative solutions based on past experiences.[7]

Solutions range from ready made to custom made.[8] Decision makers who search for **ready-made solutions** use ideas they have seen or tried before or follow the advice of others who have faced similar problems. **Custom-made solutions,** on the other hand, must be *designed for* the specific problems. This technique requires combining ideas into new, creative solutions. For example, the Sony Walkman was created by combining

Innovation

FIGURE 4.2

The stages of
decision making

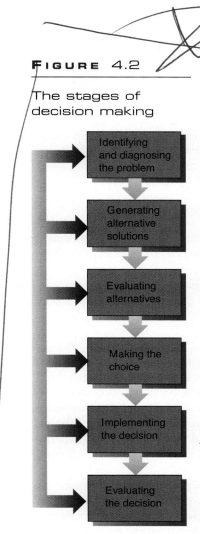

Identifying
and diagnosing
the problem

Generating
alternative
solutions

Evaluating
alternatives

Making the
choice

Implementing
the decision

Evaluating
the decision

two existing products: earphones and a tape player.[9] Techniques for enhancing creativity will be discussed later in this chapter.

Choosing a ready-made alternative is much easier than designing a custom-made solution. Therefore, most decision makers use the ready-made approach, sometimes even when the ready-made alternative is inappropriate. If this approach fails to uncover an acceptable solution, the harder work of devising a unique solution will begin. For important, irreversible decisions, custom-made alternatives should be developed because they are more likely to lead to higher-quality solutions.[10]

EVALUATING ALTERNATIVES

The third stage involves determining the value or adequacy of the alternatives that were generated. Which solution will be the best?

Too often, alternatives are evaluated with little thought or logic. After Walter P. Chrysler died, Chrysler's lawyer sometimes contacted the ghost of Walter P. for advice. The lawyer would excuse himself from the meeting, go into Chrysler's office, close the door and drapes, turn off the lights, and conjure up Chrysler's spirit. Then the lawyer would return to the meeting and reveal his findings, which the Chrysler executives would use to make the final decision.[11]

Alternatives obviously should be evaluated more carefully than this. Fundamental to this process is to predict the consequences that will occur if the various options are put into effect.

Managers should consider several types of consequences. Obviously they must attempt to predict the effects on financial or other performance measures. But there are other, less clear-cut consequences to address.[12] Decisions set a precedent; will this precedent be a help or a hindrance in the future? Also, the success or failure of the decision will go into the track records of those involved in making it.

Refer again to your original goals. What goals does each alternative meet, and fail to meet? Which alternatives are most acceptable to you and to other important stakeholders? If several alternatives may solve the problem, which can be implemented at the lowest cost? If no alternative achieves all your goals, perhaps you can combine two or more of the best ones.

Of course, the future cannot be forecast with perfect accuracy. But sometimes decision makers can build in safeguards against an uncertain future by considering the potential consequences of several different scenarios. Then they generate *contingency plans*—alternative courses of action that can be implemented based on how the future unfolds.

ECONOMIC SCENARIOS FOR THE YEAR 2000

What will the economic landscape look like in the year 2000? Anything can happen, of course, but most forecasters expect one of these four scenarios:

1. The last half of the 1990s will see a full-scale economic boom. Unemployment will be much lower, and growth will average 5 to 6 percent annually. The U.S. government will invest heavily in high-tech information, environmental, and transportation industries, and the United States will be much stronger than its global competitors. Consumers will enjoy increased spending power, and a surge of technological innovations will propel economic growth.
2. The rest of the 1990s will show a moderately strong economy. Growth will be between 2 and 3 percent annually. The United States comes out of recession with more efficient, flexible companies, although demographics dictate fewer people entering the labor force so productivity growth is modest.

3. A more pessimistic outlook is that the late 1990s will be characterized by no economic growth, rising unemployment, and recession. Potential causes for this struggling economy include excessive government spending, an inability to control the budget deficit, partisan politics, higher interest rates, and global trade war.

4. A worse scenario yet includes global depression, massive unemployment, and widespread social unrest. Possible causes include overseas upheaval in the former Soviet Union or the Middle East, the United States' inability to compete internationally, and the widening economic gap between rich and poor.

Source: K. Labich, "Four Possible Futures," *Fortune,* January 25, 1993, pp. 40–48. ●

All of these won't come true, of course; one of these scenarios will prove to be more accurate than the others. They raise important "what if?" questions for decision makers and highlight the need for preparedness and contingency plans.

As you read this, what scenario is unfolding? What are the important current events and trends? How will *you* prepare for the turn of the century?

MAKING THE CHOICE

Once you have considered the possible consequences of your options, it is time to make your decision. Important concepts here are maximizing, satisficing, and optimizing.[13]

To **maximize** is to make the best possible decision. The maximizing decision realizes the greatest positive consequences and the fewest negative consequences. In other words, maximizing results in the greatest benefit at the lowest cost, with the largest expected total return. Maximizing requires searching thoroughly for a complete range of alternatives, carefully assessing each alternative, comparing one to another, and then choosing the very best.

To **satisfice** is to choose the first option that is minimally acceptable or adequate; the choice appears to meet a targeted goal or criterion. When you satisfice, you compare your choice against your goal, not against other options. Satisficing means a search for alternatives stops at the first one that is okay. Commonly, people do not expend the time or energy to gather complete information. Instead, they make the expedient decision based on readily available information. Satisficing is sometimes a result of laziness; other times, there is no other option because time is short, information is unavailable, or other constraints make it impossible to maximize.

Let's say you are purchasing new equipment and your goal is to avoid spending too much money. You would be maximizing if you checked out all your options and their prices, and then bought the cheapest one that met your performance requirements. But you would be satisficing if you bought the first one you found that was within your budget, and failed to look for less expensive options.

Optimizing is a type of maximizing that means that you achieve the best possible balance among several goals. Perhaps, in purchasing equipment, you are interested in quality and durability as well as price. So, instead of buying the cheapest piece of equipment that works, you buy the one with the best combination of attributes, even though there may be options that are better on the price criterion and others that are better on the quality and durability criteria.

The same idea applies to achieving business goals: one marketing strategy could maximize sales, while different strategies might maximize profit or market share. An optimizing strategy is the one that achieves the best balance among all three goals.

IMPLEMENTING THE DECISION

The decision-making process does not end once a choice is made. The chosen alternative must be implemented. Sometimes the people involved in making the choice must put it into effect. At other times, they delegate the responsibility for implementation to others, such as when a management team changes a policy or operating procedures and has first-line supervisors carry out the change.

Those who implement the decision must *understand* the choice and why it was made. They also must be *committed* to its successful implementation. These needs can be met by involving those people in the early stages of the implementation process. At Steelcase, the world's largest manufacturer of office furniture, new concepts are put through simultaneous design, engineering, and marketing scrutiny.[14] This is in contrast to an approach whereby designers design and the concept is later relayed to other departments for implementation. In such cases, understanding and commitment of all departments are less likely to result.

Managers should plan implementation carefully. Adequate planning requires several steps:[15]

1. Determine how things will look when the decision is fully operational.
2. Chronologically order, perhaps with a flow diagram, the steps necessary to achieve a fully operational decision.
3. List the resources and activities required to implement each step.
4. Estimate the time needed for each step.
5. Assign responsibility for each step to specific individuals.

EVALUATING THE DECISION

The final stage in the decision-making process is evaluating the decision. This means collecting information on how well the decision is working. Quantifiable goals—a 20 percent increase in sales, an 80 percent reduction in accidents, 100 percent on-time deliveries—can be set even before the solution to the problem is put into effect. Then objective data can be gathered to accurately determine the success (or failure) of the decision.

Decision evaluation is useful whether the feedback is positive or negative. Feedback that suggests the decision is working implies that the decision should be continued and perhaps applied elsewhere in the organization. Negative feedback, which indicates failure, means that either (1) implementation will require more time, resources, effort, or thought; or (2) the decision was a bad one.

If the decision appears inappropriate, it's back to the drawing board. Then the process cycles back to the first stage: (re)definition of the problem. The decision-making process begins anew, preferably with more information, new suggestions, and an approach that attempts to eliminate the mistakes made the first time around.

THE BEST DECISION

How can managers tell whether they have made the best decision? One approach is to wait until the results are in. But what if the decision has been made but not yet implemented? While nothing can guarantee a "best" decision, managers should at least be confident that they followed proper *procedures* that will yield the best possible decision under the circumstances. This means that the decision makers were appropriately vigilant in making the decision. **Vigilance** occurs when the decision makers carefully and conscientiously execute all six stages of decision making, including making provisions for implementation and evaluation.[16]

Even if managers reflect on these decision-making activities and conclude that they were executed conscientiously, they still will not know whether the decision will work; after all, nothing guarantees a good outcome. But they *will* know that they did their best to make the most rational decision.

Most of the causes of business failures described below are a result of inadequate vigilance. Consider them decision traps; if you find yourself thinking in the following ways, you are making poor decisions.

WHY BUSINESSES FAIL

Why do firms fail? According to *Inc.* magazine, the most common reason has nothing to do with products, market knowledge, or effort. What kills companies is poor judgment at the top. Once entrepreneurs decide to start a business, they put all their hearts into it but fail to use their heads.

- *Is this a great product, or what?* If you love it, or it's clever, that doesn't mean it meets a market need.

- *What a business! It's easy—and cheap—to start right away.* This may be true, but if it's true for you, it is true for competitors as well. You'd better find a way to be *better* than the others.

- *My forecasts are conservative.* You may think you can make your plan work because you have made cautious predictions. But you'd better have contingency plans in case your forecasts prove wrong. A rule of thumb is that start-ups take twice as long or need three times as much money as their founders predict. Sales projections are almost never met.

- *With this much money to work with, we can't miss.* It's tough to have to pinch pennies. But too much money may make for risky or poorly thought-out decisions, and you will lose control of costs.

- *Fortunately, our biggest customer is General Motors (or Xerox, or IBM).* Traditionally, many managers would have loved to be in such a position. Today, they'd better be ready in case they suddenly lose their biggest customer—it happens all the time.

- *My people aren't afraid of me. They tell me what they think all day long.* They may be telling you what they think you want to hear. You need honest, valid information, and trusted advisors. These things don't fall into your lap automatically; you have to work to get them.

- *Actually, our important numbers have never looked better.* Don't ignore signs of trouble; don't assume problems are temporary. Look constantly for trouble signs, and act on them immediately.

Source: B. G. Posner, "Why Companies Fail," *Inc.,* June 1993, pp. 102–6. ●

BARRIERS TO EFFECTIVE DECISION MAKING

Vigilance and sequential execution of the six-stage decision-making process are the exception rather than the rule in managerial decision making. Real decisions are influenced by subjective psychological biases, time pressures, and social realities.

PSYCHOLOGICAL BIASES

Decision makers are far from objective in the way they gather, evaluate, and apply information toward making their final choice. People have biases that interfere with objective rationality. The examples that follow represent only a few of the many documented subjective biases.[17]

The **illusion of control** is a belief that one can influence events even when one has no control over what will happen. Gambling is one example: Some people believe they have the skill to beat the odds even though most people, most of the time, cannot. In business, such overconfidence can lead to failure because the decision maker ignores risks and fails to objectively evaluate the odds of success.

Framing effects refer to how problems or decision alternatives are phrased. In one example, managers indicated a desire to invest more money in a course of action that was reported to have a 70 percent chance of profit than in one said to have a 30 percent chance of loss.[18] The choices were equivalent in their chances of success; it was the way

Professional gambling establishments count on people's willingness to try to beat the odds. This illusion of control is a major contributor to the high profits earned by most casinos.

(Jose Fuste Raga/The Stock Market)

the options were framed that determined the managers' choices. Thus, framing can exert an undue, irrational influence on people's decisions.

Often decision makers **discount the future.** That is, in their evaluation of alternatives, they weigh short-term costs and benefits more heavily than longer-term costs and benefits. Consider your own decision about whether or not to go for a dental checkup (see Figure 4.3). The choice to go poses short-term financial costs, anxiety, and perhaps physical pain. The choice not to go will inflict even greater costs and more severe pain if dental problems worsen. How do you choose? Many people decide to avoid the short-term costs by not going for regular checkups but end up facing much greater pain in the long run.

The same bias applies to students who don't study, weight watchers who sneak dessert or skip an exercise routine, and working people who take the afternoon off to play golf. It can also affect managers who hesitate to invest funds in research and development programs that may not pay off until the future. In all these cases, the avoidance of short-term costs or the seeking of short-term rewards results in negative long-term consequences.

The Japanese have been lauded for their attention to long-run considerations. When U.S. companies sacrifice present value to invest for the future—such as when

FIGURE 4.3

Going to the dentist (short-term versus long-term consequences)

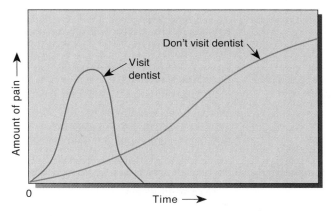

Source: From *Introduction to Modern Behaviorism,* 2nd ed., by Howard Rachlin. Copyright © 1970, 1976. W. F. Freeman and Company. Used with permission.

Weyerhaeuser incurs enormous costs for its reforestation efforts that won't lead to harvest until 60 years in the future—it seems the exception rather than the rule.

TIME PRESSURES

In today's rapidly changing business environment, the premium is on acting quickly and keeping pace. The most conscientiously made business decisions can become irrelevant and even disastrous if managers take too long to make them.

How can managers make decisions quickly? Some natural tendencies, at least for North Americans, might be to skimp on analysis (not be too vigilant), suppress conflict, and make decisions on your own without consulting other managers.[19] These strategies might speed up decision making, but they reduce decision *quality.* Can managers under time pressure make both timely and high-quality decisions?

A recent study of decision-making processes in microcomputer firms—a high-tech, fast-paced industry—showed some important differences between fast-acting and slower-acting firms.[20] The fast-acting firms realized significant competitive advantages—and did not sacrifice the quality of their decisions.

What tactics do such companies use? First, instead of relying on long-range planning and futuristic information, they focus on *real-time information:* current information obtained with little or no time delay. For example, they constantly monitor daily operating measures like work in process rather than checking periodically the traditional accounting-based indicators such as profitability.

Second, they *involve people more effectively and efficiently* in the decision-making process. They rely heavily on trusted experts, which yields both good advice and the confidence to act quickly despite uncertainty. They also take a realistic view of conflict: They value differing opinions, but they know that if disagreements are not resolved, the top executive must make the final choice in the end. Slow-moving firms, in contrast, are stymied by conflict. Like the fast-moving firms they seek consensus, but when disagreements persist they fail to come to a decision.

SOCIAL REALITIES

As the description of decision making in the microcomputer industry implies, many decisions are made by a group rather than by an individual manager. In the slow-moving firms, interpersonal factors decrease decision-making effectiveness. Even the manager acting alone is accountable to the boss and to others and must consider the preferences and reactions of many people. Important managerial decisions are marked by conflict among interested parties. Therefore, many decisions are the result of intensive social interactions, bargaining, and politicking.

The remainder of this chapter focuses on the social context of decisions, including decision making in groups and the realities of decision making in organizations.

DECISION MAKING IN GROUPS

Sometimes a manager finds it necessary to convene a group of people for the purpose of making an important decision. And ongoing work teams make decisions together constantly. Managers therefore must understand how groups and teams operate and how to use them to improve decision making. For this discussion, we will use the term "groups." You will learn much more about how teams work later in the book.

The basic philosophy behind using a group to make decisions is captured by the adage "two heads are better than one." But is this statement really valid? Yes, it is—*potentially.*

If enough time is available, groups usually make higher-quality decisions than most individuals acting alone. However, groups often are inferior to the *best* individual.[21] How well the group performs depends on how effectively it capitalizes on the potential advantages and minimizes the potential problems of using a group. Table 4.2 summarizes these issues.

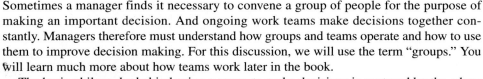

TABLE 4.2

Pros and cons of
using a group to
make decisions

Potential Advantages	Potential Disadvantages
1. Larger pool of information.	1. One person dominates.
2. More perspectives and approaches.	2. Satisficing.
3. Intellectual stimulation.	3. Groupthink.
4. People understand the decision.	4. Goal displacement.
5. People are committed to the decision.	

POTENTIAL ADVANTAGES OF USING A GROUP

If other people have something to contribute, using groups to make a decision offers at least five potential advantages.[22]

1. More *information* is available when several people are making the decision. If one member doesn't have all the facts or the pertinent expertise, another member might.

2. A greater number of *perspectives* on the issues, or different *approaches* to solving the problem, are available. The problem may be new to one group member but familiar to another. Or the group may need to consider other viewpoints—financial, legal, marketing, human resources, and so on—to achieve an optimal solution.

3. Group discussion provides an opportunity for *intellectual stimulation.* It can get people thinking and unleash their creativity to a far greater extent than would be possible with individual decision making.

These three potential advantages of using a group improve the chance that a more fully informed, higher-quality decision will result. Thus, managers should involve people with different backgrounds, perspectives, and access to information, not just their cronies who think the same way they do.

4. People who participate in a group discussion are more likely to *understand* why the decision was made. They will have heard the relevant arguments both for the chosen alternative and against the rejected alternatives.

5. Group discussion typically leads to a higher level of *commitment* to the decision. Buying into the proposed solution translates into high motivation to ensure that it is implemented successfully.

The last two advantages improve the chances that the decision will be executed effectively. Therefore, managers should involve the people who will be responsible for implementing the decision as early in the deliberations as possible.

POTENTIAL PROBLEMS IN USING A GROUP

Things *can* go wrong when groups make decisions. Most of the potential problems concern the process through which group members interact with one another.[23]

1. Sometimes one group member *dominates* the discussion. When this occurs—such as when a strong leader makes his or her preferences clear—the result is the same as if the dominant individual made the decision alone. Individual dominance has two disadvantages. First, the dominant person does not necessarily have the most valid opinions, and may even have the most unsound ideas. Second, even if that person's preference leads to a good decision, convening as a group will have been a waste of everyone else's time.

2. *Satisficing* is more likely with groups. Most people don't like meetings and will do whatever they can to end them. This may include criticizing members who want to continue exploring new and better alternatives. The result is a satisficing rather than an optimizing or maximizing decision.

3. *Pressure to avoid disagreement* can lead to a phenomenon called *groupthink.* **Groupthink** occurs when people choose not to disagree or raise objections because they

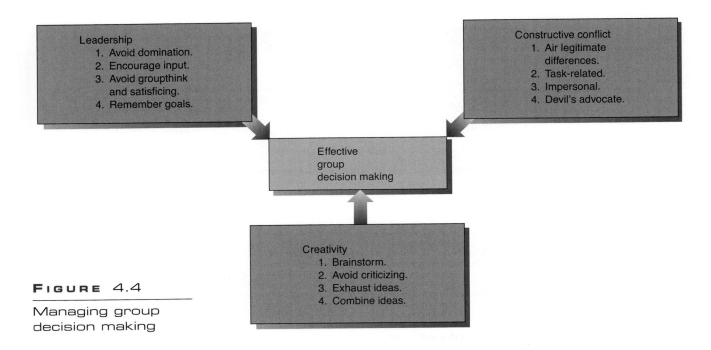

FIGURE 4.4

Managing group
decision making

don't want to break up a positive team spirit. Some groups want to think as one, tolerate no dissension, and strive to remain cordial. Such groups are overconfident, complacent, and too willing to take risks. Pressure to go along with the group's preferred solution stifles creativity and the other behaviors characteristic of vigilant decision making.

4. *Goal displacement* often occurs in groups. The goal of group members should be to come up with the best possible solution to the problem. But when **goal displacement** occurs, new goals emerge to replace the original ones. It is common for two or more group members to have different opinions and present their conflicting cases. Attempts at rational persuasion become heated disagreement. The new goal becomes winning the argument. Saving face and defeating the other person's idea become more important than solving the problem.

Effective managers pay close attention to the group process; they manage it carefully. The following sections and later chapters provide suggestions for the effective management of group meetings.

MANAGING GROUP DECISION MAKING

Figure 4.4 illustrates the requirements for effectively managing group decision making: (1) an appropriate leadership style; (2) the constructive use of disagreement and conflict; and (3) the enhancement of creativity.

LEADERSHIP STYLE

The leader of a decision-making body must attempt to minimize process-related problems. The leader should avoid dominating the discussion or allowing another individual to dominate. This means encouraging less vocal group members to air their opinions and suggestions and asking for dissenting viewpoints.

At the same time, the leader should not allow the group to pressure people into conforming. The leader should be alert to the dangers of groupthink and satisficing. Also, she or he should be attuned to indications that group members are losing sight of the primary objective: to come up with the best possible solution to the problem.

This implies two things. First, don't lose sight of the problem. Second, make a decision! Keep in mind the slow-moving microcomputer firms that were paralyzed when group members couldn't come to an agreement.

CONSTRUCTIVE CONFLICT

Total and consistent agreement among group members can be destructive. It can lead to groupthink, uncreative solutions, and a waste of the knowledge and diverse viewpoints that individuals bring to the group. Thus, a certain amount of *constructive* conflict should exist. Some companies, including Sun Microsystems, Xerox, Compaq, and United Parcel Service, take steps to ensure that conflict and debate are generated within their management teams.[24]

Of course, conflict is destructive to the group if the result is emotionalism, bitterness, and goal displacement. Conflict is constructive, on the other hand, if it is used to air legitimate differences of opinion and develop better ideas and problem solutions. Conflict, then, should be task related rather than personal.

Conflict can arise from true disagreement surfacing in an open, participative work environment, or it can be generated formally through structured processes.[25] Two techniques that purposely program conflict into the decision-making process are devil's advocacy and the dialectic method.

A **devil's advocate** has the job of criticizing ideas. The group leader can formally assign people to play this role. Requiring people to present contrary arguments can lessen inhibitions about disagreeing and make the conflict less personal and emotional.

An alternative to devil's advocacy is the dialectic. The **dialectic** goes a step beyond devil's advocacy by requiring a structured debate between two conflicting courses of action.[26] The philosophy of the dialectic stems from Plato and Aristotle, who advocated synthesizing the conflicting views of a thesis and an antithesis. Structured debates between plans and counterplans can be useful prior to making a strategic decision. For example, one team might present the case for acquiring a firm while another team advocates not making the acquisition.

ENCOURAGING CREATIVITY

As you've already learned, ready-made solutions to a problem can be inadequate or unavailable. In such cases, custom-made solutions are necessary. This means the group must be creative in generating ideas.

Innovation

Some say we are in the midst of the next great business revolution: the "creative revolution."[27] Said to transcend the agricultural, industrial, and information revolutions, the most fundamental unit of value in the creativity revolution is ideas. Creativity is more than just an option; it is essential to survival. Allowing people to be creative may be one of the manager's most important and challenging responsibilities.

You might be saying to yourself, "I'm not creative; I'm not an artist or a musician." But you do have potential to be creative in countless other ways. You have done something creative if you: (1) bring a new thing into being (creation); (2) join two previously unrelated things (synthesis); or (3) improve something or give it a new application (modification). You don't need to be a genius in school, either—Thomas Edison and Albert Einstein were not particularly good students. Nor does something need to change the world to be creative; the "little things" the business does can always be done in new, creative ways that add value to the product and the customer.

How do you "get" creative?[28] First, recognize the almost infinite "little" opportunities to be creative. Second, assume you can do it if you give it a try. Third, obtain sufficient resources, including facilities, equipment, information, and funds.

How do you "get" creativity out of other people?[29] Give creative efforts the credit they are due, and don't punish creative failures. Stimulate and challenge people intellectually, and give people some creative freedom. Provide deadlines, but also enough time to explore different ideas. Get your people in touch with customers, and let them bounce ideas around. Protect them from managers who demand immediate payoffs, who don't understand the importance of creative contributions, or who try to take credit for others' successes. Perhaps most important of all, strive to be creative yourself and you'll set a good example.

A technique that is commonly used is brainstorming. In **brainstorming,** group members generate as many ideas about a problem as they can. As the ideas are presented, they are posted so that everyone can read them, and people can use these ideas as building blocks. The group is encouraged to say anything that comes to mind, except for one thing: No criticism of other people or their ideas is allowed. This rule was violated at the Walt Disney Company when, during a brainstorming session for the design of Euro Disneyland, two architects began shoving each other and almost came to blows.[30]

In the proper brainstorming environment—free of criticism—people are less inhibited and more likely to voice their unusual, creative, or even wild ideas. By the time people have exhausted their ideas, a long list of alternatives has been generated. Only then does the group turn to the evaluation stage. At that point, many different ideas can be considered, modified, or combined into a creative, custom-made solution to the problem.

ORGANIZATIONAL REALITIES

To understand decision making in organizations, a manager must consider a number of additional concepts and processes, including (1) the constraints decision makers face; (2) negotiations and politics; and (3) decision making during a crisis.

CONSTRAINTS ON DECISION MAKERS

Organizations—or, more accurately, the people who make important decisions—cannot do whatever they wish. They face various constraints—financial, legal, market, human, and organizational—that inhibit certain actions. Capital or product markets may make an expensive new venture impossible. Legal restrictions may restrain the kinds of international business activities in which a firm can participate. Labor unions may successfully defeat a contract proposed by management, contracts may prevent certain managerial actions, and managers and investors may block a takeover attempt.

In addition, ethical considerations must be thought out carefully. You will have plenty of opportunity to think about ethical issues in Chapter 6. Decision makers *must* consider ethics and the preferences of many constituent groups—the realities of life in organizations.

NEGOTIATIONS AND POLITICS

Innovation

Decision makers often need to negotiate, bargain, or compromise. Some decisions must be negotiated with parties outside the organization, such as local government, consumer groups, or environmental groups. Even inside the organization, many decisions are negotiated among a number of people.

Suppose you have a great idea that will provide a revolutionary service for your bank's customers. You won't be able to put your idea into action immediately. You will have to sell it to the people who can give you the go-ahead and also to those whose help you will need to carry out the project. You might start by convincing your boss of your idea's merit. Next, the two of you may have to hash it out with a vice president. Then the president has to be sold. At each stage, you must listen to these individuals' opinions and suggestions and often incorporate them into your original concept. Ultimately, you will have to negotiate a proposal acceptable to everyone.

The fact that decisions often must be negotiated implies that they are political; that is, they galvanize the preferences of competing groups and individuals. The decision that is best on objective grounds may lose out because powerful individuals push through their preferred alternatives.

Consider a company that is pursuing a strategy of growth through acquisitions. Such activity constitutes a favorite power game of a powerful coalition of top executives. These

TABLE 4.3

Two disasters

Union Carbide	Johnson & Johnson
Failed to identify as a crisis the public perception that the company was a negligent, uncaring killer.	Identified the crisis of public perception that Tylenol was unsafe and J&J was not in control.
No planning before reaction: CEO immediately went to India to inspect damage. All executives involved.	Planned before reacting: CEO picked one executive to head crisis team. Rest of company involved only on a strict need-to-know basis.
Set no goals.	Set goals to: Stop the killings. Find reasons for the killings. Provide assistance to the victims. Restore Tylenol's credibility.
Action: Damage control/stonewalling. Distanced itself. Misrepresented safety conditions. Spokespeople uninformed. Adopted bunker mentality.	Action: Gave complete information. Worked with authorities. Pulled Tylenol from shelves (first-year cost: $150 million). Used strong marketing program. Reissued Tylenol with tamper-proof packaging.
Chronic problems continued: Public confidence low. Costly litigation. No formal crisis plan resulted.	Crisis resolved: Public confidence high. Sales high again. Well-documented crisis management plan.

executives may prefer to acquire another company even if their own company really needs to focus its efforts on strengthening its internal operations. Decisions on pay raises, promotions, and budget also may be made (and criticized) on the basis of politics.

Most managers accept such political realities and consider them a basic challenge of organizational life.[31] Such an outlook probably is more useful for managing the decision-making process effectively than a view of organizational politics as evil and unnecessary. For any important decision that you wish to influence, it is essential that you identify and marshal the support of powerful individuals or interest groups.

DECISION MAKING IN A CRISIS

Speed

In crisis situations, managers must make some decisions under a great deal of pressure.[32] A VIP customer threatens to cancel his contract if your company doesn't get his computer lines operating within the hour. A wildcat strike shuts down your plant. People are killed or injured in a crash of one of your airline's jets or in an explosion in one of your company's mines. What actions will you take? Whatever you decide, you must do it quickly.

You have no doubt heard of some of the most famous recent crises: Tylenol, Three Mile Island, Bhopal, the space shuttle *Challenger,* the Exxon *Valdez.* Union Carbide's gas leak in Bhopal, India, killed thousands of people; several people were killed in the cyanide poisonings of Johnson & Johnson's Tylenol. As outlined in Table 4.3, the two companies handled their crises in very different ways. To this day, J&J is known for its effective handling of the crisis, as outlined in the table.

■
_____

Companies handle crisis
decision making in different
ways. Union Carbide's
mishandling of the gas leak in
Bhopal, India, resulted in the
perception that the company
was negligent and uncaring.
Ten years after the tragic
accident, people demonstrated
vigorously against the company.
(AP/Wide World Photos)

Commonly a crisis makes effective decision making less likely. Psychological stress and lack of time cause decision makers to think in simplistic terms, to fail to consider an adequate number of alternatives, and to ignore the long-term implications of their actions.

Some crises can be prevented by clarifying the corporation's values and social responsibilities, and monitoring people's behavior and ethical conduct. You will read more about this in Chapter 6. Your firm should be prepared for crises in advance.

Table 4.4 lists some common rationalizations that prevent companies from preparing for and managing crises properly. Effective managers do not allow these evasions to prevent them from preparing carefully for crisis.

TABLE 4.4

Mistaken
assumptions: how
not to handle crisis
management

We don't have a crisis.

We can handle a crisis.

Crisis management is a luxury we can't afford.

If a major crisis happens, someone else will rescue us.

Accidents are just a cost of doing business.

Most crises are the fault of bad individuals; therefore, there's not much we can do to prevent them.

Only executives need to be aware of our crisis plans; why scare our employees or members of the community?

We are tough enough to react to a crisis in an objective and rational manner.

The most important thing in crisis management is to protect the good image of the organization through public relations and advertising campaigns.

Source: Abridged from C. M. Pearson and I. I. Mitroff, "From Crisis Prone to Crisis Prepared: A Framework for Crisis Management," *The Executive*, February 1993, pp. 48–59.

An effective plan for crisis management (CM) should include the following elements:[33]

1. *Strategic actions* such as integrating CM into strategic planning and official policies.
2. *Technical and structural actions* such as creating a CM team and dedicating a budget to CM.
3. *Evaluation and diagnostic actions* such as conducting audits of threats and liabilities, conducting environmental impact audits, and establishing tracking systems for early warning signals.
4. *Communication actions* such as providing training for dealing with the media, local communities, and police and government officials.
5. *Psychological and cultural actions* such as showing a strong top management commitment to CM and providing training and psychological support services regarding the human and emotional impacts of crises.

Ultimately, it is imperative that management be able to answer the following qestions:[34]

- What kinds of crises could your company face?
- Can your company detect a crisis in its early stages?
- How will it manage a crisis if one occurs?
- How can it benefit from a crisis after it has passed?

The last question makes an important point: a crisis, managed effectively, can have *benefits*. Old as well as new problems can be resolved, new strategies and competitive advantages may appear, and positive change can emerge. And if someone steps in and manages the crisis well, a hero is born.

K E Y   T E R M S

brainstorming, p. 94
certainty, p. 83
conflict, p. 84
custom-made solutions, p. 84
devil's advocate, p. 93
dialectic, p. 93
discounting the future, p. 89
framing effects, p. 88
goal displacement, p. 92
groupthink, p. 91

illusion of control, p. 88
maximize, p. 86
nonprogrammed decisions, p. 83
optimize, p. 86
programmed decisions, p. 83
ready-made solutions, p. 84
risk, p. 83
satisfice, p. 86
uncertainty, p. 83
vigilance, p. 87

S U M M A R Y   O F   L E A R N I N G   O B J E C T I V E S

Now that you have studied Chapter 4, you should know:

The kinds of decisions you will face as a manager.

Most important managerial decisions are ill structured and characterized by uncertainty, risk, and conflict. Yet managers are expected to make rational decisions in the face of these challenges.

How to make "rational" decisions.

The ideal decision-making process involves six stages. The first, identifying and diagnosing the problem, requires recog-

nizing a discrepancy between the current state and a desired state and then delving below surface symptoms to uncover the underlying causes of the problem. The second stage, generating alternative solutions, requires adopting ready-made or designing custom-made solutions. The third, evaluating alternatives, means predicting the consequences of different alternatives, sometimes through building scenarios of the future. Fourth, a solution is chosen; the solution might maximize, satisfice, or optimize. Fifth, decision makers implement the decision; this stage requires more careful planning than it often receives. Finally, managers should evaluate how well the decision is working. This means gathering objective, valid information about the impact the decision is having. If the evidence suggests the problem is not getting solved, either a better decision or a better implementation plan must be developed.

The pitfalls you should avoid when making decisions.

Situational and human limitations lead most decision makers to satisfice rather than maximize. Psychological biases, time pressures, and the social realities of organizational life may prevent sequential, rational execution of the six decision-making stages. But vigilance and an understanding of how to manage decision-making groups and organizational constraints will improve the process and result in better decisions.

The pros and cons of using a group to make decisions.

Advantages include more information, perspectives, and approaches brought to bear on problem solving; intellectual stimulation; greater understanding by all of the final decision; and higher commitment to the decision once it is made. Potential dangers or disadvantages of groups or teams include individual domination of discussions, satisficing, groupthink, and goal displacement.

The procedures to use in leading a decision-making team.

Effective leaders in decision-making teams or groups avoid dominating the discussion; encourage people's input; avoid group-think and satisficing; and stay focused on the group's goals. They encourage constructive conflict through devil's advocacy and the dialectic, posing opposite sides of an issue or solutions to a problem. They also encourage creativity through a variety of techniques.

How to encourage creative decisions.

When creative ideas are needed, leaders should set a good example by being creative themselves. They should recognize the almost infinite "little" opportunities for creativity, and have confidence in their own creative abilities. They can inspire creativity in others by pushing for creative freedom, rewarding creativity, and not punishing creative failures. They should encourage interaction with customers, stimulate discussion, and protect people from managers who might squelch the creative processes. Brainstorming is one of the most popular techniques for generating creative ideas.

How to make decisions in a crisis.

Crisis conditions make sound, effective decision making more difficult. However, it is possible for crises to be managed well. A strategy for crisis management can be developed beforehand, and the mechanisms put into readiness, so that if crises do arise, decision makers are prepared.

DISCUSSION QUESTIONS

1. Setting the Stage highlighted some gutsy decisions. What are some other gutsy decisions you have read about lately? Do you think the decisions were the right ones? Why or why not?

2. Identify some gutsy decisions *you* have made. Why did you make them? How did they work out? Looking back, what did you learn?

3. Review the "Economic Scenarios for the Year 2000" (pp. 85–86). Discuss the questions raised after the section.

4. Review Figure 4.3. What other decisions could you analyze in terms of short-range versus longer-range consequences?

5. Recall a recent decision that you had difficulty making. Describe your situation in terms of the characteristics of managerial decisions.

6. Do you think managers can use computer technology to improve the rationality of their decisions? Why (and how?) or why not?

7. Do you think that when managers make decisions they follow the decision-making steps as presented in this chapter? Which steps are apt to be overlooked or given inadequate attention? What can people do to make sure they do a more thorough job?

8. Discuss the potential advantages and disadvantages of using a team or group to make decisions. Give examples in your experience.

9. Suppose you are the CEO of a major corporation and one of your company's oil tanks has erupted, spilling thousands of gallons of oil into a river that empties into the ocean. What should you do to handle the crisis?

10. Look at the mistaken assumptions described in Table 4.4. Why do such assumptions arise, and what can be done to overcome these biases?

11. Identify some problems you want to solve. Brainstorm with others a variety of creative solutions.

CONCLUDING CASE

BAD DECISIONS AT EURO DISNEY

Two years after Walt Disney Co. opened its new park in France, Euro Disney was losing $1 million day, despite over a million visitors per month. What had gone wrong?

Disney was overly ambitious, and had made serious strategic and financial miscalculations. It relied too heavily on debt, just as interest rates started to rise. It assumed a real estate boom would continue, allowing it to sell some properties to pay off its debts. It made mistakes in the park itself, including cost overruns, a no-alcohol policy (in a country where a glass of wine for lunch is standard), too few bathrooms, and a mistaken assumption that the French would not want breakfast at the hotel restaurants.

The company blamed its problems on a severe European recession, high interest rates, and the devaluation of several currencies against the French franc. But it had alienated the people it needed to work with. Disney thought it knew best, and persistently imposed its will on others. "They were always sure it would work because they were Disney," said one French construction-industry official. Disney's European executives felt they were always playing second fiddle to corporate executives.

Disney showed its overconfidence in many ways. Executives boasted they could predict future living patterns in Paris; they predicted people would move to the east near Euro Disney. They believed they could change European habits. For instance, Europeans are more reluctant than Americans to let their kids skip school, and prefer longer vacations to short breaks. Disney believed it could change these preferences.

"There was a tendency to believe that everything they touched would be perfect," said a former Disney executive. Disney believed that what it could do in Florida, it could do in France. The perceived arrogance, and a critical press, demoralized the workforce, and initially kept visitors away.

The risky financing of Euro Disney was based on a highly optimistic scenario with little margin for error. When critics said the financial structure was far too clever for its own good, Disney's attitude was that cautious, old-world European thinking couldn't comprehend U.S.–style, free-market financing.

The Walt Disney Company made a host of bad decisions regarding its Euro Disney theme park in France. In the end, the park remained open, but observers say it will take extreme measures to make the project profitable. (Sichov/SIPA)

Eventually, the park had as many visitors as projected. But costs were way too high, and the economic environment changed. To cover costs, park admission was set at $42.45, higher than in the United States. But Disney failed to see the warnings of a European depression. Said one executive, "Between the glamour and the pressure of opening and the intensity of the project itself, we didn't realize a major recession was coming."

Michael Eisner, chairman of Disney, vowed to make Euro Disney the company's most lavish project ever. He was obsessed with maintaining Disney's reputation for quality, but he went way over budget to do things that critics considered frivolous.

When things were at their bleakest, Disney threatened to close the park, but negotiated last-minute, new favorable financing arrangements. The crisis seemed solved, at least temporarily. Many observers maintained, however, that Euro Disney was not really in danger of shutting down—too much was at stake, for the company, its creditors, and the French government, which initially had provided road and rail networks to the park and $750 million in loans at below-market rates.

Prices have been dropped, and some costs have also been reduced by new management. But more development and a second theme park are needed for Euro Disney to recover.

QUESTIONS

1. How many decisions can you count in this case? What others can you think of that needed to be made for such an ambitious undertaking?

2. What principles from the chapter can you spot in this case? What mistakes do you see by Disney executives?

3. With the benefit of hindsight, what could Disney have done differently?

4. What steps should Disney have taken to solve the crisis?

5. How is Euro Disney doing now? And why?

Source: P. Gumbel and R. Turner, "Fans Like Euro Disney, but Its Parent's Goofs Weigh the Park Down," *The Wall Street Journal,* March 10, 1994, pp. A1, A12.

VIDEO CASE

DECISION MAKING

In a global economy, sound business decisions depend on a number of important factors. The quality of managerial decisions can determine a company's success or failure. A recent study concluded that managers spend approximately 50 percent of their time dealing with the consequences of bad decision making.

In this video case study two successful businesses—the Second City Theater in Chicago and Heavenly Ski Resort in Lake Tahoe—explore the following decision making topics:

1. Managers make different decisions under different business conditions;
2. When managers take steps to explore and evaluate alternatives it leads to more effective decisions; and
3. All managers need to be aware of the many factors that can affect the decision making process.

Broadly defined, decision making is a process of choosing among alternative courses of action. In the business world, this process takes place under varying conditions of certainty and risk. Decision making is more likely to be effective when approached in a series of steps that explore and evaluate alternatives.

1. Identify the problem;
2. Generate alternative solutions;
3. Evaluate the alternatives;
4. Select the best alternative;
5. Implement the decision; and
6. Evaluate the decision.

To evaluate a decision, managers must gather information that can shed light on its effectiveness. Although most managers would prefer to follow all of these decision making steps, time and circumstances don't always allow it. This decision making process can also be influenced by other important factors such as intuition, emotion, stress, confidence, and risk propensity.

Second City has grown from its roots as a small "mom and pop" theater, to a large, internationally known corporate enterprise. Rather than investing all its resources into its immensely popular old-town Chicago improv theater, the Second City has decided to translate its expertise into other ventures, such as television, corporate training, and other theaters in Toronto, suburban Chicago, and Detroit.

Heavenly Lake Tahoe accommodates nearly 750,000 skiers per year, and competes as one of eight large Tahoe-area resorts. Like the Second City Theater, managers at Heavenly must make decisions affecting the growth of the company in less than ideal conditions.

Although following the six decision making steps may lead to a sounder decision making process, theory doesn't always play out in practice. Management may follow some steps, but perhaps not all of them, depending on the factors affecting the decision making process. "Most of the managers are encouraged to make a decision right away and don't hold on to the problem. It's such a fast pace that I want them to just go on to the next thing and not hold the problem back. I've empowered them to pretty much make their own decisions," said Steve Jacobson, director of food and beverage at Heavenly.

Making people laugh takes a lot of hard work and courage, as well as creativity and insight. Decisions about artistic design don't always fit the mold of the decision making model. Kelly Leonard, associate producer at Second City, said, "We did a show which was a parody of *Our Town* and it was at times brilliant and at times not. It got great reviews, it was very intricate in its knowledge of *Our Town*. However, it demanded a certain understanding of the play and of the Second City form to really get all the jokes. What we found is that though critics loved it and many of us loved it here, the audience didn't understand it. We tried an advertising campaign to support it, which to that time we had not advertised much and it didn't work and people wouldn't come. So we had to switch over the show."

Both the Second City Theater and Heavenly Lake Tahoe face the challenge of providing entertainment to consumers. In their day-to-day operations, both companies experience the need to make decisions in varying conditions of certainty, uncertainty, and risk. Both companies follow the steps of the decision making model when feasible. Identifying a problem, generating alternatives, evaluating the alternatives, selecting the best alternative, implementing the decision, and evaluating the decision. Factors such as intuition, emotion and stress, and confidence or risk propensity can also have an impact on the decision making process. Awareness of the nature of decision making, its important steps and influential factors may help managers minimize the time they spend responding to the consequences of poor decision making. This can enable managers to spend more time maximizing opportunities for growth.

CRITICAL THINKING QUESTIONS

1. Decision making is described in the video as a series of steps. Do you agree with the six steps as outlined in the video? What additional procedures might be added to the process?

2. There are situations where decision making requires input from many people, and times when decisions have to be made by an individual. Describe a situation that would require wide input, and one where an individual should make a decision without outside input. How do these situations differ?

3. Managerial decision making is affected by something called "risk propensity." What does this term mean? How can managers improve their risk propensity?

EXPERIENTIAL EXERCISES

4.1 Competitive Escalation: The Dollar Auction

Objective

To explore the effects of competition on decision making.

Instructions

Step 1: 5 Minutes. The instructor will play the role of auctioneer. In this auction, the instructor will auction off $1 bills (the instructor will inform you whether this money is real or imaginary). All members of the class may participate in the auction at the same time.

The rules for this auction are slightly different from those of a normal auction. In this version, *both the highest bidder and the next highest bidder will pay their last bids* even though the dollar is only awarded to the highest bidder. For example, if Bidder A bids 15 cents for the dollar and Bidder B bids 10 cents, and there is no further bidding, then A pays 15 cents for the dollar and receives the dollar, while B pays 10 cents and receives nothing. The auctioneer would lose 75 cents on the dollar just sold.

Bids must be made in multiples of 5 cents. The dollar will be sold when there is no further bidding. If two individuals bid the same amount at the same time, ties are resolved in favor of the bidder located physically closest to the auctioneer. *During each round, there is to be no talking except for making bids.*

Step 2: 15 Minutes. The instructor (auctioneer) will auction off five individual dollars to the class. Any student may bid in an effort to win the dollar. A record sheet of the bidding and winners can be kept in the worksheet that follows.

Discussion Questions

1. Who made the most money in this exercise—one of the bidders or the auctioneer? Why?
2. As the auction proceeded, did bidders become more competitive or more cooperative? Why?
3. Did two bidders ever pay more for the money being auctioned than the value of the money itself? Explain how and why this happened.
4. Did you become involved in the bidding? Why?
   a. If you became involved, what were your motivations? Did you accomplish your objectives?
   b. If not, why didn't you become involved? What did you think were the goals and objectives of those who did become involved?
5. Did people say things to one another during the bidding to influence their actions? What was said, and how was it influential?

DOLLAR AUCTION WORKSHEET

	Amount Paid by Winning Bidder	Amount Paid by Second Bidder	Total Paid for This Dollar
First dollar			
Second dollar			
Third dollar			
Fourth dollar			
Fifth dollar			

Source: Excerpted from R. Lewicki, *Experiences in Management and Organizational Behavior* (New York: John Wiley and Sons, 1991), pp. 91–92, 27–28, and 225–227. Reprinted by permission of John Wiley and Sons, Inc.

4.2 Group Problem-Solving Meeting at the Community Agency

Objective

Through role playing a meeting between a chairman and his subordinates, to understand the interactions in group decision making.

Instructions

1. Gather role sheets for each character and instructions for observers.
2. Set up a table in front of the room with five chairs around it arranged in such a way that participants can talk comfortably and have their faces visible to observers.
3. Read the introduction and cast of characters.
4. Five members from the class are selected to role play the five characters. All other members act as observers. The participants study the roles. All should play their roles without referring to the role sheets.
5. The observers read the instructions for observers.
6. When everyone is ready, John Cabot enters his office, joins the others at the table, and the scene begins. Allow 20 minutes to complete the meeting. The meeting is carried to the point of completion unless an argument develops and no progress is evident after 10 or 15 minutes of conflict.

Discussion Questions

1. Describe the group's behavior. What did each member say? Do?
2. Evaluate the effectiveness of the group's decision making.
3. Did any problems exist in leadership, power, motivation, communication, or perception?
4. How could the group's effectiveness be increased?

Introduction

The Community Agency is a role-play exercise of a meeting between the chairman of the board of a social service agency and four of his subordinates. Each character's role is designed to recreate the reality of a business meeting. Each character comes to the meeting with a unique perspective on a major problem facing the agency as well as some personal impressions of the other characters developed over several years of business and social associations.

The Cast of Characters

John Cabot, the Chairman, was the principal force behind the formation of the Community Agency, a multi-service agency. The agency employs 50 people, and during its 19 years of operations has enjoyed better client relations, a better service record, and a better reputation than other local agencies because of a reputation for high-quality service at a moderate cost to funding agencies. Recently, however, competitors have begun to overtake the Community Agency, resulting in declining contracts. John Cabot is expending every possible effort to keep his agency comfortably at the top.

Ron Smith, Director of the Agency, reports directly to Cabot. He has held this position since he helped Cabot establish the agency 19 years ago.

Joan Sweet, Head of Client Services, reports to Smith. She has been with the Agency 12 years, having worked before that for HEW as a contracting officer.

Tom Lynch, Head Community Liaison, reports to Joan Sweet. He came to the Community Agency at Sweet's request, having worked with Sweet previously at HEW.

Jane Cox, Head Case Worker, also works for Joan Sweet. Cox was promoted to this position two years ago. Prior to that time, Jane had gone through a year's training program after receiving an MSW from a large urban university.

TODAY'S MEETING

John Cabot has called the meeting with these four managers in order to solve some problems that have developed in meeting service schedules and contract requirements. Cabot must catch a plane to Washington in half an hour; he has an appointment to negotiate a key contract which means a great deal to the future of the Community Agency. He has only 20 minutes to meet with his managers and still catch the plane. Cabot feels that getting the Washington contract is absolutely crucial to the future of the agency.

Source: J. Gordon, *A Diagnostic Approach to Organizational Behavior* (Englewood Cliffs, N.J.: Prentice-Hall, 1983), pp. 340–41. Reprinted by permission of Prentice-Hall, Inc., Englewood Cliffs, N.J.

TAMPA PUMP & VALVE COMPANY

Tampa Pump & Valve Company is a subsidiary of Florida Chemical & Equipment Corporation. Its operations have been quite successful. Beginning with a capital investment of slightly less than $750,000 shortly after the end of World War II, its capital investment today exceeds $65 million. Tampa Pump & Valve Company has a newly constructed office building and a manufacturing and assembly plant. There are two sales outlets, one in Tampa and one in Jacksonville.

The company, excluding top management, currently is staffed with 60 engineers and 32 technicians. Approximately 1,000 persons are employed in the production department and work two 40-hour shifts a week.

Joe O'Malley is the general superintendent in charge of production. All valves and pump assemblies and components that are not purchased are manufactured and assembled in the production department according to job and design specifications. These are shipped to various locations according to orders, or they are stored in the company's two warehouses in Jacksonville and Tampa.

The research and development division, currently under the direction of Tom Everts, has grown from 2 engineers to 30 engineers and 12 technicians and draftspeople. Partly because of the plant manager's intense interest, 10 percent of the company's profits are allocated to research and development. The research division recently developed a less expensive and longer-lasting rust inhibitor than that manufactured previously.

In addition to being the controller, Bill Marshall is general counsel for the plant. A staff of two attorneys and three legal assistants report directly to him, as does the chief accountant and his staff. The accounting department employs approximately 15 people.

The industrial and employee relations department, under A. C. Cushwell, has a staff of about 15. A total of 82 employees work in the marketing department, which is headed by James Barber.

Plant manager John Manners suffered a severe heart attack on April 12 and died. At this time, Richard West was transferred from the Orlando Pump and Valve Plant, which is a slightly smaller subsidiary of Florida Chemical & Equipment Corporation, to fill the position.

Instructions

Today is Sunday, April 14. Richard West has just come into the office, for the first time, at 6:45 P.M. He must leave in time to catch the 10 P.M. plane for Caracas, Venezuela, for an important meeting. He will not be back until next Monday, April 22. His secretary is Pearl Powell, who was secretary to John Manners before he died.

The materials at the end of this case were left in his in-basket. You are to assume the role of Richard West and go through the entire packet of materials, taking whatever action you deem appropriate for each item. Write down every action you wish to take, including memos to the secretary, memos to "yourself," and so on. These memos may be in rough draft form.

Remember: The day is Sunday, April 14; the time is 6:45 P.M. You cannot call on anyone for assistance. You must work with the materials at hand. You will be out of the office from 9:45 tonight until Monday, April 22. Be sure to record every action, whether memo, letter, meeting plan, and so forth.

Memos to Use with the Tampa Pump & Valve Company Integrating Case

Use the following memos to complete the Tampa Pump & Valve Company Integrating Case. This in-basket exercise will help you test and develop your managerial decision-making skills.

Source: R. E. Dutton and R. C. Sherman, "The Tampa Pump & Valve Company," in *Action in Organizations,* ed. D. D. White and H. W. Vroman (Boston: Allyn & Bacon, 1978), pp. 441–49.

April 7

OFFICE MEMORANDUM

TO: John Manners

FROM: A.C. Cushwell, Industrial and Employee Relations

SUBJECT: Testing Program

You recently suggested that we institute a testing program for hiring secretarial and clerical personnel. The following are some suggested tests and other criteria that we might want to consider. Do you have any further suggestions for types of tests or other hiring procedures which we might want to look into before we finalize a program?

(1) Clerical Personnel:

   (a) Whitney General Clerical Survey (includes measures on spelling, arithmetic, alphabetizing, and general aptitude)

   (b) Mann-Watson Typing Test

   (c) Age to 40

(2) Secretarial Personnel:

   (a) Whitney General Clerical Survey

   (b) Mann-Watson Typing Test

   (c) Collins Shorthand Skill Inventory (via recording)

   (d) High School Diploma

   (e) Age to 40

A.C. Cushwell

PERSONAL

April 10

OFFICE MEMORANDUM

TO: John Manners

FROM: A.C. Cushwell, Industrial and Employee Relations

SUBJECT: Frank Batt

I have heard through the grapevine and "unimpeachable" sources that Frank Batt has been looking around and has had an outside job offer on which he is going to give a firm answer next week. I don't think anyone else knows this yet. I just happened to run on to it. I understand that he has been offered more money than we can offer him now based on present wage and salary policy. As you know, Batt has only been with the company a short time and is already making somewhat more than others at his rank. This presents a problem which needs to be ironed out. I am afraid I mentioned the possibility of just such a situation as this when you instituted the plan last November. Perhaps we need to reconsider some of the aspects of your plan before we make offers to June graduates.

I know that you and Everts feel that Frank is one of the most valuable men in research and development, and I thought I would let you know about this for whatever action you want to take.

A.C. Cushwell

April 10

OFFICE MEMORANDUM

TO: John Manners

FROM: Bill Marshall

SUBJECT: Termination of Robert Roberts, Employee #6897

This is a summary of my reasons for terminating Robert Roberts. As you know, Mr. Roberts was employed as a legal assistant on March 4, 19xx. For almost two years he has been working for us on a full-time basis while attending law school at night. He has continually been a source of irritation to those who have been working closely with him. The problem in general has been one of overstepping his authority. He has frequently been involved in controversies with the legal staff over problems we felt he was not adequately prepared to deal with and were none of his concern since they did not involve his own work assignments. In general, he did an adequate job on the work he was assigned, but many of the staff felt that he was not putting forth a full effort because he seemed to have a lot of free time which he spent in the coffee bar or in conversations with others in the department. The incident that caused his termination took place about three days before his termination. He was told to contact a party concerning a pending contract. All he was to do was to secure the necessary signatures from the other party. The attorney handling the contract for our company in the particular case was George Slavin. Mr. Roberts, instead of simply securing signatures, evidently discussed the contract with the outside party, recommending changes, and in general so disrupted proceedings that now the whole contract is in question. After the customer contacted George, George immediately discussed the occurrence with me, and we felt that the incident was serious enough to warrant dismissal.

Bill

April 6

OFFICE MEMORANDUM

TO: John Manners

FROM: James Barber

SUBJECT: Sales Promotion of Rust Inhibitor

As you know, we are moving into our campaign to push the new rust inhibitor. I would like to have your permission to set up a contest among our sales representatives with a trip to Hawaii for the sales representative who sells the highest dollar volume in the next six-month period. I want to make the prize good enough to tempt the sales force.

Jim

April 9

OFFICE MEMORANDUM

TO: John Manners

FROM: Bill Marshall

SUBJECT: Annual Budget Requests

We are late in turning in our budget proposal to Florida Chemical &
Equipment Company for the next fiscal year since the report from R&D is
still not in. All other department heads have turned in sound budgets which,
if approved, should greatly facilitate the cutting of costs next year. Can
you do something to speed up action?

Bill Marshall

April 6

OFFICE MEMORANDUM

TO: John Manners

FROM: Bill Marshall

SUBJECT: Coffee Breaks

This morning I timed a number of people who took 40 minutes standing in line
and drinking their coffee. These people were mainly from the production and
research departments. I am able to control this in my department, and I feel
you should see that this matter is taken care of by the heads of the other
departments. I estimate that the waste amounts to 125,000 man-hours
(approximately $500,000) a year.

Bill

                                                              April 9

OFFICE MEMORANDUM

TO: John Manners

FROM: Tom Everts

SUBJECT: Allocations for Research

This department has been successful in developing an efficient method for extracting certain basic compounds from slag and other similar by-products that are currently classified as waste by a large number of chemical plants within this area.

It is my recommendation that this company take every step necessary to commercially develop this extraction method. I have brought this matter to Bill Marshall's attention on two separate occasions, requesting that the necessary funds be allocated to fully develop this program. I have been advised by him both times that the funds could not possibly be made available within the next fiscal year. He has also indicated that we should deemphasize research in the chemical area, since this is unnecessary duplication of functions with the Orlando and Lake City plants.

It is my opinion that this company should capitalize on its advantageous position now, before our competitors are able to perfect a similar method.

The above is for your consideration and recommendations.

                                                              Tom Everts

cc: Mr. O.J. Thompson, Vice President
    Research & Development

OFFICE MEMORANDUM

TO: John Manners

FROM: Joe O'Malley

SUBJECT: Pay rate for maintenance men who worked on the U.S. National Day of
         Mourning

It was necessary for me to bring in seven maintenance men last Monday in spite of your order that we would observe the National Day of Mourning due to the sudden death of President Harris.

The question has arisen as to whether these men should be paid straight time for the work or double time, which is customary for work during holidays. I also had 40 people on vacation during this period. Ordinarily, when a legal holiday falls during their vacation they are given an extra day. Since this was an unusual situation I am not sure how to handle it and would like your recommendation.

                                                              Joe

AMERICAN FEDERATION OF FOUNDARY WORKERS
Local 801
Tampa, Florida

April 6

Mr. John Manners
Tampa Pump & Valve Company
Tampa, Florida 33601

Dear Sir:

On several recent occasions, I have noticed that you and your staff have
employed your company newspaper as a vehicle for undermining the present
union administration.

In addition, a series of supervisory bulletins have been circulated that
were designed to cause supervisory personnel to influence the thinking of
union members in the forthcoming union election. I am also well aware of
your "support" for Jessie Sims and others, who have been more than
sympathetic toward company management.

As you know, such behavior as I have described is in direct violation of
Section 101, Subsection 9(a), of the Labor-Management Relations Act, as well
as being a violation of Article 21 of our contract with your company. I am
sure that you are also aware of the negative impact the filing of a charge
of unfair management practices could have on future elections and
negotiations.

I trust such action will not become necessary and that you will take steps
to prevent any further discrimination against this administration.

Sincerely yours,

R.L. Loper, President
A.F.F.W., Local 801

RLL: jg
cc: Mr. A.C. Cushwell

April 10

OFFICE MEMORANDUM

TO: John Manners

FROM: Joe O'Malley

SUBJECT: Quality Control

The marketing department has put pressure on us to increase production for
the next two months so that promised deliveries can be made. At the present
time we cannot increase production without some risk in terms of quality.
The problem is that marketing does not check with us before committing us to
specific delivery dates. This problem has come up before, but nothing has
been done. Could I meet with you in the near future to discuss the
situation?

Joe

EMPLOYEE RAIDING

Litson Cotton Yarn Manufacturing Company, located in Murray, New Jersey, decided as a result of increasing labor costs to relocate its plant in Fairlee, a southern community of 4,200. Plant construction was started, and a human resources office was opened in the state employment office, located in Fairlee.

Because of ineffective HR practices in the other three textile mills located within a 50-mile radius of Fairlee, Litson was receiving applications from some of the most highly skilled and trained textile operators in the state. After receiving applications from approximately 500 people, employment was offered to 260 male and female applicants. These employees would be placed immediately on the payroll with instructions to await final installation of machinery, which was expected within the following six weeks.

The managers of the three other textile companies, faced with resignations from their most efficient and best-trained employees, approached the Litson managers with the complaint that their labor force was being "raided." They registered a strong protest to cease such practices and demanded an immediate cancellation of the employment of the 260 people hired by Litson.

Litson managers discussed the ethical and moral considerations involved in offering employment to the 260 people. Litson clearly faced a tight labor market in Fairlee, and management thought that if the 260 employees were discharged, the company would face cancellation of its plans and large construction losses. Litson management also felt obligated to the 260 employees who had resigned from their previous employment in favor of Litson.

The dilemma was compounded when the manager of one community plant reminded Litson that his plant was part of a nationwide chain supplied with cotton yarn from Litson. He implied that Litson's attempts to continue operations in Fairlee could result in cancellation of orders and the possible loss of approximately 18 percent market share. It was also suggested to Litson managers that actions taken by the nationwide textile chain could result in cancellation of orders from other textile companies. Litson's president held an urgent meeting of his top subordinates to (1) decide what to do about the situation in Fairlee, (2) formulate a written policy statement indicating Litson's position regarding employee raiding, and (3) develop a plan for implementing the policy.

Source: J. Champion and J. James, *Critical Incidents in Management: Decision and Policy Issues,* 6th ed. (Burr Ridge, Ill.: Richard D. Irwin, 1988).

EFFECTIVE MANAGEMENT

Dr. Sam Perkins, a graduate of the Harvard University College of Medicine, had a private practice in internal medicine for 12 years. Fourteen months ago, he was persuaded by the Massachusetts governor to give up private practice to be director of the State Division of Human Services.

After one year as director, Perkins recognized he had made little progress in reducing the considerable inefficiency in the division. Employee morale and effectiveness seemed even lower than when he had assumed the position. He realized his past training and experiences were of a clinical nature with little exposure to effective management techniques. Perkins decided to research literature on the subject of management available to him at a local university.

Perkins soon realized that management scholars are divided on the question of what constitutes effective management. Some believe people are born with certain identifiable personality traits that make them effective managers. Others believe a manager can learn to be effective by treating subordinates with a personal and considerate approach and by giving particular attention to their need for favorable working conditions. Still others emphasize the importance of developing management style characterized by either authoritarian, democratic, or laissez-faire approaches. Perkins was further confused when he learned that a growing number of scholars advocate that effective management is contingent on the situation.

Since a state university was located nearby, Perkins contacted the dean of its college of business administration. The dean referred him to the director of the college's management center, Professor Joel McCann. Discussions between Perkins and McCann resulted in a tentative agreement that the management center would organize a series of management training sessions for the State Division of Human Services. Before agreeing on the price tag for the management conference, Perkins asked McCann to prepare a proposal reflecting his thoughts on the following questions:

1. How will the question of what constitutes effective management be answered during the conference?
2. What will be the specific subject content of the conference?
3. Who will the instructors be?
4. What will be the conference's duration?
5. How can the conference's effectiveness be evaluated?
6. What policies should the State Division of Human Services adopt regarding who the conference participants should be and how they should be selected? How can these policies be best implemented?

Source: J. Champion and J. James, *Critical Incidents in Management: Decision and Policy Issues,* 6th ed. (Burr Ridge, Ill.: Richard D. Irwin, 1989).

PART II

PLANNING AND STRATEGY

FOUNDATIONS OF MANAGEMENT

Managers and Organizations
The Evolution of Management
The External Environment
Managerial Decision Making

PLANNING AND STRATEGY

Planning and Strategic Management
Ethics and Corporate Responsibility
Managing in our Natural Environment
International Management
New Ventures

STRATEGY IMPLEMENTATION

ORGANIZING AND STAFFING

Organization Structure
The Responsive Organization
Human Resources Management
Managing the Diverse Workforce

LEADING

Leadership
Motivating for Performance
Managing Teams
Communicating

CONTROL AND CHANGE

Managerial Control
Operations Management
Managing Technology and Innovation
Becoming World Class

Part II introduces key concepts of planning and strategy. The topics emphasize the strategic decisions made by top managers and their implications for the entire organization. Chapter 5 presents a summary of the planning process and an overview of how senior executives conduct strategic management. The next three chapters treat subjects that have recently emerged as vital considerations for modern managers. Chapter 6 examines the impact of ethical concerns and social and political factors on major decisions. Chapter 7 focuses on how managerial decisions are affected by concern for our natural environment. Chapter 8 addresses the pressing reality of managing in a competitive international environment. Finally, Chapter 9 describes entrepreneurs and the new ventures they create. These chapters will provide you with a clear understanding of the strategic directions that effective organizations pursue.

5

PLANNING AND STRATEGIC MANAGEMENT

Manage your destiny, or someone else will.

Jack Welch, CEO General Electric

After studying Chapter 5, you will know:

1. How to proceed through the basic steps in any planning process.

2. How strategic planning differs from tactical and operational planning.

3. Why it is important to analyze both the external environment and internal resources of the firm before formulating a strategy.

4. The choices available for corporate strategy.

5. How companies can achieve competitive advantage through business strategy.

6. How core competencies provide the foundation for business strategy.

7. The keys to effective strategy implementation.

STRATEGIC CHANGE AT GENERAL ELECTRIC

*I*n 1981, Jack Welch, at age 45, became chair and chief executive officer of General Electric. Since then, he has completely overhauled GE's strategy, structure, and culture, transforming GE from a conservative organization operating in mature industries to an aggressive, entrepreneurial company pursuing growth and technological dominance. He sold off old businesses, such as mining, housewares, and television manufacturing, and diversified into new businesses, including broadcasting, financial services, investment banking, and high-tech manufacturing. At the same time, he has sought to maximize the competitive capability of each business unit. Early in his tenure, he decreed that all GE's businesses needed to be first or second in market share, and focused on productivity growth as key to competitiveness. He noted, "Without productivity growth, it is possible to lose in 24 months businesses that took a half-century or a century to build." Welch's ultimate goal is to make GE the most competitive business enterprise in the world.

He realized that altering the mix of business was not enough, and that strategic changes needed to be complemented by a different approach to management. Welch's six rules for success are:

- Control your destiny, or someone else will.
- Face reality as it is, not as it was or as you wish it were.
- Be candid with everyone.
- Don't manage, lead.
- Change before you have to.

Because of Jack Welch's approach to strategic management, General Electric continues to be among the most competitive corporations in the world. *(Courtesy General Electric Company)*

- If you don't have a competitive advantage, don't compete.

To transform GE management, Welch has streamlined the corporate bureaucracy, eliminated two senior management levels, and pushed decision-making authority farther down the ranks. He has tried to make the organization "boundaryless" by blurring internal divisions, encouraging teamwork, making suppliers and customers GE partners, and eliminating the separation between foreign and domestic operations.

To tap the wealth of knowledge and expertise within GE, Welch devised an organizationwide employee involvement program called "Work-Out." Work-Out focuses on four goals: (1) building trust, (2) empowering employees, (3) eliminating unnecessary work, and (4) creating a new management paradigm. Work-Out has been a resounding success at GE, and now includes customers and suppliers as well. Welch views Work-Out as a formal mechanism for sustaining a revolutionary process, and a way to transfer real power to employees.

Because of Jack Welch's approach to strategic management, GE continues to be among the most competitive corporations in the world. And despite success, change will be a way of life for GE, its managers, and its employees.

Sources: John F. Welch, Jr., "Working Out of a Tough Year," *Executive Excellence,* April 1992, pp. 14–16; Noel M. Tichy and Stratford Sherman, *Control Your Destiny or Someone Else Will* (New York: Doubleday, 1993); Noel M. Tichy and Stratford Sherman, "Walking the Talk at GE," *Training & Development,* June 1993, pp. 26–35; Joseph F. McKenna, "Take the 'A' Training," *Industry Week,* May 21, 1990, pp. 22–29; and "Jack Welch Reinvents General Electric—Again," *Economist,* March 30, 1991, pp. 59–62.

*F*or several decades, General Electric operated on the frontier of a planning field now called *strategic management.* Under Jack Welch, GE continues to be a leader in this area. In this chapter, we examine the important concepts and processes involved in planning and strategic management. You will learn about the current approaches to the strategic management of today's organizations.

AN OVERVIEW OF PLANNING

Planning is the conscious, systematic process of making decisions about goals and activities that an individual, group, work unit, or organization will pursue in the future. Planning is not an informal or haphazard response to a crisis; it is a purposeful effort, directed and controlled by managers, often drawing on the knowledge and experience of employees throughout the organization. Planning provides individuals and work units with a clear map to follow in their future activities, at the same time this map may allow for individual circumstances and changing conditions.

The importance of formal planning in organizations has grown dramatically. During the first half of this century, most planning was unstructured and fragmented, and formal planning was restricted to a few large corporations. Although management pioneers such as Alfred Sloan of General Motors instituted formal planning processes, planning became a widespread management function only during the last 30 years. While larger organizations adopted formal planning initially, even small firms operated by aggressive, opportunistic entrepreneurs now engage in formal planning.[1]

THE FORMAL PLANNING PROCESS

Because planning is a decision process, the important steps followed during formal planning are similar to the basic decision-making steps discussed in Chapter 4. Figure 5.1 shows these formal planning steps and their decision process counterparts.

Situational Analysis

As the contingency approach advocates, planning begins with a **situational analysis.** Within their time and resource constraints, planners should gather, interpret, and summarize all information relevant to the planning issue in question. A thorough situational analysis studies past events, examines current conditions, and attempts to forecast future trends. It focuses on the internal forces at work in the organization or work unit and, consistent with the open-systems approach, examines influences from the external environment. The outcome of this step is the identification and diagnosis of planning assumptions, issues, and problems.

A recent situational analysis conducted by a major medical center gathered extensive information from external groups such as consumers, physicians, government and regulatory agencies, insurance companies, and other hospitals. The analysis included information from all departments in these organizations. Historical trends in financial data and the use of various hospital services were examined, and projections were developed based on assumptions about the future. The situational analysis took 10 months, and the information was summarized in a planning document 250 pages long. To give you an idea of the importance of this step to the planning process, the remaining steps took only three months, and the final set of goals and plans was only 50 pages long!

Alternative Goals and Plans

Based on the situational analysis, the planning process should generate alternative goals that may be pursued in the future and the alternative plans that may be used to achieve those goals. This step in the process should stress creativity and encourage managers and employees to assume a broad perspective about their jobs. Evaluation of the merits of these alternative goals and plans should be delayed until a range of alternatives has been developed.

FIGURE 5.1

Decision-making
stages (Chapter 4)
and formal planning
steps (Chapter 5)

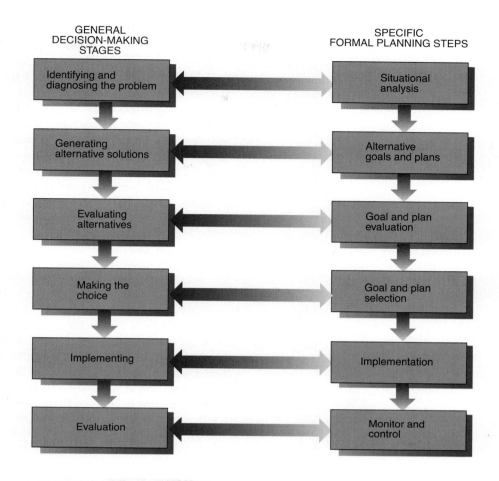

Goals are the targets or ends the manager wants to reach. Goals should be specific, challenging, and realistic. Jack Welch's goal of making General Electric first or at least second in all its markets is specific and challenging. When appropriate, goals should also be quantified and linked to a time frame. They should be acceptable to the managers and employees charged with achieving them, and they should be consistent both within and among work units.

Plans are the actions or means the manager intends to use to achieve goals. At a minimum, this step should outline alternative actions that may lead to the attainment of each goal, the resources required to reach the goal through this means, and the obstacles that may develop. Elizabeth Arden's plan to achieve its goal of becoming the fastest-growing prestigious cosmetics company in America focused on new products that meet the needs of baby boomers worried about lines, wrinkles, and skin damage from the sun. The five-year plan has Arden's sales growing an average 25 percent a year since 1989 (versus the industry's 6 percent).[2]

Goal and Plan Evaluation

Next, decision makers must evaluate the advantages, disadvantages, and potential effects of each alternative goal and plan. The decision maker must prioritize those goals or even eliminate some from further consideration. At the same time, the manager needs to consider the implications of alternative plans designed to meet high-priority goals.

In some companies, special teams of managers with diverse backgrounds conduct this evaluation. During major planning efforts at Atlantic Richfield Company (ARCO), senior executives meet with planning groups from strategic planning, public and government affairs, operations, marketing, and other areas. Often the different perspectives and ideas such groups generate lead to a more balanced and comprehensive review of company goals and plans. This approach often identifies new alternatives or refines existing ones.

Goal and Plan Selection

The planner is now in a position to select the most appropriate and feasible goals and plans. The evaluation process should identify the priorities and trade-offs among goals and plans and leave the final choice to the decision maker. Experienced judgment always plays an important role. However, as you will discover later in the chapter, relying on judgment alone may not be the best way to proceed.

Typically, a formal planning process leads to a written set of goals and plans that are appropriate and feasible within a predicted set of circumstances. In some organizations, the alternative generation, evaluation, and selection steps generate planning **scenarios,** as discussed in Chapter 4. A different contingency plan is attached to each scenario. The manager pursues the goals and implements the plans associated with the most likely scenario. However, the work unit is prepared to switch to another set of plans if the situational contingencies change and another scenario becomes relevant. This approach helps avoid crises and allows greater flexibility and responsiveness.

Implementation

Once managers have selected the goals and plans, they must implement the plans designed to achieve the goals. The best plans are useless unless they are implemented properly. Managers and employees must understand the plan, have the resources necessary to implement it, and be motivated to do so. If both managers and employees have participated in the previous steps of the planning process, the implementation phase probably will be more effective and efficient. Employees usually are better informed, more committed, and more highly motivated when a goal or plan is one that they helped develop.

Finally, successful implementation requires that the plan be linked to other systems in the organization, particularly the budget and reward systems. If the budget does not provide the manager with sufficient financial resources to execute the plan, the plan is probably doomed. Similarly, goal achievement must be linked to the organization's reward system. Many organizations use incentive programs to encourage employees to achieve goals and to implement plans properly. Commissions, salaries, promotions, bonuses, and other rewards are based on successful performance.

Monitor and Control

Although it is sometimes ignored, the final step in the formal planning process—monitor and control—is essential. Because planning is an ongoing, repetitive process, managers must continually monitor the actual performance of their work units according to the unit's goals and plans. Also, they must develop control systems that allow the organization to take corrective action when the plans are implemented improperly or when the situation changes. You will study control systems in greater detail later in this chapter and in Chapter 18.

LEVELS OF PLANNING

In Chapters 1 and 2, you learned about the three major types of managers and subsystems found in most organizations: strategic, tactical, and operational. Because planning is an important management function, managers at all three levels use it. However, the scope and activities of the planning process at each level of the organization often differ.

STRATEGIC PLANNING

Strategic planning involves making decisions about the organization's long-term goals and strategies. Strategic plans have a strong external orientation and cover major portions of the organization. Senior executives are responsible for the development and execution of the strategic plan, although they usually do not personally formulate or implement the entire plan.

Strategic goals are major targets or end results that relate to the long-term survival, value, and growth of the organization. Strategic managers usually establish goals that reflect both effectiveness (providing appropriate outputs) and efficiency (a high ratio of outputs to inputs). Typical strategic goals include various measures of return to shareholders, profitability, quantity and quality of outputs, market share, productivity, and contribution to society.

A **strategy** is a pattern of actions and resource allocations designed to achieve the goals of the organization. The strategy an organization implements is an attempt to match the skills and resources of the organization to the opportunities found in the external environment; that is, every organization has certain strengths and weaknesses. The actions, or strategies, the organization implements should be directed toward building strengths in areas that satisfy the wants and needs of consumers and other key actors in the organization's external environment. Also, some organizations may implement strategies that change or influence the external environment, as discussed in Chapter 3.

TACTICAL AND OPERATIONAL PLANNING

Once the organization's strategic goals and plans are identified, they become the basis of planning undertaken by tactical and operational managers. Goals and plans become more specific and involve shorter periods of time as planning moves from the strategic level to the operational level. **Tactical planning** translates broad strategic goals and plans into specific goals and plans that are relevant to a definite portion of the organization, often a functional area like marketing or human resources. Tactical plans focus on the major actions that a unit must take to fulfill its part of the strategic plan. **Operational planning** identifies the specific procedures and processes required at lower levels of the organization. Operational managers usually develop plans for very short periods of time and focus on routine tasks such as production runs, delivery schedules, and human resources requirements.

The organization's strategic, tactical, and operational goals and plans must be consistent and mutually supportive. For example, a major *strategic* goal of McDonald's Corporation is to increase sales growth, particularly in the dinner market. A key *tactical* planning issue is the menu McDonald's will offer for dinner. McDonald's will experiment with menus offering carrot sticks, corn on the cob, fajitas, and egg rolls. The new products must fit consumers' demands for dinnertime food. Another tactical concern is the advertising campaign that will lure consumers to McDonald's for dinner. Recent TV ads focus on price and service, two important concerns for helping the chain increase its dinner trade.

McDonald's must also fit the new items into its franchise *operating* system so that quality control, consistency, and speed are not sacrificed. The kitchens of its restaurants already employ a 600-page operations manual that stresses mass production and absolute uniformity. If McDonald's is to achieve its growth objectives, it must carefully link its strategic, tactical, and operational plans.[3]

McDonald's tactical planning efforts have resulted in a menu that now includes everything from the renowned Big Mac to pizza, tacos, and egg rolls.
(Michael Abramson)

STRATEGIC PLANNING AND STRATEGIC MANAGEMENT

Using this overview of planning as background, we will devote the remainder of this chapter to strategic issues, concepts, and processes. Strategic decision making is one of the most exciting and controversial topics in management today. In fact, many organizations currently are changing the ways they develop and execute their strategic plans.

STRATEGIC PLANNING: 1960 TO 1985

From the 1960s through the early 1980s, strategic planning often emphasized a top-down approach to goal setting and planning.[4] That is, senior managers and specialized strategic planning units developed goals and plans for the entire organization. Tactical and operational managers often received goals and plans from staff members, and their own planning activities were limited to specific procedures and budgets for their units.

During this period, individual companies and consulting firms innovated a variety of analytical techniques and planning approaches, many of which became corporate fads. These techniques often were used inappropriately and led to strategic decisions based on simplistic conclusions and evaluations. In many instances, senior managers spent more time with their planning staffs and consultants than with the managers who worked for them. Often a wide gap developed between strategic managers and tactical and operational managers. Managers and employees throughout their organizations felt alienated and lost their commitment to the organization's success.

STRATEGIC MANAGEMENT IN THE 1990S

Senior executives increasingly are involving managers throughout the organization in the strategic planning process.[5] The problems just described and the rapidly changing environment of the 1980s and 1990s have forced executives to look to all levels of the organization for ideas and innovations to make their firms more competitive. Although the CEO and other top managers continue to furnish the strategic direction or "vision" of the organization, tactical and even operational managers often provide valuable inputs to the organization's strategic plan. In some cases, these managers also have substantial autonomy to formulate or change their own plans. This increases flexibility and responsiveness, critical requirements of success in the modern organization.

Because of this trend, a new term for the strategic planning process emerged: *strategic management.* **Strategic management** involves managers from all parts of the organization in the formulation and implementation of strategic goals and strategies. It integrates strategic planning and management into a single process. Strategic planning becomes an ongoing activity in which all managers are encouraged to think strategically and to focus on long-term, externally oriented issues as well as short-term tactical and operational issues.

THE STRATEGIC MANAGEMENT PROCESS

Figure 5.2 shows the six major components of the strategic management process: (1) establishment of a mission and vision; (2) environmental analysis; (3) internal assessment, (4) strategy formulation; (5) strategy implementation; and (6) strategic control. Because this process is a planning and decision process, it is similar to the planning framework discussed earlier. Although organizations may use different terms or emphasize different parts of the process, the components and concepts described in this section are found either explicitly or implicitly in every organization.

ESTABLISHING A MISSION AND VISION

The first step in strategic planning is establishing a mission and vision for the organization. The **mission** is the basic purpose and values of the organization, as well as its scope of operations. It is a statement of the organization's reason to exist. The mission often is written in terms of the general clients it serves. Depending on the scope of the organization, the

FIGURE 5.2   The strategic management process

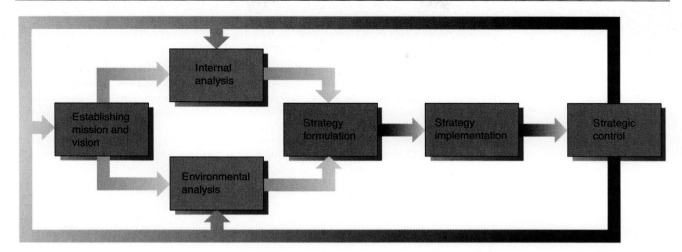

mission may be broad or narrow. For example, the mission of Kellogg Company is to be the world's leading producer of ready-to-eat cereal products and to manufacture frozen pies and waffles, toaster pastries, soups, and other convenience foods. On the other hand, the local bar found next to most campuses has the implicit mission of selling large quantities of inexpensive beer to college students.

The **strategic vision** moves beyond the mission statement to provide a perspective on where the company is headed and what the organization can become. Although the terms mission and vision often are used interchangeably, the vision statement ideally clarifies the long-term direction of the company and its *strategic intent*. Delta Airlines, for example, has a stated vision of becoming the "Worldwide Airline of Choice." This vision conveys Delta's dedication to pursuing new routes and strategic alliances while providing the very best service to its customers.[6]

Strategic goals evolve from the mission and vision of the organization. The chief executive officer of the organization, with the input and approval of the board of directors, establishes both the mission and the major strategic goals. The mission and the strategic goals influence everyone who has contact with the organization. The following statements from three respected companies demonstrate how the companies' mission and goals incorporate a strong global orientation.

THREE GLOBAL MISSIONS

Johnson & Johnson, with over 82,000 employees and $11.23 billion in sales, is the world's largest and most comprehensive manufacturer of health care products serving the consumer, pharmaceutical, and professional markets. Johnson & Johnson has 172 operating companies in 54 countries around the world. Ralph S. Larsen, chair and CEO, states that Johnson & Johnson's objective is to be "the best and most competitive health care company in the world . . . [An] important characteristic of our business is its extensive global reach. More than half our revenues come from outside the United States, and we now sell our products in more than 150 countries. This allows us to expand our new product introductions quickly and efficiently around the world."

The mission of Morgan Stanley Group Inc. is to be "the premier global securities firm," providing services to a large and diversified group of clients and customers that includes multinational corporations, governments, emerging growth companies, financial institutions, and individual investors. Morgan Stanley provides worldwide service through more than 7,000 employees, with offices in such diverse locations as New York, Toronto, London, Tokyo, Luxembourg, Hong Kong, and Singapore. Its strategy focuses on "a commitment to positioning the Firm for a truly global marketplace . . . reflecting the worldwide integration of capital markets . . . [and] expansion into promising new markets."

BellSouth is the largest provider of local telephone service in the United States and one of the largest wireless communications companies in the world. With operations spanning five continents, BellSouth is one of the world's largest telecommunications companies. The company's common stock is the second most widely held in the United States. Through BellSouth International, the firm's global marketing and business development arm, it has a diversified worldwide presence in cellular, paging, directory advertising and publishing, public and private networks, and software applications. Chair and CEO John L. Clendenin states, "We've made tough strategic decisions that strike the right balance between short-term earnings and sustainable long-term growth."

Sources: Johnson & Johnson, 1990 annual report; Morgan Stanley, 1990 annual report; BellSouth, 1991 annual report. ●

ENVIRONMENTAL ANALYSIS

After establishing a mission and vision, the second component of the strategic management process is the analysis of the external environment. Successful strategic management depends on an accurate and thorough evaluation of the environment. The various components of the environment were introduced in Chapter 3.

Table 5.1 lists some of the important activities in an environmental analysis. The analysis begins with an examination of the industry. Next, organizational stakeholders are examined. **Stakeholders** are groups and individuals who affect and are affected by the achievement of the organization's mission, goals, and strategies. They include buyers, suppliers, competitors, government and regulatory agencies, unions and employee groups, the financial community, owners and shareholders, and trade associations. The environmental analysis provides a map of these stakeholders and the ways they influence the organization.[7]

The environmental analysis should also examine other forces in the environment, such as macroeconomic conditions and technological factors. One critical task in environmental analysis is forecasting future trends. Forecasting techniques range from simple judgment to complex mathematical models that examine systematic relationships among many variables. Even simple quantitative techniques outperform the intuitive assessments of experts. Judgment is susceptible to bias, and managers have a limited ability to process information. Managers should use subjective judgments as inputs to quantitative models or when they confront new situations.[8]

The example of Compaq Computer Corporation shows the power of understanding the external environment, and correctly forecasting future trends in the industry.

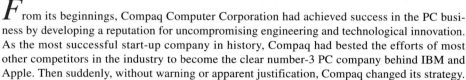

I GUESS COMPAQ KNEW WHAT IT WAS DOING AFTER ALL

*F*rom its beginnings, Compaq Computer Corporation had achieved success in the PC business by developing a reputation for uncompromising engineering and technological innovation. As the most successful start-up company in history, Compaq had bested the efforts of most other competitors in the industry to become the clear number-3 PC company behind IBM and Apple. Then suddenly, without warning or apparent justification, Compaq changed its strategy.

By 1993, Compaq had restructured its business and transformed itself from a performance-is-king company with a high-priced line of products into an aggressive, branded, low-cost producer with multiple product lines. Many experts argued the strategy was too risky and predicted that Compaq was doomed as a consequence of its abandoning the principles that had made it successful in the first place.

But unbeknownst to the critics, Compaq had devised a way to build its computers at a lower cost than previously without sacrificing quality. In essence, executives had discovered that cost and

TABLE 5.1

Environmental
analysis

Industry and market analysis

Industry profile: major product lines and significant market segments in the industry.

Industry growth: growth rates for the entire industry, growth rates for key market segments, projected changes in patterns of growth, and the determinants of growth.

Industry forces: threat of new industry entrants, threat of substitutes, economic power of buyers, economic power of suppliers, and internal industry rivalry (recall Chapter 3).

Competitor analysis

Competitor profile: major competitors and their market shares.

Competitor analysis: goals, strategies, strengths, and weaknesses of each major competitor.

Competitor advantages: the degree to which industry competitors have differentiated their products or services or achieved cost leadership.

Political and regulatory analysis

Legislation and regulatory activities and their effects on the industry.

Political activity: the level of political activity that organizations and associations within the industry undertake (see Chapter 6).

Social analysis

Social issues: current and potential social issues and their effects on the industry.

Social interest groups: consumer, environmental, and similar activist groups that attempt to influence the industry (see Chapters 6 and 7).

Human resources analysis

Labor issues: key labor needs, shortages, opportunities, and problems confronting the industry (see Chapters 12 and 13).

Macroeconomic analysis

Macroeconomic conditions: economic factors that affect supply, demand, growth, competition, and profitability within the industry.

Technological analysis

Technological factors: scientific or technical methods that affect the industry, particularly recent and potential innovations (see Chapter 20).

Speed

quality were not strategic trade-offs as many had assumed—a company could and should pursue both fervently. Compaq also had correctly identified that the market was changing and it was time to segment its product lines to fit different kinds of customers. It was the first company to offer three kinds of desktop computers, and two kinds of notebook computers. The overall result has been that Compaq now sells more computers in any one of its product lines than it used to sell in total.

Source: Stewart Alsop, "I Guess Compaq and Lotus Know What They're Doing After All," *Infoworld,* July 19, 1993, p. 4. ●

INTERNAL ANALYSIS

At the same time external analysis is conducted, the strengths and weaknesses of major functional areas within the organization are assessed. Internal analysis provides strategic decision makers with an inventory of the organization's skills and resources as well as its

TABLE 5.2

Internal resource analysis

Financial analysis

Examines financial strengths and weaknesses through financial statements such as a balance sheet and an income statement and compares trends to historical and industry figures (see Chapter 18).

Human resources assessment

Examines strengths and weaknesses of all levels of management and employees and focuses on key human resources activities, including recruitment, selection, placement, training, labor (union) relationships, compensation, promotion, appraisal, quality of work life, and human resources planning (see Chapters 12 and 13).

Marketing audit

Examines strengths and weaknesses of major marketing activities and identifies markets, key market segments, and the competitive position (market share) of the organization within key markets.

Operations analysis

Examines the strengths and weaknesses of the manufacturing, production, or service delivery activities of the organization (see Chapter 19).

Other internal resource analyses

Examine, as necessary and appropriate, the strengths and weaknesses of other organizational activities, such as research and development (product and process), management information systems, engineering, and purchasing.

---

overall and functional performance levels. Many of your other business courses will prepare you to conduct internal analysis. Table 5.2 lists some of the major components of the internal resource analysis.

Core Competence

 Without question, effective internal analysis requires a clear grasp and understanding of a company's **core competencies.** A core competence is something a company does especially well relative to its competitors. Examples might include such things as technological innovation, engineering, quality assurance, post-sales service, or marketing. Typically, a core competence refers to a set of skills or expertise in some activity, rather than physical or financial assets. For example, among U.S. automobile manufacturers, General Motors has traditionally been viewed as having a core competence in marketing while Ford has established quality as its number 1 strength. Recently Chrysler redefined its core competence to be in engineering.

When a company has a core competence in some area important to market success, those skills are the foundation for developing a competitive advantage. Companies develop partnerships or strategic alliances with other companies that have complementary competencies, enabling them to gain access to new markets, develop new technologies, or introduce new products. For example, Motorola, IBM, and Apple recently teamed up to develop the PowerPC family of microprocessors designed to compete head to head with Intel.[9]

Benchmarking

 Benchmarking is the process of assessing how well one company's basic functions and skills compare to those of some other company or set of companies. The goal of bench-

Quality

marking is to thoroughly understand the "best practices" of other firms, and to undertake actions to achieve both better performance and lower costs. For example, Xerox Corporation, a pioneer in benchmarking, established a program to study 67 of its key work processes against "world class" companies. Many of these companies were not in the copier business. For example, in an effort to improve its order fulfillment process, Xerox studied L. L. Bean, the clothing mail-order company. Benchmarking programs have helped Xerox and a myriad of other companies such as Ford, Corning, Hewlett-Packard, and Anheuser-Busch make great strides in eliminating inefficiencies and improving competitiveness. Perhaps the only downside of benchmarking is that it only helps a company perform as well as its competitors—strategic management is ultimately about surpassing those companies.[10]

STRATEGY FORMULATION

After analyzing the external environment and internal resources, strategic decision makers have the information they need to formulate corporate, business, and functional strategies of the organization. The strategy formulation process begins with a summary of the major facts and forecasts derived from the external and internal analyses. This summary leads to a series of statements that identify the primary and secondary strategic issues confronting the organization. Strategy formulation involves establishing a course of action for addressing these issues.

Corporate Strategy

Corporate strategy identifies the set of businesses, markets, or industries in which the organization competes and the distribution of resources among those businesses. An organization has four basic corporate strategy alternatives, ranging from very specialized to highly diverse. A **concentration** strategy focuses on a single business competing in a single industry. In the food-retailing industry, Kroger, Safeway, and A&P all pursue concentration strategies. Frequently companies pursue concentration strategies to gain entry into an industry, when industry growth is good, or when the company has a narrow range of competencies.

Cost

A **vertical integration** strategy involves expanding the domain of the organization into supply channels or to distributors. At one time, Henry Ford had fully integrated his company from the ore mines needed to make steel all the way to the showrooms where his cars were sold. Vertical integration is generally used to eliminate uncertainties and reduce costs associated with suppliers or distributors.

Innovation

A strategy of **concentric diversification** involves moving into new businesses that are related to the company's original core business. William Marriott expanded his original restaurant business outside Washington, D.C., by moving into airline catering, hotels, and fast food. Each of these businesses within the hospitality industry are related in terms of the services they provide, the skills necessary for success, and the customers they attract. Often companies such as Marriott pursue a strategy of concentric diversification to take advantage of their strengths in one business to gain advantage in another. Because the businesses are related, the products, markets, technologies, or capabilities used in one business can be transferred to another.

In contrast to concentric diversification, **conglomerate diversification** is a corporate strategy that involves expansion into unrelated businesses. Union Pacific Corporation has diversified from its original base in railroads to such wide-ranging industries as oil and gas exploration, mining, microwave and fiber optic systems, hazardous waste disposal, trucking, and real estate. Typically, companies pursue a conglomerate diversification strategy to minimize risks due to market fluctuations in one industry.

The corporate strategy of an organization is sometimes called its business portfolio. One of the most popular techniques for analyzing and communicating corporate strategy has been the BCG matrix.

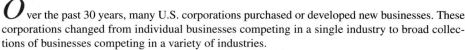

THE BCG MATRIX

*O*ver the past 30 years, many U.S. corporations purchased or developed new businesses. These corporations changed from individual businesses competing in a single industry to broad collections of businesses competing in a variety of industries.

In response to senior executives' needs to understand and manage complex, modern organizations, the Boston Consulting Group (BCG) introduced the growth/share matrix.

The BCG Matrix is shown here. Each business in the corporation is plotted on the matrix based on the growth rate of its market and the relative strength of its competitive position in that market (market share). The business is represented by a circle whose size depends on the business's contribution to corporate revenues.

High-growth, weak-competitive-position businesses are called *question marks,* They require substantial investment to improve their position; otherwise, divestiture is recommended. High-growth, strong-competitive-position businesses are called *stars.* These businesses require heavy investment, but their strong position allows them to generate the needed revenues. Low-growth, strong-competitive-position businesses are called *cash cows.* These businesses generate revenues in excess of their investment needs and therefore fund other businesses. Finally, low-growth, weak-competitive-position businesses are called *dogs.* The remaining revenues from these businesses are realized, and then the businesses are divested.

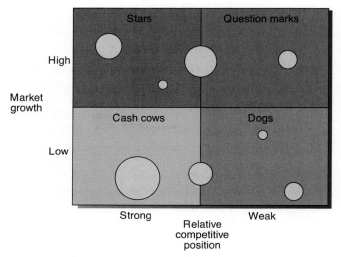

Although the BCG Matrix helps identify businesses that should be sold, it does not help managers of an individual business develop strategies to improve its competitiveness. Furthermore, the nicknames can lead to self-fulfilling prophecies. For example, a mature business may receive inadequate investment and be abandoned despite its potential for long-term profits and growth. This is particularly a problem for a business labeled a *dog.*

The BCG Matrix and similar tools can help both the corporation and the businesses if they are used as vehicles for discussion rather than as bases for major strategic decisions. The matrix should be applied with other techniques, and strategic managers must emphasize the development of long-term competitive advantages for all businesses. No single technique is a substitute for creativity, insight, or leadership.

Sources: P. Haspeslagh, "Portfolio Planning: Uses and Limits," *Harvard Business Review* 60, no. 1 (1982), pp. 58–67; and R. Hamermesh, *Making Strategy Work* (New York: John Wiley & Sons, 1986). ●

Trends in Corporate Strategy

In recent years, corporate America was swept by a wave of mergers and acquisitions. Such mergers and acquisitions often influence the organization's corporate strategy, either by concentrating in one industry or by diversifying its portfolio.

The value of implementing a diversified corporate strategy depends on individual circumstances. Many critics argue that unrelated diversification hurt the companies involved more often than it helped them. During the early 1980s, U.S. Steel acquired Marathon Oil Company, changed its federal industry classification from steel to petroleum refining, and changed its name to USX. Unfortunately, the payoff from this purchase still has not been realized, because the oil business declined soon after this acquisition. Other companies sold peripheral businesses so they could concentrate on a more focused portfolio. For example, Merck & Company sold its consumer products business to focus on the application of biotechnology in the pharmaceutical industry.[11] Sears recently sold Allstate Insurance to concentrate more on the core business of retail merchandizing. Kodak sold off Eastman Chemical to boost profitability and concentrate more on their imaging business.[12]

On the other hand, the diversification efforts of an organization competing in a slow-growth, low-profit, or threatened industry often are applauded. Many recent bank mergers, such as the creation of NationsBank from NCNB and C&S/Sovran, were designed to yield greater efficiencies and increased market share in the banking industry. Although the merits of diversification are an issue for continued study, most researchers agree that organizations usually perform better if they implement a more concentric diversification strategy in which businesses are somehow related or similar to one another.

Business Strategy

After the top management team and board make the corporate strategic decisions, executives must determine how they will compete in each business area. **Business strategy** defines the major actions by which an organization builds and strengthens its competitive position in the marketplace. A competitive advantage typically results from one of two generic business strategies introduced here and elaborated in Chapter 9.[13]

First, an organization may pursue a competitive advantage through differentiation. With a **differentiation strategy,** a company attempts to be unique in its industry or market segment along some dimensions that customers value. This unique or differentiated position within the industry often is based on high product quality, excellent marketing and distribution, or superior service. L. L. Bean's commitment to quality and service in the mail-order apparel industry is an excellent example of a differentiation strategy.

Second, a low-cost strategy may be implemented. Businesses using a **low-cost strategy** attempt to be efficient and offer a standard, no-frills product. They often are large and try to take advantage of economies of scale in production or distribution. In many cases, the large size allows them to sell their products and services at a lower price, which leads to higher market share, volume, and, ultimately, profits. To succeed, an organization using this strategy often must be the cost leader in its industry or market segment. However, even a cost leader must offer a product that is acceptable to customers when compared to competitors' products. In the toy retailing industry, Toys 'Я' Us has successfully used a low-cost strategy in the United States, emphasizing large stores and prices that are 10 to 15 percent lower than competitors'. The company is now using this strategy to penetrate overseas markets, including Japan.[14]

COOPER TIRE: HOW DO THEY DO THAT?!

*A*lthough Cooper Tire & Rubber, based in Findlay, Ohio, is clearly not the market leader in automobile tire manufacturing—it ranks only ninth in market share—this quiet little company consistently achieves the highest financial performance among all its competitors. In fact, among Fortune 500 companies, Cooper ranks 28th in total returns to investors (44.7 percent).

How does Cooper do it? According to CEO Ivan W. Gorr, Cooper prospers by forging a low-profile strategy in a many-sided marketplace. While the major tire manufacturers such as Goodyear, Michelin, and Bridgestone/Firestone battle with one another for low-profit original-equipment sales to Detroit's Big-3 automakers, Cooper instead concentrates on the replacement market where margins are higher. Since today's cars are more durable and owners keep them

longer, the replacement market is growing faster than the new-tire segment. Rather than selling through its own retail chain like Goodyear and Bridgestone/Firestone do, Cooper distributes half its production as private-label merchandise through oil companies, large independent distributors, and mass marketers such as Western Auto and Pep Boys. The other half goes to independent dealers, who account for 67 percent of replacement-tire sales.

In addition to having a solid understanding of its market niche, Cooper also has an unwavering focus on reducing costs and improving efficiency. The company saves a good deal of money on R&D by waiting to see what sells well in the new-car market and then simply producing the "winners" for the replacement market. Since new tires last up to four years, Cooper has plenty of time to produce its own version. To squeeze out even higher efficiency, Cooper runs its plants at 100 percent capacity while others in the industry are running at only about 80 percent. When Cooper wants to add capacity, it does so cheaply by buying old plants and retrofitting them.

While Cooper's strategy is not particularly elegant or sophisticated, it shows how well a company can perform when executives understand core competencies and position the company well in its competitive environment. While more than 40 U.S. tire and rubber plants have closed since the 1970s, Cooper's stock has risen an amazing 6,800 percent.

Source: Alex Taylor III, "Now Hear This, Jack Welch!" *Fortune,* April 6, 1992, pp. 94–95.   ●

Functional Strategy

The final step in strategy formulation is to establish the major functional strategies. **Functional strategies** are implemented by each functional area of the organization to support the business strategy. The typical functional areas include production, marketing, research and development, finance, and distribution. For example, the marketing function of Carnival Cruise Lines, Inc., supports the firm's share-increasing strategy with an upbeat advertising campaign that appeals to the 25- to 39-year-old market segment. This group has been largely ignored by competitors, but it has responded well to ads that feature popular personalities singing and dancing their way through the nightclubs and recreation areas of Carnival ships.[15]

Functional strategy decisions are made by the functional area executives with the input and approval of the executives responsible for business strategy. Senior strategic decision

Cooper Tire and Rubber Company not only understands its own niche in the tire market, but the company focuses strongly on reducing cost and improving efficiency. *(Courtesy Cooper Tire & Rubber Company)*

makers review the functional strategies to ensure that each major department is operating in a manner consistent with the business strategies of the organization.

STRATEGY IMPLEMENTATION

As with any plan, formulating the appropriate strategy is not enough. Strategic managers also must ensure that the new strategies are implemented effectively and efficiently. Recently corporations and strategy consultants have been paying more attention to implementation. They realize that clever techniques and a good plan do not guarantee success. This greater appreciation is reflected in two major trends.

First, organizations are adopting a more comprehensive view of implementation. The strategy must be supported by decisions regarding the appropriate organization structure, technology, human resources, reward systems, information systems, organization culture, and leadership style. Just as the strategy of the organization must be matched to the external environment, it also must fit the multiple factors responsible for its implementation. The remainder of this text discusses these factors and the ways they can be used to implement strategy.

Second, many organizations are extending the more participative strategic management process to implementation. Managers at all levels are involved with strategy formulation and the identification and execution of the means to implement the new strategies. Senior executives still may orchestrate the overall implementation process, but they place much greater responsibility and authority in the hands of others in the organization.

STRATEGY IMPLEMENTATION AT BECTON DICKINSON

*I*mplementing major strategic change requires a fundamental shift in top management's approach to organizing and managing. At Becton Dickinson (BD), the $2.5 billion medical technology company, executives have put in place a planning process designed to forge and then benefit from a partnership with employees throughout the organization. This partnership is designed to fulfill the three major requirements of strategy implementation: (1) *competence*—to have the business, technical, analytical, and interpersonal skills required to perform well; (2) *coordination*—to have the teamwork needed to respond to cost, quality, and innovation opportunities; and (3) *commitment*—to have high levels of motivation at all levels directed at achieving the new vision.

Executives at BD understand that deficiencies in any of these areas can undermine strategy implementation. In their view, the underlying obstacles to successful implementation often are deep-seated problems that are rarely discussed publicly, what they refer to as "iceberg issues." To help surface these issues, BD's implementation process facilitates open, fact-based communication among employees at all organizational levels. Since employees at lower levels are the ones most involved in actually implementing strategy, and the ones who best know where hidden icebergs lie, effective implementation depends on their involvement.

Defining strategic tasks. The first step in BD's implementation process is articulating in simple language what must be done in a particular business to create or sustain a competitive advantage. For example, BD's Diabetes Health Care business developed the following list:

- Maintain the core insulin syringe business by providing superior service and products.
- Sense new industry trends and develop new services or products to meet those trends.
- Achieve both of the above on a worldwide basis.

Defining strategic tasks helps employees understand how they each contribute to the organization, and can also redefine relationships between the parts of the organization.

Assessing the organization's capabilities. After defining strategic tasks, BD's management creates an employee task force composed of respected individuals from various parts of the organization to assess the organization's capacity to implement the strategic tasks. The task force interviews employees and managers to identify specific practices or organizational arrangements that help or hinder effective strategy implementation. Results of these interviews are summarized for top management.

Developing an implementation agenda. Once organizational capabilities are assessed, top management reaches consensus on: (1) how they will change their management pattern; (2) how critical interdependencies will be managed; (3) what skills and which individuals are needed in key roles; and (4) what structural, measurement, information, and reward systems might ultimately support specified behavior. A philosophy statement—communicated in value terms—is the natural outcome of this process.

Implementation planning. Finally a plan is developed jointly between the top management team, the employee task force, and the rest of the organization to modify, refine, and implement the vision. As organizational changes are implemented, progress is monitored by the top management team. The employee task force is charged with providing feedback about how members of the organization are responding to the changes.

According to executives at BD, their implementation process works well because it addresses, in an integrated way, all the critical dimensions of aligning a business enterprise and its strategy.

Source: Russell A. Eisenstat, "Implementing Strategy: Developing a Partnership for Change," *Planning Review,* September–October 1993, pp. 33–36. ●

STRATEGIC CONTROL

The final component of the strategic management process is strategic control. A **strategic control system** is designed to support managers in evaluating the organization's progress with its strategy and, when discrepancies exist, in taking corrective action.[16] The system must encourage efficient operations that are consistent with the plan while allowing the flexibility to adapt to changing conditions. As with all control systems, the organization must develop performance indicators, an information system, and specific mechanisms to monitor progress.

Most strategic control systems include some type of budget to monitor and control major financial expenditures. The dual responsibilities of a control system—efficiency and flexibility—often seem contradictory with respect to budgets. The budget usually establishes limits on spending, but changing conditions or innovation may require different financial commitments during the budgetary period. To solve this dilemma, some companies have responded with two separate budgets: strategic and operational. For example, managers at Texas Instruments Incorporated control two budgets under the OST (objectives-strategies-tactics) system. The strategic budget is used to create and maintain long-term effectiveness, and the operational budget is tightly monitored to achieve short-term efficiency.[17]

K E Y   T E R M S

SUMMARY OF LEARNING OBJECTIVES

Now that you have studied Chapter 5, you should know:

How to proceed through the basic steps in any planning process.

The planning process begins with a situation analysis of the external and internal forces affecting the organization, This will help identify and diagnose issues and problems, and may surface alternative goals and plans for the firm. Next the advantages and disadvantages of these goals and plans should be evaluated against one another. Once a set of goals and a plan have been selected, implementation involves communicating the plan to employees, allocating resources, and making certain that other systems such as rewards and budgets are supporting the plan. Finally, planning requires that control systems are put in place to monitor progress toward the goals.

How strategic planning differs from tactical and operational planning.

Strategic planning is different from operational planning in that it involves making long-term decisions about the entire organization. Tactical planning translates broad goals and strategies into specific actions to be taken within parts of the organization. Operational planning identifies the specific short-term procedures and processes required at lower levels of the organization.

Why it is important to analyze both the external environment and internal resources of the firm before formulating a strategy.

Strategic planning is designed to leverage the strengths of a firm while minimizing the effects of its weaknesses. It is difficult to know the potential advantage a firm may have unless external analysis is done well. For example, a company may have a talented marketing department or an efficient production system. However, there is no way to determine whether these internal characteristics are sources of competitive advantage until something is known about how well the competitors stack up in these areas.

The choices available for corporate strategy.

Corporate strategy identifies the breadth of a firm's competitive domain. Corporate strategy can be kept narrow, as in a concentration strategy, or can move to suppliers and buyers via vertical integration. Corporate strategy can also broaden a firm's domain via concentric (related) diversification or conglomerate (unrelated) diversification.

How companies can achieve competitive advantage through business strategy.

Companies gain competitive advantage in two primary ways. They can attempt to be unique in some way by pursuing a differentiation strategy or they can focus on efficiency and price by pursuing a low-cost strategy.

How core competencies provide the foundation for business strategy.

A core competence is something a company does especially well relative to its competitors. When this competence, say in engineering or marketing, is in some area important to market success, it becomes the foundation for developing a competitive advantage.

The keys to effective strategy implementation.

Many good plans are doomed to failure because they are not implemented correctly. Strategy must be supported by structure, technology, human resources, rewards, information systems, culture, leadership, and so on. Ultimately the success of a plan depends on how well employees at low levels are able and willing to implement it. Participative management is one of the more popular approaches used by executives to gain employees' input and ensure their commitment to strategy implementation.

DISCUSSION QUESTIONS

1. This chapter opened with a quote by GE's Jack Welch: "Manage your destiny, or someone else will." What does this mean for strategic management? What does it mean when Welch adds, " . . . or someone else will"?
2. How do strategic, operational, and tactical planning differ? How might the three levels complement one another in an organization?
3. What accounts for the shift from strategic planning to strategic management? In which industries would you be most likely to observe these trends?
4. In your opinion, what are the core competencies of companies in the auto industry such as General Motors, Ford, and Chrysler? How do these competencies help them compete against foreign competitors such as Honda, Toyota, Nissan, Mercedes Benz, BMW, etc.?
5. What are the key challenges in strategy implementation? In the example of Becton Dickinson, are each of these challenges addressed effectively?

CONCLUDING CASE

SOUTHWEST AIRLINES

While the airline industry consistently posts billions of dollars in losses annually, Southwest Airlines has turned a profit every year since 1973, something no other major carrier can claim. How does a small company such as Southwest compete in this highly competitive and volatile industry?

Southwest is a master of low-cost, no-frills flying. There are several features to Southwest's low-cost strategy. While other major carriers fight over "prestige-building" routes to Europe and Asia, Southwest has instead concentrated on short-haul, frequent, point-to-point domestic routes that lend themselves to reliable, more profitable business. Southwest does not accept interline traffic (passengers from other carriers), nor does it provide seat reservations or serve in-flight meals.

Instead of using major airports, Southwest seeks out small, overlooked airports such as Dallas's Love Field that are less expensive and often more convenient for business travelers. It fills its planes by consistently offering rock-bottom fares and it concentrates on local marketing. While Southwest spends about $25 million a year on advertising, it targets cheaper, local spot media instead of expensive network time.

By defying popular trends, Southwest has established a low-cost structure that is the envy of the industry. Its operating cost per revenue mile is about 5 cents cheaper than the industry average. And while this doesn't guarantee Southwest a profit, it puts them in a unique position to handle price wars brought on by the competition.

A good deal of the credit for Southwest's success goes to CEO Herbert D. Kelleher. Just as the airline has never conformed to industry norms, Kelleher does not fit the standard profile of a chief executive. He is wildly enthusiastic about his company, his employees, and his customers—and even periodically works as an attendant on Southwest's flights. But for all Kelleher's flamboyance, he is an inherently conservative businessperson. Before Southwest opens a new route, Kelleher and his staff carefully research the business viability of the proposal, and then if they decide to move, they do so with considerable force. From its base in Texas, Southwest is now the 7th largest carrier in the United States, and has expanded to more than half the United States.

Kelleher's goal is to increase the number of Southwest's seats by 15 percent each year—and, of course, to watch the costs. To achieve such an aggressive growth target requires deep commitment and capability from Southwest's 14,500 employees.

Southwest Airlines CEO Herbert Kelleher takes part in every aspect of the airline's operation. Here, he serves as a flight attendant, passing out peanuts to passengers.
(Courtesy Southwest Airlines)

Although 90 percent of Southwest's employees are unionized, Kelleher inspires loyalty at even the lowest ranks of the company. Through his vision and management style, he has built a culture of enthusiasm and devotion to customer service. Based on criteria such as opportunities for advancement, job security, pride in work and the company, the degree of openness and fairness, pay and benefits, and the level of camaraderie among employees, Southwest has been rated one of the 10 best companies to work for in America. Its 7 percent turnover rate is further evidence that Southwest's employees feel committed to their organization. Kelleher even established the industry's first profit-sharing plan, 87 percent of which employees have pumped back into company stock. The 24 percent of the employees who participate in the company's stock purchase plan pour about $500,000 per month into it. These are all indicators that Southwest has built an enormously loyal and dedicated workforce that sustains the company's competitive advantage.

QUESTIONS

1. What major opportunities in the airline industry has Southwest capitalized on? What threats has it avoided?

2. What strengths and core competencies has Southwest leveraged to be successful? Does Southwest have any weaknesses? Are these detrimental to its success? Why or why not?

3. How do Southwest's corporate, business, and functional strategies tie together? How does Southwest implement its strategies?

4. If you were asked to compete against Southwest, how would you do it?

Sources: Patricia B. Limbacher, "Southwest Workers Flying to the Stock," *Pensions & Investments,* August 1993, pp. 3, 29; Colleen Barrett, "Pampering Customers on a Budget," *Working Woman,* April 1993, pp. 19–22; Robert Levering and Milton Moskowitz, "The Ten Best Companies to Work for in America," *Business & Society Review,* Spring 1993, pp. 26–38; Edward O. Wells, "E.O.Y. 1992: Captain Marvel," *Inc.,* January 1992, pp. 44–47; Charles A. Jaffe, "Moving Fast by Standing Still," *Nation's Business,* October 1991, pp. 57–59; Elaine Underwood, "Just Plane Hot: Southwest Airlines Wins Big by Concentrating on Local Marketing and No-Frills Flying," *Brandweek,* August 1992, pp. 16–18; and Danna K. Henderson, "Southwest Luvs Passengers, Employees, Profits," *Air Transport World,* July 1991, pp. 32–41.

VIDEO CASE

PLANNING AND STRATEGIC MANAGEMENT AT FORD MOTOR COMPANY

Ford Motor Company, like the other two major automobile manufacturers in the United States, experienced difficult times during the early 1980s. Ford and the others had seen their market share severely eroded by better-quality cars from international competitors. Ford was able to weather the competitive storm, and has seen its fortunes rebound, through effective strategic planning.

Donald Peterson was Ford's CEO during the company's recovery period. To create an atmosphere of trust among employees, and between employees and management, Peterson and his fellow managers at Ford emphasized the use of employee teams to solve corporate problems. This emphasis, according to Peterson, was based on the assumption that employees want to contribute, and want to do the right thing.

As the environment at Ford began to change for the better, the leadership initiated a process to establish a strategic vision for the company. Out of this process came a written statement of the company's mission, values, and guiding principles (MVGP) that would provide strategic focus for all the company's employees. The mission is a definition of the purpose of the company. The key values were defined as people, process, and profits. The guiding principles are the code of conduct for Ford's people as they conduct the company's business worldwide.

Reflecting on how he was able to steer Ford through the thicket of intense competition, employee skepticism, and consumer dissatisfaction characterizing the early part of the decade, Peterson said, "As we were working through the extraordinarily difficult early 1980s, when we were losing so much money, we had many gatherings of our employees, talking about our problems and talking about what we had to do to solve them. And it became very clear that there was a pattern in these conversations of a request from people in the company to understand clearly what it is we stand for—what is the basic, core culture of this company. We set about the process of letting the people think about that very question. And then they in turn selected a team of themselves to continue the process in a series of meetings with top Ford executives to work out what we call our mission, values, and guiding principles."

In a video presentation to all Ford employees in 1985, Peterson introduced the MVGP statement. He explained that he wanted the statement to be a "basic platform" upon which the board and all Ford employees would stand together. Peterson told the video audience that he hoped all employees would understand and embrace what the statement meant, what was behind it, and what it would take to live the values and guiding principles in day-to-day work.

As a result of the broad acceptance of the MVGP statement, Ford has made employee involvement and teamwork a way of life at the company. People at all levels of the organization have learned new skills to help them contribute to the continuous improvement of quality. The Taurus project team, for example, is legendary for its efficiency in the design, development, manufacture, and marketing of the Ford Taurus. The new employee spirit was captured by chip-and-scratch coordinator Leon Garner when he said, "I look at each car as if I'm buying it."

The MVGP statement led to a renewed emphasis on quality throughout the company. Terry Holcomb, statistical process control coordinator in the trim department at Ford's Atlanta assembly plant, noted, "There's always room for improvement. The day that there's no room for improvement I guess I'll quit." Holcomb's plant won Ford's internal Q1 (the "Q" stands for "quality") award in 1991. One improvement that Holcomb's plant made during 1990 was in the placement of the moonroof control relay. The relay had been located behind the glove box and had interfered with the smooth functioning of the glove box door. Using a "management by facts" approach, Holcomb's team determined the best way to fix the problem. Their improvement lowered the plant's TGW (things gone wrong) rate from 18 in the second quarter of 1990, to just 2 in the first quarter of 1991.

Bob Anderson, the Atlanta plant manager, said, "When management and the workforce settle on a common goal, with that goal being productivity and quality, you end up with [that] result. But you've got to have that common goal and everyone willing to get behind that common goal." Harold Poling, chairman of the board and chief executive officer, summarized the impact of the MVGP statement on Ford's operations: "I think that if our employees recommit themselves to the basics of the business, which were the things that helped us achieve our success in the 80s, quality, product, cost, and employee relations and relations with our dealers and suppliers, then we'll be successful in the years ahead. It's a team effort and that's what we had in the decade of the 80s. And I'm confident that with that same teamwork we'll be successful in the decade of the 90s."

CRITICAL THINKING QUESTIONS

1. Ford is a complex organization with a highly diverse workforce and worldwide operations. Do you think it is possible that the statement of mission, vision, and guiding principles can be applied in all of the company's transactions? What are the limits of such a statement?

2. According to the video, Ford put together its MVGP statement through lengthy discussions with employees. Why do you think it was desirable for Ford executives to include employees in the drafting of the statement? Do you think this was the most *efficient* way to complete this project? Explain.

3. One of the reasons the automobile industry in America lost its competitive standing to foreign competition was that the

internal organizational structure of each of the Big Three auto manufacturers had become stagnant. One lesson that has been learned by many companies in a variety of industries is that stagnation leads to competitive decline. Do you think a statement such as Ford's MVGP will help the company continue to change? Explain.

EXPERIENTIAL EXERCISES

5.1 Strategic Planning

Objective

To study the strategic planning of a corporation recently in the news.

Instructions

Business Week magazine has frequent articles on the strategies of various corporations. Find a recent article on a corporation in an industry of interest to you. Read the article and answer the questions below.

STRATEGIC PLANNING WORKSHEET

1. Has the firm clearly identified what business it is in and how it is different from its competitors? Explain.

_____

_____

_____

_____

_____

2. What are the key assumptions about the future that have shaped the firm's new strategy?

_____

_____

_____

_____

_____

_____

3. What key strengths and weaknesses of the firm influenced the selection of the new strategy?

_____

_____

_____

_____

_____

_____

4. What specific objectives has the firm set in conjunction with the new strategy?

_____

_____

_____

_____

_____

Source: R. R. McGrath, Jr., *Exercises in Management Fundamentals* (Englewood Cliffs, N.J.: Prentice-Hall, 1985), p. 15. Reprinted by permission of Prentice-Hall, Inc.

5.2 Formulating Business Strategy

Objectives

1. To illustrate the complex interrelationships central to business strategy formulation.
2. To demonstrate the use of SWOT (Strengths-Weaknesses-Opportunities-Threats) analysis in a business situation.

Instructions

1. Your instructor will divide the class into small groups and assign each group with a well-known organization for analysis.
2. Each group will
   a. Study the SWOT Introduction and the SWOT Worksheet to understand the work needed to complete the assignment.
   b. Obtain the needed information about the organization under study through library research, interviews, etc.
   c. Complete the SWOT Worksheet.
   d. Prepare group responses to the discussion questions.
3. After the class reconvenes, group spokespersons present group findings.

Discussion Questions

1. Why would most organizations not develop strategies for matches between opportunities and strengths?
2. Why would most organizations not develop strategies for matches between opportunities and weaknesses?
3. Why do most organizations want to deal from strength?

SWOT INTRODUCTION

One of the more commonly used strategy tools is SWOT (Strengths-Weaknesses-Opportunities-Threats) analysis, which is accomplished in four steps:

Step 1: Analyze the organization's internal environment, identifying its strengths and weaknesses.

Step 2: Analyze the organization's external environment, identifying its opportunities and threats.

Step 3: Match (1) strengths with opportunities, (2) weak-nesses with threats, (3) strengths with threats, and (4) weaknesses with opportunities.

Step 4: Develop strategies for those matches that appear to be of greatest importance to the organization. Most organizations give top priority to strategies that involve the matching of strengths with opportunities and second priority to strategies that involve the matching of weaknesses with threats. The key is to exploit opportunities where the organization has a strength and to defend against threats where the organization has a weakness.

SWOT WORKSHEET

Organization being analyzed: _____

Internal Analysis   **External Analysis**

<table>
<tr><td>Strengths</td><td>Opportunities</td></tr>
<tr><td>Weaknesses</td><td>Threats</td></tr>
</table>

Strategies That Match Strengths with Opportunities   **Strategies That Match Weaknesses with Threats**

ETHICS AND CORPORATE RESPONSIBILITY

It is truly enough said that a corporation has no conscience; but a
corporation of conscientious men is a corporation with a conscience.

Henry David Thoreau

After studying Chapter 6, you will know:

1. How ethical perspectives guide decision making.

2. How companies use ethical codes.

3. The options you have when confronting ethical issues.

4. The important issues surrounding the corporate social responsibility debate.

5. How the political and social environment affects your firm's competitive position and legitimacy.

6. The strategies corporations use to manage the political and social environment.

WHO'S TO BLAME?

A securities trader at Kidder Peabody allegedly created about $350 million in phony profits for the firm. By engaging in these illegalities, he made $9 million in salary and bonuses. By playing it straight and honest, he would have made $2 or $3 million. The profits he claimed were outrageous; $5 million to $10 million per month on government bonds seemed impossible. Yet Kidder executives consistently ignored, evaded, or answered incorrectly questions about his profits.

Kidder's CEO had joined the firm in 1989 when it was suffering heavy losses and was recovering from an earlier scandal. His first and most important goal was to reestablish integrity. And General Electric, Kidder's parent corporation headed by Jack Welch, was famous for its tough internal auditors and controls. Critics could not understand why it took so long to uncover the trader's misdeeds, and maintained that he could not have pulled it off if top management had been paying attention.

White-collar crime has become a serious problem. A securities trader at Kidder Peabody allegedly created about $350 million in phony profits for the firm.
(Jay Brousseau/The Image Bank)

So how could the scandal have happened? Was it just a renegade trader? The trader's immediate boss claimed he could not monitor the records of all 750 traders in his department. Kidder's CEO said the same thing could have happened anywhere on Wall Street. Supporters said that in a company as big as GE, there are bound to be some bad apples. And Kidder top executives, according to Welch, were open and candid and worked hard to get at the truth once the scandal was uncovered.

Without doubt, the environment was one of high-performance pressure, high-risk gambles, low morale, and uninformed executives. Was the work environment to blame, as much as the people? Or was it just a few unethical or careless people?

Sources: W. Carley, M. Siconolfi, and A. K. Naj, "How Will Welch Deal with Kidder Scandal?" *The Wall Street Journal,* May 3, 1994, pp. A1, A6; T. P. Paré, "Jack Welch's Nightmare on Wall Street," *Fortune,* September 5, 1994, pp. 40–48.

*A*s illustrated by the Kidder Peabody example, unethical corporate behavior may be the responsibility of an unethical individual; but it often also reveals a company culture that is ethically lax.[1] Likewise, ethical individuals are likely to behave ethically, but all the more so in organizations that infuse a sense of ethics into their people.

In another example of mutual individual–company responsibility, Sears, Roebuck, did not set out to defraud its automotive service customers in the early 1990s. Nor did one individual necessarily intend to cheat consumers. But when the company instituted high-pressure, unrealistic quotas and incentives, people's judgment was affected. Management did not make clear the distinction between unnecessary service and legitimate preventive maintenance. Moreover, customers were often ignorant or oblivious. A vast gray area of repair options was exaggerated, overinterpreted, and misrepresented. The company may not have intended to deceive customers, but the result of the work environment was that consumers and attorneys general in more than 40 states accused the company of fraud. The total cost of the settlement was an estimated $60 million.[2]

This chapter will help you understand the complex issues associated with business ethics and corporate social responsibility. Business is in the center of a controversy; although most agree that corporations should avoid illegal actions and decisions that significantly harm society, there is no agreement about the extent of their responsibility for the overall impact of their activities.

ETHICS

The aim of ethics is to identify both the rules that should govern people's behavior and the "goods" that are worth seeking. All ethical decisions are guided by the underlying values of the individual. *Values* are principles of conduct such as caring, honesty, accountability, keeping promises, pursuit of excellence, loyalty, fairness, integrity, respect for others, and responsible citizenship.[3] Most people would agree that all these values are admirable guidelines for behavior. However, ethics becomes a more complicated issue when a situation dictates that one value overrule others. Thus, **ethics** is the system of rules that governs the ordering of values. Ethics scholars have pointed to four major ethical systems as guides.[4]

The first ethical system, **universalism,** states that individuals should uphold certain values, such as honesty, regardless of the immediate result. The important values are those society needs to function. For instance, people should always be honest because otherwise communication would break down.

The next three systems fall under the broad heading of utilitarianism. **Utilitarianism** states that the greatest good for society should be the overriding concern of decision makers. Utilitarianism takes various forms. **Egoism** places self-interest first as long as others are not harmed. If everyone follows this system, the well-being of society as a whole should increase. This notion is similar to Adam Smith's concept of the invisible hand in business. Smith argued that if every organization follows its own economic self-interest, the total wealth of society will be maximized.

Rule utilitarianism uses societal rules and customs to weigh the importance of conflicting values. Finally, **act utilitarianism** seeks the greatest good for the greatest number. Individuals should choose among conflicting values by calculating the total goodness (and badness) that would result from each specific act. In this way, societal well-being is maximized. This ethical standard is relative because in one instance honesty may prevail, while in another loyalty may overrule the need for honesty.

These major ethical systems underlie both personal moral choices and corporate stances on social responsibility.

BUSINESS ETHICS

Questions of ethics in business have been prominent in the news in recent years. Insider trading, illegal campaign contributions, bribery, and other scandals have created a perception

TABLE 6.1

Some ethically
questionable acts

- A bar owner runs an "All You Can Drink Special" but does not provide transportation home for intoxicated patrons because of the high cost.

- A manager fires several long-time employees because the business is undergoing financial difficulties.

- An executive collects frequent-flyer miles from company-paid business trips to use for her personal air travel.

- Instead of relying on the traditional "blind" bidding procedure, a building contractor negotiates an agreement with other major contractors so that all bids submitted will provide a reasonable profit.

- A supplier sends expensive Christmas gifts to purchasing agents in an attempt to influence their future purchase decisions.

- An owner of a small business obtains a free copy of a computer software program from a friend instead of paying the $500 licensing fee to the software manufacturer.

- A manufacturer of violence-oriented children's toys buys time on television cartoon programs to create demand for its product.

Source: S. Burton, M. Johnston, and E. Wilson, "An Experimental Assessment of Alternative Teaching Approaches for Introducing Business Ethics to Undergraduate Business Students," *Journal of Business Ethics*, July 1991, pp. 507–17.

that corporate leaders use illegal means to gain competitive advantage, increase profits, or improve their personal positions. The public had little tolerance for Ivan Boesky, Dennis Levine, and those implicated in the S&L crisis. Neither young managers[5] nor consumers[6] believe top executives are doing a good job of establishing high ethical standards. Some even joke that *business ethics* has become a contradiction in terms.

Most business leaders believe they uphold ethical standards in business practices.[7] Nevertheless, many managers and their organizations are reexamining their personal business ethics. On a daily basis, they must deal with ethical dilemmas such as those illustrated in the following example and in Table 6.1.

ETHICAL DECISION MAKING IN THE INTERNATIONAL CONTEXT

*W*hat would you do in each of these true-life situations, and why?

- You are a sales representative for a construction company in the Middle East. Your company wants very much to land a particular project. The cousin of the minister who will award the contract informs you that the minister wants $20,000 in addition to the standard fees. If you do not make this payment, your competition certainly will—and will get the contract.

- You are international vice president of a multinational chemical corporation. Your company is the sole producer of an insecticide that will effectively combat a recent infestation of West African crops. The minister of agriculture in a small, developing African country has put in a large order for your product. Your insecticide is highly toxic and is banned in the United States. You inform the minister of the risks of using your product, but he insists on using it and claims it will be used "intelligently." The president of your company believes you should fill the order, but the decision ultimately is yours.

- You are a new marketing manager for a large automobile tire manufacturer. Your company's advertising agency has just presented plans for introducing a new tire into the Southeast Asia market. Your tire is a truly good product, but the proposed advertising is deceptive. For example, the "reduced price" was reduced from a hypothetical amount that was established only so it could be "reduced," and claims that the tire was tested under the "most adverse" conditions ignore the fact that it was not tested in prolonged tropical heat and humidity. Your superiors are not concerned about deceptive advertising, and they are counting on you to see that the tire does extremely well in the new market. Will you approve the ad plan?

Source: N. Adler, *International Dimensions of Organizational Behavior* (Boston: Kent, 1991). ●

The fundamental ethical issues in business are the same as those in any other context. However, the situation may be more complex for the corporate decision maker. In most organizations, individual decision makers are agents rather than principals; that is, they act in the interests of others rather than solely on their own. Therefore, the corporate decision maker must somehow blend his or her personal ethical system with the organization's values and performance criteria. In addition, the stakes often seem higher in business because the decision may affect many groups of people in profound ways.

Corporate Ethical Standards

Because individuals have differing personal ethical codes, organizations must be explicit regarding their corporate ethical standards and expectations. Many companies have simply adopted the "golden rule": Do unto others as you would have them do unto you. IBM uses a guideline for business conduct that asks employees to determine whether under the "full glare of examination by associates, friends, and family they would remain comfortable with their decisions." However, others argue that current or accepted business practice should govern behavior. Their motto is "Everyone else does it." A more extreme attitude is that organizations should seek every possible advantage without regard for traditional social laws and customs—a "might equals right" philosophy. Finally, some believe that ethics should be determined by intuition, that is, by doing whatever "feels right."

Danger Signs

In organizations it is a challenge to maintain consistent ethical behavior by all employees. What are some danger signs that an organization may be allowing or even encouraging unethical behavior among its people? Many factors create a climate conducive to unethical behavior, including (1) excessive emphasis on short-term revenues over longer-term considerations; (2) failing to establish a written code of ethics; (3) looking for simple, "quick fix" solutions to ethical problems; (4) an unwillingness to take an ethical stand that may impose financial costs; (5) looking at ethics solely as a legal issue or a public relations tool; (6) lacking clear procedures for handling ethical problems; and (7) responding to the demands of shareholders at the expense of other constituencies.[8]

Reducing Unethical Behavior

Integrity-based programs go beyond the mere enactment of a law. The Americans with Disabilities Act requires companies to change the physical work environment to allow persons with disabilities to function on the job.
(David Young Wolff/Tony Stone Images)

As we have seen, unethical behavior is not always the sole responsibility of those who engage in it. This is true in a legal sense as well. Under new federal guidelines, a company's fines are based in part on whether it has taken actions to prevent the misconduct. Thus, responsibility is shared by those who fail to provide proper ethical leadership and controls.

Ethics programs can range from compliance-based to integrity-based.[9] **Compliance-based ethics programs** are designed by corporate counsel to prevent, detect, and punish legal violations. **Integrity-based ethics programs** go beyond the mere avoidance of illegality; they are concerned with the law but also with instilling in people a personal responsibility for ethical behavior. With such a program, companies govern themselves through a set of guiding principles that they embrace.

For example, the Americans with Disabilities Act (ADA) attempts to protect the rights of persons with both visible and invisible (for example, psychiatric) disabilities. The law requires companies to change the physical work environment so it will allow people with disabilities to function on the job. Mere compliance would involve making the necessary changes to avoid legal problems. Integrity-based programs would go farther, by training people to understand and perhaps change attitudes toward people with disabilities, and sending clear signals that people with disabilities also have valued abilities. Making people feel important to the company goes far beyond taking action to stay out of trouble with the law.

The Compliance Strategy. Compliance-based programs increase surveillance and controls on people and impose punishments on wrongdoers. Program elements include establishing and communicating legal standards and procedures, assigning high-level managers to oversee compliance, auditing and monitoring compliance, reporting criminal misconduct, punishing wrongdoers, and taking steps to prevent offenses in the future.

Such programs should reduce illegal behavior and help the company stay out of court. But they do not create a moral commitment to ethical conduct; they merely ensure moral mediocrity. As Richard Breeden, former chairman of the SEC, said, "It is not an adequate ethical standard to aspire to get through the day without being indicted."[10]

The Integrity Strategy. Integrity-based programs view ethics as a driving force in the enterprise. The company's ethics help define what it is and what it cares about. Programs based on integrity have the elements of compliance-based programs, *but also* an articulated set of values developed not by counsel but by managers throughout the organization. The elements of an integrity strategy include:

1. The guiding values are shared and clearly understood by everyone.
2. Company leaders are personally committed to the values and willing to take action on them.
3. The values are considered in decision making and reflected in all important activities.
4. Information systems, reporting relationships, and performance appraisals support and reinforce the values. At some companies, like Levi Strauss, people's raises depend in part on the ethics of their decisions.
5. People at all levels have the skills and knowledge to make ethically sound decisions on a daily basis.

Companies with strong integrity-based programs include Martin Marietta, NovaCare (a provider of rehabilitation services to hospitals and nursing homes), and Wetherill Associates (a supplier of electrical parts to the automotive market). These companies believe that their programs contribute to competitiveness, higher morale, and sustainable relationships with key stakeholders.[11]

ETHICAL CODES

One of the most visible signs of corporate commitment to ethical behavior is a code of ethics. Corporate ethics or values statements are much more common today than they used to be. They became popular in the 1980s, and then tough new federal sentencing guidelines in 1991 increased fines for illegal activities and specified more lenient fines for those companies that had an ethics statement in place. Often, the statements are just for show, but when done well they can change a company for the better and truly encourage ethical behavior.

Ethical codes must be carefully written and tailored to individual companies' philosophies. Hewlett-Packard is dedicated to the dignity and worth of its employees. Aetna Life & Casualty believes that tending to the broader needs of society is essential to fulfilling its economic role. Johnson & Johnson has one of the most famous ethical codes (see Table 6.2). J&J consistently receives high rankings for community and social responsibility in *Fortune*'s annual survey of corporate reputations.

Most ethical codes address subjects such as employee conduct, community and environment, shareholders, customers, suppliers and contractors, political activity, and technology. Often the codes are drawn up by the organizations' legal departments and

TABLE 6.2

Johnson &
Johnson's ethical
code

We believe our first responsibility is to the doctors, nurses, and patients, to mothers and all others who use our products and services. In meeting their needs everything we do must be of high quality. We must constantly strive to reduce our costs in order to maintain reasonable prices. Customers' orders must be serviced promptly and accurately. Our suppliers and distributors must have an opportunity to make a fair profit.

We are responsible to our employees: the men and women who work with us throughout the world. Everyone must be considered as an individual. We must respect their dignity and recognize their merit. They must have a sense of security in their jobs. Compensation must be fair and adequate, and working conditions clean, orderly, and safe. Employees must feel free to make suggestions and complaints. There must be equal opportunity for employment, development, and advancement for those qualified. We must provide competent management, and their actions must be just and ethical.

We are responsible to the communities in which we live and work and to the world community as well.

We must be good citizens—support good works and charities and bear our fair share of taxes. We must encourage civic improvements and better health and education.

We must maintain in good order the property we are privileged to use, protecting the environment and natural resources.

Our final responsibility is to our stockholders. Business must make a sound profit. We must experiment with new ideas. Research must be carried on, innovative programs developed, and mistakes paid for. New equipment must be purchased, new facilities provided, and new products launched. Reserves must be created to provide for adverse times.

When we operate according to these principles, the stockholders should realize a fair return.

Source: Reprinted with permission of Johnson & Johnson.

begin with research into other companies' codes. The Ethics Resource Center in Washington assists companies interested in establishing a corporate code of ethics.[12]

To make an ethics code truly effective, do the following:[13] (1) involve *everyone*, meaning every person who has to live with it, in writing the statement; (2) have a corporate statement, but also allow separate statements by different units throughout the organization; (3) keep it short and therefore easily understood and remembered; (4) don't make it too corny—make it something important, that people really believe in; and (5) set the tone at the top, having executives talk about and live up to the statement. When reality differs from the statement—as when a motto says people are our most precious asset or a product is the finest in the world, but in fact people are treated poorly or product quality is weak—the statement becomes a joke to employees rather than a guiding light.

ETHICAL DECISION MAKING

Corporate policies can help ensure ethical decision making. In addition, some guidelines for decision making may help individuals avoid inadvertent breaches of ethics.[14]

First, *define the issue clearly.* What is the context of the issue? Who are the affected stakeholders? Talk to various stakeholders to ensure that all the facts are considered. Often a decision maker omits this step, assuming she or he already understands the problem without stopping to consider all the components of the decision.

Second, *identify the relevant values in the situation.* Any ethical dilemma involves multiple values: the various consequences of your choices, what you care about the most, and what others care about the most. Clearly stating these values focuses attention on the ethical component of the decision.

Third, *weigh the conflicting values and choose an option that balances them*, with greatest emphasis on the most important values. At this stage, the decision maker must decide which values are more important than others. Companies that have clearly defined their values through a code of ethics and other actions already have clarified the value priorities. In organizations in which values are unclear or inconsistent, balancing the values is a more difficult challenge.

Fourth, *implement the decision*. This step may require justifying the organization's actions. Because the short- and long-term ethical consequences already have been assessed, the decision maker can effectively defend the decision to stakeholders.

What can you do if you see managers in your company behaving in ways that go against your ethical principles? Your options include the following, among others:[15] (1) Don't think about it; (2) go along with it to avoid conflict; (3) object, verbally or via memo; (4) quit; (5) privately or publicly blow the whistle—that is, inform others inside or outside the organization about what you have observed; or (6) negotiate and build a consensus for changing the unethical behavior. What are the advantages and disadvantages of each of these options? What other options can you think of? What do you think determines which option a person chooses?

Think about your reaction to the advice given in *The Wall Street Journal* article discussed below. Consider the issue in the context of your own personal ethics, and then use it as a springboard to thinking about the next section on corporate social responsibility.

 VOLUNTEER WORK: GOOD OR BAD FOR YOUR CAREER?

*D*on't do too much volunteer community service, because it could harm your career.

This was the message of an article in *The Wall Street Journal*. A few years ago, many companies urged people to get involved in volunteer work. But in the 1990s, said the article, more companies want more than 40 hours of work per week out of you, and want your extra hours spent working for them, not others.

In today's environment, people are not necessarily viewed as assets to be developed; they can also be seen as costs to be cut. To some bosses, if you are doing a lot of volunteer work, you must not be spending enough time on your paid job. Said one consultant, "If I were a manager today and had an employee who was extraordinarily task-oriented and another who was a mediocre performer but a great citizen in the community, I'd promote the person getting the important things done in the company. Who's kidding whom? The very survival of the corporation is at stake."

Some companies, like Schnucks Supermarkets in St. Louis and General Mills in Minneapolis, consider community involvement in performance reviews and pay raises. But this is uncommon. Community services can help you meet business contacts, acquire leadership experience, and develop other skills. But some experts say it's not worth the risk if your company doesn't value outside activities.

What do you think? How should you make decisions about your own volunteer activities?

Source: T. D. Schellhardt, "Fewer Good Deeds Go Unpunished in 90s Corporate Climate," *The Wall Street Journal*, October 6, 1993, p. B1. ●

CORPORATE SOCIAL RESPONSIBILITY

Should business be responsible for social concerns lying beyond its own economic well-being? Do social concerns *affect* a corporation's financial performance? The extent of business's responsibility for noneconomic concerns has been hotly debated. In the 1960s and 1970s, the political and social environment became more important to U.S. corporations as society turned its attention to issues like equal opportunity, pollution control, energy and natural resource conservation, and consumer and worker protection.[16] Public debate addressed these issues and how business should respond to them. This controversy focused on the concept of corporate social responsibility.

ADVOCATES OF CORPORATE SOCIAL RESPONSIBILITY

Corporate social responsibility is the extension of the corporate role beyond economic pursuits.[17] Advocates of corporate social responsibility argue that organizations have a wide range of responsibilities that extend beyond the production of goods and services at a profit. As members of society, organizations should actively and responsibly participate in the community and in the larger environment.

Others contend that socially responsible actions have long-term advantages for organizations. For example, organizations can improve their images and avoid unnecessary and costly regulation if they are perceived as socially responsible. Also, society's problems can offer business opportunities, and profits can be made from systematic and vigorous efforts to solve these problems. In other words, it pays to be good.[18]

CRITICS OF CORPORATE SOCIAL RESPONSIBILITY

On the other hand, critics of corporate social responsibility believe this perspective exceeds the limits of what is appropriate and beneficial to the organization and society. They support the view that managers are responsible primarily to the shareholders who own the corporation. The importance of other corporate stakeholders (e.g., employees, customers, and local community residents) depends on their contributions to shareholder wealth. Nobel prize–winning economist Milton Friedman champions this perspective with his now famous dictum "The social responsibility of business is to increase profits." Friedman contends that organizations may help improve the quality of life as long as such actions are directed at increasing profits.

These critics argue that in a capitalistic society, economic performance is an organization's primary social responsibility. If corporations do not serve shareholders first, they will fail to serve society. Society relies on the profit incentive to motivate organizations to create jobs and make investments. Without investments, economic growth is impossible. Also, if organizations do not directly pursue economic success in highly competitive national and international markets, the chance of failure increases significantly. Corporate decline and failure benefit no one (except possibly the competition).

PHILOSOPHIES OF CORPORATE SOCIAL RESPONSIBILITY

Organizations have adopted a wide range of stances to balance economic returns and social responsibility. Each of these positions reflects one of the ethical perspectives discussed earlier in the chapter.

Some organizations take to heart the Friedman position on corporate social responsibility, actively resisting legislative interference with their freedom of operations. This *resistance* is rooted in the utilitarian ethics of egoism. Proponents of this view claim that following the organization's self-interest will yield the greatest social good.

A second approach to the corporate social responsibility debate is corporate social *responsiveness*.[19] Proponents of corporate social responsiveness allow laws and regulations to guide their behavior. Rather than vague considerations based on individual conscience, moral judgment, or special-interest pressures, responsiveness is based on the idea that public policy, through laws and regulation, defines corporate responsibility. Thus, responsiveness uses rule utilitarianism by allowing social rules and customs to guide the achievement of maximum social good.

Third, some organizations go beyond the law by reacting to specific requests or concerns on a *discretionary* basis. Act utilitarianism is the underlying ethical perspective. Proponents of this approach believe that values beyond legal constraints can be emphasized within the bounds of the organization's economic interests to increase total social good.

Hanna Anderson receives awards for its community commitment, including a program called Hannadowns that donates customers' out-grown clothing to local charities, disaster relief, and a tree-planting program tied to the amount of paper used in printing catalogs.
(Robbie McClaran)

Finally, some organizations embrace many social responsibilities as part of their ethical philosophies. Their behavior is *proactive*. These companies follow the universalist perspective that certain values must be upheld regardless of their effects on other values, such as economic interests. Johnson & Johnson, and the small companies discussed below, are good examples of organizations that proactively pursue an array of social responsibilities.

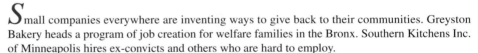

HOW SMALL COMPANIES CONTRIBUTE TO THEIR COMMUNITIES

*S*mall companies everywhere are inventing ways to give back to their communities. Greyston Bakery heads a program of job creation for welfare families in the Bronx. Southern Kitchens Inc. of Minneapolis hires ex-convicts and others who are hard to employ.

Many companies begin their philanthropy by giving money. Over time, they begin more ambitious programs. Such initiatives have the *potential* to do a lot of good, but like anything else, they must be well-managed. Programs will fail if employees aren't interested, if the results are discouraging, or if they are simply run poorly.

But when programs work, it is immensely satisfying for employees, customers, and communities. Here are a few ideas:

- *Donate your product*—Laury Hammel of the Longfellow Clubs in Massachusetts donates the use of its health-club facilities to children with special needs. Saint Louis Bread Co. donates its unsold goods at the end of each day to homeless shelters. Harper/Connecting Point Computer Center of Portland, Maine, donates computers and training services to members of the community who can benefit most from them.

- *Involve your employees*—This magnifies the effect of anything you do. Rhino Records gives its people a week off with pay if they contribute 16 hours of personal time per year of community service. Many companies target certain charities and also give employees a chance to work for a cause of their own choosing.

- *Involve other companies*—Longfellow organized an environmental task force at the Chamber of Commerce, and got 50 local businesses to commit to 10 environmentally sound practices.

Just Desserts, the San Francisco bakery, involved 35 other companies in adopting a local school in a low-income area.

- *Leverage your company's expertise*—Gilbert Tween Associates, an executive search firm, teaches nonprofit organizations how to recruit, select, and retain good volunteers. Gardener's Supply in Vermont composts food scraps, provides the nutrient-rich compost to gardeners, and uses the compost to grow produce for a medical-center cafeteria.

- *Enlist suppliers and customers*—Yakima Products of California created an easy way for customers to mail the packaging materials back to the company, for free. The company then reuses and recycles the materials. Some firms are more likely to do business with suppliers having good records of social responsibility, all else equal. And many companies announce to customers that a percentage of their purchases will be donated to a charitable cause.

Source: E. E. Spragins, "Making Good," *Inc.,* May 1993, pp. 114–22.   ●

THE POLITICAL ENVIRONMENT

The explosive growth of regulation in the late 1960s and early 1970s imposed a vast body of laws and public policy on organizations. Through this regulation, government decision makers exerted increasing control over key areas of managerial decision making—areas where managers often did not want to lose control. While managers may use public policy to define their social responsibilities, they also may recognize the need to influence the laws and regulations that constitute public policy. Therefore, organizations attempt to influence the political environment to achieve two principal goals within their ethical structures: competitive advantage and corporate legitimacy.

COMPETITIVE ADVANTAGE

In many cases, the corporate community sees government as an adversary. However, many progressive organizations realize that government may be the source of competitive advantages for an individual company or an entire industry.[20] For example, public policy may prevent or limit entry into an industry by new foreign or domestic competitors. Government may subsidize failing companies or provide tax breaks to some. Federal patents may be used to protect innovative products or production process technologies. Legislation may be passed to support industry prices, thereby guaranteeing profits or survival. Finally, regulation may favor competitors in one region of the country.

Specific examples of public policy beneficial to business are numerous. Government loan guarantees saved Chrysler Corporation from probable bankruptcy and gave it the opportunity to become a viable, profitable corporation. The utility industry entered into the nuclear power business only after the government provided insurance through the Price-Anderson Act. Since the Great Depression, farmers have been the beneficiaries of government aid and subsidies. Several airlines received help from the government or employed various regulatory and legal maneuvers to promote their survival.

CORPORATE LEGITIMACY

The second motive for corporate involvement in the public process is to increase **corporate legitimacy.**[21] Corporations are legitimate to the extent that their goals, purposes, and methods are consistent with those of society. Because the broader social system is the source of corporate support and allows organizations to pursue their goals, corporations must be sensitive to the expectations and values society establishes. These expectations, in the form of social norms, laws, and regulations, act as controls on the organization's behavior. Gross or frequent violations of these expectations will cause the corporation to lose its support and will limit its discretion.

Corporations sometimes face threats that challenge the legitimacy of their existence or their actions. They may be criticized for their efforts to gain competitive advantage, or questions regarding their social responsibility or ethical behavior may be raised. Activity intended to counter challenges to the organization's legitimacy is called **domain defense.**[22]

It is designed to strengthen the corporation's right to exist and to operate freely. Domain defense is corporations, acting in their own self-interest, using socially responsible and ethical behavior to maintain and enhance their legitimacy.

STRATEGIES FOR INFLUENCING THE POLITICAL ENVIRONMENT

Managers have an array of strategic options for dealing with the political environment. Many corporations have specialized units for managing these activities. The **public affairs department** of a corporation monitors key events and trends in the political and social environment, analyzes their effects on the organization, recommends the appropriate corporate responses, and implements political strategies. A successful public affairs program enhances an organization's credibility, facilitates a timely and appropriate response to issues, and has a positive financial impact (although this impact may be difficult to measure accurately).[23]

Depending on the needs of an industry or of an individual campaign, the public affairs department performs a variety of important activities:[24]

- *Issues management.* It identifies important social, political, economic, and technological developments and integrates this information into strategic planning.

- *Government relations (federal, state, and local).* It monitors legislative and regulatory developments, assesses their implications, and tries to affect the course of public policy.

- *Public relations.* It communicates information about the organization to the media.

- *International relations.* It promotes company interests in foreign capitals and in international forums.

- *Investor and stockholder relations.* It is often in charge of company communications with investors, brokerage houses, and other financial institutions.

- *Corporate contributions.* It frequently coordinates company contributions to the community.

- *Institutional advertising.* To heighten public awareness, it often engages in image building through nonproduct advertising.

SMALL BUSINESS AND GOVERNMENT REGULATORS

*L*arge corporations may have public affairs departments, but what can small companies do about government regulations? Here are a few approaches:

Work around the legislation: States have the right to regulate the sale and distribution of alcoholic beverages. Small California wineries must register in other states and are not allowed to sell directly to consumers, wine shops, restaurants, or hotels; they must sell through a distributor. Large wineries can afford this, but small ones cannot. One strategy for the small California winery, then, is to sell only in California and in states that have no licensing fees, like New York and New Jersey. Thus, they are regional—on the two separate coasts.

Work with the regulators: Regulators enforce the law, but they are also human beings. If small business owners explain their compliance problem, they may get helpful advice.

Change product strategies: Blockbuster products in the health care industry can take up to six or seven years to gain approval from the FDA. Small companies therefore cannot devote all their attention to developing big products with substantial market impact. They must have a development mix including small products that are easier to gain approval for, and don't have great potential, but can generate some cash flow and enhance financing opportunities. And instead of selling unapproved products to customers, which is illegal, firms can sell them to other companies that can afford to wait through the approval success.

Small California wineries are subject to the same government regulations as large wineries, which makes it difficult for wineries such as the one pictured here to sell and distribute their products. *(David Ball/The Stock Market)*

Be a voice in the wilderness: When the Bell system was broken up and the Baby Bells were prohibited from getting into manufacturing and a variety of services, many small companies were hurt because they couldn't sell to the Bells. Small-business people wrote letters to the editor, testified before Congress, and took other actions to make their plight known. It wasn't just whining—they also made the case that small businesses thrive around large companies, not only for sales but also in joint ventures. The result was a relaxation of some of the regulations and a number of new business opportunities.

Source: J. Seglin, "How Can You Survive the Regulators?" *Inc.,* September 1994, pp. 62–64. ●

Some specific strategies and vehicles used for managing the political environment are lobbying, PACs, corporate constituency programs, coalition building, stonewalling, and strategic retreat.[25]

Lobbying

Lobbying is the most traditional form of influencing the political environment. **Lobbying** involves efforts by political professionals or company executives to establish communication channels with regulatory bodies, legislators, and their staffs. It is designed to monitor legislation, provide issues papers and other information on the anticipated effects of proposed legislation, convey the company's sentiments on legislative issues to elected officials and their staffs, and attempt to influence the decisions of legislators and key advisers.

Political Action Committees (PACs)

In recent years, many businesses created corporate **political action committees (PACs).** PACs make donations to candidates for political office. Under reforms in federal election laws passed after the Watergate scandal, companies are allowed to ask their employees and shareholders for contributions for political candidates, subject to a set of limitations.

The PAC system has received much criticism. Some opponents complain that it gives large donors an unfair advantage both in an election and when their interests are brought before the elected legislator. Others claim PAC contributions are not an effective or efficient way for corporations to influence the legislative process. Because political candidates often accept contributions from many diverse and even opposing interests, the impact of any specific contribution is offset by other donations. As a result, the PAC contribution may be "protection money"—a corporation may donate funds to a candidate to ensure that it does not start at a disadvantage during the legislative process. Because of such criticisms, a number of reforms are now being discussed.

Corporate Constituency Programs

In the 1980s, many organizations started political action programs called **corporate constituency programs.** Constituency programs encourage interested stakeholders to engage in grassroots political activity on behalf of the corporation. These actions may include writing a letter to a congressperson or local politician, signing a petition, marching in a demonstration, or expressing an opinion on a television or radio talk show. Some companies spend a great amount of time and money identifying interested stakeholders and educating them on the issues.

Of the common political strategies, a comprehensive corporate constituency program probably requires the greatest commitment of organizational resources. However, many experts believe this strategy may have the most significant long-term potential to influence the political environment. Instead of providing money to politicians, constituency programs may deliver an even more valuable commodity to elected officials: votes!

Coalition Building

Many corporations and senior executives participate in cooperative efforts to manage the political and social environment. **Coalition building** involves efforts to find other organizations or groups of voters who share interest in a particular legislative issue.

Stonewalling

The final two political strategies—stonewalling and strategic retreat—are less opportunistic and proactive than the strategies just discussed, but they are viable options for managing the political and social environment. **Stonewalling** is the use of public relations, legal action, and administrative processes to delay legislation and regulation that may have an adverse impact on the organization. Legal suits or campaigns that improve the company's public image may help protect the organization against threat.

However, stonewalling has disadvantages. Although it may prevent certain problems, it rarely changes the conditions that led to the adverse law or regulation. The organization may constantly be in court or waging a continuous, losing battle for favorable public opinion. This strategy does not create opportunities for the company. Stonewalling often consumes considerable time and money that could be spent on activities leading to long-term positive outcomes. It also may undermine relations with key stakeholders, including customers.

Strategic Retreat

In some situations, top management and public-affairs executives decide the organization will be better served by accepting legislative or regulatory changes even if the changes may hurt the company. **Strategic retreat** involves an organization's efforts to adapt its products and processes to changes in the political and social environment while minimizing the negative effects of these changes. Senior managers may realize that the new law or regulation has support in most segments of society. Political action or stonewalling to oppose the change could have more negative consequences for the company, particularly in the long term, than would adapting to the environment or implementing more proactive strategies.[26]

KEY TERMS

act utilitarianism, p. 138
coalition building, p. 149
compliance-based ethics programs, p. 140
corporate constituency programs, p. 149
corporate legitimacy, p. 146
corporate social responsibility, p. 144
domain defense, p. 146
egoism, p. 138
ethics, p. 138

integrity-based ethics programs, p. 140
lobbying, p. 148
political action committees (PACs), p. 148
public affairs department, p. 147
rule utilitarianism, p. 138
stonewalling, p. 149
strategic retreat, p. 149
universalism, p. 138
utilitarianism, p. 138

SUMMARY OF LEARNING OBJECTIVES

Now that you have studied Chapter 6, you should know:

How ethical perspectives guide decision making.

The purpose of ethics is to identify the rules that govern human behavior and the "goods" that are worth seeking. Ethical decisions are guided by the individual's values, or principles of conduct such as honesty, fairness, integrity, respect for others, and responsible citizenship.

The four major ethical systems are universalism and three types of utilitarianism: egoism, rule utilitarianism, and act utilitarianism. These philosophical systems underlie the ethical stances of individuals and organizations.

How companies use ethical codes.

Ethics programs can range from compliance-based to integrity-based. An increasing number of organizations are adopting ethical codes. Such codes address employee conduct, community and environment, shareholders, customers, suppliers and contractors, political activity, and technology.

The options you have when confronting ethical issues.

Individuals have a variety of options when they witness unethical behavior. Their choice of action will depend on both their beliefs about the action's likely outcomes and on their own moral judgment. When faced with ethical dilemmas, you should define the issue clearly, identify relevant values, weigh conflicting values and choose an appropriate option, and implement your decision.

The important issues surrounding the corporate social responsibility debate.

Corporate social responsibility is the extension of the corporate role beyond economic pursuits. Advocates believe managers should consider societal and human needs in their business decisions because corporations are members of society and carry a wide range of responsibilities. Critics of corporate responsibility believe managers' first responsibility is to increase profits for the shareholders who own the corporation.

How the political and social environment affects your firm's competitive position and legitimacy.

Corporations have two goals within their ethical structures: competitive advantage and corporate legitimacy. Progressive organizations realize that the government can be an ally and a source of advantage rather than just an adversary. Corporate legitimacy comes from goals, purposes, and methods that are consistent with those of society. Thus, organizations must be sensitive to the expectations and values of society.

The strategies corporations use to manage the political and social environment.

The public affairs department monitors the political and social environment, analyzes its impact on the organization, and implements political strategies. Strategies include lobbying, political action committees, corporate constituency programs, coalition building, stonewalling, and strategic retreat. Generally, strategies that adapt to or change the environment are most effective in the long run.

DISCUSSION QUESTIONS

1. Who is to blame at Kidder Peabody in Setting the Stage? Could these problems have been prevented?
2. What kinds of questions concern ethical thinkers? Provide concrete examples and discuss.
3. What would you do in each of the scenarios described in "Ethical Decision Making in the International Context" (pp. 139–40)?

4. Which of the acts in Table 6.1 are most unethical? Least unethical? Discuss.
5. Identify and discuss illegal, unethical, and socially responsible business actions in the current news.
6. Does your school have a code of ethics? If so, what does it say? Is it effective? Why or why not?

7. You have a job you like at which you work 40 to 45 hours per week. How much off-the-job volunteer work would you do? What kinds of volunteer work? How will you react if your boss makes it clear he or she wants you to cut back on the outside activities and devote more hours to your job?

8. What are the arguments for and against the concept of corporate social responsibility? Where do you stand, and why?

9. How can the political and social environment both constrain and help the corporation in its pursuit of competitive advantage? Give examples.

10. Under what conditions might stonewalling and strategic retreat be the most appropriate political strategies? Have you seen these tactics work?

CONCLUDING CASE

DISNEY AND BULL RUN

"I was dragged to Washington as a kid and it was the worst weekend of my life. I promise you 90 percent of the kids in American don't know who lived in Mount Vernon, Montpelier, or Monticello." The speaker was Michael Eisner, chairman of the Walt Disney Co.

The company had announced plans to build Disney America, a theme park, near Manassas, Virginia. American history was to be the theme of the park. Expecting controversy over urban development and other local issues, the company instead encountered charges it would commercialize and vulgarize a noble and revered national historical landmark.

The park site was close to Bull Run, the Civil War battleground where 30,000 Americans were killed or wounded. The toll for D day in WWII was only one-sixth as high.

The park would bring traffic, crowds, motels, restaurants, malls, trash, and air pollution to an historic landscape. Disney responded to these concerns by pointing out that the park would be much smaller than its parks in Orlando and Anaheim.

The problems didn't stop with the landscape. When criticized for the Civil War exhibits' not adequately addressing slavery, a Disney spokesman disagreed, saying, "We want to make you feel what it was like to be a slave." The protests escalated, and the company began reworking its original plans. Meanwhile, the Black History Action Coalition asked that the Civil War and slavery exhibits be excluded. Disney called this censorship.

The Disney America theme park, planned for Manassas, Virginia, was so heavily criticized, for its content, location, and potentially damaging effects on the environment, that the project was ultimately abandoned. *(AP/Wide World Photos)*

Disney dropped its proposed battle reenactments and Mr. Eisner himself met with Native American chiefs to discuss the park's content. Members of both houses of Congress, including Civil War preservationists, threatened to fight the project.

On the other hand, Virginia politicians, including all the gubernatorial candidates, did everything they could to pave the way for the new theme park. And having backed out of a $2 billion project in Long Beach, California, when environmental concerns per-sisted, Disney vowed it would not back down again. The company announced that changing sites would be impossibly impractical and ex-pensive. Controversy raged, as Disney in its public pronouncements tried to walk the balance between notions of patriotism, political correctness, the value of entertainment, and the educational mission of its project as the company saw it.

Then, in late 1994, Disney officials announced they were giving up. They didn't like it, but they had decided enough was enough. They would try to find another site for their park.

QUESTIONS

1. What are the ethical and social responsibility issues in this case?

2. Should Disney have built the park at its preferred site?

3. How should Disney proceed to secure a new location?

Sources: T. Horwitz and R. Turner, "Disney and Academics Escalate Battle over the Entertainment Value of History," *The Wall Street Journal,* June 21, 1994, pp. B1, B2; J. D. Podolsky and J. S. Podesta, "An Uncivil War," *Time,* July 18, 1994, p. 70; and S. C. Fehr and S. S. Hsu, "The Fly in Walt Disney's Formula," *Washington Post,* July 31, 1994, p. B1.

VIDEO EXERCISE

THE HIGH
BID DILEMMA

Purpose

This exercise provides students with the opportunity to view the possibility of conflict of interest when dealing with an outside vendor.

A purchasing agent (PA) and his assistant are reviewing bids from seven companies to determine which company should receive a contract for bronze facing a clutch. The PA's assistant proposes that the bid should be awarded to Metaltech, the low bidder, which is located some 300 miles away. His boss, the PA agent, leans toward Spin Cast Systems, a nearby company, which has submitted a much higher bid. Both companies submitting bids have the ability to provide a quality product complete with delivery and support capabilities.

The PA attempts to persuade his assistant that the contract award should be awarded to Spin Cast Systems despite its higher bid that will create a budgetary problem. He informs his assistant that he has used Spin Cast's services previously. Moreover, Greg Sommers, the president of Spin Cast, is his personal friend, his fraternity brother, and his sailing companion. The PA tells his assistant, "You take care of your suppliers and they'll take care of you." In fact, to show his assistant that Sommers is a "nice guy," the PA will ask Sommers to invite the assistant to a house party.

CRITICAL THINKING QUESTIONS

1. Does the issue of a "conflict of interest" surface in this exercise? If so, how? If not, why not?
2. Will the purchasing assistant compromise his own ethics if he allows his boss to award the bid to Spin Cast Systems even though such an award will create a budget overrun and does not follow company regulations?
3. Does the purchasing agent's assistant have any possible options if his boss decides to award the bid to Spin Cast?

VIDEO EXERCISE

A VERY
FRIENDLY FELLOW

Purpose

This exercise demonstrates the problems of sexual harassment on the job.

Bill and Shelly are having a conversation in the hallway. Shelly feels a certain degree of discomfort because Bill is standing very close to her. Ginny, another worker, meets them in the hallway, and Bill begins talking about the good time he had at a night club. He tells Shelly and Ginny that they should meet him and his friends after work at the Steak and Cap. Although Shelly, upset by his invitation, tells him she is busy and cannot make it, Ginny sees his invitation as a friendly social gesture from a co-worker.

When Shelly tells Ginny that she has to talk with her about a work project, Bill decides to return to his office. Shelly informs Ginny that Bill will not leave her alone. She believes that he has been making sexual advances toward her and that she will be unable to work with him. The problem is that he can not seem to keep his hands off of her. He "touches" her by massaging her neck or by squeezing her arm even though she has repeatedly told Bill to stop.

CRITICAL THINKING QUESTIONS

1. What should Shelly do when she meets Bill at work?
2. What impact will Bill's "advances" have on their ability to work together on a new project?
3. Does Shelly have responsibility to report Bill's actions to the personnel office?

VIDEO EXERCISE

COMPENSATION ISSUE

Purpose

This exercise discusses the possible problems that can occur when employees discuss their pay levels among themselves, and presents some of the possible issues of pay discrimination.

After Brenda, an African-American woman, and Sandy, a white woman, exchange pleasantries early on Friday morning, Brenda reveals to Sandy that she has just learned that another employee, June, who works in bookkeeping, receives $.30 an hour more pay. Brenda is upset by this information because both she and June began their employment with the company at the same time and they both perform similar functions.

Brenda believes that the company has "discriminated" against her because she is an African-American woman. She tells Sandy that she will hire an attorney to sue the company. Sandy suggests that the difference in pay, even for performing the same job functions, may be a result of other considerations. For example, even though both women were hired at the same time, June may have had previous experience that allows the company to pay her a slightly higher salary. Brenda counters Sandy's argument by saying that a similar job within the same company should mean that each employee receives the same salary.

CRITICAL THINKING QUESTIONS

1. Is it ethical for employees to compare salaries when working for the same company? If so, why? If not, why not?

2. Do you believe that Brenda has been discriminated against by her company? If so, what type of discrimination?

3. Are there times when people working in the same company, hired at the same time, and doing the same work should be paid different salaries? Explain your answer?

VIDEO EXERCISE

COMPETITION OR REVENGE

Purpose

This exercise questions the ethics of an ex-employee to compete with his former employer for the same client.

A group of salespeople are discussing the impact a former employee is having on their current sales. Jack Rebeck, who was recently fired from his position, is now soliciting former clients. In one instance he has been successful in underbidding his old firm. The members of the sales group are concerned with Rebeck's competing for the same client pool.

Because Rebeck has limited financial resources, George, one member of the sales group, suggests that the company underbid Rebeck on projects. Jean, another former colleague, suggests that the group spread stories within the industry about the reasons Rebeck was terminated by the company, and finally, Jeff, the last member of the sales group, believes that bad-mouthing and undermining Rebeck is fruitless and will not have an impact on the company's business.

CRITICAL THINKING QUESTIONS

1. Is it ethical for an ex-employee to compete with a former company? If so, when? Under what circumstances?

2. Is it ethical for a company to attempt to undermine a former employee who is now a competitor?

3. If a company discusses the reason(s) an employee was terminated, does it violate employee confidentiality?

VIDEO EXERCISE

CREATIVE EXPENSE REPORTING

Purpose

This video raises the issues of padding the expense account by submitting unsubstantiated expense vouchers to a company for reimbursement.

Jim, a salesperson, enters Ken's workstation to discuss a problem. He apparently has lost the hotel room receipt for his last stay in New York. Ken tells him the cost of his larger suite. Jim also asks Ken about the cost of a taxi ride so that he can prepare his expense voucher. Ken informs him of the cost of his taxi ride.

Jim, after some deliberation, decides to pad both his hotel room and his taxi ride by settling on an "odd-dollar" amount that will appear more realistic to those reviewing the submission of his voucher. Finally, Jim informs Ken of his intention to pad the lunch and dinner bills to cover entertainment costs he incurred during the trip. Since Jim considers entertainment as a part of conducting business, no one would question an expense of a few extra dollars on the voucher.

CRITICAL THINKING QUESTIONS

1. Should Ken tell his superiors that Jim has padded the expense voucher?

2. Is padding a business expense ever justified? If so, when? Why?

3. If he wanted to submit an accurate expense voucher, what possible options are available to Jim to secure the correct information?

EXPERIENTIAL EXERCISES

6.1 Measuring Your Ethical Work Behavior

Objectives

1. To explore a range of ethically perplexing situations.
2. To understand your own ethical attitudes.

Instructions

Make decisions in the situations described in the Ethical Behavior Worksheet. You will not have all the background information on each situation, and, instead, you should make whatever assumptions you feel you would make if you were actually confronted with the decision choices described. Select the decision choice that most closely represents the decision you feel you would make personally. You should choose decision choices even though you can envision other creative solutions that were not included in the exercise.

ETHICAL BEHAVIOR WORKSHEET

Situation 1. You are taking a very difficult chemistry course, which you must pass to maintain your scholarship and to avoid damaging your application for graduate school. Chemistry is not your strong suit, and, because of a just-below failing average in the course, you will have to receive a grade of 90 or better on the final exam, which is two days away. A janitor, who is aware of your plight, informs you that he has found the master stencil for the chemistry final in a trash barrel and saved it. He will make it available to you for a price, which is high, but which you could afford. What would you do?

_____ (a) I would tell the janitor thanks, but no thanks.

_____ (b) I would report the janitor to the proper officials.

_____ (c) I would buy the exam and keep it to myself.

_____ (d) I would not buy the exam myself, but I would let some of my friends, who are also flunking the course, know that it is available.

Situation 2. You have been working on some financial projections manually for two days now. It seems that each time you think you have them completed your boss shows up with a new assumption or another "what-if" question. If you only had a copy of a spreadsheet software program for your personal computer, you could plug in the new assumptions and revise the estimates with ease. Then, a colleague offers to let you make a copy of some software which is copyrighted. What would you do?

_____ (a) I would really accept my friend's generous offer and make a copy of the software.

_____ (b) I would decline to copy it and plug away manually on the numbers.

_____ (c) I would decide to go buy a copy of the software myself, for $300, and hope I would be reimbursed by the company in a month or two.

_____ (d) I would request another extension on an already overdue project date.

Situation 3. Your small manufacturing company is in serious financial difficulty. A large order of your products is ready to be delivered to a key customer when you discover that the product is simply not right. It will not meet all performance specifications, will cause problems for your customer, and will require network in the field; but this, you know, will not become evident until after the customer has received and paid for the order. If you do not ship the order and receive the payment as expected, your business may be forced into bankruptcy. And if you delay the shipment or inform the customer of these problems, you may lose the order and also go bankrupt. What would you do?

_____ (a) I would not ship the order and place my firm in voluntary bankruptcy.

_____ (b) I would inform the customer and declare voluntary bankruptcy.

_____ (c) I would ship the order and inform the customer, after I received payment.

_____ (d) I would ship the order and not inform the customer.

Situation 4. You are the cofounder and president of a new venture, manufacturing products for the recreational market. Five months after launching the business, one of your suppliers informs you it can no longer supply you with a critical raw material since you are not a large-quantity user. Without the raw material the business cannot continue. What would you do?

_____ (a) I would grossly overstate my requirements to another supplier to make the supplier think I am a much larger potential customer in order to secure the raw material from that supplier, even though this would mean the supplier will no longer be able to supply another, non-competing small manufacturer who may thus be forced out of business.

_____ (b) I would steal raw material from another firm (noncompeting) where I am aware of a sizable stockpile.

_____ (c) I would pay off the supplier, since I have reason to believe that the supplier could be "persuaded" to meet my needs with a sizable "under the table" payoff that my company could afford.

_____ (d) I would declare voluntary bankruptcy.

Situation 5. You are on a marketing trip for your new venture for the purpose of calling on the purchasing agent of a major prospective client. Your company is manufacturing an electronic system that you hope the purchasing agent will buy. During the course of your conversation, you notice on the cluttered desk of the purchasing agent several copies of a cost proposal for a system from one of your direct competitors. This purchasing agent has previously reported mislaying several of your own company's proposals and has asked for additional copies. The purchasing agent leaves the room momentarily to get you a cup of coffee, leaving you alone with your competitor's proposals less than an arm's length away. What would you do?

_____ (a) I would do nothing but await the man's return.

_____ (b) I would sneak a quick peek at the proposal, looking for bottom-line numbers.

_____ (c) I would put the copy of the proposal in my briefcase.

_____ (d) I would wait until the man returns and ask his permission to see the copy.

Source: Jeffry A. Timmons, *New Venture Creation,* 3rd ed. (Burr Ridge, Ill.: Richard D. Irwin, 1994), pp. 285–86.

6.2 Social Responsibility

Objectives

1. To have a look at a socially responsible undertaking of a firm.
2. To examine the pros and cons of firms' taking on the role of trying to solve social ills.

Instructions

Social responsibility refers to the organization's taking on a role in solving social and community problems. There are many arguments for and against firms' taking a role in trying to alleviate community or social ills. Find an example of a business acting in a manner that is clearly socially responsible, such as providing job training programs for the unemployed or providing financial support for urban renewal. You may be able to find your own example of this locally, or in articles in business periodicals.

ETHICAL BEHAVIOR WORKSHEET

1. Briefly describe the firm and its program(s).

_____

_____

_____

_____

_____

_____

_____

2. What is the rationale the firm uses to support this program?

_____

_____

_____

_____

_____

_____

_____

_____

3. What is the response from those affected by the program?

_____

_____

_____

_____

_____

_____

_____

4. What is the response, if any, from those who oppose the program?

_____

_____

_____

_____

_____

_____

_____

5. Do you think the company is benefiting from the program to the extent of the program's cost?

_____

_____

_____

_____

_____

_____

_____

Source: R. R. McGrath, Jr., *Exercises in Management Fundamentals* (Englewood Cliffs, N.J.: Prentice-Hall, 1985), p. 192. Reprinted by permission of Prentice-Hall, Inc.

MANAGING IN OUR NATURAL ENVIRONMENT

Never doubt that a small group of thoughtful, committed citizens can change the world. Indeed, it is the only thing that ever has.

Margaret Mead

LEARNING OBJECTIVES

After studying Chapter 7, you will know:

1. The relationship between the natural environment and business.

2. The importance of managing with the environment in mind.

3. The important perspectives on our natural environment.

4. Constructive actions managers can take to both protect the environment and benefit the firm.

STRATEGIC ENVIRONMENTALISM AT PITNEY BOWES

As with many manufacturers, Pitney Bowes's approach to considering environmentalism in its decisions initially focused on staying out of trouble with the law. The company studied regulations, and to comply with them it fixed problems in its underground storage tanks, air toxin releases, and asbestos in old buildings.

Over time, the number of regulations grew, and complying with them became more and more complex. Compliance also became more expensive; over a five-year period, the per-drum cost of hazardous waste disposal increased by a factor of five.

But after tremendous effort and investment, the company still never really knew whether and when it was in full compliance with the law. Therefore, it began taking a more strategic approach to environmental management.

Pitney Bowes works hard to identify and understand the full economic costs and benefits of proposed changes. For example, an internal task force worked with Ernst & Young, the public accounting firm, to design a method to assess waste minimization programs. Program goals are set, and technical and financial feasibility tests are conducted. The best programs are approved and implemented, and completed programs are thoroughly evaluated so the company learns lessons for future projects.

The company's overall strategic approach is called "Design for Environmental Quality." The purpose is to consider environmental issues from the moment new products are first conceived, and design environmental problems out of the products. Thus, the company chooses materials and processes that do not generate environmentally harmful waste.

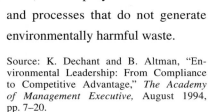

At Pitney Bowes, the best environmental programs are approved and implemented, and completed programs are thoroughly evaluated so the company learns lessons for future projects. Pitney Bowes has learned that paying attention to environmental issues is now an essential part of doing business.
(Jake Wyman)

Source: K. Dechant and B. Altman, "Environmental Leadership: From Compliance to Competitive Advantage," *The Academy of Management Executive,* August 1994, pp. 7–20.

*T*he Pitney Bowes example illustrates the fact that dealing with environmental issues is now an essential part of doing business; it is not a mere "side issue." In the end, management has no viable option but to get involved. This realization has led to a new corporate perspective on environmentalism as a part of strategic management, affecting product development, process technology, and total quality. Companies like AT&T, Amoco, Exxon Chemicals, ABB Flakt, Shell International, Rohn and Hass, and British Gas are leading the way.

Managers operating in today's world face a new and urgent imperative: to create a new relationship between business activity and our natural environment that will halt environmental damage and clean up the effects of past practices.[1] James Post, professor of management and public policy at Boston University, states, "[E]nvironmental issues will be . . . a force of such power as to literally transform the way managers manage their businesses and think about the relationship of the firm to its internal and external stakeholders." Table 7.1 gives just a few examples of things U.S. corporations are doing to help solve environmental problems.

The range of environmental issues is broad, and the impact huge. Effectively managing with the environment in mind requires attention to efficiency, effectiveness, and long-term goals. Environmental management must consider a mix of technical, ethical, social, and competitive issues.[2]

A McKinsey survey found that 92 percent of CEOs and board members stated the environment should be one of the top three management priorities; 85 percent said one of their major goals should be integrating environment into strategy, but only 37 percent said they do so successfully.[3] Richard A. Clarke, CEO of Pacific Gas and Electric Company, puts it this way: "A strong global economy is sustained only if it integrates economic, social, and environmental well-being."[4]

BUSINESS AND THE ENVIRONMENT: CONFLICTING VIEWS

Some people believe everyone wins when business tackles environmental issues. Others disagree.

THE WIN-WIN MENTALITY

Business used to look at environmental issues as a no-win situation: You either help the environment and hurt your business, or help your business only at a cost to the environment. Fortunately, things have changed. "When Americans first demanded a cleanup of the environment during the early 1970s, corporations threw a tantrum. Their response ran the psychological gamut from denial to hostility, defiance, obstinacy, and fear. But today, when it comes to green issues, many U.S. companies have turned from rebellious underachievers to active problem solvers."[5]

Being "green" is potentially a catalyst for innovation, new market opportunities, and wealth creation. Advocates believe that this is truly a win-win situation; actions can be taken that benefit both business and the environment. Only win-win companies will survive; they will come out ahead of those companies that have an us-versus-them, we-can't-afford-to-protect-the-environment mentality.

Or is this an unrealistic vision? Is the easy part over? Companies have found a lot of easy-to-harvest, "low-hanging fruit"—that is, overly costly practices that were made environmentally friendlier and that saved money at the same time. Many big companies have made these easy changes, and reaped benefits from them. Many small companies still have such low-hanging fruit to harvest.[6]

THE DISSENTING VIEW

The critics of environmentalism in business are vocal. Some economists maintain that not a single empirical analysis supports the "free lunch view" that spending money on envi-

TABLE 7.1

What companies
are doing to
enhance the
environment

- Ben & Jerry's Homemade feeds the sludge left over from the manufacture of ice cream to pigs; it also pours it on farmland as fertilizer.

- Texaco created a new division for the environment, health, and safety; the head of the division reports directly to the CEO.

- Kodak is recycling its disposable cameras and spending $46 million to cut methylene chloride emissions 70 percent.

- Monsanto has pledged to reduce toxic air emissions 90 percent from 1988 levels.

- Procter & Gamble is experimenting with recycling disposable diapers into drywall backing and selling Spic 'n Span Pine in containers made entirely from used pop bottles.

- ARCO and Pacific Gas & Electric have prominent environmentalists on their boards of directors.

- Nissan enlisted a group of ecologists, energy experts, and science writers to brainstorm about how an environmentally responsible car company might behave. Among the ideas: to produce automobiles that snap together into electrically powered trains for long trips and then detach for the dispersion to final destinations.

- BMW and Volkswagen have efforts under way to make cars entirely recyclable.

Sources: C. Garfield, *Second to None: How Our Smartest Companies Put People First* (Burr Ridge, Ill.: Business One–Irwin, 1992); C. Morrison, *Managing Environmental Affairs: Corporate Practices in the U.S., Canada, and Europe* (New York: The Conference Board, 1991); A. Kleiner, "What Does It Mean to Be Green?" *Harvard Business Review,* July–August 1991, pp. 38–47; and E. Smith and V. Cahan, "The Greening of Corporate America," *Business Week,* April 23, 1990, pp. 96–103.

ronmental problems provides full payback to the firm.[7] Skepticism should continue, they say; the belief that everyone will come out a winner is naive.

What really upsets many businesspeople is the financial cost of complying with environmental regulations.[8] Consider a few examples:

- GM is spending $1.3 billion to comply with California requirements that 10 percent of the cars sold there be emission-free. European automakers spent $7 billion to install pollution-control equipment in all new cars between 1989 and 1993.

- The data are not in yet, but projections are of a $200 billion expenditure in the United States on pollution abatement in 1995.

- At Bayer, 20 percent of manufacturing costs are for the environment. This is approximately the same amount spent for labor.

- The Clean Air Act alone is expected to cost U.S. petroleum refiners $37 billion, more than the book value of the entire industry.

- Executives expect environmental expenditures to double as a percentage of sales in the next few years.

- California's tough laws are a major reason manufacturers move to Arkansas or Nevada.

In industries like chemicals and petroleum, already plagued by fierce competition and declining profit margins, the ability to respond to environmental regulations may determine their very survival.[9]

BALANCE

A more balanced view is that business must weigh the environmental benefits of an action against value destruction. The advice here is, don't obstruct progress, but pick your

IBM was one of *Fortune* magazine's top 10 winners for attentiveness to the environment. The company eliminated CFCs seven years before the regulatory deadline. *(Courtesy International Business Machines Corporation)*

environmental initiatives carefully. J. Ladd Greeno of Arthur D. Little believes that compliance and remediation efforts will protect, but not increase, shareholder value.[10] And it is shareholder value, rather than compliance, emissions, or costs, that should be the focus of objective cost/benefit analyses. Such an approach is environmentally sound but also hardheaded in a business sense, and is the one approach that is truly sustainable over the long term.

Johan Piet maintains, "Only win-win companies will survive, but that does not mean that all win-win ideas will be successful."[11] In other words, rigorous analysis is essential. Thus, Polaroid maintains continuous improvement in environmental performance, but funds only projects that meet financial objectives.

Most people understand that business has the resources and the competence to bring about constructive change, and that this creates great opportunity—if well managed—for both business and the environment.

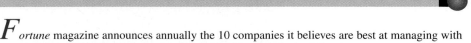

AND THE WINNERS ARE . . .

*F*ortune magazine announces annually the 10 companies it believes are best at managing with the environment in mind. The environmental leaders include the following:

Sun Co., parent of Sunoco, was the first major company to sign the Coalition for Environmentally Responsible Economies (CERES) principles. Sunoco gas stations were the first outside California to install pumps for methanol, which produces less smog than regular gasoline.

IBM was one of the first major corporations to embrace a four-tiered approach to waste: reduce, reuse, recycle, and landfill as a last resort. This shifts the focus to waste prevention. A major focus of IBM's effort is CFCs, used widely in the industry as solvents and cleaning agents. In 1989, the regulatory deadline for eliminating CFCs was the year 2000; IBM responded by announcing its own deadline of 1993—a fortunate move, since the required deadline later changed to 1995. IBM is also committed to the EPA's Energy Star program, which proposes to cut the energy consumption of PCs 50 to 75 percent. EPA estimates are that converting two-thirds of all PCs to meet these requirements will save electricity equivalent to that consumed annually by Vermont, Maine, and New Hampshire combined.

AT&T developed an alternative to CFC solvents for cleaning electronic circuit boards, and is now selling the technology to other companies. Another breakthrough eliminates the need for another ozone-depleting solvent; AT&T is *giving* the technology to its competitors for free. The most universal office pollution problem is too much paper. AT&T formed a corporate TQM team to alleviate its paper blizzard. The team initiated a corporatewide study, and created TQM teams throughout the company. Now, by implementing simple ideas like eliminating cover pages, using electronic media, and compressing spacing on bills, paper use is way down and cost savings are well into the millions annually.

Source: F. Rice, "Who Scores Best on the Environment?" *Fortune,* July 26, 1993, pp. 114–22. ●

WHY MANAGE WITH THE ENVIRONMENT IN MIND?

Business is turning its full attention to environmental issues for many reasons, including legal compliance, cost effectiveness, competitive advantage, public opinion, and long-term thinking.

LEGAL COMPLIANCE

Table 7.2 shows just some of the most important U.S. environmental laws. Government regulations and liability for damages provide strong economic incentives to comply with environmental guidelines. Most industries already have made environmental protection regulation and liability an integral part of their business planning.[12] The U.S. Justice Department is handing out tough prison sentences to executives whose companies violate hazardous-waste requirements.

TABLE 7.2

Some U.S.
environmental laws

Superfund [Comprehensive Environmental Response, Compensation, and Liability Act (CER-CLA)]: Establishes potential liability for any person or organization responsible for creating an environmental health hazard. Individuals may be prosecuted, fined, or taxed to fund cleanup.

Clean Water Act [Federal Water Pollution Control Act]: Regulates all discharges into surface waters, and affects the construction and performance of sewer systems. The Safe Drinking Water Act similarly protects ground waters.

Clean Air Act: Regulates the emission into the air of any substance that affects air quality, including nitrous oxides, sulfur dioxide, and carbon dioxide.

Community Response and Right-to-Know Act: Mandates that all facilities producing, transporting, storing, using, or releasing hazardous substances provide full information to local and state authorities and maintain emergency-action plans.

Federal Hazardous Substances Act: Regulates hazards to health and safety associated with consumer products. The Consumer Product Safety Commission has the right to recall hazardous products.

Hazardous Materials Transportation Act: Regulates the packaging, marketing, and labeling of shipments of flammable, toxic, and radioactive materials.

Resource Conservation and Recovery Act: Extends to small-quantity generators the laws regulating generation, treatment, and disposal of solid and hazardous wastes.

Surface Mining Control and Reclamation Act: Establishes environmental standards for all surface-mining operations.

Toxic Substances Control Act: Addresses the manufacture, processing, distribution, use, and disposal of dangerous chemical substances and mixtures.

Source: D. C. Kinlaw, *Competitive and Green* (Amsterdam: Pfeiffer, 1993).

Many businesspeople consider the regulations to be too rigid, inflexible, and unfair. In response to this concern, regulatory reform may become more creative. The Aspen Institute Series on the Environment in the Twenty-First Century is trying to increase the cost-effectiveness of compliance measures through more flexibility in meeting standards and relying on market-based incentives. Such mechanisms, including tradable permits, pollution charges, and deposit refund systems, provide positive financial incentives for good environmental performance.[13]

COST EFFECTIVENESS

Environmentally conscious strategies can be cost effective. In the short run, company after company is realizing cost savings from repackaging, recycling, and other approaches. Union Carbide, for instance, faced costs of $30 a ton for disposal of solid wastes and $2,000 a ton for disposal of hazardous wastes. By recycling, reclaiming, or selling its waste, it avoided $8.5 million in costs *and* generated $3.5 million in income during a six-month period.

Environmentally conscious strategies also offer long-run cost advantages. Companies that are functioning barely within legal limits today may incur big costs—being forced to pay damages or upgrade technologies and practices—when laws change down the road.

A few of the other cost savings include fines, cleanups, and litigation; lower raw materials costs; reduced energy use; less-expensive waste handling and disposal; lower insurance rates; and possibly higher interest rates.

COMPETITIVE ADVANTAGE

Corporations gain a competitive advantage by channeling their environmental concerns into entrepreneurial opportunities and by producing higher-quality products that meet consumer demand. Business opportunities abound in pollution protection equipment and processes, waste cleanup, low-water-use plumbing, new light bulb technology, and marketing environmentally safe products like biodegradable plastics. With new pools of venture capital, government funding, and specialized investment funds available, environmental technology is becoming a major sector of the venture-capital industry.[14]

In addition, companies that fail to innovate in this area will be at a competitive *disadvantage*. Environmental protection is not only a universal need; it is also a major export industry. U.S. trade has suffered as other countries—notably Germany—have taken the lead in patenting and exporting anti–air pollution and other environmental technologies. If the United States does not produce innovative, competitive new technologies, it will forsake a growth industry and see most of its domestic spending for environmental protection go to imports.[15]

In short, competitive advantage can be gained by maintaining market share with old customers, and by creating new products for new market opportunities. And, if you are an environmental leader, you may set the standards for future regulations—regulations that you are prepared to meet, while your competitors are not.

PUBLIC OPINION

The majority of the U.S. population believes business must clean up; few people think it is doing its job well. Gallup surveys show that more than 80 percent of U.S. consumers consider environmentalism in making purchases. An international survey of 22 countries found that majorities in 20 countries gave priority to environmental protection even at the risk of slowing economic growth. Consumers seem to have reached the point of routinely expecting companies to come up with environmentally friendly alternatives to current products and practices.[16]

Companies also receive pressure from local communities and from their own employees. Sometimes the pressure is informal and low key, but much pressure is exerted by environmental organizations, aroused citizen groups, societies and associations, international codes of conduct, and environmentally conscious investors.[17]

Another important reason for paying attention to environmental impact is TRI, the Toxic Release Inventory.[18] Starting in 1986, the EPA required all the plants of approximately 10,000 U.S. manufacturers to report annual releases of 317 toxic chemicals into air, ground, and water. The substances include freon, PCBs, asbestos, and lead compounds. Hundreds of others are being added to the list. The releases are not necessarily illegal, but they provide the public with an annual environmental benchmark. TRI provides a powerful incentive to reduce emissions.

Finally, it is useful to remember that companies recover very slowly in public opinion from the impact of an environmental disaster. Adverse public opinion may affect sales as well as the firm's ability to attract and retain talented people. You can see why companies like P&G consider concern for the environment a new consumer need, making it a basic and critical business issue.

LONG-TERM THINKING

Long-term thinking about resources helps business leaders understand the nature of their responsibilities with regard to environmental concerns. Economic arguments, sustainable growth, and the tragedy of the commons highlight the need for long-term thinking.

Economic Arguments

In Chapter 4, we discussed long-term versus short-term decision making. We stated that it is common for managers to succumb to short-term pressure for profits and to avoid spending now when the potential payoff is years down the road. In addition, some economists maintain that it is the responsibility of management to maximize returns for shareholders, implying the preeminence of the short-term profit goal.

But other economists argue that such a strategy caters to immediate profit maximization for stock speculators and neglects serious investors who are with the company for the long haul. Attention to environmental issues enhances the organization's long-term viability because the goal is the long-term creation of wealth for the patient, serious investors in the company[19]—not to mention the future state of our planet and the new generations who will inhabit it.

Sustainable Growth

Today many companies are moving beyond the law to be truly environmentalist in their philosophies and practices. Their aim is to jointly achieve the goals of economic growth and environmental quality in the long run by striving for sustainable growth. **Sustainable growth** is economic growth and development that meets the organization's present needs without harming the ability of future generations to meet their needs.[20] Sustainability is fully compatible with the natural ecosystems that generate and preserve life.

Some believe that the concept of sustainable performance offers[21] (1) a framework for organizations to use in communicating to all stakeholders; (2) a planning and strategy guide; and (3) a tool for evaluating and improving the ability to compete. The principle can begin at the highest organizational levels, and be made explicit in performance appraisals and reward systems.

The Tragedy of the Commons

In a classic article in *Science*, Garrett Hardin described a situation that applies to all business decisions and social concerns regarding scarce resources like clean water, air, and land.[22] Throughout human history, a commons was a tract of land shared by communities of people on which they grazed their animals. A commons has limited **carrying capacity,** or the ability to sustain a population, because it is a finite resource. For individual herders, short-term interest lies in adding as many animals to the commons as they can. But problems develop as more herders add more animals to graze the commons. This leads to tragedy: As each herder acts in his short-term interest, the long-run impact is the destruction of the commons. The only solution is to make choices according to long-run rather than short-run consequences (recall Chapter 4).

In many ways, we are witnessing this **tragedy of the commons.** Carrying capacities are shrinking as precious resources, water chief among them, become scarcer. Inevitably, conflict arises—and solutions are urgently needed.

▌ RECYCLING: SUPPLY AND DEMAND

Some products, like steel and aluminum containers, couldn't survive without recycled materials. But in 1993 paper, plastics, and other industries were struggling to make recycling work. What was the problem?

The success of recycling efforts will depend not on saved landfill space, but on economic sense. In order for recycling to make economic sense, the demand for recycled materials must increase.

Recycling had been highly successful in creating a huge supply of recycled materials. But in 1993 demand for the products made from these materials was too low. The cost of collecting and processing recycled materials far outweighed their value as a commodity to be sold. Mountains of recycled materials remained in storage, waiting for prices to rise to cover costs of collection, transportation, processing, packaging, and storing—not to mention the need for profit.

Costs would come down over time, but companies also went to work stimulating demand. Some companies devised creative marketing strategies on their own. And many companies are

Companies recycle both out of a sense of environmental responsibility and because recycling programs are becoming profitable. *(Courtesy National Office Paper Recycling Project, Photography by Koji Yamashita/Panoramic Images, Chicago)*

banding together to motivate others to use recycled materials. Bank of America, Anheuser-Busch, Bell Atlantic, American Airlines, and Coca-Cola have participated actively in campaigns organized by the Buy Recycled Business Alliance. The alliance now has thousands of members.

By 1994 and 1995, things had changed. Prices of cardboard, plastics, and mixed paper were up dramatically, although glass prices remained low. Demand was higher, and the unused piles of recycled materials disappeared.

Still, towns were paying for recycling programs only because collection costs remained higher than the value of recycled materials. But as other costs are lowered, the programs begin breaking even or making a profit. Although prices are expected to remain volatile (like all commodities), Weyerhaeuser and other big companies are acquiring recycling centers. Recycling once again is expected to become a huge business.

Sources: D. Biddle, "Recycling for Profit: The New Green Business Frontier," *Harvard Business Review,* November–December 1993, pp. 145–56; and D. Stripp, "Cities Couldn't Give Away Their Trash; Now They Get Top Dollar from Recyclers," *The Wall Street Journal,* September 19, 1994, pp. B1, B9. ●

THE ENVIRONMENTAL MOVEMENT

The 1990s have been labeled the "earth decade" when a "new environmentalism" with new features is emerging.[23] For example, proponents of the new environmentalism are asking companies to reduce their wastes, use resources prudently, market safe products, and take responsibility for past damages. These requests have been formalized in the *Valdez* principles (see Table 7.3).

The new environmentalism combines many diverse viewpoints, but initially it did not blend easily with traditional business values. Some of the key aspects of this philosophy are noted in the following discussion of the history of the movement.[24]

Conservation and Environmentalism

A strand of environmental philosophy that is not at odds with business management is **conservation.** The conservation movement is anthropocentric (human centered), technologically optimistic, and concerned chiefly with the efficient use of resources. The movement seeks to avoid waste, promote the rational and efficient use of natural resources, and maximize long-term yields, especially of renewable resources.

The **environmental movement,** in contrast, historically has posed dilemmas for business management. Following the lead of early thinkers like George Perkins Marsh (1801–1882), it has shown that the unintended negative effects of human economic activi-

TABLE 7.3

The *Valdez* principles

- **Protection of the biosphere:** Minimize the release of pollutants that may cause environmental damage.

- **Sustainable use of natural resources:** Conserve nonrenewable resources through efficient use and careful planning.

- **Reduction and disposal of waste:** Minimize the creation of waste, especially hazardous waste, and dispose of such materials in a safe, responsible manner.

- **Wise use of energy:** Make every effort to use environmentally safe and sustainable energy sources to meet operating requirements.

- **Risk reduction:** Diminish environmental, health, and safety risks to employees.

- **Marketing of safe products and services:** Sell products that minimize adverse environmental impact and are safe for consumers.

- **Damage compensation:** Accept responsibility for any harm the company causes the environment; conduct bioremediation; and compensate affected parties.

- **Disclosure of environmental incidents:** Public dissemination of accidents relating to operations that harm the environment or pose health or safety risks.

- **Environmental directors:** Appoint at least one board member who is qualified to represent environmental interests; create a position for vice president for environmental affairs.

- **Assessment and annual audit:** Produce and publicize each year a self-evaluation of progress toward implementing the principles and meeting all applicable laws and regulations worldwide. Environmental audits will also be produced annually and distributed to the public.

Sources: *Chemical Week,* September 20, 1989; *CERES Coalition Handbook.*

ties on the environment often are greater than the benefits. For example, there are links between forest cutting and soil erosion and between the draining of marshes and lakes and the decline of animal life.

Other early environmentalists, such as John Muir (1838–1914) and Aldo Leopold (1886–1948), argued that humans are not above nature but a part of it. Nature is not for humans to subdue but is sacred and should be preserved not simply for economic use but for its own sake—that is, for what people can learn from it.

Science and the Environment

Rachel Carson's 1962 best-selling book *The Silent Spring* helped ignite the modern environmental movement by alerting the public to the dangers of unrestricted pesticide use.[25] Carson brought together the findings of toxicology, ecology, and epidemiology in a form accessible to the public. Blending scientific, moral, and political arguments, she connected environmental politics and values with scientific knowledge.

Barry Commoner's *Science and Survival* (1963) continued in this vein. Commoner expanded the scope of ecology to include everything in the physical, chemical, biological, social, political, economic, and philosophical worlds.[26] He argued that all these elements fit together, and have to be understood as a whole. According to Commoner, the symptoms of environmental problems are in the biological world, but their source lies in economic and political organizations.

Economics and the Environment

Economists promote growth for many reasons: to restore the balance of payments, to make the nation more competitive, to create jobs, to reduce the deficit, to provide for the elderly and the sick, and to reduce poverty. Environmentalists criticize economics for its notions of efficiency and its emphasis on economic growth.[27] For example, environmentalists argue that economists do not adequately consider the unintended side effects of efficiency. Environmentalists hold that economists need to supplement estimates of the economic costs and benefits of growth with estimates of other factors that historically were not measured in economic terms.[28]

Economists and public policy analysts argue that the benefits of eliminating risk to the environment and to people must be balanced against the costs. Reducing risk involves determining how effective the proposed methods of reduction are likely to be and how much they will cost. There are many ways to consider cost factors. Analysts can perform cost effectiveness analyses, in which they attempt to figure out how to achieve a given goal with limited resources, or they can conduct more formal risk-benefit and cost-benefit analyses, in which they quantify both the benefits and the costs of risk reduction.[29]

Qualitative Judgments in Cost-Benefit Analysis

Formal, quantitative approaches to balancing costs and benefits do not eliminate the need for qualitative judgments. For example, how does one assess the value of a magnificent vista obscured by air pollution? What is the loss to society if a given genetic strain of grass or animal species becomes extinct? How does one assess the lost opportunity costs of spending vast amounts of money on air pollution that could have been spent on productivity enhancement and global competitiveness?

Fairness cannot be ignored when doing cost-benefit analysis.[30] For example, the costs of air pollution reduction may have to be borne disproportionately by the poor in the form of higher gasoline and automobile prices. Intergenerational fairness also plays a role.[31] Future generations have no representatives in the current market and political processes. Therefore, to what extent should the current generation hold back on its own consumption for the sake of posterity? This question is particularly poignant because few people in the world today are well off. To ask the poor to reduce their life's chances for the sake of a generation yet to come is asking for a great sacrifice.

As you can see, cost-benefit analysis usually revolves around technical matters when sensitivity to ethical issues is also needed.

International Perspectives

Environmental problems present a different face in various countries and regions of the world. The United States and Great Britain lag behind Germany and Japan in mandated emissions standards.[32] In Europe the Dutch, the Germans, and the Danes are among the most environmentally conscious. Italy, Ireland, Spain, Portugal, and Greece are in the early stages of developing environmental policies. Poland, Hungary, the Czech Republic, and former East Germany are the most polluted of the world's industrialized nations.[33]

The environmental movement is a worldwide phenomenon. The "Greens," pictured here demonstrating in LePuy, France, are a fast-growing European political party.
(Maillac/REA–SABA)

U.S. companies need to realize that there is a large growth market in Western Europe for environmentally "friendly" products. The German government stamps these products with a "Blue Angel" insignia (see Figure 7.1).

U.S. managers also need to be fully aware of the environmental movement in Western Europe. Environmentalists in Europe have been successful in halting many projects.[34] Along with events like Chernobyl, the Greens—a political party—have played an important role in stopping the further expansion of nuclear power. They also have had local successes in halting development. It is now impossible to plan a large-scale project in Western Europe without considering an adverse reaction by the Greens.

Industries that pollute or make polluting products will have to adjust to the new reality, and companies selling products in this part of the world must take into account a growing consumer consciousness about environmental protection. Manufacturers may even be legally required to take products and packaging back from customers after use, to recycle or dispose of. In order to meet these requirements in Germany, and be prepared for similar demands in other countries, Hewlett-Packard redesigned its office-machine packaging worldwide.

FIGURE 7.1

International
environmental labels

Germany's "Blue Angel"

Japan's "Ecomark"

Canada's "Environmental Choice"

Germany's "Blue Angel" program has existed since 1978.

Japan's and Canada's programs are based on the German Program.

Industry, scientific, and consumer organization representatives identify different product categories.

Products are included that are made, used, or disposed of in the least environmentally harmful way.

The certification programs are authoritative, independent, and federally approved.

Source: Environmental Protection Agency.

WHAT MANAGERS CAN DO

Innovation

To be truly "green"—that is, a cutting-edge company with respect to environmental concerns—legal compliance is not enough. Progressive companies stay abreast *and* ahead of the laws by going beyond marginal compliance and anticipating future requirements and needs. But companies can go further still by experimenting continually with innovations that protect the environment. McDonald's, for example, is conducting tests and pilot projects in composting food scraps and in offering refillable coffee mugs and starch-based (biodegradable) cutlery.[35]

SYSTEMS THINKING

The first thing managers can do to better understand environmental issues in their companies is to engage in systems thinking. Recalling the systems model discussed in Chapters 1 and 2, we can see that environmental considerations relate to the organization's inputs, processes, and outputs.[36] *Inputs* include raw materials and energy. Environmental pressures are causing prices of some raw materials, such as metals, to rise. This greatly increases the costs of production. Higher energy costs are causing firms to switch to more fuel-efficient sources.

Cost

Firms are considering new *processes* or methods of production that will reduce water pollution, air pollution, noise and vibration, and waste. They are incorporating technologies that sample and monitor (control) these by-products of business processes. Some

TABLE 7.4

Procter & Gamble's environmental quality policy

Procter & Gamble is committed to providing products of superior quality and value that best fill the needs of the world's consumers. As part of this, Procter & Gamble continually strives to improve the environmental quality of its products, packaging, and operations around the world. To carry out this commitment, it is Procter & Gamble's policy to:

- Ensure our products, packaging, and operations are safe for our employees, consumers, and the environment.

- Reduce or prevent the environmental impact of our products and packaging in their design, manufacture, distribution, use, and disposal whenever possible.

- Meet or exceed the requirements of all environmental laws and regulations.

- Continually assess our environmental technology and programs, and monitor programs toward environmental goals.

- Provide our consumers, customers, employees, communities, public interest groups, and others with relevant and appropriate factual information about the environmental quality of P&G products, packaging, and operations.

- Ensure every employee understands and is responsible and accountable for incorporating environmental quality considerations in daily business activities.

- Have operating policies, programs, and resources in place to implement our environmental quality policy.

Source: K. Dechant and B. Altman, "Environmental Leadership: From Compliance to Competitive Advantage," *The Academy of Management Executive*, August 1994, p. 10.

Innovation

chemical plants have a computerized system that flashes warnings when a maximum allowable pollution level is soon to be reached. Many companies keep only minimal stocks of hazardous materials, making serious accidents less likely.

Outputs have environmental impact, whether the products themselves or the waste or by-products of processes. To reduce the impact of its outputs, Herman Miller recycles or reuses nearly all waste from the manufacturing process. It sells fabric scraps to the auto industry, leather trim to luggage makers, and vinyl to stereo and auto manufacturers. It buys back its old furniture, refurbishes it, and resells it. Its corporatewide goal by 1995 was to send zero waste to landfills. Environmental manager Paul Murray says, "There is never an acceptable level of waste at Miller. There are always new things we can learn."[37]

STRATEGIC INTEGRATION

Systems thinking reveals that environmental issues permeate the firm, and therefore should be addressed in a comprehensive, integrative fashion. Perhaps the first step is to create the proper mindset. Does your firm see environmental concerns merely in terms of a business versus environment trade-off, or does it see in it a potential source of competitive advantage and an important part of a strategy for long-term survival and effectiveness? The latter attitude, of course, is more likely to set the stage for the following strategic actions.

These basic steps help to fully integrate environmental considerations into the firm's ongoing activities:[38]

1. *Develop a mission statement and strong values supporting environmental advocacy.* Table 7.4 shows Procter & Gamble's environmental quality policy.

2. *Establish a framework for managing environmental initiatives.* J&J has an Environmental Responsibility Program consisting of two initiatives:[39] Environmental Regulatory Affairs ensures that regulations are followed worldwide, and uses external

audit teams to conduct environmental audits. The Community Environmental Responsibility Program incudes emergency preparedness, strategy and planning, and the development of products and processes with neutral environmental impact.

3. *Engage in "green" process and product design.* The core concept of TQM is that products will cost more to fix after manufacture than if the defects are prevented in the first place. With respect to the environment, a similar concept is pollution prevention as opposed to "end-of-pipe" cleanup strategies. Such programs strive for zero emissions or at least continuous improvement toward that goal. Olin Corporation, the chemical company, announced in 1994 a 70 percent reduction since 1987 of reportable emissions through source reduction, recycling, treatment, and other pollution prevention techniques.[40]

4. *Establish environmentally focused stakeholder relationships.* Many firms work closely with the FDA and receive technical assistance to help convert to more energy-efficient facilities. And to defray costs as well as develop new ideas, small companies like WHYCO Chromium Company establish environmental management partnerships with firms like IBM and GM.[41]

5. *Provide internal and external education.* Engage employees in environmental actions. Dow's WRAP program has cut millions of pounds of hazardous and solid waste and emissions, and achieved annual cost savings of over $10 million, all through employee suggestions.[42] At the same time, inform the public of your firm's environmental initiatives. For example, eco-labeling can urge consumers to recycle and communicate the environmental friendliness of your product.

LIFE CYCLE ANALYSIS

Increasingly, firms are paying attention to the pollution caused by their manufacturing processes in the context of the total environmental impact throughout the entire life cycle of their products. **Life-cycle analysis (LCA)** is a process of analyzing all inputs and outputs to determine the total environmental impact of the production and use of a product.[43] LCA quantifies the total use of resources, and the releases into the air, water, and land.

With this in mind, green design considers the extraction of raw materials, product packaging, transportation, and disposal. Consider packaging alone. Goods make the journey from manufacturer to wholesaler to retailer to customer, and are then recycled back to the manufacturer. They may be packaged and repackaged several times, from bulk transport to large crates to cardboard boxes to individual consumer sizes. Repackaging not only creates waste—it costs *time.* The design of initial packaging in sizes and formats adaptable to the final customer can minimize the need for repackaging, cut waste, and realize many benefits.

IMPLEMENTATION

How can companies implement "greening" strategies? A fundamental requirement for effective environmentalism is a commitment by top management. Specific actions could include commissioning an environmental audit in which an outside company checks for environmental hazards, drafting (or reviewing) the organization's environmental policy, communicating the policy and making it highly visible throughout the organization, having environmental professionals within the company report directly to the president or CEO, allocating sufficient resources to support the environmental effort, and building bridges between the organization and other companies, governments, environmentalists, and local communities.

Ultimately, it is essential to make employees accountable for any of their actions that have environmental impact.[44] Texaco, Du Pont, and other companies evaluate managers on their ideas for minimizing pollution and for new, environment-friendly products. Kodak ties some managers' compensation to the prevention of chemical spills; the company attributes to this policy a dramatic reduction in accidents.[45]

Companies can employ all areas of the organization to meet the challenges posed by pollution and environmental problems. A variety of companies have responded creatively to these challenges[46] and may serve as models for other organizations. The following sections describe more specific actions companies can take to address environmental issues.

Strategy

Actions companies can take in the area of strategy include the following:

1. *Cut back on environmentally unsafe businesses.* Du Pont, the leading producer of CFCs, has announced it will voluntarily pull out of this $750 million business by the year 2000, if not sooner.[47]

2. *Carry out R&D on environmentally safe activities.* Du Pont claims it is spending up to $1 billion on the best replacements for CFCs.

3. *Develop and expand environmental cleanup services.* Building on the expertise gained in cleaning up its own plants, Du Pont is forming a safety and environmental resources division to help industrial customers clean up their toxic wastes. The projected future revenues are $1 billion by the year 2000.[48]

4. *Compensate for environmentally risky projects.* Applied Energy Services, a power plant management firm, donated $2 million in 1988 for tree planting in Guatemala to compensate for a coal-fired plant it was building in Connecticut. The trees were meant to offset emissions that might lead to global warming.

5. *Make your company accountable to others.* Danish health care and enzymes company Novo Nordisk has purposely asked for feedback from environmentalists, regulators, and other interested bodies from around Europe. Its reputation has been enhanced, its people have learned a lot, and new market opportunities have been identified.[49]

6. *Make every new product environmentally better than the last.* This is IBM's goal. IBM aims to use recyclable materials, reduce hazardous materials, reduce emissions, and use natural energy and resources in packaging.[50]

Public Affairs

In the area of public affairs, companies can take several actions:

1. *Attempt to gain environmental legitimacy and credibility.* Edgar Woolard, CEO of Du Pont, delivers speeches on corporate environmentalism. The cosponsors of Earth Day 1990 included Apple Computer, Hewlett-Packard, Shaklee, and the Chemical Manufacturers Association. McDonald's has made efforts to show that it is a proponent of recycling; it has tried to become a corporate environmental "educator."

2. *Try to avoid losses caused by insensitivity to environmental issues.* As a result of Exxon's apparent lack of concern after the *Valdez* oil spill, 41 percent of Americans polled said they would consider boycotting the company.[51]

3. *Collaborate with environmentalists.* Executives at Pacific Gas & Electric seek discussions and joint projects with any willing environmental group. They have teamed up with environmental groups to study energy efficiency, and the company rented a computer model from the Environmental Defense Fund (EDF) that showed the relationship between conservation and electricity costs.

The Legal Area

Actions companies can take in the legal area include the following:

1. *Try to avoid confrontation with state or federal pollution control agencies.* W. R. Grace faced expensive and time-consuming lawsuits as a result of its toxic dumps. Browning-Ferris, Waste Management Inc., and Louisiana-Pacific have been charged with pollution control violations, which has damaged their reputations.

2. *Comply early.* Since compliance costs only increase over time, the first companies to act will have lower costs. This will enable them to increase their market share and profits and win competitive advantage. 3M's goal was to meet government requirements to replace or improve underground storage tanks by 1993 instead of 1998, the legally mandated year.

3. *Take advantage of innovative compliance programs.* Instead of source-by-source reduction, the EPA's bubble policy allows factories to reduce pollution at different sources by different amounts provided the overall result is equivalent. Therefore, 3M has installed equipment on only certain production lines at its tape-manufacturing facility in Pennsylvania, thereby lowering its compliance costs.[52]

4. *Don't deal with fly-by-night subcontractors for waste disposal.* They are more likely to cut corners, break laws, and do a poor job. Moreover, the result for you will be bad publicity and legal problems.[53]

Operations

The actions companies can take in the area of operations include the following:

1. *Promote new manufacturing technologies.* Louisville Gas and Electric took the lead in installing smokestack scrubbers, Consolidated Natural Gas has pioneered the use of clean-burning technologies, and Nucor developed state-of-the-art steel mills. Pacific Gas & Electric agreed to rely on combinations of smaller-scale generating facilities like windmills or cogeneration plants alongside aggressive conservation efforts. It has canceled plans to build large coal and nuclear power plants.

2. *Aim for zero waste or zero discharge, just as much as zero defects.* This may be unachievable, but it is a useful target. It imposes discipline and encourages continuous improvement.

3. *Encourage technological advances that reduce pollution from products and manufacturing processes.* 3M's "Pollution Prevention Pays" program is based on the premise that it is too costly for companies to employ add-on technology and instead they should attempt to eliminate pollution at the source.[54] Add-on technology is expensive because it takes resources to remove the pollution; the pollution removal in turn generates new wastes, which requires more resources for their removal.

4. *Develop new product formulations.* One way to accomplish source reduction is to develop new product formulations. 3M's rapid fire-extinguishing agent for petroleum fires did not meet EPA requirements. Thus, the company had to develop a new formulation. The new formulation was one-fortieth as toxic as the former, but it was equally effective and less expensive to produce.

5. *Eliminate manufacturing wastes.* With fewer wastes, add-on equipment becomes less necessary. 3M's philosophy is to invest in reducing the number of materials that can trigger regulation. For example, it has replaced volatile solvents with water-based ones, thereby eliminating the need for costly air pollution control equipment. Amoco and Polaroid have implemented similar programs.

6. *Find alternative uses for wastes.* When Du Pont halted ocean dumping of acid iron salts, it discovered that the salts could be sold to water treatment plants at a profit.

7. *Insist that your suppliers have strong environmental performance.* IBM, British Telecom, Wal-Mart, British supermarkets, and many others do this. Scott Paper discovered that many of its environmental problems were "imported" through the supply chain. Initially focusing on pulp suppliers, the company sent questionnaires asking for figures on air, water, and land releases, energy consumption, and energy sources. Scott was astonished at the variance. For example, carbon dioxide emissions varied by a factor of 17 among different suppliers. Scott dropped the worst performers and announced that the best performers would in the future receive preference in its purchasing decisions.[55]

8. *Assemble products with the environment in mind.* Make them easy to snap apart, sort, and recycle, and avoid glues and screws.

Marketing

Companies can also take actions in the marketing area:

1. *Cast products in an environment-friendly light.* Most Americans believe a company's environmental reputation influences what they buy.[56] Companies such as Procter & Gamble, Arco, Colgate-Palmolive, Lever Brothers, 3M, and Sunoco have tried to act on the basis of this finding. Wal-Mart has made efforts to provide customers with recycled or recyclable products.

2. *Avoid attacks by environmentalists for unsubstantiated or inappropriate claims.* British Petroleum claimed that a new brand of unleaded gasoline caused no pollution, a claim that it had to withdraw after suffering much embarrassment. The degradable-plastics controversy should serve as another warning to consumers about the perils of unsubstantiated or inappropriate claims. Companies should be honest with their employees and the public and educate them continuously.

3. *Differentiate your product via environmental services.* ICI takes back and disposes of customers' waste as a customer service. Disposal is costly, but the service differentiates the firm's products. Teach customers how to use and dispose of products; for instance, farmers inadvertently abuse pesticides. Make education a part of a firm's after-sales service.

Accounting

Actions companies can take in the accounting area include the following:

1. *Collect useful data.* The best current reporters of environmental information are Dow Europe, Danish Steel Works, BSO/Origin, 3M, and Monsanto. BSO/Origin has begun to explore a system for corporate environmental accounting.[57]

2. *Make polluters pay.* CIBA-GEIGY has a "polluter pays principle" throughout the firm, so managers have the incentive to combat pollution at the sources they can influence.[58]

3. *Demonstrate that antipollution programs pay off.* 3M's "Pollution Prevention Pays" program is based on the premise that only if the program pays will there be the motivation to carry it out. Environmental pressures have forced U.S. companies to spend large sums of money that otherwise could have been used for capital formation, new-product research and development, and process improvements. Thus, every company owes it not only to itself but also to the nation to be cost effective in its pollution reduction efforts.

4. *Use an advanced waste accounting system.* Do this in addition to standard management accounting, which can hinder investment in new technologies. Waste accounting makes sure all costs are identified and better decisions can be made.

5. *Adopt full cost accounting.* This approach, called for by Frank Popoff, Dow's chairman, ensures that the price of a product reflects its full environmental cost.[59]

6. *Show the overall impact of the pollution reduction program.* Companies have an obligation to account for the costs and benefits of their pollution reduction programs. 3M claims half a *billion* dollars in savings from pollution prevention efforts.[60]

Finance

In the area of finance, companies can do the following:

1. *Gain the respect of the socially responsible investment community.* Socially responsible rating services and investment funds try to help people invest with a "clean conscience."[61] Their motto is that people should be able to do well while they are doing good. They believe socially responsible investments are likely to be profitable because if the companies can deal creatively with pollution, safety, and employment problems, they will tend to be innovative in other areas .

2. *Recognize true liability.* Smith Barney, Kidder Peabody & Company, and other investment houses employ environmental analysts who search for companies' true environmental liability in evaluating their potential performance.

3. *Recognize business opportunities.* The prospects for solid-waste companies (for example, Waste Management, Laidlaw Industries, and Browning-Ferris) are favorable because of a scarcity of landfill in parts of the United States, and because cities like New York have no alternative ways to get rid of their garbage. The prospects for hazardous-waste companies look promising because the Departments of Defense and Energy will have to clean up toxic wastes they have created in various parts of the country.

KEY TERMS

carrying capacity, p. 165
conservation, p. 166
environmental movement, p. 166

life-cycle analysis (LCA), p. 171
sustainable growth, p. 165
tragedy of the commons, p. 165

SUMMARY OF LEARNING OBJECTIVES

Now that you studied Chapter 7, you should know:

The relationship between the natural environment and business.

Environmental issues affect efficiency, effectiveness, and long-term goals, and entail technical, ethical, social, and competitive considerations. A mistaken belief is that you can either help the environment and hurt your business, or help your business at a cost to the environment. In contrast, the win-win mentality is that companies can take actions that help both themselves and the environment. A balanced view is that business has the resources to help the environment, but should do so in ways that protect and increase shareholder value.

The importance of managing with the environment in mind.

Today's managers make decisions that incorporate environmental considerations for reasons that include legal compliance, cost effectiveness, competitive advantage, public opinion, and long-term thinking. Managers who think long term strive to ensure the organization's viability over time and maximize shareholder wealth over the long haul rather than focus solely on short-term

costs and profits. Long-term thinking is consistent with the goals of sustainable growth and avoiding the tragedy of the commons.

The important perspectives on our natural environment.

Over time conservationists, environmentalists, and author-scientists have joined the debate over the state of our environment. The public policy and economic approaches apply cost-benefit analysis to environmental problems. However, cost-benefit analysis must be tempered by qualitative judgments.

Today the environmental movement is worldwide. Some parts of the world are more progressive than others. The Greens of Western Europe are gaining political power, and the European Community has been active in establishing environmental policies that affect the conduct of business.

Constructive actions managers can take to both protect the environment and benefit the firm.

Many companies have made significant contributions toward solving environmental challenges by employing all aspects of the organization, including strategy, legal compliance, public affairs, operations, marketing, accounting, and finance.

DISCUSSION QUESTIONS

1. To what extent can we rely on government to solve environmental problems? What are some of government's limitations? Take a stand on the role and usefulness of government regulations on business activities.
2. To what extent should managers today be responsible for cleaning up mistakes from years past that have hurt the environment?
3. How would you characterize the environmental movement in Western Europe? How does it differ from the U.S. movement? What difference will this make to a multinational company that wants to produce and market goods in many countries?
4. What business opportunities can you see in meeting environmental challenges? Be specific.
5. You are appointed environmental manager of XYZ Company. Describe some actions you will take to address environmental challenges. Discuss obstacles you are likely to encounter in the company and how you will manage them.
6. Interview a businessperson about environmental regulations and report your findings to the class. How would

you characterize their attitudes? How constructive are their attitudes?
7. Interview a businessperson about actions they have taken that have helped the environment. Report your findings to the class and discuss.
8. Identify and discuss some examples of the tragedy of the commons. How can the tragedies be avoided?
9. Discuss the status of recycling efforts in your community, your perspectives on it as a consumer, and what business opportunities could be available.
10. What companies currently come to mind as having the best and worst reputations with respect to the environment? Why do they have these reputations?
11. Choose one product and discuss its environmental impact through its entire life cycle.
12. What are you, your college or university, and your community doing about the environment? What would you recommend doing?

CONCLUDING CASE

ECOTOURISM

Each year, more than 5 million Americans take ecotourism trips. The industry's growth rate is almost 30 percent per year, faster than the travel industry in general and faster than any other type of tourism.

Just what is ecotourism? Generally, the term refers to nature and adventure travel. In its ideal form, it means traveling to a natural environment to promote conservation, support local inhabitants, and develop a new awareness of other cultures and natural environments. But critics say much of what passes for ecotourism is just big ships and hotels that happen to operate in fragile ecosystems.

With annual revenues topping $1 billion, ecotourism is the world's biggest source of funding for conservation. But some experts see the industry doing more environmental harm than good. Ecotourism is a controversial industry because of its potential impact both on environments and cultures and on other industries. Consider a few examples:

- In Antarctica, tourists increased from 800 to 7,000 per year in less than a decade. Helicopters land in penguin rookeries. One ship carrying 300 tourists and crew members went aground and was deemed too expensive to move. The wrecked ship has spilled 250,000 gallons of oil.

- In the Aguarico River region of the Ecuadorian rain forest, visitors marvel at the freshwater dolphins, butterflies, anteaters, tapirs, and other wildlife. If ecotourism in the region grows, it may postpone the government drilling permits that oil companies have been waiting and hoping for.

- Kenya has valued each lion at $27,000 a year in tourism revenues, and each elephant herd at $610,000. The net value from wildlife viewing is $40 per hectare, compared with $0.80 generated from agriculture. The money flow encourages locals to protect their resources rather than pursue activities like wildlife poaching and land clearing. But guides seeking big tips drive off the road, harass wildlife, and surround families of cheetahs, sometimes preventing them from hunting.

- In Rwanda, thanks to the mountain gorillas, tourism had become the number-3 industry before the recent political tur-

moil. Both the gorillas and their environment are now protected, and farmers stopped clearing the habitats.

- Ecotourism is a staple of the economy in Costa Rica, and has helped stop the conversion of rain forest into cattle-grazing grounds.

Ecotourism, or nature and adventure travel, is growing at the rate of 30 percent a year. Here, people visit a Brazilian rain forest.
(The Stock Market)

- Studies indicate the Galapagos Islands can handle 25,000 visitors per year. But 87,000 visitors' permits are sold annually.

- Nepal receives 250,000 visitors per year. The biggest resulting problems are litter and deforestation. Trekkers use wood to build fires, and lodges use it to heat water. Once-green areas are now bare, and the tree line has moved up several hundred feet.

- Critics describe ecotourism as a new form of colonialism. Visitors with time and money believe the local people are there to serve them, and the locals put on "sideshows" to entertain. Handing out goods and money encourages begging and creates dependence.

QUESTIONS

1. Going beyond the information in the case, generate a list of the potential advantages and disadvantages of ecotourism.

2. Discuss the ethics of ecotourism and take a stand on whether you approve or disapprove of the industry's current practices.

3. Would your position be any different if you worked for an oil company, a hotel developer, or some other big company interested in beginning operations in an area frequented by ecotourists?

4. If you were with such a company, how would you proceed?

5. If you were in the business of ecotourism, what policies would guide your operations?

6. If you were interested in going on an ecotourism trip, how would you decide which agency or outfitter to use?

Source: K. Koontz, "Is Ecotourism Killing the Golden Goose?" *Chicago Tribune,* August 14, 1994, p. C1

VIDEO EXERCISE

MANAGEMENT AND THE NATURAL ENVIRONMENT

Environmental awareness is a growing concern among corporations in the United States, and in many foreign countries as well. In this video tape, the environmental protection practices of Mobil Oil Corporation are reviewed. The company is actively involved in a number of initiatives aimed at protecting and preserving the natural environment. Mobil tries to integrate environmental awareness into its entire operation, from exploration and drilling to its "downstream" businesses, including its retail dealerships.

While most people will agree that concern for the natural environment should be an important consideration for businesses, balancing the costs of environmental concern with the pressures to turn a profit is never easy. It is also difficult to determine what level of "pollution" is acceptable. Should companies strive for zero pollution? Doing so may be so costly as to prohibit business activity entirely.

Complex issues about appropriate levels of pollution, environmental cost accounting, and free market approaches to environmental control are in the early stages of discussion across the United States. Some states are now in the business of allocating **effluent securities**. Companies are allowed a fixed amount of securities that they use to pay for effluents they produce. Companies are allowed to trade these securities with other companies, enabling them to exceed their original allotment, but keeping total discharge within specified limits.

Purpose:

The purpose of this exercise is to provide you with an opportunity to explore the environmental practices of a company near you. Companies take a variety of approaches to involvement in the natural environment, from producing so-called *green* products to supporting environmental causes through charitable donations. This exercise will help you understand the struggle managers must face when balancing the costs of environmental programs with their benefits.

Procedure:

Identify a manufacturing company in your area that you would be interested in learning about. You will contact a representative

of that company to determine the extent of environmental initiatives the company undertakes. Gather information about state and federal environmental laws and guidelines the company must comply with and the costs of compliance. After you have identified a representative of the company, proceed through the following steps:

1. Contact the representative and set up a meeting at a mutually convenient time to discuss the company's environmental practices.

2. Before going to the meeting, prepare a set of questions. Your questions should focus on determining three things: the types of environmental initiatives the company currently pursues; the state and federal regulations the company must comply with; and the cost of compliance with these regulations.

3. Arrive on time for the scheduled meeting. Proceed through your prepared questions. Tape record the interview if your interviewee agrees. Take good notes whether or not taping is allowed. If the company representative offers to give you a tour of the company's environmental projects, go along if you have the time.

4. Use your notes to begin to compile a brief report on your findings for presentation to the class. Provide a chart that outlines environmental regulations the company is subject to, and the procedures the company uses to comply with those regulations.

5. Now conduct library research to benchmark the company you studied against another company that has been recognized for environmental excellence. If you can't find any data in the library for benchmarking, as an alternative, think of some ways on your own that the company might go beyond its current environmental practices.

6. In your final report for the class, contrast the company's practices with those of the benchmark company or with those you have developed. Consider the costs and benefits of adopting these more extensive practices. Conclude with a recommendation for the company.

7. If possible, invite your interviewee to class on the day you are scheduled to report your findings and recommendations. If the person is able to attend, provide him or her with an opportunity to respond to your report.

EXPERIENTIAL EXERCISES

7.1 Strategy for Dealing with Toxic Waste in the River

Objectives

1. To examine your attitude toward managing in our natural environment.
2. To explore new strategies for dealing with natural-environment challenge.

Instructions

1. Read the scenario below about discovery of a toxic effluent by a firm's chemist.
2. You are the manager and must decide on how to respond to the discovery of the unsuspected toxic by-product.

DISCOVERY OF A TOXIC BY-PRODUCT

You are the plant manager of a small chemical plant north of St. Louis. For years your firm dumped its untreated effluents into the Mississippi as a matter of everyday business. Recently, Environmental Protection Agency standards have required you to install a treatment system to minimize the level of several specific contaminants. Your firm has abided by the ruling; only treated sewage is being dumped into the river. However, you have just received a report from your head chemist, who has discovered that a by-product of a new chemical being produced by the firm is highly toxic. Moreover, the present filtration system utterly fails to filter out the toxic substance. It is all headed downstream toward St. Louis.

STRATEGY WORKSHEET

Now that you have this report, what do you plan to do? Consider your alternatives and develop a strategy. If part of your strategy is to get in touch with your boss at company headquarters in Chicago, state what recommendation you intend to make.

_____

_____

_____

_____

_____

_____

_____

_____

_____

_____

Source: Excerpted from Robert B. Carson, *Enterprise: An Introduction to Business* (Orlando, Fla.: Harcourt Brace, 1985), p. 51. Copyright © 1985 by Harcourt Brace and Company. Reprinted by permission of the publisher.

7.2 An Environmental Protection Code of Ethics

Objectives

1. To further clarify the role business plays in environmental pollution.
2. To identify codes of ethics that business adopt to minimize the potential adverse impact of their activities on the environment.

Instructions

1. Your instructor will divide the class into small groups and assign each group one or more environmental problems to investigate.

2. For each environmental problem assigned, the groups will complete the Environmental Code of Ethics Worksheet by investigating the things business does that affect the environment and developing "code of ethics" statements by which businesses can deal with the problems in a positive, socially responsible manner.
3. After the class reconvenes, group spokespersons present group findings.
4. The class may proceed to the development of an overall Environmental Code of Ethics for businesses.

THE ENVIRONMENTAL CODE OF ETHICS WORKSHEET

In the space provided below, identify business activities that contribute to the environmental problem(s) assigned by your instructor and develop code of ethics statements that can be adopted to deal with the problem(s).

Environmental Pollution Problem: _____

Business Activity	Corresponding Code of Ethics Statement

8

INTERNATIONAL MANAGEMENT

It was once said that the sun never sets on the British Empire. Today, the sun does set on the British Empire, but not on the scores of global empires, including those of IBM, Unilever, Volkswagen, and Hitachi.

Lester Brown

After studying Chapter 8, you will know:

1. Why the world economy is becoming more integrated than ever before.

2. What integration of the global economy means for individual companies and for their managers.

3. The strategies organizations use to compete in the global marketplace.

4. The various entry modes organizations use to enter overseas markets.

5. How companies can approach the task of staffing overseas operations.

6. The skills and knowledge managers need to manage globally.

7. Why cultural differences across countries influence management.

FOR DISNEY, IT'S A SMALL WORLD AFTER ALL

*T*he Walt Disney Company has achieved an enviable level of success in the U.S. entertainment industry, and in 1994 it cracked *Fortune's* Top 10 List of Most Admired Companies. The company is renowned for its creativity, and long-term vision. For over half a century, familiar Disney characters, from Mickey Mouse and Donald Duck to the Lion King and Pocahontas, have become icons of American pop culture. And Disney has been a veritable machine of new-product development, churning out movies, videos, merchandise, and theme parks. But can a company whose formula for success rests on cartoon characters, stories, and songs transfer its magic to other countries and cultures around the world? Well, yes and no.

Disney expanded its enterprise to Asia in 1962 when it opened a Tokyo office and introduced the Japanese to *Mickey Ma-u-su.* On April 15, 1983, Tokyo Disneyland opened and from the first day, Disney had an enormous hit. By the time Tokyo Disneyland was five years old, it had averaged over 19 million visitors annually, more than 70 percent of whom were repeat customers. In May 1991, Tokyo Disneyland passed the major milestone of 100 million visitors. Just like Disney in the United States, Tokyo Disneyland has had a major impact on Japan's leisure lifestyle and forged an unrivaled position as king of the domestic amusement industry. Interestingly, while Disney made some adaptations to Japanese culture, most observers agree that the principal reason for Disney's success in Japan has been that the original concept of Disneyland was authentically recreated. Merchandising, restaurants, and hotel divi-

Tokyo Disneyland has been a tremendous success since it opened in 1983. Here, Japanese people delight in the Asian Mickey Mouse—Micky Ma-u-su.
(Reuters/Bettmann)

sions have all done well, and in 1989 Disney signed an agreement with Fujisankei Communications Group, the world's fifth-largest radio, television, and newspaper company, to distribute Disney home videos to consumers in Japan. Retail sales of goods licensed by Disney have risen to nearly $4 billion in Japan and the rest of Asia. Even in China, where the name Mickey Mouse translates to "Mickey the Rat" (Chinese do not distinguish between mice and rats), sales growth has risen to about $800 million. Observers have suggested that the warmth and humor of Disney characters play to the Confucian values of family that are paramount in Asian countries.

Contrast this with Euro-Disneyland. Disney applied the same formula that worked in Japan to its $4 billion theme park near Paris, but the park has been a huge disappointment. Since its opening in 1992, Euro-Disney has lost over $1.2 billion, and the park is still in deep financial difficulty. Part of the problem has been timing. Euro-Disney opened as Europe was heading into a recession. Only about 9 million guests visit the park each year, far less than the 11 million needed for Euro-Disney to break even. In contrast to visitor behavior in other Disney parks, penny-pinching guests have not spent much on food or merchandise. Nor have they stayed for extended vacations in the surrounding hotels as visitors do at the U.S. and Tokyo parks.

Because of these financial difficulties, and Disney's $3.4 billion debt load, CEO Michael Eisner and his staff discussed the possibility of closing the park in 1993. But while Disney owns only 49 percent of the venture (the other 51 percent is held by a consortium of French banks), French law prohibits Disney from walking away since it is deemed to be the operator of the park. To address its problems, Disney revamped its British management team and appointed the U.K.'s Bill Jones as managing director. Disney recently negotiated with Saudi Arabian Prince Al-Walid to inject $400 million to rescue the theme park, by giving him 24 percent interest in the deal.

Prospects for the future of Euro-Disney are unclear. As the recession has cleared, attendance has been better, and the 1994 opening of the English Channel tunnel has helped to bring in more British tourists. Disney has put forward plans to build an MGM Studios film tour site next to Euro-Disney to encourage visitors to stay longer and boost revenues. However, the French government appears unwilling to go beyond the $350 million investment it has already made in infrastructure improvements. In the meantime, Disney has entered into a joint venture with Luxembourg-based CLT Multi Media to launch Super RTL, a family-oriented cable/satellite channel in 33 million homes in Germany.

Although the outcome for Disney in Europe is not yet clear, what is clear from these contrasting stories is that managing across borders is neither easy nor predictable. Disney's success in Asia—with a culture very different from the United States—is no guarantee that it will succeed in Europe.

Sources: David Hulme, "Ex-Cop in Mickey Mouse Job," *Asia Business* 30, no. 6 (1994), p. 70; Robert Warren, "Theme Parks Flourish in Japan," *Japan 21st* 38, no. 7 (July 1993), pp. 35–39; Mitsuhiko Kato, "Tokyo Disneyland: Magic Kingdom Attracts 100 Million," *Tokyo Business Today* 60, no. 3 (March 1992), pp. 26–29; Jonathan Karp, "Disney's World of Fantasy," *Far Eastern Economic Review,* January 6, 1994, p. 40; Stewart Toy and Paul Dwyer, "Is Disney Headed for the Euro-Trash Heap?" *Business Week,* January 24, 1994, p. 52; Harriot Lane Fox, "Disney Opts for Lead UK Man," *Marketing,* Oct. 27, 1994, p. 4; Merrideth Amdur, "Disney, CLT Plan Germany Family Channel," *Broadcasting and Cable* 124, no. 25 (Aug. 29, 1994), p. 16; Thomas G.

*A*s the story of Disney shows, today's managers must constantly make decisions about whether and how to pursue opportunities all over the globe. Of course, opportunities must be evaluated carefully. In many industries competition is now a global game in which the same competitors confront one another in a variety of markets around the world. In this chapter, we review the reasons for the globalization of competition, examine why international management differs from domestic management, consider how companies expand globally, and see how companies can develop individuals to manage across borders.

COMPETITION IN THE GLOBAL ECONOMY

As we approach the next millennium, the global economy is becoming more integrated than ever before. Today's world is composed of three spheres of economic influence: the triad of North America, Europe, and Asia. Years of emphasis on international commerce within these regions by major industrial countries, as well as recent liberalized trading brought about by NAFTA, EU, and APEC (discussed in Chapter 3), have resulted in lowering the barriers to the free flow of goods, services, and capital among nation-states.

The impact of these trends is staggering. For example, the General Agreement on Tariffs and Trade (GATT) alone is expected to add $330 billion to the world economy by allowing companies to sell and invest in markets that were closed to them before. Most experts expect competition to increase as trade is liberalized, and as is so often the case, the more efficient players will survive. To succeed in this industrial climate, managers need to study opportunities in existing markets, as well as work to enhance the competitiveness of their firms.[1]

Companies both large and small now view the world, rather than a single country, as their marketplace. As Table 8.1 shows, the United States has no monopoly on international business. Nearly half of the top 50 corporations in the world are based in countries outside the United States.

Also, companies have dispersed their manufacturing, marketing, and research facilities to those locations around the globe where cost and skill conditions are most favorable. This

TABLE 8.1

The global 1000—
the leaders

Rank 1994	Rank 1993		Market Value (billions of U.S. dollars)
1	1	Nippon Telegraph & Telephone (Japan)	128.94
2	3	Royal Dutch/Shell Group (Neth./Britain)	91.93
3	5	General Electric (U.S.)	84.94
4	6	Mitsubishi Bank (Japan)	77.05
5	4	Exxon (U.S.)	75.92
6	13	Toyota Motor (Japan)	75.06
7	2	AT&T (U.S.)	73.87
8	9	Industrial Bank of Japan (Japan)	73.25
9	7	Sumitomo Bank (Japan)	67.53
10	11	Fuji Bank (Japan)	66.99
11	10	Sanwa Bank (Japan)	63.19
12	12	Dai-Ichi Kangyo Bank (Japan)	59.64
13	8	Wal-Mart Stores (U.S.)	54.01
14	14	Coca-Cola (U.S.)	52.24
15	15	Sakura Bank (Japan)	47.26
16	24	Roche Holding (Switzerland)	47.26
17	20	Nomura Securities (Japan)	45.38
18	17	Philip Morris (U.S.)	43.19
19	21	DuPont (U.S.)	42.01
20	16	Tokyo Electric Power (Japan)	41.34
21	33	General Motors (U.S.)	38.70
22	22	Procter & Gamble (U.S.)	38.43
23	18	Merck (U.S.)	38.25
24	27	International Business Machines (U.S.)	36.67
25	47	Matsushita Electric Industrial (Japan)	36.65
26	NR	Singapore Telecommunications (Singapore)	34.81
27	19	British Telecommunications (Britain)	33.89
28	43	Hitachi Ltd. (Japan)	33.87
29	38	Bank of Tokyo (Japan)	32.31
30	34	Mobil (U.S.)	32.25
31	41	British Petroleum (Britain)	31.78
32	28	Nestlé (Switzerland)	31.49
33	42	Microsoft (U.S.)	30.51
34	40	Allianz Holding (Germany)	30.16
35	36	American International Group (U.S.)	29.59
36	45	BellSouth (U.S.)	29.52
37	23	GTE (U.S.)	29.51
38	35	Amoco (U.S.)	29.23
39	26	Unilever (Neth./Britain)	29.15
40	46	Ford Motor (U.S.)	28.82
41	30	PepsiCo (U.S.)	28.76
42	29	Johnson & Johnson (U.S.)	28.45
43	32	Chevron (U.S.)	28.34
44	25	Bristol-Myers Squibb (U.S.)	28.30
45	50	HSBC Holdings (Britain)	27.97
46	58	Long-Term Credit Bank of Japan (Japan)	27.21
47	49	Tokai Bank (Japan)	26.37
48	52	Intel (U.S.)	26.13
49	60	Motorola (U.S.)	26.05
50	59	Toshiba (Japan)	25.95

Source: *Business Week,* July 11, 1994, p. 56

FIGURE 8.1

Foreign direct
investment flows

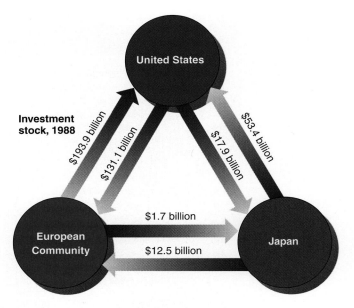

Source: "Foreign Investment and the Triad," *The Economist*, August 24, 1991, p. 57.

trend is now so pervasive in industries such as automobiles, aerospace, and electronics that it is becoming increasingly irrelevant to talk about "American products" or "British products" or "Japanese products."

Consider what happens when an American consumer buys a Pontiac Le Mans from General Motors. Most people probably perceive this model as an "American product." Of the $20,000 paid for the car, about $6,000 goes to South Korea, where the Le Mans is assembled; $3,500 goes to Japan for advanced components (engines, transaxles, and electronics); $1,500 goes to Germany, where the Le Mans was designed; $800 goes to Taiwan, Singapore, and Japan for small components; $500 goes to Britain for advertising and marketing services; and about $100 goes to Ireland for data processing services. The remainder, about $8,000, goes to GM and to the lawyers, bankers, and insurance agents that GM uses in the United States. So is the Le Mans an "American product"? Obviously not—but neither is it a "Korean product," a "Japanese product," or a "German product." Like an increasing number of the products we buy today, it is an *international* product.[2]

Internationalization is not limited to large corporations like General Motors. An increasing number of medium-size and small firms also engage in international trade. Some companies have limited their involvement to exporting, while others have taken the process a step further by setting up production facilities overseas. Consider Lubricating Systems Inc. of Kent, Washington. In 1991 Lubricating Systems, which manufactures lubricating fluids for machine tools, employed 25 people and generated sales of $6.5 million. The company is hardly an industrial giant, yet over $2 million of its total sales were generated by exports to a score of countries, from Japan to Israel and the United Arab Emirates. Moreover, Lubricating Systems is now setting up a joint venture with a German company to serve the European market.[3]

CONSEQUENCES OF THE GLOBAL ECONOMY

The increasing integration of the global economy has had many consequences. First, over the last decade the volume of world trade grew at a faster rate than the volume of world output. Between 1978 and 1990, world output grew by 30 percent while world trade grew by over 50 percent.[4] These figures imply that more and more companies are doing what GM does with the Pontiac Le Mans: dispersing manufacturing, marketing, and design services around the

TABLE 8.2

U.S.: A healthy
share of the world
market

Shares of global
corporate profits
and sales, 1987-92

Industry	U.S.		Japan		Europe	
	Profits	**Sales**	**Profits**	**Sales**	**Profits**	**Sales**
Energy equipment and services	99.6%	92.7%	0.8%	1.0%	−0.4%*	6.3%
Aerospace and military technology	81.6	75.8	0	0.4	18.4	23.8
Data processing and reproduction	65.1	73.2	10.7	22.2	24.2	4.6
Electronic components and instruments	65.0	61.8	30.5	35.8	4.5	2.4
Beverages and tobacco	63.0	63.4	3.6	16.4	33.4	20.2
Health and personal care	61.9	48.9	8.2	20.3	29.9	30.8
Leisure and tourism	60.3	45.7	7.4	16.3	32.3	38.1
Forest products and paper	59.7	51.0	7.0	17.4	33.3	31.6
Energy source	50.4	45.8	2.8	13.5	47.0	40.7
Metals—nonferous	45.7	30.2	11.9	30.8	42.4	39.0
Recreation and other consumer goods	44.0	33.2	46.4	60.7	9.7	6.1
Food and household products	42.6	32.6	7.8	21.7	49.6	45.7
Electrical and electronics	41.1	21.4	25.7	50.7	33.2	27.9
Chemicals	41.0	28.2	13.3	30.3	45.7	41.5
Industrial components	38.2	24.5	32.5	44.7	29.3	30.8
Automobiles	23.6	37.0	31.0	35.3	45.5	27.6
Machinery and engineering	19.2	18.9	34.4	46.3	46.3	34.9
Appliances and household durables	16.5	7.6	74.4	66.6	9.1	25.7
Metals—steel	2.3	10.1	51.2	57.0	46.5	32.9
All industries	47.7%	37.4%	15.5%	31.5%	38.8%	31.1%

*Europe's businesses in this sector had a net loss.

Source: Daniel Strickberger, "Sharing World Markets," *The Wall Street Journal*, Feb. 15, 1994.

globe. Second, *foreign direct investment (FDI)* is playing an ever-increasing role in the global economy as companies of all sizes invest in overseas operations. The major investors have been U.S. companies investing in Europe and (increasingly) Japan and Japanese and European companies investing in the United States (see Figure 8.1).[5] Thus, for example, Japanese auto companies have been investing rapidly in U.S.–based auto assembly operations (Britain, *not* Japan, has been the largest investor in the United States in recent years).

A third consequence of an increasingly integrated global economy is that imports are penetrating deeper into the world's largest economies. For the first time manufactured goods rather than raw materials account for more than half of Japan's imports.[6] The growth of imports is a natural by-product of the growth of world trade and the trend toward the manufacture of component parts, or even entire products, overseas before shipping them back home for final sale.

Finally, the growth of world trade, foreign direct investment, and imports implies that companies around the globe are finding their home markets under attack from foreign competitors. This is true in Japan, where Kodak has taken market share in the photographic film industry away from Fuji; in the United States, where Japanese auto makers have captured market share from GM, Ford, and Chrysler; and in Western Europe, where the once dominant Dutch company Philips N. V. has lost market share in the consumer electronics industry to Japan's JVC, Matsushita, and Sony. U.S. companies, in general, have faired well in this environment and, as shown in Table 8.2, enjoy a healthy share of the world market in many industries.

What does all of this mean for the manager? Compared with only a few years ago, *opportunities are greater* because the movement toward free trade has opened up many formerly protected national markets. The potential for export, and for making direct investments overseas, is greater today than ever before. *The environment is more complex* because today's manager often has to deal with the challenges of doing business in countries with radically different cultures and of coordinating globally dispersed operations. Finally, *the environment is more competitive* because in addition to domestic competitors the manager must deal with cost-efficient overseas competitors.

BEER GAMES OF EUROPE

*N*orth American breweries have a vital interest in selling in the Unified Europe. With more favorable trade laws, the European beer market is up for grabs, and prospects for expansion and revenue generation are quite good. But the competition is stiff. Heineken, the Dutch beer company, anticipated a single European market back in the late 1970s and began buying smaller breweries in France, Greece, Italy, and Spain. BSN and Guiness have been doing much the same.

Anheuser Busch and Philip Morris, makers of Budweiser and Miller beers, have been making a big push to strengthen their foothold in Europe. Budweiser is currently being brewed in the United Kingdom, and to increase sales throughout Europe, Anheuser Busch has recently increased its advertising budget 50 percent to $18 million—all other U.K. brewers together spend only $180 million. In addition, Anheuser Busch has been trying to buy the Budvar brewery in the Czech Republic, the home of the original Budweiser beer.

Phillip Morris, meanwhile, has been working with partners and distributors in Europe. In 1991, executives at Miller signed an agreement with the Italian food broker, Eurofood, to distribute Miller High Life. Another company that has done well in Europe is the Boston Brewing Company, makers of Samuel Adams Beer. Currently, Boston Brewing ships more than 3,000 barrels of beer annually throughout Europe.

These examples indicate that U.S. brewers recognize the opportunities that free trade and European unification provide. And with the growing trend among Europeans to drink lighter beers that are more characteristic of U.S. brewers, the market seems to be opening up. However, most observers say that if U.S. brewers don't acquire local breweries of their own, they will never have the distribution networks and consumer acceptance they need.

Sources: J. F. Siler, "Wooing Jacques and Fritz Six-Pack," *Business Week,* February 4, 1991, pp. 92–93; "Budvar Beer in Legal Limbo," *East European Markets* 13, no. 18 (September 3, 1993), pp. 16–17; and Ira Teinowitz, "A-B Turns Up Heat under UK Marketing," *Advertising Age,* July 20, 1992, p. 38. ●

GLOBAL STRATEGY

One of the critical tasks an international manager faces is to identify the best strategy for competing in a global marketplace. To approach this issue, it is helpful to plot a company's position on an integration-responsiveness grid (see Figure 8.2). The vertical axis measures pressures for *global integration,* and the horizontal axis measures pressures for *local responsiveness.*

PRESSURES FOR GLOBAL INTEGRATION

Universal needs create strong pressure for a global strategy. Universal needs exist when the tastes and preferences of consumers in different countries with regard to a product are similar. Products that serve universal needs require little adaptation across national markets; thus, global integration is facilitated. This is the case in many industrial markets. Electronic products such as capacitors, resistors, and semiconductor chips are products that meet universal needs.

Competitive *pressures to reduce costs* may force a company to globally integrate manufacturing. This can be particularly important in industries in which price is the main competitive weapon and competition is intense (for example, hand-held calculators and semiconductor chips). It is also important in industries in which key international competitors are based in countries with low factor costs (e.g., low labor and energy costs).

The presence of competitors engaged in *global strategic coordination* is another factor that creates pressure for global integration. Reacting to global competitive threats calls for

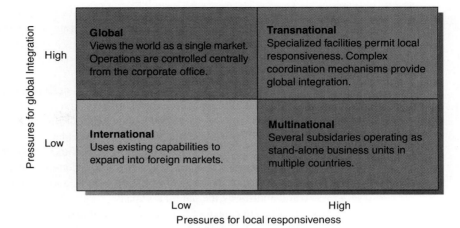

FIGURE 8.2

Organizational
models

Sources: "Christopher A. Bartlett and Sumantra Ghoshal, *Managing across Borders: The Transnational Solution* (Boston: Havard Business School Press, 1991); and Sumantra Ghoshal and Nitin Nohria, "Horses for Courses: Organizational Forms for Multinational Corporations," *Sloan Management Review,* Winter 1993, pp. 23–35.

global strategic coordination, which creates pressure to centralize decisions regarding the competitive strategies of different national subsidiaries at corporate headquarters. Thus, once one multinational company in an industry adopts global strategic coordination, its competitors may be forced to respond in kind.

PRESSURES FOR LOCAL RESPONSIVENESS

In some circumstances, companies must be able to adapt to different needs in different locations. Strong pressures for local responsiveness emerge when *consumer tastes and preferences differ significantly* among countries. In such cases, product and/or marketing messages have to be customized.

In the automobile industry, for example, demand by U.S. consumers for pickup trucks is strong. This is particularly true in the South and West, where many families have a pickup truck as a second or third car. In contrast, in Europe pickup trucks are viewed as utility vehicles and are purchased primarily by companies rather than by individuals. As a result, automakers must tailor their marketing messages to the differences in consumer demand.

Pressures for local responsiveness also emerge when there are *differences in traditional practices* among countries. For example, in Great Britain people drive on the left side of the road, creating a demand for right-hand-drive cars, whereas in neighboring France people drive on the right side of the road. Obviously automobiles must be customized to accommodate this difference in traditional practices.

Differences in distribution channels and sales practices among countries may also create pressures for local responsiveness. In the pharmaceutical industry, the Japanese distribution system differs radically from the U.S. system. Japanese doctors will respond unfavorably to an American-style, high-pressure sales force. Thus, pharmaceutical companies have to adopt different marketing practices in Japan (soft versus hard sell).

Finally, *economic and political demands* imposed by host country governments may necessitate a degree of local responsiveness. Most important, threats of protectionism, economic nationalism, and local content rules (rules requiring that a certain percentage of a product be manufactured locally) dictate that international companies manufacture locally. For Japanese auto companies setting up U.S. production operations, increasing threats of protectionism by Congress are a major concern.

CHOOSING A GLOBAL STRATEGY

Figure 8.2 shows the integration-responsiveness grid implying the existence of four approaches to international competition: the international model, the multinational model, the global model, and the transnational model. Each of these types of organizations differs in terms of its approach to strategy as well as the structure and systems that drive operations.

The International Model

The **international organization model** is designed to help companies exploit their existing core capabilities to expand into foreign markets. The international model uses subsidiaries in each country in which the company does business, with ultimate control exercised by the parent company. In particular, while subsidiaries may have some latitude to adapt products to local conditions, core functions such as research and development tend to be centralized in the parent company. Consequently, subsidiary dependence on the parent company for new products, processes, and ideas requires a great deal of coordination and control by the parent company.

The advantage of this model is that it facilitates the transfer of skills and know-how from the parent company to subsidiaries around the globe. For example, IBM, Xerox, and Kodak all profited from the transfer of their core skills in technology and R&D overseas. The overseas success of Kellogg, Coca-Cola, Heinz, and Procter & Gamble is based more on marketing know-how than on technological expertise. During the 1970s, many Japanese companies, including Toyota and Honda, successfully penetrated U.S. markets with their core competencies in manufacturing relative to local competitors. Still others have based their competitive advantage on general management skills. These factors explain the growth of international hotel chains such as Hilton International, Intercontinental, and Sheraton.

One disadvantage of the international model is that it does not provide maximum latitude for responding to local conditions. In addition, it frequently does not provide the opportunity to achieve a low-cost position via scale economics.

The Multinational Model

In contrast to the international model, the **multinational organization model** uses subsidiaries (i.e., independent companies) in each country in which the company does business, and provides a great deal of discretion to those subsidiaries to respond to local conditions. Each local subsidiary is a self-contained unit with all the functions required for operating in the host market. Thus, each subsidiary has its own manufacturing, marketing, research, and human resources functions. Because of this autonomy, each multinational subsidiary can customize its products and strategies according to the tastes and preferences of local consumers, the competitive conditions, and political, legal, and social structures.

The multinational model was widespread among many of the early European corporations such as Unilever and Royal Dutch Shell. One advantage of allowing local responsiveness is that there is less need for coordination and direction from corporate headquarters.

Heinz is especially skilled at overseas marketing. This prominent billboard is displayed in Guangdong, China.
[Greg Girard/Contact Press Images]

Since each subsidiary is a self-contained unit, few transfers of goods and services occur among subsidiaries, thus alleviating problems with transfer pricing and the like.

A major disadvantage of the multinational form is higher manufacturing costs and dupliction of effort. Although a multinational can transfer core skills among its international operations, it cannot realize scale economies from centralizing manufacturing facilities and offering a standardized product to the global marketplace. Moreover, since a multinational approach tends to decentralize strategy decisions (discussed further in Chapter 10), it is difficult to launch coordinated global attacks against competitors. This can be a significant disadvantage when competitors have this ability.

The Global Model

The **global organization model** is designed to enable a company to market a standardized product in the global marketplace and to manufacture that product in a limited number of locations where the mix of costs and skills is most favorable. The global model has been adopted by companies that view the world as one market and assume that there are no tangible differences among countries with regard to consumer tastes and preferences. Procter & Gamble, for example, has been successful in Europe against Unilever because it has approached the entire continent as a unified whole.

Companies that adopt the global model tend to become the low-cost players in any industry. These companies construct global-scale manufacturing facilities in a few selected low-cost locations so that they can realize scale economies. These scale economies come from spreading the fixed costs of investments in new-product development, plant and equipment, and the like over worldwide sales. By using centralized manufacturing facilities and global marketing strategies, Sony was able to push down its unit costs to the point where it became the low-cost player in the global television market. This enabled Sony to take market share away from Philips, RCA, and Zenith, all of which traditionally based manufacturing operations in each major national market (a characteristic of the multinational approach). Because operations are centralized, subsidiaries usually are limited to marketing and service functions.

On the downside, because a company pursuing a purely global approach tries to standardize its products and services, it may be less responsive to consumer tastes and demands in different countries. Attempts to lower costs through global product standardization may result in a product that fails to satisfy anyone. For example, while Procter & Gamble has been quite successful using a global approach, the company experienced problems when it tried to market Cheer in Japan. Unfortunately for P&G, the product did not "suds up" as promoted in Japan because the Japanese use a great deal of fabric softener, which suppresses suds. Moreover, the claim that Cheer worked in all water temperatures was irrelevant in Japan, where most washing is done in cold water.

Companies pursuing a pure global approach to strategy require increased coordination, paperwork, and additional staff. Moreover, such companies must decide how to price transfers of goods and services among parts of the company based in different countries. Transfer pricing problems are difficult enough to resolve within just one country; in a global company, transfer pricing can be further complicated by volatile exchange rates.

The Transnational Model

In today's global economy, achieving a competitive advantage often requires the *simultaneous* pursuit of gains from local responsiveness, transfer of know-how, and cost economies.[7] This raises the question of whether it is possible to design an organization that enables a company to simultaneously reap all the benefits of global expansion. Recently a number of companies, including Unilever, Caterpillar, and Philips, have been experimenting with a new organization model—the transnational organization model—that is designed to do just that.

In companies that adopt the **transnational organization model,** certain functions, particularly research, tend to be centralized at home. Other functions are also centralized, but not necessarily in the home country. To achieve cost economies, companies may base global-scale production plants for labor-intensive products in low-wage countries such as Mexico or Singapore and locate production plants that require a skilled work force in high-skill countries such as Germany or Japan.

Other functions, particularly marketing, service, and final-assembly functions, tend to be based in the national subsidiaries to facilitate greater local responsiveness. Thus, major components may be manufactured in centralized production plants to realize scale economies and then shipped to local plants, where the final product is assembled and customized to fit local needs.

Caterpillar Tractor is a transnational company.[8] The need to compete with low-cost competitors such as Komatsu has forced Caterpillar to look for greater cost economies by centralizing global production at locations where the factor cost/skill mix is most favorable. At the same time, variations in construction practices and government regulations across countries mean that Caterpillar must be responsive to local needs. On the integration-responsiveness grid in Figure 8.2, therefore, Caterpillar is situated toward the top right-hand corner.

To deal with these simultaneous demands, Caterpillar has designed its products to use many identical components and invested in a few large-scale component manufacturing facilities to fill global demand and realize scale economies. But while the company manufactures components centrally, it has assembly plants in each of its major markets. At these plants Caterpillar adds local product features, tailoring the finished product to local needs. Thus, Caterpillar is able to realize many of the benefits of global manufacturing while managing pressure for local responsiveness by differentiating its product among national markets.

Perhaps the most important distinguishing characteristic of the transnational organization is the fostering of communications among subsidiaries. National subsidiaries communicate better with one another so that they can transfer technological expertise and skills among themselves to their mutual benefit. At the same time, centralized manufacturing plants coordinate their production with local assembly plants, thereby facilitating the smooth operation of an integrated, worldwide production system.

Achieving such communications across subsidiaries requires elaborate formal mechanisms, such as transnational committees staffed by people from the various subsidiaries who are responsible for monitoring coordination among subsidiaries. Equally important is to transfer managers among subsidiaries on a regular basis. This enables international managers to establish a global network of personal contacts in different subsidiaries with whom they can share information as the need arises. Finally, achieving coordination among subsidiaries requires that the head office play a proactive role in coordinating their activities.

RETAILERS GO GLOBAL

Something mega is happening in retailing. Armed with the best logistics and operational know-how in the world, American retailers like Wal-Mart and Kmart are busting across borders, setting up stores for eager consumers from Mexico to South China. Saturated U.S. markets and freer trade abroad have given urgency to the global expansion. It is estimated that U.S. retailers will spend a minimum of $5 billion over the next few years on new stores in foreign countries. Office Depot, Saks Fifth Avenue, and JC Penney have already kicked off major Mexican expansion, and the number of retailers on the ground in Europe has increased from 14 in 1992 to over 50 today. These companies include the Gap, Pier 1, and Foot Locker. Even Woolworth—itself a global pioneer—plans to operate nearly 1,000 stores in Europe within the next several years.

Clearly this level of growth is explosive—and risky. Companies such as Wal-Mart and Kmart are banking on superior operating ability and brand names to safeguard their overseas moves. Executives in these companies are confident that the survival skills they have honed in the ferocious U.S. markets will give them a leg up on the competition overseas. So far so good. Kmart's international sales growth has already outpaced its growth domestically. The company, which runs 13 stores in Eastern Europe and a SuperK in Singapore, plans to open 7 stores in Mexico by 1996.

Wal-Mart, the world's largest retailer, now operates 67 discount stores and Sam's Clubs in Mexico, along with its Mexican partner, Cifra. By 1996, the company plans to open 3 stores in Brazil, 2 in Argentina, and 3 joint venture stores in Hong Kong. In three years Wal-Mart's international sales should top $10 billion—amazingly, that is less than 10 percent of projected total sales. Rob Walton, chairman of Wal-Mart, acknowledges that the Asian component of their business has not taken off as well as he had hoped, but views those stores as training centers for the company's eventual expansion into China.

All over the world, customer wants and needs are converging, not just for designer jeans and children's toys, but also for convenience, wider selection, and sharper pricing. If these retailers can manage costs, bring down prices, and offer a broader set of choices to customers, their chances for success are very good.

Source: Carla Rapport and Justin Martin, "Retailers Go Global," *Fortune*, February 20, 1995, pp. 102–8. ●

ENTRY MODE

When considering global expansion, international managers must decide on the best means of entering an overseas market. There are five basic ways to expand overseas: exporting, licensing, franchising, entering into a joint venture with a host country company, and setting up a wholly owned subsidiary in the host country.[9] Table 8.3 compares the entry modes.

EXPORTING

Most manufacturing companies begin global expansion as exporters and later switch to one of the other modes for serving an overseas market. Advantages of exporting are that it (1) provides scale economies by avoiding the costs of manufacturing in other countries and (2) is consistent with a pure global strategy. By manufacturing the product in a centralized location and then exporting it to other national markets, the company may be able to realize substantial scale economies from its global sales volume.

On the other hand, exporting has a number of drawbacks. First, exporting from the company's home base may be inappropriate if other countries offer lower-cost locations for manufacturing the product. An alternative is to manufacture in a location where the mix of factor costs and skills is most favorable and then export from that location to other markets to achieve scale economies. Several U.S. electronics companies have moved some manufacturing operations to the Far East, where low-cost, high-skill labor is available, then export from that location to other countries, including the United States.

TABLE 8.3

Comparison of entry modes

	Exporting	**Licensing**	**Franchising**	**Joint Venture**	**Wholly Owned Subsidiary**
Advantages	Scale economies	Lower development costs	Lower development costs	Local knowledge	Maintains control over technology
	Consistent with pure global strategy	Lower political risk	Lower political risk	Shared costs and risk	Maintains control over operations
				May be the only option	
Disadvantages	No low-cost sites	Loss of control over technology	Loss of control over quality	Loss of control over technology	High cost
	High transportation costs			Conflict between partners	High risk
	Tariff barriers				

A second drawback of exporting is that high transportation costs can make it uneconomical, particularly in the case of bulk products. Chemical companies get around this by manufacturing their products on a regional basis, serving several countries in a region from one facility.

A third drawback is that host countries can impose (or threaten to impose) tariff barriers. As noted earlier, Japanese automakers reduced this risk by setting up manufacturing plants in the United States.

LICENSING

International licensing is an arrangement whereby a licensee in another country buys the rights to manufacture a company's product in its own country for a negotiated fee (typically, royalty payments on the number of units sold). The licensee then puts up most of the capital necessary to get the overseas operation going. The advantage of licensing is that the company need not bear the costs and risks of opening up an overseas market.

On the other hand, a problem arises when a company licenses its technological expertise to overseas companies. Technological know-how is the basis of the competitive advantage of many multinational companies. But RCA Corporation lost control over its color TV technology by licensing it to a number of Japanese companies. The Japanese companies quickly assimilated RCA's technology and then used it to enter the U.S. market. Now the Japanese have a bigger share of the U.S. market than the RCA brand does.

FRANCHISING

In many respects, franchising is similar to licensing. However, whereas licensing is a strategy pursued primarily by manufacturing companies, franchising is used primarily by service companies. McDonald's, Hilton International, and many other companies have expanded overseas by franchising.

In franchising, the company sells limited rights to use its brand name to franchisees in return for a lump-sum payment and a share of the franchisees' profits. However, unlike most licensing agreements, the franchisee has to agree to abide by strict rules as to how it does business. Thus, when McDonald's enters into a franchising agreement with an overseas company, it expects the franchisee to run its restaurants in a manner identical to those run under the McDonald's name elsewhere in the world.

The advantages of franchising as an entry mode are similar to those of licensing. The most significant disadvantage concerns quality control. The company's brand name guarantees consistency in the company's product. Thus, a business traveler booking into a Hilton International hotel in Hong Kong can reasonably expect the same quality of room, food, and service that he or she would receive in New York. But if overseas franchisees are less concerned about quality than they should be, the impact can go beyond lost sales in the local market to a decline in the company's reputation worldwide. If a business traveler has an unpleasant experience at the Hilton in Hong Kong, she or he may decide never to go to another Hilton hotel—and urge colleagues to do likewise. To make matters worse, the geographical distance between the franchisor and its overseas franchisees makes poor quality difficult to detect.

JOINT VENTURES

Establishing a joint venture (a formal business agreement discussed in more detail in Chapter 11) with a company in another country has long been a popular means for entering a new market. Joint ventures benefit a company through (1) the local partner's knowledge of the host country's competitive conditions, culture, language, political systems, and business systems; and (2) the sharing of development costs and/or risks with the local partner. In addition, many countries' political considerations make joint ventures the only feasible entry mode. For example, historically many U.S. companies found it much easier to get permission to set up operations in Japan if they went in with a Japanese partner rather than entering on their own.

There are two major disadvantages to joint ventures. First, as in the case of licensing, a company runs the risk of losing control over its technology to its venture partner. Second, because control is shared with the partner, the company may lose control over its subsidiaries. Indeed, conflict over who controls what within a joint venture is a primary reason many joint ventures fail.

WHOLLY OWNED SUBSIDIARIES

Establishing a wholly owned subsidiary, that is, an independent company owned by the parent corporation, is the most costly method of serving an overseas market. Companies that use this approach must bear the full costs and risks associated with setting up overseas operations (as opposed to joint ventures, in which the costs and risks are shared, or licensing, in which the licensee bears most of the costs and risks).

Nevertheless, setting up a wholly owned subsidiary offers two clear advantages. First, when a company's competitive advantage is based on technology, a wholly owned subsidiary normally will be the preferred entry mode because it reduces the risk of losing control over the technology. Wholly owned subsidiaries tend to be the favored entry mode in the semiconductor, electronics, and pharmaceutical industries.

Second, a wholly owned subsidiary gives a company tight control over operations in other countries, which is necessary if it chooses to pursue a global strategy. Establishing a global manufacturing system requires world headquarters to have a high degree of control over the operations of national affiliates. Unlike licensees or joint venture partners, wholly owned subsidiaries usually accept centrally determined decisions about how to produce, how much to produce, and how to price output for transfer among operations.

EUROPE'S FAST-FOOD FRANCHISES

Speed

*T*he fast-food revolution has finally hit Europe, and companies such as McDonald's, Pizza Hut, and Kentucky Fried Chicken are pouring tens of millions of dollars annually into expanding their number of franchises. McDonald's, for example, opened its first restaurant in England 20 years ago. Since that time, its number of U.K. restaurants has grown to 525 and company chairman Michael Quinlan plans to double this number within the decade. KFC International, with even more ambitious growth plans, hopes to triple its number of European units over the next five years. As of December 1994, KFC has close to 348 restaurants in the U.K., and plans to open restaurants in Spain, France, Germany, and Eastern Europe. In Germany alone, Pizza Hut plans to open 30 to 50 restaurants each year.

Franchising is the key to this breakneck pace of expansion. Franchising offers fast-food companies a relatively low-risk investment while facilitating a low-cost transfer of know-how, technology, training, and management skills to other parts of the world. Franchising has been especially successful for U.S.–based companies trying to expand into parts of Eastern Europe. Unification and the elimination of customs barriers have made it much easier for companies to open fast-food franchises and conduct business across borders. However, while an integrated Europe makes free market transactions easier, there is no such thing as a *homogeneous* European market—U.S.–based operators have had to alter their concept of fast food for each region. KFC's first restaurant in Europe, for example, included a menu of sandwiches, salads, and desserts, while providing a more country French decor. Pizza Hut also has made extensive menu changes, from bigger salads to a broader dessert selection. McDonald's, which rightfully prides itself on providing a consistent and standardized fare, has made adjustments to accommodate local preferences. Here again is an advantage of franchising—local knowledge helps to fine-tune each company's product line and provide ways of integrating fast food into the European culture. No longer just fish 'n chips or croissants, fast-food franchises are changing the way Europeans eat.

Sources: David Lennon, "Goodbye Fish and Chips," *Europe,* July–August 1994, pp. 43–44; "Franchising Catches On in Eastern Europe," *Business America,* June 28, 1993, p. 10; John McLaughlin, "The Dollar's Fall Has a Bright Spot," *Restaurant Business,* October 10, 1992, p. 46; and John McLaughlin, "Tromping across Europe," *Restaurant Business,* May 1, 1992, pp. 70–87. ●

American fast-food franchises have taken European markets by storm, as evidenced by this Kentucky Fried Chicken store in France.

(Courtesy Kentucky Fried Chicken (KFC))

MANAGING ACROSS BORDERS

When establishing operations overseas, headquarter executives have a choice among sending **expatriates** (individuals from the parent country), using **host-country nationals** (natives of the host country), or deploying **third-country nationals** (natives of a country other than the home country or the host country). While most corporations use some combination of all three types of employees, there are advantages and disadvantages of each. Colgate-Palmolive, for example, uses expatriates in an effort to shorten the delivery time of products-to-market, while AT&T uses expatriates to help transfer the company's culture. On the other hand, companies such as Chevron and Texas Instruments make more limited use of expatriates. Chevron typically sends a management team to review the skills of local employees, and sends expatriates only if their technical skills are needed. If expatriates are sent, it is expected that operational control will be passed over to local employees. Texas Instruments uses very few expatriates, but relies on phone, fax, and computers to facilitate communication. However, TI frequently sends people on extended travel so they meet their cohorts around the world.[10]

In recent years, the use of expatriate managers has been declining as more companies make use of host-country nationals (see Table 8.4). These local employees tend to be readily

TABLE 8.4

Employees of U.S. multinationals (in thousands)

Nationals of:	1977	1982	1985	1990
Britain	1,069.3	830.7	809.5	846.7
China	N.A.	N.A.	N.A.	14.4
Germany*	587.4	541.3	541.1	590.5
India	94.6	75.2	71.8	38.3
Ireland	27.6	38.4	35.2	45.5
Jamaica	N.A.	8.8	6.2	8.7
Japan	389.1	302	331	407.8
Mexico	370.1	470.3	466	551.6
Singapore	44.2	46.1	49	85.8
Thailand	27.3	29.4	29.1	64.4

*East and West Germany combined for 1990.
Note: The number of foreign workers employed by U.S. companies declined in the early eighties as conglomerates sold off acquisitions made earlier, but rose by half a million between 1986 and 1990 to 6.7 million.

Source: Brian O'Reilly, "Our New Global Work Force," *Fortune,* December 14, 1992.

available, tend to have familiarity with the culture and language, and usually cost less because they do not have to be displaced. In addition, local governments often provide incentives to companies that create good jobs for their citizens (or they may place restrictions on the use of expatriates). For these reasons, executives at Allen Bradley, a division of Rockwell International, believe that building a strong local workforce is critical to their success overseas, and they transport key host-country nationals to the United States for skills training. The trend away from using expatriates in top management positions is especially apparent in companies that truly want to create a multinational culture.[11] In Honeywell's European division, for example, 12 of the top executive positions are held by non-Americans.[12]

Over the years, U.S.–based companies, in particular, have tended to use more third-country nationals to work in a country different from their own, and different from the parent company's. When Eastman Kodak assembled a management team to devise a launch strategy for its new Photo-CD line in Europe, the team members were based in London, but the leader was from Belgium. Because third-country nationals can soften the political tensions between the parent country and the host country, they often represent a convenient compromise.

COLGATE-PALMOLIVE'S GLOBAL WORKFORCE

*C*olgate-Palmolive has been operating internationally for more than 50 years. Its products, such as Colgate toothpaste, Palmolive soap, Fab detergent, and Ajax cleanser, are household names in more than 170 countries. Since more than 70 percent of the company's $7 billion in sales comes from overseas markets, Colgate requires a certain type of manager who understands not only the particular niches and communities in which the company operates locally, but who also has a global perspective and understands the benefits of a global product line. Since 1960, two of its last four CEOs have come from outside the United States, and all of the top executives speak at least two languages. As a routine element of their business operations, important meetings are regularly scheduled in various places around the globe.

But having a cadre of *globalite executives*—as Colgate-Palmolive calls them—is not enough. Fully 60 percent of the company's expatriates are from places other than the United States, and the company goes to great lengths to attract and develop individuals who want international careers anywhere in the world. One example of Colgate's commitment to recruiting and staffing globally is its Global Marketing Program. The program takes approximately 15 high-potential MBA graduates and rotates them through various departments for 18 to 24 months. Recruits gain experience in the global business development group and, after their stint in Colgate's headquarters, they are deployed overseas. The success of this program extends beyond its training value. The Global Marketing Program also serves as an excellent recruiting device—more than 15,000 candidates apply for the 15 slots each year.

Once on board, employees are provided an array of overseas assignments: long term, short term, and stopgap for addressing particular competency needs. While the programs vary based on the individual's interests and needs, they are all designed to provide exposure to the corporate—as well as local—culture. Ultimately Colgate's objective is to generate an international core of managers who will be the future leaders of the company.

Source: Charlene Marmer Solomon, "Staff Selection Impacts Global Success," *Personnel Journal,* January 1994, pp. 88–101. ●

SKILLS OF THE GLOBAL MANAGER

It is estimated that by the year 2000, nearly 15 percent of all employee transfers will be to an international location. However, a recent survey of 1,500 senior executives showed that there is a critical shortage of U.S. managers equipped to run global businesses.[13] Indicative of this fact is the **failure rate** among expatriates (defined as those who come home early), which has been estimated to range from 25 to 50 percent. The average cost of each of these failed assignments ranges from $40,000 to $250,000.[14] Typically the causes for failure overseas extend beyond technical capability, and include personal and social issues as well. Interestingly, one of the biggest problems is a spouse's inability to adjust to his or her new surroundings.[15] For both the expatriate and the spouse, adjustment requires flexibility, emotional stability, empathy for the culture, communication skills, resourcefulness, initiative, and diplomatic skills.[16]

Interestingly, while many U.S. companies have hesitated to send women abroad—believing that women either do not want international assignments or that other cultures would not welcome women—their success rate has been estimated at 97 percent (far greater than their male counterparts).[17] Ironically, for a country which had been viewed as not welcoming foreign women, in Japan U.S. women are first viewed as foreigners (*gaijin* in Japanese), and only second as women. And because it is unusual for women to be sent on foreign assignments, their distinctiveness and visibility tend to increase their chances for success.[18]

Executives at Levi-Strauss have pointed out that if individuals are to function effectively in an international setting, regardless of gender, they need the following six attributes: (1) the ability to seize strategic opportunities; (2) the ability to manage a highly decentralized organization; (3) awareness of global issues; (4) sensitivity to issues of diversity; (5) interpersonal competency; and (6) ability to build the community.[19] Other companies, such as Colgate-Palmolive, Whirlpool, and Dow Chemical, have identified a set of *core skills* that are critical for success abroad, as well as a set of *augmented skills* that help boost the chances of a manager's success abroad. These skills are summarized in Figure 8.3.

Companies such as Amoco, Bechtel, 3M, Hyatt, Honeywell, and others with large international staffs have extensive training programs to prepare employees for international assignments. Other organizations such as Coca-Cola, Motorola, Chevron, and Mattel have extended this training to include employees who may be located in the United States, but who nevertheless deal in international markets. These programs focus on areas such as language, culture, and career development.

UNDERSTANDING CULTURAL ISSUES

In many ways, cultural issues represent the most elusive aspect of international business. In an era when modern transportation and communication technologies have created a "global village," it is easy to forget how deep and enduring the differences among nations actually can be. The fact that people everywhere drink Coke, wear blue jeans, and drive Toyotas doesn't mean we are all becoming alike. Each country is unique for reasons rooted in history, culture, language, geography, social conditions, race, and religion. These differences complicate any international activities, and represent the fundamental issues that inform and guide how a company should conduct business across borders.

Ironically, while most of us would guess that the trick to working abroad is learning about the foreign culture, in reality our problems often stem from our being oblivious to our own cultural conditioning. Most of us pay no attention to how culture influences our everyday behavior, and because of this we tend to adapt poorly to situations that are unique or foreign to us. This is one reason why people traveling abroad frequently experience **culture shock**—the disorientation and stress associated with being in a foreign environment. Managers who ignore culture put their organizations at a great disadvantage in the global marketplace. Since each culture has its own norms, customs, and expectations for behavior, success in an international environment depends on one's ability to understand one's own and the other culture and to recognize that abrupt changes will be met with resistance.

A wealth of cross-cultural research has been conducted on the differences and similarities between various countries. Geert Hofstede, for example, has identified four dimensions along which managers in multinational corporations tend to view cultural differences:

- *Power distance:* the extent to which a society accepts the fact that power in organizations is distributed unequally.
- *Individualism/collectivism:* the extent to which people act on their own or as a part of a group.

FIGURE 8.3

The 21st-century expatriate manager profile

Core Skills	Managerial Implications
Multidimensional perspective	Extensive multiproduct, multi-industry, multifunctional, multicompany, multicountry, and multienvironment experience.
Proficiency in line management	Track record in successfully operating a strategic business unit(s) and/or a series of major overseas projects.
Prudent decision-making skills	Competence and proven track record in making the right strategic decisions.
Resourcefulness	Skillful in getting himself or herself known and accepted in the host country's political hierarchy.
Cultural adaptability	Quick and easy adaptability into the foreign culture—An individual with as much cultural mix, diversity, and experience as possible.
Cultural sensitivity	Effective people skills in dealing with a variety of cultures, races, nationalities, genders, religions. Also, sensitive to cultural difference.
Ability as a team builder	Adept in bringing a culturally diverse working group together to accomplish the major mission and objective of the organization.
Physical fitness and mental maturity	Endurance for the rigorous demands of an overseas assignment.
Augmented skills	**Managerial Implications**
Computer literacy	Comfortable exchanging strategic information electronically.
Prudent negotiating skills	Proven track record in conducting successful strategic business negotiations in multicultural environment.
Ability as a change agent	Proven track record in successfully initiating and implementing strategic organizational changes.
Visionary skills	Quick to recognize and respond to strategic business opportunities and potential political and economic upheavals in the host country.
Effective delegatory skills	Proven track record in participative management style and ability to delegate.

Source: C. G. Howard, "Profile of the 21st-Century Expatriate Manager," *HRMagazine,* June 1992, pp. 93–100.

- *Uncertainty avoidance:* the extent to which people in a society feel threatened by uncertain and ambiguous situations.
- *Masculinity/femininity:* the extent to which a society values quantity of life (e.g., accomplishment, money) over quality of life (e.g., compassion, beauty).

Figure 8.4 offers a graphic depiction of how 40 different nations differ on the dimensions of individualism/collectivism and power distance. Clearly, cultures such as the United States' that emphasize "rugged individualism" differ significantly from collectivistic cultures such as those of Pakistan, Taiwan, and Colombia. In order to be effective in cultures that exhibit a greater power distance, managers often must behave more autocratically, perhaps being less participative in decision making. Conversely, in Scandinavian cultures, in Sweden, for instance, where power distance is low, the very idea that management has the prerogative to make decisions on their own may be called into question. Here managers tend to work more toward creating processes that reflect an "industrial democracy."

FIGURE 8.4

The position of the 40 countries on the power distance and individualism scales

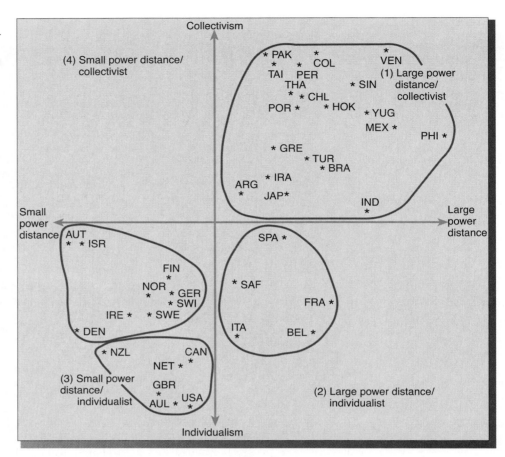

The 40 Countries
(Showing Abbreviations used above)

ARG Argentina	FRA France	JAP Japan	SIN Singapore
AUL Australia	GBR Great Britain	MEX Mexico	SPA Spain
AUT Austria	GER Germany (West)	NET Netherlands	SWE Sweden
BEL Belgium	GRE Greece	NOR Norway	SWI Switzerland
BRA Brazil	HOK Hong Kong	NZL New Zealand	TAI Taiwan
CAN Canada	IND India	PAK Pakistan	THA Thailand
CHL Chile	IRA Iran	PER Peru	TUR Turkey
COL Colombia	IRE Ireland	PHI Philippines	USA United States
DEN Denmark	ISR Israel	POR Portugal	VEN Venezuela
FIN Finland	ITA Italy	SAF South Africa	YUG Yugoslavia

Source: Geert Hofstede, "Motivation, Leadership, and Organization: Do American Theories Apply Abroad?" *Organizational Dynamics* 9, no.1 (Summer 1980), pp. 42–63.

ETHICAL ISSUES IN INTERNATIONAL MANAGEMENT

If managers are to function effectively in a foreign setting, they must understand how culture influences both how they are perceived as well as how others behave. One of the most sensitive issues in this regard is understanding how culture plays out in terms of ethical behavior.[20] Issues of right and wrong are often culturally determined, and actions that may be normal and customary in one setting may be unethical—even illegal—in another. The use of bribes, for example, is an accepted part of commercial transactions in many Asian, African, Latin American, and Middle Eastern cultures. In the United States, of course, such behavior is illegal, but what should a U.S. businessperson do when working abroad?

TABLE 8.5

Is this ethical?

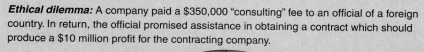

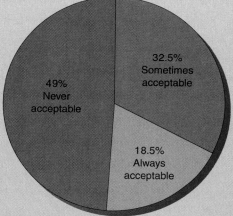

Ethical dilemma: A company paid a $350,000 "consulting" fee to an official of a foreign country. In return, the official promised assistance in obtaining a contract which should produce a $10 million profit for the contracting company.

49%
Never
acceptable

32.5%
Sometimes
acceptable

18.5%
Always
acceptable

Percentage of respondents who said the payments were:

49.0% "never acceptable"

32.5% "sometimes acceptable"

18.5% "always acceptable"

Source: J. G. Longenecker, J. A. McKinney, and C. W. Moore, "The Ethical Issue of International Bribery: A Study of Attitudes among U.S. Business Professionals," *Journal of Business Ethics* 7 (1988), pp. 341–46.

Though most Americans prefer to conduct business in a way consistent with prevailing U.S. laws, many people feel that we should not impose our cultural values on others. As a consequence, opinions differ widely on what is acceptable behavior when confronted with certain ethical dilemmas. Table 8.5 shows the results of a recent survey that asked managers about the ethicality of payments to foreign officials. Surprisingly, less than half of the respondents said that the bribes were never acceptable, and in many cases managers suggested that such behavior would be acceptable if it was the local custom. In reality, these particular views are somewhat naive—while giving and receiving business gifts may be acceptable, the Foreign Corrupt Practices Act (1977) strictly prohibits U.S. employees from providing payments to foreign officials. While small "grease payments" to lower-level figures are permissible under the act, if the dollar amount of the payments is significant and would influence the outcome of negotiations, the transaction would be illegal.

Without an understanding of local customs, ethical standards, and applicable laws, an expatriate might be woefully unprepared to work internationally. To safeguard against these and other ethical problems, companies such as Caterpillar Tractor, General Dynamics, and United Technologies have established codes of conduct for international business. The codes lay out precisely what kinds of actions are permissible, and provide procedures and support systems that individuals can use in ambiguous situations.

To a large extent, the challenge of managing across borders comes down to the philosophies and systems used to manage people. In moving from domestic to international management, managers need to develop a wide portfolio of behaviors along with the capacity to adjust their behavior for a particular situation. This adjustment, however, should not compromise the values, integrity, and strengths of their home country. When managers can transcend national borders, and move among different cultures, then they will finally be in a position to leverage the strategic capabilities of the organization, and take advantage of the opportunities that our global economy has to offer.

KEY TERMS

culture shock, p. 196
expatriates, p. 194
failure rate, p. 195
global organizational model, p. 189
host-country nationals, p. 194

international organization model, p. 188
multinational organization model, p. 188
third-country nationals, p. 194
transnational organization model, p. 189

SUMMARY OF LEARNING OBJECTIVES

Now that you have studied Chapter 8, you should know:

Why the world economy is becoming more integrated than ever before.

The gradual lowering of barriers to free trade is making the world economy more integrated. This means that the modern manager operates in an environment that offers more opportunities but is also more complex and competitive than that faced by the manager of a generation ago.

What integration of the global economy means for individual companies and for their managers.

In recent years, rapid growth in world trade, foreign direct investment, and imports has occurred. One consequence is that companies around the globe are now finding their home markets under attack from international competitors. The global competitive environment is becoming a much tougher place in which to do business. However, companies now have access to markets that were previously denied to them.

The strategies organizations use to compete in the global marketplace.

The *international corporation* builds on its existing core capabilities in R&D, marketing, manufacturing, and so on, to penetrate overseas markets. A *multinational* is a more complex form that usually has fully autonomous units operating in multiple countries. Subsidiaries are given latitude to address local issues such as consumer preferences, political pressures, or economic trends in different regions of the world. The *global organization* pulls control of overseas operations back into the headquarters and tends to approach the world market as a "unified whole" by combining activities in each country to maximize efficiency on a global scale. A *transnational* attempts to achieve both local responsiveness and global integration by utilizing a network structure that coordinates specialized facilities positioned around the world.

The various entry modes organizations use to enter overseas markets.

There are five ways to enter an overseas market: exporting, licensing, franchising, entering into a joint venture, and setting up a wholly owned subsidiary. Each mode has advantages and disadvantages.

How companies can approach the task of staffing overseas operations.

Most executives use a combination of *expatriates, host-country nationals,* or *third-country nationals.* Expatriates are sometimes used to quickly establish new country operations, transfer the company's culture, and bring in a specific technical skill. Host-country nationals have the advantages that they are familiar with local customs and culture, may cost less, and are viewed more favorably by local governments. Third-country nationals are often used as a compromise in politically touchy situations or when home-country expatriates are not available.

The skills and knowledge managers need to manage globally.

The causes for failure overseas extend beyond technical capability, and include personal and social issues as well. Success depends on a manager's *core skills* such as having a multidimensional perspective, having proficiency in line management and decision-making, and having resourcefulness, cultural adaptability, sensitivity, team building skills, and mental maturity. In addition, helpful *augmented skills* include computer literacy, negotiating skills, strategic vision, and ability to delegate.

Why cultural differences across countries influence management.

Culture influences our actions and perceptions as well as the actions and perceptions of others. Unfortunately, we are often unaware of how culture influences us, and this can cause problems. Today, managers must be able to change their behavior to match the needs and customs of local cultures. For example, in various cultures, employees expect a manager to be either more or less autocratic or participative. By recognizing their cultural differences, people can find it easier to work together collaboratively and benefit from the exchange.

DISCUSSION QUESTIONS

1. Why is the world economy becoming more integrated? What are the implications of this integration for international managers?
2. Imagine you were the CEO of a major company. What approach to global competition would you choose for your firm: international, multinational, global, or transnational? Why?
3. Why have franchises been so popular as a method of international expansion in the fast-food industry? Contrast this with high-tech manufacturing where joint ventures and partnerships have been more popular. What accounts for the differences across industries?

4. What are the pros and cons of using expatriates, host-country nationals, and third-country nationals to run overseas operations? If you were expanding your business, what approach would you use?
5. If you had entered into a joint venture with a foreign company, but knew that women were not treated fairly in that culture, would you consider sending a female expatriate to handle the startup? Why or why not?
6. What are the biggest cultural obstacles that we must overcome if we are to work effectively in Mexico? Are there different obstacles in France? Japan?

CONCLUDING CASE

FORD'S $6 BILLION WORLD CAR

On July 19, 1994, the world's most expensive car rolled off Ford's Kansas City assembly line and marked the final stage of an 11-year, $6 billion project code-named CDW27. The car, known in the United States as the Ford Contour and Mercury Mystique, had been introduced to the European market in February 1993 as the Ford Mondeo, proving a smash-hit there, achieving sales of over 470,000 cars, and becoming the leader in the mid-sized segment of the European market. Initial response to the Contour and Mystique has been quite favorable as well.

In many ways, project CDW27 is more than a car; it represents a platform for how Ford wants to compete in the future. Most experts agree that national borders mean less and less in the world auto industry, and that building a world car—one that can be made and marketed around the world—can provide the ultimate in economies of scale. But actually pulling off this achievement is difficult, and building a world car has been the holy grail for automakers. Only Volkswagen's classic Beetle, and perhaps the Toyota Corolla, have come close.

To organize the design and manufacture of CDW27, Ford had to reconcile divergent European and American engineering standards, fly hundreds of technicians back and forth across the Atlantic, and spend tens of millions of dollars on late design changes. Four design studios in Italy, California, Germany, and Michigan worked on the project. And although Ford's European operations maintained the project leadership, key responsibilities

Ford Motor Company's "global" car, the Ford Mondeo, has become a leader in the mid-sized segment of the European market. Its U.S. versions (Contour and Mystique) are doing well, too.
(Courtesy Ford Motor Company)

were divided. Engineers in Detroit designed the all-new 2.5 liter V-6 engine, the automatic transmission, and the heating and air-conditioning units. A team in Dunton, England, contributed the interior, the steering, the suspension, the electronics, the manual transmission, and the new four-cylinder engine. Employees in Cologne, Germany, did the basic structural engineering and also designed three sheet-metal bodies for the car tailored to different markets.

In addition to design requirements, the CDW27 project required renovations and retooling at nine factories, including engine parts in Wales, Cologne, Cleveland, and Chihuahua, Mexico. To ensure quality, Ford created a team of troubleshooters to check and solve defects and other quality problems. The company airlifted some 150 engineers from England and Germany to mobile offices outside the production plant in Genk, Belgium. Ford's goal was to have no more defects at the beginning of production for the new model than it had at the end of the old one. The troubleshooting team worked tirelessly and efficiently, and solved at least half the problems within 48 hours of their occurrence.

The executive in charge of CDW27, John Oldfield, was British and based in Cologne, Germany. But final responsibility for the program rested at Ford's world headquarters in Dearborn, Michigan. So Oldfield traveled back and forth across the Atlantic about once a month for six years. During one nine-month stretch, he made the round trip once a week. Other top executives flew to Europe three times a year to test-drive CDW27 prototypes. Preparing for production in Kansas City, Oldfield began airlifting the launch team there in September 1993. The launch took 10 months and cost about $150 million for training and production lost during the changeover. It was also accompanied by a $110 million advertising campaign, the biggest the industry has known for a single model.

With all the obstacles that had to be overcome, as well as the expense, why did Ford create CDW27? The "one size fits all" approach of a world car may seem counter to conventional wisdom in the 1990s regarding getting close to your customers. Ford executives point to the economics of the project as a primary rationale. A global car saves money in areas such as engineering. By having one 800-person engineering team produce the car for both Europe and the United States, Ford was able to deploy the rest of its people and facilities to other projects. By using identical production tools at both Genk and Kansas City, Ford saved an estimated 25 percent on custom-built factory items. Ford's goal for CDW27 was to save $75 per car. In fact, they saved closer to $150. Those savings spread over 700,000 units result in a total gain of $100 million a year.

A second reason for CDW27 was that it was a learning experience. If the project is a success, it will become the nucleus for other vehicles. In reality, CDW27 lays the foundation for a decade's worth of products, all built from a common design and with great economies of scale. Ford's chairman, Alex Trotman, points out that for $6 billion the company got three new models, two new engines, two new transmissions, and nine new or revamped factories. Currently, Ford can crank out 800,000 cars of this type each year.

Even so, most executives at Ford acknowledge that developing a world car was a bit too ambitious for a company whose European and American operations were distinct. Ford has since reorganized its worldwide operations, merging North America and Europe, in order to make global product launches cheaper and easier in the future. The goal is for engineers and executives to talk with each other daily across the Atlantic through video conference and computer nets. And Ford will pick its global battles carefully. Future global products will all be focused on mid-range cars. Europeans, for instance, will never buy huge Lincoln town cars or pickup trucks, but both are important in North American markets.

Even cars that are developed globally will be customized regionally in order to ensure details of styling and specifications tailored to regional markets. The CDW27, while sharing 75 percent common parts across its three versions, has been customized in the United States so that the Contour and Mystique are slightly longer and have more chrome. Despite all Ford has learned, its new strategy remains something of a gamble—one of the biggest and most interesting in the automotive industry.

QUESTIONS

1. Why does Ford believe that it needs to produce a "world car"?
2. How would you describe Ford's aproach to global strategy?
3. What has Ford learned from CDW27?

Sources: Richard A. Melcher, "Meet Ford's Brave New 'World Car,' " *Business Week,* January 18, 1993, p. 46; Richard A. Melcher, "Ford of Europe: Slimmer, but Maybe Not Luckier," *Business Week,* January 18, 1993, pp. 45–46; Steve Kichen, "Will the Third Time Be the Charm?" *Forbes,* March 15, 1993, p. 54; Alex Taylor III, "Ford's $6 Billion Baby," *Fortune,* June 28, 1993, pp. 76–81; "Enter the McFord," *The Economist,* July 23, 1994, p. 69; and Jerry Flint, "Will It, or Won't It?" *Forbes,* February 28, 1994, p. 18.

VIDEO CASE

INTERNATIONAL MANAGEMENT AT COCA-COLA

Over the past several decades, many large corporations have developed international markets for their products and services. Today, it is commonplace to speak of a global economy, where goods and services flow across international borders and across vast oceans with few impediments. Although international trade has for centuries been a source of wealth creation for a few of the most developed countries, the modern global economy is distinguished by the number of countries now participating. American companies are finding great opportunities abroad for their products and services. At the same time, new competitors have entered the contest for global market share.

Coca-Cola is a well-established American company that has aggressively pursued foreign markets. One of the most attractive foreign markets is Japan. Although Coca-Cola has been bottling its flagship Coke since 1915, it was not widely available in Japanese markets until 1960. Today, Japan is the company's most important international market.

Originally, the license to distribute Coke in Japan was purchased by a Japanese businessman. This approach of partnering with a foreign businessperson wasn't common practice at the time. As it turned out, the partnering strategy was vital to Coke's success in the Japanese market, and was a precursor to the partnering strategy that is widely used today by large, multinational corporations. Over the years, Coke has applied the partnering approach with companies like Mitsui and Mitsubishi to build up its bottling and distribution operations across the country. Today, Coca-Cola Japan calls itself a "multilocal," rather than a multinational, company. Local expertise offered by the Japanese bottlers was essential in introducing the new products to Japanese products. Local expertise also allowed the company to circumvent the traditional mode of distribution of foreign products in Japan, bypassing wholesalers and selling directly to retailers.

Frank Kelly, Jr., senior vice president and marketing director, Coca-Cola (Japan) Co., Ltd., said, "When we introduced Coca-Cola we introduced the 'store door' delivery system. In the beginning, we had a very difficult time convincing the local population that this was the way to go. The second major hurdle was that, in the beginning, all of our products were sold for cash. In Japan, based on cultural experiences, bills were only paid once or twice per year." Because of these different expectations, the Japanese retailers would send Coke's drivers away and tell them to come back when they had returned to their senses and were ready to behave like "normal people."

Despite these difficulties, Coke persisted, and within a few years the company was able to convince the Japanese of the value of its style of doing business. Still, the company made a few concessions to Japanese traditions. For example, at the Fuji Bottling plant, most of the workers have a lifetime employment contract. This reflects the Japanese belief that long-term commitments result in more-productive workers. Inside the plant, decision making is based on consensus. Kelly says that Coca-Cola Japan operates as a "hybrid" company. "Here in Japan we do things such as assist our employees in purchasing a home with low interest loans. We have a number of social clubs within the company. What we have here is a lot of group activities. We do a lot of things as a team rather than as individuals."

Another key factor in the success of Coca-Cola Japan is that it creates and tailors new products to meet the tastes of local consumers. For example, the company has created an entirely new line of soft-drink products that are distributed only in Japan. Coke's advertising strategy in Japan also tries to cultivate its image as a good citizen, and to demonstrate the fact that its products have become a part of everyday life throughout Japan.

Over the years Coke has strengthened its position in Japan to a point where it now holds over 30 percent of the soft drink market share, and over 90 percent of the cola market. Its distribution system sells to over a million retailers, and it operates over 700,000 vending machines. Summarizing Coke's success in Japan, Kelly said, "I think that the most important thing that you have to learn as a foreigner in Japan is to develop, or to have, patience. Patience is very important because consensus building is a key to success here. So you have to be patient and you have to let things develop."

As Coke learned, doing business in international markets is a delicate balancing act. Companies must maintain the integrity of their products and leverage their knowledge of effective production processes, but they must also pay attention to the needs and demands of the foreign culture and of the foreign workers who operate their plants. Perhaps the key to Coke's success in Japan is that it never lost track of its need to be a good citizen.

CRITICAL THINKING QUESTIONS

1. The lessons in this video case pertain to the Japanese market. With other foreign markets in Asia, Latin America, and elsewhere developing rapidly, do you think the keys to successful business in Japan apply in these markets? Explain your answer.

2. One of the keys to success for Coke in Japan is the adoption of traditional Japanese practices, such as lifetime employment, in its local plants. Why do you think this is important?

3. Coke entered the Japanese market by developing partnerships with local businesspeople. What are some other potential modes of entry to the Japanese market that Coke might have used instead? What do you think would have been the outcome of these alternative approaches?

4. Frank Kelly, Coke's senior vice president and marketing director in Japan, said that one of the most important things for doing business in Japan is patience. What did he mean?

EXPERIENTIAL EXERCISES

8.1 Understanding Multinational Corporations

Objective

To gain a more thorough picture of how a multinational corporation operates.

Instructions

Perhaps the best way to gain an understanding of multinational corporations is to study a specific organization and how it operates throughout the world. Select a multinational corporation and find several articles on that company and answer the questions on the Multinational Worksheet.

MULTINATIONAL WORKSHEET

1. What is the primary business of this organization?

_____

_____

_____

_____

_____

2. To what extent does the company engage in multinational operations? For example, does it only market its products/services in other countries or does it have manufacturing facilities? What portion of the firm's operating income comes from overseas operations?

_____

_____

_____

_____

_____

3. What percentage of the managers in international activities are American (or from the country the corporation considers home)? Are these managers given any special training prior to their international assignment?

_____

_____

_____

_____

_____

4. What characteristics of the organization have contributed to its success or lack of success in the international marketplace?

_____

_____

_____

_____

Source: R. R. McGrath, Jr., *Exercises in Management Fundamentals* (Englewood Cliffs, N.J.: Prentice-Hall, 1985), p. 177. Reprinted by permission of Prentice-Hall, Inc.

8.2 Expatriates versus Locals

Objectives

1. To help you understand the various advantages and disadvantages of using expatriates and locals as managers and professional staffers.
2. To broaden your understanding of the difficult human resources management problems the multinational enterprise faces.

Instructions

1. Working alone, read the Expatriates versus Locals Situation.
2. Go to the library and research the pros and cons of using expatriates versus locals.
3. Complete the Expatriates versus Locals Worksheet.
4. When the class reconvenes, your instructor can organize a debate on the expatriates versus locals issue.

Expatriates versus Locals Situation

Your company is planning to open a number of manufacturing and distribution centers in other countries to become a true multinational enterprise. There has been considerable controversy among top management as to how to staff the overseas operations. It's agreed that for nonmanagerial and nonprofessional staff positions, locals should be hired and trained whenever possible. However, for managerial and professional staff positions, there is considerable and sometimes emotional disagreement. You are to investigate the various advantages and disadvantages in using expatriates versus locals in overseas operations.

EXPATRIATES VERSUS LOCALS WORKSHEET

Advantages of Using Expatriates

_____
_____
_____
_____
_____
_____
_____

Advantages of Using Locals

_____
_____
_____
_____
_____
_____
_____

9

NEW VENTURES

A man is known by the company he organizes.

Ambrose Bierce

LEARNING OBJECTIVES

After studying Chapter 9, you will know:

1. The activities of entrepreneurship.

2. How to find and evaluate ideas for new business ventures.

3. What it takes to be a successful entrepreneur.

4. The important management skills, resources, and strategies needed to avoid failure and achieve success.

5. The process of spinning off new ventures.

6. How to foster intrapreneurship in large companies.

HUMBLE BEGINNINGS

Succcessful business people have to start somewhere:

- Abby Margalith was waiting tables, and her brother Ethan had just finished high school and needed a summer job. He borrowed a truck and hauled a few items, made some cash, and realized he had his summer job. Abby joined him in the moving business. Their first real moving truck was a 1944 weapons carrier they dug out of a mud slide. After painting "Starving Students" and their phone number on the side, they parked it at a Beverly Hills street corner. The phone rang off the hook. Today, Starving Students has 14 locations in five states, and sales have reached $15 million.

Abby Margalith and her brother started their Starving Students moving company with one 50-year-old truck. Today their sales have reached $15 million.
(Rocky Thies)

- One day, Dan Hoard cut off a pants leg and put it on his head. He and his buddy, Tom Bunnell, laughed so hard they said, "We have to sell this. We have to at least try." Thus was born Mambosoks. They made five more and gave them to Bunnell's wedding party in 1990, who did the polka in them at the reception. Next, in 1991, they contracted with a manufacturer to make 1,000 Mambosoks. Tom sold them to patrons of the bar where he worked. The partners expanded production, and by year two their sales reached $1 million. In response to Mambosoks knockoffs, they have diversified into dozens of other items, including the Mambohead Shirt, the Chubby Summer Snowboarding Shorts, and the three-foot Polar Dunce Cap. By 1993 Mambosoks was serving 1,000 accounts all over the world.

- A young inventor named Masaru Ibuka decided to start his own company. The year was 1945, he had $1,600, and he hired seven employees. But he did not have a product, or an idea for a product. His group sat in a small room for weeks, trying to figure out what kind of business to enter. The first product was a rice cooker that didn't work. Its next offering was a tape recorder, but it struck out as well. The company stayed afloat by stitching wires to cloth to make cheap but marketable heating pads. The company today is known as Sony Corp.

Sources: T. Ehrenfeld, P. Hise, R. Mamis, and A. Murphy, "Where Great Ideas for New Businesses Come From," *Inc.,* September 1993, pp. 54–62; and J. C. Collins, "Sometimes a Great Notion," *Inc.,* July 1993, pp. 90–91.

*G*reat opportunity, in both large and small companies, is available to those who develop a vitally important skill: entrepreneurship. **Entrepreneurship** is the act of forming a new organization of value.[1]

Entrepreneurs generate new ideas and turn them into business ventures.[2] But entrepreneurship is frequently misunderstood. Read Table 9.1 to start you thinking about the myths and realities of this important career option.

As you read this chapter, you will learn about the three primary sources of new venture creation: independent entrepreneurship, corporate spin-offs, and intrapreneurship. **Independent entrepreneurship** occurs when an individual establishes a new organization

TABLE 9.1

Some myths about entrepreneurs

Myth #1: Entrepreneurs are born, not made.

Reality: The making of an entrepreneur occurs by accumulating the relevant skills, know-how, experiences, and contacts over a period of years and includes large doses of self-development.

Myth #2: Anyone can start a business.

Reality: The easiest part is starting up. What is hardest is surviving, sustaining, and building a venture so its founders can realize a harvest.

Myth #3: Entrepreneurs are gamblers.

Reality: Successful entrepreneurs take very careful, calculated risks. They do not deliberately take unnecessary risk, nor do they shy away from unavoidable risk.

Myth #4: Entrepreneurs want the whole show to themselves.

Reality: Solo entrepreneurs make a living, but it is extremely difficult to grow a higher-potential venture by working single-handedly. Higher-potential entrepreneurs build a team, an organization, and a company.

Myth #5: Entrepreneurs are their own bosses and completely independent.

Reality: Entrepreneurs have to serve many masters and constituencies, including partners, investors, customers, suppliers, creditors, employees, and families. Entrepreneurs can, however, make free choices of whether, when, and what they respond to.

Myth #6: Entrepreneurs experience a great deal of stress and pay a high price.

Reality: No doubt about it: being an entrepreneur is stressful and demanding. But there is no evidence that it is any more stressful than numerous other highly demanding professional roles, and entrepreneurs find their jobs very satisfying.

Myth #7: Entrepreneurs should be young and energetic.

Reality: These qualities may help, but age is no barrier. The average age of entrepreneurs starting high-potential businesses is in the mid-30s, and many start businesses in their 60s.

Myth #8: If an entrepreneur has enough start-up capital, he or she can't miss.

Reality: The opposite is often true. Too much money often creates euphoria, lack of discipline, and impulsive spending, leading to serious problems.

Myth #9: If an entrepreneur is talented, success will happen in a year or two.

Reality: An old maxim among venture capitalists says that the lemons ripen in two and a half years, but the pearls take seven or eight. Rarely is the new business established solidly in less than three or four years.

Source: J. Timmons, *New Venture Creation* (Burr Ridge, Ill.: Richard D. Irwin, 1994), pp. 23–24.

without the benefit of corporate support. In **spin-offs,** corporate managers become entrepreneurs by creating new, independent business units with assets purchased from the corporation. **Intrapreneurs** are new venture creators working in big corporations; they are corporate entrepreneurs.[3]

In the computer industry, independent entrepreneurs founded Apple Computer and Microsoft. Data General resulted from a corporate spin-off. IBM's personal computer line emerged from an intrapreneurial effort within "Big Blue."

In this chapter, our primary emphasis will be on *growth*-oriented businesses. These companies create a disproportionate share of job and export growth. Thus, they drive a nation's economic development.

INDEPENDENT ENTREPRENEURS

Our discussion of independent entrepreneurs will answer questions about why people start their own business, what kind of business a person should start, what it takes to be successful, planning and decision making, effective strategy, and the hazards of entrepreneurship.

WHY DO PEOPLE BECOME INDEPENDENT ENTREPRENEURS?

Entrepreneurs start their own firms because of the challenge, the profit potential, and the enormous satisfaction they hope lies ahead.[4] People starting their own businesses are seeking a better quality of life than they might have at big companies. They seek independence, and a feeling of being part of the action. They feel tremendous satisfaction in building something from nothing, seeing it succeed, and watching the market embrace their ideas and products.

Limited opportunities elsewhere can inspire people to become independent entrepreneurs. People start their own companies when they see their progress blocked at big corporations. When people are laid off, they often try to start businesses of their own. And when employed people believe there is no promotion in their future, or are frustrated by bureaucracy or other features of corporate life, they may quit and become entrepreneurs.

New immigrants may find existing paths to economic success closed to them.[5] Blocked from conventional means of advancement, these newcomers turn to the alternative paths entrepreneurship provides. For example, the Cuban community in Miami has produced many entrepreneurs, as has the Vietnamese community throughout the United States.

The timing is good for starting new companies at present. According to *Fortune,* "Now is a great time to start a new venture . . . we've entered a particularly fertile era for entrepreneurism . . . [This is] an age in which nimble and often smaller organizations will perform best. In this new environment, entrepreneurs will flourish as in no time since the onset of the Industrial Age."[6]

Other factors in the environment also play a role in business formation.

Economic Conditions

Money is a critical resource for all new businesses. As the money supply and the supply of bank loans increase, a larger number of loan applicants can secure funds. The result is a rise in the rate of business formation. Conversely, as the supply of money and loans decreases, fewer aspiring business owners can find funding. The rate of business formation then declines.

Other economic factors contribute to an improved climate for business formation. Real economic growth and improved stock market performance lead to both improved prospects and increased sources of capital. In turn, the prospects and the capital increase the rate of business formation. However, the economy is a double-edged sword; the same factors have a long-term effect on business failure.[7] Under favorable conditions, many aspiring entrepreneurs find early success. However, economic cycles dictate that favorable conditions will change. To succeed, entrepreneurs must have the foresight and talent to survive when the environment becomes more hostile.

Sometimes areas with weak economies but potential for growth are overlooked by entrepreneurs. But those who understand the potential can achieve business success. The inner city is an example.

ENTREPRENEURSHIP IN THE INNER CITY

*T*oday's inner cities hold tremendous business opportunity. Retailers have fled the cities and located in the suburbs, and now the suburbs are saturated. Inner-city residents have to travel long distances for many of their shopping needs. Woolworth is one company that is capitalizing on the inner-city vacuum. It operates 450 of its 1,000 stores in minority areas and recently opened two outlets in New York City's Harlem. Another example is the Tops supermarket chain. A well-run supermarket in a low-income neighborhood faces virtually no competition.

Big opportunity can mean big risk, however. Security in crime-ridden areas is an ongoing problem. Finding skilled labor also can be difficult. Woolworth has no trouble filling sales jobs, but trained managers are harder to come by. Furthermore, capital is often difficult to find. Immigrants frequently start businesses in inner cities through informal credit sources. Korean grocers get start-up capital from revolving credit associations, and West Indians have a *sou sou*— a traditional group savings plan in which members make periodic donations and take turns receiving the whole pot.

But the right kind of banker will inject capital into inner cities. Ronald Grzywinski bought an ailing bank in a poor area of Chicago and transformed it into a comprehensive neighborhood development corporation. He lends money to entrepreneurs and developers in struggling neighborhoods, has a nonprofit business development center, and acquires or renovates 1,000 apartments a year in deteriorating neighborhoods. Small developers follow—without the need for public subsidies.

James Rouse is a for-profit developer who is revitalizing a blighted area in Baltimore. He organized the neighborhood into task forces to tackle issues of education, crime, family support, community spirit, and health care. He sees the plight of the central cities as a severe threat to our civilization, and feels that if the dreadful conditions are not changed our country will not be able to compete economically and our standard of living will drop precipitously. People who don't live in the inner cities don't know the extent of the threat; the cost of these conditions, according to Mr. Rouse, is about $750 billion a year. Mr. Rouse wants to show that it is both possible and economical to alleviate the conditions of poverty.

Fortune calls these people and others like them social entrepreneurs. They pursue social objectives through private enterprise practices that earn money, create jobs, and save tax dollars.

Sources: M. Alpert, "The Ghetto's Hidden Wealth," *Fortune,* July 29, 1991, pp. 167–74; and J. Huey, "Finding New Heros for a New Era," *Fortune,* January 25, 1993, pp. 62–69. ●

WHAT BUSINESS SHOULD YOU START?

Technology and marketing are two areas particularly good for spawning new enterprises.[8] And often, people set themselves up as consultants to other businesses. But whether a business idea is viable is not so much a function of what industry it's in as much as it is a function of (1) your capabilities and desires and (2) the quality of the opportunity.

Your Capabilities and Desires

Your capabilities include technical competence, business competence, contacts who can help, and resources like capital, time, and commitment. You are more likely to commit, and therefore succeed, if you truly love your idea and love working to make it happen. You also must be willing and able to *take action.* Those who sit back hoping for the perfect idea, or fretting about risks, will never act and therefore never succeed as entrepreneurs.

Opportunities

Entrepreneurs spot opportunities in a variety of ways.[9] For starters, it is useful to *always be on the lookout.* Talk to consumers, business associates, and technical people. Monitor and evaluate products currently on the market. Think about how current needs can be filled in new ways, and how current products can be improved.

Think carefully about events and trends as they unfold. Consider, for example:[10]

- *Technological discoveries.* Start-ups in biotechnology, microcomputers, and electronics followed.

- *Demographic changes.* Medical and nursing organizations have sprung up to serve an aging population.

- *Lifestyle and taste changes.* Start-ups have capitalized on new clothing trends, desire for fast food, and public interest in sports.

- *Economic dislocations,* such as booms or failures. The oil boycott spawned new drilling firms. Steel industry collapse was accompanied by mini-mill start-ups.

- *Calamaties* such as wars and natural disasters. Henry Kaiser's business expanded to shipbuilding in World War II. Mt. St. Helen's eruption spawned new tourism companies.

- *Rule changes by government.* Environmental legislation created opportunities for new consulting firms and cleanup machinery firms. The Small Business Innovation Research Program underwrote new product innovation firms. Deregulation spawned new airlines and trucking companies.

- *Resource discoveries.* North Slope oil production spawned new construction firms in Alaska. When the price of gold rose, new companies in Colorado and Nevada started to reprocess the tailings of old mines.

There also exists a useful role for trial and error. Some entrepreneurs start their enterprises and then let the market announce whether it likes their ideas or not. This is risky, of course, and should be done only if you can afford the risks. But even if the original idea doesn't work, you may be able to capitalize on the *side street effect:*[11] As you head down a road, wondering where it will lead, you come to unknown places, and unexpected opportunities begin to appear.

And, while you are looking, *prepare* so you are able to act quickly and effectively on the opportunity when it does present itself.

WHAT DOES IT TAKE TO BE SUCCESSFUL?

Successful entrepreneurs exhibit the following characteristics:[12]

1. *Commitment and determination:* They are decisive, tenacious, disciplined, willing to sacrifice, and able to immerse themselves totally in their enterprises.

Trial and error is also known as the side street effect where, like Dorothy in *The Wizard of Oz,* you head down a road and the unexpected begins to appear.

(MGM/Courtesy Kobal)

2. *Leadership:* They are self-starters, team builders, superior learners, and teachers.
3. *Opportunity obsession:* They have an intimate knowledge of customers' needs, are market driven, and are obsessed with value creation and enhancement.
4. *Tolerance of risk, ambiguity, and uncertainty:* They are calculated risk takers, risk minimizers, tolerant of stress, and able to resolve problems.
5. *Creativity, self-reliance, and ability to adapt:* They are open-minded, restless with the status quo, able to learn quickly, highly adaptable, creative, skilled at conceptualizing, and attentive to details.
6. *Motivation to excel:* They have a clear results orientation, set high but realistic goals, have a strong drive to achieve, know their own weaknesses and strengths, and focus on what can be done rather than on the reasons things can't be done.

If you see yourself in these descriptions, you have attitudes and behavior that will help you be a successful entrepreneur. If you do not fit the description, it does not mean you should give up all dreams of becoming an entrepreneur. But it does suggest that you carefully assess yourself in these terms, and then take steps to become more decisive, to learn to be a better leader, to think about market opportunity and value creation, to become more self-reliant, to strive for excellence, or to develop other useful attitudes and behaviors.

PLANNING

So, you think you have spotted a business opportunity. Now what? Should you act on your idea? Where should you begin?

Your excitement and intuition may convince you that you are on to something. But they might not convince anyone else. You will need more thorough planning and analysis. This will help convince other people to get on board, and help you avoid costly mistakes.

The first formal planning step is to do an opportunity analysis. An **opportunity analysis** includes a description of the product or service, an assessment of the opportunity, an assessment of the entrepreneur (you), a specification of activities and resources needed to translate your idea into a viable business, and your source(s) of capital.[13] Table 9.2 shows the questions you should answer in an opportunity analysis.

The opportunity analysis, or opportunity assessment plan, focuses on the opportunity, not the entire venture. It provides the basis for making a decision on whether to act. It is the **business plan** that describes all the elements involved in starting the new venture.[14]

TABLE 9.2

Opportunity analysis

What market need does my idea fill?

What personal observation have I experienced or recorded with regard to that market need?

What social condition underlies this market need?

What market research data can be marshaled to describe this market need?

What patents might be available to fulfill this need?

What competition exists in this market? How would I describe the behavior of this competition?

What does the international market look like?

What does the international competition look like?

Where is the money to be made in this activity?

Source: R. Hisrich and M. Peters, *Entrepreneurship: Starting, Developing, and Managing a New Enterprise* (Burr Ridge, Ill.: Richard D. Irwin, 1995), p. 33.

The business plan describes the venture and its market, strategies, and future directions. It often includes functional plans including marketing, finance, manufacturing, and human resources.

Table 9.3 shows an outline for a typical business plan. The business plan (1) helps determine the viability of your enterprise; (2) guides you as you plan and organize; and (3) helps you obtain financing. It is read by potential investors, suppliers, customers, and others. Get help in writing up a sound plan!

CRITICAL RESOURCES

In a small business, the key resources are financial and nonfinancial resources such as the entrepreneur's time and the people who work for the company.

TABLE 9.3

Outline of a business plan

I. Introductory Page
   A. Name and address of business
   B. Name(s) and address(es) of principals
   C. Nature of business
   D. Statement of financing needed
   E. Statement of confidentiality of report

II. Executive Summary—Three to four pages summarizing the complete business plan

III. Industry Analysis
   A. Future outlook and trends
   B. Analysis of competitors
   C. Market segmentation
   D. Industry forecasts

IV. Description of Venture
   A. Product(s)
   B. Service(s)
   C. Size of business
   D. Office equipment and personnel
   E. Background of entrepreneurs

V. Production Plan
   A. Manufacturing process (amount subcontracted)
   B. Physical plant
   C. Machinery and equipment
   D. Names of suppliers of raw materials

VI. Marketing Plan
   A. Pricing
   B. Distribution
   C. Promotion
   D. Product forecasts
   E. Controls

VII. Organizational Plan
   A. Form of ownership
   B. Identification of partners or principal shareholders
   C. Authority of principals
   D. Management-team background
   E. Roles and responsibilities of members of organization

VIII. Assessment of Risk
   A. Evaluate weakness of business
   B. New technologies
   C. Contingency plans

IX. Financial Plan
   A. Pro forma income statement
   B. Cash flow projections
   C. Pro forma balance sheet
   D. Break-even analysis
   E. Sources and applications of funds

X. Appendix (contains backup material)
   A. Letters
   B. Market research data
   C. Leases or contracts
   D. Price lists from suppliers

Source: R. Hisrich and M. Peters, *Entrepreneurship: Starting, Developing, and Managing a New Enterprise* (Burr Ridge, Ill.: Richard D. Irwin, 1994).

Financial Resources

Many unsuccessful entrepreneurs blame their failure on inadequate financial resources. Yet failure due to a lack of financial resources indicates *either* a real lack of money *or* the failure to properly use the resources available. Entrepreneurs who fail to use their resources wisely usually make one of two mistakes: They apply financial resources to the wrong uses, or they maintain inadequate control over their resources.

One aspiring entrepreneur borrowed $100,000 and used $25,000 of that money to buy a dating service. He then used the remaining $75,000 to buy radio advertising for the business. A few months later, bankrupt and bitter, he blamed his failure on a lack of financial resources. But a more objective view might reveal that he did not use his resources wisely. In this case, he should not have spent $25,000 to purchase the business; he could have entered the business at a lower cost by starting his own operation. In addition, he should not have spent $75,000 on advertising without specific knowledge about how that advertising would affect his business. This entrepreneur failed because he applied his financial resources to the wrong uses.

Even when financial resources are applied correctly, improper control of money can cause business failures. One common entrepreneurial malady is an aversion to record-keeping. Expenses mount, but records do not keep pace. Pricing decisions are based on intuition without adequate reference to costs. As a result, the company earns inadequate margins to support growth. With accurate records, the entrepreneur could identify those areas where costs could be cut or prices increased. Without them, the entrepreneur can only guess. Guesses are nearly always inaccurate, and when made too often they guarantee failure.

Nonfinancial Resources

Nonfinancial resources also are crucial to the success of a new business. Well-planned management of time and people allows the new enterprise to counteract the advantages large organizations enjoy. The entrepreneur can realize efficiencies by using a network composed of suppliers and customers. For example, entrepreneurs often delegate work to a network of subcontractors. The subcontractors work only part-time for the entrepreneurs, but as full-time specialists at their jobs, they give the entrepreneur some of the advantages of specialization.[15]

The top management team is another crucial resource. The board of directors improves the company's image, develops longer-term plans for expansion, supports day-to-day activities, and develops a network of information sources. Michael Dell, founder of Dell Computer at age 19, knows the importance of surrounding himself with talent. He hires managers who are far more experienced than he, and prominent and powerful board members. In 1995, at age 30, Michael Dell held the longest tenure of any chief executive in the industry.[16]

Anita Brattina thought after two or three years of running her own marketing firm she would have lots of cash, no debt, and time to enjoy her independence.[17] Eight years later, she still worked 50 to 60 hours a week and was not making much money. So, she got an advisory board. They taught her how to do cash-flow analysis, suggested some strategic changes, and encouraged her to cultivate relationships with a banker, an accountant, and an attorney. In addition, they helped her interview salespeople, develop a long-term marketing strategy, and reorganize operations. They also vetoed a number of her ideas. Sales are now up, after one year of listening to the board and implementing its ideas. She is confident that she is well on her way to the coveted goal of $1 million in sales.

Often, two people go into business together as partners. Traditionally, partners are family members or friends. Nowadays, partnerships form between people from among the millions laid off, who meet each other and discover they have common interests and complementary skills. Partners can help one another access capital, spread the workload, share the risk, and furnish expertise.

INCOMPATIBLE PARTNERS

*D*espite the potential advantages of finding a compatible partner, partnerships are not always marriages made in heaven.

- One partner in a plastics fabricator learned that his partners scheduled business meetings without telling him, took customers to lunch and didn't invite him, hired assistants for themselves but not for him, and finally forced him out. "If people's moral intentions are no good, the best legal document in the world is hooey," he says.

- "Mark" talked three of his friends into joining him in starting his own telecommunications company because he didn't want to try it alone. He learned quickly that while he wanted to put money into growing the business, his three partners wanted the company to pay for their cars and meetings in the Bahamas. The company collapsed. "I never thought a business relationship could overpower friendship, but this one did. Where money's involved, people change."

- An insurance broker, a lawyer, and a contractor bought a small mall. Only the insurance broker found the time to make decisions and take action; the others "just couldn't get to it." But they did find time to complain about everything the broker did. The broker quit in disgust.

To be successful, partners need to acknowledge one another's talents, let each other do what they do best, communicate honestly, and listen to one another. And they must learn to trust each other by making and keeping agreements. If they must break an agreement, it is crucial that they give early notice and clean up after their own mistakes.

Source: R. A. Mamis, "Partner Wars," *Inc.*, June 1994, pp. 36–44. ●

COMPETITIVE ADVANTAGE AND BUSINESS STRATEGY

One theme guides entrepreneurs as they balance critical resources and blend organizational elements: the search (and struggle) for competitive advantage. If the organization gains advantage, the business will survive. If that advantage is distinctive, the organization will thrive.

In Chapter 5, you learned about two approaches to building competitive advantage: a differentiation strategy and a low-cost strategy. As you recall, a company that uses a *differentiation strategy* competes on the basis of its ability to do things differently from its major competitors. Ray Kroc differentiated McDonald's Corporation from its original competition through his emphasis on burgers and fries, and Steven Jobs differentiated Apple Computer from major competition by emphasizing that the Apple is fun to use. An organization that uses a *low-cost strategy* attempts to provide a good or service at the lowest possible cost. Dell Computer Corporation uses a high-quality, low-cost strategy. While competitors criticize Michael Dell for not furthering innovation, he seems to have found just the right mix of service and price for his customers.[18]

Entrepreneurs as well as large corporations can use these strategies to gain competitive advantage. Entrepreneurs frequently use a third approach: a niche strategy.[19] Competitors that use **niche strategies** are specialists. They serve a narrow market segment that may be local, national, or international. A company might gain a market by serving only one narrow segment of a market. Niche strategists build special skills that are uniquely matched to a specific market; they are rewarded with high profit margins. Many of the country's budding biotechnology companies are playing in niche markets while they stabilize their operations and build a base from which to expand.

Companies with a single competitive advantage seldom prosper if they wander from their expertise. For example, Triangle Industries built a reputation for producing custom-built special-application packages (a niche strategy). Triangle designed special packaging to move sophisticated astronaut suits from its Connecticut manufacturing site to the Florida launching pad. The business was profitable but had a low sales volume. A national company offered the entrepreneur a contract to package thousands of toasters (a cost strategy). Faced with the opportunity for more volume, the entrepreneur accepted the contract. However, his organization could not change its stripes. His designers, accustomed to specialty work, were unable to design an inexpensive package, and his workers, all strong team performers, could not work in a mass production mode. In the end, the entrepreneur had to hire new labor and pay supervisors overtime. Therefore, his costs exceeded his revenue. For Triangle Industries, the niche strategy worked; leaving its niche was a strategic error.

Successful strategies do not require a cutting-edge technology or a unique new product. Even companies offering the most mundane products can gain competitive advantage by doing basic things differently from and better than competitors, as the following examples show.

MASTERS OF THE ORDINARY

*E*very year, *Inc.* magazine publishes its list of the 500 fastest-growing companies in the United States. As you might guess, many companies on the list are high-tech enterprises. But the list also includes a baker, a candlemaker, a plumber, an antiques gallery, and an exterminator.

These are not hot growth industries. But they are industries. And knowing a lot about business and management, in any industry, provides a competitive edge. So your company can grow, even if your industry is not growing.

Larry Harmon of Demar Plumbing, Heating & Air-Conditioning strives to do business like Mary Kay, Walt Disney, Nordstrom's, and Federal Express. The way he sees it, people are not too enamored of plumbing—but would love a plumber who provides world-class customer service. He gives same-day service, trains his staff in customer relations, and makes his customers want to come back to him year after year.

Jim Jeffrey of Pest Control Technologies creates a professional image with white trucks and white uniforms for his employees, while his competitors work in blue jeans and T-shirts. Bear Barnes, a house painter, offers two-year guarantees and maintains a detailed database to target his market, track bids, and record every shade of paint on every house his company services.

In other words, many of the *Inc.* 500 are masters of the ordinary. They are in ordinary, dull (on the face of it) businesses, but they manage them extraordinarily well compared to their competitors.

Source: A. Murphy, "*Inc.* 500 Masters of the Ordinary," *Inc.,* October 1993, pp. 70–71. ●

ENTREPRENEURIAL HAZARDS

The hazards of striking out on your own are many. First, you may start your own company and find out that you don't enjoy it. One person who quit a large company to start his own small one stated, "As an executive in a large company, the issues are strategic. You're implementing programs that affect thousands of people. In a small business the issues are less complex . . . you worry about inventory every day, because you may not be in business next week if you have negative cash flow." His most unpleasant surprise: "How much you have to sell. You're always out selling . . . I didn't want to be a salesman. I wanted to be an executive."[20]

And survival is difficult. As *Fortune* put it, "Misjudgments are punished ruthlessly. When competition gets tougher, small businesses feel it first. Financing is hard to find, sometimes impossible . . . 'In small business there are no small mistakes'—it's a phrase that comes up time and again when you talk to the owners."[21] But, says *Fortune,* most are proud of this description of entrepreneurial hazards.

Many entrepreneurs fail when economic conditions change. The causes of failure may include (1) poor management; (2) an inadequate business plan; (3) unclear goals;

(4) ineffective sales strategies; (5) overdependence on a single customer; (6) undercapitalization; (7) lack of teamwork; or (8) failure to obtain sound business advice.[22]

Failure can be devastating. "I remember thinking I was very comfortable financially, and the crystal chandelier hit the floor . . . I remember trying to find enough money to buy groceries. You never forget that."[23] So stated David Pomije, CEO and founder of Funco, a chain that buys and resells used and new Nintendo and Sega videogames. Fortunately, he has turned the corner; he now operates over 100 stores with sales of $50 million.

Failure can be traced to several hazards; the most common are mortality, the inability to delegate, and poor planning and controls.

Mortality

One long-term measure of an entrepreneur's success is the fate of the venture after the founder's death. The organization can outlive the entrepreneur under one of two conditions: (1) if the entrepreneur has gone public, or (2) if the entrepreneur has planned an orderly family succession. Both conditions are relatively rare.

Entrepreneurs often fail to seek public capital because equity capital is scarce and expensive or because they want to maintain control. One entrepreneur's comment suggests how important the business is to a founder: "The satisfaction of starting and operating a successful business is one of life's most rewarding experiences, and the loss or sale of an enterprise can be a fate worse than death."[24] An entrepreneur who is funded with public equity risks losing the business if stockholders are not satisfied. To avoid this risk, the entrepreneur maintains private control over the business. But founding entrepreneurs often fail to plan for succession. When death occurs, estate tax problems and/or the lack of a skilled replacement for the founder can lead to business failure.

Management guru Peter Drucker offers the following advice to help family-managed businesses survive and prosper:[25] Family members working in the business must be at least as capable and hard-working as other employees; at least one key position should be filled by a nonfamily member; and someone outside the family and the business should help plan succession. Family members who are mediocre performers are resented by others; outsiders can be more objective and contribute expertise the family might not have; and issues of management succession are often the most difficult of all, causing serious conflict and possible breakup of the firm.

Inadequate Delegation

Although mortality contributes to some new venture failures, the founder's death usually cannot be blamed. Most new businesses collapse before their owners do. In these cases, the cause of the demise often can be traced to the entrepreneur's desire to personally control every aspect of the business.

Just as entrepreneurs resist loss of control of the company to either public investors or heirs, they often hesitate to delegate work to people within the business. This managerial flaw is not unique to the entrepreneurial company, but it is a critical problem. The entrepreneur's desire for control fosters a climate in which managers and workers depend too heavily on the entrepreneur's decisions. When this happens, opportunities are lost and the employees (and the organization) fail to develop. Once the organization reaches a certain size, the entrepreneur's attempt to exert personal control becomes dysfunctional. The company's competitive advantage may be lost, and the company ultimately may fail.

Poor Planning and Controls

Entrepreneurs, in part because they are very busy, often fail to use formal planning and control systems. Planning takes time from activities that entrepreneurs may find more enjoyable, such as selling, producing, and buying. Unfortunately, many entrepreneurs fail because they don't anticipate predictable problems such as cash flow shortages and the loss of key customers. Such entrepreneurs learn too late that prevention is the best cure.

In part because they don't plan, many entrepreneurs fail to develop adequate controls over the resources they manage. Common problems include excessive inventories and excessive receivables. The initial growth of a business can mask problems if controls are not developed. If expenses grow more quickly than sales, the entrepreneur will encounter problems. Blinded by the light of growing sales, many entrepreneurs fail to maintain vigilance over other aspects of the business. In the absence of controls, the business veers out of control. Because these hazards are so critical, pay close attention to the more detailed discussions of delegation in Chapter 10 and control systems in Chapter 19.

ENTREPRENEUR'S CREED

When asked what are the most critical concepts and skills for running a business, here's what entrepreneurs have to say. When the statements are considered together, they might be considered a creed.

- Do what gives you energy—have fun.
- Figure out how to make it work.
- Say "can do" rather than "cannot" or "maybe."
- Tenacity and creativity will triumph.
- Be dissatisfied with the way things are—and look for improvement.
- Do things differently.
- Make opportunity and results—not money—your obsession.
- Take pride in your accomplishments—it's contagious.
- Sweat the details that are critical to success.
- Play for the long haul—it is rarely possible to get rich quickly.

Source: Abridged from J. Timmons, *New Venture Creation* (Burr Ridge, Ill.: Richard D. Irwin, 1994), p. 202. ●

SPIN-OFFS

The independent entrepreneur is the initiating agent of the new business, but many established organizations also play an important role in new venture creation. These organizations give most entrepreneurs their initial professional experience and contacts.[26] In some cases, aspiring entrepreneurs remain with their employers and act as intrapreneurs. But often, the entrepreneurs leave their employers and become owners of a *spin-off*—a division of a company that splits from its parent company to become an independent company that offers a product similar to those of the owners' former employers.

WHY SPIN-OFFS OCCUR

Spin-offs occur frequently and may take place with the original employer's approval. The approved spin-off occurs when the established company senses an opportunity but does not pursue the opportunity with internal resources. However, the company recognizes that it might still profit from the idea by selling the patents to a new entity or by investing in a new enterprise.

Employer approval is not necessary to create a spin-off. Often spin-offs occur when entrepreneurs disagree with their former employers. An entrepreneur may sense an opportunity that the employer considers unprofitable. Or both the entrepreneur and the employer may see an opportunity for gain, but the employer has other attractive opportunities.

Stories abound about the flight of the entrepreneur from the stifling handcuffs of the corporation. Thomas Watson left National Cash Register to become the founder of IBM. Ross Perot quit IBM to start EDS. And there are countless success stories of people whose names you've never heard.

Often, spin-offs occur when employees feel stifled by the corporate environment. Thomas Watson (left) and Ross Perot are two well-known examples of people who quit jobs and became immensely successful founders of new companies.

(Courtesy International Business Machines Corporation)

THE SPIN-OFF PROCESS

Figure 9.1 summarizes the stages of the spin-off process. Factors such as the stage of the product life cycle and the type of industry contribute to the frequency of spin-offs. The entrepreneur's ability to attract capital and build a team determines the ultimate destiny of the new venture. If the spin-off successfully wards off competition, both the company's survival and the entrepreneur's wealth are ensured.

Early Stage

Spin-offs occur most often at the early stages of the product life cycle. When an industry is first formed, real demand often outstrips supply, promising excellent opportunities. At the same time, the absence of product standards provides the opportunity for a variety of competitive approaches to the market.

The computer industry offers many examples of spin-off activity in a new industry. Amdahl was created by an IBM executive. Data General grew out of Digital Equipment Corporation. Countless software companies spun off from the major hardware producers and their customers. Route 128 in Massachusetts and Silicon Valley in California had exponential growth as one company grew into two, two branched into four or more, and so on.

FIGURE 9.1

Stages of the spin-off process

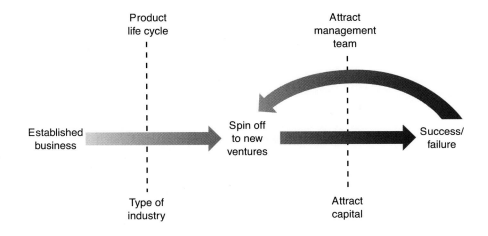

Industry Types

New industries are not the only source of spin-offs. Mature industries that are fragmented or undergoing change and declining industries also generate significant spin-off activity.

A *fragmented industry* has few barriers to entry and therefore has many competitors. Such an industry offers great opportunity for spin-offs. In the restaurant industry, for example, a talented chef can make more money by owning a bistro than by working for another owner. Thus, good restaurants—and stores, consulting firms, travel agencies, and so on—often spin off new competitors.

In a *mature industry* undergoing change, new competitors may have an advantage over established competitors. For example, the cable industry is mature. Established cable companies were slow to respond to the demands of networked computers. Cabletron, a new company, was started by two entrepreneurs (one a sales representative for an established company) to provide cables for computer networks. In a few years, the company became a dominant producer.[27]

A different logic explains spin-offs in *declining industries.* Established organizations, frustrated by stagnant conditions in their industry, often seek opportunity in newer industries. A company can fund new opportunities by selling its older businesses. The original companies encourage management or employees to purchase aging plants through employee stock ownership plans (ESOPs). Unburdened by corporate overhead and neglect, the new owners are able to revitalize the business while the former owners invest the funds from the buyout elsewhere.

Regardless of the situation, the spin-off entrepreneur faces key challenges. Specifically, the entrepreneur needs to build a management team and raise sufficient amounts of capital.

Attracting Management Teams and Capital

Unlike the entrepreneur of classical folklore, today's entrepreneur who is involved in a spin-off usually is a highly educated professional. Many spin-off entrepreneurs have undergraduate or graduate training in science. But as a specialist, the entrepreneur in the spin-off has limited knowledge of some business functions. Moreover, the entrepreneur's time usually is spent pursuing his or her specialty. Therefore, the entrepreneur must build a strong management team.

Consider the two research biologists who helped form Electro-Biology, Inc. They discovered a new method for healing bone fractures by using electronic processes. Although each was a highly skilled researcher, neither had a working knowledge of finance, marketing, and medical law. However, they quickly recognized their weaknesses and found specialists to supervise each area. The company prospered, while the biologists returned to the lab to search for new (and better) products.

The search for capital is the greatest challenge for spin-off owners. For company-sponsored spin-offs, favorable purchase terms and long-term loans provide some of this capital. But like managers in all ventures, spin-off managers need to be creative in their pursuit and use of capital. Although the company was not a spin-off, Performance Inc.'s owner Garry Snook provides an excellent example of the creative use of capital. Snook minimized his need for capital by convincing a supplier to rent him unused factory space. Similarly, he lowered the cost of retail space by renting ski equipment supply stores during their off season.

Once the entrepreneur builds a management team and obtains capital, the spin-off faces the hazards of competition and change. Just as the entrepreneur sensed opportunity, so will other potential entrepreneurs establish spin-offs and become competitors.

CHANGE IN INDUSTRY STRUCTURE

A change in industry structure may be the most critical hazard for the spin-off businesses. While this change is most likely to arise in the early stages of an industry's evolution, it can occur at any time. During its early stages, the industry has a wide variety of product types, production methods, and distribution methods. As the personal computer industry developed, some companies offered stand-alone units, while others offered modular units. Various companies offered different software packages. In the production area, some companies produced the majority of their components, while others assembled purchased goods. In the marketing area, companies sold through catalogs, established their own retail outlets, sold through specialty stores, or sold through department stores. Department stores sold the machines as toys, electronic goods, or business machines. Confusion reigned!

However, a pattern emerged from the chaos. The modular unit became the market leader and was distributed primarily through retail specialists. PC-DOS captured the operating system market, and a narrow band of software applications became the standard fare for initial sales. This emerging pattern changed the structure of the industry. Competitors that initially chose a different product design, a different software system, or a different distribution network faced a competitive disadvantage. Those companies could only change, or fail. Changes in industry structure are common hazards in entrepreneurial environments, and the spin-off entrepreneur should be prepared to face them.

INTRAPRENEURSHIP

Established corporations have observed with interest the rise in entrepreneurial activity. Some of these companies are looking for new sources of growth. Thus, today's large corporations are more than passive bystanders in the entrepreneurial explosion. For example, even established companies try to find new and profitable ideas. Table 9.4 provides some help in deciding which new ideas are worth pursuing.

BUILDING SUPPORT FOR YOUR IDEA

A manager who has a new idea to capitalize on a market opportunity or an innovative solution to a problem will need to get others in the organization to buy in or sign on. In other words, the manager needs to build an informal network of allies who support and will help the manager implement the idea.

If you need to build support for a project idea, the first step involves *clearing the investment* with your immediate boss or bosses.[28] At this stage, you explain the idea and seek approval to look for wider support.

Higher executives often want evidence that the project is backed by your peers before committing to it. This involves *making cheerleaders*—people who will support the manager before formal approval from higher levels. Managers at General Electric refer to this strategy as "loading the gun"—lining up ammunition.

Next, *horse trading* begins. You can offer promises of payoffs from the project in return for support, time, money, and other resources that peers and others contribute.

Finally, you should *get the blessing* of relevant higher-level officials. This usually involves a formal presentation. The more specific the request, the easier it is to get support. You will also need to guarantee the project's technical and political feasibility. Higher management's endorsement of the project and promises of resources help convert potential supporters into a solid team. At this point, you can go back to your boss and make specific plans for going ahead with the project.

Along the way, expect resistance and frustration—and use passion and persistence to persuade others to get on board.[29]

BUILDING INTRAPRENEURSHIP

Can corporations foster intrapreneurship? If so, how? Two common approaches used to stimulate intrapreneurial activity are skunkworks and bootlegging. **Skunkworks** refers to project teams designated to produce a new product. A team is formed with a specific goal within a specified time frame. A respected person is chosen to be manager of the skunkworks. In this approach to corporate innovation, risk takers are not punished for taking risks because their jobs are held for them. The risk takers also have the opportunity to earn large rewards.

Bootlegging refers to informal efforts on the part of managers and workers to create new products and new processes. "Informal" can mean "secretive," such as when a bootlegger

TABLE 9.4

Checklist for
choosing ideas

Fit with your skills and experience

Do you believe in the product or service?

Does the need it fits mean something to you personally?

Do you like and understand the potential customers?

Do you have experience in this type of business?

Do the basic success factors of this business fit your skills?

Are the tasks of the enterprise ones you could enjoy doing yourself?

Are the people the enterprise will employ ones you will enjoy working with and supervising?

Has the idea begun to take over your imagination and spare time?

Fit with the market

Is there a real customer need?

Can you get a price that gives you good margins?

Would customers believe in the product coming from your company?

Does the product or service you propose produce a clearly perceivable customer benefit that is significantly better than that offered by competing ways to satisfy the same basic need?

Is there a cost-effective way to get the message and the product to the customers?

Fit with the company

Is there a reason to believe your company could be very good at the business?

Does it fit the company culture?

Does it look profitable (high margin/low investment)?

Will it lead to larger markets and growth?

What to do when your idea is rejected

As an intrapreneur, you will frequently find that your idea has been rejected. There are a few things you can do.

1. Give up and select a new idea.

2. Listen carefully, understand what is wrong, improve your idea and your presentation, and try again.

3. Find someone else to whom you can present your idea by considering:
    a. Who will benefit most if it works? Can they be a sponsor?
    b. Who are potential customers? Will they demand the product?
    c. How can you get to the people who really care about intrapreneurial ideas?

Source: G. Pinchot, *Intrapreneuring* (New York: Harper & Row, 1985).

believes the company will frown on these activities. But the intrapreneurial organization should tolerate and even encourage bootlegging.

Innovation

Decentralization, which you will read more about in Chapter 10, is another way to encourage intrapreneurship. Although decentralization is not an attractive option for all companies, the decentralized company is a natural laboratory for new ideas. The decentralized company, in which individuals and units have a high degree of autonomy and discretion, can allocate capital to fund new ideas. The internal capital allocation process mimics the private venture capital market. Ideas compete in an open arena for capital funding. The competition fuels the engines of innovation.

ORGANIZING NEW CORPORATE VENTURES

Innovation

For large-scale innovation, strategic alliances, or cooperation among different organizations, can be a useful route. By engaging in joint efforts, organizations can minimize their investment and risk. You will learn more about strategic alliances in Chapter 11.

However, innovation often takes place on a small scale. Aspiring intrapreneurs need access to small amounts of capital. At Teleflex, intrapreneurs can apply for grants of $1,000 to $200,000. At Kodak, innovation offices located throughout the company help intrapreneurs find sponsors within the organization. Also committees will provide seed money for new ideas.[30]

Technical assistance can be as valuable to the intrapreneur as money. In recognition of this fact, Raytheon maintains a new-products center (NPC). The job of an NPC is to develop products for internal clients. Scientists in the NPC work for a variety of internal clients, providing a cross-fertilization of ideas among divisions. The flow of product ideas goes both ways: Clients ask the NPC to develop certain products, while the NPC advises its internal clients about opportunities they might miss.

The encouragement of intrapreneurship gives these large companies two advantages. First, their policies encourage aspiring entrepreneurs within the company to pursue their ideas. Second, they help the companies attract people interested in intrapreneurial pursuits. Companies that institutionalize innovation are, like great Broadway musicals, assured a long run. Innovation is so important to an organization—and so central to the process of change—that an entire chapter (Chapter 20) is devoted to it in Part V of the text.

HAZARDS IN INTRAPRENEURSHIP

Organizations that encourage intrapreneurship face an obvious risk: The effort can fail. One author noted, "There is considerable history of internal venture development by large firms, and it does not encourage optimism."[31] However, this risk can be managed. In fact, failing to foster intrapreneurship may represent a subtler but greater risk than encouraging it. The organization that resists intrapreneurial initiative may lose its ability to adapt when conditions dictate change.

The most dangerous risk in intrapreneurship is the risk of overreliance on a single project. Many companies fail while awaiting the completion of one large, innovative project.[32] The successful intrapreneurial organization avoids overcommitment to a single project and relies on its entrepreneurial spirit to produce at least one winner from among several projects.

Organizations also court failure when they spread their intrapreneurial efforts over too many projects.[33] If there are many intrapreneurial projects, all their efforts may be too small in scale. Managers will consider the projects unattractive because of their small size. At the least, those recruited to manage the projects may have difficulty building power and status within the organization.

The hazards in intrapreneurship, then, are related to scale. One large project is a threat, as are too many underfunded projects. But a carefully managed approach to this strategically important process will upgrade an organization's chances for long-term survival.

KEY TERMS

SUMMARY OF LEARNING OBJECTIVES

Now that you have studied Chapter 9, you should know:

The activities of entrepreneurship.

Entrepreneurship is the act of forming a new organization. The independent entrepreneur is the individual who establishes a new organization. Spin-offs are businesses founded by innovators who leave their organizations to start firms producing and selling similar products. Intrapreneurs are new venture creators who work within the boundaries of their established companies.

In recent years, both small and large organizations have been involved in the creation of new ventures. Environmental factors, such as the economy, create or close off start-up opportunities, and play a role in the success or failure of the new venture.

How to find and evaluate ideas for new business ventures.

You should always be on the lookout for new ideas, talking to other people and monitoring current products and the business environment. Trial and error and preparation play important roles. Ideas should be carefully assessed via opportunity analysis and a thorough business plan.

What it takes to be a successful entrepreneur.

Successful entrepreneurs are determined, effective leaders; obsessed with the opportunity; tolerant of risk, ambiguity, and uncertainty; creative; self-reliant; adaptable; and motivated to excel.

The important management skills, resources, and strategies needed to avoid failure and achieve success.

Successful entrepreneurs also understand how to plan their new venture, obtain financial resources, and develop a network of other people including suppliers, customers, partners, and boards of directors. They use a low-cost, differentiating strategy, or niche strategy that sets them apart from their competitors. Through effective use of their skills, resources, and appropriate strategy, they avoid major causes of failure including poor financial controls, inadequate delegation, and failure to plan for succession.

The process of spinning off new ventures.

A spin-off occurs when an employee with a new-product idea quits his or her employer and starts an independent business offering a product similar to those of the former parent company. Typically spin-offs occur in new industries, but they are also found in mature or declining industries that are fragmented or undergoing change. To be successful, the spin-off must attract a strong management team and adapt to changes in the structure of the industry.

How to foster intrapreneurship in large corporations.

Intrapreneurs work within established companies to develop new goods or services that allow the corporation to reap the benefits of innovation. To facilitate intrapreneurship, organizations use skunkworks—project teams designated to develop a new product—and allow bootlegging—informal efforts by managers and employees to create new products and processes. Businesses also may work together through strategic alliances to create new ventures. Whatever the approach, the organization must select its projects carefully and fund them appropriately.

DISCUSSION QUESTIONS

1. What is your level of personal interest in becoming an independent entrepreneur? Why did you rate yourself as you did?
2. How would you assess your *capability* of being a successful entrepreneur? What are your strengths and weaknesses? How would you increase your capability?
3. Brainstorm a list of ideas for new business ventures. Where did the ideas come from? Which ones are most and least viable, and why?
4. Identify some businesses that have recently opened in your area. What are their chances of survival, and why? How would you advise the owners or managers of those businesses to enhance their success?
5. Assume you are writing a story about what it's *really* like to be an entrepreneur. To whom would you talk, and what questions would you ask?
6. Conduct interviews with two entrepreneurs, asking whatever questions most interest you. Share your findings with the class. How do the interviews differ from one another, and what do they have in common?
7. Read Table 9.1, some myths about entrepreneurs. Which myths did you believe? Do you still? Why or why not? Interview two entrepreneurs by asking each myth as a true-or-false question. What did they say? What do you conclude from their answers?
8. With your classmates, form small teams of skunkworks. Your charge is to identify an innovation that you think would benefit your school, college, or university, and to outline an action plan for bringing your idea to reality.
9. Identify some bootlegging activities in which you have engaged or you have seen others engage. What resulted from the activities? Were the efforts successful? Why or why not?
10. Identify a business that recently folded. What were the causes of the failure? What could have been done differently to prevent the failure?

CONCLUDING CASE

AMERICA ONLINE

Stephen M. Case was a consumer marketer for PepsiCo Inc. in 1982. When he discovered online services that year, he naturally wanted something user-friendly.

That's not what he found.

Case believed online services had a huge potential market if they simply could be easier to use, so in 1985 he cofounded America Online. His marketing strategy was the pursuit of niches instead of the mass approach used by competitors such as Prodigy, the joint venture of IBM and Sears, Roebuck.

"The others are like *Time* magazine or *USA Today*," he said. "We see ourselves as a series of specialized magazines catering to specific interests."

America Online became profitable within two years of start-up. It reached 180,000 subscribers by mid-1992, and by the end of 1994, the company was claiming 1.25 million subscribers.

Despite its astonishing growth, entrepreneurial thinking has remained with the company.

In November 1994, America Online announced a competition allowing entrepreneurs to apply for The AOL Greenhouse, an initiative giving them a chance to launch their business ideas using the online service, the Internet, and other interactive media.

"Entrepreneurs are often the most creative force in any new medium. In fact, we know that members of our online community have some of the best ideas for expanding our service . . . We hope to identify and support the best, most creative infopreneurs and help them offer their content and ideas to over 1.25 million AOL members and to the entire Internet community," said a spokesperson for the company.

America Online wanted to recruit individuals and organizations who understand market segments and are able to deliver what those customers want. Winning applicants would be independent contractors with knowledge of online media and especially a great idea.

In return, AOL promised seed equity, production support, and online promotion. Winners would gain access to AOL members and participation in Internet initiatives. Significantly, the company said that winners were expected to think about alternative sources of revenue and financing.

The company's announcement came at the same time that software giant Microsoft Inc. was preparing to introduce its own online service in 1995 as part of the next version of its Windows operating system. In response, AOL, Prodigy, and CompuServe are experimenting with new pricing models, better interfaces, and connections to the Internet, a global collection of 45,000 computer networks.

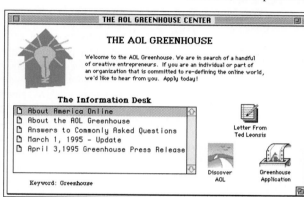

The America Online Greenhouse, announced in 1994, is an initiative that allows AOL members to share business ideas via the online service.

(Copyright 1995 America Online; used with Permission)

QUESTIONS

1. What infopreneurial ideas would you submit to The AOL Greenhouse?

2. Entrepreneurs take chances and often act independently. If you were an entrepreneur, would you apply with AOL or go it alone? Why?

3. Why do you think AOL is looking for outside partners when it already is a success?

4. If you led a mid-sized firm, how would you respond to potential competition from a company as big as Microsoft?

Sources: America Online; *PC Week,* December 5, 1994; *Business Week,* June 21, 1993; *Business Week,* September 14, 1992.

VIDEO EXERCISE

MANAGING NEW VENTURES: INVESTIGATE A NEW VENTURE IDEA

Purpose

To introduce you to the basic procedures that entrepreneurs use to determine the viability of new product or service ideas.

Procedure

View the Irwin videotape that features the start-up story of the children's food company My Own Meals, Inc. Note in particular the five steps needed for managing new ventures: Problem Recognition, Information Search, Alternative Evaluation, Purchase Decision, and Postpurchase Behavior. Over the next two weeks develop a product or service idea and conduct the research necessary on each of the five steps to determine whether it is a viable business concept. Keep track of your findings in a log book, and be prepared to discuss what you have learned in class. Below is a guide for each step of your research:

1. *Problem recognition:* Identify problems that could be solved through the introduction of a new product or service. Think about ordinary problems in your day-to-day life that could be made easier if a product or service were available. Make a list of these ideas. Ask your friends how much they would be willing to pay for the product or service and list that next to the idea. Recall that, in the video, Mary Ann Jackson created My Own Meals, Inc., out of her recognition of the problem that there were no nutritious meals for children that could be served quickly from the microwave oven. *Identify one idea that you intend to investigate further.*

2. *Information search:* Decide whether it is feasible to bring your product or service idea to market. Several issues that should be addressed include the potential market for the product or service, and the cost of each product or service unit. Identify resources you can use to find reasonable answers to these questions. Be aware that new start-up ventures often

can't find certainty on some issues, but must make reasonable assumptions based on available data. Note how the video emphasizes the need for objective data as it discusses in detail the statistics about the percentage of homes with microwave ovens, the percentage of working mothers with school-age children, and the percentage of children who eat less-nutritious foods—such as McDonald's. Gather objective data about the potential market for your product or service idea.

3. *Alternative evaluation:* One of the major issues entrepreneurs must address is competition. Most products and services are able to be produced and delivered by many competitors, and it is essential for new-venture start-ups to know who their competitors are or, if there currently are none, who they are likely to be if the business succeeds. My Own Meals, Inc., created a new product category in which there were no existing competitors. However, as the video stated, the concept was quickly copied by some major food producers. Determine how your product or service will maintain its distinctiveness from existing or potential competition. Determine your advertising strategy.

4. *Purchase decision:* Identify several factors that will be important to consumers in making a purchase decision about your product or service. Note in the videotape how My Own Meal's shelf-stable packaging affects the purchase decision. Also note that the company essentially created a new product category and how that affects the purchase decision. Finally, be aware that some things beyond your control can affect the purchase decision. For example, in the video, the grocer's decision about where to place My Own Meals on the shelves affects buyer behavior.

5. *Postpurchase behavior:* Customer satisfaction is the ultimate goal of any company. Without customers, there is no business. Therefore, all companies must be concerned about whether their customers are satisfied with the products or services they provide. With the information about your product or service that you have already developed, determine ways in which customer postpurchase behavior could be evaluated. Identify some key factors that should be evaluated, and also identify some tools or techniques that could be used to measure those factors.

EXPERIENTIAL EXERCISES

9.1 Take an Entrepreneur to Dinner

Objectives

1. To get to understand what an entrepreneur does, how she or he got started, and what it took to succeed.
2. To interview a particular entrepreneur in depth about her or his career and experiences.
3. To acquire a feeling for whether you might find an entrepreneurial career rewarding.

Instructions

1. Identify an entrepreneur in your area you would like to interview.
2. Contact the person you have selected and make an appointment. Be sure to explain why you want the appointment and to give a realistic estimate of how much time you will need.
3. Identify specific questions you would like to have answered and the general areas about which you would like information. (See suggested interview below.) Using a combination of open-ended questions, such as general questions about how the entrepreneur got started, what happened next, and so forth, and closed-ended questions, such as specific questions about what his or her goals were, if he or she had to find partners, and so forth, will help to keep the interview focused and yet allow for unexpected comments and insights.
4. Conduct the interview. If *both* you and the person you are interviewing are comfortable, using a small tape recorder during the interview can be of great help to you later. Remember, too, that you most likely will learn more if you are an "interested listener."
5. Evaluate what you have learned. Write down the information you have gathered in some form that will be helpful to you later on. Be as specific as you can. Jotting down direct quotes is more effective than statements such as "highly motivated individual." And be sure to make a note of what you did not find out.
6. Write a thank you note. This is more than a courtesy; it will also help the entrepreneur to remember you favorably should you want to follow up on the interview.

SUGGESTED INTERVIEW

Questions for Gathering Information

- *Would you tell me about yourself before you started your first venture?*

  Were your parents, relatives, or close friends entrepreneurial? How so?

  Did you have any other role models?

  What was your education/military experience? In hindsight, was it helpful? In what specific ways?

  What was your previous work experience? Was it helpful? What particular "chunks of experience" were especially valuable or irrelevant?

  In particular, did you have any sales or marketing experience? How important was it or a lack of it to starting your company?

- *How did you start your venture?*

  How did you spot the opportunity? How did it surface?

  What were your goals? What were your lifestyle or other personal requirements? How did you fit these together?

  How did you evaluate the opportunity in terms of the critical elements for success? The competition? The market?

Did you find or have partners? What kind of planning did you do? What kind of financing did you have?

Did you have a start-up business plan of any kind? Please tell me about it.

How much time did it take from conception to the first day of business? How many hours a day did you spend working on it?

How much capital did it take? How long did it take to reach a positive cash flow and break-even sales volume? If you did not have enough money at the time, what were some ways in which you "bootstrapped" the venture (i.e., bartering, borrowing, and the like). Tell me about the pressures and crises during that early survival period.

What outside help did you get? Did you have experienced advisors? Lawyers? Accountants? Tax experts? Patent experts? How did you develop these networks and how long did it take?

What was your family situation at the time?

What did you perceive to be your own strengths? Weaknesses?

What did you perceive to be the strengths of your venture? Weaknesses?

What was your most triumphant moment? Your worst moment?

Did you want to have partners or do it solo? Why?

- *Once you got going, then:*

What were the most difficult gaps to fill and problems to solve as you began to grow rapidly?

When you looked for key people as partners, advisors, or managers, were there any personal attributes or attitudes you were especially seeking because you knew they would fit with you and were important to success? How did you find them?

Are there any attributes among partners and advisors that you would definitely try to avoid?

Have things become more predictable? Or less?

Do you spend more/same/less time with your business now than in the early years?

Do you feel more managerial and less entrepreneurial now?

In terms of the future, do you plan to harvest? To maintain? To expand?

Do you plan ever to retire? Would you explain.

Have your goals changed? Have you met them?

Has your family situation changed?

Questions for Concluding (choose one)

- What do you consider your most valuable asset—the thing that enabled you to "make it"?

- If you had it to do over again, would you do it again, in the same way?

- Looking back, what do you feel are the most critical concepts, skills, attitudes, and know-how you needed to get your company started and grown to where it is today? What will be needed for the next five years? To what extent can any of these be learned?

- Some people say there is a lot of stress being an entrepreneur. What have you experienced? How would you say it compares with other "hot seat" jobs, such as the head of a big company or a partner in a large law, consulting, or accounting firm?

- What are the things that you find personally rewarding and satisfying as an entrepreneur? What have been the rewards, risks, and trade-offs?

- Who should try to be an entrepreneur? Can you give me any ideas there?

- What advice would you give an aspiring entrepreneur? Could you suggest the three most important "lessons" you have learned? How can I learn them while minimizing the tuition?

Source: Jeffry A. Timmons, *New Venture Creation,* 3d ed. (Burr Ridge, Ill.: Richard D. Irwin, Inc., 1994), p. 33.

9.2 Starting a New Business

Objectives

1. To introduce you to the complexities of going into business for yourself.
2. To provide hands-on experience in making new-business decisions.

Instructions

1. Your instructor will divide the class into teams and assign each team the task of investigating the start-up of one of the following businesses:
   a. Submarine sandwich shop
   b. Day care service
   c. Bookstore
   d. Gasoline service station
   e. Other

2. Each team should research the information necessary to complete the New-Business Start-Up Worksheet. The following agencies or organizations might be of assistance:
   a. Small Business Administration
   b. Local county/city administration agencies
   c. Local chamber of commerce
   d. Local small-business development corporation
   e. U.S. Department of Commerce
   f. Farmer's Home Administration
   g. Local realtors
   h. Local businesspeople in the same or a similar business
   i. Banks and S&Ls
3. Each team presents its findings to the class.

NEW-BUSINESS START-UP WORKSHEET

1. *Product*

    What customer need will we satisfy?   _____

    How can our product be unique?   _____

2. *Customer*

    Who are our customers? What are their profiles?   _____

    Where do they live/work/play?   _____

What are their buying habits?   _____

    What are their needs?   _____

3. *Competition*

    Who/where is the competition?   _____

    What are their strengths and weaknesses?   _____

    How might they respond to us?   _____

4. *Suppliers*

    Who/where are our suppliers?   _____

    What are their business practices?   _____

    What relationships can we expect?   _____

5. *Location*

    Where are our customers/competitors/suppliers?   _____

    What are the location costs?   _____

    What are the legal limitations to location? _____

6. *Physical Facilities/Equipment*

    Rent/own/build/refurbish facilities?   _____

    Rent/lease/purchase equipment?   _____

    Maintenance?   _____

7. *Human Resources*

    Availability?   _____

    Training?   _____

    Costs?   _____

8. *Legal/Regulatory Environment*

    Licenses/permits/certifications?   _____

    Government agencies?   _____

    Liability?   _____

9. *Cultural/Social Environment*

   Cultural issues?   _____

   Social issues?   _____

10. *International Environment*   _____

    International issues?   _____

11. *Other*   _____

    _____

    _____

    _____

CHAPTER APPENDIX

INFORMATION FOR ENTREPRENEURS

If you are interested in starting or managing a small business, you have access to many sources of information.

The **Small Business Administration (SBA)** is an agency of the federal government charged with promoting the growth of small businesses. It provides financial, educational, and lobbying services. The SBA defines a small business as a business that has fewer than 500 employees or lacks dominant market power.

The SBA's most visible services are its direct loans and loan guarantees. Under the direct loan program, the SBA acts as a lender of last resort to small businesses. In recent years, these loans generally have been used for special target populations. Under the loan guarantee program, the SBA protects the lender in the event the loan holder defaults. Each loan program is designed to improve the environment for small business by expanding the sources of capital. Many states offer similar lending programs to encourage investment in certain industries or geographic areas.

The SBA sponsors and delivers training programs and provides a wide range of booklets and brochures on small-business management. Many SBA training programs are delivered through community colleges and universities. Some of these programs, such as the Small Business Institute and Small Business Development Centers, involve students and faculty in special consulting projects designed to help specific clients. In addition to its college-based programs, the SBA uses SCORE (Service Corps of Retired Executives) to provide services for struggling new businesses. Most of these services are free; for others, a small fee is charged.

Several publications are produced specifically for the entrepreneurial audience. *Inc.* publishes articles about the management problems of growing businesses. *Venture Capital Journal* caters to entrepreneurs and the venture capital industry at large. Pratt's *Guide to Venture Capital* is a "must-have" for any entrepreneur; it covers not only the how-to's of starting a business and obtaining venture capital but also profiles every major venture capital organization in the country.

Still other sources of help are available. Private groups, universities, and government agencies supply technical and managerial assistance to entrepreneurs. For example, several organizations in various parts of the country offer the services of a board of directors for an evening. One such program, the MIT Forum, is offered by volunteers in cities nationwide. At each meeting of the Forum, a business presents its plan to an audience and preselected panelists provide feedback on the plan. Then the audience reacts to both the plan and the panelists. Most presenters find they obtain more advice than they could purchase on the open market.

In addition, several of the Big Six accounting firms have groups specifically geared to the needs of smaller, emerging companies. Most publish guides to new-business formation and management as a service to their current and prospective clientele. These companies can provide professional consulting and financial services and also make critical introductions within the financial community. One screened introduction can save months of effort and thousands of dollars in lost opportunities.

Small-business ownership or management can provide a challenging and rewarding career. The interested student should start looking in the local community for sources of ideas and assistance. Planning can't begin too soon!

INTEGRATING CASE

UNIVERSITY MEDICAL CENTER

Stan Ferguson, executive director of University Medical Center (UMC), sat back from his report-cluttered desk and contemplated the current and future competitive environment of his institution. Recently he had been hired to formulate and implement a strategic plan that would guide UMC through the turbulent conditions facing the health care industry in the 1990s.

Industry Overview

As the chief officer of a large, not-for-profit teaching and research hospital, Ferguson was aware of the many complex changes affecting the health care industry. Federal and state governments were trying to cap health care spending. Hospitals were hit with $55 billion in proposed cuts in federal health programs from 1986 to 1990, after absorbing $40 billion in cuts over the previous five years. Private health insurers and employers also were clamping down, forcing health care providers to compete with one another and to seek new ways to cut costs and deliver their services.

As government and private insurance spending growth slowed, many hospitals were losing business. Nonessential surgery often was delayed, and minor procedures were performed in doctors' offices and outpatient clinics. Patients often left the hospital sooner to stay under the medicare reimbursement ceiling. Hospital occupancy rates fell from 75 percent in 1980 to 65 percent in 1985 and below 60 percent by 1990. Many experts argued that the U.S. hospital industry simply suffered from excess capacity, with at least 25 percent too many beds.

Many not-for-profit hospitals were experiencing the worst problems. Dozens were being purchased at bargain prices by for-profit hospital chains such as Hospital Corporation of America (HCA) and Humana. Many industry observers believed the for-profit hospitals were likely to be the strongest survivors of the industry shakeout. Traditionally, these hospitals had kept their costs low. However, even the for-profit hospitals were feeling the pressure.

Competitive pressure came not only from the for-profit hospitals but from health maintenance organizations (HMOs) and a variety of outpatient and nursing facilities. For a single fee paid in advance, usually by an employer or an insurance company, an HMO contracts to provide its members with complete health care, from routine physical exams to major surgery. Employers like HMOs and often encourage their workers to join.

The emphasis on HMOs and other forms of group practice was also changing traditional referral patterns. Not only were hospital admissions dropping, but fewer were coming through primary care physicians. In an effort to "lock up" new referral patterns, hospital management companies and those not-for-profits that could afford it were starting or buying HMOs, getting into the health insurance business, and building freestanding emergency and surgical centers (often called "docs-in-a-box").

However, the not-for-profit hospital often operates at a disadvantage in its efforts to open an HMO or similar facility. The initial costs are high, and the competition, particularly in certain areas, can be frantic.

Some hospitals have begun to specialize to a greater degree, emphasizing profitable services that give them a distinctive competence in the marketplace. For example, some hospitals stress psychiatric care and alcohol and drug treatment programs. This area of growth is supported by government, consumer, church, and law enforcement groups, not to mention all professional sports and entertainment. Several hospitals around the country have provided unique services tailored to the needs and preferences of women. Many of these programs have been successful.

Alternatively, because many patients are leaving the hospital sooner, some health care institutions were diversifying into nursing homes and home health care programs. The changing demographics in the aging of America favor nursing homes. One trend was for greater luxury in nursing homes, thus giving retirees and established patients with adequate incomes an attractive option over either hospital or home care. Providing home health care through the delivery of equipment, supplies, and services was another alternative, but this diversification alternative, like others, entailed high start-up costs.

Hospital supply companies, which sell sutures, solutions, and syringes to hospitals, were feeling the pressure as well. In response, suppliers have diversified into other businesses, often competing directly with hospitals, and have engaged in mergers to strengthen their competitive positions. Many pharmaceutical companies also faced potential problems as hospitals turned away from high-priced brand name drugs and toward generic drugs to cut costs. Also, manufacturers of expensive diagnostic equipment were feeling the squeeze.

Finally, physicians, the ultimate supplier of health care services, were beginning to feel the effects of the new environment. Large physician surpluses arose by 1990. This situation encouraged the formation of large group practices and clinics, which created additional competition for hospitals. Ironically, the individuals who controlled hospital usage, the physicians, became serious competitors. Hospitals sought to improve this relationship by constructing medical office buildings adjacent to hospitals and engaging in a variety of joint ventures (e.g., surgery and radiology centers) with physicians.

Despite all these economic, regulatory, and competitive shocks, Stan Ferguson knew that the health care system remained under attack. Critics claimed that hospitals still were not addressing the problem. Although national health expenditures were declining in current dollars, national health spending in real terms (dollars deflated by the consumer price index) had accelerated since 1980. Others suggested hospitals were covering their inefficiency and overcapacity with slick marketing programs designed to attract customers. Ferguson realized that the competitive pressures from both outside and within the industry were likely to worsen before they improved.

UMC Location, Background, and Facilities

UMC was located on the southern edge of a major city on the East Coast (see the map). The city was divided into Northside and Southside by a major river, which also divided the city's downtown area. The primary service area for UMC was the Southside and the suburbs located to the south and west of the city. The Southside included most of the city's major industrial plants, two major universities, several high-crime areas, and many of the city's oldest and poorest neighborhoods. The western suburbs consisted primarily of moderate-income families and the affluent southern suburbs of single professionals and high-income families. The secondary service area included the Northside and the northern suburbs.

UMC was founded in 1920 by a teaching hospital affiliated with the medical and nursing schools of a well-respected private university. Since that time, UMC had grown in both size and prestige and often was rated one of the better health care facilities in the country. Today UMC consists of six interconnected buildings with a variety of services and a total of 933 beds.

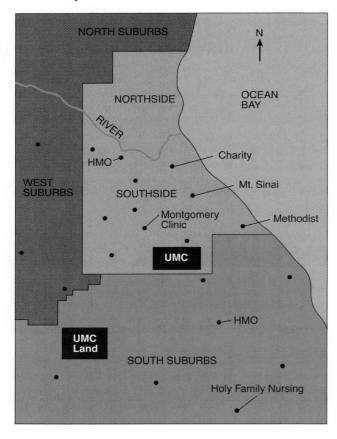

UMC was not affiliated with an HMO or nursing home, and it did not operate any satellite units or nursing facilities. It was involved in a home health care program in a limited way. Some of the large employers and insurance companies in the area had discussed the possibility of developing a prepaid program, but these talks were still in the planning stages. UMC also owned an undeveloped, 10-acre tract of land in the southern suburbs, and several ideas had been proposed for its use. Ferguson realized that UMC should consider some of the options more seriously in the near future.

UMC Patient Care

Approximately 85 percent of all patients admitted came from the primary service area, a slight increase over the past few years. The remaining 15 percent were admitted to take advantage of services not available in other locations. Of all patients admitted, 7 percent of private patients came from the Southside, 30 percent from the western suburbs, and 47 percent from the southern suburbs. The remaining private patients came from the secondary service area. The Southside contributed 79 percent of the staff patients, and 16 percent of the staff patients came from the western and southern suburbs. Ninety-eight percent of the ambulatory care clinic patients and emergency ward patients came from the primary service area. Eighty-seven percent of the clinic patients and 60 percent of the emergency ward patients came from the Southside.

The number of beds had not changed in the past 10 years, but inpatient activity had changed dramatically over the last year. The number of beds devoted to staff patients had increased, although overall admissions to the institution were down slightly. Pediatric patients were holding steady, medicine and surgery patients were down slightly, but serious drops in volume were reported for ob-gyn patients. Newborn inpatient activity had declined 28 percent in the past four years. Psychiatric inpatient activity was up 24 percent, partially because of a new substance abuse program. Overall, private inpatient days declined 9 percent, and staff inpatient days were down 3 percent. The average length of stay for all patients declined sharply, causing a lower occupancy rate. Overall, occupancy at UMC had declined from 74 percent to 69 percent.

Visits to the emergency ward and ambulatory care clinic were increasing, but at a decreasing rate. These trends were attributed to the Southside community's greater use of HMOs and other free-standing clinics. Although UMC continued to be the largest provider of ambulatory care in its primary service area, Ferguson was concerned that this trend was responsible for some recent declines in inpatient admissions and would threaten the institution's ability to attract patients for its inpatient care and related teaching programs. The ambulatory care clinic was the primary source of staff inpatients, followed by the emergency ward.

UMC Medical staff, Personnel, and Finances

The full-time medical staff had increased from 210 to 240 physicians (14 percent) in the past five years, while the part-time staff had increased from 307 to 379 physicians (23 percent). However, the staff had lost several of its better-known and respected physicians to other hospitals and a number of the younger staff to HMOs and other facilities. UMC relied heavily on a group of older, full-time physicians for a disproportionate share of private patient admissions. Obviously, this concerned Ferguson.

The number of other personnel employed by the hospital had held steady, including the nursing staff. The only real increases had been in the ambulatory care clinic and the emergency ward. Unemployment in the area had made recruiting unskilled employees to cover normal turnover relatively easy. A recruitment program was used to identify and attract qualified nurses, an essential activity given the nationwide shortage.

The changes confronted by UMC and the rest of the health care industry had an adverse impact on the financial picture of the institution. Although total income had increased from $162 million to approximately $169 million during the last five years, total expenses had increased from $166 million to $172 million. Endowment income, which stood at about $2 million, failed to cover the deficit.

Service Area Characteristics

Demographic data contained a number of trends that, if continued, would have a significant impact on the volume and types of demand for UMC patient care programs. The population of the Southside had declined 5 percent over the past five years to 496,000, a trend that could reduce the number of patients using the clinic and the emergency ward. This trend eventually could have serious implications for the demand for staff services, because the residents of the Southside were older, poorer, and less healthy. On the other hand, the population of the more affluent southern suburbs had increased 15 percent over the past five years to 250,000 and that of the western suburbs had increased approximately 7 percent to 300,000.

Competition

The UMC service area map indicates the location of other health care facilities in UMC's service area. Competition within the UMC service area had increased dramatically. Several area hospitals had constructed major additions in the past five years, thereby increasing the number of inpatient beds for the service area. Given the decline in occupancy rates for most hospitals, the entire region suffered from excess capacity. Despite UMC's history of drawing patients from the suburbs, many health care experts believed its competitive position in the suburbs was under serious attack. Suburban hospitals were newer, more convenient, and attracting both new physicians and more affluent patients.

The area was experiencing a birthrate decline of 20 percent. This decline was lower than the drop in demand for obstetric services at UMC, indicating a loss of market share. Fewer suburban woman were using UMC. The demand for ambulatory care had increased greatly within the service area, although this increase was being met by several alternative channels of health care delivery. Three hospitals in the suburbs had opened outpatient clinics, all with surgical units. Two of these clinics were operating in the western suburbs and one in the southern suburbs. A major HMO in the southern suburbs was attracting an increasing number of patients, particularly among younger singles and families. A variety of freestanding primary care clinics had opened throughout the area, although most did not have a formal affiliation with a hospital.

Among the Southside hospitals, UMC was the second largest. Mt. Sinai had slightly over 1,000 beds. With the exception of the Montgomery Clinic, these hospitals were experiencing the same problem as UMC, but most were in much worse financial condi-

tion. A relatively large, although not very successful HMO operated in the center of the city, and several freestanding clinics had opened in different neighborhoods.

Charity Hospital, perhaps the most aggressive hospital in the Southside, was planning an HMO facility. Montgomery Clinic was considered a hospital for the "rich and famous," specializing primarily in expensive and sophisticated procedures. This hospital had no financial problems and was considered among the five best hospitals in the country (if not the world). However, it had no outpatient or emergency facilities, and it devoted limited space to obstetrics and pediatrics.

Methodist Hospital, located near the southeastern boundary of the Southside, represented a special problem. Three years ago, Methodist had undertaken an expansion and renovation program that placed a tremendous strain on the financial condition of the hospital. Although the hospital had an excellent physical plant, it suffered from management problems, a difficult union, and a restless medical staff. Ferguson knew that the for-profit hospital management companies considered Methodist an attractive target, and one was beginning negotiations for a management contract or purchase.

Two nursing care facilities operated in the Southside. Three nursing homes were located in the suburbs, and a fourth, owned by a national chain, was a possibility. All essentially were filled, but the cost and quality of care varied greatly. Only one nursing home—Holy Family, in the extreme southern suburbs—was considered well above average in quality of care. It was also more expensive than the others, but it had a long waiting list.

The Future

Ferguson knew that UMC was in a difficult position, but he now had a greater appreciation for some of the essential competitive issues facing the institution. He was anxious to develop a strategic plan for the institution. Once he fully understood the sources of competitive pressure, he could develop a coherent and integrated strategy with which to respond.

Questions

1. Using Porter's competitive forces model (described in Chapter 3), conduct an analysis of the health care industry.

2. Based on your analysis of the health care industry, what strategies would you recommend for UMC? How would you recommend that UMC gain a competitive advantage in its market?

3. What are the important social and political issues confronting UMC? What should UMC do to deal with these issues?

WHISTLE-BLOWING

Albert Higgenbotham, a 48-year-old middle manager for United Fibers, Inc., discovered that the company's owners were cheating the government out of several thousand dollars in taxes annually. Albert believed he had an obligation to do something about the situation, but he also had a sense of loyalty to the firm and to his superiors. He also desired to keep his job. Thus far, Albert had not done anything except worry.

Needing to talk with someone helpful and "safe," Albert thought of his brother, Richard, who worked at the same company as a quality assurance manager. One Tuesday after work, Albert drove over to his brother's house and accepted a seat on the patio and a beer. Wanting to ease into the discussion of his concerns, Albert mentioned an item printed in that day's newspaper entitled "Pentagon Whistle-Blower Wins Promotion and Legal Fees." Albert had read the article carefully and had learned that years earlier, whistle-blower Earnest Fitzgerald had blown the whistle on a $2 billion cost overrun on the giant C-5A military transport plane project. Because of his action, Fitzgerald was fired from the Air Force. The brothers exchanged views and agreed that it had taken great personal courage for Fitzgerald to blow the whistle, be ousted from his job, then struggle through the long and expensive battle to obtain a reinstatement order from the Civil Service Commission and back pay, and win a legal suit for recovery of $200,000 in legal costs he had sustained. The brothers agreed that volunteering for those experiences bordered on the heroic. They speculated that Fitzgerald had expected better treatment than he received.

While trying to work up to presenting his ethic problem to Richard, Albert referred to several other examples of ethical puzzles and whistle-blowing in business organizations he had read about. He mentioned the B. F. Goodrich Company employee who allegedly was pressured by superiors to misrepresent test results on a new brake designed for military planes. Albert also recalled a senior design engineer for Ford Motor Company who, after objecting to the hazardous design features of the Ford Pinto's gas tank and windshield, was demoted and terminated and then sued the company. After relating these examples of conflict between employees' personal values and company goals and practices, Albert shifted the conversation to his ethical problem, described it fully to Richard, and asked for his brother's thoughts.

Richard responded by describing his own ethical predicament to a dismayed Albert:

Our company has been selling defective parachute cord to the federal government for the past six months. When my chief quality control inspector first discovered the parachute cord flaws and informed me, I immediately informed my superior. He suggested that my data must be erroneous and instructed me to run the tests again. I did. The results of the second round of tests were similar to the earlier ones. Learning the results, my superior told me that the statistical incidence of cord failure was acceptable to our company, that the parachute cord we were selling to the government was being stockpiled anyway, and that it probably would never be used. He suggested that I not worry unnecessarily. I have continued to worry a lot. It looks like you and I are in the same boat, brother. Do you think we should blow the whistle? If we do blow the whistle, what will be the consequences? What should we do?

Albert had no ready answers to Richard's questions. Indeed, Albert had come expecting to ask similar questions, and he was dismayed to find Richard with similar problems. Albert felt pulled in three directions. First were his personal values, his own interests, and his sense of professional integrity. Second was a sense of loyalty to the company and to its owners. Third was a moral obligation to prevent serious injuries and injustice to the public. The pressures of these unresolved forces tugging at him were beginning to make Albert's stomach ache.

At work, Albert had discreetly inquired about company policy regarding actions an employee should take in the situation he and Richard were in. No such policy existed. Albert needed to decide about blowing the whistle. Also, he needed a list of prudent guiding steps he could take that might make it unnecessary to blow the whistle. Finally, before acting he needed a comparison of desirable and undesirable consequences likely to be generated by his whistle-blowing.

It wasn't easy to know the right thing to do, nor was it easy to know if it was worth doing or not. Albert did know that he and his brother needed relief from the uncertainty and indecision.

Source: J. Champion and J. James, *Critical Incidents in Management: Decision and Policy Issues,* 6th ed. (Homewood, Ill.: Richard D. Irwin, 1989).

PART III

ORGANIZING
AND STAFFING

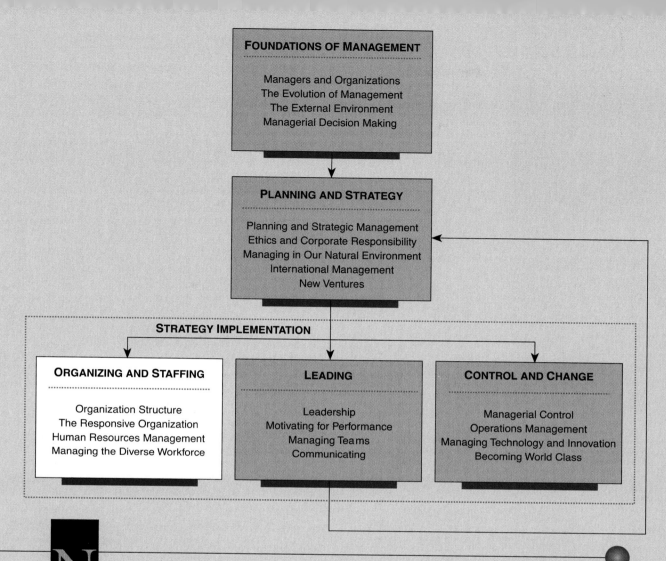

FOUNDATIONS OF MANAGEMENT

Managers and Organizations
The Evolution of Management
The External Environment
Managerial Decision Making

PLANNING AND STRATEGY

Planning and Strategic Management
Ethics and Corporate Responsibility
Managing in Our Natural Environment
International Management
New Ventures

STRATEGY IMPLEMENTATION

ORGANIZING AND STAFFING

Organization Structure
The Responsive Organization
Human Resources Management
Managing the Diverse Workforce

LEADING

Leadership
Motivating for Performance
Managing Teams
Communicating

CONTROL AND CHANGE

Managerial Control
Operations Management
Managing Technology and Innovation
Becoming World Class

N ow that you know about planning and strategy, the remaining three parts correspond to the other three functions of management: organizing, leading, and controlling. Parts III, IV, and V discuss issues pertaining to *implementing* strategic plans. In Part III, we describe how to organize and staff for maximum effectiveness. Chapter 10 introduces you to different organization structures and explains how to group and delegate tasks. Chapter 11 builds on those basic concepts by describing more complex organization designs. This chapter discusses how firms can adapt quickly to rapidly changing environments and how "corporate America" is restructuring. Chapter 12 addresses the management of human resources. Its focus is on staffing the firm with capable employees and the issues surrounding employee reward systems. Finally, Chapter 13 discusses the challenge of managing today's workforce, one composed of diverse groups of people. Chapters 12 and 13 set the stage for Part IV, which further elaborates on how to manage people.

10

ORGANIZATION STRUCTURE

*Take my assets—but leave me my organization and in five years
I'll have it all back.*

Alfred P. Sloan, Jr.

LEARNING OBJECTIVES

After studying Chapter 10, you will know:

1. How specialization and coordination influence your organization's structure.

2. How authority operates.

3. The roles of the board of directors and the chief executive officer.

4. How span of control affects structure and managerial effectiveness.

5. How to delegate work effectively.

6. The difference between centralized and decentralized organizations.

7. How to allocate jobs to work units.

8. How to manage the unique challenges of the matrix organization.

9. The nature of important organizational roles: line, staff, integrating, and boundary roles.

DIFFERENT "TAKES" ON ORGANIZING

- In multinational corporations, it used to be common to allow local managers to make decisions in the countries where their offices were located. Foreign subsidiaries often had a great deal of independence. But now, power is moving away from the field and returning to corporate headquarters. At IBM, 14 global divisions are run by global specialists in different categories of international expertise, and these executives call the shots more than the country managers. In Japan as well, multinationals have reorganized such that Tokyo headquarters are all-powerful. But a contrasting example lies with Johnson & Johnson, in which the heads of foreign subsidiaries are so independent of corporate headquarters they are called kings of their own countries.

Although Rupert Murdoch certainly gets the job done, his autocratic style frequently strikes fear in the hearts of his managers. *(AP/Wide World Photos)*

- Rupert Murdoch is chairman of News Corp., and owner of the Fox television network and many other businesses. Murdoch is the consummate "micromanager"— an autocrat who makes virtually all decisions and monitors others very closely. He believes (rightly) that he is a fast decision maker who can act quickly and seize an opportunity before others see it. But his managers sometimes are paralyzed into inaction as they wait to hear from him first. No one would call Murdock a "delegator."

- Randy Kirk is founder and president of AC International, which now manufacturers and distributes bicycle accessories to countries all over the world. He started in 1981 with one partner and no employees, preferring to operate like many wholesalers: he ran marketing and advertising, and contracted with other firms to manufacture and distribute his products. But one by one, for various reasons, he stopped using other firms and brought these functions under his own roof. He bought production equipment, and by 1990 he had 35 employees. Costs have gone down dramatically, and customer service and product quality have improved. This entrepreneur believes firmly in the value of having himself and his own people, not outside suppliers and service providers, do as much of the work as possible.

Sources: R. W. Kirk, "It's about Control," *Inc.*, August 1994, pp. 25–26; R. Hudson and J. Lublin, "Power at Multinationals Shifts to Home Office," *The Wall Street Journal*, September 9, 1994, pp. B1, B6; M. Cox, "How Do You Tame the Global Company: Murdoch Does It Alone," *The Wall Street Journal*, February 14, 1994, pp. A1, A6; B. O'Reilly, "J&J Is on a Roll," *Fortune*, December 26, 1994, pp. 178–92.

What do you think are the pros and cons of these approaches to management? The examples in Setting the Stage might not offer enough information for you to answer these questions with confidence. But they touch upon important issues about how managers organize companies and use authority. These issues, which you will learn about in this chapter, will say a lot about the company you work for, and determine in part how satisfied and successful you will be there.

This chapter presents some fundamental concepts that help you understand an organization's structure. It begins by covering the most basic principles of organization structure, starting with *specialization,* or the division of labor, and *coordination* of different jobs. Next, it discusses *authority,* or the right of some people to tell others what to do. Then it describes the different *parts* of an organization, such as the board of directors, the president, and the various departments that form the building blocks of the company.

Next, the chapter discusses how *responsibilities* are assigned and the degree to which *decisions* are centralized. Finally, it illustrates the broad categories of organizational *roles:* line, staff, integrating, and boundary roles.

SPECIALIZATION AND COORDINATION

Two fundamental concepts around which organizations are structured are specialization and coordination. **Specialization** means that the work of the organization is subdivided into smaller tasks. Various individuals and units throughout the organization perform different tasks.[1] The assignment of different tasks to different people or groups is often referred to as **division of labor.** Secretaries and accountants specialize in, and perform, different jobs; similarly, marketing, finance, and human resources tasks are divided among those respective departments. The numerous tasks that must be carried out in an organization make specialization a necessity.

However, all these specialized tasks cannot be performed completely independently. Because the different units are part of the larger organization, some degree of communication and cooperation must exist among them. **Coordination** refers to the procedures that link the various parts of the organization to achieve the organization's overall mission.

Harvard professors Paul Lawrence and Jay Lorsch made an important contribution in this regard.[2] They described organization structures according to two key dimensions: differentiation (which stems from specialization and the division of labor) and integration (their term for coordination).

DIFFERENTIATION

Differentiation is created by job specialization and the division of labor. Differentiation means that people in various units work on very different kinds of tasks, using different skills and work methods. Differentiation is high when there are many subunits and many kinds of specialists who think differently.

Lawrence and Lorsch found that organizations in complex, dynamic environments (plastics firms, in their study) developed a high degree of differentiation in order to cope with the complex challenges. Companies in simple, stable environments (container companies) had low levels of differentiation. Companies in intermediate environments (food companies) had intermediate differentiation.

Lawrence and Lorsch went one step further: they determined the structural difference that distinguished successful from unsuccessful firms. Highly differentiated firms were successful *if* they also had high levels of integration.[3]

INTEGRATION

Integration is the degree to which differentiated units work together and coordinate their efforts. Organizations are more likely to fail if they exist in complex environments and are highly differentiated, but fail to adequately integrate their activities.[4]

Integration is achieved through structural mechanisms that enhance collaboration and coordination. Any job activity that links different work units performs an integrative function. Remember, the more highly differentiated your firm, the greater the need for integration among the different units.

These concepts permeate the rest of the chapter. We will discuss specialization and differentiation with respect to the authority structure of organizations (that is, *vertical* differentiation among different hierarchical levels), departmentalization (*horizontal* differentiation among different units at similar levels), and organizational roles. We will discuss techniques of coordination and integration toward the end of the chapter and in parts of future chapters.

▮▼ AUTHORITY IN ORGANIZATIONS

Fundamental to the functioning of every organization is **authority:** the legitimate right to make decisions and to tell other people what to do. For example, a boss has the authority to give an order to a subordinate.

Authority resides in positions rather than in people. Thus, the job of vice president of a particular division has authority over that division, regardless of how many people come and go in that position and who presently holds it.

In private business enterprises, the owners have ultimate authority. In most small, simply structured companies, the owner also acts as manager. Sometimes the owner hires another person to manage the business and its employees. The owner gives this manager some authority to oversee the operations, but the manager is accountable to—that is, reports and defers to—the owner. Thus, the owner still has the ultimate authority.

Traditionally authority has been the primary means of running an organization. An order that a boss gives to a lower-level employee is usually carried out. As this occurs throughout the organization day after day, the organization can move forward toward achieving its goals.

We will discuss the authority structure of organizations from the top down, beginning with the board of directors.

THE BOARD OF DIRECTORS

In corporations, the owners are the stockholders. But because there are numerous stockholders, and these individuals generally lack timely information, few are directly involved in managing the organization. Stockholders elect a board of directors to oversee the organization. The board, led by the chair, makes major decisions affecting the organization, subject to corporate charter and bylaw provisions. However, even board members have other interests, meet on a limited basis, and give only intermittent attention to managing the company. Also, the chair is often the CEO, so the other members of the board may be relatively powerless.[5]

Authority rests in positions, not people. Here, the woman in authority clearly holds the attention of her subordinates. *(Walter Hodges/Tony Stone Images)*

Nevertheless, boards of directors perform important functions. Directors have three major sets of duties: (1) selecting, assessing, rewarding, and perhaps replacing the CEO; (2) determining the firm's strategic direction and reviewing financial performance; and (3) assuring ethical, socially responsible, and legal conduct.[6]

Some board members, or inside directors, are top managers inside the company. Outside members of the board are executives at other companies. The trend in recent years has been toward reducing the number of insiders and increasing the number of outsiders.[7] Today, most companies have a majority of outside directors. Boards made up of strong, independent outsiders are more likely to provide different information and perspectives and to prevent big mistakes.

Boards of directors are not just for large corporations. Small companies have them too. However, many entrepreneurs do not know how to use their boards to maximum advantage.

HOW TO USE YOUR BOARD

*T*he role of the board is not to police your company but to advise you. Your company needs a board in large part because the directors add value to the company. Some advice to entrepreneurs:

- *Treat your directors as resources.* The board can complement your strengths. When your company falters, the board members can be of great help, not only in providing advice but in imparting credibility to customers and lenders.

- *Always be honest with your directors.* Don't give them unrealistically optimistic reports. If your directors are unaware of important problems, you will cut yourself off from valuable advice.

- *Create a compensation committee.* This will help depersonalize the compensation negotiations between you and your managers, reducing the you-versus-them conflict.

- *Create an audit committee.* A tough audit committee will help establish effective financial controls early on.

- *Manage board meetings effectively.* Prepare thoroughly so that you won't be stumped by questions. Appoint a devil's advocate to avoid groupthink (recall Chapter 4).

Source: "Confessions of a Director," *Inc.,* April 1991, pp. 119–21. ●

THE CHIEF EXECUTIVE OFFICER

The authority officially vested in the board of directors is assigned to a chief executive officer, who occupies the top of the organizational pyramid. The chief executive is personally accountable to the board and to the owners for the organization's performance.

It is estimated that in 15 percent of Fortune 500 corporations, one person holds all three positions of CEO, chair of the board of directors, and president.[8] More commonly, however, one person holds two of those positions, with the CEO serving also as either the chair of the board or the president of the organization. When the CEO is president, the chair may be honorary and may do little more than conduct meetings. In other cases, the chair may be the CEO and the president is second in command.

HIERARCHICAL LEVELS

In Chapter 1, we discussed the three broad levels of the organizational pyramid, commonly called the **hierarchy.** The CEO occupies the top position and is the senior member of top management. The top managerial level also includes presidents and vice presidents. These are the strategic managers in charge of the entire organization. The second broad level is middle management. At this level, managers are in charge of plants or departments. The lowest level is made up of lower management and workers. It includes office managers, sales managers, supervisors, and other first-line managers, as well as the employees who report directly to them. This level is also called the *operational level* of the organization.

An authority structure is the glue that holds these levels together. Generally (but not always), people at higher levels have the authority to make decisions and to tell lower-level people what to do. For example, middle managers can give orders to first-line supervisors; first-line supervisors, in turn, direct operative-level workers.

In the 1980s, a powerful trend for U.S. businesses was to reduce the number of hierarchical layers. General Electric used to have 29 levels; today, following a major reorganization, it has only 5. Most executives today believe that fewer layers create a more efficient, fast-acting, and cost-effective organization. This also holds true for the **subunits** of major corporations. A study of 234 branches of a financial services company found that branches with fewer layers tended to have higher operating efficiency than branches with more layers.[9]

THE ORGANIZATION CHART

The **organization chart** depicts the positions in the firm and how they are arranged. The chart provides a picture of the reporting structure (who reports to whom) and the division of labor. Most companies have official organization charts drawn up to give people this information.

Figure 10.1 shows the traditional organization chart. Note the information that it conveys:[10]

1. *The division of work.* The boxes represent work units.
2. *The work performed by each unit.* The titles in the boxes show this.
3. *Reporting relationships.* The solid lines indicate superior–subordinate relationships—who has authority over whom.
4. *Levels of management.* The number of levels is not indicated by the number of horizontal layers in the chart. Rather, all persons or units that are of the same rank and report to the same person are on one level.

FIGURE 10.1

A conventional organization chart

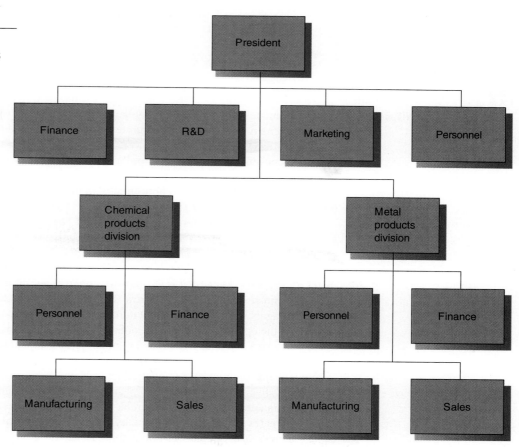

Figure 10.2 depicts a more complex chart of a large downtown hotel. What are the different work units and the nature of their tasks? How many people report directly to the resident manager, food and beverage manager, and executive assistant manager? How many levels are there?

AN UPSIDE-DOWN ORGANIZATION CHART

Who should really run the organization? The organization charts of companies like Dana Corporation, Wal-Mart, and Nordstrom look like this:

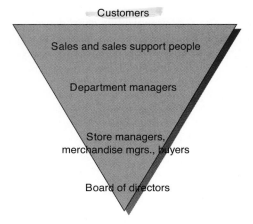

What is the point of an upside-down chart? Who runs the organization according to this chart? What are the benefits of this kind of chart?

Sources: T. Peters and N. Austin, *A Passion for Excellence* (New York: Random House, 1985); J. Collins and J. Porras, *Built to Last* (New York: Harper Business, 1994), p. 117; and Nordstrom Orientation Packet. ●

SPAN OF CONTROL

As the organization chart shows, people report to a manager of their unit. The number of people under a manager is an important feature of the organization's structure. The number of subordinates who report directly to an executive or supervisor is called the **span of control.** This concept has implications for the shape of the entire organization.

Figure 10.3(*a*) shows an organization whose managers have narrow spans of control, that is, few subordinates who report directly to them. The organization in Figure 10.3(*b*), on the other hand, has wide spans of control.

The implications of differences in the span of control for the shape of an organization are straightforward. Narrow spans build a *tall* organization that has many reporting levels. Wide spans create a flat organization with fewer reporting levels.

The span of control can be too narrow or too wide. The optimal span of control maximizes effectiveness because it is (1) narrow enough to permit managers to maintain control over subordinates, but (2) not so narrow that it leads to overcontrol and an excessive number of managers who oversee a small number of subordinates.

What is the optimal number of subordinates? Five, according to Napoleon.[11] Some managers today still consider five a good number. At one Japanese bank, in contrast, several hundred branch managers report to the same boss.

Actually, the optimal span of control depends on a number of factors.[12] The span should be wider when (1) the work is routine, (2) subordinates are highly trained, (3) the manager is highly capable, (4) the jobs are similar and performance measures are comparable, and (5) subordinates prefer autonomy to close supervisory control. If the opposite conditions exist, a narrow span of control is more appropriate.

FIGURE 10.2

The organization
chart of a large
hotel

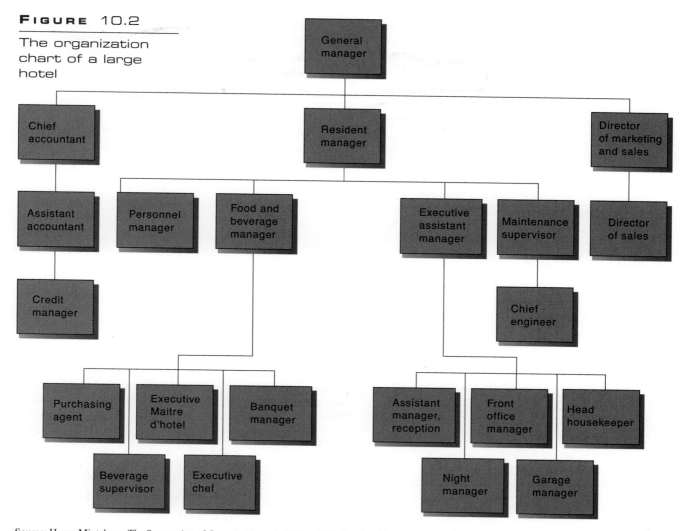

Source: Henry Mintzberg, *The Structuring of Organizations,* © 1979, p. 330. Reprinted by permission of Prentice-Hall, Inc., Englewood Cliffs, New Jersey.

FIGURE 10.3

Span of control and
tall versus flat
structures

a. Tall structure with a
   narrow span of control.

b. Flat structure with a
   wide span of control.

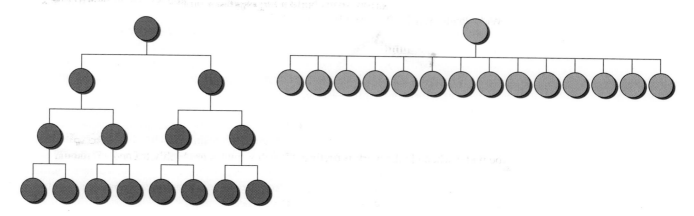

DELEGATION

A basic characteristic of organizations and work units is how much authority is granted, or delegated, to people at lower hierarchical levels. Specifically, **delegation** is the assignment of additional responsibilities to a subordinate. It requires that the subordinate report back to his or her boss as to how effectively the assignment was carried out. Delegation is perhaps the most fundamental feature of management, because it entails getting work done through others. Thus, delegation is important at all hierarchical levels. The process can occur between any two individuals in any type of structure with regard to any task.

Some managers are comfortable delegating to subordinates; others are not. Consider the differences between the two office managers and the ways they gave out the same assignment in the following example.

CONTRASTING STYLES OF DELEGATION

*M*anager A: Call Jones Office Equipment and the Wilson Supply Store. Get them to quote you prices on all their office dictation equipment. Ask them to give you a demonstration. Invite two managers to the demonstration, Ellis and Conrad, and let them try it out. Get them to put their reactions on paper. Then prepare me a report with the costs and specifications of all the equipment. Oh yes, be sure to ask for information on repair cost . . . .

Manager B: I'd like to do something about our stenographic system. Managers who don't have secretaries of their own are complaining that it takes them too long to get someone to handle their dictation. Could you evaluate the various kinds of dictating machines and give me a recommendation on what we should do? I think we can spend $2,000. Possibly you could talk to some of the managers to get their ideas.

Source: G. Strauss and L. Sayles, *Behavioral Strategies for Managers* (Englewood Cliffs, N.J.: Prentice-Hall, 1980). ●

RESPONSIBILITY, AUTHORITY, AND ACCOUNTABILITY

When delegating work, it is helpful to keep in mind the important distinctions among responsibility, authority, and accountability.

Responsibility means that a person is assigned a task that he or she is supposed to carry out. When delegating work responsibilities, the manager should also delegate to the subordinate enough authority to get the job done. **Authority** means that the person has the power and the right to make decisions, give orders, draw upon resources, and do whatever else is necessary to fulfill the responsibility. Commonly, though, people have more responsibility than authority and must perform as best they can through informal influence tactics instead of relying purely on authority. More will be said about informal power and how to use it in Chapter 14.

As the manager delegates responsibilities, subordinates are held accountable for achieving results. **Accountability** means that the subordinate's manager has the right to expect the subordinate to perform the job, and the right to take corrective action in the event the subordinate fails to do so. The subordinate must report upward on the status and quality of his or her performance of the task.

On the other hand, the ultimate responsibility—accountability to higher-ups—lies with the manager doing the delegating. Managers remain responsible and accountable not only for their own actions but for the actions of their subordinates. Thus, managers should not resort to delegation to others as a means of escaping their own responsibilities. In many cases, however, managers refuse to accept responsibility for subordinates' actions. Managers often "pass the buck" or take other evasive action to ensure they are not held accountable for mistakes.[13]

ADVANTAGES OF DELEGATION

Delegating work offers important advantages. The manager saves time by giving some of his or her own responsibilities to someone else. Then the manager is free to devote energy to important, higher-level activities like planning, setting objectives, and monitoring performance.

Delegation essentially gives the subordinate a more important job. The subordinate acquires an opportunity to develop new skills and to demonstrate potential for additional responsibilities and perhaps promotion. In essence, the subordinate receives a vital form of on-the-job training that could pay off in the future.

The organization also receives payoffs. Allowing managers to devote more time to important managerial functions while lower-level employees carry out assignments means that jobs are done in a more efficient and cost-effective manner.

HOW TO DELEGATE

To achieve these advantages, delegation must be done properly. As Figure 10.4 shows, effective delegation proceeds through several steps.[14]

The first step in the delegation process, defining the goal, requires that the manager have a clear understanding of the outcome he or she wants. Then the manager should select a person who is capable of performing the task.

The person who gets the assignment should be given the authority, time, and resources needed to successfully carry out the task. Throughout the delegation process, the manager

FIGURE 10.4

The steps in effective delegation

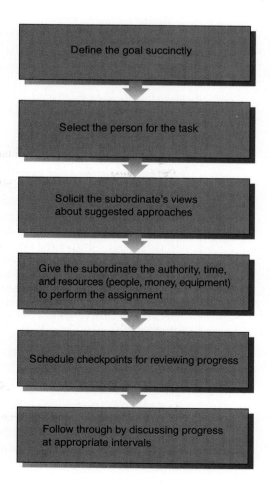

Define the goal succinctly

Select the person for the task

Solicit the subordinate's views about suggested approaches

Give the subordinate the authority, time, and resources (people, money, equipment) to perform the assignment

Schedule checkpoints for reviewing progress

Follow through by discussing progress at appropriate intervals and the subordinate must work together and communicate about the project. The manager should know the subordinate's ideas at the beginning and should inquire about progress or problems at periodic meetings and review sessions. Thus, even though the subordinate performs the assignment, the manager is available and aware of its current status.

Some tasks, such as disciplining subordinates and conducting performance reviews, should not be delegated. But when managers err, it usually is because they delegated too little rather than too much. The manager who wants to learn how to delegate more effectively should remember this distinction: If you are not delegating, you are merely *doing* things; but the more you delegate, the more you are truly *building* and *managing* an organization.[15]

DECENTRALIZATION

The delegation of responsibility and authority "decentralizes" decision making. In a **centralized organization,** important decisions usually are made at the top. In **decentralized organizations,** more decisions are made at lower levels. Ideally, decision making occurs at the level of the people who are most directly affected and have the most intimate knowledge about the problem. This is particularly important when the business environment is fast-changing and decisions must be made quickly and well.

For example, CBS used to have a vice president for program practices whose department censored controversial television programs like the "Smothers Brothers Comedy Hour." Today (and when CBS aired a Smothers Brothers reunion show), the program practices department no longer exists; individual departments use their own judgment to monitor program content. Thus, CBS decentralized censorship decisions.

Most American executives today understand the advantages of pushing decision-making authority down to the point of the action—the level that deals directly with problems and opportunities, has the most relevant information, and can best foresee the consequences of decisions. They also see how the decentralized approach allows people to take more timely action.[16]

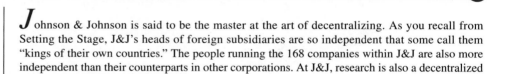

DECENTRALIZED DECISIONS

*J*ohnson & Johnson is said to be the master at the art of decentralizing. As you recall from Setting the Stage, J&J's heads of foreign subsidiaries are so independent that some call them "kings of their own countries." The people running the 168 companies within J&J are also more independent than their counterparts in other corporations. At J&J, research is also a decentralized activity, with small units specializing in particular niches.

But decentralization at J&J is not anarchy. Auditors and product-quality checkers monitor results. Also, top management can trust people because of the strength of the company's credo, which de-emphasizes profits and focuses attention on ethics, integrity, and the people the company serves. You read J&J's credo in Chapter 6.

Nucor provides another good example of a decentralized approach. Nucor is a $2 billion steelmaker that has only 23 people at its headquarters in Charlotte, North Carolina. Its 21 plant managers are responsible for virtually every aspect of the business. The plants do their own purchasing, set their own production quotas, and sell their own products. Many of these functions are often centralized at other companies. Nucor knows it would cost less to centralize these functions, but believes that decentralization makes the company more responsive to the marketplace.

Sources: B. O'Reilly, "J&J Is on a Roll," *Fortune,* December 26, 1995, pp. 178–92; W. Zellner, "Go-Go Goliaths," *Business Week,* February 13, 1995, pp. 64–70. ●

DEPARTMENTAL-
IZATION

The organization must be subdivided, or *departmentalized,* into smaller units. In this section, we will examine four basic means of **departmentalization:** functional, product, customer, and geographical. In the following section, we will discuss the matrix structure, which combines these basic forms.

FUNCTIONAL DEPARTMENTALIZATION

In a functional organization, jobs are specialized and grouped according to *business functions* and the skills they require: production, marketing, human resources, research and development, finance, accounting, and so forth. **Functional departmentalization** is common in small organizations. Large companies may organize along several different functional groupings, including groupings unique to their business. For example, General Cinema Theaters has vice presidents of marketing, engineering, finance, controller, operations, and concessions and a vice president who is the head film buyer. Figure 10.5 shows an organization chart of a manufacturing company that is organized by function.

The traditional functional approach to departmentalization has a number of potential advantages:[17]

1. *Economies of scale can be realized.* When people with similar skills are grouped, more efficient equipment can be purchased, and discounts for large purchases can be used.
2. *Monitoring of the environment* is more effective. Each functional group is more closely attuned to developments in its own field and therefore can adapt more readily.
3. *Performance standard*s are better maintained. People with similar training and interests may develop a shared concern for performance in their jobs.
4. People have greater opportunity for *specialized training* and *in-depth skill development.*
5. Technical specialists are relatively *free of administrative work.*
6. *Decision making* and *lines of communication* are simple and clearly understood.

The functional form has disadvantages as well as advantages. People may care more about their own function than about the company as a whole, and their attention to functional tasks may make them lose focus on overall product quality and customer satisfaction. Managers develop functional expertise but do not acquire knowledge of the other areas of the business; they become specialists, but not generalists. Between functions, conflicts arise, and communication and coordination fall off.

In this fragmented environment, it becomes difficult to develop and bring new products to market, and difficult to respond quickly to customer demands and other changes. Particularly when companies are growing and business environments changing, the need arises to integrate work areas more effectively so that the organization can be more flexible and responsive. Other forms of departmentalization can be more flexible and responsive than the functional structure.

For a time, some observers believed that the functional structure was disappearing—that in today's complex, rapidly changing business environment, the functional form had to

FIGURE 10.5

Functional departments in a manufacturing company

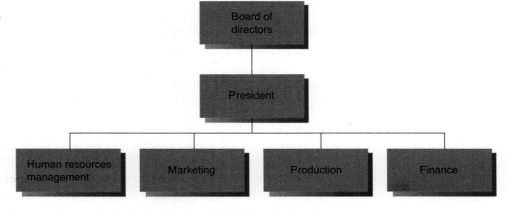

Source: D. Robey and C. Sales, *Designing Organizations,* 4th ed. (Burr Ridge, Ill.: Richard D. Irwin, 1994), p. 185.

give way to alternative forms discussed later. But in the early 1980s, pressures to reduce costs brought a resurgence of the more cost-effective functional structure.[18]

Nonetheless, recent demands first for total quality, then customer service, and now speed have made clear the shortcomings of the functional form. Functional organizations are highly differentiated, and create barriers to coordination across functions. Cross-functional coordination is essential for total quality, customer service, and speed. The functional organization will not disappear, in part because functional specialists will always be needed, but functional managers will make fewer decisions. The more important units will be cross-functional teams that have integrative responsibilities for products or customers.[19]

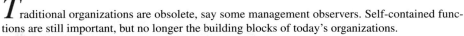

TOMORROW'S ORGANIZATION?

*T*raditional organizations are obsolete, say some management observers. Self-contained functions are still important, but no longer the building blocks of today's organizations.

Because today's environment poses new challenges, we need new organizational entities. Among the units proposed for tomorrow's organizations are:

1. A *knowledge/learning center,* which asks what we need to know and how we can come to know it.
2. A *recovery/development center,* which asks how we can aid the development of healthy employees and a healthy company.
3. A *world services/spiritual center,* which asks how we can aid the development of a healthy outside world, and focuses on our company's meaning and purpose.
4. An *operations center,* which asks how we can implement world-class manufacturing and service operations.
5. A *leadership institute,* comprising the CEO, the directors of the centers, and the CEO's staff.

In response to these suggestions, T. H. Davenport of Ernst & Young observed, " . . . the predictions are plausible . . . my greatest questions involve not whether but how rapidly some of the organizational innovations will appear."

On the other hand, June E. K. Delano of Eastman Kodak maintains, " . . . the model looks like an assemblage of staff organizations with unusual names and familiar functions, heavily tainted by old-fashioned paternalism . . . If something is critical to the survival of an organization in today's world, it must be widely diffused and owned; it cannot be relegated to a staff or a management group set apart from the day-to-day work of the organization."

Sources: I. Mitroff, R. Mason, and C. Pearson, "Radical Surgery: What Will Tomorrow's Organizations Look Like?" *The Executive,* May 1994, pp. 11–21; "On Tomorrow's Organizations: Moving Forward, or a Step Backwards?" *The Executive,* August 1944, pp. 93–98. ●

PRODUCT DEPARTMENTALIZATION

As organizations grow and become increasingly diversified, they may change to a **product** form of **departmentalization.** Because functional departments have difficulty managing a wide variety of products, all the functions that contribute to a given product are organized under one manager. Table 10.1 presents examples of how the same tasks would be organized under functional and product structures.

Figure 10.6 shows a product structure. In the product organization, managers in charge of functions for a particular product report to a product manager.

In large organizations, the product structure is sometimes called a *divisionalized* structure. Johnson & Johnson is one example of this form. J&J has 168 independent divisions in 33 groups, each responsible for a handful of products worldwide. Another example is 3M, at which a new product or product line typically becomes an independent division once it reaches a certain size.

FIGURE 10.6

Product departments in manufacturing

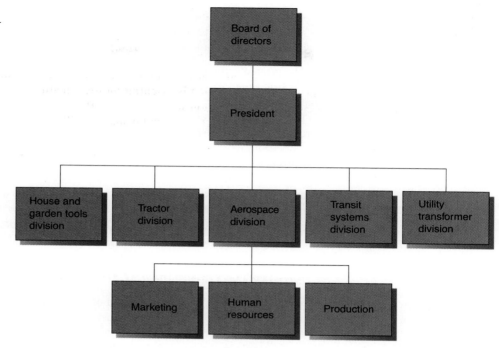

Source: D. Robey and C. Sales, *Designing Organizations,* 4th ed. (Burr Ridge, Ill.: Richard D. Irwin, 1994), p. 188.

The product or divisionalized approach to departmentalization offers a number of advantages:[20]

1. *Information needs are managed more easily.* Less information is required, because people work closely on one product and need not worry about other products.
2. *People have a full-time commitment to a particular product line.* They develop a greater awareness of how their jobs fit into the broader scheme.
3. *Task responsibilities are clear.* When things go wrong in a functional organization, functional managers can "pass the buck" ("that other department is messing up, making it harder for us to do our jobs"). In a product structure, managers are more independent and accountable because they usually have the resources they need to perform their tasks. Also, the performances of different divisions can be compared by contrasting their profits and other measures.

TABLE 10.1

Examples of functional and product organization

Functional Organization	Product Organization
A typing pool.	Each typist is assigned to one boss.
A central purchasing department.	Each division has its own purchasing unit.
Separate companywide marketing, production, design, and engineering departments.	Each product group has experts in marketing, design, production, and engineering.
A central-city health department.	The school district and the prison have their own health units.
Plantwide inspection, maintenance, and supply departments.	Production Team Y does its own inspection, maintenance and supply.
A university statistics department teaches statistics for the entire university.	Each department hires statisticians to teach its own students.

Source: George Strauss and Leonard R. Sayles, *Strauss & Sayles's Behavioral Strategies for Managers,* © 1980, p. 221. Reprinted by permission of Prentice-Hall, Inc., Englewood Cliffs, New Jersey.

4. *People receive broader training.* General managers develop a wide variety of skills, and they learn to be judged by results. Many top executives received crucial early experience in product structures.

The product structure is more flexible than the functional structure. The product structure is best suited for unstable environments, when an ability to rapidly adapt to change is important.

But the product or divisional structure also has disadvantages. It is difficult to coordinate across product lines and divisions. And, although managers learn to become generalists, they may not acquire the depth of functional expertise that develops in the functional structure.

Furthermore, functions that are not centralized at headquarters—where they can be done *for* all product lines or divisions—are done *by* each division. Such duplication of effort is expensive. Also, decision making is decentralized in this structure, so top management can lose some control over decisions made in the divisions. Proper management of all the issues surrounding decentralization and delegation, as discussed earlier, is essential for this structure to be effective.

CUSTOMER AND GEOGRAPHICAL DEPARTMENTALIZATION

Organizations can be departmentalized on bases other than function and product. Some companies are built around groups of customers or around geographical distinctions.

Many organizations are departmentalized by *client*s or **customers.** Universities have different people in charge of undergraduate, master's, doctoral, and night or part-time programs. These distinctions depend on the mix of students the university serves. A hospital may organize its services around child, adult, psychiatric, and emergency cases. Bank loan departments commonly allocate assignments based on whether customers are requesting consumer, mortgage, small-business, corporate, or agricultural loans.

Sears, Roebuck traditionally organized its stores by *geography.* **Geographical** distinctions include district, territory, region, and country. In companies like the industrial wholesaler diagrammed in Figure 10.7, different managers are in charge of the Southwest, Pacific, Midwest, Northeast, and Southeast regions. Seagram International is one of many companies that assign managers to Europe, the Far East, and Latin America.

The primary advantage of these approaches to departmentalization is the ability to focus on customer needs and provide faster, better service. But again, duplication of activities across many customer groups and geographic areas is expensive.

FIGURE 10.7

Geographical organization

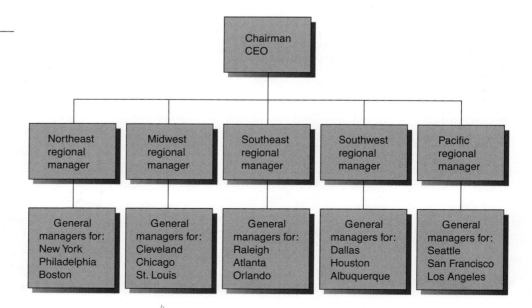

MIXED FORMS OF DEPARTMENTALIZATION

In many organizations, several forms of departmentalization exist simultaneously. Different *divisions* can have different structures. The same is usually true of different *levels,* such as when the top level is organized by product divisions and the divisions are organized on a functional basis. How would you describe the organizational structure shown in Figure 10.8? To further complicate things, more than one form can coexist within the same division *and* level. This is the matrix organization.

MATRIX ORGANIZATIONS

A **matrix organization** is a hybrid form of organization in which functional and product forms overlap. Managers and staff personnel report to two bosses—a functional manager and a product manager. Thus, matrix organizations have a dual rather than single line of command. Figure 10.9 illustrates the basic matrix structure.

FIGURE 10.8

Hybrid structure of a retailing organization

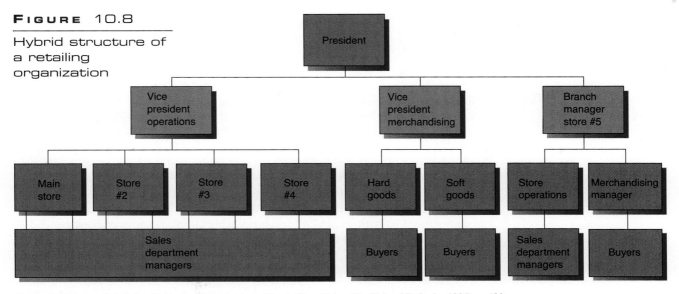

Source: D. Robey and C. Sales, *Designing Organizations,* 4th ed. (Burr Ridge, Ill.: Richard D. Irwin, 1994), p. 199.

FIGURE 10.9

Matrix organizational structure

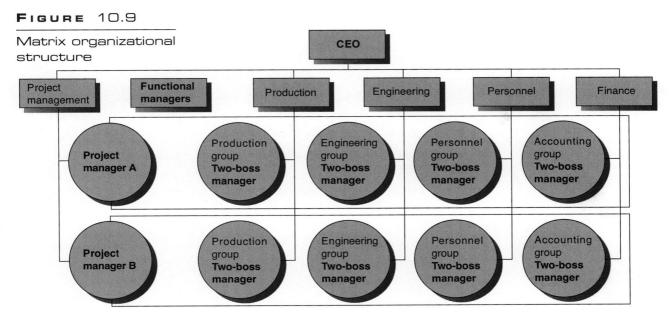

Source: D. Robey and C. Sales, *Designing Organizations,* 4th ed. (Burr Ridge, Ill.: Richard D. Irwin, 1994), p. 222.

NASA successfully used the matrix organization to organize and implement the launch of the legendary Mercury astronauts in the late 1950s. *(Courtesy NASA)*

The matrix form originated in the aerospace industry, first with TRW in 1959 and then with NASA. Applications now occur in hospitals and health care agencies, entrepreneurial organizations, government laboratories, financial institutions, and multinational corporations.[21] Companies that have used or presently use the matrix form include Chase Manhattan Bank, General Electric, Dow Chemical, Xerox, Shell Oil, Texas Instruments, Bechtel, Phillips Petroleum, Dow Corning, and Martin Marietta.

PROS AND CONS OF THE MATRIX FORM

Like other organization structures, matrix has both strengths and weaknesses. Table 10.2 summarizes the advantages of using a matrix structure. The major potential advantage is a higher degree of flexibility and adaptability.

Table 10.3 summarizes the potential shortcomings of the matrix form. Many of the disadvantages stem from the matrix's inherent violation of the unity-of-command principle, which states that a person should have only one boss. Reporting to two superiors can create confusion and a difficult interpersonal situation.

MATRIX SURVIVAL SKILLS

To a large degree, problems can be avoided if the key managers in the matrix learn the behavioral skills demanded in the matrix structure.[22] These skills vary depending on the job in the four-person diamond structure shown in Figure 10.10.

The *top executive,* who heads the matrix, must learn to balance power and emphasis between the product and functional orientations. *Product or program managers* and *functional managers* must learn to collaborate and manage their conflicts constructively. Finally, the *two-boss managers* or employees at the bottom of the diamond must learn how to be responsible to two superiors. This means prioritizing multiple demands and sometimes even reconciling conflicting orders. Some people function poorly under this ambiguous, conflictual circumstance; sometimes this signals the end of their careers with the company. Others learn to be proactive, communicate effectively with both superiors, rise above the difficulties, and manage these work relationships constructively.

THE MATRIX FORM TODAY

The matrix organization was popular in the 1970s and lost favor in the 1980s when many companies had difficulty implementing it. But in the 1990s it came back strong. Reasons for this resurgence included pressures to consolidate costs and be faster to market, creating

TABLE 10.2

Advantages of the matrix design

- Decision making is decentralized to a level where information is processed properly and relevant knowledge is applied.

- Extensive communications networks help process large amounts of information.

- With decisions delegated to appropriate levels, higher management levels are not overloaded with operational decisions.

- Resource utilization is efficient, because key resources are shared across several important programs or products at the same time.

- Employees learn the collaborative skills needed to function in an environment characterized by frequent meetings and more informal interactions.

- Dual career ladders are elaborated as more career options become available on both sides of the organization.

Source: H. Kolodny, "Managing in a Matrix," *Business Horizons,* March–April 1981, pp. 17–24.

TABLE 10.3

Disadvantages of
the matrix design

- Confusion can arise because people do not have a single superior to whom they feel primary responsibility.

- The design encourages managers who share subordinates to jockey for power.

- The mistaken belief can arise that matrix management is the same thing as group decision making—in other words, everyone must be consulted for every decision.

- Too much democracy can lead to not enough action.

Source: H. Kolodny, "Managing in a Matrix," *Business Horizons,* March–April 1981, pp. 17–24.

a need for better coordination across functions in the business units, and a need for coordination across countries for firms with global business strategies. Many of the challenges created by the matrix are particularly acute in an international context.[23]

The structure of the matrix hasn't changed, but our understanding of it has. The key to managing today's matrix is not the formal structure itself but the realization that the matrix is a *process.* Companies that have had trouble adopting the matrix form may have been correct in creating such a multidimensional structure to cope with environmental complexity, but they needed to go further than try to construct a flexible organization simply by changing the structure. The formal structure is merely the organization's anatomy. Executives must also attend to its physiology—the relationships that allow information to flow through the organization—and its psychology—the norms, values, and attitudes that shape how people think and behave.[24] We will address these issues in the next chapter when we discuss corporate culture and in Part IV, which focuses on how to lead and manage people.

ORGANIZATIONAL ROLES

Specialized organizational jobs include line, staff, integrating, and boundary roles.

LINE MANAGERS

Line managers are responsible for the principal activities of the firm. Line units deal directly with the organization's primary goods or services; they make things, sell things, or

FIGURE 10.10

The matrix diamond

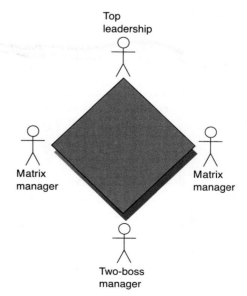

Source: Reprinted, by permission of the publisher, from *Organizational Dynamics* (Summer 1977) © 1977 American Management Association, New York. All rights reserved.

provide customer service. At General Motors, for example, the predominant line organization is the manufacturing divisions that produce the products GM sells.

Line managers typically have much authority and power in the organization. They have the ultimate responsibility for making major operating decisions. They also are accountable for the "bottom-line" results of their decisions.

STAFF

To run effectively, an organization needs **staff** people to carry out administrative procedures. For example, accounting procedures must be designed and managed, although accounting is tangential to the operational activities of most organizations. Other examples of staff units are research, personnel or human resources, public relations, and legal. Each of these specialized units often has its own vice president.

Some staff units are vested with great authority, as when accounting or finance staff groups approve and monitor budgetary activities or financial performance. For a time, staff in many organizations acquired a great deal of power as they closely monitored and controlled line performance. This role for staff provided coordination by specifying formal plans, goals, standard procedures, and measures of performance.

Innovation

But today, most staff units are moving away from a control orientation and toward one of strategic support and expert advice.[25] Staff add value by being supportive business partners to the line. Staff provide strategic information, expertise, and other services. They provide coordination across units by creating and supporting cross-functional teams. They look ahead to the future, and help the firm prepare for change. Successfully helping the organization change, in order to cope with new realities, is perhaps the ultimate value added by staff.

Line and staff are the two primary organizational roles. But within these two types are two other very important roles: integrating and boundary roles.

INTEGRATING ROLES

Because of specialization and the division of labor, different groups of managers and employees develop different orientations. Depending on whether employees are in a functional department or in a product group, are line or staff, and so on, they will think and act in ways that are geared toward their particular work units.

This high degree of *differentiation* among work units within the same organization creates a need for *coordination* among them. To achieve coordination among widely diverse departments, **integrating roles** must be created and performed. Such roles help reduce conflict and enhance the quality of collaboration among groups.

Some integrative functions are carried out by committees and task forces composed of representatives from different departments. Job titles like *product manager, project manager,* and *program manager* also imply integrative responsibilities. People in these roles must understand the work of different groups, manage conflict among them, and strive for coordination and unified performance.[26] Some of these roles are discussed more fully in Chapters 11 and 15.

BOUNDARY ROLES

Some managers and employees spend a lot of time interacting with people from other organizations. Such jobs are called **boundary roles,** and they are vital to the organization. Examples of boundary roles include jobs in sales, purchasing, customer service, public relations, advertising, and human resources (e.g., recruiting activities).

People in boundary roles fill two important functions for the organization. First, they *represent the company;* they provide information about the company to the outside world. In fact, the performance of the people in boundary roles often is the most visible part of an organization to customers and other outsiders. In this capacity, crucial performers are salespersons, advertisers, and public relations people. For example, people in the key boundary roles for MTV or ABC news have a big impact on public perception of their organizations.

Second, people in boundary roles *acquire information about the environment.* Salespersons, product managers, and others keep in touch with the competition and with customers' needs, concerns, and suggestions. On a more formal level, market researchers seek the same information. Purchasing agents attend to changes in the supply of raw materials. Engineers keep up with technological advances. Attorneys monitor changes in the organization's legal environment.

Boundary roles are like integrating roles, except that they involve interfacing between the organization and its external environment rather than among different groups within the organization.

LOOKING AHEAD

Lines of authority, the organization chart, the bases of departmentalization, and organizational roles like line and staff convey fundamental information about an organization's structure. However, the organization chart is just a snapshot, while the real organization is a motion picture. More complex forms of the modern organization have evolved.

No organization is merely a set of static work relationships. Because organizations are composed of people, they are hotbeds of social relationships. Networks of individuals cutting across departmental boundaries interact with one another. Various friendship groups or cliques band together to form *coalitions*—members of the organization who jointly support a particular issue and try to ensure that their viewpoints determine the outcome of policy decisions.[27]

Thus, the formal organization structure does not describe how the company really works. Even if you know departments and authority relationships, there is still much to understand. How do things really get done? Who influences whom, and how? Which managers are the most powerful? How effective is the top leadership? Which groups are most and which are least effective? Who interacts with whom? What is the nature of communication patterns throughout the organization? These issues are discussed throughout the rest of the book.

Now you are familiar with the basic organizing concepts discussed in this chapter. In the next chapter, we will discuss the current challenges of designing the modern organization with which the modern executive constantly grapples.

KEY TERMS

accountability, p. 246
authority, p. 241, 246
boundary roles, p. 257
centralized organization, p. 248
coordination, p. 240
customer departmentalization, p. 252
decentralized organizations, p. 248
delegation, p. 246
departmentalization, p. 249
differentiation, p. 240
division of labor, p. 240
functional departmentalization, p. 249
geographic departmentalization, p. 252

hierarchy, p. 242
integrating roles, p. 256
integration, p. 240
line managers, p. 256
matrix organization, p. 253
organization chart, p. 243
product departmentalization, p. 250
responsibility, p. 246
span of control, p. 244
specialization, p. 240
staff, p. 256
subunits, p. 243

SUMMARY OF LEARNING OBJECTIVES

Now that you have studied Chapter 10, you should know:

How specialization and coordination influence your organization's structure.

Specialization means that various individuals and units throughout the organization perform different tasks. The assignment of tasks to different people or groups is often referred to as the division of labor. But the specialized tasks in an organization cannot all be performed independently of one another. Coordination links the various tasks in order to achieve the organization's overall mission. When there are many different specialized tasks and work units, the organization is highly differentiated; the more differentiated the organization, the more integration or coordination is required.

How authority operates.

Authority is the legitimate right to make decisions and tell other people what to do. Authority is exercised throughout the hierarchy, as bosses have the authority to give orders to subordinates. Through the day-to-day operation of authority, the organization proceeds toward achieving its goals. Owners or stockholders have ultimate authority.

The roles of the board of directors and the chief executive officer.

Boards of directors report to stockholders. The board of directors controls or advises management, considers the firm's legal and other interests, and protects stockholders' rights. The chief executive officer reports to the board, and is accountable for the organization's performance.

How span of control affects structure and managerial effectiveness.

Span of control is the number of people who report directly to a manager. Narrow spans create tall organizations, and wide spans create flat ones. No single span of control is always appropriate; the optimal span is determined by characteristics of the work, the subordinates, the manager, and the organization.

How to delegate work effectively.

Delegation is the assignment of tasks and responsibilities. Delegation has many potential advantages for the manager, the subordinate, and the organization. But to be effective, the process must be managed carefully. The manager should define the goal, select the person, solicit opinions, provide resources, schedule checkpoints, and discuss progress periodically.

The difference between centralized and decentralized organizations.

In centralized organizations, most important decisions are made by top managers. In decentralized organizations, many decisions are delegated to lower levels.

How to allocate jobs to work units.

Jobs can be departmentalized on the basis of function, product, customers, or geography. Most organizations use several different types of departmentalization.

How to manage the unique challenges of the matrix organization.

The matrix is a complex structure with a dual authority structure. A well-managed matrix enables organizations to adapt to change. But it can also create confusion and interpersonal difficulties. People in all positions in the matrix—top executives, product and function managers, and two-boss managers—must acquire unique survival skills.

The nature of important organizational roles: line, staff, integrating, and boundary roles.

Line managers deal directly with the primary goods and services of the organization; they make things, sell things, or provide customer service. Staff people monitor or support and facilitate the work of line managers. Integrating roles enhance coordination among different units within the organization. Boundary roles form the interface between the organization and its external environment.

DISCUSSION QUESTIONS

1. Using the concepts in the chapter, discuss the advantages and disadvantages of the management approaches described in Setting the Stage.
2. What are some advantages and disadvantages of being in the CEO position?
3. Would you like to sit on a board of directors? Why or why not? If you did serve on a board, what kind of organization would you prefer? As a board member, in what kinds of activities do you think you would most actively engage?
4. Interview a member of a board of directors and discuss the member's perspectives on his or her role.
5. Discuss the questions under the upside-down organization chart on page 244.
6. Pick a job you have held and describe it in terms of span of control, delegation, responsibility, authority, and accountability.
7. Why do you think managers have difficulty delegating? What can be done to overcome these difficulties?

8. Consider an organization in which you have worked, draw its organization chart, and describe it using terms in this chapter. How did you like working there, and why?

9. Would you rather work in a functional or product organization? Why?

10. If you learned that a company had a matrix structure, would you be more or less interested in working there? Explain your answer. How would you prepare yourself to work effectively in a matrix?

11. Brainstorm a list of people in boundary roles. Discuss the activities they perform and the impression they give about their organizations.

CONCLUDING CASE

CODETERMINATION

In Germany and some Scandinavian countries, a company's board of management operates under a framework different from that of U.S. boards of directors. All publicly traded German companies operate under the principle of codetermination. Under codetermination, companies have both a board of management and a supervisory board including owner and employee representatives. The supervisory board oversees the board of management.

As in the United States, the board of management is responsible for the management and operation of the company. Each board member has responsibility for a function, a business, or both. Germany's codetermination law specifies one position on the management board as "works director." Responsibilities of the works director include personnel and employee relations.

Board chairs can be quite powerful, but their authority is not nearly as absolute as that of U.S. CEOs. The chair is more a colleague than a boss of the board members. The chair has one vote, just like the other members, and a great deal of time is devoted to reaching consensus decisions.

Members of the board of management are not allowed to serve on the supervisory board. In large companies half the members of the supervisory board must be employee representatives; the other half, owner representatives. The supervisory board has sole power to appoint members of the board of management, and it reviews board members' performance at the end of their one- to five-year contracts. The supervisory board then decides whether to renew the management board members' contracts.

Although appointing members to the board of management is the most important responsibility of the supervisory board, it also participates in important decisions affecting employment. For example, the supervisory board participates in any plant closing

German companies like Mercedes-Benz operate under the principle of codetermination. Each company has both a board of management and a supervisory board.
(David Pollack/The Stock Market)

decisions and can approve or veto plans to set up foreign operations or acquire foreign firms.

Critics argue that the system of codetermination has made it too difficult for German companies to lay off workers; in other words, it places jobs before profits. Such a system may sound compassionate, say the critics, but it is not capitalism and it hinders management's authority to act. It also hinders stockholders and potential acquirers from getting rid of ineffective, entrenched managers.

Carl H. Hahn, chairman of the board of management at Volkswagen AG, believes emphatically in the value of union representation on supervisory boards. Hahn maintains that decision making with labor participation can be faster, not slower, if employees understand the issues. The important thing, says Hahn, is open communication and continuous information.

QUESTIONS

1. What do you see as the advantages of codetermination? The disadvantages?

2. How does the system of codetermination differ from the framework within which boards of directors operate in the United States?

3. How effective could codetermination be in the United States? Which stakeholders would support the idea, and which would oppose? Why?

4. Propose a structure for a U.S.–based firm to realize some of the potential benefits of codetermination.

Sources: J. W. Lorsch, "The Workings of Codetermination," *Harvard Business Review,* July–August, 1991, p. 108; B. Avishai, "A European Platform for Global Competition," *Harvard Business Review,* July–August 1991, pp. 103–13; S. Hanke and Sir A. Walters, "As We See It," *Forbes,* April 11, 1994, p. 87.

EXPERIENTIAL EXERCISES

10.1 The Business School Organization Chart

Objectives

1. To clarify the factors that determine organization structure.
2. To provide insight into the workings of an organization.
3. To examine the working relationships within an organization.

Instructions

1. Draw an organization chart for your school of business. Be sure to identify all the staff and line positions in the school. Specify the chain of command and the levels of administration. Note the different spans of control. Are there any advisory groups, task forces, or committees to consider?

2. Review the chapter material on organization structure to help identify both strong and weak points in your school's organization. Now draw another organization chart for the school, incorporating any changes that you believe would improve the quality of the school. Support the second chart with a list of recommended changes and reasons for their inclusion.

Discussion Questions

1. Is your business school well organized? Why or why not?
2. Is your school's organization organic or mechanistic? In what ways?
3. In what ways is the school's structure designed to suit the needs of students, faculty, staff, the administration, and the business community?

10.2 Mechanistic and Organic Structures

Objectives

1. To think about your own preferences when it comes to working in a particular organizational structure.
2. To examine aspects of organizations using as an example *this class* you are a member of.

Instructions

1. Complete the Mechanistic and Organic Worksheet below.
2. Meet in groups of four to six persons. Share your data from parts 1 and 2 of the worksheet. Discuss the reasons for your responses, and analyze the factors that probably encouraged your instructor to choose the type of structure that now exists.

MECHANISTIC AND ORGANIC WORKSHEET

1. Indicate your general *preference* for working in one of these two organizational structures by circling the appropriate response:

Mechanistic	1	2	3	4	5	6	7	8	9	10	**Organic**

2. Indicate your perception of the form of organization that is used in *this class* by circling the appropriate response for each item:

A. **Task-role definition**

Rigid	1	2	3	4	5	6	7	8	9	10	**Flexible**

B. **Communication**

Vertical	1	2	3	4	5	6	7	8	9	10	**Multidirectional**

C. **Decision making**

Centralized	1	2	3	4	5	6	7	8	9	10	**Decentralized**

D. **Sensitivity to the environment**

Closed	1	2	3	4	5	6	7	8	9	10	**Open**

Source: Keith Davis and John. W. Newstrom, *Human Behavior at Work,* 9th ed. (New York: McGraw-Hill, 1993), p. 358. Reprinted by permission of McGraw-Hill, Inc.

11

THE RESPONSIVE ORGANIZATION

Bureaucracy defends the status quo long past the time when the quo has lost its status.

Laurence J. Peter

LEARNING OBJECTIVES

After studying Chapter 11, you will know:

1. The market imperatives your firm must meet to survive.

2. The potential advantages of creating an organic form of organization.

3. How your firm can "be" both small and big.

4. How to manage information-processing demands.

5. How to diagnose and manage your firm's culture.

6. The activities and impact of corporate restructuring.

7. The new types of dynamic organizational concepts and forms.

TWO VASTLY DIFFERENT COMPANIES

Consider two very different, successful companies:

- Zurich-based ABB Asea Brown Boveri is a huge industrial firm. It is broken down into eight major business segments, 65 business areas, 1,300 independent companies, and about 5,000 autonomous profit centers of about 50 people each. The profit centers are further broken down into 10-person teams. Each profit center performs multiple business functions, has its own balance sheet and profit-and-loss statement, and directly serves its own customers. Every employee is part of a team that is itself a small business.

- Paul Farrow started Walden Paddlers in 1992. In a very short period of time he has designed, produced, and marketed a high-tech kayak made from recycled plastic. The kayak costs less than its competition—and performs better. How many employees does Mr. Farrow have? One: him-

self. Why? Because he figured that building a company to design, manufacture, and market kayaks would take forever and cost over $1 million, which he did not have.

How has he pulled all this off? He became a customer to a talented molder who would take on custom work from the outside—and the molder was a serious whitewater kayaker. Then, he found a talented designer with the same passion. And then, he contacted successful retailers and gave them demonstration kayaks for 30 days, allowing them to paddle them, take them apart, or sell them. All the people involved are talented, share a passion for the product, and have personal or business reasons to trust one another. And they share the costs, as well as the profits, of Paul Farrow's business dream.

Paul Farrow realized his business dream, to manufacture a high-tech kayak, with only himself on the payroll. Walden Paddlers is a network organization, which is one of the many new forms today's businesses are taking.
(Gary Moss)

Sources: E. O. Welles, "Virtual Realities," *Inc.*, August 1993, pp. 50–58; T. Peters, *Liberation Management* (New York: Alfred A. Knopf, 1992); G. E. Schares, "Percy Barnevik's Global Crusade," *Business Week,* 1993 Special Issue, pp. 204–11.

*A*s you can see from the two examples above, there are different routes to success. One organization is huge, the other small. One is organized around teams, the other is a one-person firm that contracts with other firms in what is called a network organization. Today's companies are taking many other approaches to organizing as well, including changing their organization cultures, restructuring, and forming strategic alliances with their competitors. In this chapter, you will learn about these developments and their impact on organizations.

Chapter 10 described the formal structure of organizations. The ideas we discussed there are traditional and basic, and fundamental to understanding organizations. But your firm's structure does not in and of itself make things happen. Organizations are not static structures, but complex systems in which many people do many different things at the same time. The overall behavior of organizations does not just pop out of a chart, but emerges out of many individual actions.

In today's modern firm, new approaches to organizing are emerging. The emphasis in this chapter is not on the formal organization, but on organizing for *action*.[1]

TODAY'S IMPERATIVES

The formal structure is put in place to *control* people, decisions, and actions. But in today's fast-changing business environment, *responsiveness*—quickness, agility, the ability to adapt to changing demands—is more vital than ever to your firm's survival.[2]

Progressive companies place a premium on being able to act, and act fast. They want to act in accord with customer needs and other outside pressures. They want to take actions to correct past mistakes, and also to prepare for an uncertain future. They want to be able to respond to threats and opportunities. To do these things, they try to operate organically, manage size effectively, process huge amounts of information, create the appropriate culture, and adopt new forms of organization.

THE ORGANIC STRUCTURE

One common conception of organizations is a simple organization chart in which pure authority rules in a rigid structure of reporting relationships. This basic idea originated in the classical school of management discussed in Chapter 2. The specific principles underlying this ideal are the basis for the most traditional type of organization: the *bureaucracy*.

Many years after Max Weber wrote about bureaucracy (Chapter 2), two British management scholars described what they called the **mechanistic organization.**[3] The common mechanistic structure they described was similar to Weber's bureaucracy. But they went on to suggest that in the modern corporation, the mechanistic structure is not the only option.

The **organic structure** is in stark contrast to the mechanistic organization.[4] It is much less rigid, and in fact, emphasizes flexibility. In the organic organization,

1. Jobholders have broader responsibilities that change as the need arises.
2. Communication occurs through advice and information rather than through orders and instructions.
3. Decision making and influence are more decentralized and informal.
4. Expertise is highly valued.
5. Jobholders rely more heavily on judgment than on rules.
6. Obedience to authority is less important than commitment to the organization's goals.
7. Employees depend more on one another and relate more informally and personally.

Figure 11.1 compares the mechanistic and organic structures in terms of who interacts with whom in the work unit.[5] People in the organic organization work more as teammates than as subordinates who take orders from the boss, thus breaking away from the traditional bureaucratic form.[6]

The organic concept underlies the newer forms of organization described in this chapter. The more organic your firm is, the more responsive it will be to changing competitive demands and market realities.

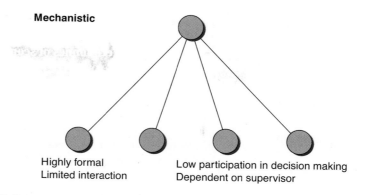

FIGURE 11.1

Mechanistic versus organic work units

Mechanistic

Highly formal
Limited interaction

Low participation in decision making
Dependent on supervisor

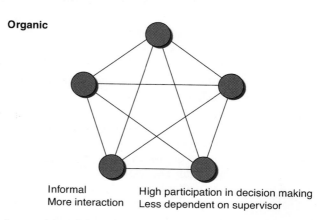

Organic

Informal
More interaction

High participation in decision making
Less dependent on supervisor

Source: Adapted from D. Nadler, J. Hackman, and E.E. Lawler III, *Managing Organizational Behavior* (Boston: Little, Brown, 1979).

MANAGING SIZE

One of the most important characteristics of an organization is its size. Large organizations are typically less organic and more bureaucratic. For example, at Hewlett-Packard, before the recent reduction of its stifling bureaucracy, it took over 90 people on nine committees more than seven months to decide what to name some new software.[7]

In large organizations, jobs become more specialized. More distinct groups of specialists get created because large organizations can add a new specialty at lower proportional expense. The complexity these numerous specialities create makes the organization harder to control. Therefore, management has traditionally added more levels to keep spans of control from becoming too large.[8]

Innovation

To cope with complexity, large companies become more bureaucratic. Rules, procedures, and paperwork are introduced. The conventional wisdom is that bureaucratization increases efficiency but decreases a company's ability to innovate. But innovation and bureaucracy can coexist if rules and regulations provide guidance but are not cast in stone, so that people are allowed to deviate from them for good reasons.[9]

Thus, with size comes greater complexity, and complexity brings a need for increased control. In response, organizations adopt bureaucratic strategies of control. But is large size a good thing or a bad thing?

THE CASE FOR BIG

Cost

Bigger was better after World War II, when foreign competition was limited and growth seemed limitless. To meet high demand for its products, U.S. industry embraced high-volume, low-cost manufacturing methods. IBM, GM, and Sears all grew into behemoths during these decades.

Alfred Chandler, distinguished professor emeritus at Harvard, believes that big companies have been the engine of economic growth throughout this century and will continue to be over the next century.[10] Professor Chandler maintains that companies *must* grow big to succeed in the long run. Size creates *scale economies,* that is, lower costs per unit of production. Size also creates **economies of scope;** materials and processes employed in one product can be used to make other, related products.

Executives and shareholders want size. Size potentially offers prestige, stability, and profits. And size can offer specific advantages like economies of scale, lowered operating costs, greater purchasing power, and easier access to capital. For example, $11.5 billion Intel spends more than $1 billion a year on research and development, far more than its rivals can afford.[11] With such advantages, huge companies with lots of money may be the best at taking on large foreign rivals in huge global markets.

THE CASE FOR SMALL

But a huge, complex organization can find it hard to manage relationships with customers and among its own units.[12] Bureaucracy can run rampant, too much success can breed complacency, and the resulting inertia hinders change—a surefire formula for being left in the dust by hungry competitors. Moreover, some economies of scale are declining; for instance, small firms now can purchase tremendous computing power at low cost, and reach niche markets through cable TV and target marketing rather than mass media.

In recent years, consumers began demanding a more diverse array of products, customized products, high quality, and better service. As you know, these offerings must be developed, marketed, and delivered *quickly.* The giants began to stumble. A new term has entered business vocabulary: *dis*economies of scale, or the *costs* of being too big. "Small is beautiful" became the cry.

Smaller companies can move fast, can provide quality goods and services to targeted market niches, and can inspire greater involvement from their people. Nimble, small firms now outmaneuver the big bureaucracies, introduce new and better products, and steal market share. The premium now is on flexibility and responsiveness—the unique potential strengths of the small firm.

For example, Ultra Pac Inc. produces recyclable plastic food containers.[13] It has only 300 employees, but competes against Mobil Corp. and Tenneco Inc. The smaller company turns out 500 different kinds of packaging and ships within three days of an order, in contrast to over a week at the larger companies.

Arthur Young, one of the former Big Eight accounting firms, used to give great service to small business. But after Young merged with Ernst & Whinney to form Ernst & Young, the firm began losing clients because of poor service.[14] In particular, smaller clients felt they had no contact with partners, had no personal relationships, and received poor advice for the stiff fees they paid. The only ones to give them priority, it seemed, were the billing departments. In accounting, as elsewhere, big companies are losing clients to smaller competitors.

SMALL WITHIN BIG

Small *is* beautiful for unleashing energy and speed. But in buying and selling, size offers market power. The challenge is to be both: big and small, to capitalize on the advantages of each. IBM is trying to do both in order to emerge from its doldrums and regain its past glory.[15] It is working together on major projects with Siemens, Motorola, and a variety of other partners. At the same time it is creating smaller, more flexible business units.

Motorola is a behemoth that has successfully maintained a "small-within-big" mentality, although it continually must struggle to do so as its sales double every five years. Motorola is considered by many to be the best-managed company in the world. It, too, is decentralized and team-based, organized around small, adaptive work units.[16]

If power is decentralized so small units can act quickly, with a minimum of bureaucratic constraints from the top, what is left to be done at the corporate level? Plenty. Corporate headquarters can still add value by virtue of its size and power.[17] It can inculcate entrepreneurism throughout the organization. Specifically, it can provide access to money (borrowing capacity is greater and costs lower for the corporation than for its individual business

Cost

units), manage key technologies, supply management talent, leverage its power by negotiating sales and purchasing contracts, manage government relations, and provide technical expertise to its units.

In these ways, a corporation can enjoy the advantages of being both big and small.

MANAGING INFORMATION

Today's environments are dynamic and uncertain. Even seemingly simple business situations may rapidly become more complex. To cope, managers must acquire, process, and act on huge amounts of information. Information flows from the external environment to the organization's decision makers. For decisions to be effective and organizations to survive and prosper, managers must develop effective mechanisms for processing information.

How can management improve decision making in these difficult situations and help ensure organizational success? Figure 11.2 shows two general strategies that can help managers cope with high uncertainty and heavy information demands. First, management can act to reduce the need for information. Second, it can increase its capacity to handle more information.[18]

REDUCING THE NEED FOR INFORMATION

Managers can use two specific methods to reduce the need for information: creating slack resources and creating self-contained tasks. *Creating slack resources* makes more time, money, or other resources available so that work units can cope smoothly when problems arise. For example, extending deadlines and increasing budgets will help prevent crises of missed deadlines and budget shortfalls.

Creating self-contained tasks refers to changing from a functional organization to a product or project organization and giving each unit the resources it needs to perform its task. Information-processing problems are reduced because each unit has its own full complement of specialties instead of functional specialties having to share their expertise among a number of different product teams. Communications then flow within each team rather than among a complex array of interdependent groups.

PROCESSING MORE INFORMATION

Organizations can use two techniques to help them process more information. First, they can *invest in information systems,* which usually means employing or expanding computer

FIGURE 11.2

Managing high information-processing demands

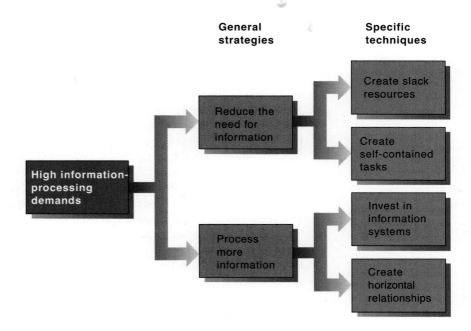

systems. Second, they can *create horizontal relationships* to foster coordination across different units. Such horizontal relationships are effective because they increase integration, which Lawrence and Lorsch suggest is necessary for managing complex environments. As uncertainty increases, the following horizontal processes may be used, ranging from the simplest to the most complex:[19]

1. *Direct contact* among managers who share a problem. In a university, for example, a residence hall adviser might call a meeting to resolve differences between two feuding students who live in adjacent rooms.
2. *Liaison roles,* or specialized jobs to handle communications between two departments. A fraternity representative is a liaison between the fraternity and the interfraternity council, the university, or the local community.
3. *Task forces,* or groups of representatives from different departments, brought together temporarily to solve a common problem. For example, students, faculty, and administrators may be members of a task force charged with bringing distinguished speakers to campus for a current-events seminar.
4. *Teams,* or permanent interdepartmental decision-making groups. An executive council made up of department heads might meet regularly to make decisions affecting a college of engineering or liberal arts.
5. *Product, program, or project managers* who direct interdisciplinary groups with a common task to perform. In a college of business administration, a faculty administrator might head an executive education program composed of professors from several disciplines.
6. *Matrix organizations,* composed of dual relationships in which some managers report to two superiors (recall Chapter 10). Your instructors, for example, may report to department heads in their respective disciplines and also to a director of undergraduate or graduate programs.

Several of these processes are discussed further in Chapter 16, where we examine managing teams and intergroup relations.

ORGANIZATION CULTURE

Management theory is continually evolving. One of the hottest management topics of the 1980s was corporate culture. And this issue is back in the 1990s, with more executives recognizing its importance and understanding better how to manage it.

Organization culture is the set of important assumptions about the organization and its goals and practices that members of the company share.[20] It is a system of shared *values* about what is important and *beliefs* about how the world works. A company's culture provides a framework that organizes and directs people's behavior on the job.

Two important examples illustrate how similar the cultures of seemingly disparate organizations can be and the dramatic contrast when cultures change. Consider the culture of AT&T before divestiture and that of organizations in the former Soviet Union before *perestroika.*[21] Despite vastly different national political and economic systems, the cultures of these organizations were remarkably similar: They were characterized by a heavily staffed bureaucracy, centralized control, nepotism, a welfare mentality in which workers were "taken care of," strong socialization processes, little concern with efficiency, and an emphasis on loyal, "right-thinking" employees. After AT&T's divestiture, and in the current environment in Russia, both cultures differ from what they were before: Entrepreneurship is encouraged, decisions are decentralized, efficiency is measured and rewarded, and individuals hold more responsibility and accountability.

Cultures can be strong or weak;[22] strong cultures can have great influence on how people think and behave. A *strong* culture is one in which everyone understands and believes in the firm's goals, priorities, and practices. A strong culture can be a real advantage to the organization if the behaviors it encourages and facilitates are appropriate ones. On the other hand, a strong culture that encourages the wrong behaviors can severely hinder the company's efforts to bring about appropriate changes.

In contrast, in a *weak* culture different people hold different values, there is confusion about corporate goals, and it is not clear from one day to the next what principles should guide decisions. As you can guess, such a culture fosters confusion, conflict, and poor performance. Most managers would agree that they want to create a strong culture that encourages and supports goals and useful behaviors that will make the company more effective.

DIAGNOSING CULTURE

Let's say that you want to understand a company's culture—because you are thinking about working there and you want a good "fit," or because you *are* working there and you want to be an effective manager. How would you go about making the diagnosis?

A variety of things will give you useful clues about culture:

- *Corporate mission statements and official goals* are a starting point, as they will tell you the firm's desired public image. But you still need to figure out whether the public statements truly reflect how the firm conducts business.

- *Business practices* can be observed. How a company responds to problems, makes strategic decisions, and treats employees and customers tells a lot about what top management *really* values.

- *Symbols, rites, and ceremonies* give further clues about culture. For instance, status symbols can give you a feel for how rigid the hierarchy is and for the nature of relationships between lower and higher levels. Who is hired and fired—and why—and the activities that are rewarded indicate the firm's real values.

- The *stories people tell* carry a lot of information about their company's culture. Every company has its myths, legends, and true stories about important past decisions and actions that convey the company's main values. Traditionally, Frito-Lay tells service stories, J&J tells quality stories, and 3M tells innovation stories.[23] The stories often feature the company's heroes: persons once or still active possessed of the qualities and characteristics that the culture especially values, who act as models for others about how to behave.

MANAGING CULTURE

Concern with organization culture seemed to be a trendy fad in the 1980s. Most companies that tried to change their cultures tried superficial "fixes" and learned that changing the culture isn't easy. But companies today know that improving quality, adopting a customer orientation, and other moves necessary to being competitive are so essential that they require deep-rooted cultural changes.[24]

Top management can take several approaches to managing culture. First, corporate leadership should *espouse lofty ideals and visions* for the company that will inspire the organization's members. (We will discuss visions more fully in Chapter 14, which focuses on leadership.) The vision, whether it concerns quality, integrity, innovation, or whatever, should be articulated over and over until it becomes a tangible presence throughout the organization.

Second, executives must give *constant attention* to the mundane details of daily affairs like communicating regularly, being visible and active throughout the company, and setting examples.[25] The CEO should not only talk about the vision; he or she should embody it day in and day out. This makes the CEO's pronouncements credible, creates a personal example others can emulate, and builds trust that the organization's progress toward the vision will continue over the long run.

Important here are the *moments of truth* when hard choices must be made. Imagine top management trumpeting a culture that emphasizes quality and then discovering that a part used in a batch of assembled products is defective. The decision whether to replace the part at great expense in the interest of quality or to ship the defective part just to save time and money will go a long way toward either reinforcing or destroying a quality-oriented culture.

All along, it is essential that the CEO and other executives *celebrate and reward* those who exemplify the new values. Another key to managing culture involves *hiring, socializing newcomers, and promoting based on the new corporate values.* In this way, the new culture will begin to permeate the organization.[26] While this may seem a time-consuming approach to building a new culture, executives must recognize that it can take years to replace a long-time culture of traditional values with one that embodies the competitive values needed in the future.

THE CULTURE OF SUCCESS

What kind of culture helps a firm to be successful? A strong culture that fosters behavior that delivers value to the customer and competitive advantage to the firm breeds success. Top executives can do a great deal to create a culture that places a high value on customers, and on competitiveness, and to make those values clear to everyone. The culture of success should emphasize several major priorities simultaneously: innovation, customer service, product quality, speed, and work that gives employees a sense of well-being and a feeling of being a part of something special. A true success culture focuses on future opportunities, not just on past accomplishments. All these things can be signaled to people, and all are discussed throughout this book.

Source: B. Schneider, S. Gunnarson, and K. Niles-Jolly, "Creating the Climate and Culture of Success," *Organizational Dynamics,* Summer 1994, pp. 17–29. ●

So far, we have discussed how companies become more effective and responsive by managing size, information, and culture. Next, we turn our attention to other approaches currently used to respond to changing environments: restructuring and new forms of organization.

THE RESTRUCTURING OF CORPORATE AMERICA

Business headlines over the past few years have had some recurring themes: mergers, acquisitions, hostile takeovers, and buyouts. The 1980s have been labeled the "deal decade." More than a third of the *Fortune* 500 industrials were swallowed up by other concerns or went private in a 10-year span. *Fortune* called the action a "ripsnorting string of shoot'em ups like nothing ever seen on Wall Street or Main Street."[27]

Today, companies are merging and acquiring at high rates once again.[28] If you are like most people, you have found all this activity quite confusing. This section will help you sort out the events and types of new deals that have restructured corporate America.

MERGERS

The first business mergers in the United States took place in the 19th century (Mr. Procter and Mr. Gamble initially had separate businesses). A **merger** occurs when two companies form one corporation by mutual agreement. Major oil company mergers occurred in the early 1980s, food and consumer products company mergers dominated the late 1980s, and bank mergers were the rage of the early 1990s.

Recently, Federated bought R. H. Macy and is now the country's largest department store company.[29] Lockheed and Martin Marietta, the nation's second- and third-largest weapons makers, merged into a huge corporation with a market value over $10 billion.[30] A number of railroads have merged, and many suppliers to large companies have merged with one another.[31] Glaxo, the pharmaceutical company, vowed in 1994 not to get into the merger game—but was bidding on other companies by 1995.[32]

Why all the activity? Much of it stems from fear and the need for survival.[33] Small companies merge to achieve economies of scale that their larger competitors already enjoy.

The first business mergers in the United States took place in the 19th century when Mr. Procter (left) and Mr. Gamble joined forces.
(© The Procter & Gamble Company; used with permission)

Lockheed and Martin Marietta were driven to merge by the massive decline in defense spending. Banks merge in order to reduce expenses or spread costs across a bigger asset base. Railroads merge to compete with the trucking industry; they have come to realize their competitors are not other railroads, but the highway and truckers. With the trend among large companies to use fewer suppliers than in the past, many small suppliers must merge to stay in business.

Innovation   Firms also merge because new technologies make it possible to offer customers a full array of services (for example, cable, local, and long-distance services).[34] Ciba-Geigy bought Chiron in 1995 to become a stronger player in biotech.[35] And markets change; drug companies squeezed by cost-conscious customers merge to cut costs and offer a wider range of products, as when Merck bought Medco, a discounter.[36]

Cost   The goals of a merger may be worthwhile, but the merger process is difficult. After undergoing the staggering expense of a merger, the new company needs to reduce its debt quickly so that it can pursue strategies aimed at long-term strength and competitiveness. "People" problems also can be severe; morale may suffer if jobs are cut and employees transferred or let go, or if excessive executive compensation creates resentment among employees.

Mergers often fail; one estimate is that 90 percent fail to meet expectations.[37] A common reason for failure is the chaos resulting from the clash of different organization cultures. Most analysts agree that for a merger to work two conditions must hold. First, the two companies must fit together from a strategic standpoint. Second, the two organization cultures must be compatible.

ACQUISITIONS

An **acquisition** is a transaction in which a firm buys all or part of another business and the transaction is agreeable to both parties. Mergers and acquisitions are similar in that, unlike takeovers and buyouts (described later), they are "friendly," that is, done by mutual consent. Also, strategic fit and culture compatibility are essential to success for both processes.

In the 1990s, a common strategy for manufacturing companies is to acquire businesses in service and technology-based industries.[38] Services are attractive to manufacturers because they are the fastest-growing sector of the economy, manufacturers need to provide services in support of their products, and services tend to be local businesses and thus less susceptible to foreign competition. Business opportunities in R&D or technology-intensive

Innovation

industries are attractive because they provide a competitive weapon against new international competitors. Moreover, companies see acquiring technology firms as a means to enter the growth industries of the future.

TAKEOVERS

Traditional mergers and acquisitions have been popular for decades. But recently a different type of acquisition has gained popularity. A **takeover** occurs when the purchasing company makes a direct bid to the target company's stockholders because the target's management opposes the purchase. The individuals who have been successful at taking over their targets are known as *corporate raiders.* Famous raiders include T. Boone Pickens, Carl Icahn, England's Sir James Goldsmith, and Canada's Robert Campeau.

Most takeovers are *hostile,* that is, the target tries to prevent the purchase. A classic defense tactic by targets is the *poison pill:* The target issues new securities to raise the cost of acquiring the firm. Another common strategy is to go private: Instead of being publicly held by stockholders, the CEO owns and has direct responsibility for the firm. Buybacks of company stock for this purpose usually occur through leveraged buyouts, discussed next.

LEVERAGED BUYOUTS

Cost

In a **leveraged buyout (LBO),** a group buys the majority of stock in their own company from shareholders. The investors borrow up to 90 percent of the money and pledge the company's assets as collateral. If the investors succeed in taking over the company, the company becomes privately rather than publicly held. Typically the investors sell subsidiaries, cut jobs, and slash costs. The result—ideally—is a smaller, better-focused company.[39]

A common motive behind going private is to avoid a takeover by hostile outsiders. Buyouts also occur because managers want to become their own bosses, running the business the way they want to instead of having to report to shareholders and deal with the Securities and Exchange Commission (SEC). Companies also go private in this way when managers are tired of low stock prices.[40] The buyout (and takeover) process raises prices, and managers often sell their personal holdings at big profits.

THE IMPACT OF RESTRUCTURING

Takeovers and LBOs were defended because allegedly they bring out the best in companies. Debt forces a company to operate with greater efficiency. According to James Bere, CEO of Borg-Warner, "There's nothing like survival mode to get humans moving." Some of the effects of restructuring are summarized in Table 11.1.

Cost

The new debt load both enabled and forced a change in management behavior.[41] It created a new toughness in labor negotiations and forced corporations to be "lean and mean" to satisfy their creditors.[42] LBOs formed in 1981 through 1984 lifted corporate cash flows considerably (although this was not true for the LBOs of the late 1980s). LBOs appear to have worked best in the manufacturing sector.[43]

TABLE 11.1

The impact of restructuring

Potential Benefits	Potential Disadvantages
A new toughness	Loss of good people
Greater efficiency	Massive debt
Stock profits	Short-term focus
Motivated managers	Fear of job loss

Another benefit of takeover activity accrues to stockholders, who profit from the activity. Also, LBOs give management a bigger stake in the company, because they purchase the company's stock. In theory, this means a more committed, motivated management team. But in fact, top management ends up with less money in the company because they take advantage of the deals to sell part of their stakes.[44]

Takeovers and LBOs also have negative consequences. Good managers may leave. The massive debt weakens the firm. Short-term attention to retiring the debt can cause top management to lose sight of long-term goals. Even companies that have not been taken over may spend more time and money trying to prevent its happening to them than they do pursuing product quality and other central goals of the firm.[45]

Finally, takeovers and LBOs strike fear in people—from the lowest levels to the very top of the organization—that they will lose their jobs. Takeovers often result in layoffs, plant closings, and the sale of plants and subsidiaries.

DOWNSIZING

Even companies not engaging in the restructuring activities described above often eliminate jobs and people in an effort to reduce their size. As long as overhead costs are high, and particularly when companies are deeply in debt, companies turn to downsizing as a strategy for reducing costs and improving their financial position.[46]

Downsizing is the planned elimination of positions or jobs. Common approaches to downsizing include eliminating functions, hierarchical levels, or units.[47] A more recent, related term is rightsizing. To some people, rightsizing is just a euphemism for laying people off so the company becomes smaller. But **rightsizing** is better described as a successful effort to achieve an appropriate size at which the company performs most effectively.[48] Thus, downsizing is a more general term, and rightsizing more specfically refers to appropriate, well-managed changes in size.

It is hard to pick up a newspaper without seeing announcements of another company downsizing; likewise, it is hard to name a major corporation that has not downsized in recent years. The list includes IBM, Citicorp, Goodyear, Exxon, CBS, ABC, Xerox, TRW, and General Motors. It also includes every conceivable type of small- and midsized company. And the practice is worldwide, with companies downsizing in Europe, China, South America, and Japan.

Historically, layoffs tended to affect manufacturing firms, and operative level workers in particular. But things are different now, as "white-collar" middle managers in many industries have been hardest hit.

Microsoft is one notable exception to the big-company downsizing trend.[49] As of 1995, they had not embarked on a downsizing effort. However, Microsoft has carefully controlled its size even as revenues have mushroomed. Its approach to head-count growth is "n-minus-one": if a task requires five extra people, Microsoft allocates four. As it turns out, the work gets done, and the company has not become bloated to the point of needing to downsize.

The people who lose their jobs because of downsizing are not the only ones deeply affected. Those who survive the process—who keep their jobs—tend to exhibit what has become known as **survivor's syndrome.**[50] They struggle with heavier workloads, wonder who will be next to go, try to figure out how to survive, lose commitment to the company and faith in their bosses, and become narrow-minded, self-absorbed, and risk averse. Morale and productivity drop.

What can be done to manage downsizing effectively—to help make it a more effective "rightsizing"? First, efforts to avoid exorbitant debt and overhead costs, and to avoid excessive hiring the way Microsoft has done, can help reduce the need to engage in major or multiple downsizings. Second, when downsizing, firms must avoid the common mistakes:[51] don't make slow, small, frequent layoffs; don't implement voluntary early retirement programs that may entice your best people to leave; don't lay off so many people that the company's work can no longer be performed; and don't place survivors in more demanding jobs without sufficient training and communication about the future of the

Downsizing is the planned elimination of jobs. The fact that layoffs are planned doesn't mean people aren't frightened and angry when they lose their jobs, as evidenced by these placard-carrying ex-employees.

[Tom McKitterick/Impact Visuals]

company. Third, firms need to engage in positive practices such as choosing positions to be eliminated based on careful analysis and strategic thinking; training people to cope with the new situation; identifying and protecting talented people; seeking recommendations from people throughout the organization about how to downsize; giving special attention and help to those who have lost their jobs; communicating constantly with people about the process; and emphasizing a positive future and people's new roles in attaining it.[52] You will learn more about some of these ideas in later chapters on leadership, motivation, communication, and managing change.

NEW ORGANIZATIONAL FORMS

In response to changing demands and new strategic requirements, new organizational forms are emerging. All represent efforts to become more organic and responsive. The new concepts include core competencies, network organizations, strategic alliances, the learning organization, the high involvement organization, and team-based organizations.

CORE COMPETENCIES

A recent, different, and important perspective on strategy, organization, and competition hinges on the concept of core competence.[53] Companies compete not just with their products, but also on the basis of their core strengths and expertise.

As you learned in Chapter 5, a *core competence* is the capability—knowledge, expertise, skill—that underlies a company's ability to be a leader in providing a range of specific goods or services. A core competence gives value to customers, makes the company's products different from (and better than) competitors', and can be used in creating new products. Think of core competencies as the roots of competitiveness, and products as the fruits.

What are some concrete examples of core competencies? And how can they be used to make firms more responsive and competitive?

| | CORE COMPETENCIES: EXAMPLES | |

Innovation

Sharp and Toshiba committed years ago to being the world's best creators of flat-screen displays. They wanted to monopolize the markets for flat screens, although they didn't yet know all the potential product applications. A business case could not be made for each application; in fact, all applications couldn't even be envisioned. But the companies knew that this would be an important technology of the future.

The applications began with calculators. Over time, flat-screen displays were needed in pocket diaries, laptop computers, miniature televisions, LCD projection televisions, and video telephones. By committing early to a *competence,* these companies were ready for new and future *products* and *markets.*

As another example, SKF is the world's largest manufacturer of roller bearings. Is roller bearings its core competence? No, this would limit its products and market access. SKF's core competencies are antifriction, precision engineering, and making perfectly spherical devices. Perhaps they could manufacture other products, for example the round, high-precision rolling heads that go inside a VCR, or the tiny balls in roller-ball pens.

Some other examples of companies with special competencies, which feed many specific products, are Hewlett-Packard (measurement, computing, communications); Sony (miniaturization); Rubbermaid (low-tech plastics); Lotus (enterprise computing or "groupware"); 3M (adhesives and advanced materials); EDS (systems integration); and Motorola (wireless communications).

Sources: G. Hamel and C. K. Prahalad, *Competing for the Future* (Boston: Harvard Business School Press, 1994); M. Loeb, "How to Grow a New Product Every Day," *Fortune,* November 14, 1994, pp. 269–70; L. Hays, S. Lipin, and W. Bulkeley, "Software Landscape Shifts as IBM Makes Hostile Bid for Lotus," *The Wall Street Journal,* June 6, 1995, pp. A1, A10. ●

Innovation

Speed

Successfully developing a world-class core competence opens the door to a variety of future opportunities; failure means being foreclosed from *many* markets. Thus, a well-understood, well-developed core competence can enhance a company's responsiveness and competitiveness.

Strategically, this means that companies should commit to excellence and leadership in competencies before they commit to winning market share for specific products. Organizationally, this means that the corporation should be viewed as a portfolio of competencies, not just a portfolio of specific businesses. Companies should strive for core competence leadership, not just product leadership.

Managers who want to strengthen their firms' competitiveness via core competencies have these tasks:[54] (1) identify existing core competencies; (2) acquire or build core competencies that will be important for the future; (3) keep investing in your competencies so they remain world-class and better than your competitors'; and (4) use your competencies to find new applications and opportunities for the markets of tomorrow.

THE NETWORK ORGANIZATION

Remember the kayak company in Setting the Stage? In contrast to the traditional, hierarchical firm performing all the business functions, the **network organization** is a collection of independent, mostly single-function firms.[55] As depicted in Figure 11.3, the dynamic network organization describes not one organization but the web of interrelationships among many firms. Network organizations are flexible, often temporary, arrangements among designers, suppliers, producers, distributors, and customers. Brokers sometimes locate and assemble the various firms in the network.

In the network, each firm is able to pursue its distinctive competence. The network as a whole, then, can display the technical specialization of the functional structure, the market responsiveness of the product structure, and the balance and flexibility of the matrix.[56]

The dynamic network—also called the modular or virtual corporation—is arranged such that its major components can be assembled and reassembled to meet a changing competitive environment. The members of the network are held together by contracts and payments for results (market mechanisms) rather than by hierarchy and authority. Poorly performing firms can be removed and replaced.

Such arrangements are common in the electronics and apparel industries, both of which create and sell trendy products at a fast pace.[57] For example, Reebok owns no plants; it designs and markets, but does not produce. Nike owns only one small factory that makes sneaker parts. Other examples include the Bombay Company, Apple Computer, Brooks Brothers, and the Registry (which markets the services of independent software engineers,

FIGURE 11.3

A dynamic network

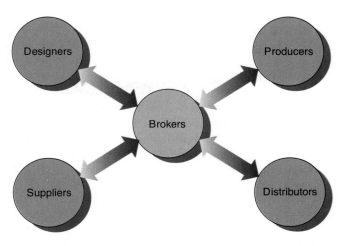

Source: R. Miles and C. Snow, "Organizations: New Concepts for New Forms," *California Management Review,* Spring 1986, p. 65.

programmers, and technical writers).[58] In biotechnology, smaller firms do research and manufacture, and the drug giants market the products.[59]

Successful networks potentially offer flexibility, innovation, quick responses to threats and opportunities, and reduced costs and risk. But for these arrangements to be successful, several things must occur. First, your firm must choose the right specialty—something the market needs and that you truly are better at than other firms. Second, you should choose collaborators that also are excellent at what they do and that provide complementary strengths that you need. Third, make sure that all parties fully understand the strategic goals of the partnership. Fourth, you must be able to trust your collaborators with strategic information about your firm, and also trust that they will deliver quality products, even if your business grows quickly and makes heavy demands on them.[60]

STRATEGIC ALLIANCES

As discussed earlier, the modern organization has a variety of links with other organizations. These links are more complex than the standard relationships with traditional stakeholders like suppliers and clients. Today even fierce *competitors* are working *together* at unprecedented levels to achieve their strategic goals.[61] For example, IBM and Apple have some cooperative arrangements; and GM, Ford, and Chrysler agreed to work together on "high-speed multiplexing," which improves the performance of a vehicle's electronic controls.[62]

A **strategic alliance** is a formal relationship created with the purpose of joint pursuit of mutual goals. In a strategic alliance, individual organizations share administrative authority, form social links, and accept joint ownership. Such alliances are blurring firms' boundaries. They occur between companies and their competitors, governments, and universities. Such partnering often crosses national and cultural boundaries.[63]

Companies form strategic alliances to develop new technologies, enter new markets, and reduce manufacturing costs. Alliances are often the fastest, most efficient way to achieve objectives. Moreover, strategic alliances can pay off not only through the immediate deal, but through creating additional, unforeseen opportunities and opening new doors to the future.[64]

Managers typically devote plenty of time to screening potential partners in financial terms.[65] But for the alliance to work, managers must also foster and develop the human relationships in the partnership. Asian companies seem to be the most comfortable with the nonfinancial, "people" side of alliances, European companies the next so, and U.S. companies the least. So, U.S. companies may need to pay extra attention to the human side of alliances.[66] Table 11.2 shows some recommendatons for how to do this. In fact, most of the ideas apply not only to strategic alliances but to any type of relationship.

THE LEARNING ORGANIZATION

Being responsive requires continually changing and learning new ways to act. This has led to a new term that is now part of the vocabulary of most managers: the learning organization.[67] A **learning organization** is "an organization skilled at creating, acquiring, and transferring knowledge, and at modifying its behavior to reflect new knowledge and insights."[68]

GE, Corning, and Honda are good examples of learning organizations. Such organizations are skilled at (1) solving problems; (2) experimenting with new approaches; (3) learning from their own experiences; (4) learning from other organizations; and (5) spreading knowledge quickly and efficiently.

How do firms become true learning organizations?[69] First, their people must engage in disciplined thinking and attention to details, making decisions based on data and evidence rather than guesswork and assumptions. Second, they search constantly for new knowledge, looking for expanding horizons and opportunities rather than quick fixes to current problems. Third, they carefully review both successes and failures, looking for lessons and deeper understanding. Fourth, learning organizations *benchmark*—they identify and implement the best business practices of other organizations, stealing ideas

TABLE 11.2

How I's can become
we's

The best alliances are true partnerships that meet these criteria:

1. *Individual excellence:* both partners add value, and their motives are positive (pursue opportunity) rather than negative (mask weaknesses).

2. *Importance:* both partners want the relationship to work because it helps them meet long-term strategic objectives.

3. *Interdependence:* the partners need each other; each helps the other reach its goal.

4. *Investment:* the partners devote financial and other resources to the relationship.

5. *Information:* the partners communicate openly about goals, technical data, problems, and changing situations.

6. *Integration:* the partners develop shared ways of operating; they teach each other and learn from each other.

7. *Institutionalization:* the relationship has formal status with clear responsibilities.

8. *Integrity:* both partners are trustworthy and honorable.

Source: R. M. Kanter, "Collaborative Advantage: The Art of Alliances," *Harvard Business Review,* July–August 1994, pp. 96–108.

shamelessly. Fifth, they share ideas throughout the organization via reports, information systems, informal discussions, site visits, education, and training.

THE HIGH-INVOLVEMENT ORGANIZATION

Participative management is becoming increasingly popular as a way to create a competitive advantage. Particularly in high-technology companies facing stiff international competition, such as Microsystems and Compaq Computer, the aim is to generate high levels of commitment and involvement as employees and managers work together to achieve organizational goals.[70]

In the **high-involvement organization,** top management ensures that there is a consensus about the direction in which the business is heading. The leader seeks input from his or her top management team and from lower levels of the company. Task forces, study groups, and other techniques are used to foster participation in decisions that affect the entire organization. Also fundamental to the high-involvement organization is continual feedback to participants regarding how they are doing compared to the competition and how effectively they are meeting the strategic agenda.

Structurally, this usually means that even lower-level employees have a direct relationship with a customer or supplier and thus they receive feedback and are held accountable for a product or service delivery. The organizational form is a flat, decentralized structure built around customer, product, or service.[71]

Employee involvement is particularly powerful when the environment changes rapidly, work is creative, complex activities require coordination, and firms need major breakthroughs in innovation and speed[72]—in other words, when companies need to be more responsive.

TEAM-BASED ORGANIZATIONS

Many organizations are more organic and responsive because they use work teams as their basic building blocks; that is, they are **team-based organizations.** Teams are made up of people from different functional units. These **cross-functional teams** of employees are organized into groups that share responsibilities and have lots of decision-making authority.[73]

The members of this Rubbermaid cross-functional work team applied their training to solve a freight charge-back problem. (© 1993 Rubbermaid Incorporated; used with permission)

Cross-functional teams commonly are used in new-product development. They are also common where people from different departments must work closely together to deliver a good or service. They often work closely with customers; in other words, teams are not hidden deep within a huge corporation, shielded from the real world. Hewlett-Packard, David Kelley Design (DKD), Johnsonville Sausage, ABB Asea Brown Boveri, Eastman Chemical, and many other companies have reorganized around teams.[74]

Cross-functional teams operate separately from traditional, vertical lines of authority. Moreover, cross-functional teams often are short-lived. Teams form, complete their tasks, disband, and then new teams are formed. People may be members of more than one cross-functional team simultaneously.

Another team-based design is the **cluster organization.**[75] Here, teams of people are arranged like grapes growing on a common vine. A **cluster** is a group of people from different disciplines who work together on a semipermanent basis. Profit centers are the primary type of cluster (as in product departmentalization), but the firm also contains other clusters like project teams and teams that work with members of other firms on joint projects. Examples of the cluster are found in British Petroleum, General Electric Canada, Du Pont's fibers department, and many consulting, accounting, and law firms.

The cluster is accountable for business results and has a customer or client orientation.[76] Even staff units (clusters such as human resources and marketing research) sell to customers inside and sometimes outside the firm. Thus, every employee is part of a team that is itself a small business.

EVERYONE A BUSINESSPERSON

Some firms today want everyone to think like a complete businessperson, not just a worker doing a particular task.[77] They want all their people thinking and behaving like entrepreneurs, looking for new business opportunities, and going anywhere and doing anything to make positive contributions to the company. They want people to seek responsibility, take initiative, provide great customer service, focus on results, be action oriented, and have a do-whatever-it-takes-to-get-the-job-done mentality.

Of course, they don't want their people to do these things chaotically, but within the context of the corporation's goals and culture.

This concept applies at the unit level as well. Since every business activity potentially can be outsourced to other firms in a network organization, each activity within your firm should provide good, low-cost service to its internal users. As noted earlier, these activities can also be sold directly to outside customers. Actually, if one of your units can't sell its services outside, it is probably not good enough for your own firm's needs.[78]

KEY TERMS

SUMMARY OF LEARNING OBJECTIVES

Now that you have studied Chapter 11, you should know:

The market imperatives your firm must meet to survive.

Organizations have a formal structure to help control what goes on within them. But to survive today, firms need more than control—they need responsiveness. They must act quickly and adapt to fast-changing demands.

The potential advantages of creating an organic form of organization.

The organic form emphasizes flexibility. Organic organizations are decentralized, informal, and dependent on the judgment and expertise of people with broad responsibilities. The organic form is not a single formal structure, but a concept that underlies all the new forms discussed in this chapter.

How your firm can "be" both small and big.

Historically, large organizations have had important advantages over small. Today, small size has advantages, including the ability to act quickly, respond to customer demands, and serve small niches. The ideal firm today combines the advantages of both: it creates many small, flexible units, while the corporate level adds value by taking advantage of its size and power.

How to manage information-processing demands.

Integrative mechanisms help coordinate the efforts of differentiated subunits. Slack resources and self-contained tasks reduce the need to process information. Information systems and horizontal relationships help the organization process information.

How to diagnose and manage your firm's culture.

Organization culture is the set of shared assumptions, values, and beliefs about the organization's goals and practices. Cultures can be strong and weak, and can be diagnosed by investigating mission statements, business practices, symbols, rites, ceremonies, and stories. Managing culture requires communicating success-oriented values, attending to details, delivering on moments of truth, rewarding appropriate behaviors, and hiring, socializing, and promoting people based on the firm's values.

The activities and impact of corporate restructuring.

A merger occurs when two companies form one corporation by mutual agreement. An acquisition is a transaction in which a firm buys all or part of another business, as agreed upon by both parties. A takeover occurs when the purchasing company makes a direct bid to the target company's stockholders because the target's management opposes the purchase. In a leveraged buyout, a group buys the majority of stock in their own company.

These activities can inspire greater efficiency and cost cutting, help firms survive, and potentially profit stakeholders. However, they also create massive debt, a short-term focus, and layoffs.

The new types of dynamic organizational concepts and forms.

New and emerging organizational concepts and forms include core competencies, network organizations, strategic alliances, learning organizations, high-involvement organizations, and team-based organizations.

DISCUSSION QUESTIONS

1. Discuss evidence *you have seen* of the imperatives for change, flexibility, and responsiveness faced by today's firms.

2. Describe large, bureaucratic organizations with which you have had contact that have not responded flexibly to customer demands. Also describe examples of satisfactory responsiveness. What do you think accounts for the differences between the responsive and nonresponsive organizations?

3. Considering the potential advantages of large and small size, would you describe the "feel" of your college or university as big, small, or small-within-big? Why? What might make it feel different?

4. Think about a job you have held. How would you describe the culture where you worked? Was it strong or weak? What behaviors were valued? What evidence did you use to diagnose the culture? On a 1-to-10 scale, to what degree was it a "success" culture? Discuss.

5. Talk to someone who has been through one or more restructurings and get her or his perspective. Share your findings with the class. Are there any common themes? What are the major differences of opinion?

6. What is a core competence? Generate some examples of companies with distinctive competencies, identifying what those competencies are. Brainstorm some creative new products and markets to which these competencies could be applied.

7. If you were going into business for yourself, what would be *your* core competencies? What competencies do you have now, and what competencies are you going to develop? Describe what your role would be in a network organization, and the competencies and roles of other firms you would want in your network.

8. Identify some recently formed alliances between competitors. What are the goals of the alliance? What brought them together? What have they done to ensure success? How are they doing now?

9. What skills will you need to work effectively in (1) a team-based organzation; (2) a learning organization; and (3) a high-involvement organization? Be specific, generating long lists. Would you enjoy working in these environments? Why or why not? What can you do to prepare yourself for these eventualities?

CONCLUDING CASE

MERGER AND DOWNSIZING AT FLEET FINANCIAL GROUP

In 1995 Fleet Financial Group bought Shawmut National Bank and became the ninth-largest bank in the United States. Fleet will dominate consumer banking in New England with 900 branches and $50 billion in deposits. Because New England's population and income growth are stagnant, the region is a difficult one for banks to grow in. Acquisitions are the better way to grow.

The deal is expected to help Fleet cut costs and increase profits and earnings. But the bank's short-term actions will include layoffs and branch closings. A stock analyst who believes the acquisition was a great move said the bank was first taking "two steps backward to take three steps forward."

This would not be the first time Fleet has downsized. A previous downsizing effort, in which 25 percent of the bank's employees were eliminated, was believed at the time of the Shawmut National acquisition to have saved almost $300 million annually.

That downsizing effort obviously took a human toll on those who lost their jobs, but also on management and others. The vice chairman called the eight-month process physically, intellectually, and emotionally exhausting. The CEO spent 50 percent of his time overseeing the project, and hundreds of other managers were heavily involved. Employees took part in 600 brainstorming sessions, and made over 21,000 suggestions for improving efficiency and saving money.

Meanwhile, board meetings continued to be held at an expensive resort hotel in Palm Beach, Florida, and management ignored

Although Fleet Financial Group's acquisition of Shawmut National Bank was generally considered good for New England's economy, the purchase resulted in major downsizing at Shawmut. *(Michael Rosenfeld/Tony Stone Images)*

the suggestion to eliminate executive perks. Worried about employees and former employees angered by the layoffs, management posted a security guard outside the executive suite and installed electronic doors.

Fleet was one of the most aggressive in the industry at eliminating jobs in 1994, and some predicted it would cut 20 percent more in 1995. Supporters of Fleet's actions say that shareholders will realize great gains over the long run, that big, national, "superregional," and small niche banks are the only ones that will survive in today's banking environment, and that midsize banks cannot survive. Shawmut, founded in 1835, was a midsize bank that probably would not have succeeded on its own.

QUESTIONS

1. What do you think of Fleet's approach to laying off employees?

2. What lessons might they learn from their previous downsizing efforts as they plan the next round of layoffs?

3. If you were managing the downsizing process, what actions would you take?

4. If you were an employee at Fleet or Shawmut, what would be your reaction to the acquisition? What actions would you take?

Sources: A. Willette, "Fleet Joins Bank Consolidation Trend," *USA Today,* February 22, 1995, p. 3B; M. Hitt, B. Keats, H. Harback, and R. Nixon, "Rightsizing: Building and Maintaining Strategic Leadership and Long-Term Competitiveness," *Organizational Dynamics,* Fall 1994, pp. 18–31.

Video Case

The Responsive Organization

In the past, a corporation was structured much like the military, with a formal chain of command and division of labor. Over time, many companies came to realize that the bureaucratic structure of the traditional corporation can often cause breakdowns in communication and lower efficiency.

Manufacturers of products in relatively unchanging environments often take a mechanistic approach to production. In such environments, employees strictly adhere to their job descriptions. However, companies that depend on their ability to continuously introduce new innovations usually take a more organic approach, giving employees more room to make decisions and communicate outside the chain of command. Some companies may choose to radically modify or reengineer their structure.

Big Apple Bagels and St. Louis Bread Company are two rapidly growing businesses that share a similar market. However, each organization is structured quite differently. Whatever the structure, for an organization to be successful, it must be responsive to its customers. This operating principle means more than just making sure the right kind of cheese gets put on a turkey sandwich.

Many companies are finding that changing the way in which they are organized improves their responsiveness. They may choose to simplify their structure and reduce the layers of management, thus reducing the layers in the chain of command. Another option is to widen the spans of control. The traditional organization has a tall structure and a narrow span of control, which means managers have few subordinates who report directly to them. A company with a flat organizational structure has a wide span of control with fewer reporting levels.

Many companies are empowering their employees and allowing them to make decisions rather than insisting that they report to various levels of management. When Paul Stolzer opened the first Big Apple Bagel store in 1985, he had no idea that in seven years his small store would grow into a franchise that boasts 75 stores with more opening all the time. Stolzer said, "The stores have changed quite extensively over the years. We are actually a fourth or fifth generation store right now. Initially the stores were set up as strictly bagel bakeries with a predominant product being bagels and cream cheese. We've progressed to a more aggressive stature, adding a few more dimensions to our operation in that we have dine-in facilities, a more extensive sandwich menu, and a very, very strong coffee program."

One thing that hasn't changed in Big Apple Bagels' open-door policy. From top management to line workers, communication channels are open. Jim Lentz, director of training said, "At Big Apple Bagels we have an open door policy between the franchisee and the franchisor, and between the ultimate consumer and the franchisor in that we encourage people to come up with suggestions, new products, new ideas."

In 1987, Ken Rosenthal opened his first St. Louis Bread Company store in Kirkwood, Missouri, with used baking equipment. Today, St. Louis Bread company operates over 50 stores in the St. Louis area, with stores opening in other midwestern markets as well. The growth happened quickly, forcing the company to change its organizational structure. Originally, it was a small store with 17 employees. When it became a large chain, employing over 1,000 people, a more traditional organizational structure was needed.

When a company is growing, it may need to use some of the concepts of reengineering. Reengineering entails the radical redesign of business processes to achieve major gains in cost, service, or time. For example, by mid-1992, St. Louis Bread was growing at a frantic pace. The partners had reached a point where the controls and information systems they had in place were inadequate for a larger operation. New equipment was purchased to automate processes on the line, and $30,000 point-of-purchase cash registers were installed to track everything from sales per hour to sales per stock keeping unit to sales by stores.

Doron Berger said, "The organization at St. Louis Bread Company is probably not atypical of many organizations. While we have a hierarchical structure in terms of someone is ultimately accountable for the results of the business. We do fight vigorously to maintain a flat organization. In other words, there aren't a lot of layers between the president CEO and the people who are on the front lines. I think we have succeeded because of the effort we have put into that."

In November of 1983, Au Bon Pain, the dominant bakery/cafe chain in the country acquired St. Louis Bread Company. David Hutkin said, "Our organizational structure had not changed dramatically. It really hasn't changed since the acquisition.

A company like Big Apple Bagels is considered to be a boundaryless organization. In such an organization, the corporate structure is more horizontal than vertical. Boundaryless businesses are typically organized around core customer oriented processes, such as communication, customer contact, and managing quality. In order to enjoy the benefits a horizontal organization offers, four boundaries must be overcome: authority, task, political, identity.

Even a relatively boundaryless company has an authority boundary. Some people lead, others follow. To overcome problems that may arise, managers must learn how to lead and still remain open to criticism. Their "subordinates" need to be trained and encouraged not only to follow but also to challenge their superiors if there is an issue worth considering.

The task boundary arises out of the "it's not my job" mentality. A task boundary can be overcome by clearly defining who does what when employees from different departments divide up work.

The political boundary derives from the differences in political agendas that often separate employees and can cause conflict. This is closely related to identity boundary, which emerges due to an employee tendency to identify with those individuals or groups with whom they have shared experiences, or with whom they share fundamental values.

To overcome the identity boundary, employees and management need to be trained to gain an understanding of the business as a whole and avoid the "us versus them" mentality. A good way to do this is by forming cross-functional teams, in which tasks are shared and cross-training simply happens as a result of employee interaction.

The new boundaryless organization relies on self-managed work teams. It reduces internal boundaries that separate functions and create hierarchical levels. A horizontal corporation is structured around core, customer-oriented processes.

CRITICAL THINKING QUESTIONS

1. If companies today are working so hard to break down boundaries, why is it that there are boundaries in the first place?

2. What are some new technologies that will help managers keep lines of communication open to employees? To customers?

3. The video mentions that St. Louis Bread Company had to use a more traditional organizational structure when it grew rapidly. Why do you think that was necessary? What do you think the company gains by adopting such a structure? What does it lose?

EXPERIENTIAL EXERCISES

11.1 Decentralization: Pros and Cons

Objective

To explore the reasons for, as well as the pros and cons of, decentralizing.

Instructions

Below in the Decentralization Worksheet are some observations on decentralization. As you review each of the statements, provide an example that illustrates why this statement is important and related problems and benefits of the situation or condition indicated in the statement.

DECENTRALIZATION WORKSHEET

A large number of factors determine the extent to which a manager should decentralize. Clearly, anything that increases a manager's workload creates a pressure for decentralization since there is only a finite level of work that can be accomplished by a single person. As with many facets of management, there are advantages and disadvantages to decentralization.

1. The greater the diversity of products, the greater the decentralization. _____

_____

_____

_____

2. The larger the size of the organization, the more the decentralization. _____

_____

_____

_____

3. The more rapidly changing the organization's environment, the more decentralization. _____

_____

_____

_____

4. Developing adequate, timely controls is the essence of decentralizing. _____

_____

_____

_____

5. Managers should delegate those decisions that involve large amounts of time but minimal erosions of their power and control. _____

_____

_____

_____

_____

6. Decentralizing involves delegating authority, and therefore, the principles of delegation apply to decentralization. (List the principles of delegation before you start your discussion). _____

_____

_____

_____

_____

Source: R. R. McGrath, Jr., *Exercises in Management Fundamentals* (Englewood Cliffs, N.J.: Prentice-Hall, 1985) pp. 59–60. Reprinted by permission of Prentice-Hall, Inc.

11.2 The University Culture

Objectives

1. To measure the culture at your university.
2. To study the nature of organization culture.
3. To understand how a culture can be changed.

Instructions

1. Working alone, complete and score the University Culture Survey.
2. In small groups, exchange survey scores and develop responses to the discussion questions.

3. Group spokespersons report group findings to the class.

Discussion Questions

1. In what respects did students agree or disagree on survey test items?
2. What might account for differences in students' experiences and attitudes with respect to the university culture?
3. How can the survey results be put to constructive use?

UNIVERSITY CULTURE SURVEY

To measure the culture of your university, complete the following survey by circling the degree to which you agree with each statement.

	Strongly Agree	Agree	Neither Agree nor Disagree	Disagree	Strongly Disagree
1. There is a feeling on this campus that everyone can communicate freely with everyone else.	5	4	3	2	1
2. This campus has leadership with a clear vision of its goals.	5	4	3	2	1
3. Everyone connected with this university seems to be loyal to the image and mission of the university.	5	4	3	2	1
4. Innovative courses and creative activities are rare here.	5	4	3	2	1
5. The administration "stays close to the customer."	5	4	3	2	1
6. The curriculum maintains high quality in all of its programs.	5	4	3	2	1
7. Students are expected to assume responsibility for their own learning.	5	4	3	2	1
8. Computer and library facilities are inadequate.	5	4	3	2	1
9. Loyalty to the university is highly rewarded.	5	4	3	2	1
10 Friendliness and warmth are valued norms.	5	4	3	2	1
11. University missions are clear, and everyone seems to understand and accept his or her role on campus.	5	4	3	2	1
12. Campus operations seem to be well organized and consistent with university goals.	5	4	3	2	1
13. The administration is people oriented, and administrators really care about the students.	5	4	3	2	1

	Strongly Agree	Agree	Neither Agree nor Disagree	Disagree	Strongly Disagree
14. The university expects high standards of performance from everyone.	5	4	3	2	1
15. Students are encouraged to be creative and nontraditional.	5	4	3	2	1
16. A strong code of ethics permeates this campus.	5	4	3	2	1
17. Student advising services are available when needed.	5	4	3	2	1
18. People on this campus can trust one another.	5	4	3	2	1
19. Students have few opportunities to take active roles in campus activities.	5	4	3	2	1
20. Relevant information, such as drop and add deadlines, is readily available to all who need it.	5	4	3	2	1
21. Performance, not politics, is rewarded at this university.	5	4	3	2	1
22. When a student has a problem, there is usually someone to help.	5	4	3	2	1
23. The university sets challenging goals and high standards for all campus activities.	5	4	3	2	1
24. Students don't feel restricted by university rules.	5	4	3	2	1
25. Channels of communication through which to air student problems are open and available.	5	4	3	2	1
26. It's very difficult to get things changed on this campus.	5	4	3	2	1
27. For a student with a problem, this campus provides an atmosphere of warmth and support.	5	4	3	2	1

Scoring

Test items 4, 8, 19, and 26 are reverse-scored. That is, if you responded with a 5 to item 4, change the response to a 1 (i.e., when reverse-scoring, 5 = 1, 4 = 2, 3 = 3, 2 = 4, 1 = 5).

Now add up your score according to each of the following dimensions of organization culture:

Communication   1. _____ + 20. _____ + 25. _____ = _____

Identification   3. _____ + 11. _____ + 12. _____ = _____

Innovation   4. _____ + 15. _____ + 26. _____ = _____

Leadership   2. _____ + 5. _____ + 13. _____ = _____

Quality standards   6. _____ + 14. _____ + 23. _____ = _____

Student role   7. _____ + 19. _____ + 24. _____ = _____

Support   8. _____ + 17. _____ + 22. _____ = _____

Values   9. _____ + 16. _____ + 21. _____ = _____

Warmth/trust   10. _____ + 18. _____ + 27. _____ = _____

Total = _____

(The higher the score, the more positive the university culture.)

12

HUMAN RESOURCES MANAGEMENT

You can get capital and erect buildings,

but it takes people to build a business.

Thomas J. Watson, Founder, IBM

LEARNING OBJECTIVES

After studying Chapter 12, you will know:

1. How companies use human resources management to gain competitive advantage.

2. Why companies recruit both internally and externally for new hires.

3. The various methods available for selecting new employees.

4. Why companies spend so much on training and development.

5. How to determine who should appraise an employee's performance.

6. How to analyze the fundamental aspects of a reward system.

7. How unions influence human resources management.

8. How the legal system influences human resources management.

WINNING BIG IN VEGAS

*L*as Vegas, Nevada—a town that somehow blends gambling halls with wedding chapels, amusement parks, and high-priced boutiques. It's a place to which approximately 25 million visitors, of all ages, from all walks of life, and from all over the globe, come to play each year. The town's 89 casino hotels that form the Las Vegas strip depend on these visitors, and they compete vigorously for them. So what gives one a competitive advantage over the others? Mirage Resorts Inc. believes it's the people who work for them.

The Las Vegas–based firm is so focused on the importance of people that it hired Arte Nathan as the vice president of human resources for The Mirage just after it chose a president, and before the hotel was even built. Nathan staffed The Mirage, then went on to assist in staffing Mirage Resorts' Las Vegas enterprise, Treasure Island, which opened in 1993. For both resorts, Nathan made finding the right people his number one priority. Before opening The Mirage, he set up a college-recruitment program at Cornell University and the University of Nevada, Las Vegas. The management candidates who come through the program must have received hotel-management degrees, earned grade point averages of 3.0 or better, served as interns, and been given high recommendations from their colleges.

Mirage applies an equally stringent selection process for all employees. Even while staffing on a large scale for hotel openings, Nathan and the human resources staff screened all applicants for personality, stability and experience. Selection began by making the candidates fill out their applications in the office. "We greeted them and shook their hands," Nathan says. "If they responded to us—shook our hands back and made eye contact—we knew they wouldn't mind talking to other people they didn't know. At The Mirage, we cut 22,000 people with a handshake." The candidates who survived the handshake test took behavioral written interviews. Department heads then chose three candidates for each opening and interviewed them using a structured questionnaire.

Once on board, employees received an abundance of training, something Nathan feels greatly contributes to the corporation's competitive advantage. Before The Mirage opened, he conducted interviews with more than 200 companies in a variety of industries that had opened in the previous 10 years. The vast majority of them regretted not having done more training prior to opening. Accordingly, The Mirage put together a strong training program, spending approximately $3.5 million for preopening training at The Mirage and almost $3 million at Treasure Island.

The effectiveness of the selective recruiting process and the commitment to training is clearly evident. Mirage enjoys a 98 percent occupancy rate. Furthermore, the hotels' turnover rate is only 13.5 percent compared with a 40 percent average in Las Vegas, and 70 percent nationwide. In recognition of their excellence in human resources management, Mirage Resorts received the 1994 Optimas Award for Competitive Advantage.

Mirage Resorts Inc. is a strong believer in training programs. Prior to launching their Las Vegas hotel, they spent about $3.5 million for preopening training.
(Courtesy Mirage Resorts Incorporated)

Source: Reprinted from Dawn Anfuso, "HR Helps The Mirage Thrive in Crowded Vegas," *Personnel Journal,* January 1994, p. 72.

*H*uman resources management (HRM), historically known as *personnel management,* deals with formal systems for the management of people within the organization. As the Mirage Resorts example demonstrates, HRM has assumed a vital strategic role because organizations are trying to transform their human resources into a source of competitive advantage.

HR managers have many concerns regarding their workers and the entire personnel puzzle for the 1990s.[1] These concerns include how to manage layoffs, address reduced employee loyalty, create a well-trained, highly motivated workforce that can deliver higher quality and productivity, manage an increasingly diverse workforce, and contain health care costs.

HRM has been undergoing a transformation. In the 1970s, the job of HR managers was to keep their companies out of court and in compliance with the increasing number of regulations governing the workplace. In the 1980s, HR managers had to address staffing costs related to mergers and acquisitions and downsizing (also known as "rightsizing"). The 1990s is characterized by economic issues related to an increasingly global and competitive workplace. Recall in Chapter 8 we discussed some of the fundamental issues associated with managing a global workforce.

We begin this chapter by describing HRM as it relates to strategic planning. We then discuss more of the functional aspects of HRM related to attracting, retaining, and maintaining an effective workforce: human resources planning and job analysis, recruitment and selection, performance appraisal, reward systems, and labor relations. Throughout the chapter, we discuss legal issues that influence each aspect of HRM.

HUMAN RESOURCES PLANNING

"Get me the right kind and the right number of people at the right time." It sounds simple enough, but meeting the organization's staffing needs requires *strategic human resources planning:* an activity with a strategic purpose derived from the organization's plans.

Thus, human resources activities must be adapted to the organization's needs. These needs vary depending on the circumstances of the organization. A steel producer facing a cutback in business may need human resources activities to assist with layoffs, whereas a semiconductor company may need more staff to produce enough microchips to meet the demands of the burgeoning personal computer market. The emphasis on different HR activities depends on whether the organization is growing, declining, or standing still. The example of Marriott Corporation shows this connection between strategy and HR planning.

STRATEGIC HRM AT MARRIOTT

*A*s a worldwide leader in the hotel industry, Marriott Corporation believes it is vital to link human resources activities to strategic planning. To create this linkage Marriott established direct reporting relationships between the top human resources executive and the president and chief executive officer. The human resources executive for each division reports to the general manager of the division. These relationships enable members of the human resources group to assist in the discussion and deliberation of strategic decisions. It also allows HR executives to assess the implications of human resources for the company's goals and objectives.

Second, the budget prepared by the HR managers is reviewed and analyzed by Marriott's top management team. The top HR executive must be able to defend the spending plans for each functional area and must show how each area contributes to the achievement of specific strategic objectives.

Third, the entire HR division is fully informed of Marriott's strategic direction. This allows the HR group to gear their activities to corporate strategy. It also enables them to realize the vital contribution they are making to Marriott.

Several major accomplishments have resulted from the HR–strategic planning linkage. A new executive staff review system projects growth and staffing requirements for the next five years. This allows Marriott to anticipate management shortages and identify leading candidates for promotion. Another example was the discovery of an opportunity for unprecedented growth contingent on the company's ability to vastly increase the number of hotel development projects. The HR group created an incentive compensation program for a select group of hotel developers, geared toward the successful closing of hotel development projects that met return-on-investment goals. The latter project in particular was an unusual one for Marriott, but it is one of the many reasons the company has pronounced the marriage between strategic planning and HR a smashing success.

Source: C. J. Ehrlich, "Marriott Benefits by Linking Human Resources with Strategy," in *The Quest for Competitiveness*, ed. Y. Shetty and V. Buehler (New York: Quorum Books, 1991). ●

THE HR PLANNING PROCESS

The HR planning process occurs in three stages: planning, programming, and evaluating. First, HR managers need to know the organization's business plans to ensure that the right number and types of people are available—where the company is headed, what businesses it plans to be in, what future growth is expected, and so forth. Few things are more damaging to morale than having to lay off recently hired college graduates because of inadequate planning for future needs. Second, the organization conducts programming of specific human resources activities, such as recruitment, training, or layoffs. In this stage, the company's plans are implemented. Third, human resources activities are evaluated to determine whether they are producing the results needed to contribute to the organization's business plans.

Figure 12.1 illustrates the components of the human resources planning process. In this chapter, we focus on human resources planning and programming. Many of the other factors listed in Figure 12.1 are discussed in future chapters. In Chapter 18, we will examine evaluation issues.

Demand Forecasts

Perhaps the most difficult part of human resources planning is conducting *demand* forecasts. Demand forecasts for people needs are derived from organizational plans. For example, suppose a pharmaceutical company develops a new drug to relieve eye problems common in the over-60 age group. The company estimates the future size of this market based on demographic projections. Based on current sales and projected future sales

■
_____

One of Marriott's HRM programs involves training and employing people with disabilities. Here, Laurie Axtell (left) coaches Jill Durbin. *(© 1991 Dennis Brack/Black Star)*

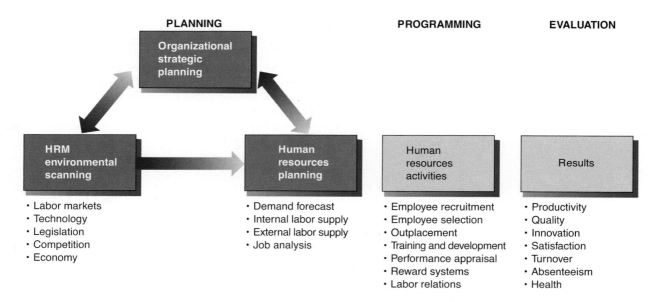

PLANNING   PROGRAMMING   EVALUATION

- Labor markets   - Demand forecast   - Employee recruitment   - Productivity
- Technology   - Internal labor supply   - Employee selection   - Quality
- Legislation   - External labor supply   - Outplacement   - Innovation
- Competition   - Job analysis   - Training and development   - Satisfaction
- Economy   - Performance appraisal   - Turnover
                                                    - Reward systems   - Absenteeism
                                                    - Labor relations   - Health

FIGURE 12.1

An overview of the HR planning process

growth, the company estimates what plant capacity it will need to meet future demand. At this point, the number of labor-hours required to operate a plant and the demand for different types of workers can be estimated.

Labor Supply Forecasts

The *supply* of labor must also be forecast. In performing a supply analysis, the organization estimates the number and quality of its current employees as well as the available external supply of workers. To estimate internal supply, the company typically relies on past experiences with turnover, terminations, retirements, or promotions and transfers. A computerized human resources information system assists greatly in supply forecasting.

Worldwide, there is a growing gap between the world's supply of labor and the demand for labor.[2] Most of the well-paid jobs are generated in the cities of the industrialized world, but many skilled and unskilled human resources are in the developing nations. This gap will lead to massive relocations of people (including immigrants, temporary workers, and retirees) and a reduction of protectionist immigration policies (as countries come to rely on and compete for foreign workers).

Forecasts of a diverse workforce have become fact. The business world is no longer the exclusive domain of white males. Minorities, women, immigrants, older and disabled workers, and other groups have made the *management of diversity* a fundamental activity of the modern manager. Because of the importance of managing the "new workforce," the next chapter is devoted entirely to this topic.

JOB ANALYSIS

Job analysis is another fundamental component of HR planning. A **job analysis** does two things.[3] First, it tells the HR manager about the job itself: the essential tasks, duties, and responsibilities involved in performing the job. This information is called a *job description.* Second, it describes the skills, knowledge, abilities, and other characteristics needed to perform the job. This is called the *job specification.*

Job analysis provides the information that virtually every human resources activity requires. It assists with the essential HR programs: recruitment, training, selection, appraisal, and reward systems. For example, a thorough job analysis helps organizations successfully defend themselves in lawsuits involving employment practices.[4] Ultimately, job analysis helps to increase the value added by employees to the organization since it clarifies what is really required to perform effectively.

STAFFING THE ORGANIZATION

The staffing function of HRM consists of three activities: recruiting, selecting, and outplacing.

RECRUITING

Recruitment is the development of a pool of applicants for a job. Recruitment may be internal to the organization (considering current employees for promotions and transfers) or external. Each approach has advantages and disadvantages.[5]

Internal Recruiting

Advantages of internal recruiting are that employers know their employees, and employees know their organization. External candidates who are unfamiliar with the organization may find they don't like working there. Also, the opportunity to move upward within the organization may encourage employees to remain with the company, work hard, and succeed. Recruiting from outside the company can be demoralizing to employees. Many companies, such as Sears Roebuck and Eli Lilly, prefer internal over external recruiting for these reasons.

Internal staffing has some drawbacks. If existing employees lack skills or talent, internal recruitment yields a limited applicant pool, leading to poor selection decisions. Also, an internal recruitment policy can inhibit a company that wants to change the nature or goals of the business by bringing in outside candidates. In changing from a rapidly growing, entrepreneurial organization to a mature business with more stable growth, Data General went outside the organization to hire managers who better fit those needs.

Many companies that rely heavily on internal recruiting use a job-posting system. A *job-posting system* is a mechanism for advertising open positions, typically on a bulletin board. Texas Instruments uses job-posting. Employees complete a request form indicating interest in a posted job. The posted job description includes a list of duties and the minimum skills and experience required.

External Recruiting

Innovation

External recruiting brings in "new blood" to a company and can inspire innovation. Among the most frequently used sources of outside applicants are newspaper advertisements, employee referrals, and college campus recruiting.

Newspaper advertisements are the most popular recruiting source for many occupations, because they are inexpensive and can generate a large number of responses. Employee referral is another frequently used source of applicants;[6] some companies actively encourage employees to refer their friends by offering cash rewards. The advantages of campus recruiting include a large pool of people from which to draw, applicants with up-to-date training, and a source of innovative ideas.[7]

It is becoming increasingly common for organizations to use electronic media such as Internet or Compuserve both to advertise job openings and to gather applicant information. E-Span, for example, is an on-line service that lists professional and managerial positions. Federal Job Opportunity Board is a similar service that lists openings in the federal government.

SELECTION

Selection decisions concern which applicants to hire. In this section we describe a number of selection instruments, because you will soon be exposed to most or all of them.

Interviews

Interviews are the most popular selection tool, and every company uses some type of interview. However, employment interviewers must be careful about what they ask and how they ask it. Questions that are not job related are prohibited.

In an *unstructured interview,* the interviewer asks different interviewees different questions. The interviewer may also use probes, that is, ask follow-up questions to learn more about the candidate.[8]

In a *structured interview,* the interviewer conducts the same interview with each applicant. There are two basic types of structured interview. One approach explores the past behavior of interviewees. In selecting college students for an officer training program, the U.S. army asks the following question to assess a candidate's ability to influence others: "What was the best idea you ever sold to a supervisor, teacher, peer, or subordinate?" The second approach focuses on hypothetical situations. Zale Corporation, a major jewelry chain, uses this type of structured interview to select sales clerks. A sample question is: "A customer comes into the store to pick up a watch he had left for repair. The watch is not back yet from the repair shop, and the customer becomes angry. How would you handle the situation?"

Reference Checks

Reference checks are another commonly used screening device. Virtually all organizations use either a reference or an employment and education record check.[9] Although reference checking makes sense, reference information is becoming increasingly difficult to obtain as a result of several highly publicized lawsuits. In one case, an applicant sued a former boss on the grounds that the boss told prospective employers the applicant was a "thief and a crook." The jury awarded the applicant $80,000.

Personality Tests

Personality tests are less popular for employee selection, largely because they are hard to defend in court.[10] However, they are regaining popularity, and chances are that at some point in your career you will complete some personality tests. A number of well-known paper-and-pencil inventories measure personality traits like sociability, adjustment, and energy. Typical questions are "Do you like to socialize with people?" and "Do you enjoy working hard?"

Biological/Physiological Tests

Biological/physiological tests are among the most controversial screening instruments. Biological tests include drug screening and genetic tests.[11] Urinalysis is the most common method of testing for the presence of drugs. A genetic test tries to identify the likelihood of contracting a disease (such as emphysema) based on genetic makeup. While genetic screening is far less common than drug testing, its popularity may increase as the technique is perfected.

Cognitive Ability Tests

Cognitive ability tests are among the oldest employment selection devices. These tests measure a range of intellectual abilities, including verbal comprehension (vocabulary, reading) and numerical aptitude (mathematical calculations). About 20 percent of U.S. companies use cognitive ability tests for selection purposes.[12] Figure 12.2 shows some examples of cognitive ability test questions.

Performance Tests

Performance tests are procedures in which the test taker performs a sample of the job. Approximately 75 percent of companies use performance tests, although many use them only for secretarial and clerical positions.[13] The most widely used performance test is the typing test. However, performance tests have been developed for almost every occupation, including managerial positions. Assessment centers are the most notable offshoot of the managerial performance test.

Assessment centers (ACs) originated during World War II. A typical **assessment center** consists of 10 to 12 candidates who participate in a variety of exercises or situations; some of the exercises involve group interactions, and others are performed individually. Each

FIGURE 12.2

Sample measures
of cognitive ability

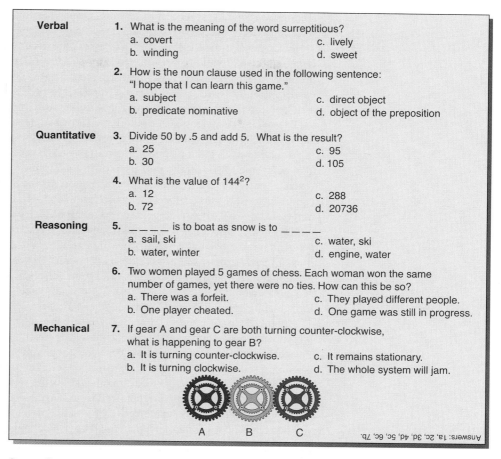

Verbal

1. What is the meaning of the word surreptitious?
   a. covert   c. lively
   b. winding   d. sweet

2. How is the noun clause used in the following sentence:
   "I hope that I can learn this game."
   a. subject   c. direct object
   b. predicate nominative d. object of the preposition

Quantitative

3. Divide 50 by .5 and add 5. What is the result?
   a. 25   c. 95
   b. 30   d. 105

4. What is the value of 144^2?
   a. 12   c. 288
   b. 72   d. 20736

Reasoning

5. _ _ _ _ is to boat as snow is to _ _ _ _
   a. sail, ski   c. water, ski
   b. water, winter   d. engine, water

6. Two women played 5 games of chess. Each woman won the same
   number of games, yet there were no ties. How can this be so?
   a. There was a forfeit.   c. They played different people.
   b. One player cheated.   d. One game was still in progress.

Mechanical

7. If gear A and gear C are both turning counter-clockwise,
   what is happening to gear B?
   a. It is turning counter-clockwise.   c. It remains stationary.
   b. It is turning clockwise.   d. The whole system will jam.

A   B   C

Answers: 1a, 2c, 3d, 4d, 5c, 6c, 7b.

Source: Sherman, Bohlander, and Snell, *Managing Human Resources* (Cincinnati: South-Western, 1995).

exercise taps a number of critical managerial dimensions, such as leadership, decision-making skills, and communication ability. Assessors, generally line managers from the organization, observe and record information about the candidates' performance in each exercise. AT&T was the first organization to use assessment centers. Since then, a number of large organizations have used or currently are using the AC technique, including Bristol-Myers, the FBI, and Sears Roebuck.

Integrity Tests

Integrity tests are used to assess a job candidate's honesty. Two forms of integrity tests are polygraphs and paper-and-pencil honesty tests. Polygraphs, or lie detector tests, have been banned for most employment purposes.[14] Paper-and-pencil honesty tests are more recent instruments for measuring integrity. These tests include questions such as whether a person has ever thought about stealing and whether he or she believes other people steal ("What percentage of people take more than $1 from their employer?"). Best Products Company, a catalog showroom chain based in Richmond, Virginia, is typical of the companies that use paper-and-pencil honesty tests; applicants must pass this test to get hired.[15] However, the accuracy of these tests is debatable.

RELIABILITY AND VALIDITY

Regardless of the method used to select employees, two crucial issues that need to be addressed are a test's **reliability** and **validity.** *Reliability* refers to the consistency of test scores over time and across alternative measurements. For example, if three different interviewers talked to the same job candidate, but drew very different conclusions about the candidate's abilities, we might suspect that there were problems with the reliability of one or more of the selection tests or interview procedures.

Validity moves beyond reliability to assess the accuracy of the selection test. The most common form of validity, *criterion-related validity,* refers to the degree that a test actually predicts or correlates with job performance. That is, is the test a true predictor of job performance? Figure 12.3 shows a scatterplot of the correlations between two different tests and job performance. Each of the dots on the scatterplots corresponds to an individual's test score relative to his or her job performance. Dots in the bottom-left corner of each scatterplot show individuals who scored poorly on the test and performed poorly on the job. Individuals in the top-right corner are those who scored well on the selection test and also performed well on the job. By plotting many individual scores, the points begin to reveal a pattern in the relationship between test scores and job performance. This pattern can be captured statistically with a correlation coefficient (i.e., a validity coefficient) that ranges from − 1.0 (a perfect negative correlation) to 1.0 (a perfect positive correlation). In reality most validity coefficients fall somewhere in between these extremes. In Figure 12.3, for example, Test A has a validity coefficient of zero (0.0) indicating that there is no relationship between test scores and job success. Test B, however, has a validity coefficient of .75 indicating that high test scores tend to be strongly predictive of good performance. Managers would not want to use Test A—it is not valid—but would be wise to use Test B for selecting employees since it has high criterion-related validity.

Another form of validity, *content validity,* concerns the degree to which selection tests measure a representative sample of the knowledge, skills, and abilities required for the job. The best-known example of a content-valid test is a typing test for secretaries, because typing is a task a secretary almost always performs. However, to be completely content valid, the selection process should also measure other skills the secretary would be likely to perform, such as answering the telephone, duplicating and faxing documents, and dealing with the public. Content validity is more subjective (less statistical) than evaluations of criterion-related validity, but is no less important, particularly when defending employment decisions in court.

OUTPLACING

Outplacement is the process of helping people who have been dismissed from the company to regain employment elsewhere. People sometimes "get fired," for poor performance or other reasons. A new twist has been added to this long-standing tradition of dismissing unwanted employees. As a result of the massive restructuring of American industry brought about by mergers and acquisitions, divestiture, and increased competition, organizations have been *downsizing*—laying off large numbers of managerial and other employees. In this section, we will discuss firing individual employees and layoffs.

Should an employer have the right to fire a worker? In 1884, a Tennessee court ruled: "All may dismiss their employee(s) at will for good cause, for no cause, or even for cause morally wrong." The concept that an employee may be fired for any reason is known as

FIGURE 12.3

Correlation scatterplots

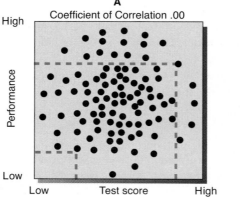

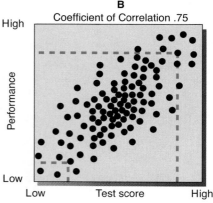

employment-at-will or termination-at-will.[16] The logic is that if the employee may quit at any time, the employer is free to dismiss at any time.

Since the mid-1970s, courts in most states have made exceptions to this doctrine. For example, *public policy* is a policy or ruling designed to protect the public from harm. One exception to the employment-at-will concept under public policy is employee whistle-blowing. For example, if a worker reports an environmental violation to the regulatory agency and the company fires him or her, the courts may argue that the firing was unfair because the employee acted for the good of the community. Another example is that employees may not be fired for serving jury duty.

Employers can avoid the pitfalls associated with dismissal by developing progressive and positive disciplinary procedures.[17] By *progressive,* we mean that a manager takes graduated steps in attempting to correct a workplace behavior. For example, an employee who has been absent receives a verbal reprimand for the first offense. A second offense invokes a written reprimand. A third offense results in employee counseling and probation, and a fourth results in a paid-leave day to think over the consequences of future rule infractions. The employer is signaling to the employee that this is the "last straw." Arbitrators are more likely to side with the employer that fires someone when they believe the company has made sincere efforts to help the person correct his or her behavior.

The Termination Interview

The **termination interview,** in which the manager discusses the employee's firing with the employee, is a stressful situation for both parties. The manager needs to determine before-hand what severance package to offer the employee. The trend in recent mass layoffs is to offer increased benefits. For example, when Stroh Brewery Company closed a facility in Detroit, workers received individualized career counseling, job search skills workshops, financial planning services, a research library, and telephone and secretarial services.[18] It is customary to have a third party, such as a representative from the HRM department, present as a witness to the interview. Table 12.1 summarizes guidelines for conducting a termination interview.

Layoffs

Dismissing any employee is tough, but when a company lays off a substantial portion of its workforce, the results can rock the foundations of the organization.[19] The victims of

TABLE 12.1

Advice on termination

Do's	Don'ts
▪ Give as much warning as possible for mass layoffs.	▪ Don't leave room for confusion when firing. Tell the individual in the first sentence that he or she is terminated.
▪ Sit down one on one with the individual, in a private office.	▪ Don't allow time for debate during a termination session.
▪ Complete a termination session within 15 minutes.	▪ Don't make personal comments when firing someone; keep the conversation professional.
▪ Provide written explanations of severance benefits.	▪ Don't rush a fired employee offsite unless security is an issue.
▪ Provide outplacement services away from company headquarters.	▪ Don't fire people on significant dates, like the 25th anniversary of their employment or the day their mother died.
▪ Be sure the employee hears about his or her termination from a manager, not a colleague.	▪ Don't fire employees when they are on vacation or have just returned.
▪ Express appreciation for what the employee has contributed, if appropriate.	

Source: S. Alexander, "Firms Get Plenty of Practice at Layoffs, but They Often Bungle the Firing Process," *The Wall Street Journal,* November 14, 1991, p. 31.

restructuring face all the difficulties of being fired—loss of self-esteem, demoralizing job searches, and the stigma of being out of work. But the impact goes even further. For many of the employees who remain with the company, disenchantment, distrust, and lethargy overshadow the comfort of still having a job. In many respects, how management deals with dismissals will affect the productivity and satisfaction of those who remain. A well-thought-out dismissal process eases tensions and helps remaining employees adjust to the new work situation.

Organizations with strong performance evaluation systems benefit because the survivors are less likely to believe the decision was arbitrary. Further, if care is taken during the actual layoff process—that is, if workers are offered severance pay and help in finding a new job—remaining workers will be comforted. Companies should also avoid stringing out layoffs, that is, dismissing a few workers at a time. AT&T has developed a unique approach to avoiding layoffs.

AT&T's Resource Link

*W*hen AT&T divested its local phone companies in 1984, it set in motion a massive change process designed to recreate the organization. And with the 1991 acquisition of NCR, AT&T dramatically transformed itself from a domestic monopoly to a formidable competitor in global telecommunications. But ever since the company restructured into 26 autonomous business units, it has faced a constant challenge in coordinating its employee staffing efforts. As some units grow and others downsize, there are sometimes huge inconsistencies in the internal demand and supply of labor.

One extremely innovative solution to this staffing problem has been the creation of Resource Link—an HR unit within AT&T that operates as an internal temporary agency, supplying business units with employees on an as-needed basis. Resource Link uses workers on the AT&T payroll who might otherwise be laid off because of downsizing as contingent workers to make up a readily available pool for the entire company. Now at-risk employees fill other jobs within the company that in the past would have gone to outside contractors.

When Harold W. Burlingame, AT&T's senior vice president of HR, and Jim L. Meadows, HR vice president for career placement alternatives, sat down and looked at the situation, they determined that beyond having created Resource Link, it was becoming urgent that the company move toward having both a core and an internal contingent workforce.

Employees wanting to be considered for Resource Link must apply and complete the selection process. Candidates tend to be high-performing candidates who have the ability and flexibility to contribute immediately in a variety of assignments. Once associates have been accepted, they have permanent positions with Resource Link—it is only their assignments that are temporary. Associates remain regular AT&T employees retaining the same salary and benefits that they had when they joined. But rather than being in a traditional job and career path, Resource Link associates move from project to project. No longer restricted to at-risk employees, Resource Link now numbers more than 600 associates.

Associates log their billable hours by calling a specific phone number and punching in the time that they have worked on a touch-tone phone. AT&T's conversant voice response system then downloads into Resource Link's billing system. Because Resource Link operates as a profit center, it bills clients for the services of its associates on an hourly rate based on the assignment.

As permanent employees, associates receive semiannual performance appraisals. All staff members participate in the performance review process to provide associates with client feedback (appraisals can be given to peers or even to those at a higher level), and these appraisals are used to determine associates' salary increases. Interestingly, Resource Link associates receive pay even when they are between assignments (for a maximum of 135 days). To date, however, idle time for workers within the organization has been less than 2 percent of total available billable hours.

AT&T gains several benefits from Resource Link. In addition to smoothing out staffing patterns, AT&T retains and develops talented employees, while spending less on severance payments and fees paid to temporary service agencies (business units within AT&T must contact Resource Link before using outside temp agencies). The savings to the company in severance pay alone outweigh the costs of the operation.

In recognition of these and other accomplishments, AT&T received *Personnel Journal's* 1994 Optimas Award for General Excellence in Human Resources.

Sources: Jim L. Meadows, "AT&T Workers Form an Internal Contingent Labor Pool," *Personnel Journal,* December 1994, p. 90; Dawn Anfuso, "AT&T Connects HR and Business Leaders for Success," *Personnel Journal,* December 1994, pp. 84–94; Dawn Anfuso, "Through AT&T Turbulent Decade, HR Excels," *Personnel Journal,* January 1994, pp. 54–55. ●

LEGAL ISSUES AND EQUAL EMPLOYMENT OPPORTUNITY

In 1964 Congress passed the Civil Rights Act, which prohibits discrimination in employment based on race, sex, color, national origin, and religion. Title VII of the act specifically forbids discrimination in employment decisions such as recruitment, hiring, discharge, layoff, discipline, promotion, compensation, and access to training.[20] In 1972, the act was amended to allow the Equal Employment Opportunity Commission (EEOC) to take employers to court. The amendments also expanded the scope of the act to cover private and public employers with 15 or more employees, labor organizations, and public and private employment agencies.

Nevertheless, employment discrimination remains a controversial and costly issue for both organizations and individuals. Opponents of the 1991 Civil Rights Act argued that the act would force companies to hire based on mandated quotas rather than on the most qualified candidates. But the new bill provides protection for many groups.

The 1991 Civil Rights Act also provides for punitive damages to workers who sue under the Americans with Disabilities Act. The latter act, passed in 1990, prohibits employment discrimination against people with disabilities. Recovering alcoholics or drug abusers, cancer patients in remission, and AIDS victims are covered by this legislation.

Thousands of court cases have challenged employment decisions and practices. Today one common reason employers are sued is *adverse impact,* in which an apparently neutral employment practice adversely affects a *group* of individuals protected by the Civil Rights Act.[21] Discrimination issues provide a means for both minority groups as well as individuals to seek Title VII protection from employment discrimination. Today the *Uniform Guidelines on Employee Selection Procedures* deal specifically with how to develop employment practices that comply with the law.[22]

Many other important staffing laws affect employment practices. The *Rehabilitation Act* of 1973 and the *Americans with Disabilities Act* of 1990 prohibit discrimination against persons with physical and mental disabilities. The *Age Discrimination in Employment Act (ADEA)* of 1967 and amendments in 1978 and 1986 prohibit discrimination against people age 40 and over. The *Immigration Act* of 1990 was designed to allow immigrants into the country based on what they can contribute to the economy. This legislation nearly tripled the cap on immigrant visas to 140,000 but limited nonimmigrant or temporary visas to 90,000 (the latter category previously was unrestricted). This new law complicates the hiring process for non–U.S. professionals under temporary visas such as investment bankers, scientists, and engineers. Finally, the *Worker Adjustment and Retraining Notification Act* of 1989, commonly known as the *WARN Act* or *Plant Closing Bill,* requires covered employers to give affected employees 60 days' written notice of plant closings or mass layoffs.

Table 12.2 summarizes many of these major equal employment laws. Table 12.3 shows the top employment discrimination issues faced by the EEOC.

DEVELOPING THE WORKFORCE

The skills and performance of employees and managers must be continually upgraded. Meeting this requirement involves training and development activities and appraising performance for the purposes of giving feedback and motivating people to perform at their best.

TRAINING AND DEVELOPMENT

Annual spending by employers on formal and informal training is over $200 billion—slightly more than annual public and private spending on elementary and secondary education.[23]

Act	Major Provisions	Enforcement and Remedies
Equal Pay Act (1963)	Prohibits gender-based pay discrimination between two jobs substantially similar in skill, effort, responsibility, and working conditions.	Fines up to $10,000, imprisonment up to 6 months, or both; enforced by Equal Employment Opportunity Commission (EEOC); private actions for double damages up to 3 years' wages, liquidated damages, reinstatement, or promotion.
Title VII of Civil Rights Act (1964)	Prohibits discrimination based on race, sex, color, religion, or national origin in employment decisions: hiring, pay, working conditions, promotion, discipline, or discharge.	Enforced by EEOC; private actions, back pay, front pay, reinstatement, restore seniority and pension benefits, attorneys' fees and costs.
Executive Orders 11246 and 11375 (1965)	Requires equal opportunity clauses in federal contracts; prohibits employment discrimination by federal contractors based on race, color, religion, sex, or national origin.	Established Office of Federal Contract Compliance Programs (OFCCP) to investigate violations; empowered to terminate violator's federal contracts.
Age Discrimination in Employment Act (1967)	Prohibits employment discrimination based on age for persons over 40 years; restricts mandatory retirement.	EEOC enforcement; private actions for reinstatement, back pay, front pay, restore seniority and pension benefits; double unpaid wages for willful violations; attorneys' fees and costs.
Vocational Rehabilitation Act (1973)	Requires affirmative action by all federal contractors for persons with disabilities; defines disabilities as physical or mental impairments that substantially limit life activities.	Federal contractors must consider hiring disabled persons capable of performance after reasonable accommodations.
Americans with Disabilities Act (1990)	Extends affirmative action provisions of Vocational Rehabilitation Act to private employers; requires workplace modifications to facilitate disabled employees; prohibits discrimination against disabled.	EEOC enforcement; private actions for Title VII remedies.
Civil Rights Act (1991)	Clarifies Title VII requirements: disparate treatment impact suits, business necessity, job relatedness; shifts burden of proof to employer; permits punitive damages and jury trials.	Punitive damages limited to sliding scale only in intentional discrimination based on sex, religion, and disabilities.
Family and Medical Leave Act (1991)	Requires 12 weeks' unpaid leave for medical or family needs: paternity, family member illness.	Private actions for lost wages and other expenses, reinstatement.

TABLE 12.2

U.S. equal employment laws

General Motors has invested more than $2 billion over the past decade on education and training, making it the largest privately funded educational institution in the United States. IBM's annual training cost of $1.5 billion exceeds Harvard University's annual operating expenses of $951.7 million. Other notable companies are shown in Table 12.4.

Although $200 billion spent on formal and informal training sounds like a lot of money, the American Society for Training and Development (ASTD) argues that as a percentage of total payroll, the average organizational investment in training is too small.[24] This is of great concern given that future jobs will require more education, but the education level of U.S. workers will not keep pace.

Another impetus for workplace training is the emphasis on total quality management or continuous improvement programs. The Department of Commerce created the Malcolm Baldrige National Quality Award in 1987 to recognize companies that have achieved excellence through adherence to quality improvement processes.[25]

Quality

TABLE 12.3

Top employment bias issues

Firing remains the top work bias issue, but sexual harassment grew fastest from 1993 to 1994.

Issue	Complaints in '94	Change from '93
Firing	42,756	− 1.9%
Working conditions	15,029	+10.4
Nonsexual harassment	11.657	+ 12.5
Sexual harassment	8,234	+ 13.2
Promotion	8,060	+ 4.5
Hiring	7,252	− 8.2
Wages	6,482	+ 2.9
Layoff	5,382	− 2.3

Source: U.S. Equal Employment Opportunity Commission.

TABLE 12.4

Benchmark companies for training

Company (employees worldwide)	Training		Comments
	Percent of Payroll Spent in 1992	Avg. Hours per Employee per Year	
Motorola 107,000	3.6%	36	The gold standard of corporate training. The company says every $1 spent on education returns $30 in productivity gains.
Target 100,000	N.A.	N.A.	Rapidly expanding retail chain has used Disney-type training to empower frontline employees and improve customer service.
Federal Express 93,000	4.5%	27	Workers take computer-based job competency tests every 6 to 12 months. Low scores lead to remedial action.
General Electric Aircraft Engines 33,000	N.A.	N.A.	Training budget has shrunk, but new focus on teamwork has helped the division boost productivity in a slumping industry.
Andersen Consulting 26,700	6.8%	109	Replaced 40-hour business practices class with interactive video, saving $4 million per year, mostly on travel and lodging.
Corning 14,000 (domestic)	3.0%	92	Ordinary employees, not professional educators, do most training. Pay of factory workers rises as they learn new skills.
Solectron 3,500	3.0%	95	Training helped this fast-growing Silicon Valley company win a Baldrige in 1991. The 1993 goal: 110 hours per worker.
Dudek Manufacturing 3,500	5.0%	25	Had to teach basic literacy and math before introducing quality management. Hefty investment has paid off in profits.

Source: Company data reprinted in *Fortune,* March 22, 1993.

TABLE 12.5

Types of training programs

Types of Training	% Providing[1]	In-House Only (%)[2]	Outside Only (%)[3]	Both (%)[4]
Management skills/development	91	12	18	61
Basic computer skills	90	21	14	55
Communication skills	87	21	12	53
Supervisory skills	86	18	12	56
Technical skills/knowledge	82	22	6	54
New methods/procedures	80	38	5	37
Executive development	77	8	26	44
Customer relations/services	76	25	9	41
Personal growth	73	14	15	45
Clerical/secretarial skills	73	23	18	32
Employee/labor relations	67	23	12	31
Customer education	65	28	5	31
Wellness	63	21	15	28
Sales skills	56	15	11	30
Remedial/basic education	48	11	21	15

[1]Percent that provide each type of training.
[2]Percent that say all training of this type is designed and delivered by in-house staff.
[3]Percent that say all training of this type is designed and delivered by outside consultants or suppliers.
[4]Percent that say training of this type is designed and delivered by a combination of in-house staff and outside suppliers.

Source: Reprinted with permission from the October 1993 issue of *Training*. Copyright © 1993. Lakewood Publications, Minneapolis, Minn. All rights reserved.

Companies invest in training to enhance individual performance and organizational productivity. Table 12.5 shows the variety of subjects covered in company training programs. Although we use the general term **training** here, training is sometimes distinguished from *development*. Training usually refers to teaching lower-level employees how to perform their present jobs, while **development** involves teaching managers and professional employees broader skills needed for their present and future jobs.

Training should begin with a **needs assessment.** An analysis should be conducted to identify the jobs, people, and departments for which training is necessary. Job analysis and performance measurements are useful for this purpose.

Several training methods are available once the organization's training needs and objectives have been determined. A basic decision for selecting a training method is whether to provide on-the-job or off-the-job training. A second decision involves determining the content of the training and then selecting an appropriate training method. Examples of training methods include lectures, role playing, programmed learning, case discussion, business simulation, behavior modeling (watching a videotape and imitating what is observed), assigned readings, conferences, job rotation, vestibule training (practice in a simulated job environment), and apprenticeship training. Ultimately, the effectiveness of the training should be carefully evaluated.

Motorola U. is a cutting-edge example of a world-class training and development facility.

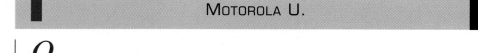

MOTOROLA U.

 *O*ver a decade ago, Motorola recognized that to compete as the industry leader in quality, it had to develop a workforce that was highly talented and flexible. However, to their chagrin, Motorola executives realized that they faced a problem common to other U.S. companies—their workforce was illiterate. To overcome this problem, the company began providing employees remedial courses in reading, writing, and arithmetic, as well as instruction in new concepts of work, quality, community, and leadership. From that beginning grew one of the most comprehensive and admired educational programs in the world. Motorola executives had created Motorola University.

Motorola U. doesn't have tenured professors or basketball teams. Instead, it establishes partnerships with established colleges and universities. Motorola supplies the students, equipment, and tuition; brings in outside faculty members; and collaborates with them on course content and design. Individuals from all over the world have attended Motorola's quality management programs. And with Motorola University Press, the company prints more than a million documents per month and a series of books on design and quality written by Motorola employees.

In an effort to push the use of technology, Motorola has begun experimenting with video equipment, computers, and satellite communications in a program they call Project SALSA (Southwest Advanced Learning Systems Applications). The program began as a six-month study in computer-assisted adult education for Motorola employees in Phoenix, Arizona. Using personal computers, Project SALSA links employees and their families to NOVAnet, an electronic education network based at the University of Illinois, so that they can access a variety of computer-based courses. Through SALSA, Motorola hopes to prove that employees can acquire skills at a faster rate using technology than they can only attending classes.

Clearly, Motorola is taking aggressive steps to reeducate its workers. Motorola's mission is to create an environment for learning that produces employees who are creative and flexible, who do high-quality work, and who not only adapt quickly to new technologies but *anticipate* them as well.

Sources: W. Wiggenhorn, "Motorola U.: When Training Becomes an Education," *Harvard Business Review,* July–August 1990, pp. 71–83; and James Goodno, "The Educated Workplace," *Technology Review* 94, no. 4 (May–June 1991), pp. 22, 24. ●

PERFORMANCE APPRAISAL

Performance appraisal (PA) is the assessment of an employees' job performance. PA has two basic HRM purposes. First, PA serves an *administrative* purpose. It provides information for making salary, promotion, and layoff decisions, as well as providing documentation than can justify these decisions in court. Second, and perhaps more importantly, PA serves a *developmental* purpose. The information can be used to diagnose training needs, career planning, and the like. Feedback and coaching based on PA provide the basis for improving day-to-day performance.

GATHERING PA INFORMATION

Performance measures fall into one of four categories: production data, personnel data, management by objectives (MBO), and judgmental measures. *Production data* consist of information such as sales volume (for a salesperson), units produced (for a line worker), and profits (for a manager). *Personnel data* include turnover rate, absenteeism rate, number of accidents, or grievances filed against a supervisor.

Management by objectives (MBO) is a process in which a subordinate and a supervisor agree on specific performance goals (objectives). Then they develop a plan that describes the time frame and criteria for determining whether the objectives have been reached. The aim is to agree on a set of objectives that are clear, specific, and reachable. For example, an objective for a salesperson might be to increase sales 25 percent during the following year. An objective for a computer programmer might be to complete two projects within the next six months. Although MBO helps focus employees on reaching specific goals and encourages planning and development, it often focuses too much on short-term achievement and ignores long-term goals.

Judgmental measures are subjective PA evaluations made by rating the individual's performance. This approach is extremely common, but unfortunately it often is not valid because subjective ratings can be inaccurate.

A number of instruments for collecting judgmental data have been developed. *Trait scales* contain dimensions such as initiative, leadership, and attitude; they ask raters to indicate how much of each trait the employee possesses. Trait scales are ambiguous, subjective, and not suitable for obtaining useful feedback.

Behavioral scales, such as the behaviorally anchored rating scale (BARS), were developed to address the problems of the trait scale. These scales focus on specific, relevant behaviors, which can help ensure that all parties understand what the ratings are really measuring. They also can help provide useful feedback. Figure 12.4 contains an example of a BARS.

Comparative scales require the manager to make comparisons among employees, often by rank ordering subordinates from lowest to highest performers. Hewlett-Packard's rank-ordering system requires the manager to put 10 percent of employees in the "exceptional" category, 40 percent in "very good," 40 percent in "good," and 10 percent in "unacceptable." Unacceptable performers are counseled and must improve or be terminated.

None of these PA systems are easy to conduct properly; all have drawbacks that must be guarded against. You will learn more about these systems if you take upper-level HRM courses. Nevertheless, some general guidelines apply in all cases:

1. Always take legal considerations into account.
2. Base performance standards on job analysis.
3. Communicate performance standards to employees.
4. Evaluate employees on specific performance-related behaviors rather than on a single global or overall measure.
5. Document the PA process carefully.
6. If possible, use more than one rater (discussed below).
7. Develop a formal appeal process.[26]

SOURCES OF APPRAISAL INFORMATION

Just as there are multiple methods for gathering PA information, there are several different sources who can provide PA information.

FIGURE 12.4

Example of BARS used for evaluating quality

Performance Dimension: Total Quality Management. This area of performance concerns the extent to which a person is aware of, endorses, and develops proactive procedures to enhance product quality, ensure early disclosure of discrepancies, and integrate quality assessments with cost and schedule performance measurement reports to maximize client's satisfaction with overall performance.

OUTSTANDING	7	Uses measures of quality and well-defined processes to achieve project goals. Defines quality from the client's perspective.
	6	Look for/identifies ways to continually improve the process.
	5	Clearly communicates quality management to others. Develops a plan that defines how the team will participate in quality. Appreciates TQM as an investment.
AVERAGE	4	Has measures of quality that define tolerance levels.
	3	Views quality as costly. Legislates quality.
	2	Focuses his/her concerns only on outputs and deliverables, ignoring the underlying processes.
POOR	1	Blames others for absence of quality. Gives lip service only to quality concerns.

Source: Landy, Jacobs, and Associates. Used by permission.

Managers and supervisors are the traditional source of appraisal information since they are often in the best position to observe an employee's performance. However companies such as Coors, General Foods, and Digital are turning to *peers and team members* to provide input to the PA. Peers and team members often see different dimensions of performance, and are often best at identifying leadership potential and interpersonal skills.

One increasingly popular source of appraisal is the person's *subordinates.* Appraisal by subordinates has been used by companies such as Xerox and IBM to give superiors feedback on how their employees view them. However, since this process gives employees power over their bosses, it is normally only used for developmental purposes.

Internal and external customers are also used as sources of performance appraisal information, particularly for companies such as Ford and Honda that are focused on total quality management. External customers have been used for some time to appraise restaurant employees, but internal customers can include anyone inside the organization who depends upon an employee's work output. Finally, it is usually a good idea for employees to evaluate their own performance. Although *self-appraisals* may be biased upward, the process of self-evaluation helps increase the employee's involvement in the review process, and is a starting point for establishing future goals.

Since each source of PA information has some limitations, and different people may see different aspects of performance, companies such as Westinghouse and Eastman Kodak have taken to using multiple-rater approaches that involve more than one source for appraisal information. By combining different sources, it is possible to obtain a more complete assessment of an employee's performance.

GIVING PA FEEDBACK

Giving PA feedback can be a stressful task for both managers and subordinates. The purposes of PA conflict to some degree. Providing growth and development requires understanding and support; however, the manager must be impersonal and be able to make tough decisions. Employees want to know how they are doing, but typically they are uncomfortable about getting feedback. Finally, the organization's need to make HR decisions conflicts with the individual employee's need to maintain a positive image.[27] These conflicts often make the PA interview difficult; therefore, managers should conduct such interviews thoughtfully.

There is no one "best" way to do a PA interview. The most difficult interviews are those with employees who are performing poorly. Here is a useful PA interview format to use when an employee is performing below acceptable standards:

1. Summarize the employee's specific performance. Describe the performance in behavioral or outcome terms, such as sales or absenteeism. Don't say the employee has a poor attitude; rather, explain which employee behaviors indicate a poor attitude.
2. Describe the expectations and standards, and be specific.
3. Determine the causes for the low performance; get the employee's input.
4. Discuss solutions to the problem, and have the employee play a major role in the process.
5. Agree to a solution. As a supervisor, you have input into the solution. Raise issues and questions, but also provide support.
6. Agree to a timetable for improvement.
7. Document the meeting.

Follow-up meetings may be needed. Here are some guidelines for giving feedback to an average employee:

1. Summarize the employee's performance, and be specific.
2. Explain why the employee's work is important to the organization.
3. Thank the employee for doing the job.
4. Raise any relevant issues, such as areas for improvement.
5. Express confidence in the employee's future good performance.

DESIGNING REWARD SYSTEMS

Cost

Reward systems are another major set of HRM activities. Most of this section will be devoted to monetary rewards like pay and fringe benefits. Although traditionally pay has been of primary interest, benefits have received increased attention in recent years. Benefits make up a far greater percentage of the total payroll than in past decades.[28] The typical employer today pays nearly 40 percent of payroll costs in benefits. Accordingly, employers are trying to find ways to reduce these costs. Another reason for the growing interest in benefits is increased complexity. Many new types of benefits are now available, and tax laws affect myriad fringe benefits, such as health insurance and pension plans.

PAY DECISIONS

Reward systems can serve the strategic purposes of attracting, motivating, and retaining people. Compensation systems are based on a complex set of forces. Beyond the body of laws governing compensation, a number of basic decisions must be made in choosing the appropriate pay plan. Three types of decisions are crucial for designing an effective pay plan: pay level, pay structure, and individual pay.

Pay level refers to the choice of whether to be a high-, average-, or low-paying company. Compensation is a major cost for any organization, so low wages can be justified on a short-term financial basis. But being the high-wage employer—the highest-paying company in the region—ensures that the company will attract many applicants. Being a wage leader may be important during times of low unemployment or intense competition.

The *pay structure* decision is the choice of how to price different jobs within the organization. Jobs that are similar in worth usually are grouped together into job families. A *pay grade,* with a floor and ceiling, is established for each job family. Figure 12.5 illustrates a hypothetical pay structure.

Finally, *individual pay* decisions concern different pay rates for jobs of similar worth within the same family. Differences in pay within job families are decided in two ways.

FIGURE 12.5

A pay structure

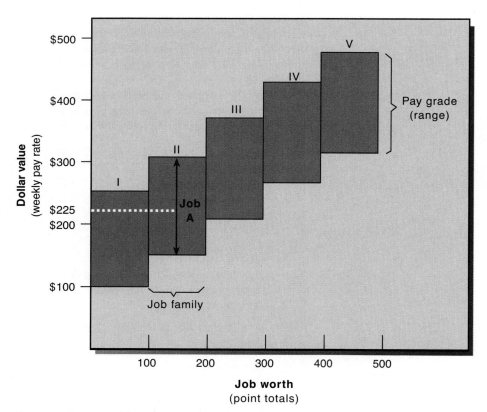

Source: *Effective Personal Management,* 3rd ed., by Randall S.Schuler, Nicholas J. Bentell and Stuart A. Youngblood. Copyright © 1989 by West Publishing Company.

First, some jobs are occupied by individuals with more seniority than others. Second, some people may be better performers, therefore deserving of a higher level of pay.

INCENTIVE SYSTEMS AND VARIABLE PAY

A number of incentive systems have been devised to encourage and motivate employees to be more productive.[29] (See Chapter 15 for more discussion of rewarding performance.) *Individual incentive plans* are the most common type of incentive plan. An individual incentive system consists of an objective standard against which a worker's performance is compared. Pay is determined by the employee's performance. Individual incentive plans frequently are used in sales jobs. If effectively designed, individual incentive plans can be highly motivating.

There are several types of group incentive plans in which pay is based on group performance. *Gainsharing plans* concentrate on saving money. The best known is the Scanlon plan, which is based on a function of the ratio between labor costs and sales value of production. An additional feature of the Scanlon plan is the use of employee committees to evaluate workers' suggestions for improving productivity.

Profit-sharing plans give employee incentives based on unit, department, plant, or company productivity. Nucor Steel, one of the nation's most profitable steel companies, relies heavily on a group-oriented profit-sharing plan. The entire company—4,000 employees— is broken down into bonus groups. For instance, each mill consists of groups of 25 to 35 employees who perform a complete task (e.g., melting and casting the steel or rolling the steel). Each group has a production standard and is paid for the amount of production over the specified level.[30]

When objective performance measures are not available but the company still wants to base pay on performance, it uses a merit pay system. Individuals' pay raises and bonuses are based on the judgmental merit rating they receive from their boss. Lincoln Electric Company has a particularly effective merit pay plan.[31] The Lincoln Electric system will be discussed further in Chapter 15.

EMPLOYEE BENEFITS

Like pay systems, employee benefit plans are subject to regulation. Employee benefits are divided into those required by law and those optional for an employer.

The three basic required benefits are workers' compensation, social security, and unemployment insurance. *Workers' compensation* provides financial support to employees suffering a work-related injury or illness. *Social security,* as established in the Social Security Act of 1935, provides financial support to retirees; in subsequent amendments, the act was expanded to cover disabled employees. The funds come from payments made by employers, employees, and self-employed workers. *Unemployment insurance* provides financial support to employees who are laid off for reasons they cannot control. Companies that have terminated fewer employees pay less into the unemployment insurance fund; thus, organizations have an incentive to keep terminations at a minimum.

A large number of benefits are not required to be employer provided. The most common are pension plans and medical and hospital insurance. Other optional employee benefits include dental insurance, life insurance, and vacation time. Because of the wide variety of possible benefits and the considerable differences in employee preferences and needs, companies often use **cafeteria** or **flexible benefit programs.** In this type of program, employees are given credits that they "spend" on benefits they desire. FinPac Corporation, a small computer software company, provides each employee with a required amount of life and disability insurance. Then employees use their credits toward individualized packages of additional benefits, including medical and dental insurance, dependent care, extra life insurance, or cash.

LEGAL ISSUES IN COMPENSATION AND BENEFITS

A number of laws affect employee compensation and benefits.[32]

The *Fair Labor Standards Act (FLSA)* of 1938 set minimum wages, maximum hours, child labor standards, and overtime pay provisions. The Department of Labor monitors and enforces the FLSA. *Nonexempt* employees are entitled to premium pay for overtime (e.g., time-and-one-half). *Exempt* employees (e.g., executives, administrators, and professionals) are not subject to the overtime and minimum wage provisions.

The *Equal Pay Act (EPA)* of 1963, now enforced by the EEOC, prohibits unequal pay for men and women who perform equal work. *Equal work* means jobs that require equal skill, effort, and responsibility and are performed under similar working conditions. The law does permit exceptions where the difference in pay is due to a seniority system, a merit system, an incentive system based on quantity or quality of production, or any other factor other than sex, such as market demand. Although equal pay for equal work may sound like common sense, many employers have fallen victim to this law by rationalizing that men, traditionally the "breadwinners," deserve more pay than women or by giving equal jobs different titles (senior assistant versus office manager) as the sole basis for pay differences.

One controversy concerns male and female pay differences within the same company. **Comparable worth** doctrine implies that women who perform *different* jobs of equal *worth* as men should be paid the same wage.[33] In contrast to the equal-pay-for-equal-work notion, comparable worth suggests that the jobs need *not* be the same to require the same pay. For example, nurses (predominantly female) were found to be paid considerably less than skilled craftworkers (predominantly male), even though the two jobs were found to be of equal value or worth.[34] Under the Equal Pay Act, this would not constitute pay discrimination because the jobs are very different. But under the comparable-worth concept, these findings would indicate discrimination because the jobs are of equal worth.

To date, no federal law requires comparable worth, and the Supreme Court has made no decisive rulings about it. However, some states have considered developing comparable-worth laws, and others already have implemented comparable-worth changes, raising the wages of female-dominated jobs. For example, Minnesota passed a comparable-worth law for public-sector employees after finding that women on average were paid 25 percent less than men. Several other states have comparable-worth laws for public-sector employees, including Iowa, Idaho, New Mexico, Washington, and South Dakota.[35]

Some laws influence mostly benefit practices. The *Pregnancy Discrimination Act* of 1978 states that pregnancy is a disability and qualifies a woman to receive the same benefits that she would with any other disability. The *Employee Retirement Income Security Act (ERISA)* of 1974 protects private pension programs from mismanagement. ERISA requires that retirement benefits be paid to those who vest or earn a right to draw benefits and ensures retirement benefits for employees whose companies go bankrupt or who otherwise cannot meet their pension obligations.

HEALTH AND SAFETY

The *Occupational Safety and Health Act (OSHA)* of 1970 requires employers to pursue workplace safety. Employers must maintain records of injuries and deaths caused by workplace accidents and submit to on-site inspections. Large-scale industrial accidents, such as the Union Carbide gas leak in Bhopal, India, and nuclear power plant accidents worldwide, have focused attention on the importance of workplace safety.

One of many examples of the importance of this issue is the coal-mining industry. Coal miners spend their workdays in three-foot-high spaces wading in mud and water. Nearly every coal miner can name a friend or family member who has been killed, maimed, or stricken with black lung disease. "You die quick or you die slow," reports one mine worker. However, according to the federal Mine Safety and Health Administration, the mines are much safer now, and catastrophic cave-ins are largely a thing of the past.[36]

LABOR RELATIONS

Labor relations is the system of relations between workers and management. As discussed in Chapter 3, labor unions recruit members, collect dues, and ensure that employees are treated fairly with respect to wages, working conditions, and other issues. When workers organize for the purpose of negotiating with management to improve their wages, hours, or working conditions, two processes are involved: unionization and collective bargaining. These processes have evolved over a 50-year period in the United States to provide important employee rights.[37]

The workers in this 1935 photo are showing support for their union. Marches such as this one are increasingly rare in today's pro-management climate.

(The Bettmann Archive)

LABOR LAWS

Try to imagine what life would be like with unemployment at 25 percent. Pretty grim, you would say. Legislators in 1935 felt that way too. Therefore, organized labor received its Magna Carta with the passage of the National Labor Relations Act.

The *National Labor Relations Act* (also called the *Wagner Act* after its legislative sponsor) ushered in an era of rapid unionization by (1) declaring labor organizations legal, (2) establishing five unfair employer labor practices, and (3) creating the National Labor Relations Board (NLRB). Today the NLRB conducts unionization elections, hears unfair labor practices complaints, and issues injunctions against offending employers. The Wagner Act greatly assisted the growth of unions by enabling workers to use the law and the courts to legally organize and collectively bargain for better wages, hours, and working conditions.

Public policy began on the side of organized labor in 1935, but over the next 25 years the pendulum swung toward the side of management. The *Labor-Management Relations Act,* or *Taft-Hartley Act* (1947), protected employers' free-speech rights, defined unfair labor practices by unions, and permitted workers to decertify (reject) a union as their representative.

Finally, the *Labor-Management Reporting and Disclosure Act,* or *Landrum-Griffin Act,* of 1959 swung the public policy pendulum midway between organized labor and management. By declaring a bill of rights for union members, establishing control over union dues increases, and imposing reporting requirements for unions, Landrum-Griffin was designed to curb abuses by union leadership and rid unions of corruption.

UNIONIZATION

How do workers join unions? Through a union organizer or local union representative, workers learn what benefits they may receive by joining.[38] The union representative distributes authorization cards that permit workers to indicate whether or not they want an election to be held to certify the union to represent them.

The National Labor Relations Board (NLRB) will conduct a certification election if at least 30 percent of employees sign authorization cards. Management has several choices at this stage: to recognize the union without an election, to consent to an election, or to contest the number of cards signed and resist an election.

If an election is warranted, an NLRB representative will conduct the election by secret ballot. A simple majority of those voting determines the winner. Thus, apathetic workers who do not show up to vote in effect support the union. If the union wins the election, it is certified as the bargaining unit representative.

FIGURE 12.6

Determinants of
union voting
behavior

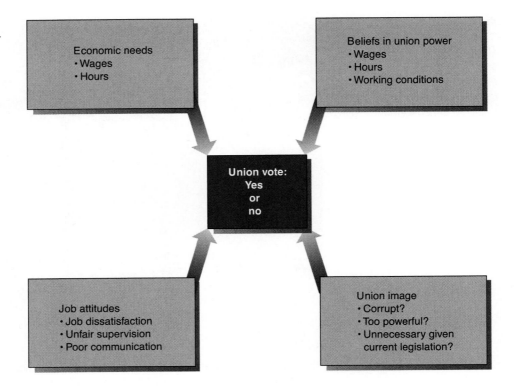

During the campaign preceding the election, efforts are made by both management and the union to persuade the workers how to vote. Most workers, though, are somewhat resistant to campaign efforts, having made up their minds well before the NLRB appears on the scene. If the union wins the election, management and the union are legally required to bargain in good faith to obtain a collective bargaining agreement or contract.

Why do workers vote for a union? Four factors play a significant role (see Figure 12.6).[39] First, economic factors are important, especially for workers in low-paying jobs; unions attempt to raise the average wage rate for their members. Second, job dissatisfaction encourages workers to seek out a union. Poor supervisory practices, favoritism, lack of communication, and perceived unfair or arbitrary discipline and discharge are specific triggers of job dissatisfaction. Third, the belief that the union can obtain desired benefits can generate a pro-union vote. Finally, the image of the union can determine whether a dissatisfied worker will seek out the union. Headline stories of union corruption and dishonesty can discourage workers from unionization.

COLLECTIVE BARGAINING

In the United States, management and unions engage in a periodic ritual (typically every three years) to negotiate an agreement over wages, hours, and working conditions. Two types of disputes can arise during this process. First, before an agreement is reached, the workers may go on strike to compel agreement on their terms. Such an action is known as an *economic strike* and is permitted by law. Once the agreement is signed, however, management and the union can still disagree over *interpretation* of the agreement. Usually they settle their disputes through arbitration. **Arbitration** is the use of a neutral third party, typically jointly selected, to resolve the dispute. The United States uses arbitration while an agreement is in effect to avoid *wildcat strikes* (in which workers walk off the job in violation of the contract) or unplanned work stoppages.

What does a collective bargaining agreement contain? In a **union shop,** a union security clause specifies that workers must join the union after a set period of time. **Right-to-work** states, through restrictive legislation, do not permit union shops; that is, workers have the right to work without being forced to join a union. The southern United States has many right-to-work states.

The wage component of the contract spells out rates of pay, including premium pay for overtime and paid holidays. Individual rights usually are specified in terms of the use of seniority to determine pay increases, job bidding, and order of layoffs.

A feature of any contract is the grievance procedure. Unions perform a vital service for their membership in this regard by giving workers a *voice* in what goes on during both contract negotiations and administration through the grievance procedure.[40] In about 50 percent of discharge cases that go to arbitration, the arbitrator overturns management's decision and reinstates the worker.[41] Unions have a legal duty of fair representation, which means they must represent all workers in the bargaining unit and ensure that workers' rights are protected.

WHAT DOES THE FUTURE HOLD?

In recent years, union membership has declined to less than 12 percent of the U.S. labor force as a consequence of changing laws concerning employee rights, global competition and decreased demand for the products of traditionally unionized industries, the rise of the service economy (which is difficult to unionize), job loss from automation, and changing expectations of the new workforce.[42] On the other hand, unions are adapting to changing workforce demographics; they are paying more attention to women, older workers, and people who work at home.

Some people applaud unions' apparent decline. Others hope for an eventual reemergence based on the potential power of management–union cooperation to help U.S. businesses regain their competitive position in the global economy.[43]

Unions may play a different role in the future, one that is less adversarial and more cooperative with management. The steel industry signed an innovative contract with the steelworkers' union that *The Wall Street Journal* and the *Washington Post* called "precedent breaking" and "a model for survival." Elimination of inefficient work rules, the introduction of profit sharing, and a guarantee of no layoffs were seen as a big step toward a fundamentally different, cooperative long-term relationship.[44]

Sometimes, as in the case of the recent baseball strike, labor–management relations can be highly destructive. In other cases, management and labor have worked to forge better relationships. Some Japanese plants in the United States have progressive labor–management practices, and Scandinavia and other European countries have long provided positive models of collaborative relationships. Things are constantly changing, as illustrated by recent union efforts to buy United Airlines. In general, constructive change within a company or industry cannot occur without the positive transformation of labor–management relations.

KEY TERMS

arbitration, p. 308
assessment center, p. 292
cafeteria programs, p. 305
comparable worth, p. 306
development, p. 300
flexible benefit programs, p. 305
human resources management (HRM), p. 288
job analysis, p. 290
labor relations, p. 306
management by objectives (MBO), p. 301
needs assessment, p. 300

outplacement, p. 294
performance appraisal (PA), p. 301
recruitment, p. 291
reliability, p. 293
right-to-work, p. 308
selection, p. 291
termination interview, p. 295
training, p. 300
union shop, p. 308
validity, p. 293

SUMMARY OF LEARNING OBJECTIVES

Now that you have studied Chapter 12, you should know:

How companies use human resources management to gain competitive advantage.

To succeed, companies must align their human resources to their strategy. Effective planning is necessary to make certain that the right number and kind of employees are available to implement a company's strategic plan. For example, in the Setting the Stage case of Mirage Resorts, it is clear that excellent service in the hotel industry depends on hiring the most competent people and training them to perform well on the job. Other companies that compete on cost, quality, innovation, and so on should also use their staffing, training, appraisal, and reward systems to elicit and reinforce the kinds of behaviors that underlie their strategies.

Why companies recruit both internally and externally for new hires.

Some companies prefer to recruit internally to make certain that employees are familiar with organizational policies and values. AT&T's Resource Link is an example of a company trying very hard to make certain that available work goes to internal candidates before looking externally. In other instances, companies prefer to recruit externally to find individuals with new ideas and fresh perspectives.

The various methods available for selecting new employees.

There are a myriad of selection techniques to choose from. Interviews and reference checks are most common. Personality tests and cognitive ability tests measure an individual's aptitude and potential to do well on the job. Other selection techniques include assessment centers and integrity tests. Regardless of the approach used, any test should be able to demonstrate reliability (consistency across time and different interview situations) and validity (accuracy in predicting job performance).

Why companies spend so much on training and development.

People cannot depend on a set of skills for all of their working lives. In today's changing, competitive world, old skills quickly become obsolete and new ones become essential for success. Refreshing or updating an individual's skills requires a great deal of continuous training. Companies such as Motorola understand that gaining a competitive edge in quality or innovation depends on having the most talented, flexible workers in the industry.

How to determine who should appraise an employee's performance.

Many companies are using multiple sources of appraisal since different people see different sides of an employee's performance. Typically a superior is expected to evaluate an employee, but peers and team members are often in a good position to see aspects of performance that a superior misses. Even an employee's subordinates are being asked more often today to give their input in order to get yet another perspective on the evaluation. Particularly in companies concerned about quality, internal and external customers are also surveyed. Finally, each employee should evaluate his or her own performance, if only to get them thinking about their own performance, as well as to engage them in the appraisal process.

How to analyze the fundamental aspects of a reward system.

Reward systems are broken down into three basic components: pay level, pay structure, and individual pay determination. To achieve an advantage over competitors, executives may want to generally pay a higher wage to their company's employees, but this decision must be weighed against the need to control costs (pay-level decisions are often tied to strategic concerns such as these). To achieve internal equity (paying people what they are worth relative to their peers within the company) managers must look at the pay structure, making certain that pay differentials are based on knowledge, effort, responsibility, working conditions, seniority, and so on. Individual pay determination is often based on merit or the different contributions of individuals. In these cases it is important to make certain that men and women receive equal pay for equal work, and managers may wish to base pay decisions on the idea of comparable worth (equal pay for equal contribution).

How unions influence human resources management.

Labor relations involves the interactions between workers and management. One mechanism by which this relationship is conducted is unions. Unions seek to present a collective voice for workers, to make their needs and wishes known to management. Unions negotiate agreements with management regarding a range of issues such as wages, hours, working conditions, job security, and health care. One important tool that unions can use is the grievance procedure established through collective bargaining. This gives employees a way to seek redress for wrongful action on the part of management. In this way, unions make certain that the rights of all employees are protected.

How the legal system influences human resources management.

The legal system influences managers by placing constraints on the ways potential and actual employees are treated. Equal opportunity laws ensure that companies do not discriminate in their hiring and training practices. The Fair Labor Standards Act and the Equal Pay Act ensure that people earn fair compensation for the contribution they make to the organization. The Occupational Safety and Health Act (OSHA) ensures that employees have a safe and healthy work environment. Labor laws seek to protect the rights of both employees and managers so that their relationship can be productive and agreeable.

DISCUSSION QUESTIONS

1. How will changes in the labor force affect HRM practices for the year 2000?
2. Describe the major regulations governing HRM practices.
3. Define *job analysis*. Why is job analysis relevant to each of the six key HRM activities discussed in the chapter (i.e. planning, staffing, training, performance appraisal, reward systems, labor relations)?
4. What are the various methods for recruiting employees? Why are some better than others? In what sense are they better?
5. What is a "test"? Give some examples of tests used by employers.

6. What purpose does performance appraisal serve? Why are there so many different methods of appraisal?
7. What are some key ideas to remember when conducting a performance interview?
8. How would you define an effective reward system? What role do benefits serve in a reward system?
9. Why do workers join unions? What implications would this have for the organization that wishes to remain nonunion?
10. Discuss the advantages and disadvantages of collective bargaining for the employer and the employee.

CONCLUDING CASE

EMPLOYEE DEVELOPMENT GIVES GRANITE ROCK A COMPETITIVE EDGE

Granite Rock is a small family-owned business, employing only about 400 people. Its headquarters is in Watsonville, California, a small town on the central coast of the Pacific. Granite Rock's HR staff is small—three people to be exact. But they think big. And nothing about the success of the multimillion-dollar company is small.

Everything Granite Rock does, it does in a big way. It has to. Not so long ago, this construction-materials supplier was competing with companies similar in size and resources to itself. That all changed when about 1987 many of those companies sold out to well-endowed, multinational corporations. Granite Rock executives realized that for their company to come out ahead of the competition, it had to offer superior customer service and quality products. So that's what it does. Granite Rock's concrete products consistently exceed the industry performance specifications by 100 times. The reliability of several of its key processes has reached the six-sigma level (3.4 errors per 1 million chances to err, a goal most high-tech companies hope to reach). And it delivers more than 90 percent of product on time, topping the on-time delivery average of a prominent national company that Granite Rock benchmarked.

Granite Rock realizes the importance of manufacturing superior products. By implementing a Total Quality Program, it earned the coveted Malcolm Baldrige National Quality Award in 1992.

(Andy Sacks/Tony Stone Images)

The strategy works. Granite Rock has been gaining market share every year since 1987; its market share today is double what it was back then. And by continuously responding to customers' needs (it surveys its customers annually, asking them to rate Granite Rock against its competitors), it aims to build a 10 percent lead over its nearest competitor for each indicator of customer satisfaction.

The company's success at serving its customers can be credited in large part to its Total Quality Program, which earned it the coveted Malcolm Baldrige National Quality Award in 1992. The cornerstone of Granite Rock's TQM program is a commitment to employee development and training. Development begins with the Individual Professional Development Plan (IPDP), a system that allows employees to set developmental goals in conjunction with the firm's needs. Together with his or her supervisor, each employee sets goals each year for skill development and job accomplishments. Management, in roundtable sessions, reviews the goals and determines educational and training needs required for meeting them. The company backs this goal setting with ample opportunity for training. Granite Rock University, its training program, offers all employees seminars, courses, and lectures on at least 50 different subjects. Types of offerings fall into five categories: quality-process skills, maintenance skills, sales and service skills, product or technical skills, and health, wellness, and personal growth. Granite Rock covers the cost of off-site training, be it college courses or professional conferences.

Granite Rock employees average 37 hours of training each year, at an average cost of nearly $2,000 per employee. This is 3 times more than the mining-industry average and 13 times more than the construction-industry average. As a result, revenue earned per Granite Rock employee has risen to approximately 30 percent above the national industry average. These efforts led to Granite Rock's receiving the 1994 Optimas Award for HR excellence. Not bad for a small company.

QUESTIONS

1. How is human resource management a source of competitive advantage for Granite Rock?

2. What training and development initiatives are used to drive quality?

3. Are there other HR issues that you believe would be important for enhancing quality and competitiveness for Granite Rock? What are they? What would you do?

Source: Dawn Anfuso, "Staying a Stone's Throw Ahead of the Competition," *Personnel Journal,* January 1994, p. 56.

VIDEO CASE

HUMAN RESOURCES MANAGEMENT

What is it about a company that allows it to attract the best employees? The first thing that usually comes to mind for most people is salary. Salary can be an effective lure to top talent, but benefits are also important when a candidate considers a position with a company. In most organizations, benefits make up a significant part of the total compensation paid to an employee. These benefits can include a variety of health insurance plans, retirement options, and life insurance choices. Employee benefits also include sick days, vacation days, holidays, and personal days. Typically, the human resources department of an organization administers benefit plans. The size of the human resources department can vary considerably depending on the size of the company, but one thing all human resources departments have in common despite their size is the need to manage large amounts of data that can be regularly updated and organized.

Efficient management of human resources data is crucial to containing costs and to providing the best possible service to employees. The computerized database is one tool HR departments commonly use to manage employee benefit information. Information systems that use databases organize data into fields. Each field contains specific information such as name, address, health insurance options, or available vacation days. Several fields make up a record. Generally, there is one record per employee. The database can be sorted by fields so that specific information on an individual employee can be extracted and analyzed alongside data from other individuals. This allows an organization to track information on a group of employees, such as total vacation days available.

Databases can be used by both large and small organizations since they can exist on large mainframes or personal computers. Two organizations that have found unique ways of using information systems for human resources management are Hewitt Associates and USX Corporation.

Hewitt Associates manages defined benefit programs such as 401(k) or other retirement plans for large companies. The company uses sophisticated technology and a customer-service orientation to excel in its industry. Account representative Laurie Caputo explained Hewitt's approach to customer service, "Whenever a call comes through to me as a representative on the phone, I feel the most important thing that I can impart to a person is personalized service and my complete attention during that call. I also want to provide accurate information. I consider myself an extension of their benefits office and the client, so it's very important that when they talk to us they get the sense that we care about them and that we are really part of their team."

Giving the right answers, performing transactions quickly and accurately, and providing professional counsel—for Laurie Caputo, these are the keys to keeping benefit plan participants and clients satisfied. Laurie is an account representative in Hewitt Associates' benefit center, a modern communications facility that lets participants find information on defined benefit, defined contribution, and flexible benefits programs. Through an interactive voice response system and a staff of account representatives, participants can get information, make transactions, and enter personal data. Brenda Sural, Hewitt's voice response system consultant, said, "Voice response provides an automated method of communicating with the plan. For the participants it's great because it provides a convenient and confidential method of getting information. When we sit down with a client to define a voice response system, we'll look very carefully at any printed material that they give to employees as well as study their plan features so we can customize a voice response system that's unique to them."

The voice response system is designed for ease of use by callers who are not necessarily familiar with the technology. A plan participant calls the voice response system and gets a professionally recorded message, which is actually a digitized audio file that is retrieved based on the caller's input. The system is linked to a mainframe database, and before any information is provided, the caller must pass security. When a caller enters the voice response system, they are first asked for their employer ID number, and a four- to six-digit personal identification number. The computer treats the voice response unit as an input device, such as a computer terminal. The caller uses a Touch-Tone phone to answer the questions and navigate through the system. When a more personal touch is needed, participants can be connected to an account representative.

When a call reaches an account representative, that representative's screen displays how far into the voice response system the caller had journeyed. Thus, if the caller had already passed security, the representative would have the caller's name and account information already displayed on the screen. Account representatives' computer terminals are linked directly to Hewitt Associates' mainframe. A graphical user interface makes it easy for them to perform transactions, and offers the capability of running two different applications simultaneously, a function known as *multitasking*. One use of multitasking is the online help feature. When an account representative needs more information, the help feature provides information for whatever application is on the screen. The representative doesn't have to search through a list of choices. The system also uses a real-time database, meaning that any information that is retrieved is up to date. Any updates made to the participant's records by the account representative occur instantly, and a letter confirming the change is automatically sent the same day.

Hewitt Associates uses information technology to provide cost effective solutions to defined benefits management for large corporations. The use of sophisticated voice response systems and databases and a focus on customer service enable Hewitt to save its clients money while making a profit. As the next example shows, some companies are using technology to let employees help themselves to important human resources data.

USX, one of the largest steel companies in the United States, also turned to computer technology to help its employees better plan their retirement investments. Bob McMaster, manager of

USX's benefits information management system, said, "Basically we were looking for a better way to communicate information and benefits to the employees. With the changing environment people are retiring at an earlier age. We wanted them to have the ability to see what the effects on an earlier pension would be."

To address this concern, USX installed an interactive retirement planning application in multimedia kiosks throughout the company. At each kiosk, employees enter their Social Security number and a personal identification number to retrieve their retirement plan data directly from a host computer. A graphical interface and audio prompting make navigation easy. Employees can input personal savings information, and obtain 401(k), and Social Security projections along with their company pension plan. After projecting through retirement, the employee can print out the results and go back and review their assumptions. McMaster said, "The employees realize that this is truly a benefit for them. We have had 85 percent of our employees actually use the system at the kiosk. Many people, of course, return time and again to update their information."

According to McMaster, the benefits from an information systems approach to human resources management can include:

- Cost savings.
- Better service for employees.
- Instant access to personnel data.
- Easy updating.

In summary, databases provide a useful tool for organizing and managing employee benefit and personal data. Fields in a database are used to group similar types of data such as last name, ZIP code, or telephone numbers. Sorting data by fields allows a human resources department to track specific types of data that can be useful in budgeting and controlling costs. A well-organized database can be instantly accessed and updated. Whether an organization uses a mainframe or personal computers, a database offers an efficient way for a human resources department to manage personnel data. As human resources management costs rise with the increasing price and number of benefit options, information systems that are well implemented can offer a way to contain costs and provide better employee service.

CRITICAL THINKING QUESTIONS

1. Most of us have had some experience with voice response technology in registering for school, contacting a local government office, or elsewhere. What have you found to be some of the limitations of such a system? How could these limitations be overcome with enhanced or additional technology?

2. People that call Hewitt Associates can speak with an account representative if their questions aren't answered by the voice response system. Do you think Hewitt should do away with this option? Explain your answer.

3. Employee benefit plans have become more complex, allowing companies the flexibility of tailoring plans to meet individual needs. What are the advantages of this increasing complexity? What are some of the disadvantages? How did USX Corporation respond to the complexity of benefit plans?

4. USX Corporation allows employees to retrieve their retirement plan and determine what payments they can expect when they retire. Explain some potential pitfalls of the approach taken by USX.

EXPERIENTIAL EXERCISES

12.1 The "Legal" Interview

Objectives

1. To introduce you to the complexities of employment law.
2. To identify interview practices that might lead to discrimination in employment.

Instructions

1. Working alone, review the text material on interviewing and discrimination in employment.
2. In small groups, complete the "Legal" Interview Worksheet.
3. After the class reconvenes, group spokespersons present group findings.

"Legal" Interview Worksheet

The employment interview is one of the most critical steps in the employment selection process. It may also be an occasion for discriminating against individual employment candidates. The following represent questions that interviewers often ask job applicants. Identify the legality of each question by circling *L* (legal) or *I* (illegal) and briefly explain your decision.

Interview Question	Legality	Explanation
1. Could you provide us with a photo for our files?	L I	_____
2. Have you ever used another name (previous married name or alias)?	L I	_____
3. What was your maiden name?	L I	_____
4. What was your wife's maiden name?	L I	_____
5. What was your mother's maiden name?	L I	_____
6. What is your current address?	L I	_____
7. What was your previous address?	L I	_____
8. What is your social security number?	L I	_____
9. Where was your place of birth?	L I	_____
10. Where were your parents born?	L I	_____
11. What is your national origin?	L I	_____
12. Are you a naturalized citizen?	L I	_____
13. What languages do you speak?	L I	_____
14. What is your religious/church affiliation?	L I	_____
15. What is your racial classification?	L I	_____
16. How many dependents do you have?	L I	_____
17. What are the ages of your dependent children?	L I	_____
18. What is your marital status?	L I	_____
19. How old are you?	L I	_____
20. Do you have proof of your age (birth certificate or baptisimal record)?	L I	_____
21. Whom do we notify in case of an emergency?	L I	_____
22. What is your height and weight?	L I	_____
23. Have you ever been arrested?	L I	_____
24. Do you own your own car?	L I	_____
25. Do you own your own house?	L I	_____
26. Do you have any charge accounts?	L I	_____
27. Have you ever had your salary garnished?	L I	_____
28. What organizations do you belong to?	L I	_____
29. Are you available to work on Saturdays and Sundays?	L I	_____
30. Do you have any form of disability?	L I	_____

12.2 The Pay Raise

Objectives

1. To further your understanding of salary administration.
2. To examine the many facets of performance criteria, performance criteria weighting, performance evaluation, and rewards.

Instructions

1. Working in small groups, complete the Pay Raise Worksheet.
2. After the class reconvenes, group spokespersons present group findings.

PAY RAISE WORKSHEET

April Knepper is the new supervisor of an assembly team. It is time for her to make pay raise allocations for her subordinates. She has been budgeted $30,000 to allocate among her seven subordinates as pay raises. There have been some ugly grievances in other work teams over past allocations, so April has been advised to base the allocations on objective criteria that can be quantified, weighted, and computed in numerical terms. After she makes her allocations, April must be prepared to justify her decisions. All of the evaluative criteria available to April are summarized as follows:

Employee	EEO Status	Seniority	Output Rating*	Absent Rate	Supervisory ratings			Personal
					Skills	Initiative	Attitude	
David Bruce	Caucasian Male	15 yrs.	0.58	0.5%	Good	Poor	Poor	Nearing retirement. Wife just passed away. Having adjustment problems.
Eric Cattalini	Caucasian Male	12 yrs.	0.86	2.0%	Excellent	Good	Excellent	Going to night school to finish his BA degree.
Chua Li	Asian Male	7 yrs.	0.80	3.5%	Good	Excellent	Excellent	Legally deaf.
Marilee Miller	Black Female	1 yr.	0.50	10.0%	Poor	Poor	Poor	Single parent with three children.
Victor Munoz	Hispanic Male	3 yrs.	0.62	2.5%	Poor	Average	Good	Has six dependents. Speaks little English.
Derek Thompson	Caucasian Male	11 yrs.	0.64	8.0%	Excellent	Average	Average	Married to rich wife. Personal problems.
Sarah Vickers	Caucasian Female	8 yrs.	0.76	7.0%	Good	Poor	Poor	Women's activist. Wants to create a union.

*Output rating determined by production rate less errors and quality problem.

13

MANAGING THE DIVERSE WORKFORCE

"e pluribus unum"

LEARNING OBJECTIVES

After studying Chapter 13, you will know:

1. How changes in the U.S. workforce are making diversity a critical organizational and managerial issue.

2. The distinction between affirmative action and managing diversity.

3. How companies can gain a competitive edge by effectively managing diversity.

4. What challenges a company is likely to encounter with a diverse workforce.

5. How an organization can take steps to cultivate diversity.

MANAGING DIVERSITY AT PRUDENTIAL

*I*n 1988, executives at The Prudential surveyed African-American employees to determine why so many were leaving the company. Turnover had been a serious problem, and Prudential executives wanted to find the underlying causes. After reviewing the results of the survey, management realized that the problem was widespread and affected more than just African-American employees. Most of the complaints about the organization's inability to meet employee needs went beyond its African-American associates and extended to issues that were also shared by females, other minority groups, and white males. In response to these concerns, Charles Thomas, then Vice President of Human Resources, and his team, devised a managing-diversity program that would "reach organizational objectives by maximizing the contribution of every segment of the employee population." The goals of the program were to extend beyond employee relations by focusing squarely on business goals. Today, organizational diversity is viewed by Prudential's management as vital for enhancing productivity and improving customer relationships. How did they accomplish such a turnaround?

The original program consisted of a two-day workshop that all 12,000 mid- to upper-level managers attended to broaden understanding and establish an agenda for action. Each of the managers was required to develop a personal action plan stating which activities and behaviors they would engage in to demonstrate their commitment to organization diversity. Activities included improving communication skills, actively recruiting the talents of their diverse associates, and strengthening work teams. The program has been expanded to all of the company's 99,000 employees and has integrated a diversity component into existing training programs from new hire orientation programs to team-building workshops to management skills training.

These Prudential employees are members of the company's diversity council, which is charged with the responsibility of monitoring and making recommendations for improvement in the company's diversity programs.
(Courtesy The Prudential)

But Prudential's commitment to diversity doesn't stop with training. All senior-level managers are now required to complete business unit action plans and submit annual progress reports stating how they have addressed diversity issues as part of their strategic planning process. Business-unit actions include developing alternative work schedules, revising performance appraisals to include diversity dimensions, and identifying emerging client markets. Further, the company holds all managers financially accountable for their stated efforts to improve their organizational climates for diversity, and this has encouraged managers to work even harder to coach and provide feedback to employees who are different from themselves. To evaluate these efforts, special diversity councils have been established to monitor and make recommendations for improvement. African-American executives, for example, have formed a forum to help Prudential measure employee attitudes towards its diversity efforts and implement change. Other groups have also formed for similar purposes including an association of gay and lesbian employees and one for individuals who are hearing disabled. Additionally, a division of the Corporate Human Resources Department, Prudential Diversity Consultants, has been formed to spearhead and support diversity efforts companywide.

Obviously, diversity initiatives have gone far beyond the status of mere programs at Prudential. But what's interesting is that the company does not measure its success using traditional affirmative-action guidelines. While Prudential is doing much better at promoting minorities and women to upper-management positions, their sensitivity to diversity goes beyond race and gender to include sexual orientation, religion, age, managerial level, work styles, employee rank, and other differences. Efforts to acknowledge diversity issues and to promote positive responses to them have become institutionalized in the company's core values. For Prudential, it is simply the best way to conduct business.

Source: "Successful Companies Realize that Diversity Is a Long-Term

*A*s the Prudential case illustrates, building a more diverse workforce is one of corporate America's biggest challenges. **Managing diversity** involves such things as recruiting, training, promoting, and utilizing to full advantage individuals with different backgrounds, beliefs, capabilities, and cultures. Managing diversity is more than just hiring minorities and women. It means understanding and appreciating employee differences to build a more effective and profitable organization.

In this chapter, we examine the meaning of diversity and the management skills and organizational processes involved in effectively managing the diverse workforce. We also explore the social and demographic changes and economic and employment shifts that are creating this changing U.S. workforce.

DIVERSITY: A BRIEF HISTORY

Managing diversity is not a new or futuristic management issue. From the late 1800s to the early 1900s, groups that immigrated to the United States were from Italy, Poland, Ireland, and Russia. Members of these groups were considered outsiders because they did not speak English and had different customs and work styles. They struggled, often violently, to gain acceptance in industries such as steel, coal, automobile manufacturing, insurance, and finance. In the 1800s, it was considered poor business practice for white-Protestant–dominated insurance companies to hire Irish, Italians, Catholics, or Jews.

By the 1960s, the struggle for acceptance by the various white ethnic and religious groups had succeeded. Once the white male members of the various ethnic and religious groups were successfully assimilated into the workforce, the stage was set for the next struggle of "outsiders": cultural and racial minorities and women. Today more than half of the U.S. workforce consists of people other than white, U.S.–born males, and this trend is expected to continue. Two-thirds of all global migration is into the United States.

The traditional American image of diversity has been one of assimilation. The United States was considered the "melting pot" of the world, a country in which ethnic and racial differences were blended into an American purée. In real life, many ethnic and most racial groups retained their identities—but they did not express them at work. Employees often abandoned most of their ethnic and cultural distinctions while at work to keep their jobs and get ahead. Many Europeans came to the United States, Americanized their names, perfected their English, and tried to enter the mainstream as quickly as possible.

Today's immigrants are predominantly Asian and South American. For example, Asian Americans—from China, Japan, the Philippines, Korea, and Vietnam—will number 9.8 million by the year 2000.[1] The majority are or will be highly skilled. These newer immigrants are willing to be part of a team, but they no longer are willing to sacrifice their cultural identities to get ahead. Nor will they have to. Companies are finding that they have to be more accommodating of differences. Companies are also beginning to realize that their customers have become increasingly diverse and that retaining a diversified workforce can provide a competitive advantage in the marketplace.

DIVERSITY TODAY

Today *diversity* refers to far more than skin color and gender. It is a broad term used to refer to all kinds of differences, summarized in Figure 13.1. These differences include reli-

FIGURE 13.1

Components of a
diversified
workforce

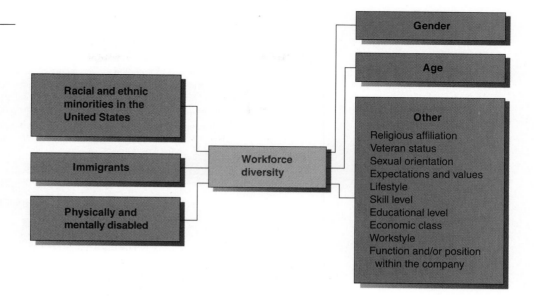

gious affiliation, age, disability status, military experience, sexual orientation, economic class, educational level, and lifestyle in addition to gender, race, ethnicity, and nationality.

Although members of different groups (white males, people born during the Depression, homosexuals, Vietnam veterans, Hispanics, Asians, women, blacks, etc.) share within their groups many common values, attitudes, and perceptions, there is also much diversity within each of these categories. Every group is made up of individuals who are unique in personality, education, and life experiences. There may be more differences among, say, three Asians from Thailand, Hong Kong, and Korea than among a Caucasian, an African-American, and an Asian, all born in Chicago. And not all white males share the same personal or professional goals and values or behave alike.

Thus, managing diversity may seem a contradiction within itself. It means being acutely aware of characteristics *common* to a group of employees, while also managing these employees as *individuals*. Managing diversity means not just tolerating or accommodating all sorts of differences but supporting, nurturing, and utilizing these differences to the organization's advantage. U.S. businesses will not have a choice of whether or not to have a diverse workforce; if they want to survive, they must learn to manage a diverse workforce sooner or better than their competitors.

A good start toward effectively managing diversity is to understand that different groups value different things. A brief preview of some of the trends and issues addressed in this chapter is given in Figure 13.2.

THE SIZE OF THE WORKFORCE

The U.S. civilian labor force totaled 125 million in 1990 and is expected to reach 151 million by 2005. Though this projected increase of 21 percent for the 15-year period may seem high, it is actually much lower than the 33 percent increase for the period 1975–90. This difference represents a slowing in both the number of people joining the labor force and the rate of labor force growth, which is now projected at 1.3 percent per year.[2] Changes in fertility, death, and immigration rates could increase the population, but probably not until later in the 21st century.

The slowing growth in the population is expected to be mirrored by a reduced growth in the labor force. Using even modest economic growth projections, the number of jobs that will be created is expected to equal or exceed the growth in the labor force by the year 2005.[3]

FIGURE 13.2

The diverse
workforce

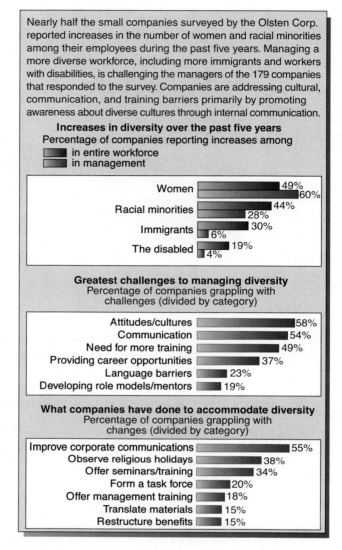

Nearly half the small companies surveyed by the Olsten Corp. reported increases in the number of women and racial minorities among their employees during the past five years. Managing a more diverse workforce, including more immigrants and workers with disabilities, is challenging the managers of the 179 companies that responded to the survey. Companies are addressing cultural, communication, and training barriers primarily by promoting awareness about diverse cultures through internal communication.

Increases in diversity over the past five years
Percentage of companies reporting increases among
■ in entire workforce
■ in management

Women — 49% / 60%
Racial minorities — 44% / 28%
Immigrants — 30% / 6%
The disabled — 19% / 4%

Greatest challenges to managing diversity
Percentage of companies grappling with
challenges (divided by category)

Attitudes/cultures — 58%
Communication — 54%
Need for more training — 49%
Providing career opportunities — 37%
Language barriers — 23%
Developing role models/mentors — 19%

What companies have done to accommodate diversity
Percentage of companies grappling with
changes (divided by category)

Improve corporate communications — 55%
Observe religious holidays — 38%
Offer seminars/training — 34%
Form a task force — 20%
Offer management training — 18%
Translate materials — 15%
Restructure benefits — 15%

Source: "Workplace Social Issues of the 1990s," Olsten Forum on Human Resource Issues and Trends, Olsten Corp., Westbury, N.Y., 1992.

During most of its history, the United States has experienced a surplus of workers. But this situation is quickly changing. Employers will have to compete for the best candidates from a smaller and more diverse labor pool. To compete effectively, employers will have to know who these new workers are—and they must be prepared to meet those workers' needs.

THE WORKERS OF THE FUTURE

Until recently, white, American-born males dominated the U.S. workforce. Businesses catered to their needs. However, this group will constitute only 15 percent of new entrants to the labor force in the 1985–2000 period. The remaining 85 percent of those joining the workforce are U.S.–born white females, immigrants, and minorities. By the year 2005, women will make up about 47 percent of workers, and minorities and immigrants will hold 27 percent of all jobs, up from 22 percent in 1990.[4]

Gender Issues

One of the most important developments in the U.S. labor market has been the growing number of women working outside the home. Social changes during the late 1960s and

Yolanda Zabala, manager of documents and billing at Connell Brothers, represents a growing trend toward more women—particularly minority women—in the U.S. workforce. *(Robert Holmgren)*

early 1970s, coupled with financial necessity, caused women to enter the workforce and redefine their role to include paid employment.

It is predicted that by the year 2000, women will constitute 65 percent of all labor force entrants.[5] Furthermore, 61 percent of U.S. women are expected to be employed by 2000.[6]

The traditional family of the 1960s represented fewer than 15 percent of U.S. families by 1990.[7] Forty percent of today's workforce consists of families in which both spouses are working, with another 6 percent being single parents.[8] In 1990, approximately 62 percent of all mothers were employed. Now women with children under age six make up the fastest-growing segment of the workforce.[9] For many such women, as well as their spouses, balancing work life with family responsibilities and parenting presents an enormous challenge.

Although men's roles in our society have been changing, women still adopt the bulk of family responsibilities, including homemaking, child care, and care of elderly parents. As employers search for new workers from a shrinking supply and try to retain experienced employees, women will be in a position to make demands and companies will be forced to make it easier to balance work and family commitments.

The average full-time working female earns much less than the average working male.[10] When she reaches the level of vice president, the average female earns over 40 percent less than a male in the same job. However, this situation is getting somewhat better. Over the past decade, average total compensation for women executives has more than doubled to $187,000. (However, this is still much less than the $289,000 average for men.)

Some of the discrepancy in compensation is the consequence of both the level and type of jobs women receive. As women—along with minorities—move up the corporate ladder, they encounter a "glass ceiling." The **glass ceiling** is an invisible barrier that makes it difficult for women and minorities to move beyond a certain level in the corporate hierarchy. In 1981, for example, only 1 percent of executives in Fortune 500 companies were women, and by 1991 this number had increased to only 3 percent. But the situation is improving, albeit too slowly. Today, the percentage of women who hold the title of executive vice president has jumped to 8.7 percent, and the number of women who are senior vice presidents is 23 percent. Across all management levels, the picture is even more encouraging; the percentage of women managers has increased from 27 percent in 1981 to 41 percent in 1991. In addition, evidence suggests that women no longer have to choose between careers and families. In 1982, only 49 percent of women executives were married and only 39 percent had children. Today, nearly 70 percent of women executives are married and 63 percent have children.[11] Table 13.1 shows a list of some very successful women in business today.

The job of balancing work and family is not just a women's issue. In some ways, the changing status of women has given men the opportunity to redefine male roles, expectations, and lifestyles. Some men are deciding that there is more to life than corporate success and are choosing to scale back work hours and commitments to spend time with their families. Worker values are shifting toward personal time, quality of life, self-fulfillment, and family. Workers today, both men and women, are looking to achieve a balance between career and family.

Name	Position	Company	Employees	Sales†	Ownership
1. Anita Axson Johnson	Chair	Axel Johnson Group	2,000	$829	100%
2. Gretchen and Liz Minyard	Co-Chairs	Minyard Food Stores	6,100	700	33
3. Linda J. Wachner	Chair, CEO, President	Warnaco Group Inc.	11,800	548	14.4
4. Jenny Craig	Vice Chair	Jenny Craig, Inc.	7,000	412	61
5. Donna W. Steigerwaldt	Chair, CEO	Jockey International	5,000	450	50
6. Susie Tompkins	Creative Director	Esprit de Corp.	1,400	450	20
7. Norma Paige	Chair, Exec. VP	Astronautics	4,700	415	100
8. Helen K. Copley	Chair, CEO	Copley Press	3,500	405	100
9. Barbara Levy Kipper	Chair	Chas. Levy Co.	1,700	350	100
10. Annabelle L. Fetterman	Chair	Lundy Packing Co.	900	350	20
11. Bettye Martin Musham	CEO, President	Gear Holdings, Inc.	30	280	20
12. Dian Graves Owen	Chair, Co-CEO	Owen Healthcare, Inc.	2,000	250	37.8
13. Carole Little	Co-Chair, Founder	Carole Little, Inc.	600	205	50
14. Lana Jane Lewis-Brent	CEO, President, V-Chair	Sunshine Jr. Stores, Inc.	1,800	203	56
15. Ellen R. Gordon	President	Tootsie Roll Industries	1,400	200	49
16. Donna Karan	CEO	Donna Kara Co.	750	200	50
17. Dorothy Owen	Chair	Owen Steel Co.	1,500	192	20
18. Christel Dehann	CEO, President	Resort Condominiums Intl.	2,300	180	100
19. Adrienne Vittadini	Chair	Adrienne Vittadini, Inc.	200	160	50
20. Lillian Vernon	CEO	Lillian Vernon Corp.	1,000	160	30
21. Helen Jo Whitsell	Chair, CEO	Copeland Lumber Yards	800	152	50
22. Judy Sims	CEO	Software Spectrum	260	146	20
23. Paula Kent Meehan	Chair, CEO	Redken Laboratories	830	140	51
24. Lois Rust	President	Rose Acre Farms	500	127	49

*Individuals listed are top executives running the day-to-day operations; ranks are based on revenues.
†Sales are shown in millions.

Source: "The Working Women Twenty-Five: America's Top Women Business Owners," *Working Women*, May 1992, pp. 63–69.

TABLE 13.1

Top women
business owners*

Minorities and Immigrants

Nonwhites will make up 35 percent of new entrants to the workforce between 1990 and 2005 and will compose 27 percent of the total work population in 2005.[12] Although whites will remain the dominant labor group in the United States, their absolute numbers will increase only 15 percent, compared with a 20 percent increase for African-Americans and a 75 percent increase for Hispanics.

English will be the second language for the majority of California's population by the year 2000. By 2020, most of that state's entry-level workers will be Hispanic. Current projections indicate that Hispanics will surpass African-Americans as the largest racial minority in the next 20 to 25 years.[13]

Since 1970, 83 percent of immigrants to the United States have come from Asia and Latin America.[14] Nearly 90 percent of recent immigrants have chosen to live in metro-

The glass ceiling is so named because it symbolizes an invisible barrier that makes it difficult for women and minorities to move beyond a certain point on the corporate ladder.

(Norman Sugimoto)

politan areas.[15] Today, more than 30 percent of New York City's residents are non–U.S.–born, Miami is two-thirds Hispanic, Detroit is 79 percent African-Americans, and San Francisco 33 percent Asian.[16] Figure 13.3 indicates the immigrant groups and the cities in which they are settling.

Mentally and Physically Disabled

The largest unemployed minority population in the United States is people with disabilities. Of the 13 million disabled persons of working age, only 34 percent worked full- or part-time in 1986. When a sample of these workers was surveyed, 66 percent reported that they wanted to work.[17]

The Americans with Disabilities Act (ADA), introduced in Chapter 12, defines a disability as a physical or mental impairment that substantially limits one or more major life activities. Examples of such physical or mental impairments include those resulting from conditions such as orthopedic, visual, speech, and hearing impairments; cerebral palsy; epilepsy; muscular dystrophy; multiple sclerosis; HIV infections; cancer; heart disease; diabetes; mental retardation; emotional illness; specific learning disabilities; drug abuse; and alcoholism.[18]

Because most disabilities are acquired, many people will become disabled in some way as they grow older. As the baby-boom generation ages, attitudes toward many disabilities may change. Mary Ann Breslin, executive director of Disability Rights Education and Defense Fund, Inc., states:

> Fifty or 100 years ago, wearing glasses was not acceptable, but today wearing corrective lenses is taken for granted, because it is a technology so ingrained in our culture. Glasses are orthopedic devices that are no different than an artificial limb or wheelchair or back brace.[19]

Individuals with disabilities have found themselves isolated from job opportunities largely because they have lacked access to educational and workplace environments. In addition, the attitudes of many employers and those of the disabled themselves have been barriers to employment. Today laws and technology are providing access to education and jobs. For most businesses, the mentally and physically disabled represent a largely unexplored labor market.

THE AGE OF THE WORKFORCE

The baby-boom generation (born between 1946 and 1964) is aging, which will cause the average age of the workforce to increase to around 40 by the year 2005. The number of

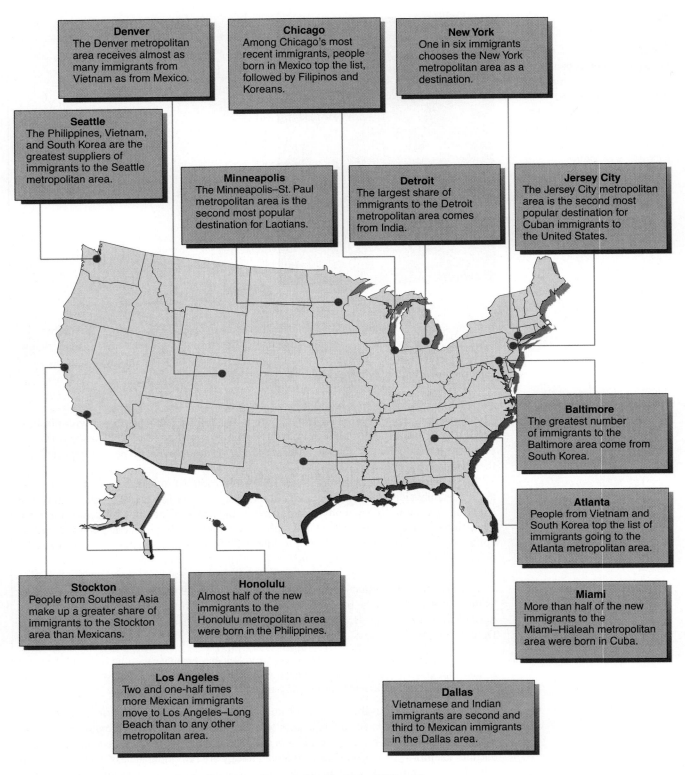

Denver
The Denver metropolitan area receives almost as many immigrants from Vietnam as from Mexico.

Chicago
Among Chicago's most recent immigrants, people born in Mexico top the list, followed by Filipinos and Koreans.

New York
One in six immigrants chooses the New York metropolitan area as a destination.

Seattle
The Philippines, Vietnam, and South Korea are the greatest suppliers of immigrants to the Seattle metropolitan area.

Minneapolis
The Minneapolis–St. Paul metropolitan area is the second most popular destination for Laotians.

Detroit
The largest share of immigrants to the Detroit metropolitan area comes from India.

Jersey City
The Jersey City metropolitan area is the second most popular destination for Cuban immigrants to the United States.

Baltimore
The greatest number of immigrants to the Baltimore area come from South Korea.

Atlanta
People from Vietnam and South Korea top the list of immigrants going to the Atlanta metropolitan area.

Stockton
People from Southeast Asia make up a greater share of immigrants to the Stockton area than Mexicans.

Honolulu
Almost half of the new immigrants to the Honolulu metropolitan area were born in the Philippines.

Miami
More than half of the new immigrants to the Miami–Hialeah metropolitan area were born in Cuba.

Los Angeles
Two and one-half times more Mexican immigrants move to Los Angeles–Long Beach than to any other metropolitan area.

Dallas
Vietnamese and Indian immigrants are second and third to Mexican immigrants in the Dallas area.

Source: J. Allen and E. Turner, "Immigrants," *American Demographics,* September 1988, p. 27.

FIGURE 13.3

The newest labor markets

people age 50 to 65 will increase at more than twice the rate of the overall population, and by 2005 over 15 percent of the workforce will be 55 years of age or older. At the same time the number of younger workers (ages 16 to 24) is expected to drop from its 24 percent level in 1975 to 16 percent in 2005.[20]

As a result of these trends, the Bureau of Labor Statistics projects that entry-level workers will be in short supply, and fewer new workers will enter the labor force than will be lost through retirement.[21] Many older employees are opting for early retirement even though there is no longer a mandatory retirement age and life expectancies have increased. Companies therefore need to retain and hire older, experienced workers.

Retirement-age workers could be encouraged to remain in or reenter the workforce on a flexible or part-time basis, whether for economic reasons, desire for social interaction, or the need to be productive. As the following examples show, creative companies are rethinking their retirement policies and solving their skilled-labor shortage by finding ways to attract and retain people over 55. These companies save on turnover and training costs and capitalize on the experience of their older employees.

IN PRAISE OF OLDER WORKERS

*H*ere are some examples of how leading organizations attract and retain older workers.

- Days Inns of America has been particularly successful at recruiting and keeping persons over age 65. Employees from this age group compose more than 25 percent of Days Inns' 650-person reservation staff. Evidence shows that older workers remain on the job longer than younger workers—annual turnover for this group is less than 2 percent versus 70 percent for younger workers (the reduction in turnover has reduced the center's recruitment and training costs by over 40 percent). Although older workers tend to be paid more than younger workers, this is because of their having been on the job longer. Performance measures show that older workers take more time talking with prospective customers and are more successful booking reservations.

- The Environmental Protection Agency (EPA) discovered the value of older workers back in 1976 when it pioneered one of the first programs for older workers. In 1984, Congress gave the EPA legislation to operate the Senior Environmental Employment (SEE) program. Enrollees in SEE are assigned to a diverse set of jobs, ranging from messengers to accountants. These full- and part-time employees have been involved in every aspect of EPA's efforts to improve the environment. Work options implemented for all employees have especially benefited older workers by providing flextime, job sharing, part-time employment, and training for changing technologies.

- Eastman Kodak has concentrated on using redeployed mature employees in its project management division (PMD). Kodak has found that mature employees with the right skills can make excellent additions to the project management teams as either controls engineers or project managers. To take advantage of this opportunity, Kodak has established special selection criteria for people in project management, modified its job posting process, and developed special training programs for new people in project management.

- Control Data Corporation in Minneapolis has developed a new business advisers' division made up of retired professionals. Employees from this division are hired by other companies as independent consultants.

- Travelers Insurance was one of the first companies to establish a retiree job bank. After discovering that 90 percent of its older employees were interested in working part-time after retirement, the company established an in-house temporary agency using retirees to fill in during peak periods, absences, and vacations. After managers requested more retirees than Travelers could provide, the company opened up the program to retirees from other companies.

- At Grumman, the $3.4 billion defense contractor in Bethpage, New York, employees have always been allowed to work past age 65 because it is difficult and costly to gain security clearance for new employees. The company also offers phased retirement programs and mid-career training programs, as well as rehiring of retirees.

Sources: Robert J. Nemes, "The Golden Years and Project Management," *American Association of Cost Engineers Transactions* (1994 Transactions, HF5.1–HF5.3); Susan Street, "EPA's Seasoned Resource," *Public Manager* 22, no. 1 (Spring 1993), p. 26; William McNaught, "Are Older Workers Good Buys? A Case Study of Days Inns of America," *Sloan Management Review,* Spring 1993, pp. 53–63; Dyan Machan, "Cultivating the Gray," *Forbes,* September 4, 1989, pp. 126, 128; Bill Stack, "Jobs Available: Homeless and Seniors Encouraged to Apply," *Management Review* 78, no. 8 (August 1989), pp. 13–16; A. Ramirez, "Making Better Use of Older Workers," *Fortune,* June 30, 1989, pp. 179–87; C. Fyock, *America's Work Force Is Coming of Age* (Lexington, Mass.: Lexington Books, 1990); and David V. Lewis, "Make Way for the Older Worker," *HRMagazine,* May 1990, pp. 75–77. ●

FUTURE JOBS AND WORKFORCE QUALIFICATIONS

U.S. Department of Labor projections indicate that the United States will be a predominantly service-oriented economy by the year 2005 and that manufacturing will represent only 12 to 15 percent of all jobs. People without high school diplomas will be at an increasing disadvantage, because their employment opportunities will be confined to the lowest-paying service jobs. Even the lower-skilled occupations of the future will require workers who can communicate well and read and comprehend instructions, and have a working knowledge of basic mathematics. For example, the job of assembly-line worker traditionally was considered a low-skilled occupation. Today many of these workers are learning statistical process control techniques, which require a solid foundation in mathematics.

There is a growing gap between the knowledge and skills jobs require and those many employees and applicants possess. Skill deficiencies are particularly acute among minority workers and many immigrant populations. Whereas 86 percent of white workers had a high school diploma in 1989, only 60 percent of Hispanics and 73 percent of African-Americans had attained this level of education. In a recent year, the high school dropout rate was 35 percent in New York and 50 percent in Washington, D.C. In major cities in which minorities are concentrated, the dropout rate is rising even though 80 percent of new jobs will require a high school education.[22]

|▼|

MANAGING DIVERSITY AND AFFIRMATIVE ACTION

The goal of affirmative action was to correct the past exclusion of women and minorities from U.S. organizations. While a good deal of progress has been made in hiring women and minorities, Table 13.2 reveals that in most industries these groups continue to be disproportionately clustered at the bottom of corporate hierarchies (recall our earlier discussion of the *glass ceiling*). In reality, employment discrimination still persists in

TABLE 13.2

Where women and minorities are now

Percentage of Managers Who Are Women		Percentage of Managers Who Are Minorities	
Industry	**Percentage**	**Industry**	**Percentage**
Finance, Insurance, real estate	41.4%	Retail trade	13.0%
Services	38.9	Transportation, communications, and public utilities	12.0
Retail trade	38.5	Services	11.0
Transportation, communications, and public utilities	25.6	Finance, insurance, and real estate	11.0
Wholesale trade	20.9	Agriculture	1.3
Manufacturing	15.9	Wholesale trade	0.9
Agriculture	14.5	Manufacturing	0.8
Construction	10.4	Mining	0.7
Mining	9.8	Construction	0.6

Source: Federal Glass Ceiling Commission.

organizations, and even after nearly three decades of government legislation, equal employment opportunity (EEO) and affirmative action laws have not adequately improved the upward mobility of women and minorities. In fact, critics argue that the laws result in *de facto* employment quotas, and those companies that conscientiously pursue affirmative action have had claims of preferential treatment and reverse discrimination leveled against them. Reverse discrimination exists when qualified white males are passed over for employment opportunities in favor of members of protected classes. For these reasons, several members of Congress have recently argued that the EEO and affirmative action laws should be dramatically changed or eliminated altogether.

In contrast to EEO and affirmative action programs, managing diversify involves organizations making changes in their systems, structures, and management practices in order to eliminate barriers that may keep people from reaching their full potential. The goal is not to treat all people the same but to treat people as individuals, recognizing that each employee has different needs and will need different things to succeed. This approach implies that different people in the workplace sometimes should be treated equally but differently. Avon's manager of diversity, Daisy Chin-Lor, has used this analogy:

> If I were planting a garden and I wanted to have a number of flowers, I would never think of giving every flower the same amount of sun, the same amount of water, and the same soil. I'd be sure to cultivate each individual type of flower differently. Does that mean that the rose or the orchid is less because I have to do more with them? Certainly not![23]

What do you think about this important issue?

BUILDING COMPETITIVE ADVANTAGE THROUGH WORKFORCE DIVERSITY

For many organizations, the original impetus to diversify their workforces was social responsibility and legal necessity (recall Chapters 6 and 12). Morally, ethically, and legally, it was the right thing to do. Today many organizations are approaching diversity efforts from a more practical, business-oriented perspective. Increasingly, diversity can be a powerful tool for building competitive advantage.

For companies facing changing demographics and business needs, diversity just makes good sense. Eastman Kodak and Toys "Я" Us, for example, are committed to diversity because as the composition of the American workforce changes, so does the customer base of these companies. Executives at Kodak are so convinced of the competitive potential of a diverse workforce that they recently tied a portion of management compensation to success in recruiting and promoting minorities and women (recall in Setting the Stage that Prudential employed a similar tactic). The business advantages of a diverse workforce are summarized in Table 13.3.

ATTRACTING, RETAINING, AND MOTIVATING EMPLOYEES

Companies with a reputation for providing opportunities for diverse employees will have a competitive advantage in the labor market and will be sought out by the most qualified

TABLE 13.3

The diverse workforce: advantages and challenges

Advantages	Challenges
▪ Fulfills social responsibility	▪ Lower cohesiveness
▪ Helps attract, retain, and motivate employees	▪ Communication problems
▪ Greater knowledge of diversified marketplace	▪ Mistrust and tension
▪ Promotes creativity, innovation, and problem solving	▪ Stereotyping
▪ Enhances organizational flexibility	

employees. In addition, when employees believe their differences are not merely tolerated but valued, they may become more loyal, productive, and committed.

Marketing

Companies are realizing that consumers, like the workforce, are changing demographically. Just as women and minorities may prefer to work for an employer that values diversity, they may prefer to patronize such organizations.

Many Asian-Americans, African-Americans, Mexican-Americans, and women have entered the middle class and now control consumer dollars. A multicultural workforce can provide a company with greater knowledge of the preferences and consuming habits of this diversified marketplace. This knowledge can assist companies in designing products and developing marketing campaigns to meet those consumers' needs. In addition, for at least some products and services, a multicultural sales force may help an organization sell to diverse groups. A diverse workforce can also give a company a competitive edge in a global economy by facilitating understanding of other customs, cultures, and marketplace needs.

Creativity, Innovation, and Problem Solving

Work team diversity promotes creativity and innovation, because people from different backgrounds hold different perspectives on issues. Diverse groups have a broader base of experience from which to approach a problem; when effectively managed, they invent more options and create more solutions than homogeneous groups do. In addition, diverse work groups are freer to deviate from traditional approaches and practices. The presence of diversity can also help minimize "groupthink" (recall Chapter 4).[24]

Flexibility

A diverse workforce can enhance organizational flexibility, because successfully managing diversity requires a corporate culture that tolerates many different styles and approaches. Less restrictive policies and procedures and less standardized operating methods enable organizations to become more flexible and thus better able to respond quickly to environmental changes (recall Chapters 10 and 11).

Challenges of a Diverse Workforce

A diverse workforce also poses many challenges. Many of these challenges, summarized in Table 13.3, can be turned into advantages if the workforce is managed effectively.

Lower Cohesiveness

Diversity can create a lack of cohesiveness. Cohesiveness refers to how tightly knit the group is and the degree to which group members perceive, interpret, and act on their environment in similar or mutually agreed-upon ways. Because of their lack of similarity in language, culture, and/or experience, diverse groups typically are less cohesive than homogeneous groups. Often mistrust, miscommunication, stress, and attitudinal differences reduce cohesiveness, which in turn can diminish productivity. Group cohesiveness will be discussed in greater detail in Chapter 16.

Communication Problems

Perhaps the most common negative effect of diversity is communication problems. These difficulties include misunderstandings, inaccuracies, inefficiencies, and slowness. Speed is lost when not all group members are fluent in the same language or when additional time is required to explain things.

Diversity also increases errors and misunderstandings. Group members may assume they interpret things similarly when in fact they do not, or they may disagree because of their different frames of reference.[25]

MISTRUST AND TENSION

People prefer to associate with others who are like themselves. This tendency often leads to mistrust and misunderstanding of those who are different because of a lack of contact and low familiarity. It also causes stress and tension, and reaching agreement on problems can be difficult.

STEREOTYPING

We learn to see the world in a certain way based on our backgrounds and experiences. Our interests, values, and cultures act as filters and distort, block, and select what we see and hear. We see and hear what we expect to see and hear. Group members often inappropriately stereotype their "different" colleagues rather than accurately perceiving and evaluating those individuals' contributions, capabilities, aspirations, and motivations.

Such stereotypes in turn affect how people are treated. Employees stereotyped as unmotivated or emotional will be given less-stress-provoking (and perhaps less-important) jobs than their co-workers. Those job assignments will create frustrated employees, perhaps resulting in lower commitment, higher turnover, and underused skills.[26]

MULTICULTURAL ORGANIZATIONS

To capitalize on the benefits and minimize the costs of a diverse workforce, organizations can strive to become **multicultural.** This term refers to the degree to which an organization values cultural diversity and is willing to utilize and encourage it.[27] Organizations can be classified as one of three types according to how much they employ and value a diverse workforce.

Some organizations are **monolithic.** This type of organization has very little *structural integration;* in other words, it employs few women, minorities, or any other groups that differ from the majority. The organization is highly homogeneous in terms of its employee population.

In monolithic organizations, if groups other than the norm are employed, they are found primarily in low-status jobs. Minority group members must adopt the norms of the majority to survive. This fact, coupled with small numbers, keeps conflicts among groups low. Discrimination and prejudice typically prevail, informal integration is almost nonexistent, and minority group members do not identify strongly with the company.

Most large U.S. organizations made the transition from monolithic to *plural* organizations in the 1960s and 1970s because of changing demographics as well as societal forces such as the civil rights and women's movements. **Plural organizations** have a more diverse employee population and take steps to involve persons from different gender, racial, or cultural backgrounds. These organizations use an affirmative action approach to managing diversity: They actively try to hire and train a diverse workforce, and to ensure against any discrimination against minority group members. They typically have much more structural integration than monolithic organizations; but like monolithic organizations, they often have minority group members clustered at certain levels or in particular functions within the organization.

Because of greater structural integration, affirmative action programs, and training programs, the plural organization has some integration of minority group members into the informal network, much less discrimination, and less prejudice. Improved employment opportunities create greater identification with the organization among minority group members. Often the resentment of majority group members, coupled with the increased number of women and minorities, creates more conflict than in the monolithic organization.

The plural organization fails to address the cultural aspects of integration. In contrast, in **multicultural organizations** diversity not only exists but is valued. These organizations fully integrate gender, racial, and minority group members both formally and informally. The multicultural organization is marked by an absence of prejudice and discrimination and by low levels of intergroup conflict. Such an organization creates an environment in which all members can contribute to their maximum potential and the advantages of diversity can be fully realized.

HOW ORGANIZATIONS CAN CULTIVATE A DIVERSE WORKFORCE

An organization's plans for becoming multicultural and making the most of its diverse workforce should include (1) securing top management support and commitment, (2) assessing the workforce, (3) attracting employees, (4) developing employees, and (5) retaining employees. Ten tips for cultivating a diverse workforce are shown in Table 13.4.

TOP MANAGEMENT SUPPORT AND COMMITMENT

Obtaining top management support and commitment is critical for diversity programs to succeed. One way to communicate this commitment to all employees—as well as to the external environment—is to incorporate the organization's attitudes toward diversity into

TABLE 13.4

Top 10 diversity tips

1. **Clarify your motivation.** Moral, social, and legal obligations are not bad reasons for learning to manage diversity, but they are not business reasons. In business terms, a diverse workforce is not something your company ought to have; it's something you must have in order to be competitive.

2. **Clarify your vision.** Away from public opinion, establish your private vision of a diverse workforce. Ideally you can move past a vision of equality or coexistence with "them," to an image of fully tapping the human potential of every member of the workforce.

3. **Expand your focus.** Let your definition of diversity go beyond race, gender, creed, and ethnicity to include age, background, education, function, and personality differences. The objective is not to assimilate minorities and women into a dominant white male culture but to create a dominant heterogeneous culture.

4. **Audit your corporate culture.** Take a long hard look at the unexamined assumptions, values, and mythologies in your company. Culture is often inherited from the founder.

5. **Modify your assumptions.** Overcoming resistance to change is difficult because you are challenging people's basic assumptions. Leaders must work hard to establish values and a sense of purpose that transcends the interests of any one group.

6. **Modify your systems.** Promotion and reward systems must be adjusted to allow people to do the work they have been charged to do.

7. **Modify your models.** Expand your ideals about how managers and employees are supposed to act.

8. **Help people pioneer.** There is no single best way to manage diversity; it is a learning process. Help pioneers to handle conflict and failure, and treat them accordingly.

9. **Apply the social consideration test.** The test consists of one question: Does this program, policy, or principle give special consideration to one group? If the answer is yes, you're probably not on the road to managing diversity.

10. **Continue affirmative action.** You must first have a workforce that is diverse at every level before you can manage the company without unnatural advantage or disadvantage to anyone. For this you will need affirmative action.

Source: Roosevelt Thomas, "From Affirmative Action to Affirming Diversity," *Harvard Business Review,* March–April 1990.

TRW is one of a growing number of companies that recognize the important relationship between workforce diversity and long-term competitiveness.
(Courtesy TRW Inc.)

the corporate mission statement and into strategic plans and objectives. Managerial compensation can be directly linked to accomplishing diversity objectives. Adequate funding must be allocated to the diversity effort to ensure its success. Also, top management can set an example for other organization members by participating in diversity programs and making participation mandatory for all managers.

Some organizations have established corporate offices or committees to coordinate the companywide diversity effort and provide feedback to top management. Digital Equipment Corporation has a "director of valuing differences," Honeywell has a "director of workforce diversity," and Avon has a "director of multicultural planning and design." Other companies prefer to incorporate diversity management into the function of director of affirmative action or EEO.

The work of managing diversity cannot be done by top management or diversity directors alone. Many companies rely on minority advisory groups or task forces to monitor organizational policies, practices, and attitudes; assess their impact on the diverse groups within the organization; and provide feedback and suggestions to top management.

For example, Digital Equipment Corporation uses Core Groups, in which employees from different backgrounds form small groups to address stereotypes and other relevant issues. At Equitable Life Assurance Society, Business Resource Groups meet regularly with the CEO to discuss issues pertaining to women, African-Americans, and Hispanics and make recommendations for improvement. U.S. West has a 33-member Pluralism Council that advises senior management on how to more effectively manage and utilize the company's diverse workforce. At Honeywell, disabled employees formed a council to discuss their needs. They proposed and accepted an accessibility program that went beyond federal regulations for accommodations of disabilities.

As you can see, progressive companies are moving from asking managers what they think minority employees need to asking the employees themselves what they need.

ORGANIZATIONAL ASSESSMENT

The next step in managing diversity is to assess the organization's workforce, culture, policies, and practices in areas such as recruitment, promotions, benefits, and compensation. In addition, the demographics of the labor pool and the customer base should be evaluated. The objective is to identify problem areas and make recommendations where changes are needed.

For example, many women and Asians are at a disadvantage when aggressiveness is a valued part of the organization's culture. After analysis, management might decide that the organizational values need to be changed so that other styles of interacting are equally acceptable. Corporate values and norms should be identified and critically evaluated regarding their necessity and their impact on the diverse workforce.

ATTRACTING EMPLOYEES

Companies can attract a diverse, qualified workforce through using effective recruiting practices, accommodating employees' work and family needs, and offering alternative work arrangements.

Recruitment

A company's image can be a strong recruiting tool. Companies with reputations for hiring and promoting all types of people will have a competitive advantage. Xerox gives prospective minority employees reprints of an article that rates the company as one of the best places for African-Americans to work. Hewlett-Packard ensures that its female candidates are familiar with its high rating by *Working Woman* magazine. Many employers are implementing policies to attract more women, ensure that women's talents are used to full advantage, and avoid losing their most capable female employees.

Many minorities and economically disadvantaged people are physically isolated from job opportunities. Companies can bring information about job opportunities to the source of labor, or they can transport the labor to the jobs. Polycast Technology in Stamford, Connecticut, contracts with a private van company to transport workers from the Bronx in New York City to jobs in Stamford. Days Inn recruits homeless workers in Atlanta and houses them in a motel within walking distance of their jobs. Burger King has done a lot to recruit and hire immigrants in its fast-food restaurants.

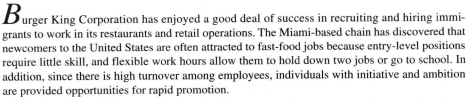

BURGER KING MAKES THE MOST OF IMMIGRANTS

*B*urger King Corporation has enjoyed a good deal of success in recruiting and hiring immigrants to work in its restaurants and retail operations. The Miami-based chain has discovered that newcomers to the United States are often attracted to fast-food jobs because entry-level positions require little skill, and flexible work hours allow them to hold down two jobs or go to school. In addition, since there is high turnover among employees, individuals with initiative and ambition are provided opportunities for rapid promotion.

To facilitate the hiring of foreign-born workers, Burger King has adopted several of its basic human resource systems. For example, employment applications are available in Spanish as well as English, an accommodation that is especially helpful in certain parts of the United States. In addition, several company videos are dubbed in Spanish. For example, one eight-minute video shown to applicants before the initial interview presents the various jobs that employees perform in Burger King restaurants. It shows crew members lifting, walking, cooking Whoppers, serving customers, and taking orders from drive-through customers. The video was developed to comply with the Americans with Disabilities Act (ADA), to describe physical characteristics of jobs, but it works well for prospective workers who don't have disabilities.

During the actual job interview, if an applicant speaks Spanish, he or she can be interviewed in that language. In addition, prospective employees can bring a family member or a friend to act as interpreter during the interview. To help applicants answer questions about employment eligibility and documentation, Burger King provides a toll-free number, staffed by people who speak Spanish. The company has contracted with an outside agency to ensure that all application forms are filled out correctly and that the company is in compliance with the law.

As part of its management training programs, Burger King teaches managers to be conscious of concerns immigrants may have, and their uneasiness with new surroundings. For example, many foreign-born workers simply don't understand the options they have regarding benefits.

While the term medical insurance may be clear to U.S.–born workers, many immigrants may not understand what it means. This is also true of workers' compensation. When foreign-born employees are injured, they often hesitate to report the injury for fear of being fired. To enable its managers to handle these situations, Burger King has extensive training programs that address these specific concerns. Although there is no language requirement at Burger King, managers take cultural sensitivity seminars so that they can work well in a bilingual setting.

Each of these efforts has helped Burger King take advantage of an important and growing sector of the workforce. With immigrants making up as much as 40 percent of the annual growth in the U.S. labor force, Burger King and other companies are learning how to manage diversity successfully.

Source: Charlene Marmer Solomon, "Managing Today's Immigrants," *Personnel Journal,* February 1993, pp. 57–65. ●

Accommodating Work and Family Needs

More job seekers are putting family needs first. Corporate work and family policies are now one of the most important recruiting tools.

Employers that have become involved in child care report decreased turnover and absenteeism and improved morale. In addition to providing child care, many companies now assist with care for elderly dependents, offer time off to care for sick family members, provide parental leaves of absence, and offer a variety of benefits that can be tailored to individual family needs. Some companies are accommodating the needs and concerns of dual-career couples by limiting relocation requirements or providing job search assistance to relocated spouses.

Alternative Work Arrangements

Another way companies accommodate diversity is to offer flexible work schedules and arrangements. The 11-branch New Haven region of People Bank based in Bridgeport, Connecticut, was having difficulty recruiting part-time tellers. The region's employee relations specialist initiated the Working Parent Program, which allowed part-timers to schedule their hours to coincide with their children's: home by 3 P.M., with summers and school holidays off. Staffing problems were solved by being flexible, using part-timers to cover peak hours, and hiring college students to fill in during holidays and summers.[28]

Other creative work arrangements include compressed workweeks (for example, four 10-hour days) and job sharing, in which two part-time workers share one full-time job. Another option to accommodate working mothers and the disabled is teleworking (working from home) or telecommuting (working from home via computer hookup to the main worksite). This option has been slow to catch on, but those organizations that have tried it report favorable results.

DEVELOPING EMPLOYEES

As you learned in Chapter 12, employees can be developed in a variety of ways. Here we will focus on skills training and diversity training.

Skills Training

It is estimated that between 20 million and 30 million adults in the U.S. workforce have problems with basic reading, writing, and math.[29] Deficiencies in these skills are most acute among African-Americans, Hispanics, and immigrants.

Employers are combating this basic-skills gap in a number of ways. One approach is in-house basic-skills training programs. Other strategies include partnerships with public schools, community colleges, and local, state, and federal agencies.

Many companies, including Esprit de Corp. and Hasbro, Inc., teach their employees English as a second language or offer second-language training to managers and employees to communicate that languages other than English are valued. Hasbro invites employees' families and friends to the classes to help reinforce the learning off the job.[30]

Diversity Training

Diversity training programs attempt to identify and reduce hidden biases and develop the skills needed to effectively manage a diversified workforce.

Traditionally, most management training has been based on the assumption that "managing" means managing a homogeneous, often white-male, full-time workforce. But gender, race, culture, and other differences create an additional layer of complexity.[31] Typically, diversity training has two components: awareness building and skill building.

Awareness Building.   *Awareness building* is designed to increase awareness of the meaning and importance of valuing diversity.[32] Its aim is not to teach specific skills but to sensitize employees to the assumptions they make about others and how these assumptions affect their behaviors, decisions, and judgment.

To build awareness, people are taught to become familiar with myths, stereotypes, and cultural differences as well as the organizational barriers that inhibit the full contributions of all employees. They develop a better understanding of corporate culture, requirements for success, and career choices that affect opportunities for advancement.

In most companies, the "rules" for success are ambiguous, unwritten, and perhaps inconsistent with written policy. A common problem for women and minorities is that they are unaware of many of the rules that are obvious to people in the mainstream. Valuing diversity means teaching the unwritten "rules" or cultural values to those who need to know them and changing the rules when necessary to benefit employees and hence the organization. It also requires inviting "outsiders" in and giving them access to information and meaningful relationships with people in power.

Skill Building.   *Skill building* is designed to allow all employees and managers to develop the skills they need to deal effectively with one another and with customers in a diverse environment. Most of the skills taught are interpersonal, such as active listening, coaching, and giving feedback.

Hewlett-Packard provides both awareness and skill building. Then it attempts to transfer the training to the job by asking managers to develop personal action plans before they leave the program. For example, a manager recognizes from training that his record of retaining African-American sales representatives is poor and plans to spend more time coaching these salespeople.[33]

Experiential exercises and videotapes often are used in the training programs to help expose stereotypes and encourage employees to discuss fears, biases, and problems. One widely used training tool is a series of seven 30-minute videotapes titled *Valuing Diversity,* produced by Copeland-Griggs with funding from 50 corporations, including Hewlett-Packard, Xerox, U.S. West, and Procter & Gamble. Table 13.5 provides a set of guidelines for designing effective diversity training.

RETAINING EMPLOYEES

As replacing qualified and experienced workers becomes more difficult and costly, retaining good workers will become much more important. Aetna estimates its annual turnover expense at more than $100 million—largely money spent on training new employees and the costs of their lower productivity during the learning period.[34] Corning found in the 1980s that its African-American and female professionals quit at roughly twice the rate of white males. Top management appointed teams to figure out why, and declared that retaining workers would become an integral part of the company's quality effort.[35] A number of policies and strategies will increase retention of all employees, especially those who are "different" from the norm. Radisson Hotels International is one example of a company that has made strides in utilizing disabled employees.

TABLE 13.5

Guidelines for
diversity training

1. **Position training in your broad diversity strategy.** Training is one important element of managing diversity, but on its own it will probably fail. Culture change means altering underlying assumptions and systems that guide organizational behavior. Training programs must be internally consistent with, and complement, other initiatives focused on culture change.

2. **Do a thorough needs analysis.** Do not start training prematurely. As with any training program, eagerness to "do something" may backfire unless you have assessed what specific aspects of diversity need attention first. Focus groups help identify what employees view as priority issues.

3. **Distinguish between education and training.** Education helps build awareness and understanding but does not teach usable skills. Training involves activities that enhance skills in areas such as coaching, conducting performance appraisals, and adapting communications styles. Education and training are both important but they're not the same.

4. **Use a participative design process.** Tap a multitude of parties to ensure that the content and tone of the program are suitable to everyone involved. Outsider consultants often provide fresh perspectives, and have credibility. Insiders have specific company knowledge, sensitivity to local issues, and long-standing relationships with company members. Balance these various sources.

5. **Test the training thoroughly before rollout.** Given the sensitivity, even volatility, of diversity issues, use diversity councils and advocacy groups to pilot the programs. Build in ample feedback time to allow these groups to address sensitive concerns, and refine the training.

6. **Incorporate diversity programs into the core training curriculum.** One-time programs do not have a lasting impact. Blend the program's content into other training programs such as performance appraisal, coaching, and so on.

Source: Adapted from Ann Perkins Delatte and Larry Baytos, "Guidelines for Successful Diversity

RADISSON MAKES A DIFFERENCE FOR THE DISABLED

*R*adisson Hotels International has a long-standing commitment to employ persons who live and work with severe disabilities. According to Sue Gordon, vice president of human resources, this commitment is a natural outgrowth of the company's philosophy "to provide meaningful work and a chance to contribute to business and society for a very special group of deserving citizens."

In the mid-1980s Radisson became involved with Supported-Employment Programs, a partnership with the government to create job opportunities for individuals with disabilities. Many of the program participants are confined to wheelchairs or have some physical, emotional, or mental disability that would otherwise prevent them from being considered for jobs in a regular work setting. But through Supported-Employment Programs, an employer pays individuals with disablilities based on their output, and the government uses grant money to reimburse the corporation for the difference so that it does not sacrifice productivity or increase labor costs.

Since Radisson began the program, the company has successfully hired and trained severely disabled individuals as housekeepers, lobby cleaners, banquet setup workers, and laundry staff at approximately 30 of the properties it manages. Currently, nearly half of the 500 individuals with disabilities on Radisson's payroll are part of the Supported-Employment Programs. Initial hesitation among managers and supervisors about how to act around persons with disabilities was quickly overcome through education and direct side-by-side work experience.

By mainstreaming persons with disabilities into a regular worksite, Radisson has created a *"win-win-win"* opportunity. The employees win because they have jobs, income, and the chance to develop higher self-esteem. The company wins because it has employees who are consistent and productive. And society wins because there is less need for public welfare of one type or another.

Juergen Bartels, president of Carlson Hospitality Group, which includes Radisson Hotels International, has been delighted with the program's success. In addition, to their level of productivity, turnover among persons with disabilities continues to be the very lowest of any employee group. As a consequence, employees with disabilities are helping Radisson solve labor shortages that continue to plague other companies in the industry. The company has won several awards for promoting diversity, and customer response has been overwhelming. Clearly, Radisson is setting the standard for employment of individuals with disabilities.

Source: Susan M. Bard, "Radisson Makes a Difference for Disabled," *Hotel and Motel Management* 206, no. 12 (July 8, 1991), pp. 2, 6. ●

Support Groups

Companies can help form minority networks and other support groups to promote information exchange and social support. Support groups provide emotional and career support for members who traditionally have not been included in the majority's informal groups. They also can help diverse employees understand work norms and the corporate culture.

At Apple headquarters in Cupertino, California, support groups include a Jewish cultural group, a gay/lesbian group, an African-American group, and a technical women's group. Avon encourages employees to organize into African-American, Hispanic, and Asian networks by granting them official recognition and providing a senior manager to provide advice. These groups help new employees adjust and provide direct feedback to management on problems that concern the groups. Avon once had a women's network, but that group disbanded years ago. With women holding 79 percent of management positions, female employees at Avon believed the group was no longer necessary.

Mentoring

Many people have been puzzled at the inability of women and minorities to move up beyond a certain point on the corporate ladder (the glass ceiling). To help these groups enter the informal network that provides exposure to top management and access to information about organizational politics, many companies have implemented formal mentoring programs. **Mentors** are higher-level managers who help ensure that high-potential people are introduced to top management and socialized into the norms and values of the organization.

Career Development and Promotions

Because they are hitting a glass ceiling, many of the most talented women and minority group members are leaving their organizations in search of better opportunities elsewhere (including starting their own companies; see Chapter 9). In response, companies can give such employees the same key developmental jobs that traditionally have led to higher-level positions for their white male counterparts. For example, Mobil Oil has a special committee of executives that selects women and minorities with high potential for high-paying and critical line positions. Honeywell has established a team to evaluate the career progress of women, minorities, and employees with disabilities and to devise ways to move them up through the ranks.

Systems Accommodation

Companies can support diversity by recognizing cultural and religious holidays, differing modes of dress, and dietary restrictions, and accommodating the needs of individuals with disabilities and workers with family responsibilities. One important disabling condition is AIDS. Bank of America, headquartered in San Francisco, is one of a growing number of companies to address AIDS as a disability. The company accommodates AIDS sufferers as it would persons with any other disability, permitting and even encouraging them to continue working for as long as they are able and, if warranted, allowing flexible scheduling. AIDS sufferers also are eligible for corporate health and disability benefits.[36]

Accountability

For diversity efforts to succeed, managers must be held accountable for workforce development. Organizations must ensure that their performance appraisal and reward systems reinforce the importance of effective diversity management. The Federal National Mortgage Association, Baxter Health Care, Coca-Cola, and Merck (as well as Prudential and Kodak mentioned earlier) all tie compensation to managers' performance in diversity efforts.[37]

For 25 years, U.S. corporations were striving to integrate their workforces because of regulatory and social responsibility pressures. Today globalization, changing demographics, and the expansion of ethnic markets at home have made managing a diverse workforce a bottom-line issue. Labor shortages are causing companies to compete with one another in hiring, developing, and retaining women, minorities, and others who differ from the norm in age, appearance, physical ability, and lifestyle. Companies now realize that to remain competitive in the coming years, they will have to make managing diversity a strategic priority.

KEY TERMS

glass ceilings, p. 323
managing diversity, p. 320
mentors, p. 338
monolithic organizations, p. 331

multicultural, p. 331
multicultural organizations, p. 332
plural organizations, p. 331

SUMMARY OF LEARNING OBJECTIVES

Now that you have studied Chapter 13, you should know:

How changes in the U.S. workforce are making diversity a critical organizational and managerial issue.

The labor force is getting older, more ethnic, with a higher proportion of women. And while the absolute number of workers is increasing, the growth in jobs is outpacing the numerical growth of workers. In addition, the jobs that are being created frequently require higher skills than the typical worker can provide—thus, we are seeing a growing skills gap. To be competitive, organizations can no longer take the traditional approach of depending on white males to form the core of the workforce. Today, managers must look broadly to make use of talent wherever it can be found. As the labor market changes, organizations that can recruit, develop, motivate, and retain a diverse workforce will have a competitive advantage.

The distinction between affirmative action and managing diversity.

Affirmative action is designed to correct past exclusion of women and minorities from U.S. organizations. But despite the accomplishments of affirmative action, it has not resulted in eliminating barriers that prevent individuals from reaching their full potential. Managing diversity goes beyond hiring people who are different from the norm and seems to support, nurture, and use employee difference to the organization's advantage.

How companies can gain a competitive edge by effectively managing diversity.

Managing diversity is a bottomline issue. If managers are effective at managing diversity, they will have an easier time attracting, retaining, and motivating the best employees. They will be more effective at marketing to diverse consumer groups in the United States and globally. They will enjoy a workforce that is more creative, more innovative, and better able to solve problems. In addition, they are likely to increase the flexibility and responsiveness of the organization to environmental change.

What challenges a company is likely to encounter with a diverse workforce.

The challenges for managers created by a diverse workforce include decreased group cohesiveness, communication problems, mistrust and tension, and stereotyping. These challenges can be turned into advantages by training and effective management.

How an organization can take steps to cultivate diversity.

To be successful, organizational efforts to manage diversity must have top management support and commitment. Organizations should first undertake a thorough assessment of their cultures, policies, and practices, as well as the demographics of their labor pools and customer bases. Only after this diagnosis has been completed is the company in position to initiate programs designed to attract, develop, motivate, and retain a diverse workforce.

DISCUSSION QUESTIONS

1. What opportunities do you see as a result of changes in our nation's workforce?
2. Is prejudice declining in our society? In our organizations? Why or why not?
3. What distinctions can you make between affirmative action and managing diversity?
4. How can we overcome obstacles to diversity such as mistrust and tension, stereotyping, and communication problems?

5. How can organizations meet the special needs of different groups (e.g., work and family issues) without appearing to show favoritism to those particular sets of employees?
6. How can diversity give a company a competitive edge? Can diversity really make a difference in the bottom line? How?

CONCLUDING CASE

PILLSBURY COOKS UP A DIVERSITY STRATEGY

In 1988, when executives at Pillsbury Inc. were desperate to thwart a takeover bid by Grand Metropolitan, they cut their affirmative action and diversity programs to save money and gain some short-term financial advantages. But the reduction went against Pillsbury's traditional approach, and raised concerns among minority employees, the media, and residents of Minneapolis–St. Paul, where the company is based. To many observers, the company had lost its focus on commitment to issues of diversity.

After Pillsbury was successfully acquired by GrandMet, executives renewed their investment in diversity. Ian Martin, the food sector's chairman and chief executive officer, launched a cultural diversity strategy for the business with the following goals:

- Create an organization where cultural diversity is a driving force.

- Improve competitiveness by reflecting in the employee population the diversity that exists in the marketplace.

- Enhance Pillsbury's management and human resource systems and practices to support the development of all employees.

One of Martin's first actions was to appoint a vice president of cultural diversity, who would be responsible for implementing diversity programs, and who would report to the senior executive vice president and chief administrative officer of Pillsbury. Today this diversity position is held by Robert Hayles.

Education and awareness are seen as fundamental elements of the diversity strategy. For example, all executives based in

Pillsbury places a high premium on diversity. Its multifaceted diversity strategy has education and awareness as one of its fundamental elements.
(Courtesy Pillsbury, Inc.)

Minneapolis are required to attend briefings and participate in the leadership education series. Martin himself participated in these sessions to gain a better understanding of the issues and to demonstrate his commitment to the process. To ensure relevance and encourage feedback, much of the training has been structured around departments, with emphasis placed on attitudes among colleagues, managers, and subordinates. While the programs include topics such as stereotyping and prejudice, they are designed to move toward valuing differences and recognizing the potential of all employees.

A second key aspect of Pillsbury's strategy is ensuring accountability and integration of diversity into normal business processes. All executives are required to develop, as part of their personal objectives, a strategy related to diversity. To reinforce the importance of diversity in real terms, managers' incentive compensation is tied to the success of the diversity program. In addition, a mentoring system has been established to involve managers directly in the program and enable them to contribute. Individual managers have volunteered to act as mentors for minority and female employees, providing coaching and development opportunities on a regular basis.

The third element in Pillsbury's diversity strategy has been to increase the level of representation of women and minorities, particularly in higher-level positions. A record of the existing mix of employees was already well established via affirmative action programs, and this provided benchmarks for measuring progress toward diversity goals. Within one year of starting the program, Pillsbury increased the number of minorities at senior levels by 1.5 percent. Representation by women increased by nearly the same amount. Ongoing progress toward diversity goals is coordinated by a cultural diversity council, made up of representatives from all areas of the business. The council acts as an advisory board, making recommendations about ways to enhance the work environment.

The success of Pillsbury's diversity initiatives has been so impressive that executives of GrandMet have taken steps to transfer Pillsbury systems and strategies to their family of businesses in the United Kingdom. Although GrandMet has always had equal opportunity policies, these efforts had been fragmented and buried in the human resources department. The high-profile successes at Pillsbury are seen as cultivating a vision of diversity that has global applicability.

QUESTIONS

1. What is your assessment of Pillsbury's diversity programs? Is the company doing enough? What suggestions do you have about changing or adding programs to enhance diversity?

2. Do you think Pillsbury is altering core assumptions and perspectives of employees in order to create a culture of diversity?

3. How easy would it be to transfer Pillsbury systems and strategies to GrandMet's family of businesses in the United Kingdom? What additional obstacles are executives likely to encounter?

4. How similar is Pillsbury's case to that of The Prudential at the beginning of this chapter in Setting the Stage? Do you see any similar trends?

Source: Malcolm Greenslade, "Managing Diversity: Lessons from the United States," *Personnel Management*, December 1991, pp. 28–32.

VIDEO EXERCISE

VALUING DIVERSITY

The modern workplace is fast becoming a microcosm of the American population. Minority groups that previously have not had access to management and leadership positions in organizations are now a significant proportion of the overall workforce. Organizations must be able to take advantage of this broader talent pool, ensuring that all people have the opportunity to contribute to the extent of their potential.

Not all organizations have evolved to the point where they are able to see beyond a person's gender or ethnic status and to appreciate people for what they are able to contribute. Eliminating barriers to merit-based advancement is a central part of valuing diversity in the modern workplace.

Purpose

To heighten your awareness of the issues that companies are facing as the workplace becomes more diverse, and to understand the issues faced by individuals who work there.

Procedure

In this exercise, you will identify and interview a corporate diversity officer, and you will identify and interview a person employed in a business or nonprofit organization whose ethnic or gender status differs from your own to learn about the issues he or she faces in the workplace.

1. *Identify and interview a corporate diversity officer:* Many organizations today have designated a staff position to handle diversity issues for the firm. You should identify a person who serves this function in a medium to large organization. Contact this person and arrange a one-hour information interview. Besides developing your own set of questions for the diversity officer, your interview should cover the following issues:

   ▪ What type of diversity training program does the company have?

   ▪ What are the major diversity issues the company faces?

   ▪ What are the major problems faced by women and minorities in the organization?

   ▪ Does the company recruit in a way that increases its diversity?

   ▪ Does the company have an active affirmative action program?

2. *Identify and interview a person of different gender or ethnicity:* Identify and interview a person of managerial rank or better in a medium to large company who is different in gender or ethnicity from you. This person should *not* be directly involved in the organization's diversity function, and preferably should be in a line position. Arrange a one-hour information interview with this person to learn more about the challenges he or she perceives are directly related to his or her gender or ethnicity. This could be a sensitive issue for some people, so you may have to guarantee anonymity to the person you are interviewing. What you want to learn from this interview is how the individual believes her or his career has been affected because of gender or ethnicity. Several issues to explore include:

   ▪ Has the person ever been passed up for career advancement based on gender or ethnic status?

   ▪ Has the person ever felt that he or she has been given special consideration based on gender or ethnic status?

   ▪ What kinds of organizational barriers does the person feel as a function of her or his gender or ethnic status?

   ▪ What strategies does the person use to overcome these barriers?

3. *Report your findings to the class:* After conducting your two informal interviews, be prepared to discuss your findings with the class. You should be able to summarize the types of diversity training programs the organization you identified is using, and describe the effect of this training on the organization. You should also be able to summarize your interview with the individual of different gender or ethnic status. What are the key issues as this person sees them? Has this person benefited from or been harmed by corporate diversity programs?

EXPERIENTIAL EXERCISES

13.1   Being Different

Objectives

1. To increase your awareness of the feeling of "being different."
2. To better understand the context of "being different."

Instructions

1. Working alone, complete the Being Different Worksheet.
2. In small groups, compare worksheets and prepare answers to the discussion questions.

3. After the class reconvenes, group spokespersons present group findings.

Discussion Questions

1. Were there students who experienced being different in situations that surprised you?
2. How would you define "being different"?
3. How can this exercise be used to good advantage?

BEING DIFFERENT WORKSHEET

Think back to a recent situation in which you experienced "being different," and answer the following questions:

1. Describe the situation in which you experienced "being different." _____

_____

_____

_____

2. Explain how you felt. _____

_____

_____

_____

3. What did you do as a result of "being different"? (That is, in what way was your behavior changed by the feeling of "being different"?) _____

_____

_____

_____

_____

4. What did others in the situation do? How do you think they felt about the situation? _____

_____

_____

_____

_____

5. How did the situation turn out in the end? _____

_____

_____

_____

_____

6. As a result of that event, how will you probably behave differently in the future? In what way has the situation changed you? _____

_____

_____

_____

_____

13.2 He Works, She Works

Instructions

1. Complete the He Works, She Works Worksheet. In the appropriate spaces, write what you think the stereotyped responses would be. Do not spend too much time considering any one item. Rather, respond quickly and let your first impression or thought guide your answer.
2. Compare your individual responses with those of other class members or participants. It is interesting to identify and discuss the most frequently used stereotypes.

HE WORKS, SHE WORKS WORKSHEET

The family picture is on *his* desk: *He's a solid, responsible family man.*

His desk is cluttered: _____

_____

He's talking with co-workers: _____

_____

He's not at his desk: _____

_____

He's not in the office: _____

_____

He's having lunch with the

boss: _____

_____

The boss criticized *him:* _____

_____

He got an unfair deal: _____

_____

He's getting married: _____

_____

He's going on a business trip: _____

_____

He's leaving for a better job: _____

The family picture is on *her* desk: *Her family will come before her career.*

Her desk is cluttered: _____

_____

She's talking with co-workers: _____

_____

She's not at her desk: _____

_____

She's not in the office: _____

_____

She's having lunch with the boss: _____

_____

The boss criticized *her:* _____

_____

She got an unfair deal: _____

_____

She's getting married: _____

_____

She's going on a business trip: _____

_____

She's leaving for a better job: _____

_____

Source: F. Luthans, *Organizational Behavior* (New York: McGraw-Hill, 1989), pp. 224–25.

THE MERGER OF FEDERAL EXPRESS AND THE FLYING TIGERS LINE

It was January 1990. Thomas R. Oliver, senior vice president of International Operations for Federal Express Corporation, was on his way to meet with the members of his "Tigerclaws" Committee. The operational merger of Flying Tigers with Federal Express was supposed to have been concluded last August. Yet anticipated and unanticipated problems kept surfacing. International operations were draining financial resources, and there were other problems that had to be immediately resolved.

Several days ago, Mr. Oliver had met with Mr. Fred Smith, the company founder and CEO, and had been assigned the job of heading a special task force whose purpose was to direct the Flying Tigers' merger efforts and resolve the resulting problems. Mr. Oliver requested, and got, representatives of senior executives from every department of the company to form what he named the Tigerclaws Committee (see exhibit "The Tigerclaws Committee"). This committee had the power to cut across departmental bureaucratic lines. It had the resources of all the departments behind it to reach fast-track solutions to any problems in existence. Even with such commitments, Mr. Oliver realized what a formidable task he and his committee were facing.

Express and Freight Forwarding Industries

In 1990, sending documents or packages by priority mail was viewed as a necessary convenience, rather than a luxury. The domestic market was led by Federal Express Corporation with 53 percent of the market, followed by United Parcel Service at 19 percent. The U.S. Postal Service had 3 to 4 percent of the market.[1] The overnight letter traffic was characterized by slow growth because of the increased use of facsimile machines.

The increasing competition between express delivery services and the traditional air freight industry was changing the face of international cargo transportation. Many independent freight carriers complained that big couriers and integrated carriers were poaching on their market niches. Others ignored the competition, believing that the more personalized relationships provided by the traditional air freight companies would keep clients coming back. Still, such companies as Federal Express were having a big effect on the air freight industry. Express couriers were building their nondocument business by 25 to 30 percent a year.

Express Services in the United States

Federal Express, United Parcel Service (UPS), Airborne Express, and the U.S. Postal Service were quickly introducing services that promised to translate the fundamentals of speed and information into a powerful competitive edge. They were stressing good service at lower costs. For example, UPS had started offering discounts to its bigger customers and shippers that shipped over 250 pieces weekly. In addition, UPS was building an $80 million computer and telecommunications center to provide support for

The Tigerclaws Committee

Departments That Are Represented
Memphis SuperHub
Business Application
Airfreight Systems
Q.A. Audits
Planning and Administration
International Clearance
Communications
Ramp Plans/Program
Hub Operations
Personnel Services
International Operations
Central Support Services
Customer Support
COSMOS/Pulsar System Division
COO/Quality Improvement

all operations worldwide. Airborne's chief advantage was that it operated its own airport and had begun operating a "commerce park" around its hub in Wilmington, Ohio.

Europe

The international document and parcel express delivery business was one of the fastest-growing sectors in Europe. Although the express business would become more important in the single European market, none of the four principal players in Europe was European. DHL, Federal Express, and UPS were United States companies while TNT was Australian. Europe was not expected to produce a challenger because the "Big Four" were buying smaller rivals at such a fast pace that the odds seemed to be heavily against a comparable competitor emerging.[2]

Pacific Rim

The Asia-Pacific air express market was expanding by 20 to 30 percent annually, and the world's major air express and air freight companies had launched massive infrastructure buildups to take advantage of this growth. Industry leader DHL strengthened its access to air service by agreeing to eventually sell 57.5 percent of the equity of its international operation to Japan Air Lines, Lufthansa, and Nissho Iwai trading company. TNT Skypak's strength was in providing niche services, and its ability to tap into the emerging Asian–East European route with its European air hub. Two new U.S. entrants, Federal Express and UPS, were engaged in an undeclared price war. Willing to lose millions of dollars annually to carve out a greater market share, Federal Express already had captured about 10 percent of Pacific express business and 15 percent of freight. UPS's strategy was to control costs and to offer no-frills service at low rates. All four companies were seeking to expand the proportion of parcels, which would yield about twice the profits of the express documents business.[3]

Major Airlines

Since the common adaptation of wide body jets, major international airlines had extra cargo space in their planes. Japan Air Lines and Lufthansa were two of the worldwide players, with most national airlines providing regional services.

Airlines were expanding and automating their cargo services to meet the challenges presented by fast-growing integrated carriers. Two strategies were being employed: (1) the development of new products to fill the gap between the demand for next-day service and traditional air cargo service, and (2) computerization of internal passenger and cargo operations.[4]

The Merging Organizations: Federal Express Corporation

Frederick W. Smith, founder of Federal Express Corporation, went to Yale University, where he was awarded a now infamous "C" on an economics paper that outlined his idea for an overnight delivery service.[5] After college and military service, Smith began selling corporate jets in Little Rock, Arkansas. In 1973, he tapped his $4 million inheritance, rounded up $70 million in venture capital, and launched Federal Express, testing his college paper's thesis. The company turned profitable after three years.

Federal Express always had taken pride in its people-oriented approach and its emphasis on service to its customers. Mr. Smith believed that, in the service industry, it is the employees that make the business.[6] The philosophy of Smith and his managing staff was manifested in many ways, including: (1) extensive orientation programs, (2) training and communications programs, (3) promotion of employees from within, and (4) a tuition reimbursement program. Federal Express's "open door policy" for the expression of employee concerns also illustrated the commitment of top management to resolve problems.[7]

As to services, Federal Express stressed the importance of on-time delivery and established a 100 percent on-time delivery goal. It has achieved a record 95 percent on-time delivery. In 1990, Federal Express was one of the five U.S. firms to win the Malcolm Baldrige National Quality Award. This award was given by the U.S. government to promote quality awareness and to recognize the quality achievements of U.S. companies.

Frederick W. Smith had a vision for the overnight express delivery business. Although Federal Express was the No. 1 express firm in the United States, Mr. Smith firmly believed that globalization was the future for the express business.[8] From 1986 to 1988, Federal struggled to become a major player in international deliveries. The company ran head-on into entrenched overseas rivals, such as DHL, and onerous foreign regulations.[9]

Frustrated with the legal processes in negotiating for landing rights that were restricted by bilateral aviation treaties,[10] Mr. Smith reversed his promise to build only from within and started on a series of acquisitions. From 1987 to 1988, Federal purchased 15 minor delivery companies, mostly in Europe. In December 1988, Mr. Smith announced the merger of Tiger International,

Inc., best known for its Flying Tigers airfreight service. On paper, the merger of Federal Express and Tiger International seemed to be a marriage made in heaven. As one Federal Express executive pointed out: "If we lay a route map of Flying Tigers over that of Federal Express, there is almost a perfect match. There are only one or two minor overlaps. The Flying Tigers' routes are all over the world, with highest concentration in the Pacific rim countries, while Federal Express's routes are mostly in domestic U.S.A." As a result of the merger, Federal Express's world routes were completed. For example, the acquisition of Flying Tigers brought with it the unrestricted cargo landing rights at three Japanese airports that Federal Express had been unsuccessful in acquiring for the last three years.[11]

One high-level Federal Express employee commented that the merger brought other benefits besides routes. He said: "We got a level of expertise with the people we brought in and a number of years of experiences in the company in handling air freight . . . You have to look at this acquisition also as a defensive move. If we hadn't bought Flying Tigers, UPS might have bought Flying Tigers."

The Merging Organizations: Tiger International, Inc.

Tiger International, Inc., better known for The Flying Tigers Line, Inc., freight service, or Flying Tigers, was founded 40 years ago by Robert Prescott. Over the years, the company became modestly profitable. But in 1977, Smith won his crusade for air-cargo deregulation over the strident objection of Prescott. Heightened competition, troubled acquisitions, and steep labor costs led to big losses at Tigers. In 1986, Stephen M. Wolf, the former chairman of Republic Airline Inc., came on board at Tigers and managed to get all employees, including those represented by unions, to accept wage cuts. As Tigers rebounded financially, it was ripe to be taken over by one of the major delivery service companies. In 1988, Federal Express announced the acquisition of Tigers to the pleasure of some and dismay of others. At the announcement, some Tigers' employees shouted, "TGIF—Thank God It's Federal" or "It's purple [Federal Express] not brown [UPS]—thank goodness," In contrast, Robert Sigafoos, who wrote a corporate history of Federal Express, commented, "Prescott must be turning over in his grave."[12]

Flying Tigers always had a distinctive culture, one that partly developed from the military image of its founders. Tigers' employees stressed "Tiger Spirit" or teamwork. Since Mr. Wolf took over as the chairman and CEO at an extremely difficult time, the general orientation of Flying Tigers was to keep the company flying.

The Merger

Federal Express announced the acquisition of Flying Tigers in December 1988. However, because of government regulations, the actual operational merging of the two companies did not occur until August 1989.

One top-level Federal Express executive, with considerable expertise in mergers, described the process in the following way: "I think that after any merger you go through three phases. You come in and you have euphoria. Everybody's happy. The second phase is the transition phase. In that phase, the primary qualification that every employee must have is sadomasochistic tendencies, because you kill yourself going through it . . . And then you start coming out of that into the regeneration and regrowth phase, where you clean up all this hazy area without knowing exactly what you are going to do or thinking this works and trying it out . . . In the meantime, going through all that turmoil creates a number of problems . . . People's morale starts to dip. People start to question all the leadership. You start to see the company reorganizing, you know, trying to figure out, well, what's the best thing to do here or there or whatever and, all of a sudden, all of the confidence that ever existed in the whole world starts to diminish."

Although the two companies were supposed to now become one, problems from the merger kept surfacing. Some of these problems were to be anticipated with the merger of two companies of these sizes. However, many problems were not anticipated and had become very costly to the company.

Human Resources Management Problems

There were union questions. Federal Express traditionally had been a nonunion shop, while the Flying Tigers' employees were predominately unionized. During the merger, the National Mediation Board could not determine a majority among the pilots at Federal Express and Flying Tigers. The board requires a majority to decide the union status at any firm. Because a majority could not be determined, the mediation board decided to allow the temporary mix of union and nonunion employees until the fall of 1989, when elections would determine if there would be union representation. The ruling had created ambiguities in employee status and raised some important financial and legal issues for Federal Express, unions, and employees.[13]

An executive in the international division described Federal Express's feelings on unions: "They [Flying Tigers] had a lot of unions. Tigers was a traditional company . . . and we [Federal Express] don't dislike unions . . . Our feelings about unions is [sic] that if you get a union, you deserve it, because you have not managed your business well. We would like to think that we could keep that old family [feeling]. We realize that we can't keep the old family. It's very difficult to keep the family spirit corporatewide [after a merger]."

Tiger people had a variety of attitudes to job offers after the merger. The employees of Federal Express believed that Federal Express was a great place to work, mainly because of its people-oriented policies. Because of this belief, most of the managers thought that the Flying Tigers' employees would "welcome the merger with open arms." A communications official said: "We tried to position Federal Express as a great place to work, a wonderful place to be—cutting edge technology, a great aircraft fleet, a great employee group, good management—all those types of things."

Flying Tigers had a rich and long history. Tiger employees prided themselves on their team spirit and their willingness to take pay cuts for the good of The Flying Tiger Line, Inc., during the lean years. Employees proudly displayed items with the Tiger logo on them.

A long-time Tiger employee and member of one of the pre-merger Tiger committees remarked on the job offers: "For the employees, it [the merger] was a spectrum, we've got all of them on a line. Up in front, we've got those employees for whom the merger was the best thing that ever happened to them. In the back, you've got the employees where it was the worst thing that ever happened—because of personal things, they decided to leave the company. And then there's the group of employees in the middle, which really composed the majority of Flying Tigers' employees, that it really didn't matter one way or the other since they never moved. All they did was change their uniforms from Friday to Monday. They're basically doing the same jobs in the same locations." A member of his family and many friends refused to accept a job with Federal Express. He explained their refusal, by saying: "Because [Federal Express was] taking the name away. You were taking the history of the Flying Tiger line away . . . because we were a small company, we were like a close-knit family." Another middle-level former Tiger said, "Although a lot of merger information was provided to people at headquarters in L.A., people at other locations, like Boston, received less information." She said that some Tigers refused the job offer for the following reason: "They left, I think, just because of the attitude that . . . you're taking Flying Tigers away and I don't want to go with you." Some Tigers hoped that Federal Express would permit them to keep the Flying Tiger name or change the company name to Federal Tigers.

There were cultural differences. A Federal Express executive on the Tigerclaws Committee commented on cultural differences by saying: "The difference was astounding. Absolutely astounding. Federal Express's employees, typically, they seem to be younger, we're all in uniforms, enthusiastic about the company. You can walk around Federal Express and everybody can tell you what the corporate philosophy is . . . I remember standing in the Los Angeles airport facility . . . it's typical Federal Express. And you go over to the Tiger facility and here are all of these much older guys standing around. None of them in any type of uniform, clothes were all over the mat, there was [sic] no apparent standards, whatsoever. You know, kicking some of the packages, tossing them, throwing. It was just . . . just terrible. I couldn't believe it. But that was part of the way they did business. They referred to a lot of the cargo that they carried as big, ugly freight. And to us . . . we go around thinking every customer's package is the most important thing we carry."

A former Tiger employee shared her perspective on the differences: "Most of the employees that you dealt with you had known for a lot of years. We used to work together side by side very closely for 20 years. And this company, Federal Express, isn't even 20 years old. You walk into a meeting or classroom or something . . . Federal Express people are introducing themselves to other Federal Express people. Tiger people found that really hard to believe—that you didn't know everybody at Federal Express."

During the announcement of the merger, Mr. Smith made a job offer to all the employees of Flying Tigers. Almost 90 percent of the 6,600 former Tiger employees took the offer. In a two-week period, from July 15 to 31, over 4,000 new jobs were to be created and Tiger employees transferred to these jobs. Many employees had to be relocated, because the old Tiger hub in Columbus, Ohio, was phased out, and primarily only freight and maintenance personnel were kept at the hub in Los Angeles. Some job placements were troublesome, because the human resources department had difficulty obtaining job descriptions and pay scales from Flying Tigers. During the haste, there were quite a number of mismatches of jobs and employees.

One of Federal Express's personnel officers remarked: "I was concerned about being able to meet employee's expectations. A lot of times people coming in from outside of Federal Express have this—I mean it's a great place, but they have this picture that it's a fairy tale place, and that there aren't any real problems and that everybody gets his own way. So I was concerned about the expectations that people brought, both positive and negative. How are we going to make people feel real good about the company?"

To help former Flying Tigers' employees determine whether to accept Federal Express's job offers, Federal Express provided the employees with detailed information about the company. Videotapes introducing Federal Express and explaining the benefits of working for the company were mailed to the homes of Tiger employees. Additionally, many Tiger employees were flown into Federal Express's headquarters in Memphis and given the "grand tour." "Express Teams," groups of four to five employees, visited Flying Tigers' locations and gave them previews of what it was like to work for Federal Express.

Regarding expectations, one long-time Tiger remarked: "There's still a lot of unhappy people in Memphis that came out of L.A., because I think they expected an awful lot. They had the option of saying no to a job and being out on the street looking for something else, or they could come to Memphis and have Federal Express be their employer. And there are a lot of people that still take offense at the fact that Federal Express bought Flying Tigers. But those people have an attitude that they have to deal with." Another former Tiger remarked: "And I honestly thought that by going from a small company to a large company, I was just going to be another number. But . . . it's also their attention to people. All of the hype and promotion they did before T-day [merger day] to Flying Tiger people that they were people oriented . . . we really didn't [know] what that meant and what it would mean to us individually until we became employees."

Summary

Since 1985, Federal Express's international business had lost approximately $74 million and given company executives a lifetime supply of headaches.[14] To improve Federal Express's competitive position with its overseas rivals and overcome the foreign regulations regarding landing rights, Frederick Smith announced in December 1988 the acquisition of Tiger International, Inc. Although the combined companies would have $2.1 billion in debt, Flying Tigers was expected to provide Federal Express with desperately needed international delivery routes. The Tiger acquisition would allow Federal Express to use its own planes for overseas package delivery where Federal Express used to contract other carriers. In addition, Tigers' sizable long-range fleet could be used to achieve dominance in the international heavy-freight business that Federal Express had yet to crack.

Suppose you had been in Thomas Oliver's shoes and were the head of the Tigerclaws Committee. What were the major problems and opportunities facing Federal Express? What should be the priorities of the Tigerclaws Committee? How would you solve or reduce the problems and exploit the opportunities?

Source: A case study by Howard S. Tu, Fogelman College of Business and Economics, Memphis State University; and Sherry E. Sullivan, Bowling Green State University.

QUESTIONABLE PURCHASING PRACTICES

Motton Electronics was widely respected in the industry as being fair, dependable, and progressive. Cy Bennett, founder of the company, was chair of the board and majority stockholder. One of the company's progressive practices was to employ professional managers as members of top management. Each carefully selected manager received an excellent salary for performing his or her job. None of the top management group served on the board.

One month ago, Bennett reported to the board that he had facts proving that the director of purchasing for the company, Russell Hale, was giving preferential treatment to certain vendors and, in turn, was receiving merchandise and money. After the chair presented the evidence, the board formally condemned such purchasing practices by unanimous vote.

Immediately following this action, a vocal board member asserted that he believed the chief executive officer was responsible for all employee behavior on the job, that such administrative negligence should not be tolerated, and that the board needed a policy on the issue. This statement triggered an extensive discussion among the directors on topics such as shared responsibility for subordinates' actions, relevant duties of the board of directors, and related policy implications.

The meeting ended with a motion, unanimously supported, that Bennett (1) decide on appropriate measures regarding the errant director of purchasing and (2) develop and implement a policy on shared responsibility.

Bennett believed his prompt action on these matters would be critical to managerial performance, to the firm's profitability, and to the value of his majority block of company stock.

Source: J. Champion and J. Hames, *Critical Incidents in Management: Decision and Policy Issues,* 6th ed. (Homewood, Ill.: Richard D. Irwin, 1989).

WORKFORCE REDUCTION POLICY

Five years ago Wireweave, Inc., moved to a rural area 25 miles outside a large southern city. The company, formerly situated in a midwestern industrial city, chose this location primarily because of the lower wage rates paid in the community, a nonunion tradition in the region, and a favorable tax situation.

Wireweave, a manufacturer of wire products, has two major high-volume product lines: aluminum wire screen and dish racks. The dish racks are supplied to several appliance manufacturers for use in automatic dishwashers.

Because of intense industry competition, Wireweave's management realized several years ago that if Wireweave was to continue manufacturing aluminum wire screen and dish racks—and even stay in business—it would have to procure up-to-date equipment, become more automated and computerized, and even use robots for some of the hottest and dustiest jobs. After a two-year evaluation of production needs and an analysis of technologically advanced manufacturing equipment (including robots), Wireweave purchased equipment that would modernize production and replace 65 employees, representing about 33 percent of the total labor force. Significant labor costs would be saved by this employment reduction. As a result, Steve Jackson, president of Wireweave, expected the company to regain its competitiveness and profitability.

The following spring, shortly after installing the new equipment, Jackson called in Muriel Fincher, human resources director, and told her that the company could no longer afford to employ the unneeded workers. He requested that she decide on an acceptable plan for reducing company employment by 65 persons, and the sooner the better in terms of company profitability. Jackson also asked that she recommend a specific operating policy covering future workforce reductions.

Fincher had successfully handled some tough challenges as human resources director, but the latest assignments from Jackson were the most difficult ones she had faced. As Fincher considered relevant options and constraints, her deliberations were dominated by three factors: (1) the company's economic and ethical responsibilities to terminated employees, (2) the potential moral problems for employees who would be retained, and (3) the pressure from Jackson for prompt decision and action.

Source: J. Champion and J. James, *Critical Incidents in Management: Decision and Policy Issues,* 6th ed. (Homewood, Ill.: Richard D. Irwin. 1989).

PART IV

LEADING

FOUNDATIONS OF MANAGEMENT

Managers and Organizations
The Evolution of Management
The External Environment
Managerial Decision Making

PLANNING AND STRATEGY

Planning and Strategic Management
Ethics and Corporate Responsibility
Managing in Our Natural Environment
International Management
New Ventures

STRATEGY IMPLEMENTATION

ORGANIZING AND STAFFING

Organization Structure
The Responsive Organization
Human Resources Management
Managing the Diverse Workforce

LEADING

Leadership
Motivating for Performance
Managing Teams
Communicating

CONTROL AND CHANGE

Managerial Control
Operations Management
Managing Technology and Innovation
Becoming World Class

N ow that you know about organizing and staffing, Part IV further elaborates on managing human resources by discussing the third function of management: leading. Effective managers know how to lead others toward unit and organizational success. Chapter 14 explores the essential components of leadership, including the use of power in the organization. Chapter 15 focuses on motivating people, with implications for enhancing job performance. Chapter 16 examines work teams, including the management of task forces and relationships among groups. Finally, Chapter 17 addresses a vital management activity: communication. Here, you will learn how to maximize your effectiveness in communicating with other people throughout the organization.

14

LEADERSHIP

Every soldier has a right to competent command.

Julius Caesar

After studying Chapter 14, you will know:

1. What it means to be a leader.

2. How vision helps you be a better leader.

3. How to understand and use power.

4. The personal traits and skills of effective leaders.

5. The behaviors that will make you a better leader.

6. What it means to be a charismatic and transformational leader.

7. How to further your own leadership development.

GM: A DINOSAUR NO MORE

*D*o you remember the "dinosaurs" you read about in Chapter 2: IBM, GM, and Sears? All struggled to survive, but General Motors is now in the best shape of any of them. Why? There is no simple answer, of course, but new CEO Jack Smith gets much of the credit. According to *Fortune,* Smith is leading "the biggest turnaround in American corporate history. In just two and a half years, he has steered [GM] down the road not just toward recovery but toward global preeminence."

Smith has candidly pointed out the attitudes and behaviors that led to GM's slide: complacency, myopia, a reliance on past success, maintenance of the status quo. He has set his eyes on the future: his vision for GM is to be the world leader in transportation products and services. He wants GM to sell the best-quality cars and trucks in the United States. He wants to challenge Toyota in manufacturing productivity. And he wants GM to learn world-class practices from companies in all industries.

General Motors CEO Jack Smith has led the company from hard times to what *Fortune* magazine has described as "global preeminence." Smith's leadership style is thoughtful and incisive.
(AP/Wide World Photos)

Smith is described as a thoughtful, incisive man who listens well and gives credit to others. He has made far-reaching changes in the way GM operates. He has cut costs, streamlined processes, improved coordination, and inspired everyone to work together for the good of the company. These represent dramatic departures from the recent past. Says one veteran GMer: "There is more excitement around here than we've had in a long time. It is more than morale; it is a real feeling that people can make a difference."

Fortune concludes that Smith succeeded where others failed because he understands the company intimately—he has spent over 30 years there—and yet was able to step back and look at the company with a fresh, objective eye.

Source: A. Taylor III, "GM's $11,000,000,000 Turnaround," *Fortune,* October 17, 1994, pp. 54–74.

*P*eople get excited about the topic of leadership. They want to know: What makes a great leader? Executives at all levels in all industries are interested in this question. They believe the answer will bring improved organizational performance and personal career success. They hope to acquire the skills that will transform an "average" manager into a true leader.

Fortunately, leadership *can* be taught—and learned. According to one source, "Leadership seems to be the marshaling of skills possessed by a majority but used by a minority. But it's something that can be learned by anyone, taught to everyone, denied to no one."[1]

What *is* leadership? To start with, a leader is one who influences others to attain goals. The greater the number of followers, the greater the influence. And the more successful the attainment of worthy goals, the more evident the leadership. But we must explore beyond this bare definition to capture the excitement and intrigue that devoted followers and students of leadership feel when they see a great leader in action, and to understand what organizational leaders really do or what it really takes to gain entry into *Fortune*'s Hall of Fame for U.S. Business Leadership.

Outstanding leaders have vision. They move people and organizations in directions they otherwise would not go. They may launch enterprises, build organization cultures, win wars, or otherwise change the course of events.[2] They are strategists who seize opportunities others overlook, but "they are also passionately concerned with detail—all the small, fundamental realities that can make or mar the grandest of plans."[3]

VISION

"The leader's job is to create a vision," states Robert L. Swiggett, chair of Kollmorgen Corporation.[4] Until a few years ago, *vision* was not a word one heard managers utter. But today, having a vision for the future and communicating that vision to others are known to be essential components of great leadership. "If there is no vision, there is no business," maintains entrepreneur Mark Leslie.[5] Joe Nevin, MIS director at Apple Computer, describes leaders as "painters of the vision and architects of the journey."[6] Practicing businesspeople are not alone in this belief; leadership scholars also have brought vision to a position of prominence in management thinking.

A **vision** is a mental image of a possible and desirable future state of the organization. Great leaders imagine an ideal future for their organizations that goes beyond the ordinary and beyond what others may have thought possible. They strive to realize significant achievements that others have not. In short, as the following examples show, leaders must be forward looking and clarify the directions in which they want their organizations and even entire industries to move.

VISIONS IN ACTION

*H*ere are some concrete examples of leaders and their visions:

- Rita Colwell of the University of Maryland is one of the world's foremost microbiologists, known for her work on the developmental changes in oyster larvae. She is also a practical person of action who wants to make the world a better place. Believing that the world's oceans offer hope for feeding, healing, and sustaining humankind, she founded the Maryland Biotechnology Institute in 1985. Among other practical applications of the research, Colwell envisions a multibillion-dollar industry using biotechnology for environmental cleanup. Her aim is to make Maryland the number one international champion of marine biotechnology. While California is ahead of Maryland as the overall leader in biotech, Maryland is better positioned to lead in the newer field of marine biotechnology.

- Ted Turner's vision is to create the first truly "global information company," the "global network of record" (his terms), seen in every nation on the planet, broadcast in most major languages. He sees CNN and its people as world citizens who just happen to be based in the United States.

- Percy Barnevik of ABB wants to sell power equipment internationally. Not just some power equipment—*all* of it. And not just in certain countries, but *everywhere.* He envisions a company that has no national boundaries, but that understands and capitalizes on local differences.

- Phil Turner was facilities manager at Raychem Corporation, fixing toilets and air conditioners. But rather than believing that the workers in the facilities were performing menial jobs and making only trivial contributions to the organization, Turner viewed their work as a mission—to make people feel good, "to lift people's spirits through beauty, cleanliness, and functionality, enthusiasm, good cheer, and excellence."

Sources: J. K. Andrews, "Lady with a Mission," *The World & I,* May 1991, pp. 304–11; E. Fennema, "Megalopolis over Tokyo," *The World & I,* July 1991, pp. 183–87; J. Kouzes and B. Posner, *The Leadership Challenge* (San Francisco: Jossey-Bass, 1987); R. Furchgott, "Maryland Sees Its Future as Mecca for Biotechnology Businesses," *Raleigh News & Observer,* August 30, 1994, p. 3D; G. E. Schares, "Percy Barnevik's Global Crusade," *Business Week,* January 11, 1994, pp. 204–11; and T. Peters, *Liberation Management* (New York: Alfred A. Knopf, 1992). ●

Visions can be small or large and can exist throughout all organizational levels as well as at the very top. The important points are that (1) a vision is necessary for effective leadership; (2) a person can develop a vision for any job, work unit, or organization; and (3) most people, including managers who do not develop into strong leaders, do not develop a clear vision—instead, they focus on performing or surviving on a day-by-day basis.

Two metaphors reinforce the important concept of vision.[7] The first is the jigsaw puzzle. It is much easier to put a puzzle together if you have the picture on the box cover in front of you. Without the picture, or vision, the lack of direction is likely to result in frustration and failure. The second metaphor is the slide projector. Imagine a projector that is out of focus. If you had to watch blurred images for a long period of time, you would get confused, impatient, and disoriented. You would stop following the presentation and lose respect for the presenter. It is the leader's job to focus the projector. That is what communicating a vision is all about: making it clear where you are heading.

Not just any vision will do, either for the leader or for the company. Whereas vision is very important for success, visions can be inappropriate, and even fail, for a variety of

In founding the Biotechnology Institute, Rita Colwell demonstrated that she was a person with a vision as well as an extraordinary researcher. *(Tom Wolff)*

reasons.[8] First, an inappropriate vision may reflect merely the leader's personal needs. Such a vision can be unethical, or may fail because of lack of acceptance by the market or by those who must implement it.

Second (and related to the first), an inappropriate vision may ignore stakeholder needs. You learned about assessing stakeholders in the earlier chapters on strategy. Third, the leader must stay abreast of environmental changes. Although effective leaders maintain confidence and persevere despite obstacles, the time may come when the facts dictate that the vision must change. You will learn more about change and how to manage it later in the text.

LEADERS AND MANAGERS

Effective managers are not necessarily true leaders. Many administrators, supervisors, and even top executives execute their responsibilities without being great leaders. But these positions afford *opportunity* for leadership. The ability to lead effectively, then, will set the excellent managers apart from the average ones.

Managers must deal with the ongoing, day-to-day complexities of organizations. True leaders manage effectively and devote their attention to orchestrating change.[9] While managers engage in planning and budgeting routines, leaders set the direction (create a vision) for the firm. Management requires structuring the organization, staffing it with capable people, and monitoring activities; leadership goes beyond these functions by inspiring people to attain the vision. Great leaders keep people focused on moving the organization toward its ideal future, motivating them to overcome whatever obstacles lie in the way.

Many observers believe that U.S. business has lost its competitive advantage because of a lack of strong leadership.[10] While managers focus on superficial activities and worry about short-term profits and stock prices, too few have emerged as leaders who foster innovation and attainment of long-term goals. And whereas many managers are overly concerned with "fitting in" and not rocking the boat, those who emerge as leaders are more concerned with making important decisions that may break with tradition but are humane, moral, and right. The leader puts a premium on substance rather than on style.

LEADERS AND FOLLOWERS

Organizations succeed or fail not only because of how well they are led but because of how well followers follow. Just as managers are not necessarily good leaders, people are not always good followers. The most effective followers are capable of independent thinking and at the same time are actively committed to organizational goals.[11]

As a manager, you will be asked to play *both* roles. As you lead the people who report to you, you will report to your boss. You will be a member of some teams and committees, and you may chair others. While the leadership roles get the glamor and therefore are the roles that many people covet, followers must perform their responsibilities conscientiously as well.

Effective followers are distinguished from ineffective ones by their enthusiasm and commitment to the organization and to a person or purpose—an idea, a product—other than themselves or their own interests. They master skills that are useful to their organizations, and they hold performance standards that are higher than required. Effective followers may not get the glory, but they know their contributions to the organization are valuable. And as they make those contributions, they study leaders in preparation for their own leadership roles.[12]

POWER AND LEADERSHIP

Central to effective leadership is **power**—the ability to influence other people. In organizations, this often means the ability to get things done or accomplish one's goals despite resistance from others.

SOURCES OF POWER

One of the earliest and still most useful approaches to understanding power suggests that leaders have five important potential sources of power in organizations.[13] Figure 14.1 shows these power sources.

FIGURE 14.1

Sources of power

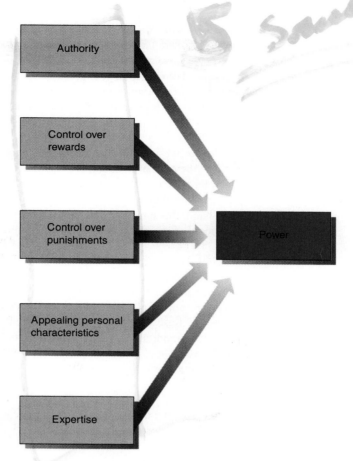

Source: Adapted from J. R. P. French and B. Raven, "The Bases of Social Power," in *Studies in Social Power,* ed. D. Cartwright (Ann Arbor, Mich.: Institute for Social Research, 1959).

Legitimate Power

The leader with *legitimate power* has the right, or the authority, to tell subordinates what to do; subordinates are obligated to comply with legitimate orders. For example, a supervisor tells an employee to remove a safety hazard, and the employee removes the hazard because he has to obey the authority of his boss. In contrast, when a staff person lacks the authority to give an order to a line manager, the staff person has no legitimate power over the manager. And, as you might guess, managers have more legitimate power over subordinates than they do over their peers, bosses, and others inside or outside their organizations.[14]

Reward Power

The leader who has *reward power* influences others because she or he controls valued rewards; people comply with the leader's wishes to receive those rewards. For example, a manager works hard to achieve her performance goals to get a positive performance review and a big pay raise from her boss. On the other hand, if company policy dictates that everyone receive the same salary increase, a leader's reward power decreases because he or she is unable to give higher raises.

Coercive Power

The leader with *coercive power* has control over punishments; people comply to avoid those punishments. For instance, a manager implements an absenteeism policy that administers harsh disciplinary actions to offending employees. A manager has less coercive power if, say, a union contract prohibits him or her from punishing employees too severely. In general, lower-level managers have less coercive and reward power than do middle- and higher-level managers.[15]

Referent Power

The leader with *referent power* has personal characteristics that appeal to others; people comply because of admiration, a desire for approval, personal liking, or a desire to be like the leader. For example, young, ambitious managers emulate the work habits and personal style of a successful, charismatic executive. An executive who is incompetent, disliked, and commands little respect has little referent power.

Expert Power

The leader who has *expert power* has certain expertise or knowledge; people comply because they believe in, can learn from, or can otherwise gain from that expertise. For example, a sales manager gives her salespeople some tips on closing a deal. The salespeople then alter their sales techniques because they respect the manager's expertise. On the other hand, this manager may lack expert power in other areas, such as finance; thus, her salespeople may ignore her advice concerning financial matters.

People who are in a position that gives them the right to tell others what to do, who can reward and punish, who are well liked and admired, and who have expertise on which other people can draw will be powerful members of the organization. *All* these sources of power are potentially important. Although it is easy to assume that the most powerful bosses are those who have high legitimate power and control major rewards and punishments, it is important not to underestimate the more "personal" sources like expert and referent power. These personal sources of power are the ones most closely related to people's motivation to perform to their managers' expectations.[16]

TRADITIONAL APPROACHES TO UNDERSTANDING LEADERSHIP

Three traditional approaches to studying leadership are the trait approach, the behavioral approach, and the situational approach.

LEADERSHIP TRAITS

The **trait approach** is the oldest leadership perspective and was dominant for several decades. This approach seems logical for studying leadership: It focuses on individual leaders and attempts to determine the personal characteristics (traits) that great leaders share. What set Winston Churchill, Alexander the Great, Gandhi, Napoleon, and Martin Luther King apart from the crowd? The trait approach assumes the existence of a leadership personality and assumes that leaders are born, not made.

From 1904 to 1948, over 100 leadership trait studies were conducted.[17] At the end of that period, management scholars concluded that no particular set of traits is necessary for a person to become a successful leader. Enthusiasm for the trait approach diminished, but some research on traits continued. By the mid-1970s, a more balanced view emerged: Although no traits ensure leadership success, certain characteristics are potentially useful. The perspective of the 1990s is that some personality characteristics—many of which a person need not be *born* with but can strive to acquire—do distinguish effective leaders from other people:[18]

1. **Drive.** *Drive* refers to a set of characteristics that reflect a high level of effort. Drive includes high need for achievement, constant striving for improvement, ambition, a high energy level, tenacity (persistence in the face of obstacles), and initiative. In several countries, the achievement needs of top executives have been shown to be related to the growth rates of their organizations.[19]
2. **Leadership motivation.** Great leaders not only have drive; they want to *lead*. They have a high need for power, preferring to be in leadership rather than follower positions.
3. **Integrity.** *Integrity* is the correspondence between actions and words. Honesty and credibility, in addition to being desirable characteristics in their own right, are especially important for leaders because these traits inspire trust in others.

4. **Self-confidence.** *Self-confidence* is important for a number of reasons. The leadership role is challenging, and setbacks are inevitable. Self-confidence allows a leader to overcome obstacles, make decisions despite uncertainty, and instill confidence in others. All of these qualities are vital to implementing decisions and attaining the leader's vision.

5. **Knowledge of the business.** Effective leaders have a high level of knowledge about their industries, companies, and technical matters. Leaders must have the intelligence to interpret vast quantities of information. Advanced degrees are useful in a career, but ultimately less important than acquired expertise in matters relevant to the organization.[20]

Finally, there is one personal skill that may be the most important: the ability to perceive the needs and goals of others and to adjust one's personal leadership approach accordingly.[21] Leadership means being able to assess others, evaluate the situation, and select or change behavior to more effectively respond to the demands of the circumstances. This quality is the cornerstone of the situational approaches to leadership, which we will discuss shortly.

LEADERSHIP BEHAVIORS

The **behavioral approach** attempts to identify what good leaders do. Should leaders focus on getting the job done or on keeping their followers happy? Should they make decisions autocratically or democratically? In the behavioral approach, personal characteristics are considered less important than the actual behaviors leaders exhibit.

Three general categories of leadership behavior have received particular attention: behaviors related to task performance, group maintenance, and employee participation in decision making.

Task Performance

Leadership requires getting the job done. **Task performance behaviors** are the leader's efforts to ensure that the work unit or organization reaches its goals. This dimension is sometimes referred to as *concern for production, directive leadership, initiating structure,* or *closeness of supervision.* It includes a focus on work speed, quality and accuracy, quantity of output, and following the rules.[22]

Group Maintenance

In exhibiting **group maintenance behaviors,** leaders take action to ensure the satisfaction of group members, develop and maintain harmonious work relationships, and preserve the social stability of the group. This dimension is sometimes referred to as *concern for people, supportive leadership,* or *consideration.* It includes a focus on people's feelings and comfort, appreciation of them, and stress reduction.[23]

What *specific* behaviors do performance- and maintenance-oriented leadership imply? To help answer this question, assume you are asked to rate your boss on these two dimensions. If a leadership study were conducted in your organization, you would be asked to fill out a questionnaire similar to the one in Table 14.1. The behaviors indicated in the first set of questions represent performance-oriented leadership; those indicated in the second set represent maintenance-oriented leadership.

Participation in Decision Making

How should a leader make decisions? More specifically, to what extent should leaders involve their people in making decisions?[24] The **participation-in-decision-making dimension** of leadership behavior can range from autocratic to democratic. **Autocratic leaders** make decisions on their own and then announce them to the group. **Democratic leaders** solicit input from others. These leaders seek information, opinions, and preferences, sometimes to the point of meeting with the group, leading discussions, and using consensus or majority vote to make the final choice.

TABLE 14.1

Questions assessing task performance and group maintenance leadership

---

Task performance leadership

1. Is your superior strict about observing regulations?

2. To what extent does your superior give you instructions and orders?

3. Is your superior strict about the amount of work you do?

4. Does your superior urge you to complete your work by a specified time?

5. Does your superior try to make you work to your maximum capacity?

6. When you do an inadequate job, does your superior focus on the inadequate way the job is done?

7. Does your superior ask you for reports about the progress of your work?

8. How precisely does your superior work out plans for goal achievement each month?

Group maintenance leadership

1. Can you talk freely with your superior about your work?

2. Does your superior generally support you?

3. Is your superior concerned about your personal problems?

4. Do you think your superior trusts you?

5. Does your superior give you recognition when you do your job well?

6. When a problem arises in your workplace, does your superior ask your opinion about how to solve it?

7. Is your superior concerned about your future benefits, such as promotions and pay raises?

8. Does your superior treat you fairly?

Source: J. Misumi and M. Peterson, "The Performance-Maintenance (PM) Theory of Leadership: Review of a Japanese Research Program," *Administrative Science Quarterly* 30, no. 2 (June 1985).

The Effects of Leader Behavior

How the leader behaves influences people's attitudes and performance. Studies of these effects focus on autocratic versus democratic decision styles or on performance- versus maintenance-oriented behaviors.

Decision Styles.   The classic study comparing autocratic and democratic styles found that a democratic approach resulted in the most positive attitudes, whereas an autocratic approach resulted in somewhat higher performance.[25] A **laissez-faire** style, in which the leader essentially made no decisions, led to more negative attitudes and lower performance. These results seem logical and probably represent the prevalent beliefs among managers about the general effects of these decision-making approaches.

However, more valid conclusions have been drawn since the early research. Whether a decision should be made autocratically or democratically depends on characteristics of the leader, the followers, and the situation.[26] Thus, a situational approach to leader decision styles, discussed later in the chapter, is appropriate.

Performance and Maintenance Behaviors.   The performance and maintenance dimensions of leadership are independent of each other. In other words, a leader can behave in ways that emphasize one, both, or neither of these dimensions. Some research indicates that the ideal combination is to engage in both types of leader behaviors.

In the well-known Ohio State studies, a team of Ohio State University researchers investigated the effects of leader behavior in a truck manufacturing plant of International Harvester.[27] Generally, supervisors who were high on *maintenance behaviors* (which the researchers termed *consideration*) had fewer grievances and less turnover in their work

FIGURE 14.2

The Leadership
Grid®

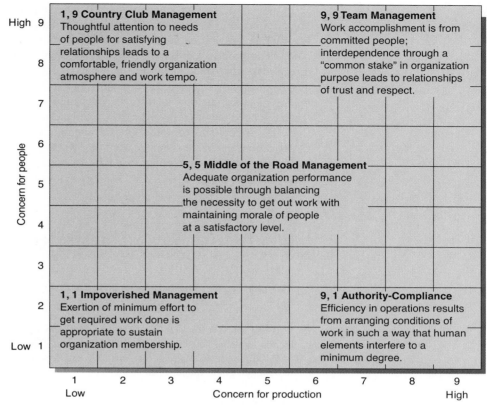

Source: The Leadership Grid® Figure from *Leadership Dilemmas—Grid Solutions,* by Robert R. Blake and Anne Adams McCanse. Houston: Grid Publishing Company, p. 29. Copyright © 1991, by Scientific Methods, Inc. Reproduced by permission of the owners.

units than supervisors who were low on this dimension. The opposite held for *task performance behaviors* (which the team called *initiating structure*). Supervisors high on this dimension had more grievances and higher turnover rates.

When maintenance and performance leadership behaviors were considered together, the results were more complex. But one conclusion was clear: When a leader must be high on performance-oriented behaviors, he or she should *also* be maintenance oriented. Otherwise the leader will have employees with high rates of turnover and grievances.

At about the same time the Ohio State studies were being conducted, an equally famous research program at the University of Michigan was studying the impact of the same leader behaviors on groups' job performance.[28] Among other things, the researchers concluded that the most effective managers engaged in what they called **task-oriented behavior:** planning, scheduling, coordinating, providing resources, and setting performance goals. Effective managers also exhibited more **relationship-oriented behavior:** demonstrating trust and confidence, acting friendly and considerate, showing appreciation, keeping people informed, and so on. As you can see, these dimensions of leader behavior are essentially the task performance and group maintenance dimensions.

After the Ohio State and Michigan findings were published, it became popular to talk about the ideal leader as one who is always both performance and maintenance oriented. The best-known leadership training model to follow this style is Blake and Mouton's Leadership Grid®.[29] In grid training, managers are rated on their performance-oriented behavior (called *concern for production*) and maintenance-oriented behavior (*concern for people*). Then their scores are plotted on the grid shown in Figure 14.2. The highest score is a 9 on both dimensions.

As the figure shows, joint scores can fall at any of 81 points on the grid. Managers who did not score a 9,9—for example, those who were high on concern for people but low on concern for production—would then receive training on how to become a 9,9 leader.

In the 1960s, grid training was warmly received by U.S. business and industry. Later, however, it was criticized for embracing a simplistic, one-best-way style of leadership and ignoring the possibility that 9,9 is not best under all circumstances. For example, even 1,1 could be appropriate if employees know their jobs (and therefore don't need to receive directions). Also, they may enjoy their jobs and their co-workers enough that whether or not the boss shows personal concern for them is not very important. Nonetheless, if the manager is uncertain how to act in a given situation, it probably is best to exhibit behaviors that are related to both task performance and group maintenance.[30]

As the following example shows, a wide range of effective leadership styles exists. Organizations that understand the need for diverse leadership styles will have a competitive advantage in the modern business environment over those that believe there is only one "best" way.

MEN AND WOMEN LEADERS: (HOW) DO THEY DIFFER?

*O*n the average, men and women are equally effective as leaders. However, the situation may make a difference: male leaders are more effective in military settings, and women are more effective in educational, social service, and government organizations. Why this is so is not completely clear.

Think about it for a moment: Do women and men behave differently in leadership roles? Is there a "male" leadership style, and, if so, does it differ from the "female" style?

According to an article in *Harvard Business Review,* the first female executives had to behave like men to get to the top. But today, women are moving into top management by drawing on unique skills and attitudes that men are less likely to possess. Men, says author Judy Rosener, are more likely to rely on their formal authority and on rewards and punishments (legitimate, reward, and coercive powers), whereas women tend to use their charisma, interpersonal skills, hard work, and personal contacts. In Rosener's study, women leaders claimed to encourage participation, share power and information, and enhance other people's self-worth.

Now consider some reactions to this article in a subsequent debate in *HBR:*

- Cynthia Fuchs Epstein, distinguished professor of the City University of New York, believes that too many articles have focused on identifying differences in how the sexes behave. Men should not be embarrassed about adopting the humanitarian styles described by the women leaders, and the "qualities of toughness and drive . . . should be prized in women who wish to express them when they are appropriate. The category is 'people,' not 'men and women.' "

- Monique R. Siegel of MRS Management Related Services AG in Zurich, Switzerland, wrote, "Haven't we all been told again and again that in a man's world we have to adjust to the male rules of the game? It is high time that we discard this myth—and Judy Rosener has done so . . . [T]op women succeed *because* they are women, not in spite of it . . . Our strength lies in *not* being like men, but—and this is good news—men's strength may very well lie in not being 'like a man' anymore."

- Jeffrey A. Sonnenfeld, professor at Emory University in Atlanta, states that the female leadership style described by Rosener also characterizes the strengths of many prominent male corporate leaders, including Thomas J. Watson, Jr., of IBM, Ken Olsen of Digital Equipment, John McElwee of John Hancock, Edwin Land of Polaroid, and Jim Casey of United Parcel Service. Sonnenfeld also criticized the study on a number of methodological grounds.

- The letters to the editor concluded with one from Carol R. Goldberg, president and CEO of The Avcar Group, Ltd., of Boston, who agreed that the participative style comes more naturally to women. However, she wrote, "the Japanese, a very male-oriented culture, seem to have perfected the art of participatory management as a critical feature of their highly productive corporations . . . [We need to build] cultures that affirm diversity of styles in managers."

Source: J. B. Rosener, "Ways Women Lead," *Harvard Business Review* 68 (May–June 1990), pp. 103–11; "Debate: Ways Men and Women Lead," *Harvard Business Review* 69 (January–February 1991), pp. 150–60; A. Eagly, S. Karom, and M. Makhijani, "Gender and the Effectiveness of Leaders: A Meta-Analysis," *Psychological Bulletin,* 1995, pp. 125–45. ●

Men are said to be more
effective in military settings
while women work better in
educational, social service, and
government organizations.
Illinois Senator Carol Moseley
Braun's effectiveness would
seem to bear out this
hypothesis.
(AP/Wide World Photos)

SITUATIONAL APPROACH TO LEADERSHIP

According to proponents of the **situational approach** to leadership, universally important
traits and behaviors don't exist. They believe effective leader behaviors vary from situation
to situation. *The leader should first analyze the situation and then decide what to do.* In
other words, look before you lead.

DEMOCRACY VERSUS DICTATORSHIP

A head nurse in a hospital described her leadership style to an interviewer:

> My leadership style is a mix of all styles. On some things I'm a dictator; I tell subordinates
> what to do. I'm a role model; I lead by example. In this environment I normally let people
> participate. . .
>
> I very much like the participatory idea, but in a code blue situation where a patient is
> dying I automatically become very autocratic: "You do this; you do that; you, out of the room;
> you all better be quiet; you, get Dr. Mansfield." The staff tell me that's the only time they see
> me like that. In an emergency like that, you don't have time to vote, talk a lot, or yell at each
> other. It's time for someone to set up the order.
>
> I remember one time, one person saying, "Wait a minute, I want to do this." He wanted
> to do the mouth-to-mouth resuscitation. I knew the person behind him did it better, so I said,
> "No, he does it." This fellow told me later that I hurt him so badly to yell that in front of all the
> staff and doctors. It was like he wasn't good enough. So I explained it to him: that's the way it
> is. A life was on the line. I couldn't give you warm fuzzies. I couldn't make you look good
> because you didn't have the skills to give the very best to that patient who wasn't breathing
> anymore.
>
> If anyone ever tells me that they're a democratic type of leader, I don't want them. In an
> emergency, if you're a democratic leader, I wouldn't want you leading the team. There come
> times when you can't stop, vote, or have participation on what's to be done. If you're doing
> that all the time, then you aren't a leader.

Source: J. Wall, *Bosses* (Lexington, Mass.: Lexington Books, 1986), pp. 103–4.

This head nurse has her own intuitive situational approach to leadership. She knows the
potential advantages of the participatory approach to decision making, but she also knows
that in some circumstances she must make decisions on her own.

The first situational model of leadership was proposed in 1958 by Tannenbaum and
Schmidt. In their classic *Harvard Business Review* article, these authors described how

managers should consider three factors before deciding how to lead: forces in the manager, forces in the subordinate, and forces in the situation.[31] *Forces in the manager* include the manager's personal values, inclinations, feelings of security, and confidence in subordinates. *Forces in the subordinate* include the employee's knowledge and experience, readiness to assume responsibility for decision making, interest in the task or problem, and understanding and acceptance of the organization's goals. *Forces in the situation* include the type of leadership style the organization values, the degree to which the group works as a unit effectively, the problem itself and the type of information needed to solve it, and the amount of time the leader has to make the decision.

Consider which of these forces make an autocratic style most appropriate and which dictate a democratic, participative style. By engaging in this exercise, you are constructing a situational theory of leadership.

Although the Tannenbaum and Schmidt article was published almost a half-century ago, most of its arguments remain valid. Since that time, other situational models have emerged. We will focus here on path-goal theory; the others are summarized in the Appendix to this chapter.

Path-Goal Theory

Perhaps the most generally useful situational model of leadership effectiveness is path-goal theory. Developed by Robert House, **path-goal theory** gets its name from its concern with how leaders influence followers' perceptions of their work goals and the paths they follow toward goal attainment.[32]

The key situational factors in path-goal theory are (1) personal characteristics of followers and (2) environmental pressures and demands with which subordinates must cope to attain their work goals. These factors determine which leadership behaviors are most appropriate.

The four pertinent leadership behaviors are (1) **directive leadership,** a form of task performance–oriented behavior; (2) **supportive leadership,** a form of group maintenance–oriented behavior; (3) **participative leadership,** or decision style; and (4) **achievement-oriented leadership,** or behaviors geared toward motivating people, such as setting challenging goals and rewarding good performance.

These situational factors and leader behaviors are merged in Figure 14.3. As you can see, appropriate leader behaviors—based on characteristics of followers and the work environment—lead to effective performance.

The theory also specifies *which* follower and environmental features are important. There are three key follower characteristics. *Authoritarianism* is the degree to which individuals respect, admire, and defer to authority. *Locus of control* is the extent to which individuals see the environment as responsive to their own behavior. People with an *internal* locus of control believe that what happens to them is their own doing; people with an *external* locus of control believe that it is just luck or fate. Finally, *ability* is people's beliefs about their own abilities to do their assigned jobs.

Path-goal theory states that these personal characteristics determine the appropriateness of various leadership styles. For example, the theory makes the following propositions:

- A directive leadership style is more appropriate for highly authoritarian people, because such people respect authority.

FIGURE 14.3

The path-goal
framework

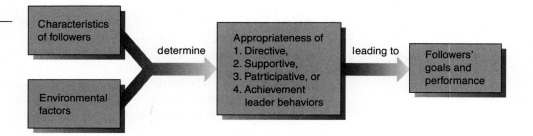

- A participative leadership style is more appropriate for people who have an internal locus of control, because these individuals prefer to have more influence over their own lives.

- A directive style is more appropriate when subordinates' ability is low. The directive style helps people understand what has to be done.

Appropriate leadership style is also determined by three important environmental factors: people's tasks, the formal authority system of the organization, and the primary work group.

- Directive leadership is inappropriate if tasks already are well structured.

- If the task and the authority or rule system are dissatisfying, directive leadership will create greater dissatisfaction.

- If the task or authority system is dissatisfying, supportive leadership is especially appropriate, because it offers one positive source of gratification in an otherwise negative situation.

- If the primary work group provides social support to its members, supportive leadership is less important.

Path-goal theory offers many more propositions. In general, the theory suggests that the functions of the leader are to (1) make the path to work goals easier to travel by providing coaching and direction; (2) reduce frustrating barriers to goal attainment; and (3) increase opportunities for personal satisfaction by increasing payoffs to people for achieving performance goals.

How best to do these things depends on your people and on the work situation. Again: Analyze, then adapt your style accordingly.

CONTEMPORARY PERSPECTIVES ON LEADERSHIP

So far, you have learned the major classic approaches to understanding leadership. Now we will discuss a number of new developments that are revolutionizing our understanding of this important aspect of management. These developments include substitutes for leadership, charismatic leadership, transformational leadership, and post-heroic leadership.

SUBSTITUTES FOR LEADERSHIP

Sometimes leaders don't have to lead—or, they can't lead. The situation may be one in which leadership is unnecessary or has little impact. **Substitutes for leadership** can provide the same influence on people that leaders otherwise would have.

Certain follower, task, and organizational factors are substitutes for task performance–oriented and group maintenance–oriented leader behaviors.[33] For example, group maintenance behaviors will have less impact if people already have a closely knit group, they have a professional orientation, the job is intrinsically satisfying, or there is great physical distance between leader and followers. Physicians who are strongly concerned with professional conduct, enjoy their work, and work independently do not need social support from hospital administrators.

Task performance leadership is less important if people have a lot of experience and ability, feedback is supplied to them directly from the task or by computer, or the rules and procedures are rigid. If these factors are operating, the leader does not have to tell people what to do or how well they are performing.

The concept of substitutes for leadership does more than indicate when a leader's attempts at influence will and will not work. It provides useful and practical prescriptions for how to manage more efficiently. If the manager can develop the work situation to the point where a number of these substitutes for leadership are operating, less time will need to be spent in direct attempts to influence people. The leader will be free to spend more time on other important roles.

CHARISMATIC LEADERSHIP

Like many great leaders, former president Ronald Reagan had charisma. Lee Iacocca of Chrysler, Thomas Watson of IBM, Alfred Sloan of General Motors, and Steve Jobs of NeXt Computers are good examples of charismatic leaders in industry.

What *is* charisma, and how does one acquire it? Charisma is a rather evasive concept; it is easy to spot but hard to define. According to one definition, "Charisma packs an emotional wallop for followers above and beyond ordinary esteem, affection, admiration, and trust. . . . The charismatic is an idolized hero, a messiah and a savior. . . ."[34] As you can see from this quotation, many people, particularly North Americans, value charisma in their leaders. But some people associate it with the negative charisma of Hitler.[35]

Charismatic leaders are dominant and self-confident and have a strong conviction in the moral righteousness of their beliefs.[36] They strive to create an aura of competence and success and communicate high expectations for and confidence in followers.

The charismatic leader articulates ideological goals. Martin Luther King had a dream for a better world, and John F. Kennedy spoke of landing a human on the moon. In other words, such leaders have a vision. The charismatic leader also arouses a sense of excitement and adventure. He or she is an eloquent speaker who exhibits superior verbal skills, which helps communicate the vision and motivate followers. Walt Disney was able to mesmerize people with his storytelling, had enormous creative talent, and instilled in his organization strong values of good taste, risk taking, and innovation.[37]

Leaders who possess these characteristics inspire in their followers trust, confidence, unquestioning acceptance, willing obedience, emotional involvement, affection for the leader, and higher performance.

TRANSFORMATIONAL LEADERSHIP

Charisma contributes to transformational leadership. **Transformational leaders** change things from what could be to what is; that is, they translate a vision into reality. They get people to transcend their personal interests for the sake of the group. They generate excitement and revitalize organizations. At Hewlett-Packard, the ability to generate excitement is an explicit criterion for selecting managers.

The transformational process moves beyond the more traditional *transactional* approach to leadership.[38] The concept of transactional leadership views management as a series of business transactions in which leaders use their legitimate, reward, and coercive powers to give commands and exchange rewards for services rendered. Unlike transformational leadership, transactional leadership is dispassionate; it does not excite, transform, empower, or inspire people to focus on the interests of the group or organization.

Transformational leaders generate excitement in three primary ways.[39] First, they are *charismatic,* as described earlier. Second, they give their followers *individualized attention.* Transformational leaders delegate challenging work, increase people's responsibilities, keep lines of communication open, and provide one-on-one mentoring to develop their people. They do not treat everyone alike, because not everyone *is* alike.

Third, transformational leaders are *intellectually stimulating.* They arouse in their followers an awareness of problems and potential solutions. They articulate the organization's opportunities, threats, strengths, and weaknesses. They stir the imagination and generate insights. Therefore, problems are recognized and high-quality solutions are identified and implemented with the full commitment of followers.

Four skills or strategies contribute to transformational leadership.[40] First, transformational leaders *have a vision*—a goal, an agenda, or a results-orientation that grabs people's attention. Second, they *communicate their vision;* through words, manner, or symbolism, they relate a compelling image of the ultimate goal. Third, transformational leaders *build trust* by being consistent, dependable, and persistent. They position themselves clearly by choosing a direction and staying with it, thus projecting organizational integrity. Finally, they have a *positive self-regard.* They do not feel self-important or complacent; rather, they recognize their personal strengths, compensate for their weaknesses, nurture their skills and continually develop their talents, and know how to learn from failure. They strive for success rather than merely trying to avoid failure.

Transformational leadership has been identified in industry, the military, and politics.[41] Examples of transformational leaders include Henry Ford, who achieved his vision of an affordable, mass-produced automobile; General George Patton, who transformed the Third Army; Lee Iacocca, who carried Chrysler from bankruptcy to success; and Jan Carlzon, who turned Scandinavian Air System (SAS) from an $8 million loss to a $71 million profit (on sales of $2 billion) in a little over a year.[42]

POST-HEROIC LEADERSHIP

A common view of leaders is that they are heroes. Phenomenally talented, they step forward in difficult times and save the day. But in these complex times, it is foolhardy to assume that a great top executive can solve all problems by himself or herself.[43] No one person can deal with all of today's rapid-fire changes, competitive threats, and escalating customer demands.

Therefore, it is a big mistake to cruise along assuming Arnold Schwarzenegger will emerge and make things right. Implicit in this way of thinking is the belief that a single leader can save the firm. But effective leadership must permeate the organization, not reside in one or two superstars at the top.

The leader's job becomes one of spreading leadership abilities throughout the firm:[44] Make people responsible for their own performance. Create an environment in which each person can figure out what needs to be done and then do it well. Point the way and clear the path so people can succeed. Give them the credit they deserve. Make heroes out of *them*.

To do this, you can paint a clear picture of great performance, and engage individuals— their hearts, minds, and hands—in making the business better. This requires the leader to coach and develop individual capability and competence, and to challenge every individual to continually improve her or his abilities and make greater contributions.

Thus, the leader must be willing to visualize greatness, and take action to achieve it— and expect the same from everyone else in the organization. *Everyone* needs to think like a complete businessperson—like an entrepreneur, recalling Chapter 9. And everyone must be willing and able to take action on behalf of the business.

METAPHORS FOR LEADERSHIP

*A*s noted above, our traditional view of leadership is of heroes who come to the fore in times of crisis. But a newer view is that the leader continually engages in subtler, more important tasks like building organizations in which people continually expand their capabilities. In other words, leaders encourage and facilitate continual learning. Three metaphors help describe the leader's role in helping people learn: leaders as designers, stewards, and teachers.

The leader as *designer:* What is the most important role of the leader of an ocean liner? The captain, who gives the orders? The navigator, who sets the direction? The engineer, who provides energy to make the ship move forward? Perhaps the most important role is that of designer. Even with orders, direction, and energy, the ship won't reach its destination if it doesn't *work*. The designer creates an organization that works. This role begins with establishing the vision, values, and mission of the organization, and creating an environment where people can do their jobs successfully and work together effectively toward achieving goals.

The leader as *steward:* A steward is a leader who exercises responsible care over the organization that is entrusted to him or her. Good leaders have a deep sense of purpose and destiny, and become stewards of their vision. They communicate the overarching explanation of why they do what they do, how their organization needs to grow, and how its development is part of a greater purpose. They convince people that their organization is a vehicle for bringing learning and change into society. They bring personal and universal meaning into the organization, and into people's work.

The leader as *teacher:* A teacher helps people achieve a richer and more accurate view of the world. Retired Herman Miller CEO Max de Pree said, "The first responsibility of a leader is defining reality." The leader as teacher helps people understand the forces shaping change, helps them learn, and inspires them to seek the truth.

Source: P. Senge, *The Fifth Discipline* (New York: Doubleday Currency, 1990). ●

A NOTE ON COURAGE

To be a good leader, you need to create a vision of greatness for your unit, identify and manage allies, adversaries, and fencesitters, and also have the *courage* required to live out your vision. This does not mean you should commit career suicide by alienating too many powerful people; it does mean taking reasonable risks, with the good of the firm at heart, in order to produce constructive change.

Specifically, some acts of courage required to fulfill your vision will include:[45] (1) seeing things as they are and facing them head-on, making no excuses and harboring no wishful illusions; (2) saying what needs to be said to those who need to hear it; and (3) putting up with, and persisting despite, resistance, criticism, abuse, and setbacks. Courage includes stating the realities, even when they are harsh, and publicly stating what you will do to help and what you want from others. This means laying the cards on the table honestly: Here is what I want from you . . . What do you want from me?[46]

DEVELOPING YOUR LEADERSHIP SKILLS

If you want to be a leader you need to learn how to do the things leaders do: the leader behaviors we have been discussing. All of these are easier said than done, but they separate leaders from the crowd.

As with other things, you must work at *developing* your leadership abilities. Great musicians and great athletes don't become great on natural gifts alone. They also pay their dues by practicing, learning, and sacrificing.

How do you go about developing your leadership abilities? In general, start by getting out of your "comfort zone." That is, don't seek out and remain in easy, nonchallenging situations; enter, create, and face situations that require you to adapt and change. This is the best way to learn, and it is the way great executives learn.

■

John Johnson, founder and CEO of Johnson Publishing, which includes *Ebony* magazine, personifies the leader as steward—someone who exercises responsible care over the organization that is entrusted to him.
(Chicago Tribune *photo by Nancy Stone)*

More specifically, here are some developmental experiences you should seek:[47]

- *Assignments:* building something from nothing; fixing or turning around a failing operation; project or task force responsibilities; international assignments.
- *Other people:* exposure to positive role models; visibility to others; working with people of diverse backgrounds.
- *Hardships:* overcoming ideas that fail and deals that collapse; confronting others' performance problems; breaking out of a career rut.
- *Other events:* formal courses; challenging job experiences; supervision of others; experiences outside work.

These experiences do not guarantee that you will develop into an effective leader. But without them, your development will surely be constrained. Seek these experiences; expect mistakes and don't beat yourself up over them; and take time to learn from your experiences.

KEY TERMS

achievement-oriented leadership, p. 364
autocratic leaders, p. 359
behavioral approach, p. 359
charismatic leaders, p. 366
democratic leaders, p. 359
directive leadership, p. 364
group maintenance behaviors, p. 359
laissez-faire, p. 360
participation-in-decision-making dimension, p. 359
participative leadership, p. 364
path-goal theory, p. 364

power, p. 356
relationship-oriented behavior, p. 361
situational approach, p. 363
substitutes for leadership, p. 365
supportive leadership, p. 364
task-oriented behavior, p. 361
task performance behaviors, p. 359
trait approach, p. 358
transformational leaders, p. 366
vision, p. 354

SUMMARY OF LEARNING OBJECTIVES

Now that you have studied Chapter 14, you should know:

What it means to be a leader.

A leader is one who influences others to attain goals. Leaders orchestrate change, set direction, and motivate people to overcome obstacles and move the organization toward its ideal future.

How vision helps you be a better leader.

Outstanding leaders have vision. A vision is a mental image that goes beyond the ordinary and perhaps beyond what others thought possible. The vision provides the direction in which the leader wants the organization to move.

How to understand and use power.

Having power and using it appropriately are essential attributes of an effective leader. Managers have five potential sources of power: legitimate, reward, coercive, referent, and expert. These power sources must be perceived by others and are potentially available to leaders at all organizational levels.

The personal traits and skills of effective leaders.

The old idea that leaders have certain traits or skills fell into disfavor but lately has been resurrected. Important leader characteristics include drive, leadership motivation, integrity, self-confidence, and knowledge of the business. Perhaps the most important skill is the ability to accurately perceive the situation and then change behavior accordingly.

The behaviors that will make you a better leader.

Important leader behaviors include task performance, group maintenance, and participation in decision making. Exhibiting more rather than fewer of these behaviors will enhance your effectiveness in the long run. Path-goal theory assesses characteristics of the followers, the leader, and the situation; it then indicates the appropriateness of directive, supportive, participative, or achievement-oriented leadership behaviors.

What it means to be a charismatic and transformational leader.

To have charisma is to be dominant and self-confident, to have a strong conviction of the righteousness of your beliefs, to create an aura of competence and success, and to communicate high expectations for and confidence in your followers. Charisma is one component of transformational leadership. Transformational leaders change things from what could be to what is; that is, they translate a vision into reality. They do this through charisma, individualized attention to followers, intellectual stimulation, forming and communicating their vision, building trust, and having positive self-regard.

How to further your own leadership development.

You can develop your own leadership skills not only by understanding what effective leadership is all about, but also by seeking out challenging developmental experiences. Such important life experiences come about from taking challenging assignments, through exposure in working with other people, by overcoming hardships and failures, by taking formal courses, and by other actions.

DISCUSSION QUESTIONS

1. Develop your own definition of leadership and compare it with the characteristics of leadership described in the chapter.
2. Is there a difference between effective management and effective leadership? Why or why not?
3. Identify someone you think is an effective leader. What traits and skills does this individual possess that make him or her effective?
4. Do you think most managers can be transformational leaders? Why or why not?
5. In your own words, define courage. What is the role of courage in leadership? Give examples of acts of leadership you consider courageous.
6. Do you think men and women differ in their leadership styles? If so, how? Do men and/or women prefer different styles in their bosses? What evidence do you have for your answers?

7. Who are your heroes? Try to identify some traditional heroes and also some that are "post-heroic." What makes them heroes, and what can you learn from them in general? What can you learn from them about leadership in particular?
8. Assess yourself as a leader based on what you have read in this chapter. What are your strengths and weaknesses?
9. Identify the developmental experiences you have had that may have strengthened your ability to lead. What did those experiences teach you? Also identify some developmental experiences you need to acquire, and how you will seek them. Be specific.

CONCLUDING CASE

ROBERT ALLEN AND AT&T

Robert Allen has the extraordinary challenge of leading one of the five largest companies in the world. The scope of his responsibilities extends far beyond running huge AT&T, which has 300,000 employees and revenues exceeding $75 billion. More than most executives, he must predict and meet long-term threats and seize opportunities that are massive in scale.

The federal government broke up AT&T in the early 1980s and split its telephone monopoly into seven regional operating companies. AT&T was left with the long-distance business, Western Electric, the telephone equipment maker, and AT&T Bell Laboratories. Since divestiture, AT&T has lost about 25 percent of the long-distance market to MCI, Sprint, and others.

Allen is a career telephone company executive who became CEO in 1988. He has responded to aggressive competitors and the impact of computers on communications with daring, high-profile decisions. Allen has vast ambitions: he thinks the company can more than double its revenues to $150 billion or $200 billion in the first decade of the new century. His vision: "To bring people together and give them easy access to each other and the information they want and need—anything, anywhere."

To help attain that vision, AT&T is trying to build the first truly nationwide cellular telephone network. Managers at AT&T no longer talk about telephones; they talk of two-way video, voice recognition, and intelligent messaging. The networks envisioned at the company will handle services for work, education, entertainment, and shopping. The goal is to have a complete and ubiquitous network, of perfect quality.

Allen's moves have included:

- Strengthening union ties. Unions now sit on planning committees at corporate and plant levels.

- Emphasizing cooperation among AT&T's mostly independent business units. Cross-unit teams search constantly for new opportunities. Allen also has made the businesses more customer-focused and accountable for results.

- Hiring and promoting strong people, and keeping them focused on company goals. Allen allows a team including the leaders of the major business groups to run the company day-to-day.

- Promoting values that Allen refers to as "our common bond." The values include respect for individuals, dedication to help-

Robert Allen, AT&T CEO, is a man with a vision: "To bring people together and give them easy access to each other and the information they want and need—anything, anywhere."
(Courtesy AT&T)

ing customers, adhering to the highest ethical standards, teamwork, and innovation. AT&T's managers now say that in discussions, Allen penetrates emotions, not just intellect. They describe the company as far less political than before, because people share values and a vision.

- Making major strategic acquisitions consistent with the vision.

AT&T spent $12 billion for McCaw Cellular Communications in late 1994. With this move, one of the world's oldest, biggest corporations, known for its old-time bureaucracy, bought a small upstart firm with a feisty, entrepreneurial, vastly different culture. In acquiring McCaw, AT&T should gain a place in wireless communications for the 21st century. The merger's success is essential to AT&T's strategy.

The two companies admire each other, their businesses fit naturally, and they have the common goal of anywhere, anytime communications. People at McCaw are excited about the possibilities created by the combination. But they are not happy about losing their independence and having to work under bureaucratic constraints. They also miss their old boss.

Speaking about mammoth AT&T, Allen said, "It's not easy to change a culture that was very control oriented and top-down. We're trying to create an atmosphere of turning the organization upside down, putting the customers on top. The people close to the customer should be doing the key decision making."

QUESTIONS

1. How will Allen's vision help AT&T?

2. What other aspects of effective leadership do you see in Robert Allen?

3. Can AT&T get an infusion of entrepreneurial spirit from McCaw?

4. What actions should Allen take from here?

5. If you were a small-business owner, what could you learn about leadership from role models like Robert Allen?

Sources: D. Kirkpatrick, "Could AT&T Rule the World?" *Fortune,* May 17, 1993, pp. 55–66; A. Kupfer, "AT&T's $12 Billion Cellular Dream," *Fortune,* December 12, 1994, pp. 100–112.

VIDEO CASE

LEADERSHIP AND MOTIVATION AT BERNARD WELDING EQUIPMENT COMPANY

Leadership is a concept that is frequently discussed, but whose meaning is unclear. What distinguishes a manager from a leader? What is power? How can a manager develop leadership skills and use power in a manner that will motivate and inspire employees to go beyond their job description? In the workplace, leadership can be defined as the application of personal attributes and abilities, such as insight, energy, and knowledge, to create a shared vision of the future. A manager must deal with the pressures of the moment, and is responsible for organizing and controlling the workforce. The means by which a manager creates lasting meaning or purpose for employees defines the manager's "leadership style."

Bernard Welding Equipment Company has garnered a large share of the world's welding accessories business. The company's success may be attributed to the application of a new style of leadership, and a quality management approach to every stage of its operation. Reflecting on the important role of leadership at Bernard, company president Pat Cunningham said, "The leader of a company becomes the personality of the company. Very often, in the old days, he was an autocratic person. If you view old-time manufacturing, you've got one guy in the corner office barking out orders and people running around doing his bidding day in and day out. Well, in today's environment, where people are much more informed and communications can happen much more rapidly, that style of management is no longer effective."

Jim Therrien, Bernard's vice president of operations, noted in the video that his company began a continuous quality improvement journey in the early 1990s. The first step in the journey involved reviewing and refining the company's mission. Therrien explained the role of leadership in the mission review process: "The only constant in life is change, and the same is true in business. People who can capture change and run with it will be tremendously successful. Those that don't won't be in tune with the ever-changing markets and will be left behind. If management is efficiently climbing the ladder, then leadership is making sure the ladder is against the right wall. Our right wall is the customer need. Starting with that, and backing into the plant and moving through the organization gives you the wherewithal and the master plan to effect the kinds of changes that we've had at Bernard. As people become part of a team, they feel like they're accomplishing something. When people are in that mode, it's very easy to lead them in the right direction. And the right direction is always based on what the customer need is. And when you're filling those customer needs, there are fewer of those complaint calls, there are fewer people coming down on people and more people being up with people and helping to move things in the proper direction."

After reviewing the mission, the second stage of Bernard's continuous improvement process was to examine its manufac-turing operations. The company's assembly line was improved through the participative leadership style. Training for both the managers and the workforce was key to the change. Managers needed to learn how to delegate and empower their workforce, and the workers needed to learn how to accept their new responsibilities.

Production supervisor Kathy Yates is enthusiastic about the changes in the workforce that resulted from Bernard's new participative leadership style: "In the past when we had problems on the assembly line the operators would come to me and ask, 'What should we do?' We're doing things a lot differently now. When problems arise on the assembly line we get together as a group, we talk it out, and we decide what the best solution is to that problem. We didn't do that in the past. We're more of a team effort now and it really shows up in the results. Our production is up, our quality is up, the morale of the people is up. It really has paid off."

Bernard's continuous improvement process has also focused on reducing costs. Using employee-driven quality improvement teams, the company changed its practice of maintaining a supply of precut, assembled cables for its welding guns because it incurred unnecessarily high inventory costs. Bernard now uses a delayed, differentiated quick response system. With this new approach, the cable needed to fill each order is cut to the customer's specifications from the spools of cable as needed. Reduced inventory lowers costs and benefits the customer through lower prices and quicker turnaround times.

Workers on the shop floor have embraced their new decision-making authority. Randy Warren, manufacturing engineer, noted another example of employee-led cost reduction: "We've been able to reduce set-up time across 65 percent of our head volume. A good example is our head forming process. A process that used to take a good set-up person 30 to 40 minutes to accomplish can now be done by the operator in less than a minute. We recognize that our most important resource is our people out there. By empowering the people to make decisions on their own we've been able to generate a lot of input right at the floor level where the process takes place. These are the experts in the manufacture of our products. They see things that we can't anticipate on the tooling side or on the process side."

Bernard's new participatory leadership style has motivated the employees to reach new levels of quality and customer satisfaction, as Kathy Yates elaborated: "We find that, on a daily basis, when problems come up, we get together as a team and we solve them. I have found that [the line workers] are the experts; they are the ones who are out there building this product day after day after day. They know more about the product than I do. So, when problems arise, we get together, we sit down, we talk it out, we brainstorm it, whatever it takes to come up with a solution. I think this has really helped the quality of our product. I think people are dedicated to their work areas, and they feel an ownership. They're very concerned about what they're putting out and how they're doing it. If they have a question, they go to whomever they need to talk to get the answer and they want it now; they're very strong on that. They feel that they've got to make the highest-quality product."

Therrien explained how his own leadership style has changed in the continuous quality improvement culture: "As I've transitioned from managing to leading in this organization, and I think the same holds true for most managers here, I've learned to listen better than I've ever listened before. I only thought I was listening. People have a lot to say. You don't always want to hear it. But when you sit quietly, and gather data from many directions, then the decisions that you make are better decisions because they're based on more information. When you have everyone in one room, then you are going to hear from all sides, and you will gather information in the same manner that it goes through the organization. Most large organizations are vertically structured, and most of the information that the customer needs, and the product, goes through horizontally. Once you have your people in tune with that, the product and the information flow moves horizontally, you will be able to look down on it and see where the bottlenecks are. Then you can bring your resources to bear to help the people do a better job."

Cunningham summarized the new leadership style being practiced at Bernard: "One of the benefits of the longer-term view that we've taken of improving the managerial capability of our people is their ability to make better decisions on improving productivity in a given product line. I can recall, some years ago, in sitting in meetings with our people, they looked to me and a couple of others to answer the key questions and communicate the direction of the company, to solve all of the problems, to take just about everything that needed to be decided and decide it. That doesn't make sense. For the CEO of a business or the top manager of a fairly sizable organization to think that he has the knowledge and capability to make all of the minute decisions that need to be made on a daily basis is kind of foolhardy. That may have been appropriate in a very small business 50 years ago, but it surely isn't appropriate in today's environment. We now bring customers and distributors right into our factories and sit them down with employees and let them communicate, let them get a better understanding of exactly what's going on in our business and what the needs of our customers are right from the horse's mouth. We provide each of our employees with access to all of our financial information regularly on exactly how this company is doing. Our employees actually have access to every piece of financial data that I have. And I'm proud to say that I think it's helped them become more informed employees, who are willing to recognize faster when change needs to be made. I think that our growth in our industry in the last couple of years, in terms of sales, earnings, and profit margins, and all the other places where you can measure the financial performance of a company, has outstripped all of our competitors as best we can judge that. And in many cases we can judge that very accurately. We think we do a better job, and the numbers are starting to prove that we do."

CRITICAL THINKING QUESTIONS

1. Continuous quality improvement processes, like the approach being used at Bernard, call for authority and power to be pushed down from the management to employee level. Why do you think this is an important part of continuous improvement?

2. Bernard President Pat Cunningham stated that all employees have access to every bit of financial data pertinent to the company's performance. What are the possible advantages of sharing these data? What are the possible disadvantages?

3. Jim Therrien, vice president of operations, said that he has learned to listen better to employees. What role do you think listening should play in leadership? What steps can you take to become a more effective listener in your life?

EXPERIENTIAL EXERCISES

14.1 Power and Influence

Objective

To explore the nature of power and influence, and your attitudes toward different kinds of power and influence.

POWER AND INFLUENCE WORKSHEET

A. Power

A number of people have made statements about power and winning (e.g., P. T. Barnum, Mao Tse-tung, Leo Durocher, Lord Action, Vince Lombardi). Some of them are listed in the table that follows. Indicate how you feel about each of the statements by circling number 1 if you strongly disagree, number 5 if you strongly agree, and so on.

	Strongly Disagree	Disagree	Neutral	Agree	Strongly Agree
Winning is everything.	1	2	3	4	5
Nice guys finish last.	1	2	3	4	5
There can only be one winner.	1	2	3	4	5
There's a sucker born every minute.	1	2	3	4	5
You can't completely trust anyone.	1	2	3	4	5
All power rests at the end of the gun.	1	2	3	4	5
Power seekers are greedy and can't be trusted.	1	2	3	4	5
Power corrupts; absolute power corrupts absolutely.	1	2	3	4	5
You get a much power as you pay for.	1	2	3	4	5

B. Influence

During the past week or so you have come in contact with many people. Some have influenced you positively (turned you on), some negatively (turned you off). Try to recall recent experiences with employers, peers, teachers, parents, clergy, and the like who may have influenced you in some way. Then try to think about how and why they influenced you as they did.

1. One the following table, list the names of all those who influenced you during the past week or so according to the kind of power that person used. The same person's name may appear under more than one type of social power if that person used multiple power bases. Also, indicate whether the influence was positive (+) or negative (–).

Social Power Base	Names and Whether (+) or (–)
Coercive	_____
Monetary	_____
Legitimate	_____
Skill/expertise	_____
Affection	_____
Respectable/rectitude	_____

2. After examining your list, check (✓) the questions below.

	Yes	No
a. Was there one person who had + marks appearing under several social power bases?	—	—
b. Was there one person who had – marks appearing under several social power bases?	—	—
c. Did you find that most of the people with + marks tended to fall under the same power bases?	—	—
d. Did you find that most of the people with – marks tended to fall under the same power bases?	—	—

3. From your answers to the last two questions list which social power bases you found to be positive (+) and which you found to be negative (−).

+   −

_____

_____

_____

_____

_____

Do you think you personally prefer to use those power bases you listed under + when you try to influence people? Do you actually use them?

C. Power and Influence

From the table in Part B, find the one person who you think had the strongest positive influence on you (Person 1), and the one who had the strongest negative influence (Person 2). These are most likely the persons whose names appear most frequently.

In the following table, place a 1 on the line for each statement that best indicates how you think Person 1 would respond to that statement. Put a 2 on the line for each statement that reflects how you think Person 2 would respond to that item.

	Strongly Disagree	Disagree	Neutral	Agree	Strongly Agree
Winning is everything.	—	—	—	—	—
Nice guys finish last.	—	—	—	—	—
There can only be one winner.	—	—	—	—	—
There's a sucker born every minute.	—	—	—	—	—
You can't completely trust anyone.	—	—	—	—	—
All power rests at the end of the gun.	—	—	—	—	—
Power seekers are greedy and can't be trusted.	—	—	—	—	—
Power corrupts; absolute power corrupts absolutely.	—	—	—	—	—
You get a much power as you pay for.	—	—	—	—	—

Now compare your responses in Part A to those in Part C. Do you more closely resemble Person 1 or Person 2? Do you prefer to use the kinds of power that person uses? Which kinds of power do you use most frequently? Which do you use least frequently? When do you feel you have the greatest power? When do you have the least power? How do these answers compare to what you found in Part B3?

Excepted from Lawrence R. Jauch, Arthur G. Bedian, Sally A. Coltin, and William F. Glueck, *The Managerial Experience: Cases, Exercises, and Readings,* 4th ed. Copyright ©1986 by The Dryden Press. Reprinted by permission of the publisher.

14.2 Evaluating Your Leadership Style

Objectives

1. To examine your personal style of leadership.
2. To study the nature of the leadership process.
3. To identify ways to improve or modify your leadership style.

Instructions

1. Working alone, complete and score the Leadership Style Survey.
2. In small groups, exchange scores, compute average scores, and develop responses to the discussion questions.

3. After the class reconvenes, group spokespersons present group findings.

Discussion Questions

1. In what ways did your experience or lack of experience influence your responses to the survey?

2. In what ways did student scores and student responses to survey test items agree? In what ways did they disagree?
3. What do you think accounts for variances in student leadership attitudes?
4. How can students make constructive use of the survey results?

LEADERSHIP STYLE SURVEY

This survey describes various aspects of leadership behavior. To measure your leadership style, respond to each statement according to the way you would act (or think you would act) if you were a work group leader.

	Always	Frequently	Occasionally	Seldom	Never
1. I would allow team members the freedom to do their jobs in their own way.	5	4	3	2	1
2. I would make important decisions on my own initiative without consulting the workers.	5	4	3	2	1
3. I would allow the team members to make their own decisions.	5	4	3	2	1
4. I would not try to socialize with the workers.	5	4	3	2	1
5. I would allow team members to do their jobs as they see fit.	5	4	3	2	1
6. I would consider myself to be the group's spokesperson.	5	4	3	2	1
7. I would be warm, friendly, and approachable.	5	4	3	2	1
8. I would be sure that the workers understand and follow all the rules and regulations.	5	4	3	2	1
9. I would demonstrate a real concern for the workers' welfare.	5	4	3	2	1
10. I would be the one to decide what is to be done and how it is to be done.	5	4	3	2	1
11. I would delegate authority to the workers.	5	4	3	2	1
12. I would urge the workers to meet production quotas.	5	4	3	2	1
13. I would trust the workers to use good judgment in decision making.	5	4	3	2	1
14. I would assign specific tasks to specific people.	5	4	3	2	1
15. I would let the workers establish their own work pace.	5	4	3	2	1
16. I would not feel that I have to explain my decisions to workers.	5	4	3	2	1
17. I would try to make each worker feel that his or her contribution is important.	5	4	3	2	1
18. I would establish the work schedules.	5	4	3	2	1
19. I would encourage workers to get involved in setting work goals.	5	4	3	2	1
20. I would be action oriented and results oriented.	5	4	3	2	1
21. I would get the workers involved in making decisions.	5	4	3	2	1
22. I would outline needed changes and monitor action closely.	5	4	3	2	1
23. I would help the group achieve consensus on important changes.	5	4	3	2	1
24. I would supervise closely to ensure that standards are met.	5	4	3	2	1
25. I would consistently reinforce good work.	5	4	3	2	1
26. I would nip problems in the bud.	5	4	3	2	1
27. I would consult the group before making decisions.	5	4	3	2	1

CHAPTER APPENDIX

Fiedler's Contingency Model

Fiedler's **contingency model of leadership effectiveness** states that effectiveness depends on two factors: the personal style of the leader and the degree to which the situation gives the leader power, control, and influence over the situation.[48] Figure 14.A.1 illustrates the contingency model. The upper half of the figure shows the situational analysis, and the lower half indicates the appropriate style. In the upper portion, three questions are used to analyze the situation:

1. Are *leader-member relations* good or poor? (To what extent is the leader accepted and supported by group members?)
2. Is the *task* structured or unstructured? (To what extent do group members know what their goals are and how to accomplish them?)
3. Is the leader's *position power* strong or weak? (To what extent does the leader have the authority to reward and punish?)

These three sequential questions create a decision tree in which a situation is classified into one of eight categories. The lower the category number, the more favorable the situation is for the leader; the higher the number, the less favorable the situation. Thus, situation 1 is the best: Relations are good, task structure is high, and power is high. In the least favorable situation, 8, relations are poor, tasks lack structure, and the leader's power is weak.

Different situations dictate different leadership styles. Fiedler considers two leadership styles. **Task-motivated leadership** places primary emphasis on completing the task. **Relationship-motivated leadership** emphasizes maintaining good interpersonal relationships. These leadership styles correspond to task performance and group maintenance leader behaviors, respectively.

The lower part of Figure 14.A.1 indicates which style is situationally appropriate. For situations 1, 2, 3, and 8, a task-motivated leadership style is more effective. For situations 4 through 7, relationship-motivated leadership is more appropriate.

Fiedler's theory was not always supported by research. It was quite controversial in academic circles; among other arguable things, it assumed that leaders cannot change their styles but must be assigned to situations that suit their styles. However, the model has withstood the test of time and still receives attention. Most important, it initiated and continues to emphasize the importance of finding a fit between the situation and the leader's style.

Hersey and Blanchard's Situational Theory

Hersey and Blanchard developed an important situational model that added another factor the leader should take into account before deciding whether task performance or maintenance behaviors are more important. Originally called the *life cycle theory of leadership,* their **situational theory** highlights the maturity of the followers as the key situational factor.[49] **Job maturity** is the level of the follower's skills and technical knowledge relative to the task being performed; **psychological maturity** is the follower's self-confidence and self-respect. High-maturity followers have both the ability and the confidence to do a good job.

The theory proposes a simple, linear relationship between a follower's maturity and the degree of task performance behaviors a leader should use. The more mature the followers, the less the leader needs to organize and explain tasks. The required amount of maintenance behaviors is a bit more complex. As in Fiedler's model, the relationship is curvilinear: Maintenance behaviors are not important with followers of low or high levels of maturity but are important for followers of moderate maturity.

FIGURE 14.A.1 Fiedler's analysis of situations in which the task- or relationship-motivated leader is more effective

Leader–member relations	Good				Poor			
Task structure	Structured		Unstructured		Structured		Unstructured	
Leader position power	High	Low	High	Low	High	Low	High	Low
	1	2	3	4	5	6	7	8

Favorable for leader → Unfavorable for leader

Type of leader most effective in the solution	Task-motivated	Task-motivated	Task-motivated	Relationship-motivated	Relationship-motivated	Relationship-motivated	Relationship-motivated	Task-motivated

Source: D. Organ and T. Bateman, *Organizational Behavior,* 4th ed. (Burr Ridge, Ill.: Richard D. Irwin, 1990).

For low-maturity followers, the emphasis should be on performance-related leadership; for moderate-maturity followers, performance leadership is somewhat less important and maintenance behaviors become more important; and for high-maturity followers, neither dimension of leadership behavior is important.

Little academic research has been done on situational theory, but the model is extremely popular in management training seminars. Regardless of its scientific validity, Hersey and Blanchard's model provides a reminder that it is important to treat different people differently. Moreover, it suggests the importance of treating the same individual differently from time to time as he or she changes jobs or acquires more maturity in her or his particular job.[50]

The Vroom-Yetton-Jago Model

The third situational model follows in the tradition of Tannenbaum and Schmidt. Developed initially by Vroom and Yetton[51] and revised by Vroom and Jago,[52] the **Vroom-Yetton-Jago model** emphasizes the participative dimension of leadership: how leaders go about making decisions. Although it focuses on leader behaviors different from Fiedler's and Hersey and Blanchard's, the model shares their approach of assessing the situation before determining the best leadership style.

Figure 14.A.2 shows the questions used to analyze problem situations. Each question is based on an important attribute of the problem the leader faces and should be answered with a yes or a no.

FIGURE 14.A.2   The Vroom-Yetton-Jago model

QR	Quality requirement:	How important is the technical quality of this decision?
CR	Commitment requirement:	How important is subordinate commitment to the decision?
LI	Leader's information:	Do you have sufficient information to make a high-quality decision?
ST	Problem structure:	Is the problem well structured?
CP	Commitment probability:	If you were to make the decision by yourself, is it reasonably certain that your subordinate(s) would be committed to the decision?
GC	Goal congruence:	Do subordinates share the organization goals to be attained in solving this problem?
CO	Subordinate conflict:	Is conflict among subordinates over preferred solutions likely?
SI	Subordinate information:	Do subordinates have sufficient information to make a high-quality decision?

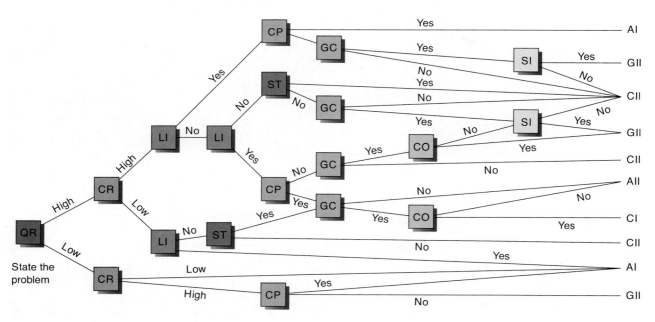

Source: Reprinted from *The New Leadership* by Victor H. Vroom and Authur G. Jago; Prentice-<None>Hall, 1988. Used by permission of the authors.

TABLE 14.A.1

Types of
management
decision styles

AI	You solve the problem or make the decision yourself, using information available to you at that time.
AII	You obtain the necessary information from your subordinate(s), then decide on the solution to the problem yourself. You may or may not tell your subordinates what the problem is in getting the information from them. The role played by your subordinates in making the decision is clearly one of providing the necessary information to you, rather than generating or evaluating alternative solutions.
CI	You share the problem with relevant subordinates individually, getting their ideas and suggestions without bringing them together as a group. Then you make the decision that may or may not reflect your subordinates' influence.
CII	You share the problem with your subordinates as a group, collectively obtaining their ideas and suggestions. Then you make the decision that may or may not reflect your subordinates' influence.
GII*	You share a problem with your subordinates as a group. Together you generate and evaluate alternatives and attempt to reach agreement (consensus) on a solution. Your role is much like that of chairman. You do not try to influence the group to adopt "your" solution, and you are willing to accept and implement any solution that has the support of the entire group.

*GI is omitted because it applies only to more comprehensive models.

Source: Reprinted from *Leadership and Decision Making* by Victor H. Vroom and Philip W. Yetton by permission of the University of Pittsburgh Press. © 1973 by University of Pittsburgh Press.

Like Fiedler's model, the Vroom-Yetton-Jago model is a decision tree. You answer the questions one at a time, skipping some questions as you follow the appropriate branch. Eventually, you reach one of ten possible endpoints. For each endpoint, the model states which of the five decision styles (labeled AI through GII) is most appropriate. Several different decision styles may work, but the style recommended is the one in the feasible set that takes the least amount of time.

Table 14.A.1 defines the types of leader decision styles. The five styles indicate that there are several shades of participation, not just autocratic or democratic.

The following example presents a managerial decision for you to work through the model tree.

APPLYING THE VROOM-YETTON-JAGO MODEL

I magine yourself in this situation. You are the head of a research and development laboratory in the nuclear reactor division of a large corporation. Often it is not clear whether a particular piece of research is potentially of commercial interest or merely of "academic" interest to the researchers. In your judgment, one major area of research has advanced well beyond the level at which operating divisions pertinent to the area could possibly assimilate or use the data being generated.

Recently two new areas with potentially high returns for commercial development have been proposed by one of the operating divisions. The team working in the area referred to in the previous paragraph is ideally qualified to research the new areas. Unfortunately, both areas are relatively devoid of scientific interest, while the project in which the team is currently engaged is of great scientific interest to all members.

At the moment, this is, or is close to being, your best research team. The team is very cohesive, has a high level of morale, and has been very productive. You are concerned not only that they would not want to switch their effort to the new areas but also that forcing them to concentrate on these two new projects could adversely affect their morale, their good intragroup working relations, and their future productivity both as individuals and as a team.

You have to respond to the operating division within the next two weeks indicating what resources, if any, can be devoted to working on these projects. It would be possible for the team to work on more than one project, but each project would need the combined skills of all the members of the team, so no fragmentation of the team is technically feasible. This fact, coupled with the fact that the team is very cohesive, means that a solution that satisfied any team member would very probably go a long way to satisfying everyone on the team.

How would you go about making this decision? Using Figure 14.A.2 and Table 14.A.1, decide which leadership approach you should apply if you were the manager in this situation. You can check the solution at the end of the appendix.

Source: V. Vroom and A. Jago, *The New Leadership: Managing Participation in Organization* (Englewood Cliffs, N.J.: Prentice-Hall, 1988). ●

Of course, not every managerial decision warrants this complicated analysis. But the model becomes less complex after one works through it once. Also, using the model for major decisions ensures that the manager considers the important situational factors and alerts the leader to the most appropriate style to use.[53]

Answer to Vroom-Yetton-Jago problem: Answers to questions are A. yes, B. yes, D. yes, E. no, F. no, G. no. The preferred decision style is C1.

APPENDIX KEY TERMS

Fiedler's contingency model of effectiveness, p. 377
Hersey and Blanchard's situational theory, p. 377
job maturity, p. 377
psychological maturity, p. 377

relationship-motivated leadership, p. 377
task-motivated leadership, p. 377
Vroom-Yetton-Jago model, p. 378

APPENDIX DISCUSSION QUESTION

1. Discuss the similarities and differences among the various situational models of leadership.

15

MOTIVATING FOR PERFORMANCE

The ability to deal with people is as purchasable a commodity as sugar or coffee. And I pay more for that ability than for any other under the sun.

John D. Rockefeller

After studying Chapter 15, you will know:

1. The kinds of behaviors managers need to motivate in people.

2. How to set challenging, motivating goals.

3. How to reward good performance.

4. The ways in which people's individual needs affect their behavior.

5. How to create a motivating, empowering job.

6. The key beliefs that affect people's motivation.

7. How people assess fairness and respond to unfair treatment.

8. The causes and consequences of a satisfied workforce.

MERIT PAY AT LINCOLN ELECTRIC

*H*arvard Business School publishes 35,000 cases worldwide. The case purchased most often is about Lincoln Electric Company of Cleveland. Lincoln Electric produces industrial electric motors and is the world's largest manufacturer of arc welding products.

The attraction of the case is Lincoln's success at motivating workers by tying pay to performance. All of its 2,300 workers participate in the company's incentive plan, and all but two share in the annual bonus—the president and the chair. The two top executives are paid based on a percentage of sales; if sales go down they take the first pay cut.

A committee evaluates each job to determine a fair hourly base rate. Lincoln also has a piecework rate, with which workers earn money based on how much they produce. All jobs in the company have pay ranges (hourly or salary) so that individuals who perform at their highest capability can move up to the top of the range for their particular job.

Every six months, the CEO personally reviews 2,300 merit ratings. Everyone is rated in four performance categories: output, quality, dependability (ability to work without supervision), and cooperation and ideas. Over the

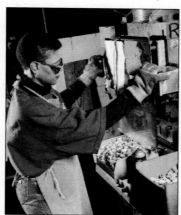

Lincoln Electric Company's merit pay plan is so successful that most workers double their base salary via their annual bonus. *(Courtesy The Lincoln Electric Company, Cleveland, Ohio)*

50-plus years in which the system has been in place, the average year-end bonus has been 95.5 percent of base. In other words, employees commonly double their annual income by virtue of the annual bonus.

Lincoln has been number one in its business worldwide for the entire life of the incentive system. Its employee turnover rate is very low, and the quality of its products is quite high. It has never faced a strike. The company has no debt. Lincoln offers Incentive Management Seminars, free of charge, as a service to industry.

Lincoln Electric has outlasted giants like Westinghouse to dominate a fiercely competitive industry. Managers attribute their company's success to a philosophy: a strong belief in the power of unfettered capitalism. The incentive system supports the philosophy with measurable goals that provide evidence of progress. Moreover, the company attracts people who believe strongly in individual accountability and the power of pure meritocracy.

Sources: R. S. Sabo, "Linking Merit Pay with Performance at Lincoln Electric," in *The Quest for Competitiveness,* ed. Y. K. Shetty and V. M. Buehler (New York: Quorum Books, 1991); C. Bartlett and S. Ghoshal, "Changing the Role of Top Management: Beyond Strategy to Purpose,"

L incoln Electric has come up with a powerful solution to the age-old question tackled in this chapter: How can a manager motivate people to work hard and perform at their best levels?

A sales manager in another company had a different approach to this problem. Each month, the person with the worst sales performance took home a live goat for the weekend. The manager hoped the goat-of-the-month employee would be so embarrassed that he or she would work harder the next month to increase sales.[1]

This sales manager may get high marks for creativity. But if he is graded by results, as he grades his salespeople, he will fail. He may succeed in motivating a few of his people to increase sales, but others will be motivated to quit the company.

MOTIVATING FOR PERFORMANCE

Understanding why people do the things they do on the job is not an easy task for the manager. *Predicting* their response to management's latest productivity program is harder yet. Fortunately, there is enough information about motivation to give the thoughtful manager practical, effective techniques for increasing people's effort and performance.

Motivation refers to forces that energize, direct, and sustain a person's efforts. All behavior, except involuntary reflexes like eye blinks (which usually have little to do with management), is motivated. A highly motivated person will work hard toward achieving performance goals. With adequate ability and understanding of the job, such a person will be highly productive.

MOTIVATED WORK BEHAVIORS

To be effective motivators, managers must know what behaviors they want to motivate people to exhibit. Although productive people appear to do a seemingly limitless number of things, most of the important activities can be grouped into five general categories.[2] The company must motivate people to: (1) *join the organization;* (2) *remain in the organization;* (3) *come to work regularly;* and (4) *perform:* Once employees are at work, they should work hard to achieve high *output* (productivity) and high *quality.* Finally, managers want employees to (5) *exhibit good citizenship.* Good citizens of the organization are committed, satisfied employees who perform above and beyond the call of duty by doing extra tasks that can help the company. The importance of citizenship behaviors may be less obvious than productivity, but these behaviors help the organization function smoothly. They also make managers' lives easier.

Now that we have identified the kinds of behaviors a manager should motivate, we will consider *how* to motivate these behaviors. Effective managers both *facilitate* and *stimulate* high performance.

FACILITATING PERFORMANCE

Many factors can prevent a person from performing at high levels. A highly motivated salesperson may work 60 hours per week but have difficulty achieving her performance goals for a number of reasons. She may not understand her customers or her products, may work for a disreputable company, have to sell inferior products at unreasonable prices, have a difficult sales territory, or be hampered by poor economic times.

Effective managers will facilitate performance by providing the things people need to do their jobs. Managers can give their people proper training, the necessary tools and equipment, adequate budget and support staff, and enough authority and information to perform their jobs well. Without these things, even highly motivated people will not perform well. Then, as they learn that the situation is inhibiting rather than helping their performance, their motivation drops.

STIMULATING PERFORMANCE

If people have everything they need to perform well, they are *able* to do the job. But they must also be *willing*.

People are willing to work hard if there is a reason to do so. Something must happen in their work environment that will prompt them to work. At the simplest level, this may be nothing more than the boss making a *request* or giving an *order*. People are even more motivated to exhibit behaviors for which they are held *accountable*. If a person knows the boss will check up on how well he carried out the order, he is more likely to do it well. If a *deadline* is imposed, he is more likely to do the task expediently. Also, people are more likely to do the things they know are assessed on their *performance appraisals*. They also will do things when they will be rewarded fairly for doing them.

Many ideas have been proposed to help managers motivate people. The most useful of these ideas are described in the following pages. The best approaches include setting goals, reinforcing performance, satisfying people's needs, designing motivating jobs, influencing people's beliefs about performance, achieving fairness, and offering a high quality of work life.

SETTING GOALS

Providing work-related goals for people is an extremely effective way to stimulate motivation. **Goal-setting theory** states that people have conscious goals that energize them and direct their thoughts and behaviors toward one end.[3] Thus, a person who wants to be a CPA has a goal that guides his or her selection of schools, courses, professional exam preparation, and job interview strategies. An individual whose goal is to become a self-employed entrepreneur will be motivated toward different, more personally appropriate actions.

What kinds of goals most effectively motivate people? How can managers set motivating goals for the people who report to them?

First, goals should be *acceptable* to employees. This means, among other things, that they should not conflict with people's personal values and that people have reasons to pursue the goals. Allowing people to participate in setting their work goals—as opposed to having the boss set goals for them—is often a great way to generate goals that people accept and pursue willingly.

Second, acceptable, maximally motivating goals should be *challenging but attainable*. In other words, they should be high enough to inspire better performance but not so high that people can never reach them. One team of consultants to an international corporation created more than 40 programs aimed at increasing quality. The company announced it did not expect significant quality improvement until the *fourth year* of the program. Such a goal obviously is not nearly demanding enough.[4]

Third, goals should be *specific, quantifiable,* and *measurable*. Ideal goals do not merely exhort employees to improve performance, start doing their best, increase productivity, or decrease the length of time that customers must wait to receive service. Goals should be more like Caterpillar Tractor's guaranteed parts delivery within 24 hours. Such deadlines, and other measurable goals, are specific, quantifiable goals that employees are motivated to achieve.

LIMITATIONS OF GOAL SETTING

Goal setting is an extraordinarily powerful management technique. But like anything else, even specific, challenging, attainable goals work better under some conditions than others. People should *not* be given individual performance goals if they work in a group and cooperation among the team members is essential to team performance.[5] Individualized goals create competition and reduce cooperation. If cooperation is essential, performance goals should be established *for the team*.

It is important that a single productivity goal not be established if there are other important dimensions of performance.[6] For instance, productivity goals will likely enhance productivity, but they may also cause employees to neglect other things like tackling new projects or developing creative solutions to job-related problems. The manager who wants to motivate creativity should establish creativity goals along with productivity goals. Even the prestigious Baldrige award for quality has been criticized as generating such zealous competitiveness that companies focus single-mindedly on winning the award at the expense of other key elements of business success.[7]

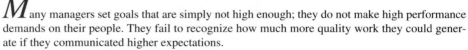

STRETCH GOALS

*M*any managers set goals that are simply not high enough; they do not make high performance demands on their people. They fail to recognize how much more quality work they could generate if they communicated higher expectations.

Even though U.S. companies know they must become more productive if they are to compete in today's global economy, too many executives continue to look to technology and other remedies and to demand too little of their people. Too much attention is placed on the latest techniques, and too little on making people accountable for measurable improvement in results.

Top firms today set "stretch goals"—targets that are exceptionally demanding, and that some people never even thought of. But, impossible though they may seem to some, they are in fact attainable.

Incremental goals, representing slight improvements over previous performance levels, represent standard management practice. Stretch goals are a major shift away from mediocrity and toward tremendous achievement.

3M was famous for its amazing innovation prowess, consistently meeting its goal of generating 25 percent of revenues from new products introduced in the last five years. But then it surpassed itself again by increasing its goal, to 30 percent and 4 years. Mead was a complacent corporation that accepted mediocre performance and cyclical downturns, but then set goals of raising long-term return on capital from 5 percent to 10-to-12 percent. And after averaging 0.3 percent annual increases in productivity, it set a goal of 3 percent—a tenfold increase. Boeing's stretch goals were to cut the cost of manufacturing an airplane 25 percent by 1998, and then it reduced the time needed to build one from 18 months to eight months. States Boeing's CEO, "We're doing things we didn't think were possible."

Sources: R. H. Schaffer, "Demand Better Results—And Get Them," *Harvard Business Review,* March–April 1991, pp. 142–49; S. Tully, "Why to Go for Stretch Targets" *Fortune,* November 4, 1994, pp. 145–58. ●

By implementing stretch goals, Boeing cut the time needed to build an airplane from 18 to 8 months.

(Courtesy The Boeing Company)

Reinforcing Performance

In 1911, psychologist Edward Thorndike formulated the **law of effect:** Behavior that is followed by positive consequences probably will be repeated.[8] This powerful law of behavior laid the foundation for countless investigations into the effects of the positive consequences, called **reinforcers,** that motivate behavior. **Organizational behavior modification** attempts to influence people's behavior by systematically managing work conditions and the consequences of people's actions.

Four key consequences of behavior either encourage or discourage people's behavior (see Figure 15.1):

1. **Positive reinforcement**—applying a valued consequence that increases the likelihood that the person will repeat the behavior that led to it. Examples of positive reinforcers include compliments, letters of commendation, favorable performance evaluations, and pay raises. Equally important, *jobs* can be positively reinforcing. Performing well on interesting, challenging, or *enriched* jobs (discussed later in this chapter) is much more reinforcing, and therefore motivating, then performing well on jobs that are routine and monotonous.

2. **Negative reinforcement**—removing or withholding an undesirable consequence. For example, a manager takes an employee (or a school takes a student) off probation because of improved performance. Nordstrom, the prominent retailer, received a great deal of negative publicity about its overreliance on negative reinforcement as a primary motivational tool. Frequent threatening memos admonished people to achieve every one of their many performance goals: "If any of these areas are not met to our expectations, you will be terminated." Another memo reminded employees that calling in sick once every three months is "a lot" and enough to "question your dedication."[9] Negative reinforcement in these examples occurs when people perform well and *don't* get punished.

3. **Punishment**—administering an aversive consequence. Examples include criticizing or shouting at an employee, assigning an unappealing task, and sending a worker home without pay. Negative reinforcement can involve the *threat* of punishment, but not delivering it when employees perform satisfactorily. Punishment is the actual delivery of the aversive consequence.

4. **Extinction**—withdrawing or failing to provide a reinforcing consequence. When this occurs, motivation is reduced and the behavior is *extinguished,* or eliminated. Examples include not giving a compliment for a job well done, forgetting to say thanks for a favor, or setting impossible performance goals so that the person never experiences success.

The first two consequences, positive and negative reinforcement, are positive for the person receiving them: The person either gains something or avoids something negative. Therefore, the person who experiences these consequences will be motivated to behave in the ways that led to the reinforcement. The last two consequences, punishment and extinction, are negative outcomes for the person receiving them: Motivation to repeat the behavior that led to the undesirable results will be reduced.

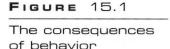

Figure 15.1

The consequences of behavior

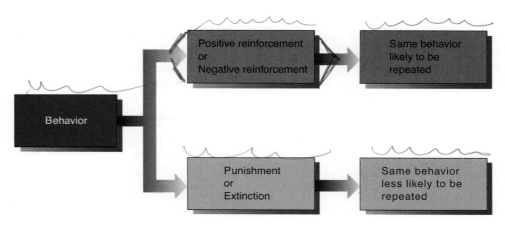

TABLE 15.1

The greatest
management
principle in
the world

"The things that get rewarded get done" is what one author calls The Greatest Management Principle in the World. With this in mind, Michael LeBoeuf offers 10 prescriptions for effectively motivating high performance. Companies, and individual managers, should reward the following:

1. *Solid solutions* instead of quick fixes.
2. *Risk taking* instead of risk avoiding.
3. *Applied creativity* instead of mindless conformity.
4. *Decisive action* instead of paralysis by analysis.
5. *Smart work* instead of busywork.
6. *Simplification* instead of needless complication.
7. *Quietly effective behavior* instead of squeaky wheels.
8. *Quality work* instead of fast work.
9. *Loyalty* instead of turnover.
10. *Working together* instead of working against.

Source: M. LeBoeuf, *The Greatest Management Principle in the World* (New York: G. P. Putnam's Sons, 1984).

Thus, effective managers give positive reinforcement to their high-performing people and negative reinforcement to low performers. They also punish or extinguish poor performance and other unwanted behavior.

Sometimes organizations or individual managers reinforce the wrong behaviors.[10] The company that bases performance reviews on short-term results is reinforcing a short-run perspective in decision making. At the same time, it is discouraging immediate sacrifices that will pay off in the future. Programs that punish employees for absenteeism beyond a certain limit may actually *encourage* them to be absent. People use up all their allowable absences and fail to come to work regularly until they reach the point where their next absence will result in punishment. Managers must identify which kinds of behaviors they reinforce and which they discourage (see Table 15.1).

The creative use of reinforcers is particularly necessary during times when money is tight and companies cannot rely on pay raises to motivate people. Whereas managers starting their careers in 1975 could expect to triple their pay in 10 years, today's managers will be lucky to double their pay in the same amount of time.[11] Promotions too are less available, as managers today can expect promotions only every three to four years—half as often as in the early 1970s. Innovative managers therefore turn to nonmonetary rewards, including intellectual challenge, greater responsibility, autonomy, recognition, flexible benefits, and greater influence over decisions. These and other rewards for high-performing employees, when creatively devised and applied, can continue to motivate when pay and other traditional reinforcers are scarce.[12]

UNDERSTANDING PEOPLE'S NEEDS

So far we have focused on forces in the environment that influence motivation. But characteristics of the person also affect motivation. People have different needs, energizing and motivating them toward different goals. The extent to which and the ways in which a person's needs can be met at work affect his or her behavior on the job.

MASLOW'S NEED HIERARCHY

Abraham Maslow organized five major types of human needs into a hierarchy, as shown in Figure 15.2.[13] The **need hierarchy** illustrates Maslow's conception of people satisfying their needs in a specified order, from bottom to top. The needs, in ascending order, are

1. *Physiological* (food, water, sex, and shelter).
2. *Safety or security* (protection against threat and deprivation).

FIGURE 15.3

The Hackman and Oldham model of job enrichment

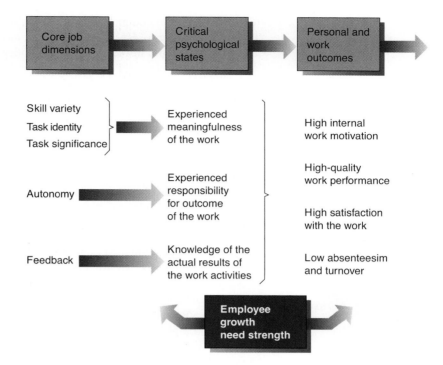

Source: © 1975 by the Regents of the University of California. Reprinted from the *California Management Review,* vol. 16, no. 4. By permission of The Regents.

other people; (2) they feel personally responsible for how the work turns out; and (3) they learn how well they performed their jobs.

These psychological states occur when people are working on *enriched* jobs, that is, jobs that offer the following five core job dimensions:

1. *Skill variety*—different job activities involving several skills and talents. For example, at Ashton Photo in Salem, Oregon, employees decide what skills they need and grade themselves on their performance. Rewards are also based on ability to teach others new skills.[28]

Task identity is the completion of a whole, identifiable piece of work. At State Farm Insurance, agents are independent contractors who sell and service only State Farm products. Agent retention and productivity exceed industry norms.

(Courtesy State Farm Insurance Companies)

2. *Task identity*—the completion of a whole, identifiable piece of work. People at Prospect Associates of Rockville, Maryland, market their ideas, and create new business.[29] At State Farm Insurance, agents are independent contractors who sell and service State Farm products exclusively. They have built and invested in their own businesses. Agent retention and productivity are far better than industry norms.[30]

3. *Task significance*—an important, positive impact on the lives of others. At Giro Sports Design, manufacturer of bicycle helmets, employees know their product saves lives.[31] Odwall is a maker of fruit and vegetable juices; its employees are proud of the nutritional value of their products. But even mundane products can generate task significance.[32]

4. *Autonomy*—independence and discretion in making decisions. At Action Instruments of San Diego, employees are urged to "make it happen": discover problems and solve them.[33] At Childress Buick in Phoenix, lot salespeople can finalize deals; they don't have to check with the sales manager.[34] In a research hospital, a department administrator told her people to do the kinds of research they wanted as long as it was within budget (and legal!). With no other guidelines—that is, complete autonomy—productivity increased six-fold in a year.[35]

5. *Feedback*—information on job performance. Many companies post charts or provide computerized data indicating productivity, number of rejects, and other data. Aspect Communications, in San Jose, ties everyone's bonuses to measures of customer satisfaction.[36] Employees pay constant attention to the customer feedback on their performance. At Great Plains Software, programmers are expected to spend time with customers.[37] This way, they learn what customers think of their products, and what kind of impact they are having.

The most effective job enrichment increases all five core dimensions in a single job.

A person's growth need strength will help determine just how effective a job enrichment program might be. *Growth need strength* is the degree to which individuals want personal and psychological development. Job enrichment would be more successful for people with high growth need strength. But very few people will respond negatively.[38]

EMPOWERMENT

Today one frequently hears managers talk about "empowering" their people. **Empowerment** is the process of sharing power with employees, thereby enhancing their confidence in their ability to perform their jobs and their belief that they are influential contributors to the organization. Empowerment results in changes in employees' beliefs—from feeling powerless to believing strongly in their own personal effectiveness. The result is that people take more initiative and persevere in achieving their goals and their leader's vision even in the face of obstacles.[39]

To foster empowerment, management must create an environment in which *everyone* feels they have real influence over performance standards and business effectiveness within their areas of responsibility.[40] Such an environment reduces costs, because fewer people are needed to supervise, monitor, and coordinate. It improves quality and service, because high performance is inspired at the source, the people who do the work. It also allows quick action, because people on the spot see problems, solutions, and opportunities on which they are "empowered" to act.

What actions can leaders take to empower their people and generate these positive beliefs? Empowering people means allowing them to participate in decision making, expressing confidence in their ability to perform at high levels, designing their jobs so they have greater freedom, setting meaningful and challenging goals, applauding outstanding performance, and encouraging people to take personal responsibility for their work. We have already discussed some of these qualities.

You should not be surprised when empowerment causes some problems, at least in the short term. This is the case with virtually any change, including changes for the better. People might make mistakes at first, especially until they have had adequate training. And since more training is needed, costs are higher. Also, because people acquire new skills and make greater contributions, they may demand higher wages. But if they are well-trained and truly empowered, they will deserve them—and both they and the company will benefit.

Significantly, empowerment does not mean allowing people to decide trivial things like what color to paint the lunchroom. For empowerment to make a difference, people must have an impact on things they *care* about like quality and productivity.[41] Companies including Lord Corporation in Dayton, Ohio (which produces engine mounts for aircraft), Herman Miller (the Michigan-based furniture manufacturer), Johnsonville Foods, and Goodyear have all been highly successful and received great acclaim for their empowerment programs.[42]

INFLUENCING PEOPLE'S BELIEFS ABOUT PERFORMANCE

So far you have learned about the motivating characteristics of the work environment and about people's needs. People's *beliefs* about their work also influence motivation. People draw conclusions about their own job performance, how their performance will be rewarded, and whether their boss and the company are treating them fairly. These and other important beliefs are discussed in the following sections.

According to **expectancy theory,** the person's work *efforts* lead to some level of *performance.*[43] Then performance results in one or more *outcomes* for the person (see Figure 15.4). People develop two important beliefs linking these three events: expectancy, which links effort to performance, and instrumentality, which links performance to rewards.

THE EFFORT-TO-PERFORMANCE LINK

The first belief, **expectancy,** is people's perceived likelihood that their efforts will enable them to successfully attain their performance goals. An expectancy can be high (up to 100 percent), such as when a student is confident that if she studies hard she can get a good grade on the final. An expectancy can also be low (down to a 0 percent likelihood), such as when a suitor is convinced that his dream date will never go out with him.

All else equal, high expectancies create higher motivation than do low expectancies. In the preceding examples, the student is more likely to study for the exam than the suitor is to pursue the dream date, even though both people want their respective outcomes.

Expectancies can vary among individuals, even in the same situation. For example, a sales manager might initiate a competition in which the top salesperson wins a free trip to Hawaii. In such cases, the few top people, who have performed well in the past, will be more motivated by the contest than will all the historically average and below-average performers. The top people will have higher expectancies—stronger beliefs that their efforts can help them turn in the top performance.

THE PERFORMANCE-TO-OUTCOME LINK

The example about the sales contest illustrates how performance results in some kind of **outcome,** or consequence, for the person. Actually, it often results in several outcomes. For example, turning in the best sales performance could lead to (1) a competitive victory, (2) the free trip to Hawaii, (3) feelings of achievement, (4) recognition from the boss, (5) prestige throughout the company, and (6) resentment from other salespeople.

FIGURE 15.4

Basic concepts of expectancy theory

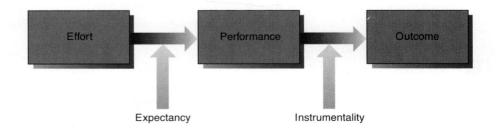

But how certain is it that performance will result in all those outcomes? Will winning the contest really lead to resentment? For that matter, will it really lead to increased prestige?

These questions address the second key belief described by expectancy theory: instrumentality. **Instrumentality** is the perceived likelihood that performance will be followed by a particular outcome. Like expectancies, instrumentalities can be high (up to 100 percent) or low (approaching 0 percent).

Also, each outcome has an associated valence. **Valence** is the value the outcome holds for the person contemplating it. Valences can be positive (up to 1.0, in the theory's mathematical formulation), like the Hawaiian vacation, or negative (down to −1.0), like the other salespeople's resentment.

IMPACT ON MOTIVATION

For motivation to be high, expectancy, instrumentalities, and total valence of all outcomes must *all* be high. A person will *not* be highly motivated if any of the following conditions exist:

1. He believes he can't perform well enough to achieve the positive outcomes that he knows the company provides to good performers (high valence and high instrumentality but low expectancy).
2. He knows he can do the job. He is fairly certain what the ultimate outcomes will be (a promotion and a transfer). However, he doesn't want those outcomes or believes other, negative outcomes outweigh the positive (high expectancy and high instrumentality but low valence).
3. He knows he can do the job. He wants several important outcomes (a favorable performance review, a raise, and a promotion). But he believes that no matter how well he performs, the outcomes will not be forthcoming (high expectancy and positive valences but low instrumentality).

MANAGERIAL IMPLICATIONS OF EXPECTANCY THEORY

Expectancy theory is complex, but it helps the manager zero in on key leverage points for influencing motivation. Three implications are crucial:

1. *Increase expectancies.* Provide a work environment that facilitates good performance, and set realistically attainable performance goals. Provide training, support, and encouragement so that people are confident they can perform at the levels expected of them. Recall from the last chapter that charismatic leaders excel at boosting their followers' confidence.
2. *Identify positively valent outcomes.* Understand what people want to get out of work. Think about what their jobs provide them and what is not, but could be, provided. Consider how people may differ in the valences they assign to outcomes. Know the need theories of motivation and their implications for identifying important outcomes.
3. *Make performance instrumental toward positive outcomes.* Make sure that good performance is followed by personal recognition and praise, favorable performance reviews, pay increases, and other positive results. Also, make sure that working hard and doing things well will have as few negative results as possible. Finally, ensure that poor performance has fewer positive and more negative outcomes than good performance.

ACHIEVING FAIRNESS

As people realize the outcomes or consequences of their actions, they develop beliefs about how just or fair those outcomes are. Basically they assess how fairly the organization treats them.

The most important theory about how people interpret their outcomes is equity theory.[44] **Equity theory** proposes that when people assess how fairly they were treated, they consider two key factors: outcomes and inputs. *Outcomes,* as in expectancy theory, refer to the various things the person receives on the job: recognition, pay, benefits, satisfaction, security, job assignments, punishments, and so forth. *Inputs* refer to the contributions the person makes to the organization: effort, time, talent, performance, extra commitment, good citizenship, and so forth. People have a general expectation that the outcomes they receive will reflect, or be proportionate to, the inputs they provide—a fair day's pay (and other outcomes) for a fair day's work.

But this comparison of outcomes to inputs is not the whole story. People also pay attention to the outcomes and inputs others receive. At salary review time, for example, most people—from executives on down—try to pick up clues that will tell them who got the high raises. As described in the following section, they compare ratios, restore equity if necessary, and derive more or less satisfaction based on how equitably they believe they have been treated.

ASSESSING EQUITY

Equity theory suggests that people compare the ratio of their own outcomes to inputs against the outcome-to-input ratio of some comparison person. The *comparison person* can be a fellow student, a co-worker, a boss, a spouse, or an average industry pay scale. Stated more succinctly, people compare

$$\text{Their own } \frac{\text{Outcomes}}{\text{Inputs}} \text{ versus Others' } \frac{\text{Outcomes}}{\text{Inputs}}$$

If the ratios are equivalent, people believe the relationship is equitable, or fair. Equity causes people to be satisfied with their treatment. But the person who believes his or her ratio is lower than another's will feel inequitably treated. Inequity causes dissatisfaction and leads to an attempt to restore balance to the relationship.

There are many examples of inequity and the negative feelings it creates. As a student, perhaps you have been in the following situation. You pull an all-nighter and get a C on the exam. Meanwhile another student studies a couple of hours, goes out for the rest of the evening, gets a good night's sleep, and gets a B on the exam. You perceive your inputs (time spent studying) as much greater than the other student's, but your outcomes are lower. You are displeased at the unfairness of the situation.

In business, the same thing happens with pay raises. One manager puts in 60-hour weeks, has a degree from a prestigious university, and believes she is destined for the top. When her archrival—whom she perceives as less deserving ("she never comes into the office on weekends, and all she does when she is here is butter up the boss")—gets the higher raise or the promotion, she experiences severe feelings of inequity.

Assessments of equity are not made objectively. They are subjective perceptions or beliefs. In the preceding example, the person who got the higher raise probably felt she deserved it. Even if she admits she doesn't put in long workweeks, she may convince herself she doesn't need to because she's so talented. The student who got the higher grade may believe it was a fair, equitable result because (1) she kept up all semester, while the other student did not, and (2) she's smart (ability and experience, not just effort, are inputs).

RESTORING EQUITY

People who feel inequitably treated and dissatisfied are motivated to do something to restore equity. They have four choices, which they carry out by actually doing something to change the ratios, or by reevaluating the situation and deciding it is equitable after all.

The equity equation shown earlier indicates a person's four options for restoring equity. People who feel inequitably treated can *reduce their inputs* by giving less effort, performing at lower levels, or even quitting ("Well, if that's the way things work around here, there's no way I'm going to work that hard [or stick around]"). Or they can attempt to *increase their outcomes* ("My boss [or teacher] is going to hear about this. I deserve more; there must be some way I can get more").

Other ways of restoring equity focus on changing the other person's ratio. A person can *decrease others' outcomes.* For example, an employee may sabotage work to create problems for his company or his boss. A person can also change her perceptions of inputs or outcomes ("That promotion isn't as great a deal as he thinks. The pay is not that much better, and the headaches will be unbelievable"). It is also possible to *increase others' inputs,* particularly by changing perceptions ("The more I think about it, the more he deserved it. He's worked hard all year, he's competent, and it's about time he got a break").

Thus, a person can restore equity in a number of ways by behaviorally or perceptually changing inputs and outcomes.

CONTRACTS, OLD AND NEW

A contract is a set of obligations between two or more parties. Contracts are based on an exchange between two parties, such as an employer and employee. What does the person owe the company, and what does the company owe the person?

Formal contracts are written, of course. But significantly, many contracts are psychological, based on beliefs about what is fair and about what parties owe each other.

In the "old days"—the 1950s, 60s, 70s, and into the 80s—the standard contract was simple: security for loyalty. The company provided steady employment, and received loyal employees in return. But this deal has been declared dead.

Today, companies do not and cannot promise job security. And most people are not as loyal to their employers. Particularly when the economy does well, people have more choices and will move to better jobs.

The new psychological contract is this: "There will never be job security. You will be employed by us as long as you add value to the organization, and *you* are continuously responsible for finding ways to add value. In return you have the right to demand interesting and important work, the freedom and resources to perform it well, pay that reflects your contribution, and the experience and training needed to be employable here or elsewhere."

The company owes only honesty. You can be notified at any time that you are "at risk" of losing your job.

For some people, this new contract is exhilarating and liberating, resulting in a series of exciting but temporary jobs. Other people find it difficult, even scary. Where will I be a year from now? How will I need to prepare myself for such an uncertain future?

But then again, the old deal caused stagnation. Unproductive workers were tolerated too long, and were kept on in demeaning jobs. Job security does not motivate people to upgrade their skills and become members of an agile, competitive work force.

Sources: D. Rousseau and J. M. Parks, "The Contracts of Individuals and Organizations," in L. L. Cummings and B. Staw, eds., *Research in Organizational Behavior* Vol. 15 (Greenwich, Conn.: JAI Press, 1992); B. O'Reilly, "The New Deal: What Companies and Employees Owe One Another," *Fortune,* June 13, 1994, pp. 44–52; W. J. Byrons, "Coming to Terms with the New Corporate Contract," *Business Horizons,* January–February 1995, pp. 8–15. ●

JOB SATISFACTION

If people feel fairly treated from the outcomes they receive, they will be satisfied. A satisfied worker is not necessarily more productive than a dissatisfied one; sometimes people are happy with their jobs because they don't have to work hard! But job dissatisfaction, aggregated across many individuals, creates a work force that is more likely to exhibit (1) higher turnover; (2) higher absenteeism; (3) lower corporate citizenship; (4) more grievances and lawsuits; (5) strikes; (6) stealing, sabotage, and vandalism; and (7) poorer mental and physical health (which can mean higher job stress, higher insurance costs, and more lawsuits).[45] All of these consequences of dissatisfaction, either directly or indirectly, are costly to organizations.

Quality of work life (QWL) programs create a workplace that enhances employee well-being and satisfaction. The general goal of QWL programs is to satisfy the full range of employee needs. QWL has eight categories.[46]

1. Adequate and fair compensation.
2. A safe and healthy environment.
3. Jobs that develop human capacities.
4. A chance for personal growth and security.
5. A social environment that fosters personal identity, freedom from prejudice, a sense of community, and upward mobility.
6. Constitutionalism, or the rights of personal privacy, dissent, and due process.
7. A work role that minimizes infringement on personal leisure and family needs.
8. Socially responsible organizational actions (discussed in Chapter 6).

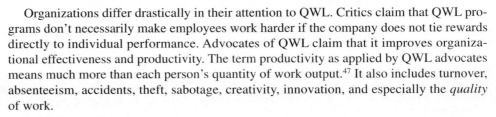

Organizations differ drastically in their attention to QWL. Critics claim that QWL programs don't necessarily make employees work harder if the company does not tie rewards directly to individual performance. Advocates of QWL claim that it improves organizational effectiveness and productivity. The term productivity as applied by QWL advocates means much more than each person's quantity of work output.[47] It also includes turnover, absenteeism, accidents, theft, sabotage, creativity, innovation, and especially the *quality* of work.

KEY TERMS

empowerment, p. 394
equity theory, p. 397
ERG theory, p. 390
expectancy, p. 395
expectancy theory, p. 395
extinction, p. 387
extrinsic reinforcers, p. 391
goal-setting theory, p. 385
hygiene factors, p. 392
instrumentality, p. 396
intrinsic reward, p. 391
job enlargement, p. 391
job enrichment, p. 391
job rotation, p. 391

law of effect, p. 387
motivation, p. 384
motivators, p. 392
need hierarchy, p. 388
negative reinforcement, p. 387
organizational behavior modification, p. 387
outcome, p. 395
positive reinforcement, p. 387
punishment, p. 387
quality of work life (QWL), p. 399
reinforcers, p. 387
[Herzberg's] two-factor theory, p. 392
valence, p. 396

SUMMARY OF LEARNING OBJECTIVES

Now that you have studied Chapter 15, you should know:

The kinds of behaviors managers need to motivate in people.

All important work behaviors are motivated. Managers need to motivate employees to join and remain in the organization and to exhibit high attendance, job performance, and citizenship. It is important to both facilitate and stimulate these behaviors.

How to set challenging, motivating goals.

Goal setting is a powerful motivator. Specific, quantifiable, and challenging but attainable goals motivate high effort and perfor-

mance. Goal setting can be used for teams as well as for individuals. Care should be taken that single goals are not set to the exclusion of other important dimensions of performance.

How to reward good performance.

Organizational behavior modification programs influence behavior at work by arranging consequences for people's actions. Most programs use positive reinforcement as a consequence, but other important consequences are negative reinforcement, punishment, and extinction. Care must be taken to reinforce appropriate, not inappropriate, behavior. Innovative managers use a wide variety of rewards for good performance.

The ways in which people's individual needs affect their behavior.

Maslow's five most important needs are physiological, safety, social, ego, and self-actualization. Alderfer's ERG theory describes three sets of needs: existence, relatedness, and growth. McClelland emphasizes three different needs: achievement, affiliation, and power. Because people are inclined to satisfy their various needs, these theories help to suggest to managers the kinds of measures to take to motivate people.

How to create a motivating, empowering job.

One approach to satisfying needs and motivating people is to create intrinsic motivation through the improved design of jobs. Jobs can be enriched by building in more skill variety, task identity, task significance, autonomy, and feedback. Empowerment is the most recent development in the creation of motivating jobs.

The key beliefs that affect people's motivation.

Expectancy theory describes three important work-related beliefs. That is, motivation is a function of people's (1) expectancies, or effort-performance links; (2) instrumentalities, or performance-outcome links; and (3) the valences people attach to the outcomes of performance. Equity theory addresses important beliefs about fairness.

How people assess fairness and respond to unfair treatment.

Equity theory states that people compare their inputs and outcomes to the inputs and outcomes of others. Perceptions of equity (fair treatment) are satisfying; feelings of inequity (unfairness) are dissatisfying, and motivate people to change their behavior or their perceptions to restore equity.

The causes and consequences of a satisfied work force.

A satisfied work force has many advantages for the firm, including lower absenteeism and turnover, fewer grievances, lawsuits, and strikes, lower health costs, and higher-quality products. One general approach to generating higher satisfaction for people is to implement a quality of work life program. QWL seeks to provide a safe and healthy environment, opportunity for personal growth, a positive social environment, fair treatment, and other improvements in people's work life.

DISCUSSION QUESTIONS

1. If a famous executive were to give a passionate motivational speech, trying to persuade people to work harder, what do you think the impact would be? Why?
2. Give some examples of situations in which you wanted to do a great job but were prevented from doing so. What was the impact on you, and what would this suggest to you in your efforts to motivate other people to perform?
3. Discuss the similarities and differences between setting goals for other people and setting goals for yourself. When does goal setting fail, and when does it succeed?
4. Identify four examples of people inadvertently reinforcing the wrong behaviors or punishing or extinguishing good behaviors.
5. Assess yourself on McClelland's three needs. On which need are you highest, and on which are you lowest? What are the implications for you as a manager?
6. Identify a job you have worked and appraise it on Hackman and Oldham's five core job dimensions. Also describe the degree to which it made you feel empowered. As a class, choose one job and discuss together how it could be changed to be more motivating and empowering.
7. Using expectancy theory, analyze how you have made and will make personal choices like a major area of study, a career to pursue, or job interviews to seek out.
8. Describe a time that you felt unfairly treated and why. How did you respond to the inequity? What other options might you have had?

CONCLUDING CASE

THE WORK ETHIC

A department store manager at J. C. Penney in suburban Washington, D.C., works 44 hours a week, often including night shifts and weekends. In addition, she takes work home at night, and is never away from work for more than a week at a time. Some of the people in her store work two jobs and 60-hour weeks.

A department store manager at Karstadt in Berlin, Germany, earns a similar salary. He works 37 hours a week and has six weeks' annual vacation. He hates the fact that his store recently started opening one night per week and Saturday mornings. When Germany introduced Thursday night shopping in 1989, retail workers went on strike.

The German, Andreas Drauschke, believes in working hard on the job and getting away from it as fast as he can. A second job is inconceivable to him. So is a promotion, because it probably would cut into his family time and might require him to move away from Berlin.

The American, Angie Clark, was born in Germany and sees a big difference between the two countries. "Germans put leisure first and work second. In America it's the other way around."

In the United States, some workers are now revolting against overtime. A few years ago, unions complained of short workshifts; but in 1994, workers struck GM's Flint, Michigan, plant in part because of mandatory overtime amounting to 66 hours per week.

Overtime pays time-and-a-half, but some workers consider the extra hours required of them to be outlandish. Companies can force people to work unlimited overtime. Those who decline overtime work sometimes are disciplined or fired.

Overtime saves money for the company, and earns extra money for workers. Some people value the opportunity for extra work.

The time clock is one symbol of the workplace and the control it can exert over people's lives.

(Murray Alcosser/The Image Bank)

Others do not, in large part because it interferes with their personal lives. But people do want the right to get it if they want it.

Some people in the United States believe that American workers today have lost the strong work ethic of the past, and that they are not loyal or committed to their companies. Others maintain that Americans have a stronger work ethic than people of other countries. Some observers maintain that the American work ethic is still very much in evidence—especially among recent immigrants, who came to this country to build a new life and create greater opportunity for their children.

QUESTIONS

1. How would you define "work ethic"? How strong is the work ethic in the United States today? Why do you believe what you do about the work ethic?

2. Assess the work ethic, and the issues in the case, with respect to the concept of psychological contract.

3. If you were a manager, how would you motivate people to work overtime? How would you motivate them to perform at their best for the company? Is there a point at which companies are demanding too much? How can an appropriate balance be struck?

Sources: D. Benjamin and T. Horwitz, "German View: 'You Americans Work Too Hard—and for What?'" *The Wall Street Journal,* July 14, 1994, pp. B1, B6; K. Deveny, "Immigrants: Still Believers after All These Years," *The Wall Street Journal,* July 12, 1994, pp. B1, B7; and J. Rigdon, "Some Workers Gripe Bosses Are Ordering Too Much Overtime," *The Wall Street Journal,* July 29, 1994, pp. A1, A6.

VIDEO CASE

EMPLOYEE MOTIVATION AT TELLABS, INC.

It's important to understand the reasons why effective managers must be concerned with employee motivation. After identifying some of the factors contributing to motivation, this video looks at how Tellabs, Inc., has successfully applied motivation theory.

Tellabs is based in the Chicago area, but is internationally known for its telecommunications products and services. However, recently the company gained fame when its stock increased 1,683 percent over a five-year period, making Tellabs the best performing stock at that time on the New York Stock Exchange, the American Stock Exchangem and Nasdaq. Tellabs was founded in 1975 by a group of engineers brainstorming at a kitchen table, and grew from 20 employees with annual sales of $312,000 to 2,600 employees with annual sales of $494 million in 1994. Tellabs currently designs, manufactures, markets, and services voice and data transport and network access systems.

One of the principal reasons for Tellabs' remarkable success has been its ability to motivate its workforce. In simple terms, employee motivation refers to an employee's willingness to perform in his or her job. Effective managers must be concerned with motivating employees toward common goals that will improve the success of the company. At Tellabs, a motivated workforce has enhanced the quality of its products and services.

Tellabs' manager of quality, Joe Taylor, explains what's behind the company's motivated workers: "In the past 10 years we've found that to improve our quality we had to invest in our employees through training programs. Specifically, they have the tools and the resources now to make a difference within our processes in the factory and provide us with process improvements."

A motivated workforce contributes to increased quality in goods and services, greater efficiency in work processes, and improved customer service. Grace Pastiak said, "When I look at the improvements that Tellabs has made since implementing just-in-time and Total Quality Commitment, by far the biggest gain has been exciting employees to do their best and giving them the opportunity to implement their own ideas."

At its core, motivation results from an individual's desire to satisfy personal needs or goals. Every person has set of needs or goals that influences their behavior. Abraham Maslow postulated that needs can be placed in a hierarchy and that as each need level in the hierarchy is satisfied, the person will concentrate on meeting needs at the next level.

Frederick Herzberg, conducted a study in the 1960s that concluded that factors pertaining to the work itself, such as achievement, recognition, and responsibility, tended to actually motivate employees. Other factors, such as supervision, pay, and company policies, might increase job satisfaction, but not necessarily employee motivation.

A third approach to motivation, developed by Douglas McGregor, involves two opposing theories about the nature of human behavior. Theory X holds that some employees are lazy or unwilling to work unless motivated by negative factors such as threats and constant supervision. Theory Y holds that employees want to work and do a good job and are motivated best by incentives, responsibility, and ownership of their work.

Maslow's hierarchy, Herzberg's factors, and McGregor's theories suggest that it's in a company's best interest to offer employees adequate rewards and to appeal to their pride of workmanship. At Tellabs, many employees say that the entrepreneurial atmosphere nurtured by managers makes them feel good about themselves. So Tellabs clearly takes a Theory Y approach.

Effective managers help create a work environment that encourages, supports, and sustains improvement in work performance. At Tellabs, mangers have implemented job rotation systems and a cadre of high performance teams to help enrich jobs and create an innovative working environment. Another innovation at Tellabs to ensure a high level of employee motivation is high performance teams.

Some companies may use a combination of motivation theories. In 1992, Tellabs presented its corporate goals, known as Strategic Initiatives, to its employees. The corporate mission statement emphasized the company's goals quality, customer satisfaction, profits, growth, its people, and its corporate integrity.

Tellabs' total compensation plan includes an Employee Stock Option Plan and retirement investments, such as 401(k). Also employees receive an annual bonus based on the company's productivity.

At Tellabs, employee motivation and performance are enhanced by an atmosphere in which employees are openly told they are valued and trusted. Managers encourage calculated risk taking and innovation. They empower workers through cross-functional teams so that they are able to identify problems and develop effective solutions.

Tellabs' Career Development System trains internal candidates for key management positions, while its competitive compensation plan shares the wealth, contributes to employee satisfaction, and encourages peak performance.

CRITICAL THINKING QUESTIONS

1. McGregor's Theory X and Theory Y have totally different views of the typical worker. Which of the two theories do you think managers should adopt? Explain. Describe how adopting Theory X would affect a managers behavior toward employees. Do the same for Theory Y.

2. What are some of the potential pitfalls of using employee empowerment as a motivational device in the workplace?

3. Herzberg's theory says workplace factors lead to employee motivation. What are some workplace factors not mentioned in the video that could affect employee motivation?

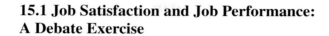

EXPERIENTIAL EXERCISES

15.1 Job Satisfaction and Job Performance: A Debate Exercise

Objective

The objective of this exercise is to explore the relationship between job satisfaction and job performance. At the conclusion of the exercise, each student should have developed her or his own opinion regarding the relationship between these two variables.

Instructions

This in-class exercise takes the form of a nontraditional four-way debate. Students will be divided by the instructor into four debating teams, each having four or five members. The remaining students will then be divided into judging teams consisting of three to six members each. The debate itself will focus on the relationship between job satisfaction and job performance

Debating Positions

Each debating team will be assigned one of the following four positions:

1. There is a direct positive relationship between job satisfaction and job performance. The higher an employee's job satisfaction, the higher will be her or his job performance and vice versa.
2. Job satisfaction is related to job performance in only the following way: A slight amount of job dissatisfaction is a prerequisite to high job performance. Thus, employees who are somewhat dissatisfied with their jobs will have higher productivity than those who are very dissatisfied or those who are completely satisfied with their jobs.
3. Job performance ultimately causes an employee's job satisfaction (high or low). If employees achieve high job performance they will receive high rewards and this, in turn, will result in high job satisfaction. If employees perform poorly on their jobs, resulting rewards will be low as will the employees' job satisfaction.
4. This position will be provided by the instructor.

The debate consists of two rounds. In round one each team first states its position and then tries to convince the judges, through the use of examples and other evidence, that its position is fully legitimate. During round two of the debate, each debating team counters the position of the other teams, i.e., team one criticizes teams two, three, and four; team two criticizes teams one, three, and four, etc. The group being countered may not rebut the criticisms made by the other teams during the debate unless specifically told to do so by the instructor. They just simply listen.

Round two, the last round of the debate, ends when team four has finished criticizing the positions of the other three teams. All debaters will be given a ten-minute recess between rounds one and two in order to finalize their criticisms of the other teams.

The judging teams' role during the debate is to "search for the truth," not select a "winner." They are to listen to all of the different arguments presented during the debate and, after it has ended, discuss the different positions among themselves until a consensus is reached regarding the "true" relationship between job satisfaction and job performance. There are no constraints placed on the judges; they are free to disagree with all of the positions presented, to agree with parts of two or more of them, etc. "After their deliberations are complete (usually about ten minutes), each judging team presents its conclusions to the class. Judges should hold preliminary discussions of the four positions during the intermission between rounds one and two.

Source: R. Bruce McAfee and Paul J. Champagne, *Job Satisfaction & Job Performance: A Debate Exercise* (St. Paul, Minn.: West, 1987), pp. 56–57. Reprinted by permission. Copyright© 1987 by West Publishing Company. All rights reserved.

15.2 What Do Students Want from Their Jobs?

Objectives

1. To demonstrate individual differences in job expectations.
2. To illustrate individual differences in need and motivational structures.
3. To examine and compare intrinsic rewards.

Instructions

1. Working alone, complete the What I Want from My Job Survey.
2. In small groups, compare and analyze differences in the survey results and prepare group responses to the discussion questions.

3. After the class reconvenes, group spokespersons present group findings.

Discussion Questions

1. Which job rewards are extrinsic, and which are intrinsic?

2. Were more response differences found in intrinsic or in extrinsic rewards?

3. In what ways do you think blue-collar workers' responses would differ from those of college students?

What I want from My Job Survey

Determine what you want from a job by circling the level of importance of each of the following job rewards.

	Very Important	Moderately Important	Indifferent	Moderately Unimportant	Very Unimportant
1. Advancement opportunities	5	4	3	2	1
2. Appropriate company policies	5	4	3	2	1
3. Authority	5	4	3	2	1
4. Autonomy and freedom on the job	5	4	3	2	1
5. Challenging work	5	4	3	2	1
6. Company reputation	5	4	3	2	1
7. Fringe benefits	5	4	3	2	1
8. Geographic location	5	4	3	2	1
9. Good co-workers	5	4	3	2	1
10. Good supervision	5	4	3	2	1
11. Job security	5	4	3	2	1
12. Money	5	4	3	2	1
13. Opportunity for self-development	5	4	3	2	1
14. Pleasant office and working conditions	5	4	3	2	1
15. Performance feedback	5	4	3	2	1
16. Prestigious job title	5	4	3	2	1
17. Recognition for doing a good job.	5	4	3	2	1
18. Responsibility	5	4	3	2	1
19. Sense of achievement	5	4	3	2	1
20. Training programs	5	4	3	2	1
21. Type of work	5	4	3	2	1
22. Working with people	5	4	3	2	1

16

MANAGING TEAMS

No one can whistle a symphony. It takes an orchestra to play it.

Halford E. Luccock

LEARNING OBJECTIVES

After studying Chapter 16, you will know:

1. How teams contribute to your organization's effectiveness.

2. What makes the new team environment different from the old.

3. How groups become teams.

4. Why teams sometimes fail.

5. How to build an effective team.

6. How to manage your team's relationships with other teams.

7. How to manage conflict.

TEAMWORK AT THERMOS

CEO Monte Peterson knew he had to reinvent his company when he took the top job at Thermos in 1990. The company was best known for its thermos bottles and lunch boxes, but its growth had stagnated. To revitalize the company, Peterson and Thermos had to innovate. The company needed a great new product, and they hoped to create one in the $1-billion-a-year barbecue grill market.

Peterson created a project team to develop an innovative new product. The team's assignment was to invent a product that would meet all of people's cookout needs. He selected six middle managers from different functions including engineering, manufacturing, marketing, and finance. He emphasized his commitment to the project, the team's opportunity to make their market grow, and the importance of the project to the entire corporation.

This Thermos work team created a new type of outdoor grill that was so successful the company now uses teams in all of its product lines.
(© James Schnepf)

Team leadership rotated among members, depending on the most pressing task. The team set strict deadlines for itself. They would have to plan, design, and build a new grill in less than two years.

The team spent a month traveling the country to find out what people really wanted in their grills. They visited families, met with focus groups, and videotaped cookouts. They learned the importance to consumers of appearance, safety, and the environment. They also learned that consumers hated electric grills because they don't provide a cookout taste, but also that they hated messy charcoal. Ultimately, the team defined its product as a new grill that looked like a piece of furniture, did not require charcoal fluid, was safe enough to use in condos and apartment buildings, and cooked food that tasted good.

While engineering worked on the technology, marketing worked on differentiating the new product, and design and manufacturing worked together on the design. The result was a completely new type of electric grill that gave food that all-important cookout taste. The product is a huge hit, growth is way up, and the functional bureaucracy is gone. The company is now using flexible, multidisciplinary teams in all its product lines.

Source: B. Dumaine, "Payoff from the New Management," *Fortune*, December 13, 1993, pp. 103–10.

*T*he 1990s have witnessed great excitement in the business community about the potential of work teams to dramatically change and improve the ways companies do business. In the Thermos case, a group of people from different functions became a team that was so successful in meeting its charge that it paved the way for a complete overhaul of the organization's structure. *Fortune* hailed well-designed teams as potentially "*the* productivity breakthrough of the 1990s."[1] Stated Jerry Junkins, CEO of Texas Instruments, "No matter what your business, these teams are the wave of the future."[2]

THE CONTRIBUTIONS OF TEAMS

It is no wonder that team-based approaches to work are generating such excitement. Used appropriately, teams can be powerfully effective as a

- *Building block for organization structure.* Organizations like Semco and Kollmorgen, manufacturer of printed circuits and electro-optic devices, are structured entirely around teams. A team-oriented structure is also in place at Kyocera Corporation, which was voted the best-managed company in Japan.

- *Force for productivity.* Shenandoah Life Insurance Company credits its new team organization with a 50 percent increase in the handling of applications and customer service requests, with fewer people.[3]

- *Force for quality.* Quality has risen 50 percent in a Northern Telecom facility, and Federal Express has reduced billing errors and lost packages by 13 percent. Boeing's engineering teams built its new 777 passenger jet with fewer than half as many design errors as earlier programs.[4]

- *Force for cost reduction.* Honeywell's teams have saved over $11 million after reducing production times and shipping over 99 percent of orders on time.[5]

- *Force for speed.* 3M, Chrysler, and many other companies are using teams to create new products quicker. Nynex is using teams to move from being a bureaucratic Baby Bell to a high-speed force on the information highway.[6]

- *Force for change.* Raymond Smith, CEO of Bell Atlantic Corporation, is transforming a formerly monopolistic bureaucracy into an entrepreneurial corporation. A major mechanism has been the creation of client service groups (CSGs). What had been a large staff organization became an array of autonomous profit centers that develop their own assortments of products or services and market them to both corporate headquarters and the various operating companies of Bell Atlantic.[7]

- *Force for innovation.* At 3M, work teams turned around one division by tripling the number of new products.[8] 3M's innovative success stories are numerous and legendary, emerging through the use of teams that are small entrepreneurial businesses within the larger corporation.

THE NEW TEAM ENVIRONMENT

Organizations have been using teams for a long time. But things are different today.[9] Teams are being more fully integrated into the organizational structure, and their authority is increasing. Managers realize more than ever that teams can provide competitive advantage and greatly improve organizational performance. They know the potential for the whole is far greater than the sum of its individual parts.

Thus, teams are used in many different ways, and to far greater effect, than in the past. Table 16.1 highlights just a few of the differences between how teams were managed in the traditional environment and how they work today. As you can see, people are far more involved, they are better trained, cooperation is higher, and the culture is one of learning as well as producing.

The trend today is toward **self-managed teams,** in which workers are trained to do all or most of the jobs in the unit, they have no immediate supervisor, and they make decisions previously made by first-line supervisors.[10] Self-managed teams are most frequently found

TABLE 16.1

The new team environment

Traditional Environment	Team Environment
Managers determine and plan the work.	Managers and team members jointly determine and plan the work.
Jobs are narrowly defined.	Jobs require broad skills and knowledge.
Cross-training is viewed as inefficient.	Cross-training is the norm.
Most information is "management property."	Most information is freely shared at all levels.
Training for nonmanagers focuses on technical skills.	Continuous learning requires interpersonal, administrative, and technical training for all.
Risk taking is discouraged and punished.	Measured risk taking is encouraged and supported.
People work alone.	People work together.
Rewards are based on individual performance.	Rewards are based on individual performance and contributions to team performance.
Managers determine "best methods."	Everyone works to continuously improve methods and processes.

Source: J. Zenger and Associates, *Leading Teams* (Homewood, Ill.: Richard D. Irwin, 1994), p. 24.

in manufacturing. Compared to traditionally managed teams, self-managed teams appear to be more productive, have lower costs, provide better customer service, provide higher quality, have better safety records, and be more satisfying for members.

SOME SELF-MANAGED TEAMS

- Josten, manufacturer of a variety of products, and from whom so many people buy their class rings, introduced self-managed teams to increase speed and productivity in the making of its class rings. Training was an essential first step. People were taught how to conduct effective meetings and how to solve problems. Everyone attended a World Class Manufacturing Seminar, and a variety of workshops on empowerment, feedback, leadership, and the like. The company established the Josten's Learning Center Computer Lab for all to use. Results have been outstanding.
- Otis Engineering's plant in Dallas makes safety equipment for surface and subsurface oil wells. Before instituting self-managed teams, the company did a thorough job of communicating the philosophy behind them, as well as articulating the new roles of team coaches and members. Since Otis has moved to self-managed teams, its products that used to take four months to build are now completed in 10 days. This *despite* an emphasis on quality above efficiency! The firm's vice president for manufacturing believes empowered teams are the *only* option for survival.
- At Texas Instrument's facility in Sherman, Texas, peers conduct performance appraisals of one another. The purpose is to create a focus on team-oriented performance rather than individual productivity. Everyone on each team receives feedback on interpersonal and administrative as well as technical skills. The teams have decided all these skills are essential to team success. The peer appraisals are used to provide constructive feedback, not for compensation decisions. Compensation is based on knowledge, skills, and team performance.

Source: D. Yeatts, M. Hipskind, and D. Barnes, "Lessons Learned from Self-Managed Work Teams," *Business Horizons,* July–August 1994, pp. 11–18. ●

The popularity of teams is on the increase. This Herman Miller work team is positively jubilant.

(Courtesy Herman Miller, Inc.)

TYPES OF TEAMS

A *working group* is a collection of people who work in the same area or have been drawn together to undertake a task but do not necessarily come together as a unit and achieve significant performance improvements. A real **team** is formed of people (usually a small number) with complementary skills who trust one another and are committed to a common purpose, common performance goals, and a common approach for which they hold themselves mutually accountable.[11] A real team is committed to working together successfully to achieve high performance.

There may be hundreds of groups and teams in your organization. Very generally, teams can be divided into three primary types.[12] **Work teams** make or do things such as manufacture, assemble, sell, or provide service. These typically are part of the formal organizational structure. These traditional teams now are becoming more self-managed.

Project and development teams work on long-term projects, often over a period of years. They have specific assignments such as research or new-product development, and disband once their work is completed. Then, new teams are formed for new projects.

Parallel teams operate separately from the regular work structure of the firm on a temporary basis. Their charge is to recommend solutions to specific problems. Examples include task forces and quality or safety teams formed to study a particular problem that has come up.

Every instance of one of these types begins as no more than a working group with the potential of becoming a team. The best ones become true teams.

HOW GROUPS BECOME TEAMS

Effective leadership of groups is central to the manager's role. As a manager, you will want your group to become an effective team. To accomplish this, it helps you to understand why groups form, how groups can become true teams, and why groups sometimes fail to become teams.

WHY PEOPLE FORM GROUPS

Groups form because they are useful. In organizations, groups serve numerous functions (see Table 16.2). Some of these functions benefit the organization directly; others benefit primarily the group's members.[13]

	For the Organization	For the Individual
TABLE 16.2 Functions served by groups in organizations	1. Accomplish tasks that could not be done by individuals working alone. 2. Bring multiple skills and talents to bear on complex tasks. 3. Provide a vehicle for decision making that permits multiple and conflicting views to be aired and considered. 4. Provide an efficient means for organizational control of individual behavior. 5. Facilitate changes in organizational policies or procedures. 6. Increase organizational stability by transmitting shared beliefs and values to new members.	1. Aid in learning about the organization and its environment. 2. Aid in learning about oneself. 3. Provide help in gaining new skills. 4. Obtain valued rewards that are not accessible through individual initiative. 5. Directly satisfy important personal needs, especially needs for social acceptance.

Source: D. Nadler, J. R. Hackman, and E. E. Lawler III, *Managing Organizational Behavior* (Boston: Little, Brown, 1979), p. 102.

The organization benefits because groups have greater *total resources* (skills, talents, information, energy) than individuals do. Therefore, they can perform jobs that can't be done by individuals working alone. They also have a greater *diversity of resources,* which enables groups to perform complex tasks. Also, groups can aid decision making, as you learned in Chapter 4. They help socialize new members, control individuals' behavior, and facilitate organizational performance, innovation, and change.

Groups also provide many benefits for their members. The group is a very useful learning mechanism. Members learn about the company and themselves, and they acquire new skills and performance strategies. The group can satisfy important personal needs, such as affiliation and esteem. Other needs are met as group members receive tangible organizational rewards that they could not have achieved working alone.

How Teams Develop

Groups become true teams via basic group activities, the passage of time, and team development activities.

Group Activities

Assume you are the leader of a newly formed group. What will you face as you attempt to develop your group into a high-performing team? As groups develop, they engage in various activities, including:[14]

- *Forming*—group members attempt to lay the ground rules for what types of behavior are acceptable.

- *Storming*—hostilities and conflict arise, and people jockey for positions of power and status.

- *Norming*—group members agree on their shared goals, and norms and closer relationships develop.

- *Performing*—the group channels its energies into performing its task.

Groups that deteriorate move to a *declining* stage, and temporary groups add an *adjourning* or terminating stage. Groups terminate when they complete their task or when they disband due to failure or loss of interest.

The Passage of Time

A key aspect of development is the passage of time. Groups pass through *critical periods,* or times when they are particularly open to formative experiences.[15] The first such critical period is the first meeting, when rules, norms, and roles are established that set long-lasting precedents. A second critical period is the midway point between the initial meeting and a deadline (e.g., completing a project or making a presentation). At this point, the group has enough experience to understand its work, it comes to realize that time is becoming a scarce resource and it must "get on with it," and there is enough time left to change its approach if necessary.

In the initial meeting, the leader should establish desired norms, roles, and other determinants of effectiveness considered throughout this chapter. At the second critical period (the midpoint), groups should renew or open lines of communication with outside constituencies. The group can use this fresh information from its external environment to revise its approach to performing its task and ensure that it meets the needs of customers and clients. Without these activities, groups may get off on the wrong foot from the beginning and members may never revise their behavior in the appropriate direction.[16]

A Developmental Sequence: From Group to Team

As a manager or group member, you should expect the group to engage in all of the activities discussed above at various times. All of these activities are natural, and all are important. But groups are not always successful. They do not always engage in the developmental activities that turn them into effective, high-performing teams.

A useful *developmental sequence* is depicted in Figure 16.1. The figure shows the various activities as the leadership of the group moves from traditional supervision, through a more participative approach, to true team leadership.[17]

It is important to understand a couple of things about this model. Groups do not necessarily keep progressing from one "stage" to the next; they may remain permanently in the supervisory level, or become more participative but never make it to true team leadership. Therefore, progress on these dimensions must be a conscious goal of the leader and the members, and all should strive to meet these goals. Your group can meet these goals, and become a true team, by engaging in the activities in the figure.

WHY GROUPS SOMETIMES FAIL

Team building does not necessarily progress smoothly through such a sequence, culminating in a well-oiled team and superb performance. Some groups never do work out. Such groups can be frustrating for managers and members, who may feel they are a waste of time, and that the difficulties outweigh the benefits.

It is not easy to build high-performance teams. Says a top consultant: "Teams are the Ferraris of work design. They're high performance but high maintenance and expensive."[18]

"Teams" is often just a word used by management to describe merely putting people into groups. "Teams" sometimes are launched with little or no training or support systems. For example, managers as well as group members need new skills to make the group work. These skills include diplomacy, the ability to tackle "people issues" head on, and walking the fine line between encouraging autonomy and rewarding team innovations without letting the team get too independent and out of control.[19] Giving up some control is very difficult for managers from traditional systems; they have to realize they will *gain* control in the long run by virtue of creating stronger, better-performing units.

Teams should be truly empowered, as discussed in Chapter 15. The benefits of teams are reduced when they are not allowed to make important decisions—in other words, when management doesn't trust them with important responsibilities. If teams must acquire permission for every innovative idea, they will revert to making safe, traditional decisions.[20] Thus, management must truly support teams by giving them some freedom and rewarding their contributions.

FIGURE   16.1

Stepping up to
team leadership

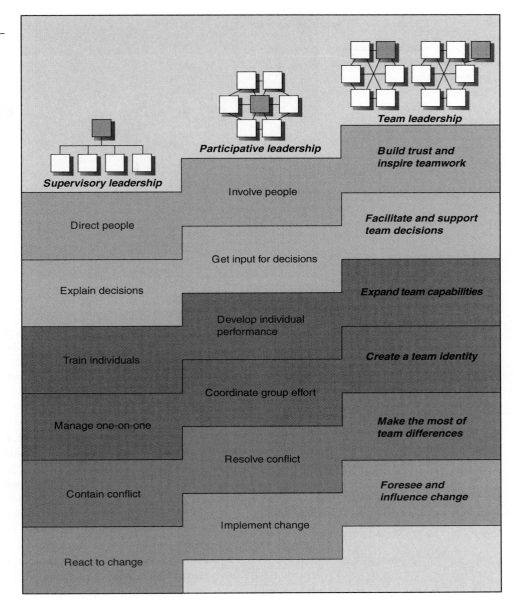

Source: J. Zenger and Associates, *Leading Teams* (Homewood, Ill.: Richard D. Irwin, 1994), p. 24.

Failure lies in not knowing and doing what makes teams successful. To be successful you must apply clear thinking and appropriate practices.[21] That is what the rest of the chapter is about.

BUILDING
EFFECTIVE TEAMS

Innovation

All the considerations just described form the building blocks of an effective work team. But what does it really mean for a team to be *effective?* What, precisely, can a manager do to design a truly effective team? Team effectiveness is defined by three criteria.[22]

First, the *productive output* of the team meets or exceeds the standards of quantity and quality; the team's output is acceptable to those customers, inside or outside the organization, who receive the team's products or services. Procter & Gamble's business teams are effective at reducing costs and at developing new products.[23] Clarence L. "Kelly" Johnson's group designed, built, and flew the first U.S. tactical jet fighter, XP80, in 143

This Hon Industry safety team addresses issues such as member training, housekeeping, safe workplace design, procedures, and personal fitness. Here, team members exercise before starting their shift.
(Courtesy Hon Industries)

Speed

Quality

days.[24] Tom West's legendary Eclipse Group at Data General worked overtime for a year and a half to create the 32-bit super minicomputer that heralded the next generation of minicomputers.[25]

Second, team members realize *satisfaction* of their personal needs. P&G's team members enjoy the opportunity to creatively participate. Johnson and West gave their teams the freedom to innovate and stretch their skills. Team members were enthusiastic and realized great pride and satisfaction in their work.

Third, team members remain *committed* to working together again; that is, the group doesn't burn out and disintegrate after a grueling project. Looking back, the members are glad they were involved. In other words, effective teams remain *viable* and have good prospects for repeated success in the future.[26]

Cost

Teams can be effective at all kinds of tasks.[27] At Colgate-Palmolive, teams handle the entire process of making bottles, filling them with detergent, and packaging the product for distribution. At Development Dimensions International in Pittsburgh, a printing, warehouse, and distribution facility, teams identify and meet customer requirements, establish improvement goals and measure results, select suppliers, identify training needs, and recommend new equipment. At K Shoes, Ltd., teams understand the business and marketplace issues that affect demand, handle materials and equipment budgeting, and control profit and loss.

A PERFORMANCE FOCUS

The key element of effective teamwork is a commitment to a common purpose.[28] The best teams are ones that have been given an important performance challenge by management, and then have come to a common understanding and appreciation of their purpose. Without such understanding and commitment, a group will be just a bunch of individuals. With a clear, strong, motivating purpose, people will pull together into a powerful force that has a chance to achieve extraordinary things.

The team's general purpose should be translated into specific, measurable performance goals.[29] You learned in Chapter 15 about how goals motivate individual performance. Team-based performance goals help define and distinguish the team's product, encourage communication within the team, energize and motivate team members, provide feedback on progress, signal team victories (and defeats), and ensure that the team focuses clearly on results.

The best team-based measurement systems will inform top management of the team's performance *and* will help the team understand its own processes and gauge its own progress.[30] Ideally, the team will play the lead role in designing its own measurement system. This is a great indicator of whether the team is truly "empowered."

WORKING TOGETHER

The best teams work hard at developing a common understanding of how they will work together to achieve their purpose.[31] They discuss and agree upon such things as how tasks and roles will be allocated, and how the group will make decisions. The team should develop norms for examining its performance strategies and be amenable to changing when appropriate.

It must be clear to all that everyone works hard, contributes in concrete ways to the team's work, and is accountable to other team members. Accountability to one another, rather than just to "the boss," is an essential aspect of good teamwork. Accountability inspires mutual commitment and trust.[32] Trust in your teammates—and their trust in you— may be the ultimate key to effectiveness.

Team effort is also generated in the first place by *designing* the team's task to be motivating. Techniques for creating motivating tasks appear in the guidelines for job enrichment discussed in Chapter 15. Tasks are motivating when they use a variety of member skills and provide high task identity, significance, autonomy, and performance feedback.

Companies that change to team-based designs must change their performance measurement system to keep pace. It is common to want teamwork but to measure individual accomplishment. Such traditional systems will fail to support the new teams. In fact, they will undermine them. A new system must focus on *team-based performance,* so that *rewards* can be team-based.

For example, at Ampex, teams are assessed against goals for continuous improvement, productivity improvement, and safety. At Miller Brewing Company, team performance is judged against team goals for production, quality, and safety. In addition, each team constantly tries to better its previous performance levels. At Texas Instruments, key team goals are improving quality, reducing costs, and meeting schedules. TI's teams also have a stretch goal tied to some specific critical need, and often have special project goals.[33]

MEMBER CONTRIBUTIONS

Team members should be selected and trained so they become effective contributors to the team. Teams often hire their new members.[34] Miller Brewing Company and Eastman Chemical teams select members on the basis of tests designed to predict how well they will contribute to team success in an empowered environment. At Hannaford Brothers Company, a retail supermarket and food distributor in New York, new employees become "team certified" and then join their teams. At Texas Instruments, Human Resources screens applicants; then team members interview them and make selection decisions.

Skills required by the team include technical or functional expertise, problem-solving and decision-making skills, and interpersonal skills. Some managers and teams mistakenly overemphasize some skills and neglect others. It is vitally important that all three types of skills are represented, and developed, among team members.

Development Dimensions International provides people with 300 hours of training, mostly about how to work in teams, but also technical cross-training. K Shoes, Ltd., trains team members in teamwork, overall business knowledge, supplier partnership development, and retail management. Kodak provides 150 hours of first-year training on team effectiveness, including teaching people to cross-train others, and 120 more hours subsequently on the same team skills plus business and financial skills.[35]

NORMS

Norms are shared beliefs about how team members should think and behave. Recall from Chapter 11 that shared beliefs form the basis for the organization culture.

From the organization's standpoint, norms can be positive or negative. In some teams, everyone works hard; in other groups, employees are antimanagement and do as little work as possible. A norm could dictate that employees speak favorably of the company in public, or criticize it. Or a norm could specify being open and honest and respecting the opinions of others, or avoiding confronting important issues and gossiping behind people's backs. Team members may show concern about poor safety practices, drug and alcohol abuse, and employee theft, or they may not care about these issues (or they may even condone such practices). Health consciousness is the norm among executives at some companies, but smoking is the norm at tobacco companies.

A professor described his consulting experiences at two companies that exhibited different norms in their management teams.[36] At Federal Express Corporation, a young manager interrupted the professor's talk by proclaiming that a recent decision by top management ran counter to the professor's point about corporate planning. He was challenging top management to defend their decision. A hot debate ensued, and after an hour everyone went to lunch without a trace of hard feelings. But at another corporation, the professor opened a meeting by asking a group of top managers to describe the company's culture. There was silence. He asked again. More silence. Then someone passed him an unsigned note that read, "Dummy, can't you see that we can't speak our minds? Ask for the input anonymously, in writing." As you can see, norms are important, and can vary greatly from one group to another.

ROLES

Roles are different sets of expectations for how various individuals should behave. Whereas norms apply generally to all team members, different roles exist for different members within the norm structure.

Two important sets of roles must be performed.[37] **Task specialist** roles are filled by individuals who have more job-related skills and abilities than do other members. These employees have more decision-making responsibilities and provide instructions and advice. They keep the team moving toward task accomplishment. **Team maintenance specialists** develop and maintain harmony within the team. They boost morale, give support, provide humor, soothe hurt feelings, and generally exhibit a concern with members' well-being.

Note the similarity between these roles and the important task performance and group maintenance leadership behaviors you learned about in Chapter 14. As suggested in that chapter, some of these roles will be more important than others at different times and under different circumstances. But these behaviors need not be carried out only by the formal leader; *any* member of the team can carry out these roles at any time. Over time, both types of roles will be performed by different individuals to maintain an effectively functioning work team.

What should be the role of the team's formal leader? The leader should keep the team's purpose, goals, and approach relevant and meaningful; build commitment and confidence; strengthen the mix and level of team members' skills; manage relationships with outsiders; remove obstacles to the team's performance; create opportunities for the team and its members; and do real work, not just supervise.[38]

Self-managed teams report to a management representative, sometimes called the coach. For example, at Wilson Sporting Goods Company, coaches facilitate and provide support and direction to teams, and hourly associates share leadership responsibilities with the coaches.[39] In true self-managed teams, the coach is *not* a true member of the team.[40] This is because the group is supposed to make its own decisions, and because the relative power of the management representative can have a dampening effect on the team's openness and autonomy.

The role of the coach, then, is to help the team understand its role in the organization, and to act as a resource for the team. The coach can provide information, resources, and opinions that team members do not or cannot acquire on their own. And, the coach should be an advocate for the team in the rest of the organization.

COHESIVENESS

One of the most important properties of a work team is cohesiveness.[41] **Cohesiveness** refers to how attractive the team is to its members, how motivated members are to remain in the team, and the degree to which team members influence one another. In general, it refers to how tightly knit the team is.

The Importance of Cohesiveness

Cohesiveness is important for two primary reasons. First, it contributes to *member satisfaction.* In a cohesive team, members communicate and get along well with one another. They feel good about being a part of the team. Even if their jobs are unfulfilling or the organization is oppressive, people gain some satisfaction from enjoying their co-workers.

Second, cohesiveness has a major impact on *performance.* Sports fans read about this all the time. When teams are winning, players talk about the team being close, getting along well, and knowing one another's games. In contrast, losing is attributed to infighting and divisiveness. It is easy to conclude that cohesiveness has a positive effect on performance.

But this interpretation is simplistic; exceptions to this intuitive relationship occur. Tightly knit work groups can be disruptive to the organization, such as when they sabotage the assembly line, get their boss fired, or enforce low performance norms.

When does high cohesiveness lead to good performance, and when does it result in poor performance? This depends on (1) the task and (2) whether the group has high or low performance norms.

The Task

If the task is to make a decision or solve a problem, cohesiveness can lead to poor performance. Groupthink (discussed in Chapter 4) occurs when a tightly knit group is so cooperative that agreeing with one another's opinions and refraining from criticizing others' ideas become norms. The following example illustrates this tendency.

THE ABILENE PARADOX

*T*he July afternoon in Coleman, Texas (population 5,607), was particularly hot—104 degrees as measured by the Walgreen's Rexall Ex-Lax temperature gauge. In addition, the wind was blowing fine-grained West Texas topsoil through the house. But the afternoon was still tolerable—even potentially enjoyable. There was a fan going on the back porch; there was cold lemonade; and finally, there was entertainment. Dominoes. Perfect for the conditions. The game required little more physical exertion than an occasional mumbled comment, "Shuffle 'em," and an unhurried movement of the arm to place the spots in the appropriate perspective on the table. All in all, it had the makings of an agreeable Sunday afternoon in Coleman—that is, it was until my father-in-law suddenly said, "Let's get in the car and go to Abilene and have dinner at the cafeteria."

I thought, "What, go to Abilene? Fifty-three miles? In this dust storm and heat? And in an unairconditioned 1958 Buick?"

But my wife chimed in with, "Sounds like a great idea. I'd like to go. How about you, Jerry?" Since my own preferences were obviously out of step with the rest, I replied, "Sounds good to me," and added, "I just hope your mother wants to go."

"Of course I want to go," said my mother-in-law. "I haven't been to Abilene in a long time."

So into the car and off to Abilene we went. My predictions were fulfilled. The heat was brutal. We were coated with a fine layer of dust that was cemented with perspiration by the time we arrived. The food in the cafeteria provided first-rate testimonial material for antacid commercials.

Some four hours and 106 miles later we returned to Coleman, hot and exhausted. We sat in front of the fan for a long time in silence. Then, both to be sociable and to break the silence, I said, "It was a great trip, wasn't it?"

No one spoke.

Finally, my mother-in-law said, with some irritation, "Well, to tell the truth, I really didn't enjoy it much and would rather have stayed here. I just went along because the three of you were so enthusiastic about going. I wouldn't have gone if you all hadn't pressured me into it."

I couldn't believe it. "What do you mean 'you all'?" I said. "Don't put me in the 'you all' group. I was delighted to be doing what we were doing. I didn't want to go. I only went to satisfy the rest of you. You're the culprits."

My wife looked shocked. "Don't call me a culprit. You and Daddy and Mama were the ones who wanted to go. I just went along to be sociable and keep you happy. I would have had to be crazy to want to go out in heat like that."

Her father entered the conversation abruptly. "Hell!" he said.

He proceeded to expand on what was already absolutely clear. "Listen, I never wanted to go to Abilene. I just thought you might be bored. You visit so seldom I wanted to be sure you enjoyed it. I would have preferred to play another game of dominoes and eat the leftovers in the icebox."

After the outburst of recrimination, we all sat back in silence. Here we were, four reasonably sensible people who, of our own volition, had just taken a 106-mile trip across a godforsaken desert in furnacelike temperatures through a cloudlike dust storm to eat unpalatable food at a hole-in-the-wall cafeteria in Abilene, when none of us had really wanted to go. In fact, to be more accurate, we'd done just the opposite of what we wanted to do. The whole situation simply didn't make sense.

Source: Reprinted by permission of the publisher, from *Organizational Dynamics,* Summer 1974. © 1974 American Management Association, New York. All rights reserved. ●

In the Abilene example, the group was exhibiting groupthink. Disagreement, which is more likely to occur in *noncohesive* groups, could have led to a better decision: to stay in Coleman. For a cohesive group to make good decisions, it should establish a norm of constructive disagreement. It could also create the role of devil's advocate, as suggested in Chapter 4.

Cohesiveness can enhance performance if the task is to produce some tangible output. In day-to-day work groups for which decision making is not the primary task, the effect of cohesiveness on performance can be positive. But that depends on the group's performance norms.[42]

Performance Norms

Some groups are better than others at ensuring that their members behave the way the group prefers. Cohesive groups are more effective than noncohesive groups at norm enforcement. But the next question is: Do they have norms of high or low performance?

As Figure 16.2 shows, the highest performance occurs when a cohesive team has high performance norms. But if a highly cohesive group has low performance norms, that group will have the worst performance. In the group's eyes, however, it will have succeeded in achieving its goal of poor performance. Noncohesive groups with high performance norms will be effective from the company's standpoint. However, they won't be as productive as they would be if they were more cohesive. Noncohesive groups with low performance norms perform poorly, but they will be less successful than cohesive groups at ruining things.

FIGURE 16.2

Cohesiveness, performance norms, and group performance

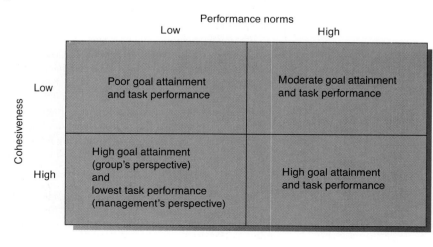

BUILDING COHESIVENESS AND HIGH PERFORMANCE NORMS

As Figure 16.2 suggests, managers should build teams that are cohesive and have high performance norms. The following actions can help create such teams:[43]

1. *Recruit members with similar attitudes, values, and backgrounds.* Similar individuals are more likely to get along with one another. *Don't* do this, though, if the team's task requires heterogeneous skills and inputs. For example, a homogeneous committee or board will make relatively poor decisions, because it will lack different information and viewpoints and may succumb to groupthink.

2. *Maintain high entrance and socialization standards.* Teams and organizations that are difficult to get into have more prestige. Individuals who survive a difficult interview, selection, or training process will be proud of their accomplishment and feel more attachment to the team.

3. *Keep the team small* (but large enough to get the job done). The larger the group, the less important members may feel. Small teams make individuals feel like large contributors.

4. *Help the team succeed, and publicize its successes.* Be a path-goal leader who facilitates success; the experience of winning brings teams closer together. Then, if you inform superiors of your team's successes, members will believe they are part of an important, prestigious unit. Teams that get into a good performance track continue to perform well as time goes on; groups that don't often enter a downward spiral in which problems compound over time.[44]

5. *Be a participative leader.* Participation in decisions gets team members more involved with one another and striving toward goal accomplishment. Too much autocratic decision making can alienate the group from management.

6. *Present a challenge from outside the team.* A deadline forces the team to draw together to beat the clock (consider how many 11th-hour agreements develop in difficult labor-management negotiations). Similarly, competition with other groups makes team members band together to defeat the enemy (witness what happens to school spirit before the big game against an archrival). But don't *you* become the outside threat. If team members dislike you as a boss, they will become more cohesive—but their performance norms will be against you, not with you.

7. *Tie rewards to team performance.* To a large degree, teams are motivated just as individuals are—they do the things that are rewarded. Make sure that high-performing teams get the rewards they deserve and that poorly producing groups get relatively few rewards. The team will become more cohesive to perform better and to reap their rewards. Performance goals will be high, the organization will benefit from higher team motivation and productivity, and the individual needs of team members will be better satisfied.

Keep in mind that these recommendations are best for teams working on tasks of productive output. If the team's task is problem solving and decision making, steps must be taken to avoid groupthink and a trip to Abilene.

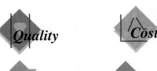

MANAGING LATERAL RELATIONSHIPS

Quality *Cost* *Innovation* *Speed*

Keep in mind that work teams are open systems (recall Chapters 1 and 2). They are not closed systems functioning in a vacuum; they are interdependent with other groups. For example, at Miller Brewing Company, major team responsibilities include coordinating with other teams and policy groups. At Texas Instruments, teams are responsible for interfacing with other teams to eliminate production bottlenecks and implement new processes, and also for working with suppliers on quality issues.[45] Thus, roles crucial to the team are those that entail dealing with people *outside* the group.

MANAGING OUTWARD

Several vital roles link teams to their external environments, that is, to individuals and groups both inside and outside the organization. You learned about *boundary-spanning roles* in Chapter 10. A specific example of a boundary spanner is the *gatekeeper,* a team member who stays abreast of technical information in scientific and other fields and informs the group of important developments. Information useful to the group can also be nontechnical, such as information about resources, trends, and political support throughout the corporation or the industry.[46]

The team's strategy dictates the team's mix of internally versus externally focused roles and how the mix changes over time. General team strategies include informing, parading, and probing.[47] The **informing** strategy entails concentrating first on the internal team process to achieve a state of performance readiness. Then the team informs outsiders of its intentions. **Parading** means the team's strategy is to simultaneously emphasize internal team building and achieve external visibility. **Probing** involves a focus on external relations. This strategy requires team members to interact frequently with outsiders, diagnose the needs of customers, clients, and higher-ups, and experiment with solutions.

The appropriate balance between an internal and external strategic focus and between internal and external roles depends on how much the team needs information, support, and resources from outside. When teams have a high degree of dependence on outsiders, probing is the best strategy. Parading teams perform at an intermediate level, and informing teams are likely to fail. They are too isolated from the outside groups on which they depend.

Informing or parading strategies may be more effective for teams that are less dependent on outside groups, for example, established teams working on routine tasks in relatively unchanging external environments. For most important work teams of the future—task forces, new-product teams, and strategic decision-making teams tackling unstructured problems in a rapidly changing external environment—effective performance in roles that involve interfacing with the outside will be vital.

LATERAL ROLE RELATIONSHIPS

Managing relationships with managers of other groups and teams means engaging in a dynamic give-and-take that ensures proper coordination throughout the management system. To many managers, this process often seems like a chaotic free-for-all. It is useful to identify the different types of lateral role relationships and take a strategic approach to building constructive relationships.

Different teams, like different individuals, have roles to perform. As teams carry out their roles, several distinct patterns of working relationships develop.[48]

1. *Work flow relationships* emerge as paperwork or materials are passed from one team to another. A team typically receives work from one unit, processes it, and sends it to the next unit in the process. Your team, then, will come before some teams and after others in the process.
2. *Service relationships* exist when top management centralizes an activity to which a large number of other units must gain access. Common examples are computing services, libraries, and clerical staff. Such units must service other people's requests.
3. *Advisory relationships* are created when teams with problems call on centralized sources of expert knowledge. For example, staff in the human resources or legal department advise work teams.
4. *Audit relationships* develop when people not directly in the chain of command evaluates the methods and performances of other teams. Financial auditors check the books, and technical auditors assess the methods and technical quality of the work.
5. *Stabilization relationships* involve auditing before the fact. In other words, teams sometimes must obtain clearance from others—for example, for large purchases—before they take action.
6. *Liaison relationships* involve intermediaries between teams. Managers often are called upon to mediate conflict between two organizational units. Public relations people, sales managers, purchasing agents, and others who work across organizational boundaries serve in liaison roles as they maintain communications between the organization and the outside world.

By assessing each working relationship with another unit ("From whom do we receive and to whom do we send work? What permissions do we control, and to whom must we go for authorizations?"), teams can better understand whom to contact and when, where, why, and how to do so. Coordination throughout the working system improves, problems are avoided or short-circuited before they get too serious, and performance in team roles improves.[49]

MANAGING INTERGROUP CONFLICT

The complex maze of interdependencies throughout organizations provides boundless opportunities for conflict to arise among groups and teams. Some conflict is constructive for the organization, as we discussed in Chapter 4. But many things cause great potential for destructive conflict: the sheer number and variety of contacts; ambiguities in jurisdiction and responsibility; differences in goals; intergroup competition for scarce resources; different perspectives held by members of different units; varying time horizons in which some units attend to long-term considerations and others focus on short-term needs; and other factors.

Tensions and anxieties are likely to arise in demographically diverse teams, or teams from different parts of the organization, or teams composed of contrasting personalities. These tensions need not be destructive influences. In fact, they can be an important source of information, new perspectives, and vitality. The team must learn not only to accept differences and conflict but to use them to advantage. The group must be willing and able to confront disagreement in direct, honest, sincere ways.[50]

Teams inevitably face conflicts and must decide how to manage them. The aim should be to make the conflict productive, that is, for those involved to believe they have benefited rather than lost from the conflict.[51] People believe they have benefited from a conflict when (1) a new solution is implemented, the problem is solved, and it is unlikely to emerge again; and (2) work relationships have been strengthened and people believe they can work together productively in the future.

Intergroup conflict can be managed through structural solutions such as the integrating roles discussed in Chapter 11. But a team in a conflict situation has several additional options regarding the style used in interactions with others.[52] These styles, shown in Figure 16.3, are distinguished based on how much people strive to satisfy their own concerns (the assertiveness dimension) and to what degree they focus on satisfying the other party's concerns (the cooperativeness dimension). For example, a common reaction to conflict is **avoidance.** In this situation, people do nothing to satisfy themselves or others. They either

FIGURE 16.3

Conflict management strategies

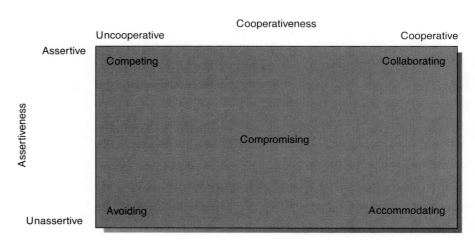

Source: K.Thomas, "Conflict and Conflict Management." In *Handbook of Industrial and Organizational Psychology,* ed. M. D. Dunnette. Copyright © 1976 John Wiley & Sons. Reprinted by permission of John Wiley & Sons, Inc.

ignore the problem by doing nothing at all or address it by merely smoothing over or deemphasizing the disagreement. This, of course, fails to solve the problem or clear the air.

Accommodation means cooperating on behalf of the other party but not being assertive about one's own interests. **Compromise** involves moderate attention to both parties' concerns, being neither highly cooperative nor highly assertive. This style therefore results in satisficing but not maximizing solutions. **Forcing** is a highly competitive response in which people focus strictly on their own wishes and are unwilling to recognize the other person's concerns. Finally, **collaboration** emphasizes both cooperation and assertiveness. The goal is to maximize satisfaction for both parties.

Quality

Cost

Innovation

Speed

Different approaches are necessary at different times.[53] For example, competition or forcing can be healthy if it promotes positive motivation and even necessary when cutting costs or dealing with other scarce resources. Compromise may be useful when under time pressure, to achieve a temporary solution, or when collaboration fails. People should accommodate when they learn they are wrong or to minimize loss when they are outmatched. Even avoiding may be appropriate if the issue is trivial or others should solve the conflict.

But when the conflict concerns important issues, when both sets of concerns are valid and important, when a creative solution is needed, and when commitment to the solution is vital to implementation, collaboration is the ideal approach. Collaboration can be achieved by airing feelings and opinions, addressing all concerns, and avoiding goal displacement by not letting personal attacks interfere with problem solving. An important technique is to invoke **superordinate goals**—higher-level organizational goals toward which all teams should be striving and that ultimately need to take precedence over unit preferences. Collaboration offers the best chance of reaching mutually satisfactory solutions based on the ideas and interests of all parties and of maintaining and strengthening work relationships.

KEY TERMS

SUMMARY OF LEARNING OBJECTIVES

Now that you have studied Chapter 16, you should know:

How teams contribute to your organization's effectiveness.

Teams are building blocks for organization structure and forces for productivity, quality, cost savings, speed, change, and innovation. They have the potential to provide many benefits for both the organization and individual members.

What makes the new team environment different from the old.

Compared to traditional work groups that were closely supervised, today's teams have more authority and often are self-managed. Teams now are used in many more ways, for many more purposes, than in the past. Types of teams include work teams, project and development teams, and parallel teams.

How groups become teams.

Groups carry on a variety of important activities including forming, storming, norming, and performing. For a group to become a team, it should move beyond traditional supervisory leadership, become more participative, and ultimately enjoy team leadership. A true team has members who complement one another; who are committed to a common purpose, performance goals, and approach; and who hold themselves accountable to one another.

Why teams sometimes fail.

Teams do not always work well. Some companies underestimate the difficulties of moving to a team-based approach. Teams require training, empowerment, and a well-managed transition to making them work. Groups may fail to become effective teams unless managers and team members commit to the idea, understand what makes teams work, and implement appropriate practices.

How to build an effective team.

Create a team with a high-performance focus by establishing a common purpose; by translating the purpose into measurable team goals; by designing the team's task so it is intrinsically motivating in the first place; then by designing a team-based performance measurement system, and providing team rewards.

Work hard to develop a common understanding of how the team will perform its task. Make it clear that everyone has to work hard and contribute in concrete ways. Establish mutual accountability and build trust among members. Examine the team's strategies periodically and be willing to adapt.

Make sure members contribute fully by selecting them appropriately, training them, and checking that all important roles are carried out. Take a variety of steps to establish team cohesiveness and high performance norms.

And don't just manage inwardly. Manage the team's relations with outsiders, too.

How to manage your team's relationships with other teams.

Perform important roles like boundary spanning, gatekeeping, informing, parading, and probing. Identify the types of lateral role relationships you have with outsiders. Build constructive relationships by thinking strategically, understanding others' perspectives, and creating trust and reciprocation through being dependable and cooperative, as appropriate.

How to manage conflict.

Conflict arises because of the sheer number of contacts, ambiguities, goal differences, competition for scarce resources, and different perspectives and time horizons. Depending on the situation, five basic interpersonal approaches to managing conflict are available: avoidance, accommodation, compromise, forcing, and collaboration. Superordinate goals offer a focus on higher-level organizational goals that can help generate a collaborative relationship.

DISCUSSION QUESTIONS

1. Why do you think some people resist the idea of working in teams? How would you deal with their resistance?
2. Consider a job you have held, and review Table 16.1 about the traditional and new team environment. Which environment best describes your job? Assess your job on each of the dimensions described in the table.
3. Assess your job as in question 2, using Figure 16.1, "Stepping Up to Team Leadership." Which leadership "stage" characterized your job environment?
4. Identify some things from a previous job that could have been done differently to move your work group closer toward the "team leadership" depicted in Figure 16.1.
5. Experts say that teams are a means, not an end. What do you think they mean? What do you think happens in a company that creates teams just for the sake of having teams because it's a fad or just because it sounds good? How can this pitfall be avoided?
6. Choose a sports team with which you are familiar. Assess its effectiveness and discuss the factors that contribute to its level of effectiveness.
7. Assess the effectiveness, as in question 6, of a student group with which you have been affiliated. Could anything have been done to make it more effective?
8. Consider the various roles that members have to perform for a team to be effective. Which roles would play to your strengths and which to your weaknesses? How can you become a better team member?
9. Can you think of any personal examples of the Abilene Paradox? Explain what happened and why.
10. What do you think are your own most commonly used approaches to handling conflict? Least common? What can you do to expand your repertoire and become more effective at conflict management?
11. Generate real examples of how superordinate goals have helped to resolve a conflict. Identify some current conflicts and provide some specific ideas for how superordinate goals could be used to help.

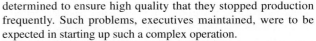

CONCLUDING CASE

GM's SATURN PLANT

GM's Saturn plant was designed when teamwork and empowerment had become the rage at GM. Saturn was to epitomize those concepts. Hourly workers got involved in virtually every decision, down to minor details. Managers and union workers went on Outward Bound-type training courses where they ran obstacle courses together and dealt with tasks that required teamwork and trust.

The organization chart was a series of interlocking circles, rather than the old GM pyramid. Each group ran its own show, and was to produce to schedule, perform to budget, create a quality product, and account for inventory control, repairs, absenteeism, scrap, and record-keeping. Moreover, teams were expected to communicate and cooperate with other teams.

Consensus and teamwork were the bywords. The Saturn plant hired exceptionally motivated workers, provided intensive train-

GM's Saturn Plant is designed around work teams and employee empowerment.

(Copyright 1995 Kevin Horan)

ing, and gave employees more say in their work. Also, it paid them salary plus performance bonuses—just as it paid executives. Even more radical was the company's bold experiment in organization structure. GM replaced its traditional line-staff hierarchy with management-union committees, as the table shows.

The first Saturn cars went on sale in selected markets in October 1990. Production at that time was far below expectations, in part because of the Gulf War and the recession and partly because of production glitches. For example, workers took longer than expected to learn to inspect their own work, and they were so

determined to ensure high quality that they stopped production frequently. Such problems, executives maintained, were to be expected in starting up such a complex operation.

Saturn is run by teams. At the most basic level, automobiles are built by the work units—teams of 6 to 15 workers, who in many respects manage themselves. Team members decide who does which job, when to order supplies, and how to control costs. Furthermore, each team maintains its own equipment, does its own inspections, sets relief and vacation schedules for its members, and tracks business data like production and freight schedules.

At the next level are work unit modules, groups of three to six work units led by a company adviser. Each module acts as a liaison between its work units and various company experts such as engineers, marketing specialists, and personnel representatives. In addition, these groups serve as a conduit of information to and from the business unit, which manages the entire plant. That group, composed of company representatives, elected workers, and various specialists, coordinates plant-level operations. Above that group are two specialty committees—one that decides on changes in salaries and benefits and one that handles long-range planning for the company.

QUESTIONS

1. What does General Motors hope to gain by using this team-dominated structure?

2. What are the possible disadvantages?

3. How would you like working at Saturn?

4. How is Saturn doing today? What do current reports say about morale, team effectiveness, quality, and productivity at the plant?

Sources: M. Edid, "How Power Will Be Balanced on Saturn's Shop Floor," in *Inside Management: A Selection of Readings from Business Week,* ed. D. R. Hampton (New York: McGraw-Hall, 1986), pp. 154–56; A. Taylor III, "Back to the Future at Saturn," *Fortune,* August 1, 1988, pp. 83–89; M. Maynard, "Enthusiasm Drives Saturn Workers," *USA Today,* August 31, 1990, p. 2B; S. C. Gwynne, "The Right Stuff," *Time,* October 29, 1990, pp. 74–84; J. B. Treece, "Are the Planets Lining Up for Saturn?" *Business Week,* April 8, 1991, pp. 32–34; P. Ingrassia and J. White, *Comeback: The Fall and Rise of the American Automobile Industry* (New York: Simon & Schuster, 1994); and E. Hitchner, *In the Rings of Saturn* (New York: Oxford University Press, 1994).

GM's Traditional Hierarchy	The Saturn Structure
Plant manager	Strategic advisory committee (long-range planning)
Production manager General superintendent	Manufacturing advisory committee (oversees Saturn complex)
Production superintendent (5 per shift)	Business unit (coordinates plant-level operations)
General supervisor (15 per shift)	Work unit module
Supervisor/foreman (90 per shift)	Work units

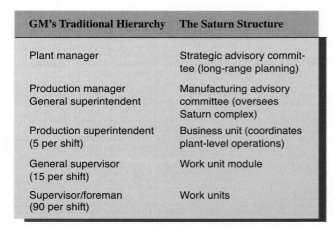

VIDEO CASE

QUALITY TEAMWORK AT THE UNIVERSITY OF MICHIGAN HOSPITALS

Foreign competition is increasing in almost every industry, and so are operating costs. Many industries have found that quality management is the solution to both of these challenges. As a result, a quality movement is sweeping across America. Teamwork is a significant part of this movement. Originally embraced by manufacturing industries, quality management and teamwork are now being used in many service industries as well. Service businesses appreciate the positive effect these practices have on employee morale, productivity, and customer satisfaction.

The University of Michigan Hospitals adopted quality management as a way to attract and keep top people in the health care profession. John Forsyth, executive director of the University of Michigan Hospitals, explained, "The three reasons the University of Michigan has become involved in total quality are: number one, to become the provider of choice; number two, to become preeminent in education in the medical sciences; and number three, to become the employer of choice. The key here is to have a diverse and motivated workforce, and we believe total quality will empower people to that end."

The development of problem-solving teams composed of both managers and employees is one highly effective aspect of a quality program. Team problem-solving techniques are proving to be a simple, effective catalyst to organizational creativity, quality improvement, and higher quality of work life. But team building in the United States requires a major culture change. Working in groups is somewhat unnatural to Americans who are instilled with a philosophy of individual achievement beginning in elementary school and continuing throughout their academic and business careers. Larry Warren, an administrator at the University of Michigan Hospitals, expressed his personal reservations about changing to a team-oriented culture: "To suggest that we change the way we do business to one of team approach, to everything that we do and do in the future, stressed me out a little bit."

For teamwork to be effective, new work relationships must be based on trust. One important way to establish this trust is through extensive training and team skills. Ellen Gaucher, senior associate hospital director, said, "We were very concerned about pushing people too hard. We thought they might think this was just another thing administration had up their sleeve for making them work harder. So we got involved with developing a training program that we thought would be the hook for us, would get them excited about total quality. And it has worked very well."

When a quality team is initially selected, it should include decision makers from several key groups: employees, peers, senior managers, customers, suppliers, and staff support. The common characteristics of any team member are interest in the team, and the ability to make decisions and commitments on behalf of the team. Joan Robinson, director of ambulatory care nursing, said, "Our nurses are next to the action. They know what our problems are, and they have been schooled on a scientific process of how to address problems. The total quality approach gives us some of the answers in terms of tools that they can use, and working with other people to solve problems, both clinical and some of the problems in the systems of how we get things done here."

Leadership is crucial for a team approach to be effective. The biggest part of a team leader's job is to keep the team together while its members solve the problem. This means developing critical-thinking skills in other team members by asking open-ended questions, or by providing business information so decisions can be made. A team leader must know when to intervene and when to stand back. The leader must avoid the temptation to jump in with solutions, allowing the team to solve the problem it has been charged with. Essentially, there are seven ground rules for effective teamwork:

1. *Time control:* Each team should have a clear, achievable deadline for resolving the problem.
2. *Be sensitive:* Each team member should be sensitive to the other members' needs and expressions.
3. *Relaxed atmosphere:* An informal, relaxed atmosphere should be fostered.
4. *Be prepared:* Material needed for team meetings should be prepared in advance.
5. *Qualified and interested members:* All team members should be qualified and have an interest in the problem the team has been assigned to solve.
6. *Keep good records:* Minutes should be kept of all team meetings.
7. *Assess team performance:* Each team should periodically stop and assess its performance.

When a company develops a quality management program, it's important to implement it slowly and in stages. Widespread team mania at the start-up of a quality program can be dangerous. Leadership by example, employee involvement, and team-building pilot projects make the transition to team problem-solving easier. After training began at the University of Michigan Hospitals, for example, management looked for an area of the hospital to pilot the new team approach. The admitting/discharge unit was selected because of its convoluted system. After examining the problem, the quality team came up with a solution: use a computer link between admitting and housekeeping. Mary Decker Staples, associate hospital administrator, said, "It was successful enough that when we initiated measuring how long it was taking us to admit patients we were averaging two hours after the patient was ready to go up to the room to actually get to the room. Last year the average was 24 minutes—a 65 percent reduction in the amount of time it takes to admit a patient."

This early success with the team approach built momentum for the future. Employees gained confidence that the approach was effective. Sally Ellis, clinical nurse, remarked, "I think the pilot program that we had with the admissions/discharge team has definitely helped. Some of the things that have come out after it are that we've all had an understanding now of what people do. It takes away some of the myths or perceptions of why something didn't happen. I think that prior to this it was easy to blame someone else why something didn't get done or why a patient didn't get out of here on time."

Once a pilot program has been implemented and employees begin to get excited about the new approach, quality teams can effectively solve all kinds of problems. At the University of Michigan Hospitals, another team tackled problems in accounts receivable. It found that the accounting department was receiving 200 to 300 calls a day—a volume so large that staff members were able to answer less than 50 percent of all calls. The quality team developed more effective means of bookkeeping, which freed up the staff so they were able to handle more calls. Pamela Chapelle, assistant manager of financial services, said, "For June, the number of calls that we answered was 74 percent. We have never, in the four years that I've been in this department, answered 74 percent of the calls that have come in."

Another quality team helped open up communication between departments for more effective patient care. A pharmacy team was reviewing the administration of drugs by the medical staff when it found that one drug could be administered on an eight-hour basis instead of the current six-hour basis. The team organized educational sessions with the medical and pharmacy staffs. Michael Ryan, assistant directory of pharmacy said, "What we find now is that 97 percent of prescribing is being done on an eight-hour basis. This has resulted in savings of labor for staff that have to compound and administer the extra dose as well as the expense of the drug which is a savings of about $30,000 per year."

The key element in effective team problem solving is employee empowerment. Teams cannot be effective if management changes or ignores the team's final recommendations. In a team situation, management must give employees wide latitude in how they go about achieving the company's goals. This requires turning the organization chart upside down, recognizing that management is there to aid the worker in overcoming problems that arise. True employee empowerment enables an employee to achieve his or her highest potential, which benefits the company and the customer.

The success of quality teams at the University of Michigan Hospitals has been recognized throughout the health care profession. In 1990, Witt and Associates, Inc., and the Health Care Forum awarded the University of Michigan Hospitals with the Commitment to Quality Award. The award was established in 1987 to recognize health care professionals committed to quality health care services. The success of the teamwork approach at the University of Michigan Hospitals has convinced many managers that it is a worthwhile endeavor. Staples said, "I think one of the biggest advantages and positive aspects of total quality is our opportunity to use the knowledge that people who are working at the front line have about what works and what doesn't work. So often we as managers sit back thinking we know what's going on. And when you begin to ask employees what's going on you get a very different picture of the process."

The employees at the University of Michigan Hospitals have embraced the philosophy of quality management, and the use of teams for solving problems, increasing work effort, and developing good employee attitudes. Not only do teams solve problems more effectively, but they allow the employees to focus on improving the processes that affect them. The result? Smoother working relationships, streamlined procedures, and reduced costs.

CRITICAL THINKING QUESTIONS

1. Producing quality services through the use of teamwork has proven an effective approach for the University of Michigan Hospitals. Why do you think team problem solving has proven to be so effective? How do teams differ from committees or task forces?

2. As discussed briefly in the video, some employees will initially resist organizational transformation to a team approach. Why do you think employees would resist this change? What are some techniques a manager might use to help overcome this resistance?

3. Teams are very effective in solving problems related to the process flow of an organization. Try to think of some organizational problems or issues that are not likely to be resolved using a team approach. Explain why you think so.

EXPERIENTIAL EXERCISES

16.1 Prisoners' Dilemma: An Intergroup Competition

Instructions

1. The instructor explains what will take place in this exercise and assigns people to groups. Two types of teams are formed and named Red and Blue (with no more than eight per group) and are not to communicate with the other team in any way, verbally or nonverbally, except when told to do so by the instructor. Groups are given time to study the Prisoner's Dilemma Tally Sheet.

2. (3 min.) Round 1. Each team has three minutes to make a team decision. Write your decisions when the instructor says time is up.

3. (2 min.) The choices of the teams are announced for Round 1. The scores are entered on the Tally Sheet.

4. (4–5 min.) Round 2 is conducted in the same manner as Round 1.

5. (6 min.) Round 3 is announced as a special round, for which the payoff points are doubled. Each team is instructed to send one representative to chairs in the center of the room. After representatives have conferred for three minutes, they return to their teams. Teams then

have three minutes, as before, in which to make their decisions. When recording their scores, they should be reminded that points indicated by the payoff schedule are doubled for this round only.

6. (8–10 min.) Rounds 4, 5, and 6 are conducted in the same manner as the first three rounds.

7. (6 min.) Round 7 is announced as a special round, in which the payoff points are "squared" (multiplied by themselves: e.g., a score of 4 would be $4^2 = 16$). A minus sign would be retained: e.g., $(-3)^2 = -9$. Team representatives meet for three minutes; then the teams meet for three minutes. At the instructor's signal, the teams write their choices; then the two choices are announced.

8. (6 min.) Round 8 is handled exactly as Round 7 was. Payoff points are squared.

9. (10–20) min.) The point total for each team is announced, and the sum of the two team totals is calculated and compared to the maximum positive or negative outcomes (+108 or –108 points). A discussion on win-lose situations, competition, etc., will be conducted.

Source: Dorothy Hai, "Prisoner's Dilemma," in *Organizational Behavior: Experiences and Cases* (St. Paul, Minn.: West, 1986), pp. 125–127. Reprinted by permission. Copyright © 1986 by West Publishing Company. All rights reserved.

PRISONERS' DILEMMA TALLY SHEET

Instructions: For 10 successive rounds, the Red team will choose either an A or a B and the Blue team will choose either an X or a Y. The score each team receives in a round is determined by the pattern made by the choices of both teams, according to the schedule below.

Payoff Schedule:

AX–Both teams win 3 points.   BX–Red team wins 6 points; Blue team loses 6 points.
AY–Red team loses 6 points; Blue team wins 6 points.   BY–Both teams lose 3 points.

Scorecard:

Round	Minutes	Choice		Cumulative Points	
		Red Team	Blue Team	Red Team	Blue Team
1	3				
2	3				
3*	3 (reps.) 3 (teams)				
4	3				
5	3				
6*	3 (reps.) 3 (teams)				
7**	3 (reps.) 3 (teams)				
8**	3 (reps.) 3 (teams)				

*Payoff points are doubled for this round.   **Payoff points are squared for this round. (Retain the minus sign.)

16.2 The Traveler's Check Scam Group Exercise

Instructions

1. (3 minutes) Group selects an observer. The observer remains silent during the group problem-solving process, recording the activities of the group on the Observer's Report Form.

2. (15 minutes) Group members read the following problem and proceed to solve it.

THE CASE OF MICKEY THE DIP

Mickey the Dip, an expert pickpocket and forger, liked to work the Los Angeles International Airport on busy days. His technique was to pick the pockets of prosperous-looking victims just before they boarded planes to the East Coast. This gave Mickey five hours to use stolen credit cards before the owners could report their losses.

One morning Mickey snatched a fat wallet from a traveler and left the airport to examine his loot. To his surprise he found no credit cards but instead $500 in traveler's checks. After 20 minutes of practice, Mickey could sign a perfect imitation of the victim's signature. He then proceeded to a large department store where all suits were being sold for 75 percent of the regular price. Mickey purchased a suit for $225 and paid for it with $300 in stolen traveler's checks. After the clerk who served him went to lunch, he bought another suit for $150 and paid for it with the remaining $200 of stolen traveler's checks. Later, Mickey switched the labels on the two suits and, using the receipt from the $225 suit, returned the $150 suit at a centralized return desk for a refund. The refund clerk took the suit and gave Mickey eleven $20 bills, which he stuffed into his pocket and disappeared.

When the department store deposited the traveler's checks, they were returned as forgeries. Assuming the store normally sold suits at twice their wholesale price and used 10 percent of sales as an overhead cost figure, what was the cash value of the loss suffered by the store as a result of Mickey's caper? Do not consider taxes in your computations.

3. (2 minutes) When the group has a solution to the problem upon which all members agree, it will be written on a note and handed to the instructor.

4. (5 minutes) The observer briefs the group on the problem-solving processes observed during the exercise.

5. (25 minutes) The small group discusses the following topics:

   a. Did the group decide on a problem solution process before it attempted to solve the problem? If so, what was it?

   b. Was the solution of the problem hindered in any way by the lack of an appropriate agreed-upon group problem-solving process? Explain.

   c. Who were the leaders of the group during the exercise? What did they do? Critique their leadership activities.

   d. What communications patterns were used by the group during the exercise? Who participated the most? Who participated the least? Describe individual behaviors.

   e. Did the group solve the problem? How many members of the group discovered the correct answer on their own?

   f. Was using the group to solve this problem better than assigning the problem to one person? Explain the rationale for your answer.

THE TRAVELER'S CHECK SCAM EXERCISE OBSERVER'S REPORT

1. What happened during the first few minutes the group met after members finished reading the problem? (List behaviors of specific group members.)

2. Identify the group role played by each group member during the exercise. Give examples of the behavior of each.

3. Were there any conflicts within or among group members during the exercise? Explain the nature of the conflicts and the behavior of the individual(s) involved.

4. How were decisions made in the group? Give specific examples.

5. How could the group improve its problem-solving skills?

Source: Peter P. Dawson, *Fundamentals of Organizational Behavior* (Englewood Cliffs, N.J.: Prentice-Hall, 1985), pp. 419–22. © 1985. Reprinted by permission of Prentice-Hall, Inc., Englewood Cliffs, N.J.

17

COMMUNICATING

Electronic engineers have yet to devise a better interoffice communications system than the water cooler.

Leo Ellis

LEARNING OBJECTIVES

After studying Chapter 17, you will know:

1. Communications problems to avoid.

2. The important advantages of two-way communications.

3. When to use, and not to use, the various communications channels.

4. Ways to become a better writer and persuasive speaker.

5. How to improve downward, upward, and horizontal communications.

6. How to work with the company grapevine.

DIALOGUE INSTEAD OF DEBATE

A steel mill in the Midwest had endured 30 years of labor-management animosity. Most recently, intensive downsizing had wrecked the company. The largest plant shrunk to 1,000 people, from a peak of 5,000.

People called each other names, threw chairs, stormed out of meetings, and staged work slowdowns. Neither management nor labor trusted the other, and both sides doubted that reconciliation was possible. But tough competition from mini-mills forced them to try to cooperate. So they agreed to try a participative total quality improvement process, and formed joint problem-solving committees.

In the initial meetings, consultants helped the groups to communicate more constructively. Instead of placing blame and resurrecting old conflicts, people tried to step away from the past and really think about the present and the future. They began talk-ing honestly about concerns, and openly considered other viewpoints.

The process was not an easy one; it took time, effort, and courage. But eventually, for the first time, managers and union personnel began to talk about the business as *theirs*. They came to recognize that they all were part of the same organization, and they began to think together rather than separately.

According to the union president, the old antagonism is a thing of the past. "That's gone. Now we're looking at the future." The CEO describes it this way: "The process became a method of exchanging thoughts and realizing that none of us have *the* answer, but together we might have a better answer."

After 30 years of labor–management conflict, this steel mill entered into a participative total quality improvement process and people finally began working together.
(Jeff Corwin/Tony Stone Images)

Source: W. Isaacs, "Taking Flight: Dialogue, Collective Thinking, and Organizational Learning," *Organizational Dynamics,* Autumn 1993, pp. 24–39.

Cost

Speed

Quality

Innovation

*T*wo types of discourse work together to help a group become a team and an organization become a more effective organization. The two types—and their impact—are illustrated in Setting the Stage above. **Discussion** is like a ping-pong match, with people hitting the ball back and forth.[1] Each person is trying to win a debate, in the sense of having his or her view accepted by the group. Discussions can be polite, and useful, but they can also work at cross-purposes and become destructive.

Dialogue, on the other hand, has the goal of going beyond one person's understanding. The goal is not to "win," but for the team to come to a common, deep understanding. Dialogue explores complex issues from many viewpoints. It requires a commitment to the truth, honesty about people's own beliefs, and true listening and open-mindedness toward others' beliefs. Free exploration of ideas helps individuals, and the group as a unit, to think and learn.[2]

Every group and organization should have both. The most common danger is plenty of discussion and argument, but not much in the way of real dialogue.

Discussion and dialogue are examples of how people communicate. Effective communication is a fundamental aspect of job performance and managerial effectiveness.[3] In this chapter, we will present important communication concepts and some practical guidelines for improving your effectiveness. We will discuss both interpersonal and organizational communication.

INTERPERSONAL COMMUNICATION

Communication is the transmission of information and meaning from one party to another through the use of shared symbols. Figure 17.1 shows a general model of the communication process.

The *sender* initiates the process by conveying information to the *receiver:* the person for whom the message is intended. The sender has a meaning he or she wishes to communicate and *encodes* the meaning into symbols (e.g., the words chosen for the message). Then the sender *transmits,* or sends, the message through some *channel,* such as a verbal or written medium.

The receiver *decodes* the message (e.g., reads it) and attempts to *interpret* the sender's meaning. The receiver may provide *feedback* to the sender by encoding a message in response to the sender's message.

The communication process often is hampered by *noise,* or interference, in the system that blocks perfect understanding. Noise could be anything that interferes with your attention to the conversation: ringing telephones, thoughts about other things, or simple fatigue or stress.

The model in Figure 17.1 is more than a theoretical treatment of the communication process: It points out the key ways in which communications can break down. Mistakes can be made at each stage of the model. A manager who is alert to potential problems can

FIGURE 17.1

A model of the communication process

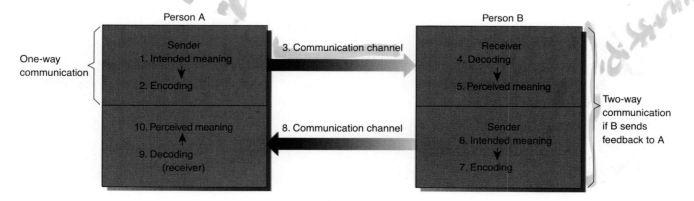

perform each step carefully to ensure more effective communication. The model also helps explain communication pitfalls, the differences between one-way and two-way communication, and the various communication channels.

COMMUNICATION PITFALLS

The sender's intended message does not always "get across" to the receiver. Here is a fact that conveys the ambiguities of communicating and possibilities for misinterpretation: For the 500 most commonly used words in the English language, there are over 14,000 definitions.[4]

Errors can occur in all stages of the communication process. In the encoding stage, words can be misused, decimal points typed in the wrong places, facts left out, or ambiguous phrases inserted. In the transmission stage, a memo gets lost on a cluttered desk, the words on an overhead transparency are too small to read from the back of the room, or words are spoken with inappropriate inflections.

Decoding problems arise when the receiver doesn't listen carefully or reads too quickly and overlooks a key point. And, of course, receivers can misinterpret the message, as a reader draws the wrong conclusion from an unclear memo, a listener takes a general statement by the boss too personally, or a sideways glance is taken the wrong way.

ONE-WAY VERSUS TWO-WAY COMMUNICATION

In **one-way communication,** only the top half of the model in Figure 17.1 is operating. Information flows in only one direction—from the sender to the receiver, with no feedback loop. A manager sends a memo to a subordinate without asking for an immediate response. A boss gives an order over the phone. A father scolds his son and then storms out of the room.

When receivers do respond to senders, completing the Figure 17.1 model, **two-way communication** has occurred. One-way communication situations like those just described can become two-way if the manager follows up her memo with a phone call and asks the receiver if he has any questions, the boss on the telephone listens to alternative suggestions for carrying out her order, and the father calms down and listens to his son's side of the story.

True two-way communication means not only that the receiver provides feedback but also that the sender is receptive to and responds to the feedback. In these constructive exchanges, information is shared between both parties rather than delivered from one person to the other.

One-way communication is much more common than it should be because it is faster and easier for the sender. The busy executive finds it easier to dash off a memo than to discuss the issue with the subordinate. Also, he doesn't have to deal with questions or be challenged by someone who disagrees with what the memo says.

Two-way communication is more difficult and time-consuming than one-way communication. However, it is more accurate; thus, fewer mistakes occur and fewer problems arise. Receivers have a chance to ask questions, share concerns, make suggestions or modifications, and consequently understand more precisely what is being communicated and what they should do with the information.[5]

Communication "breakdowns" often occur when business transactions take place between people from different countries. Chapter 8 introduced you to the importance of these cultural issues. Table 17.1 offers suggestions for communicating effectively with someone who speaks a different language.

COMMUNICATION CHANNELS

Communication can be sent through a variety of channels (steps 3 and 8 in the Figure 17.1 model) including oral, written, and electronic. Each channel has advantages and disadvantages.

TABLE 17.1

What do I do if they do not speak my language?

Verbal Behavior

- *Clear, slow speech.* Enunciate each word. Do not use colloquial expressions.
- *Repetition.* Repeat each important idea using different words to explain the same concept.
- *Simple sentences.* Avoid compound, long sentences.
- *Active verbs.* Avoid passive verbs.

Nonverbal Behavior

- *Visual restatements.* Use as many visual restatements as possible, such as pictures, graphs, tables, and slides.
- *Gestures.* Use more facial and hand gestures to emphasize the meanings of words.
- *Demonstration.* Act out as many themes as possible.
- *Pauses.* Pause more frequently.
- *Summaries.* Hand out written summaries of your verbal presentation.

Attribution

- *Silence.* When there is a silence, wait. Do not jump in to fill the silence. The other person is probably just thinking more slowly in the non-native language or translating.
- *Intelligence.* Do not equate poor grammar and mispronunciation with lack of intelligence; it is usually a sign of second-language use.
- *Differences.* If unsure, assume difference, not similarity.

Comprehension

- *Understanding.* Do not just assume they understand; assume they do not understand.
- *Checking comprehension.* Have colleagues repeat their understanding of the material back to you. Do not simply ask if they understand or not. Let them explain what they understand to you.

Source: N. Adler, *International Dimensions of Organizational Behavior,* 2nd ed. (Boston: Kent, 1991), pp. 84–85.

Oral Communication

Oral communication includes face-to-face discussion, telephone conversations, and formal presentations and speeches. Advantages are that questions can be asked and answered; feedback is immediate and direct; the receiver(s) can sense the sender's sincerity (or lack thereof); and oral communication is both more persuasive and less expensive than written. However, oral communication also has disadvantages: It can lead to spontaneous, ill-considered statements (and regret), and there is no permanent record of it (unless an effort is made to record it).

Written Communication

Written communication includes memos, letters, reports, computer printouts, and other written documents. Advantages to using written messages are that the message can be revised several times; it is a permanent record that can be saved; the message stays the same even if relayed through many people; and the receiver has more time to analyze the message. Disadvantages are that the sender has no control over where, when, or if the message is read; the sender does not receive immediate feedback; the receiver may not understand parts of the message; and the message must be longer to contain enough information to answer anticipated questions.[6]

You should weigh these considerations when deciding whether to communicate orally or in writing. Also, consider when it may be necessary to use *both* forms, such as when following up a meeting with a confirming memo or writing a letter to prepare someone for your phone call.

Electronic Media

A special category of written communications occurs via electronic media. Managers use computers not only to gather and distribute quantitative data but to "talk" with others via *electronic mail (e-mail)*. For people who don't have direct access to one another's computer terminals, *facsimile (fax) machines* can transmit messages in seconds through telephone lines all over the world. Other means of electronic communication include *teleconferencing,* in which groups of people in different locations interact over telephone lines (audioconferencing) and perhaps also see one another on television monitors as they participate in group discussions (videoconferencing).

Advantages of electronic communication technology include speed and efficiency in delivering routine messages to large numbers of people across vast geographic areas. Also, it can reduce time spent traveling to and interacting in group meetings. One study indicated that e-mail at a large office equipment corporation reduced time spent on the phone by 80 percent, interoffice mail by 94 percent, photocopying by 60 percent, and paper memos by 50 percent.[7] Electronic channels allow people to participate more equally than they can in face-to-face settings and to share more information.[8] Electronic mail also leads people to interact more frequently, providing not necessarily a substitute for face-to-face communication but a supplement.

Disadvantages include the difficulty of solving complex problems, which require more extended, face-to-face interaction, and the inability to pick up subtle, nonverbal, or inflectional clues about what the communicator is thinking or conveying. E-mail is most appropriate, then, for routine messages that do not require the exchange of large quantities of complex information. It is less suitable for confidential information, resolving conflicts, or negotiating.[9]

One inevitable consequence of electronic mail is "flaming": hurling insults, sending "nastygrams," venting frustration, snitching on co-workers to the boss, and otherwise breaching bureaucratic protocol.[10] E-mail liberates people to type and send things they would not say to a person's face. The lack of nonverbal cues can result in "kidding" remarks being taken seriously; this can cause resentment and regret if the sender's identity is known. It is not unheard of for confidential messages, including details about people's personal lives and insulting, embarrassing remarks, to become public knowledge through electronic leaks.

TV AT WORK

*M*any companies have their own satellite or cable networks. They use them to send information, handle emergencies, create more worker involvement, train people, reduce travel costs, and provide briefings on new products. Electronic "town meetings" allow people to hear and ask questions of top executives.

For example, Federal Express kept its people informed via live reports when fog at the Memphis airport stranded thousands of packages. Chrysler broadcasts to thousands of its dealers, and trains mechanics over its private TV network. Ford's daily news program—which televises press conferences after quarterly financial reports are released—is watched by 60 percent of its blue-collar workers.

But a potential disadvantage was illustrated vividly when Frank Borman, chairman of Eastern Airlines, told Eastern employees in 1983 over internal cable TV that they had better make concessions or the airline might go bankrupt. Word leaked out, and within two days customers had redeemed $2 million in tickets.

The benefits of company TV and electronic media are tremendous, but what about the potential downside? What lessons can be learned from the Eastern example? Was the problem the nature of the technology, or how the communication episode was managed?

Source: N. Templin, "Companies Use TV to Reach Their Workers," *The Wall Street Journal,* December 7, 1993, pp. B1, B10. ●

Media Richness

As you can see, some communication channels convey more information than others. The more information or cues a medium sends to the receiver, the "richer" the medium is. The richest media are more personal than technological, provide quick feedback, allow lots of descriptive language, and send different types of cues. Thus, face-to-face communication is the richest medium because it offers a variety of cues in addition to words: tone of voice, facial expression, body language, and other nonverbal signals. It also allows more descriptive language than, say, a memo does. In addition, it affords more opportunity for the receiver to give feedback to and ask questions of the sender, turning one-way into two-way communication.

The telephone is less rich than face-to-face communication, electronic mail is less rich yet, and memos are the least rich medium. In general, you should send difficult and unusual messages through richer media, transmit simple and routine messages through less rich media like memos, and use multiple media for important messages that you want to ensure people attend to and understand.[11] You should also consider factors such as which medium your receiver prefers, the preferred communication style in your organization, and cost.[12] Table 17.2 gives some sample situations for choosing channels based on the message and the audience.

TABLE 17.2

Sample situations of media choice

Situation 1: A midsize construction firm wants to announce a new employee benefit program.

Poor choice: Memo   **Better choice:** Small group meetings

Rationale: The memo does not offer the feedback potential necessary to explain what may be seen as obscure information. Moreover, with these employees there is a possibility of literacy problems. A group meeting will allow for an oral explanation after which participants can more easily ask questions about any of the complex materials.

Situation 2: A manager wishes to confirm a meeting time with 10 employees.

Poor choice: Phone   **Better choice:** Voice mail or e-mail

Rationale: For a simple message like this, there is no need to use a rich medium when a lean one will do the job.

Situation 3: Increase enthusiasm in midsize insurance company for a program that asks employees from different departments to work on the same project teams.

Poor choice: E-mail, voice mail   **Better choice:** Face-to-face, telephone

Rationale: In situations requiring persuasion the sender must be able to quickly adapt the message to the receiver in order to counter objections. This is not a feature of either e-mail or v-mail. Face-to-face communication offers the sender the greatest flexibility. The phone is the next best alternative.

Situation 4: A group of engineers who are geographically dispersed want to exchange design ideas with one another.

Poor choice: Teleconference   **Better choice:** Fax, computer conference

Rationale: A teleconference is apt to overly accentuate the status and personality differences among the engineers. Fax or computer conferencing would allow the quality of the ideas to be the central focus of interaction. Moreover, quick feedback is still possible with these media.

Situation 5: Describe a straightforward but somewhat detailed and updated version of a voice mail system to 1,000 employees who are geographically dispersed.

Poor choice: Newsletter   **Better choice:** Videotape

Rationale: If employees are already persuaded of the updated system's merit, you can probably use the newsletter. But a videotape graphically conveys information that requires demonstration, and will educate people better about procedures.

Source: P. G. Clampitt, *Communicating for Managerial Effectiveness* (Newbury Park, Calif.: Sage, 1991).

EFFICIENCY AND EFFECTIVENESS

Some managers believe they should choose only one channel to communicate a message because doing so is more efficient.[13] But for important or complex messages, multiple channels may be appropriate. Consider how Citicorp communicated its new flexible benefits plan to its 56,000 employees: through software, workbooks, videos, seminars and other teaching tools, a telephone hotline, and hundreds of trained human resources people who traveled to different sites to explain the benefits in person. The total cost was several million dollars, but Citicorp understands that different people are more likely to attend to and understand messages from different channels—and it wants *all* its employees to fully understand the new benefits program.[14] In this case, by spending time and money to make sure everyone understood the plan, costly problems were avoided. Citicorp's communication efforts were both efficient and effective.

MIXED SIGNALS AND MISPERCEPTION

A common thread underlying the topics we have discussed so far is that people's perceptions can undermine attempts to communicate. People do not pay attention to everything going on around them. They inadvertently send mixed signals that can undermine their intended messages. Different people attend to different things, and people interpret the same thing in different ways. All of this creates problems in communication.

For example, a bank CEO knew that to be competitive he had to downsize his organization, and the employees who remained would have to commit to customer service, become more empowered, and really *earn* customer loyalty.[15] Knowing that his employees would have doubts and concerns about the coming reorganization, he decided to make a promise to them that he would do his best to guarantee employment, growth, and training.

What signals did the CEO communicate to his people by his promises? One positive signal was that he cared about his people. But he also signaled that *he* would take care of *them,* thus undermining his goal of giving them more responsibility and empowering them. The employees wanted management to take responsibility for the market challenge that *they* needed to face—to handle things for them when *they* needed to learn the new ways of doing business. Inadvertently, the CEO spoke to their backward-looking need for security when he had meant to make them see that the bank's future depended on *their* efforts.

Another CEO of another firm talked repeatedly about the importance of empowerment throughout the organization.[16] And yet during one meeting, when a young manager brought up a problem that the home office was not handling for him as he had requested, the CEO thanked the manager, told him whom to talk to, and assured him that he would pave the way. Many executives in attendance even praised the CEO for empowering the manager.

But the CEO could have given a better, much more empowering response. The CEO could have taken the opportunity to ask the manager how the organization could be redesigned so that he and other people like him felt they had the freedom to take the initiative and get results on their own. Promising to help one person on one issue, by invoking CEO power, does not communicate to people the goal of their true and permanent empowerment to make positive things happen on their own.[17]

Consider how many problems could be avoided—and how much more effective communication could be—if people took the time to (1) ensure that the receivers will attend to the message they are sending; (2) consider the other party's frame of reference and attempt to convey the message from that perceptual viewpoint; (3) take concrete steps to minimize perceptual errors and improper signals, in both sending and receiving; and (4) send *consistent* messages. You should make an effort to predict people's interpretations of your messages and think in terms of how they could *misinterpret* your messages. It helps to say not only what you mean but also what you *don't* mean. Every time you say, "I am not saying X, I am saying Y," you eliminate a possible misinterpretation.[18]

IMPROVING COMMUNICATION SKILLS

In recent years, employers have been dismayed by college graduates' poor communication skills. A demonstrated ability to communicate effectively makes a job candidate more attractive and distinguishes her or him from others. You can do many things to improve your communications skills, both as a sender and as a receiver.

IMPROVING SENDER SKILLS

Senders can improve their skills in making persuasive presentations, writing, language use, and sending nonverbal messages.

Presentational and Persuasion Skills

As a manager, you will be called on frequently to "state your case" on a variety of issues. You will have information and perhaps an opinion or proposal to present to others. Typically, your goal will be to "sell" your idea. In other words, your challenge will be to persuade others to go along with your personal preference. As a leader, some of your toughest challenges will arise when people do not want to do what has to be done. Leaders have to be persuasive to get people "on board."[19]

In some organizations, as often in life, how you say things may count for more than what you say. If this is the case in your organization, you might strive for style and entertainment in your presentations. But as a manager, you should establish a communication culture that emphasizes accuracy, integrity, fairness, and objectivity rather than mere showmanship and image projection.[20]

Knowing a few fundamental principles of persuasion will help you convince others to adopt your viewpoint.[21] As the *sender* you must have credibility. This means that your audience must know about your expertise and believe you are trustworthy. Issues concerning your *message* include whether to voice opposing arguments and the order in which to present your arguments. How you solve these issues depends on characteristics of the *audience.* You should present only your side of the argument when the audience is friendly and unaware of opposing arguments. But if the audience is initially hostile to your position and aware of counterarguments, you should bring up and refute the opposing view. Also, when you present both arguments, you probably will be more effective if you present your viewpoint last.

It is generally effective to be *repetitive*. This is not to say that you should stand in front of your audience and repeat yourself over and over again. It means you should state your viewpoint in a variety of ways and at different times with different audiences. Great leaders convey their visions by seizing every opportunity to talk about them and communicate them tirelessly until their followers "buy into" the message.

Writing Skills

Effective writing is more than correct spelling, punctuation, and grammar, although these help! Good writing above all requires clear, logical thinking.[22] The act of writing can be a powerful aid to thinking, because you have to think about what you really want to say.

Your first draft rarely is as good as it could be. If you have time, revise it. In the process strive for clarity, organization, readability, and brevity.[23] Take the reader into consideration.

You want people to find your memos and reports readable and interesting. Use specific, concrete words rather than abstract phrases. Instead of saying, "A period of unfavorable weather set in," say, "It rained every day for a week." Use a dictionary and a thesaurus, and avoid fancy words.

Go through your entire letter, memo, or report and delete all unnecessary words, sentences, and paragraphs. Brevity is much appreciated by readers who are overloaded with documents, including wordy memos.

Be critical of your own writing. If you want to improve, start by reading *The Elements of Style* by William Strunk and E. B. White and the latest edition of *The Little, Brown Handbook*.[24]

Language

Jargon is actually a form of shorthand and can make communication more effective when both the sender and the receiver know the buzzwords. But when the receiver is unfamiliar with the jargon, misunderstandings result. When people from different functional areas or disciplines communicate with one another, misunderstandings often occur because of "language" barriers.

Therefore, whether speaking or writing, you should consider the receiver's background and adjust your language accordingly. When conducting business overseas, try to learn something about the other country's language and customs. Americans are less likely to do this than people from some other cultures, but those who do will have a big edge over their competitors who do not.[25]

Nonverbal Skills

Except when you intend to convey a negative message, you should give nonverbal signals that express warmth, respect, concern, a feeling of equality, and a willingness to listen. Undesirable nonverbal signals show coolness, disrespect, lack of interest, and a feeling of superiority.[26] The following suggestions can help you send positive nonverbal signals.

First, use *time* appropriately. Avoid keeping your employees waiting to see you. Devote sufficient time to your meetings with them, and communicate frequently with them to signal your interest in their concerns. Second, make your *office arrangement* conducive to open communication. A seating arrangement that avoids separation of people helps establish a warm, cooperative atmosphere (in contrast, an arrangement in which you sit behind your desk and your subordinate sits before you creates a more intimidating, authoritative environment).[27] Third, remember your *body language.* Research indicates that facial expression and tone of voice can account for 90 percent of the communication between two people.[28] Several nonverbal body signals convey a positive attitude toward the other person: assuming a position close to the person; gesturing frequently; maintaining eye contact; smiling; having an open body orientation, such as facing the other person directly; uncrossing arms; and leaning forward to convey interest in what the other person is saying.

NONVERBAL SIGNALS IN DIFFERENT COUNTRIES

When doing business in a foreign country, you should learn the language and the culture. If you develop only a basic knowledge, use the language for socializing but not for business. In business, use English very carefully, or get an excellent interpreter whom you have briefed thoroughly in advance.

But by no means is language the only source of communication problems. Nonverbal communication can be of vital importance.

Here are just a few nonverbal mistakes that Americans might make in other countries: Nodding the head up and down in Bulgaria means no. The American thumb-and-first-finger circular A-OK gesture is vulgar in Brazil, Singapore, Russia, and Paraguay. The head is sacred in Buddhist cultures, so you must never touch someone's head. In Muslim cultures, never touch or eat with the left hand, which is thought unclean. Crossing your ankle over your knee is rude in Indonesia, Thailand, and Syria. Don't point your finger toward yourself in Germany or Switzerland—it insults the other person.

You also need to correctly interpret the nonverbal signals of others. Chinese scratch their ears and cheeks to show happiness. Greeks puff air after they receive a compliment. Hondurans touch their fingers below their eyes to show disbelief or caution. Japanese indicate embarrassment or "no" by sucking in air and hissing through their teeth. Vietnamese look to the ground with their heads down to show respect. Compared to Americans, Russians use fewer facial expressions, and Scandinavians fewer hand gestures, whereas people in Mediterranean and Latin cultures may gesture and touch more. Brazilians are more likely than Americans to interrupt, Arabs to speak loudly, and Asians to respect silence.

Source: M. Munter, "Cross-Cultural Communication for Managers," *Business Horizons*, May–June 1993, pp. 69–78. ●

Knowing the meaning of body signals in other cultures is imperative to the success of doing business outside of the United States.
(Robert E. Daemmrich/Tony Stone Images)

IMPROVING RECEIVER SKILLS

Once you become effective at sending oral, written, and nonverbal messages, you are halfway home toward becoming a complete communicator. However, you must also develop adequate receiving capabilities. Receivers need good listening, reading, and observational skills.

Listening

A basic technique called *reflection* will help a manager listen effectively.[29] **Reflection** is a process whereby a person attempts to repeat and clarify what he or she believes the other person is saying. This technique places a greater emphasis on listening than on talking. When both parties actively engage in reflection, they get into each other's frame of reference rather than listening and responding from their own. The result is more accurate two-way communication.

Sperry Corporation, now part of Unisys, introduced the best-known corporate effort to heighten managers' listening skills.[30] Sperry had an advertising theme—"We understand how important it is to listen"—that reflected a basic philosophy and way of doing business. The company's senior management development specialists created listening training seminars for company personnel, drawing from a study of the 100 best and 100 worst listeners in the freshman class at the University of Minnesota. Table 17.3 summarizes these effective listening techniques.

Reading

Illiteracy is a serious problem in the United States. Even if illiteracy is not a problem in your organization, reading mistakes are common and costly. As a receiver, for your own benefit, read memos as soon as possible, before it's too late to respond. You may skim most of your reading materials, but read important memos, documents, and passages slowly and carefully. Note important points for later referral. Consider taking courses to increase your reading speed and comprehension skills. Finally, don't limit your reading to items about your particular job skill or technical expertise; read materials that fall outside of your immediate concerns. You never know when a creative idea that will help you in your work will be inspired by a novel, a biography, a sports story, or an article about a problem in another business or industry.

Observing

Effective communicators—senders as well as receivers—are also capable of observing and interpreting nonverbal communications. (As Yogi Berra said, "You can see a lot by observ-

TABLE 17.3

Ten keys to
effective listening

1. *Find an area of interest.* Even if you decide the topic is dull, ask yourself, "What is the speaker saying that I can use?"

2. *Judge content, not delivery.* Don't get caught up in the speaker's personality, mannerisms, speaking voice, or clothing. Instead, try to learn what the speaker knows.

3. *Hold your fire.* Rather than getting immediately excited by what the speaker seems to be saying, withhold evaluation until you understand the speaker's message.

4. *Listen for ideas.* Don't get bogged down in all the facts and details; focus on central ideas.

5. *Be flexible.* Have several systems for note taking, and use the system best suited to the speaker's style. Don't take too many notes or try to force everything said by a disorganized speaker into a formal outline.

6. *Resist distractions.* Close the door, shut off the radio, move closer to the person talking, or ask him or her to speak louder. Don't look out the window or at papers on your desk.

7. *Exercise your mind.* Some people tune out when the material gets difficult. Develop an appetite for a good mental challenge.

8. *Keep your mind open.* Too many people get overemotional when they hear words referring to their most deeply held convictions, for example, *communist, union, subsidy, import, Republican* or *Democrat* and *big business.* Try not to let your emotions interfere with comprehension.

9. *Capitalize on thought speed.* Take advantage of the fact that most people talk at a rate of about 125 words per minute, but most of us think at about four times that rate. Use those extra 400 words per minute to think about what the speaker is saying rather than turning your thoughts to something else.

10. *Work at listening.* Spend some energy. Don't just pretend you're paying attention. Show interest. Good listening is hard work, but the benefits outweigh the costs.

Source: Ralph G. Nichols, "Listening Is a 10-Part Skill," *Nation's Business* 45 (July 1957), pp. 56–60. Cited in R. C. Huseman, C. M. Logue, and D. L. Freshley, eds., *Readings in Interpersonal and Organizational Communication* (Boston: Allyn & Bacon, 1977).

ing.") For example, by reading nonverbal cues a presenter can determine how her talk is going and adjust her approach if necessary. Some companies train their sales forces to interpret the nonverbal signals of potential customers. People can also decode nonverbal signals to determine whether a sender is being truthful or deceitful. Deceitful communicators maintain less eye contact, make either more or fewer body movements than usual, and smile either too much or too little. Verbally, they offer fewer specifics than truthful senders do.[31]

Of course, you must *accurately interpret* what you observe. A Canadian conducting business with a high-ranking official in Kuwait was surprised that the meeting was held in an open office and was interrupted constantly.[32] He interpreted the lack of a big, private office and secretary to screen out unwanted visitors to mean that the Kuwaiti was of low rank and uninterested in doing business, and he lost interest in the deal. The Canadian observed the facts accurately, but his perceptual biases and lack of awareness regarding how norms differ across cultures caused him to misinterpret what he saw.

The Japanese are particularly skilled at interpreting every nuance of voice and gesture, putting most Westerners at a disadvantage.[33] When conducting business in Asian or other countries, local guides can be invaluable not only as language interpreters but to "decode" behavior at meetings, subtle hints and nonverbal cues, who the key people are, and how the decision-making process operates.

EFFECTIVE SUPERVISION

Many studies have compared good and poor supervisors' communications skills.[34] Supervisors who receive higher evaluations from their bosses exhibit several key characteristics. First, they *communicate more information.* For example, they give advance notice of impending changes, explain the reasons behind policies and regulations, and enjoy conversing with their subordinates. Second, effective supervisors *prefer asking and persuading* to telling and demanding (but are capable of using both styles if necessary). Third, they are *sensitive to people's feelings and needs.* For example, they are careful to reprimand privately rather than publicly. Finally, they are *willing, empathic listeners.* They respond with understanding to all questions from employees and give fair consideration to, and are willing to take appropriate action on, complaints and suggestions.

Thus, effective managers are more "communication minded" than ineffective managers. People who lack confidence in their communication skills, both oral and written, tend to avoid communication situations altogether. This tendency would be a severe handicap for any manager who wanted to enhance her or his unit's performance.[35]

ORGANIZATIONAL COMMUNICATION

Being a skilled communicator is essential to being a good manager and team leader. But communication must also be managed throughout the organization. Every minute of every day, countless bits of information are transmitted through an organization. We will discuss downward, upward, horizontal, and informal communication in organizations.

DOWNWARD COMMUNICATION

Downward communication refers to the flow of information from higher to lower levels in the organization's hierarchy. Examples include a manager's giving an assignment to a secretary, a supervisor's making an announcement to his subordinates, and a company president's delivering a talk to her management team. Employees must receive the information they need to perform their jobs and become (and remain) loyal members of the organization.

DOWNWARD COMMUNICATION DURING A MERGER

*A*dequate downward communication can be particularly valuable during difficult times. During corporate mergers and acquisitions, employees are anxious as they wonder how the merger will affect them. Ideally—and ethically—top management communicates with employees about the change as early as possible.

But some argue against that approach, maintaining that informing employees about the reorganization might cause them to quit too early. Then too, top management often cloisters itself, prompting rumors and anxiety. CEOs and other senior execs are surrounded by lawyers, investment bankers, and so on—people who are paid merely to make the deal happen, not to make it work. Yet with the people who are affected by the deal, you must increase, not decrease, communication.

In a merger of two Fortune 500 companies, two plants received very different information. All employees at both plants received the initial letter from the CEO announcing the merger. But after that, one plant was kept in the dark while the other was continually filled in about what was happening. Top management gave employees information about layoffs, transfers, promotions and demotions, and changes in pay, jobs, and benefits.

Which plant do you think fared better as the difficult transitional months unfolded? In both plants, the merger decreased employees' job satisfaction and commitment to the organization and increased their belief that the company was untrustworthy, dishonest, and uncaring. In the plant whose employees got little information, these problems persisted for a long time. But in the plant whose employees received complete information, the situation stabilized and attitudes improved toward their normal levels. Full communication not only helped employees survive an anxious period; it served a symbolic value by signaling care and concern for employees. Without such communications, employee reactions to a merger or acquisition may be so negative as to undermine the corporate strategy.

Sources: D. Schweiger and A. DeNisi, "Communication with Employees Following a Merger: A Longitudinal Field Experiment," *Academy of Management Journal* 34 (1991), pp. 110–35; and J. Gutknecht and J. B. Keys, "Mergers, Acquisitions, and Takeovers: Maintaining Morale of Survivors and Protecting Employees," *Academy of Management Executive,* August 1993, pp. 26–36. ●

Employees often lack adequate information.[36] One problem is *information overload:* They are bombarded with so much information that they fail to absorb everything. Much of the information is not very important, but its volume causes a lot of relevant information to be lost.

A second problem is a *lack of openness* between managers and employees. Managers may believe "No news is good news," "If only they knew what I know, they wouldn't be upset about this decision," "I don't have time to keep them informed of everything they want to know," or "It's none of their business, anyway." In other words, some managers withhold information even if sharing it is extremely important.

A third problem is *filtering.* When messages are passed from one person to another, some information is left out. When a message passes through many people, each transmission may cause further information losses. The message can also be distorted as people add their own words or interpretations.

Filtering poses serious problems in organizations. As messages are communicated downward through many organizational levels, much information is lost. The data in Figure 17.2 suggest that by the time messages reach the people for whom they are intended, the receivers may actually get very little information.

The fewer the number of authority levels through which communications must pass, the less information will be lost or distorted. Recall from Chapter 10 that companies are reducing the number of hierarchical layers. You can now see that the flatter organization offers another advantage: fewer problems caused by filtering of information as it cascades through many layers.

Managing Downward Communication

For downward communication, the manager should remember several things. First, most managers probably do not give their subordinates enough important information. Employees often are dismayed at how poorly informed their bosses keep them. This is especially true during a crisis or a major change.

Second, only certain kinds of information need to be communicated downward. Generally, people want—and deserve—to know about things that affect them and their work. The manager should consider the consequences of *not* sharing a piece of information and make sure that relevant information is delivered.

Top managers often are proud of their newsletters, staff meetings, videos, and other vehicles of downward communication. More often than not, the information provided concerns company sports teams, birthdays, and new copy machines. But today a more

FIGURE 17.2

Information loss in downward communication

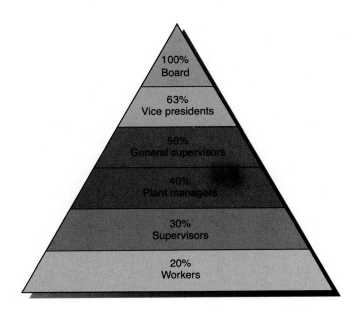

100%
Board

63%
Vice presidents

56%
General supervisors

40%
Plant managers

30%
Supervisors

20%
Workers

unconventional philosophy is gathering steam. At companies like Springfield Remanufacturing Center Corporation in Springfield, Missouri, line workers know virtually everything the company president knows. In fact, they are *taught* to understand revenues and costs, productivity, and strategic priorities.

These practices, often called **open-book management,** are controversial. Many managers prefer to keep such information to themselves. Sharing strategic plans and financial information with employees can lead to leaks to competitors or to employee dissatisfaction with their compensation. But the companies that share this information point to favorable impact on motivation and productivity. Cecil Ursprung, president and CEO of Reflexite Corporation in New Britain, Connecticut, says, "Why would you tell 5 percent of the team what the score was and not the other 95 percent?"[37] Jack Stack of SRC, an engine remanufacturing company, agrees. He taught "anyone who moved a broom or operated a grinder everything [our bank] knew. That way they could really understand how every nickel saved could make a difference."[38]

Managers can do many things to improve downward communication.[39] First, management should develop communication policies and procedures. Second, information must be available to those who need it. Third, information must be communicated accurately and efficiently. Lines of communication should be as direct, short, and personal as possible. The information should be clear, consistent, and timely—neither too early nor (a more common problem) too late.

UPWARD COMMUNICATION

Upward communication travels from lower to higher ranks in the hierarchy. Upward communication is important for several reasons.[40] First, managers learn what's going on. Management gains a more accurate picture of subordinates' work, accomplishments, problems, plans, and attitudes. Management also gains subordinates' ideas. Second, employees gain from the opportunity to communicate upward. People can relieve some of their frustrations, achieve a stronger sense of participation in the enterprise, and improve morale. Third, effective upward communication facilitates downward communication as good listening becomes a two-way street.

The problems common in upward communication are similar to those for downward communication. Managers, like their subordinates, are bombarded with information and may neglect or miss information from below. Furthermore, some employees are not always open with their bosses; in other words, filtering occurs upward as well as downward. People tend to share only good news with their bosses and suppress bad news, because they (1) want to appear competent; (2) mistrust their boss and fear that if he or she finds out about something they have done they will be punished; (3) fear the boss will punish the messenger, even if the reported problem is not that person's fault; or (4) believe they are helping their boss if they shield him or her from problems. For these and other reasons, managers may not learn about important problems.

Managing Upward Communication

Generating useful information from below requires doing two things. First, managers should *facilitate* upward communication. For example, they could have an open-door policy and encourage people to use it; have lunch or coffee with employees; pass out surveys that ask specific questions of people; or institute a program for productivity suggestions. These mechanisms are just a few possibilities that will make upward communication easier.

But managers must also *motivate* people to provide valid information. Useful upward communication must be reinforced and not punished. The person who tries to talk to the manager about a problem must not be brushed off consistently. An announced open-door policy must truly be open-door. Also, people must trust their supervisor and know that the manager will not hold a grudge if they give him or her some negative information.

Upward communication systems need not be formal; they can also be informal. For example, executives at many companies practice MBWA (management by wandering around). The term, coined by Ed Carlson of United Airlines, refers simply to getting out of the office, walking around, and talking frequently and informally with employees.[41]

HORIZONTAL COMMUNICATION

Much information needs to be shared among people on the same hierarchical level. Such **horizontal communication** can take place among people in the same work team. Other important communication must occur between people in different departments. For example, a purchasing agent discusses a problem with a production engineer and a task force of department heads meet to discuss a particular concern.

Horizontal communication has several important functions.[42] First, it allows sharing of information, coordination, and problem solving among units. Second, it helps solve conflicts. Third, by allowing interaction among peers, it provides social and emotional support to people. All these factors contribute to morale and effectiveness.

Managing Horizontal Communication

The need for horizontal communication is similar to the need for integration, discussed in Chapter 10. Particularly in complex environments, in which decisions in one unit affect another, information must be shared horizontally. In Chapters 10 and 11, we discussed numerous techniques for enhancing horizontal communication and integration: direct contact among managers, integrative roles, task forces, project teams, and so forth. Management information systems are another mechanism for making information available to all areas of the organization.

GE offers a great example of how to use productive horizontal communications as a competitive weapon.[43] GE consists of 14 divisions, including plastics, major appliances, medical systems, financial services, and NBC. CEO Jack Welch uses the term "integrated diversity" to describe how GE coordinates its 14 different businesses.

GE's businesses could operate completely independently. But each is supposed to help the others. They transfer technical resources, people, information, ideas, and money among themelves. GE accomplishes this high level of communication and cooperation through easy access between divisions and to the CEO; a culture of openness, honesty, trust, and mutual obligation; and quarterly meetings in which all the top executives get together informally to share information and ideas. The same kinds of things are done at lower levels as well.

THE VIRTUAL OFFICE

*E*very employer wants to cut costs and raise productivity. Modern communications technologies may now offer a new way to achieve these goals: the **virtual office.**

Companies are slashing office space and giving people laptops, portable phones and beepers, and orders to work out of their homes, cars, and customers' offices. IBM, AT&T, Xerox, GE, Chiat/Day, and many others are moving to these mobile offices. One consultant calls it "the most radical redefinition of the workplace since the Industrial Revolution."

In the short run, at least, the benefits appear substantial. Compaq Computer has reduced sales costs and administrative expenses from 22 percent of revenue to 12 percent. Perkin-Elmer, which makes scientific equipment, was able to close 35 branch offices. AT&T says mobile offices allow salespeople to spend 15 to 20 percent more time with customers. And most people like the flexibility it gives them.

But what will be the long-term impact on productivity and morale? Some people hate being forced to work at home. Some valuable people have quit. Some send faxes, e-mail, and voice mail in the middle of the night—and some receive them. Some work around the clock and still feel they are not doing enough. The long hours of being constantly close to the technical tools of work can cause burnout.

At the moment, it appears that most people are pleased to have changed to mobile offices, and that they believe they are being more productive. But questions have arisen, and some companies are being careful with the new idea. Automatic Data Processing, Inc., is trying out mobile offices for a year, hoping to win people's approval. And AT&T no longer makes mobile offices mandatory.

Source: S. Shellenbarger, "Overwork, Low Morale Vex the Mobile Office," *The Wall Street Journal*, August 17, 1994, pp. B1, B4. ●

While the trend toward home offices is growing, companies are keeping a watchful eye on productivity and worker morale. To look at the man pictured here, however, the home or virtual office seems like the ultimate in the good life. *(Reed Rahn)*

FORMAL AND INFORMAL COMMUNICATION

Organizational communications differ in formality. *Formal communications* are official, organization-sanctioned episodes of information transmission. They can move upward, downward, or horizontally and often involve paperwork, are prearranged, and are necessary for performing some task.

Informal communication is more unofficial. Gossip and rumors run wild on the corporate grapevine; employees complain about their boss; everyone talks about his or her favorite sports teams; people whisper secrets about their co-workers.

The **grapevine** helps people interpret the organization, translates management's formal messages into "employee language," and conveys information that the formal system leaves unsaid or wishes kept under wraps. On the other hand, the grapevine can be destructive when irrelevant or erroneous gossip and rumors proliferate and harm operations.[44]

Managing Informal Communication

Most of the suggestions for improving personal skills and organizational communication—writing, speaking, listening, facilitating and reinforcing upward communication, and so on—typically are applied to improving formal communication. But they can also help improve informal communication. Other considerations also apply to managing informal communication effectively.

Rumors start over any number of topics, including who's leaving, who's getting a promotion, salaries, job security, and costly mistakes. Rumors can destroy people's faith and trust in the company, and in each other. But the grapevine cannot be eliminated. Therefore, managers need to *work with* the grapevine.

The grapevine can be managed in several ways.[45] First, if the manager hears a story that could get out of hand, he or she should talk to the key people involved to get the facts and their perspectives.

Second, suggestions for *preventing* rumors from starting include:[46] explain things that are important but have not been explained; dispel uncertainties by providing facts; and work to establish open communications and trust over time.

Third, *neutralize* rumors once they have started:[47] disregard the rumor if it is ridiculous (has no credence with others); openly confirm any parts that are true; do make public comments (no-comment is seen as a confirmation of the rumor); deny the rumor, if the denial is based in truth (don't make false denials); make sure communications about the issue are consistent; select a spokesperson of appropriate rank and knowledge; and hold town meetings if needed.

KEY TERMS

communication, p. 432
dialogue, p. 432
discussion, p. 432
downward communication, p. 442
grapevine, p. 446
horizontal communication, p. 445
media richness, p. 433

one-way communication, p. 433
open-book management, p. 444
reflection, p. 440
two-way communication, p. 433
upward communication, p. 444
virtual office, p. 445

SUMMARY OF LEARNING OBJECTIVES

Now that you have studied Chapter 17, you should know:

Communications problems to avoid.

The communication process involves a sender who conveys information to a receiver. Problems in communication can occur in all stages: encoding, transmission, decoding, and interpreting. Noise in the system further complicates communication, creating more distortion. Moreover, feedback may be unavailable or misleading.

The important advantages of two-way communications.

One-way communication flows from the sender to the receiver, with no feedback loop. In two-way communication, each person is both a sender and a receiver as both parties provide and react to information. One-way communication is faster and easier but less accurate than two-way; two-way communication is slower and more difficult, but is more accurate and results in better performance.

When to use, and not to use, the various communications channels.

Communication occurs through oral and written channels. Electronic mail is a relatively new communication channel that is having a huge impact on organizational communications. Each channel has advantages and disadvantages. Media richness, or how much and what sort of information a channel conveys, is one factor to consider as you decide which channel to use.

Ways to become a better writer and persuasive speaker.

Work at being a better writer and speaker. Practice writing, be critical of yourself, and revise. Train yourself as a speaker. In preparing a presentation, consider your own credibility and ways to get it across; the content of your message and its clarity; and characteristics of your audience. Follow the basic guidelines presented in this chapter, and use other sources of help as well.

How to improve downward, upward, and horizontal communications.

Manage communications in all directions. Common problems for people include lack of relevant information, information overload, lack of openness, and filtering. Practice dialogue more than discussion, and two-way communication more than one-way. Make information available, and make sure it is presented accurately and efficiently. But don't let efficiency impede effectiveness. Be repetitive if you need to for emphasis and clarity, and use multiple channels as necessary.

How to work with the company grapevine.

The informal flow of information can contribute as much as formal communication can to organizational effectiveness and morale. Managers must understand that the grapevine cannot be eliminated, and should be actively managed. Many of the suggestions for managing formal communications apply also to managing the grapevine. Moreover, managers can take steps to prevent rumors or neutralize the ones that do arise.

DISCUSSION QUESTIONS

1. Think of an occasion when you faced a miscommunication problem. What do you think caused the problem? How do you think it should have been handled better?
2. Why do people withhold information from others? In cases where sharing information is important, what can be done to overcome people's reluctance to share it?
3. Think back to "discussions" and "dialogues" you have heard. Talk about the differences between a discussion and a dialogue. How can a discussion be turned into a constructive dialogue?
4. Share with the class some of your experiences—both good and bad—with electronic media.
5. Report examples of "mixed signals" you have received (or sent). How can you reduce the potential for misunderstanding and misperception as you communicate with others?
6. What makes you want to say to someone, "You're not listening!"
7. What do you think about the practice of "open-book management"? What would you think about it if you were running your own company?

8. Discuss rumors you have heard: what they were about, how they got started, how accurate they were, and how people reacted to them. What lessons can you learn from these episodes?

9. Refer to "The Virtual Office" on page 445. What do you think will be the long-term impact of the mobile office on job satis-faction and performance? If you were a manager, how would you maximize the benefits and minimize the drawbacks? If you worked in this environment, how would you manage *yourself* to maximize your performance and avoid burnout?

CONCLUDING CASE

LANGUAGE BARRIERS

Many employers in the United States are wrestling with these questions: Should they hire people with limited English skills? If they do, what should they do about the language barrier?

In the past, many employers hired only people who spoke English. Those that did hire immigrants did not need to communicate with them much because jobs were simple. If a message had to be conveyed, someone would find an interpreter. Today, however, immigrants make up a rapidly rising share of the workforce. Moreover, jobs are more complex; even the lowest-level jobs often require people to read blueprints, operate computers, and participate actively in meetings.

Some companies are responding with formal policies and programs. Motorola is spending about $30 million to provide language training to its workers. Pace Foods of San Antonio translates handbooks into Spanish and provides Spanish-speaking interpreters at staff meetings. But different problems arise when people communicate informally among themselves in their native languages.

For example, the day after Florida passed a referendum making English the official state language, an Anglo manager for Publix Supermarkets fired a cashier when she spoke Spanish to a co-worker (the company claims she was fired simply for talking on the job). A nurse is suing a hospital for prohibiting Filipino nurses from speaking Tagalog in front of patients and even among themselves at lunch or on the phone. The Equal Employment Opportunity Commission has ruled that English-only policies are discriminatory except when business reasons make them necessary.

Here's another twist: Bosses may exploit bilingual employees even while forbidding them to speak their native languages. For instance, Spanish is banned among workers, but the same workers are asked to translate when managers need them to do

Communication in the workplace is becoming increasingly complex. For example, some companies are instituting formal language training programs, and many bilingual workers are requesting extra pay for their translation skills. *(Jeff Zaruba/Tony Stone Images)*

so—say, with a non–English-speaking customer. Contel Corporation was sued for penalizing bilingual employees by pulling them from the work on which they were rated to translate for customers. And some bilingual workers are now demanding that they be paid extra for their language skills. At higher organizational levels, bilingual skills are often prized.

This issue is not merely a matter of convenience, preference, or customers. In extreme cases, it can be a matter of life and death. Pilots, copilots, and first officers sometimes speak different languages and have only a rudimentary knowledge of their partners' languages. And in Korea, few ground controllers speak English, so American pilots are required by law to be paired with a Korean first officer. But what if a crisis arises, and the American and Korean have trouble understanding each other?

The problem goes beyond language to cultural norms. Korea's rigid, hierarchical, authoritarian culture means that those of lower rank or younger age hesitate to volunteer information, ask questions, or make suggestions.

QUESTIONS

1. Contrast and evaluate the policies at Motorola, Pace Foods, and Publix.

2. Do you think bilingual employees should receive extra pay? Explain.

3. Propose a corporate policy regarding English and foreign-language use.

4. What else can be done to minimize problems in cross-cultural communications?

Sources: J. Solomon, "Firms Grapple with Language Barriers," *The Wall Street Journal,* November 7, 1989, pp. B1, B5; and S. Glain, "Language Barrier Proves Dangerous in Korea's Skies," *The Wall Street Journal,* October 4, 1994, pp. B1, B16.

VIDEO EXERCISE

COMMUNICATION

Communication and information technology are advancing at a rapid pace. AT&T has revealed its vision for revolutionizing workplace communication in a futuristic style video. The impact of these advances will have a tremendous effect on the role of communication management in business.

The process of communications in organizations has been studied by management scholars for almost 100 years. The accumulation of knowledge in this important area of management is extensive. Yet, it is questionable whether much of it will apply as the new communications technologies take over the workplace. After viewing the AT&T video, complete the following exercise.

Purpose:

To stimulate your thinking about current communication technologies, their direction, and the challenges they pose for managers.

Procedure:

Identify one currently popular tool for communications in the workplace that was not widely available 20 years ago. Your task will be to examine how this device became popular in the workplace, its uses, and the new problems that it has created. Some examples of communications tools that have entered the workplace in the last 20 years are fax machines, cellular telephones, computer networks, pagers, and voice mail. After you have identified the communications tool that interests you, write a briefing for class presentation that covers the following issues.

1. When was the device invented? Often times new inventions take many years to disseminate and become widely used. Try to track down when the tool was invented. Next, give a brief history of how the device came to its current rate of usage.
2. How is the device currently being used in the workplace? Describe the primary and secondary uses of the device. What are its primary functions? Is it a money saver? A time saver? Has the device displaced any human workers? How do managers use the device to improve productivity, quality, and competitiveness?
3. What new workplace problems have been created by the device? Often, new tools for the workplace are created to solve specific problems. Usually, the solution of those problems leads to new problems or issues. For example, the invention of the automobile was to solve the problem of travel, and it has led to the new problems of congestion and air pollution.
4. What new communication tools do you think lie on the horizon? To finish your class presentation, describe what new communication tools you think will be available in the workplace in 20 years. Be creative. Remember that, 20 years ago, not many people would have been able to envision the communication tools that we now take for granted.

EXPERIENTIAL EXERCISES

17.1 Nonverbal Communication

Objective

To become more conscious of nonverbal messages.

Instructions

Below is a list of nonverbal communication "methods." Pick a day on which you will attempt to keep track of these methods. Think back at the end of the day to three people you communicated with in some way. Record how you responded to these people in terms of their nonverbal communication methods. Identify those that had the greatest and least effect on your behavior.

NONVERBAL COMMUNICATION WORKSHEET

Medium	What was the message?	How did you respond?	Which affected your behavior most and least?
How they shook hands			
Their posture			
Their facial expressions			
Their appearance			
Their voice tones			
Their smiles			
The expressions in their eyes			
Their confidence			
The way they moved			
The way they stood			
How close they stood to you			

Symbols or gestures they used   _____   _____   _____

                                   _____   _____   _____

How loudly they spoke   _____   _____   _____

Source: Excerpted from Lawrence R. Jauch, Arthur G. Bedian, Sally A. Coltrin, and William F. Glueck, *The Managerial Experience: Cases, Exercises, and Readings,* 4th ed. Copyright © 1986 by The Dryden Press. Reprinted by permission of the publisher.

17.2 Listening Skills Survey

Objectives

1. To measure your skills as a listener.
2. To gain insight into the factors that determine good listening habits.
3. To demonstrate how you can become a better listener.

Instructions

1. Working alone, complete the Listening Skills Survey.
2. In small groups, compare scores, discuss survey test items, and prepare responses to the discussion questions.

3. After the class reconvenes, group spokespersons present group findings.

Discussion Questions

1. In what ways did students' responses on the survey agree or disagree?
2. What do you think accounts for the differences?
3. How can the results of this survey be put to practical use?

LISTENING SKILLS SURVEY

To measure your listening skills, complete the following survey by circling the degree to which you agree with each state-

	Strongly agree	Agree	Neither agree nor Disagree	Disagree	Strongly Disagree
1. I tend to be patient with the speaker, making sure she or he is finished speaking before I respond in any fashion.	5	4	3	2	1
2. When listening I don't doodle or fiddle with papers and things that might distract me from the speaker.	5	4	3	2	1
3. I attempt to understand the speaker's point of view.	5	4	3	2	1
4. I try not to put the speaker on the defensive by arguing or criticizing.	5	4	3	2	1
5. When I listen, I focus on the speaker's feelings.	5	4	3	2	1
6. I let a speaker's annoying mannerisms distract me.	5	4	3	2	1

	Strongly agree	Agree	Neither agree nor Disagree	Disagree	Strongly Disagree
7. While the speaker is talking, I watch carefully for facial expressions and other types of body language.	5	4	3	2	1
8. I never talk when the other person is trying to say something.	5	4	3	2	1
9. During a conversation, a period of silence seems awkward to me.	5	4	3	2	1
10. I want people to just give me the facts and allow me to make up my own mind.	5	4	3	2	1
11. When the speaker is finished, I respond to his or her feelings.	5	4	3	2	1
12. I don't evaluate the speaker's words until she or he is finished talking.	5	4	3	2	1
13. I formulate my response while the speaker is still talking.	5	4	3	2	1
14. I never pretend that I'm listening when I'm not.	5	4	3	2	1
15. I can focus on message content even if the delivery is poor.	5	4	3	2	1
16. I encourage the speaker with frequent nods, smiles, and other forms of body language.	5	4	3	2	1
17. Sometimes I can predict what someone is going to say before she or he says it.	5	4	3	2	1
18. Even if a speaker makes me angry, I hold my temper.	5	4	3	2	1
19. I maintain good eye contact with the speaker.	5	4	3	2	1
20. I try to focus on the speaker's message, not her or his delivery.	5	4	3	2	1
21. If I am confused by a statement someone makes, I never respond until I have asked for and received adequate clarification.	5	4	3	2	1

FRANK PERRIMAN'S APPOINTMENT

Indefatigable Mutual Insurance is a large, national company with more than 10,000 employees in the 50 states and Canada. Its basic organization has been as shown in the organization chart. Each divisional vice president has access to the president if so desired, but most communications between the field and home office are with the functional vice presidents, who set policy and monitor performance in their respective functional areas. Two senior vice presidents have acted as staff to the president in their areas of expertise—one in actuarial and statistical matters and the other in investments and finance. In general, Indefatigable has been a highly centralized, regionally dispersed organization.

Frank Perriman has had exceptional success at Indefatigable. After experience primarily in sales, Frank was appointed vice president of the Middle Division at age 35—the youngest such appointment in the company's history. One annual report contained an individual picture of Perriman (the only divisional vice president so honored) with a caption describing him as an example of what could happen to young people at Indefatigable. However, most executives were old.

After eight years as division vice president Perriman was promoted to senior vice president (thus making three senior vice presidents) and transferred to the home office. The president sent the bulletins shown on page 454.

At times Perriman thought he had no problem. After all, he had been given a significant promotion. Nonetheless, he was concerned because he feared resentment from others and was unclear about what the president wanted. Perriman had recently attended an executive program in which they had discussed a case titled "The Dashman Company," which told about a new vice president who failed to exert any impact on the organization (see the Dashman Company case on page 454). Accordingly, he decided to see Professor Eagleson, who had conducted various management training programs for the company.

During the conversation, Eagleson pointed out that there was a disparity in the managerial styles of the various division vice presidents. For example, when conducting a training program for managers in the Northern Division, he had the divisional functional managers draw an organization chart (illustrated on page 455). When sitting in the Northern Division's vice president's office one day, a divisional functional manager had come in with a problem about how to treat a certain policyholder. The vice president had asked the manager to read the relevant home office regulation on the matter and then directed the functional manager to adhere exactly to the home office rule.

By chance, Professor Eagleson had once been sitting in Perriman's office when a similar event occurred. After listening to the divisional manager and reading the home office regulation, Perriman had advised the manager that the regulation didn't exactly apply, so they were free to handle the matter as they deemed best. If headquarters would later complain to the manager, Perriman promised to say the action was his responsibility. When the Middle Division divisional managers had drawn the organization chart in their training session, it was as pictured on page 455. In general, Eagleson felt that the Northern Division's vice president's behavior was more typical of the division vice presidents than Perriman's.

When Perriman asked Eagleson what he thought the president expected of the new position, the professor said he wasn't sure. Nonetheless, he mentioned that when he recently had seen the president about the company training programs, the executive had expressed concern about his age, next year's 100th anniversary celebration of the firm, and the company's expense

Organizational chart

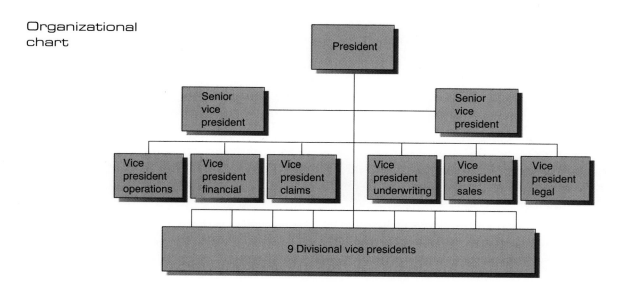

<table>
<tr><td>

HOME OFFICE ADMINISTRATION
June 29
ORGANIZATIONAL BULLETIN—GENERAL No. 349

Effective August 1, Mr. Frank Perriman, Vice President and Division Manager, Middle Division, will transfer to the President's staff at the home office.

Perriman will be responsible to the President for achieving division performance in accordance with company policies and objectives.

Mr. Perriman will assist Division Managers in obtaining well-coordinated efforts by all departments and will establish and use measurements of results for each Division.

Divisional Vice Presidents will report to and be responsible to Mr. Perriman.

Thomas Achison
President

</td><td>

HOME OFFICE ADMINISTRATION
July 14
ORGANIZATIONAL BULLETIN—GENERAL No. 351

Effective July 14, the Board of Directors made the following election: Mr. Frank Perriman—Senior Vice President

Thomas Achison
President

</td></tr>
</table>

Dashman Company

The Dashman Company was a large concern making many types of equipment for the armed forces of the United States. It had over 20 plants, located in the central part of the country, whose purchasing procedures had never been completely coordinated. In fact, the head office of the company had encouraged each of the plant managers to operate with their staffs as separate independent units in most matters. Late in 1940, when it began to appear that the company would face increasing difficulty in securing certain essential raw materials, Mr. Manson, the company's president, appointed an experienced purchasing executive, Mr. Post, as vice president in charge of purchasing, a position especially created for him. Mr. Manson gave Mr. Post wide latitude in organizing his job, and he assigned Mr. Larson as Mr. Post's assistant. Mr. Larson had served the company in a variety of capacities for many years and knew most of the plant executives personally. Mr. Post's appointment was announced through the formal channels usual in the company, including a notice in the house organ published by the company.

One of Mr. Post's first decisions was to begin immediately to centralize the company's purchasing procedure. As a first step he decided that he would require each of the executives who handled purchasing in the individual plants to clear with the head office all purchase contracts which they made in excess of $10,000. He felt that if the head office was to do any coordinating in a way that would be helpful to each plant and to the company as a whole, he must be notified that the contracts were being prepared at least a week before they were to be signed. He talked his proposal over with Mr. Manson, who presented it to his board of directors. They approved the plan.

Although the company made purchases throughout the year, the beginning of its peak buying season was only three weeks away at the time this new plan was adopted. Mr. Post prepared a letter to be sent to the 20 purchasing executives of the company. The letter follows:

Dear_____:

The board of directors of our company has recently authorized a change in our purchasing procedures. Hereafter, each of the purchasing executives in the several plants of the company will notify the vice president in charge of purchasing of all contracts in excess of $10,000 they are negotiating at least a week in advance of the date on which they are to be signed.

I am sure that you will understand that this step is necessary to coordinate the purchasing requirements of the company in these times when we are facing increasing difficulty in securing essential supplies. This procedure should give us in the central office the information we need to see that each plant secures the optimum supply of materials. In this way the interests of each plant and of the company as a whole will best be served.

Yours very truly,

Mr. Post showed the letter to Mr. Larson and invited his comments. Mr. Larson thought the letter an excellent one but suggested that, since Mr. Post had not met more than a few of the purchasing executives, he might like to visit all of them and take the matter up with each of them personally. Mr. Post dismissed the idea at once because, as he said, he had so many things to do at the head office that he could not get away for a trip. Consequently he had the letters sent out over his signature.

During the two following weeks replies came in from all except a few plants. Although a few executives wrote at greater length, the following reply was typical:

Dear Mr. Post:

Your recent communication in regard to notifying the head office a week in advance of our intention to sign contracts has been received. This suggestion seems a most practical one. We want to assure you that you can count on our cooperation.

Yours very truly,

During the next six weeks the head office received no notices from any plant that contracts were being negotiated. Executives in other departments who made frequent trips to the plants reported that the plants were busy, and the usual routines for that time of year were being followed.

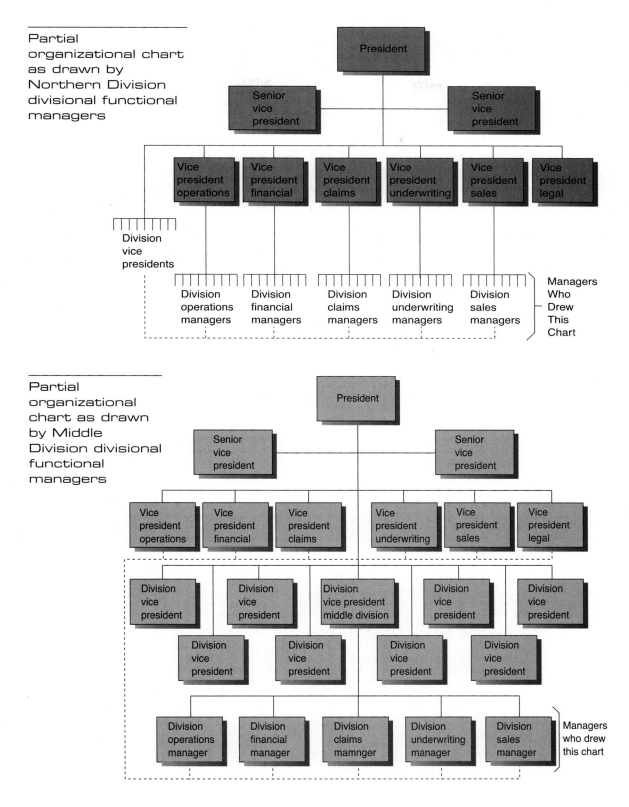

Partial organizational chart as drawn by Northern Division divisional functional managers

Partial organizational chart as drawn by Middle Division divisional functional managers

position. He had remarked on the way to lunch that the only thing wrong with the company was that the field personnel "just didn't follow home office rules." The president indicated that the company was losing money on automobile insurance policies, especially because sales was selling to less desirable risks—con-trary to the company's long-standing strategy of preferred risks. Perhaps, the president concluded, the field staff should be reduced and sales curtailed.

Pondering these points, Perriman wondered if one of his first steps as a senior vice president should be to pick a fight with one of the home office functional vice presidents to impress the division vice presidents with his willingness to battle on their behalf.

QUESTIONS

1. Discuss any problems Perriman might have in establishing authority and influence in his new post.

2. What factors should aid Perriman?

3. How do you think the divisional vice presidents will react to this appointment? Why?

4. How do you think the functional vice presidents will react to this appointment? Why?

5. How do you think Achison should have proceeded?

6. How do you interpret the differences in the organization charts as drawn by the division functional managers in the Northern Division compared with the Middle Division?

7. What do the president's remarks to Professor Eagleson suggest about his intentions for Perriman as the new senior vice president?

8. What recommendations would you offer Perriman now? Why?

Source: R. Weber, M. Morgan, and P. Brown, *Management,* 3rd ed. (Homewood, Ill.: Richard D. Irwin, 1985), pp. 253–57.

SUGGESTION SYSTEM POLICY

OFFICE OF THE PRESIDENT
Memorandum
Date: Friday, November 18, 1988
From: Bob Adams, president
To: John Sullens, vice president for human resources

Employee suggestion systems have been around for a long time. The positive financial impact of suggestion systems is significant in some organizations, according to my reading. For example, the National Association of Suggestions Systems estimates that 80 percent of the 500 largest U.S. corporations have such programs and that employee suggestions save the nation's companies more than $500 million a year.

The negative aspect of the suggestion system is that employees may become disgruntled about how the company runs the system. You may recall that two United Airlines employees charged in court that United stole their suggestion for a reduced-fare plan for employees of all airlines, that United successfully implemented the plan, and that United cheated them out of hundreds of thousands of dollars that they had coming under the company's suggestion system. They cited a provision of United Airlines' suggestion system rules that stated, "An employee is entitled to 10 percent of a typical year's profits resulting from an idea submitted through the suggestion system and successfully implemented."

During the trial, expert witnesses testified that in a typical year of operations under the reduced-fare plan, United earned $3 million attributable to the plan, of which 10 percent, or $300,000, rightfully belonged to the two employees who submitted the suggestion. The jury found that the company acted in bad faith by failing to pay off under the suggestion system and assessed $1.8 million in damages against the airline, which a judge later reduced to $368,000.

We can't afford to risk such financial peril! It's critical, therefore, that you promptly review our suggestion system rules and policies and that you give me recommendations on the following issues. Include advantages and disadvantages associated with your policy recommendations.

1. *Calculation of award amount.* Should we offer a flat amount of money for each accepted suggestion, or should the award be based on a percentage of the savings (earnings) during some period? What percentage? What period?
2. *Maximum award.* Should we have a maximum limit on the payoff for any single suggestion (perhaps $10,000), or should it be open ended?
3. *Time of award payment.* Should we pay the award in full when the suggestion is accepted or as the savings (earnings) are realized annually?
4. *Joint award allocation.* When two or more employees combine on a suggestion, how should we allocate the award among them?
5. *Originality.* Should we pay off for suggestions that help us, even if they aren't original with the employee(s) making the suggestion?
6. *Impetus award.* Are you in favor of an "impetus award" in the range of $100 to $500 to recognize a suggestion that hastens an action initiated by the company before receipt of the suggestion?
7. *Written rules.* Do you think we need to spell out in writing every aspect of our suggestion system, or will an informal approach be more conducive to employee participation?
8. *Proof of knowledge.* Should we require all employees to sign a form stating that they have read and understand the suggestion system's rules (if we decide to write them up)?
9. *Another limitation.* Should an employee be limited to suggestions relating only to his or her area of the organization?
10. *An exclusion.* Should our marketing function and financial policy (including product and service pricing) be excluded from the suggestion system?
11. *Evaluation.* Do you have any suggestions on a procedure for evaluating suggestions?
12. *Abandonment.* Maybe dropping the suggestion system would be easier. What do you think?

We are reviewing all aspects of our suggestion system policy. Our attorney recommends abandonment. Let me hear from you as soon as possible. Treat this as a priority item.

Source: J.M. Champion and J.H. James, *Critical Incidents in Management: Decision and Policy Issues,* 6th ed. (Homewood, Ill.: Richard D. Irwin, 1989).

QUALITY CIRCLE CONSEQUENCE

John Stevens, plant manager of the Fairlead Plant of Lockstead Corporation, which manufactures structural components for aircraft wings and bodies, became interested in using quality circles to improve performance in his plant. *Quality circles* was the name used to describe joint labor-supervision participation teams operating at the shop-floor level at Lockstead. Other companies called quality circles by names such as "productivity groups," "people involvement programs," and "departmental teams." Whatever the name, the purpose of quality circles was to improve the quality of manufacturing performance.

The subject of quality circles was a hot topic in the press. Stevens had seen books on Japanese management and productivity successes, which featured the use of quality circles. All these books featured the slogan "None of us is as smart as all of us."

Other books related quality circles to productivity gains. Articles on quality circles appeared often in trade journals and in business magazines, including *Business Week.*

Stevens also had a pamphlet from a management consulting firm announcing a "new and improved" training course for quality circle leaders, scheduled consecutively in Birmingham, Alabama; Williamsburg, Virginia; and Orlando, Florida. Another consultant offered "a program that will teach your managers and supervisors how to increase productivity and efficiency without making costly investments . . . by focusing on techniques germane to the quality circle process." Stevens was impressed enough to attend an advanced management seminar at a large midwestern university. A large part of the program concentrated on quality circles.

Professor Albert Mennon particularly impressed Stevens with his lectures on group discussion, team problem solving, and group decision making. Mennon convinced Stevens that employees meeting in quality circle teams with adequate leaders could effectively consider problems and formulate quality decisions that would be acceptable to employees. The staff conducting this state-of-the-art seminar covered five areas: (1) how to train quality circle members in the six-step problem sequence; (2) a description of what leaders and facilitators should do during the quality circle sessions; (3) planning and writing a policy guide; (4) developing an implementation plan; and (5) measuring quality circle progress and success.

Both the company and its employees were expected to benefit from a successfully implemented quality circle program. The list of payoffs included increased job satisfaction, productivity improvements, efficiency gains, and improved performance and labor relations. Moreover, it was expected that a reduction would occur in areas such as grievance loads, absenteeism, and costs.

Returning to his plant after the seminar, Stevens decided to practice some of the principles he had learned. He called together the 25 employees of Department B and told them that production standards established several years ago were too low in view of the recent installation of automated equipment. He gave the workers the opportunity to discuss the mitigating circumstances and to decide among themselves, as a group, what their standards should be. On leaving the room, he believed that the workers would establish much higher standards than he would have dared propose.

After an hour of discussion, the group summoned Stevens and notified him that, contrary to his opinion, they had decided the standards already were too high and, since they had been given the authority to establish their own standards, they were making a reduction of 10 percent. Stevens knew these standards were far too low to provide a fair profit on the owner's investment. Yet he believed his refusal to accept the group decision would be disastrous. Stevens thought of telephoning Professor Mennon for consultation on the quality circle dilemma, but he chose to act on his own.

Several options filled Stevens' mind: (1) He could accept the blame for the quality circle experiment having gone awry and tell them to begin anew; (2) he could establish incentive pay adjustment linkages between the quality circle's decisions and productivity improvements; (3) he might even operate at a loss for a short while to prove that the original quality circle decision had been unacceptable; or (4) he might abandon the participative team program. Stevens needed a decision, an operational policy for the quality circle program, and an implementation plan.

Source: J.H. Champion and J.H. James, *Critical Incidents in Management: Decision and Policy Issues,* 6th ed. (Burr Ridge, Ill.: Richard D. Irwin, 1989).

CONTROL
AND CHANGE

FOUNDATIONS OF MANAGEMENT

Managers and Organizations
The Evolution of Management
The External Environment
Managerial Decision Making

PLANNING AND STRATEGY

Planning and Strategic Management
Ethics and Corporate Responsibility
Managing in Our Natural Environment
International Management
New Ventures

STRATEGY IMPLEMENTATION

ORGANIZING AND STAFFING

Organization Structure
The Responsive Organization
Human Resources Management
Managing the Diverse Workforce

LEADING

Leadership
Motivating for Performance
Managing Teams
Communicating

CONTROL AND CHANGE

Managerial Control
Operations Management
Managing Technology and Innovation
Becoming World Class

I n Parts I through IV, you learned about the foundations of management, planning and strategy, and how to implement plans by organizing, staffing, and leading. Part V concludes with four chapters about controlling and changing what the organization and its people are doing. Chapter 18 describes managerial control, including techniques for ensuring that intended activities are carried out and goals are accomplished. Chapter 19 examines operations management; in that chapter, you will learn about managing manufacturing and service operations.

The last two chapters focus on change and renewal. Chapter 20 discusses technology and innovation, including a strategic approach to new technologies and the creation of a culture for innovation. Chapter 21 examines an ongoing challenge for the modern executive: Becoming world class through the management of change. In that chapter, we describe the nature of this challenge and how managers can deal with it. Some of the topics you learned about in earlier chapters play central roles in the change process; Chapter 21 should remind you how your understanding of them will continually benefit your managerial career.

18

MANAGERIAL CONTROL

More than at any time in the past, companies will not be able to hold themselves together with the traditional methods of control: hierarchy, systems, budgets, and the like . . . The bonding glue will increasingly become ideological.

Collins & Porras[1]

Use your good judgment in all situations. There will be no additional rules.

Nordstrom's employee manual

LEARNING OBJECTIVES

After studying Chapter 18, you will know:

1. Why companies develop control systems for employees.

2. How to design a basic control system.

3. The purposes for using budgets as a control device.

4. How to intrepret financial ratios and other financial controls.

5. The procedures for implementing effective control systems.

6. How the process of control can be approached in an empowered organization.

MANAGING THE MAGIC

*H*ave you seen what robots are doing at theme parks such as Disney World, MGM, and Universal Studios? From the Hall of Presidents, to E.T.'s Adventure, and the Ghostbusters' dark ride, humanoid creations are coming to life through a process known as *animatronics,* which merges art and technology to produce some truly amazing special effects. Many of these entertainment robots have been created by the people at Sally Corporation, a small company of about 40 employees in Jacksonville, Florida. Sally was founded in 1977 and is one of a few companies that build these creatures and their props.

This huge T-Rex (entertainment robot) from Sally Corp. terrifies visitors to the "Voyage to the Center of the Earth" dark ride at *Water World* in Colorado. Creating robots requires the ability to balance a myriad of complex elements. *(Courtesy Sally Corporation)*

Success in such an unusual field such as animatronics depends on a company's ability to balance conflicting demands of creativity and efficiency. The robots are the product of an exacting mix of latex, wires, and tubes, on the one hand, and on the other, a distinctive form of artistry that must be managed carefully. Many of Sally's artisans would be just as happy painting a sunset on the beach as they would arranging features on a robot's face. But the company can't be run as a laid-back creative operation—this labor-intensive work must be conducted in a business environment of fixed-price contracts and strict production schedules. Cost overruns or project delays can be disastrous with multimillion-dollar contracts with clients such as Disney and Universal.

Sally Corporation has designed a rather sophisticated management control system that provides employees with a good deal of flexibility and choice in their work, while maintaining strict accountability for their time. Each morning as employees arrive, they log onto the computer and review a menu of projects available to work on. Employees assign themselves to projects, and the starting time for their work is automatically recorded in the system's database. Employees might work on a particular task for only a few minutes or for the rest of the day. If they stop working on a task, they can simply log off one task and onto another. Meanwhile, the system automatically updates the hours worked on the project, and the terminal displays the budgeted hours remaining on all projects. At the end of the day, employees log off the system, and their time allocation is automatically recorded for each project.

For a small company, such as Sally, this control represents a significant investment. Nevertheless, company president Howard Kelley argues that the system has paid for itself in a number of ways:

- Employees are conscious of how they use their time, and they can see how their time fits into the time budgeted for a project—they work "smarter."
- Because the system is on-line, real-time managers can review project status instantaneously.
- The system flags on screen any tasks or projects that are over budget, thereby allowing managers to give these items special attention.
- Time records are more accurate since employees don't have to rely on their memories or fill out time sheets.

Source: Thomas L. Barton and Frederick M. Cole, "Accounting for Magic: A Potent Mix of Art, Technology, and Professional Management," *Management Accounting* 72, no. 7 (January 1991), pp. 27–31.

*E*nsuring creativity, enhancing quality, reducing costs—managers must figure out ways to control what occurs in their organizations. Some means of control are necessary because once managers form strategies and plans, they must ensure the plans are carried out. This means making sure that other people are doing what needs to be done and not doing inappropriate things.

If plans are not carried out properly, management must take steps to correct the problem. This is the primary control function of management. Ineffective control systems result in problems ranging from employee theft to financial losses from unauthorized foreign exchange speculation. Employees simply wasting time costs U.S. employers over $100 billion a year![2]

Control has been called one of the Siamese twins of management. The other twin is planning. Not surprisingly, effective planning facilitates control, and control facilitates planning. Planning lays out a framework for the future, and in this sense, provides a blueprint for control. Control systems, in turn, regulate the allocation and utilization of resources, and in so doing, facilitate the process of planning. In today's complex organizational environment, both functions have become more difficult to implement at the same time they have become more important in every department of the organization. Managers today must control their people, inventories, quality, and costs, to mention just a few of their responsibilities.

CONTROL DEFINED

Control is typically defined as any process that directs the activities of individuals toward the achievement of organizational goals. Left on their own, people may knowingly or unknowingly act in ways that they perceive to be beneficial but that may work to the detriment of the organization as a whole. In this sense, control is one of the fundamental forces that keep the organization together. Without some means of regulating what people do, the organization would literally fall apart.

Some managers don't want to admit it (see Table 18.1), but control problems will cause unwanted deviations from intended goals. Companies use control systems to minimize such problems. In this regard, control is not a hindrance but a managerial necessity.

TABLE 18.1

The leadership symptoms of an out-of-control company

David Ferrari, president of Argus Management Corporation, maintains that many businesses are in big trouble without the CEO even knowing it. The symptoms:

- **Misplaced confidence**—believing that everything they do is right and they cannot make mistakes.

- **Blame deflection**—if they admit they are in trouble, they blame everything but themselves.

- **Avoidance**—doing "busy work" that is easy to handle rather than tackling the big, company-wide issues.

- **An eye to the past**—justifying current practices by saying, "We've always done it that way."

- **Blind optimism**—refusing to believe bad numbers and believing that things will take care of themselves.

- **Setting a poor example**—spending lavishly on perks for themselves rather than living up to the same stringent standards expected of others.

- **Isolation**—other people—subordinates, directors, outsiders—don't send warning signals or stand up to the CEO to convince him or her that things are perilously out of control.

Source: B. Posner, "Squeeze Play," *Inc.,* July 1990, pp. 68–75.

THE CONTROL SYSTEM

Control systems are designed to measure progress toward planned performance and, if necessary, to apply corrective measures to ensure that performance is in line with managers' objectives. Control systems detect and correct significance variations, or discrepancies, in the results obtained from planned activities.

Figure 18.1 shows a typical control system with four major steps: (1) setting performance standards, (2) measuring performance, (3) comparing performance against the standards and determining deviations, and (4) taking corrective action.

SETTING PERFORMANCE STANDARDS

Every organization has goals, including profitability, innovation, satisfaction of constituencies, and so on. A **standard** is the level of expected performance for a given goal.[3] Standards are performance targets that establish desired performance levels, motivate performance, and serve as benchmarks against which to assess actual performance. Standards can be set for any activity—financial activities, operating activities, legal compliance, charitable contributions, and so on.

We have discussed setting performance standards in other parts of the text. For example, employee goal setting for motivation is built around the concept of specific, measurable performance standards. Such standards should be challenging and typically should aim for improvement over past performance. Thus, useful performance targets for control purposes would include increasing market share by 20 percent, cutting costs by 15 percent, answering all customer complaints within 24 hours, achieving a return on investment of 8 percent, or producing 800,000 units in a year.

Job requirements and objective data can provide guidance in setting standards. For example, to keep sales expenses under control, expense standards can be based on salespersons' need to travel and on the number of nights on the road. A small number of experienced people could keep track of their actual expenses to provide data for future standard setting.[4]

Performance standards can be set with respect to (1) quantity, (2) quality, (3) time used, and (4) cost. For example, production activities include volume of output (quantity), defects (quality), on-time availability of finished goods (time use), and dollar expenditures for raw materials and direct labor (cost). Many important aspects of performance, such as customer service, can be measured by the same standards—for example, adequate supply and availability of products, quality of service, speed of delivery, and so forth.

FIGURE 18.1

The control process

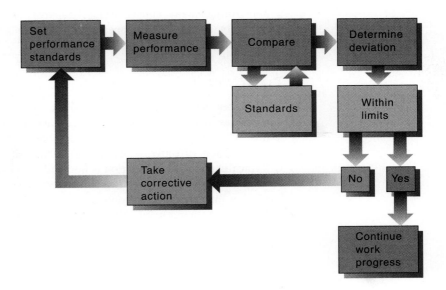

MEASURING PERFORMANCE

The second step in the control process is to measure performance levels. For example, managers can count units produced, days absent, papers filed, samples distributed, and dollars earned. Performance data commonly are obtained from three sources: written reports, oral reports, and personal observations.

Written reports include computer printouts. Thanks to computers' increasing capabilities and decreasing cost, both large and small companies can gather huge amounts of performance data.

One common example of *oral reports* occurs when a salesperson contacts his or her immediate manager at the close of each business day to report the accomplishments, problems, or customers' reactions during the day. The manager can ask questions to gain additional information or clear up any misunderstandings. When necessary, tentative corrective actions can be worked out during the discussion.

Personal observation involves going to the area of activities and watching what is occurring. The manager can observe work methods, employees' nonverbal signals, and the general operation. Personal observation gives an intimate picture of what is going on. But it also has some disadvantages. It does not provide accurate quantitative data; the information usually is general and subjective. Also, employees can misconstrue personal observation as mistrust or a lack of confidence. Nevertheless, many managers believe there is no good substitute for firsthand observation. As you learned in earlier chapters, personal contact can increase leadership visibility and upward communication. It also provides valuable information about performance to supplement written and oral reports.

COMPARING PERFORMANCE WITH THE STANDARD

The third step in the control process is comparing performance with the standard. In this process, the manager evaluates the performance. For some activities relatively small deviations from the standard are acceptable, while in others a slight deviation may be serious. Managers who perform the controlling work therefore must carefully analyze and evaluate the results.

The managerial **principle of exception** states that control is enhanced by concentrating on the exceptions, or significant deviations, from the expected result or standard. In comparing performance with the standard, managers need to direct their attention to the exception. For example, controlling the prices at which 100 items are purchased might show that only five prices are out of line. These five prices are the exceptions and should be investigated further.

Only exceptional cases require corrective action. The manager should not be concerned with performance that equals or closely approximates the expected results. This principle is important in controlling. Managers can save much time and effort if they apply the principle of exception.

TAKING CORRECTIVE ACTION

The last step in the control process is to take action to correct significant deviations. This step ensures that operations are adjusted where necessary to achieve the initially planned results. Where significant variances are discovered, the manager should take immediate and vigorous action. Effective control cannot tolerate needless delays, excuses, or exceptions.

Typically the corrective action is initiated by those who have authority over the actual performance. For example, United Parcel Service (UPS) uses tight controls over its drivers. Every day, management compares each driver's performance (number of miles, deliveries, and pickups) with a computerized projection of what performance should have been. When drivers fail to meet standards, a supervisor rides with them and provides suggestions for improvement. Drivers who do not improve are warned, then suspended, and finally dismissed.[5]

An alternative approach is for the corrective action to be taken not by higher-ups but by the operator at the point of the problem. In computer-controlled production technology, two basic types of control are feasible: specialist control and operator control. With **specialist control,** operators of computer-numerical-control (CNC) machines must notify engineering specialists of malfunctions. With this traditional division of labor, the specialist takes corrective action. With **operator control,** multiskilled operators can rectify their own problems as they occur. Not only is this strategy more efficient, because deviations are controlled closer to their source; operators benefit by virtue of a more enriched job.[6]

Quality

The appropriate corrective action depends on the nature of the problem. The corrective action may involve a change in a procedure or method, a disciplinary action, a new way to check the accuracy of manufactured parts, or a major organizational modification. Or it may simply be an inexpensive investment in employee training. At Corning, the source of major quality and production problems was traced to minute drafting errors by the engineering group. One of the solutions was quite simple: An engineer was sent to a proofreading class.[7]

TYPES OF CONTROL

The three types of control are feed forward, concurrent, and feedback.[8] **Feedforward control** takes place before operations begin and includes policies, procedures, and rules designed to ensure that planned activities are carried out properly. Examples include inspection of raw materials and proper selection and training of employees. **Concurrent control** takes place while plans are being carried out. It includes directing, monitoring, and fine-tuning activities as they occur. **Feedback control** focuses on the use of information about results to correct deviations from the acceptable standard after they arise.

You may notice a connection between the three types of control and two important models described elsewhere in the text. First, feedforward, concurrent, and feedback control focus on the inputs, transformation processes, and outputs, respectively, of the systems model described in Chapters 1 and 2. Second, they also correspond to the A-B-C model of motivation described in Chapter 15. Preliminary control sets antecedents that dictate how people should behave. Concurrent control monitors behavior as it takes place. Feedback control occurs after the fact, and the corrective action can include rewards and punishments for proper and improper performance.

FEEDFORWARD CONTROL

Feedforward control (sometimes called *preliminary control*) is future oriented; its aim is to prevent problems before they arise. Instead of waiting for results and comparing them with goals, a manager can exert control by limiting activities in advance. For example, companies have policies defining the scope within which decisions are made. A company may dictate that managers adhere to clear ethical and legal guidelines when making decisions. Formal rules and procedures also prescribe people's actions before they occur. Stating that a financial officer must approve expenditures over $1,000 or that only components that pass all safety tests can be used in a product specifies in advance which actions can and cannot be taken. To prevent loan defaults, banks may require extensive loan documentation, reviews, and approvals by bank officers before authorizing a loan.

Cost

Japan has a unique cost management system that provides preliminary cost control. In the United States and Europe, accountants set a product's cost after various departments have built in their cost specifications. But in Japan, the price at which the product will appeal to potential buyers is determined *first,* and *then* each department is assigned a cost that it must meet. Such *target costing* prevents costs from soaring so high that products must be priced beyond what consumers are willing to pay.[9]

CONTROL AND QUALITY AT GE AIRCRAFT ENGINES

Quality

*I*n recent years, much as been said about "the quality revolution" as if no one had ever taken a rational approach to quality control in the past. Nothing could be further from the truth at General Electric Aircraft Engines, where quality and safety have always been fundamental requirements and major competitive strengths. But while emphasis on quality has been constant, GE's approach to *controlling* quality has changed in recent years.

In the past—from the 1950s through the 1980s—GE Aircraft Engines was a classic quality control organization; an independent internal group audited the work of the rest of the organization by inspecting products, both hardware and other deliverables, to detect defects. Since quality at 30,000 feet is critical, Aircraft Engines did a lot of inspections, often 200 or 300 percent inspections of critical characteristics. By the time the product reached the customer, it was safe and met stringent specifications for performance.

Speed

But the cost of quality and the lead times needed to deliver it were heavy burdens. To stay competitive, GE redesigned its quality initiatives to focus on speed or cycle time as well as traditional quality metrics. To achieve this goal, quality control has shifted from defect detection (a feedback system) to defect prevention (a feedforward system). To achieve continuous reduction of process variation, customers and suppliers are integrated with a team of designers, project engineers, purchasing agents, and manufacturing employees. Design for manufacturability has become a whole new approach to enhancing quality and customer value. The essence of quality is "doing it right the first time."

Along with control system changes designed to enhance quality, GE has also focused on the cultural aspects of change associated with continuous improvement—teamwork and empowerment are viewed as vital elements of total quality management. As a result of the culture changes, quality control is no longer the province of a backroom quality department; it has become an "up-front" responsibility of each supplier, manager, and employee within the organization.

Source: Adapted from Al Parker, "The Changing Role of Quality at GE Aircraft Engines," *Quality,* September 1993, pp. 18–21. ●

CONCURRENT CONTROL

Concurrent control, which takes place while plans are carried out, is the heart of any control system. On the production floor, all efforts are directed toward producing the correct quantity of the right products in the specified amount of time. In an airline terminal, the

While General Electric Aircraft Engines has always emphasized quality, most recently the company has focused on speed or cycle time as well as traditional quality metrics. This shift reflects the importance to this company of *controlling* quality.
(Courtesy GE Aircraft Engines)

baggage must get to the right airplanes before flights depart. In factories, materials must be available when and where needed, and breakdowns in the production process must be repaired immediately. Concurrent control also is in operation when supervisors watch employees to ensure they work efficiently and avoid mistakes.

Advances in information technology have created powerful concurrent controls. Computerized systems give managers immediate access to data from the most remote corners of their companies. For example, managers can continuously update budgets based on an ongoing flow of performance data. In production facilities, monitoring systems that track errors per hour, machine speeds, and other measures allow managers to continuously correct small production problems before they become disasters.[10]

FEEDBACK CONTROL

Feedback control implies that performance data were gathered and analyzed and the results returned to someone (or something) in the process to make corrections. When supervisors monitor behavior, they are exercising concurrent control. When they point out and correct improper performance, they are using feedback as a means of control.

Timing is an important aspect of feedback control. Long time lags often occur between performance and feedback, such as when actual spending is compared against the quarterly budget or when some aspect of performance is compared to the projection made a year ago. If feedback on performance is not timely, managers cannot quickly identify and eliminate the problem and prevent more serious harm.

Some feedback processes are under real-time (concurrent) control, such as a computer-controlled robot on an assembly line. Such units have sensing units, which continually determine whether they are in the correct position to perform their functions. If not, a built-in control device makes immediate corrections.

MANAGEMENT AUDITS

Over the years, **management audits** have developed as a means for evaluating the effectiveness and efficiency of various systems within an organization, from social responsibility to accounting control.[11] Management audits may be external or internal. Managers conduct external audits of other companies and internal audits of their own company. Some of the same tools and approaches are used for both types of audits.

EXTERNAL AUDITS

An **external audit** occurs when one organization evaluates another organization. Typically an external body such as a CPA firm conducts financial audits of an organization (accounting audits are discussed later). But any company can also conduct external audits of competitors or other companies for strategic decision-making purposes. This type of analysis (1) investigates other organizations for possible merger or acquisition; (2) determines the soundness of a company that will be used as a major supplier; or (3) discovers the strengths and weaknesses of a competitor to maintain or better exploit the competitive advantage of the investigating organization. Publicly available data usually are used for these evaluations.[12]

External audits were used in feedback control in the discovery and investigation of the savings and loan scandals. They also are useful for preliminary control because they can prevent problems from occurring. If a company gathers adequate, accurate information about acquisition candidates, it is more likely to acquire the most appropriate companies and avoid unsound acquisitions.

INTERNAL AUDITS

Internal audits improve the planning process and the organization's internal control systems. Periodic assessment of a company's own planning, organizing, leading, and controlling is the essential function of an internal management audit. The audit reviews the company's past, present, and future.

Cost

Among the more common undesirable practices uncovered by a management audit are the performance of unnecessary work; duplication of work; poor inventory control; uneconomical use of equipment and machines; procedures that are more costly than necessary; and wasted resources. Square D, the electrical equipment manufacturer, discovered it could throw away four manuals with 760 rules and regulations in favor of 11 policy statements. At Heinz, a quality program aimed mostly at eliminating waste and rework is estimated to save $250 million over three years.[13] Oryx, the world's largest independent oil and gas producer, now takes six weeks instead of seven months to produce the annual budget and has cut in half the average time and cost of finding new oil and gas reserves.[14]

To perform a management audit, a list of desired qualifications is drawn up and weights are attached to each qualification. The audit assesses (1) what the company has done for itself and (2) what it has done for its customers or other recipients of its goods or services. The company can be evaluated on a number of factors, including financial stability, production efficiency, sales effectiveness, human resources development, earnings growth, public relations, civic responsibility, or other criteria of organizational effectiveness.

BUDGETARY CONTROL

Budgetary control is one of the most widely recognized and commonly used methods of managerial control. It ties together feedforward control, concurrent control, and feedback control, depending on the point at which it is applied. *Budgetary control* is the process of finding out what's being done and comparing the results with the corresponding budget data to verify accomplishments or to remedy differences. Budgetary control commonly is called **budgeting.**

FUNDAMENTAL BUDGETARY CONSIDERATIONS

In private industry, budgetary control begins with an estimate of sales and expected income. Table 18.2 shows a budget with estimates for sales and expenses for the first three months of the year. There is space to enter the actual accomplishments to expedite comparison between expected and actual results. Note that the total expenses plus estimated gross profit equal the total sales expectancy.

Budgeting information is supplied to the entire enterprise or to any of its units; it is not confined to financial matters. Units other than dollars typically can be used. For example, industry uses budgeting of production in physical units and of labor by different skills.

A primary consideration of budgeting is the length of the *budget period*. All budgets are prepared for a definite time period. Many budgets are for one, three, or six months or for

TABLE 18.2

A sales-expense budget

	January		February		March	
	Expectancy	Actual	Expectancy	Actual	Expectancy	Actual
Sales	$1,200,000		$1,350,000		$1,400,000	
Expenses						
General						
overhead	310,000		310,000		310,000	
Selling	242,000		275,000		288,000	
Producing	327,000		430,500		456,800	
Research	118,400		118,400		115,000	
Office	90,000		91,200		91,500	
Advertising	32,500		27,000		25,800	
Estimated gross						
profit	80,100		97,900		112,900	

one year. The length of time selected depends on the primary purpose of the budgeting. The period chosen should include the enterprise's complete normal cycle of activity. For example, seasonal variations should be included both for production and for sales. The budget period commonly coincides with other control devices, such as managerial reports, balance sheets, and statements of profit and loss. In addition, the extent to which reasonable forecasts can be made should be considered in selecting the length of the budget period.

Budgetary control proceeds through several stages. *Establishing expectancies* starts with the broad plan for the company and the estimate of sales, and it ends with budget approval and publication. The *budgetary operations* stage, then, deals with finding out what is being accomplished and comparing the results with expectancies. The last stage, as in any control process, involves taking corrective action when necessary.

Although practices differ widely, a member of top management often serves as the chief coordinator for formulating and using the budget. Usually the treasurer, controller, or chief accountant has these duties. He or she needs to be less concerned with the details than with resolving conflicting interests, recommending adjustments when needed, and giving official sanction to the budgetary procedures.

TYPES OF BUDGETS

There are many types of budgets. Some of the more common types are as follows:

- **Sales budget.** Usually data for the sales budget are prepared by month, sales area, and product.
- **Production budget.** The production budget commonly is expressed in physical units. Required information for preparing this budget includes types and capacities of machines, economic quantities to produce, and availability of materials.
- **Cost production budget.** The information in the cost production budget sometimes is included in production budgets. Comparing production cost with sales price shows whether or not profit margins are adequate.
- **Cash budget.** The cash budget is essential to every business. It should be prepared after all other budget estimates are completed. The cash budget shows the anticipated receipts and expenditures, the amount of working capital available, the extent to which outside financing may be required, and the periods and amounts of cash available.
- **Master budget.** The master budget includes all major activities of the business. It brings together and coordinates all the activities of the other budgets and can be thought of as a "budget of budgets."

Accounting records must be inspected periodically to ensure they were properly prepared and are correct. **Accounting audits,** which verify accounting reports and statements, are essential to the control process. This audit is performed by members of an outside firm of public accountants. Knowing that accounting records are accurate, true, and in keeping with generally accepted accounting practices (GAAP) creates confidence that a reliable base exists for sound overall controlling purposes.

ACTIVITY-BASED COSTING

It is now widely recognized that traditional methods of cost accounting may be inappropriate in today's business environment because they are based on outdated methods of rigid hierarchical organization. Instead of assuming that organizations are bureaucratic "machines" that can be separated into component functions such as human resources, purchasing, or maintenance, companies such as Chrysler, Hewlett-Packard, and GE have begun using **activity-based costing (ABC)** to allocate costs across business processes.

ABC starts with the assumption that organizations are collections of people performing many different but related activities to satisfy customer needs. The ABC system is designed to identify those streams of activity, and then to allocate costs across particular

FIGURE 18.2

How Dana discovers what its true costs are

Old way

Old-style accounting identifies costs according to the category of expense. The new math tells you that your real costs are what you pay for the different tasks your employees perform. Find that out and you will manage better.

Salaries
$371,917

Fringes
$118,069

Supplies
$76,745

Fixed Costs
$23,614

Total $590,345

New way

Activity-based costing

	Salaries	Fringes	Supplies	Fixed costs
Process sales order				$144,846
Source parts				$136,320
Expedite supplier orders				$72,143
Expedite internal processing				$49.945
Receive supplier quality				$47,599
Reissue purchase orders				$45,235
Expedite customer orders				$27,747
Schedule intracompany sales				$17,768
Request engineering change				$16,704
Resolve problems				$16,648
Schedule parts				$15,390
Total				$590,345

Source: Dana Corp.

business processes. The basic procedure works as follows (see Figure 18.2): First, employees are asked to break down what they do each day in order to define their *basic activities*. For example, employees in Dana Corporation's material control department engage in a number of activities ranging from processing sales orders and sourcing parts to requesting engineering changes and solving problems. These activities form the basis for ABC. Second, managers look at total expenses computed by traditional accounting—such as fixed costs, supplies, salaries, fringe benefits, and so on—and spread total amounts over the activities according to the amount of time spent on each activity. At Dana, customer service employees spend nearly 25 percent of their time processing sales orders and only about 3 percent on scheduling parts. So 25 percent of the total cost ($144,846) goes to order processing and 3 percent ($15,390) goes to scheduling parts. As can be seen in Figure 18.2, both the traditional and ABC systems reach the same bottom line. However, because the ABC method allocates costs across business processes, it provides a more accurate picture of how costs should be charged to products and services.[15]

Perhaps more important than the accuracy of ABC, the system highlights where wasted activities are occurring or if activities cost too much relative to the benefits they provide to customers. By providing this type of information, ABC has quickly become a valuable method for streamlining business processes. The example below from GE Medical shows how.

THE ABCs OF GE MEDICAL

*A*t General Electric Medical Systems, activity-based costing (ABC) has been particularly helpful for streamlining business processes. Case in point: Field engineers, the people who service the huge imaging machines GE manufactures, used to lug around a trunk full of manuals that weighed nearly 200 pounds on each service call. While on the job, these technicians frequently had to make several trips to their cars to check procedures or get information to help diagnose problems. If they had not updated their manuals, which they were supposed to do periodically, they had to call the office for information. All in all, the field engineers estimated they spent as much as 15 percent of their time during service calls shuttling back and forth to their cars.

ABC provided some insights to this problem. By allocating expenses over each activity field engineers undertook, it was possible to isolate the costs of wasted activities. As the people in the field saw it, the remedy to their problem was to issue laptop computers with CD-ROM readers that would allow them to carry all reference information right to the job site. But with 2,500 field engineers in the U.S. alone, switching to laptops was a major capital expenditure. However, once the ABC activity analysis was completed, the decision was easy.

Switching to laptops has helped GE Medical raise productivity 9 percent—the equivalent of a $25 million increase in sales with no increase in cost. One unexpected benefit: The field engineers' cars are 200 pounds lighter, which improves their gas mileage. Eventually GE believes that use of laptops will help technicians channel service information back to the manufacturing units so that design improvements can be approached with an eye toward servicing costs. When this connection occurs, ABC will be helping to improve the design process for million-dollar pieces of medical equipment.

Source: Terence P. Pare, "A New Tool for Managing Costs," *Fortune,* June 14, 1993, pp. 124–29. ●

FINANCIAL CONTROL

In addition to budgets, businesses commonly use other statements for financial control. Two financial statements that help control overall organizational performance are the balance sheet and the profit and loss statement.

BALANCE SHEET

The **balance sheet** shows the financial picture of a company at a given time. This statement itemizes three elements: (1) assets, (2) liabilities, and (3) stockholders' equity. **Assets** are the values of the various items the corporation owns. **Liabilities** are the amounts the corporation owes to various creditors. **Stockholders' equity** is the amount accruing to the corporation's owners.

The relationships among these three elements is as follows:

$$\text{Assets} = \text{Liabilities} + \text{Stockholders' equity}$$

Table 18.3 shows an example of a balance sheet. During the year, the company grew because it enlarged its building and acquired more machinery and equipment by means of long-term debt in the form of a first mortgage. Additional stock was sold to help finance the expansion. At the same time, accounts receivable were increased and work in process reduced. Observe that Total assets ($3,053,367) = Total liabilities ($677,204 + $618,600) + Stockholders' equity ($700,000 + $981,943 + $75,620).

Summarizing balance sheet items over a long period of time uncovers important trends and gives a manager further insight into overall performance and areas in which adjustments need to be made.

PROFIT AND LOSS STATEMENT 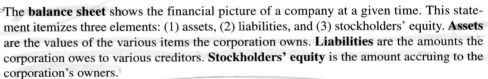 or Income Statement

The **profit and loss statement** is an itemized financial statement of the income and expenses of the company's operations. Table 18.4 shows a comparative statement of profit and loss for two consecutive years. In this illustration, the operating revenue of the enterprise has increased. Expense also has increased, but at a lower rate, resulting in a higher net income. Some managers draw up tentative profit and loss statements and use them as goals. Then performance is measured against these goals or standards. From comparative statements of this type, a manager can identify trouble areas and correct them.

Controlling by profit and loss is most commonly used for the entire enterprise and, in the case of a diversified corporation, its divisions. However, if controlling is by departments, as in a decentralized organization in which department managers have control over both revenue and expense, a profit and loss statement is used for each department. Each department's output is measured, and a cost, including overhead, is charged to each department's operation. Expected net income is the standard for measuring a department's performance.

TABLE 18.3

A comparative
balance sheet

Comparative Balance Sheet
For the Years Ending December 31

Assets	This Year	Last Year
Current assets:		
Cash	$ 161,870	$ 119,200
U.S. Treasury bills	250,400	30,760
Accounts receivable	825,595	458,762
Inventories:		
Work in process and finished products	429,250	770,800
Raw materials and supplies	251,340	231,010
Total current assets	1,918,455	1,610,532
Other assets:		
Land	157,570	155,250
Building	740,135	91,784
Machinery and equipment	172,688	63,673
Furniture and fixtures	132,494	57,110
Total other assets before depreciation	1,202,887	367,817
Less: Accumulated depreciation and amortization	67,975	63,786
Total other assets	1,134,912	304,031
Total assets	$3,053,367	$1,914,563

Liabilities and Stockholders' Equity

	This Year	Last Year
Current liabilities:		
Accounts payable	$ 287,564	$ 441,685
Payrolls and withholdings from employees	44,055	49,580
Commissions and sundry accruals	83,260	41,362
Federal taxes on income	176,340	50,770
Current installment on long-term debt	85,985	38,624
Total current liabilities	667,204	622,021
Long-term liabilities:		
15-year, 9 percent loan, payable in each of the years		
1988 to 2001	210,000	225,000
5 percent first mortgage	408,600	
Registered 9 percent notes payable		275,000
Total long-term liabilities	618,600	500,000
Stockholders' equity:		
Common stock: authorized 1,000,000 shares, outstanding last year 492,000 shares, outstanding this year 700,000 shares at $1 par value	700,000	492,000
Capital surplus	981,943	248,836
Earned surplus	75,620	51,706
Total liabilities and stockholders' equity	$3,053,367	$1,914,563

FINANCIAL RATIOS

An effective approach for checking on the overall performance of an enterprise is to use key financial ratios. Ratios help indicate possible strengths and weaknesses in the company's operations. Key ratios are calculated from selected items on the profit and loss

TABLE 18.4

A comparative statement of profit and loss

Comparative Statement of Profit and Loss For the Years Ending June 30	This Year	Last Year	Increase or decrease
Income:			
Net sales	$253,218	$257,636	$ 4,418*
Dividends from investments	480	430	50
Other	1,741	1,773	32
Total	255,439	259,839	4,400*
Deductions:			
Cost of goods sold	180,481	178,866	1,615
Selling and administrative expenses	39,218	34,019	5,199
Interest expense	2,483	2,604	121*
Other	1,941	1,139	802
Total	224,123	216,628	7,495
Income before taxes	31,316	43,211	11,895*
Provision for taxes	3,300	9,500	6,200*
Net income	$ 28,016	$ 33,711	$ 5,695*

*Decrease.

statement and the balance sheet. We will briefly discuss three categories of financial ratios: liquidity, leverage, and profitability.

Liquidity Ratios

Liquidity ratios indicate the company's ability to pay short-term debts. The most common liquidity ratio is *current assets to current liabilities,* called the **current ratio** or *net working capital ratio.* This ratio indicates the extent to which current assets can decline and still be adequate to pay current liabilities. Some analysts set a ratio of 2 to 1, or 2.00, as the desirable minimum.

Leverage Ratios

Leverage ratios show the relative amount of funds in the business supplied by creditors and shareholders. An important example is the **debt-equity ratio,** which indicates the company's ability to meet its long-term financial obligations. If this ratio is less than 1.5, the amount of debt is not considered excessive.

Profitability Ratios

Profitability ratios indicate management's ability to generate a financial return on sales or investment. For example, **return on investment (ROI)** is a ratio of profit to capital used, or a rate of return from capital.

Using Financial Ratios

Although ratios provide both performance standards and indicators of what has occurred, exclusive reliance on financial ratios can have negative consequences as well. Because ratios usually are expressed in compressed time horizons (monthly, quarterly, or yearly), they often cause **management myopia**—managers focus on short-term earnings and profits at the expense of their longer-term strategic obligations.[16] Control systems using long-term (e.g., three-to-six-year) performance targets can reduce management myopia and focus attention farther into the future.

A second negative outcome of ratios is that they relegate other important considerations to a secondary position. Research and development, management development, progressive human resources practices, and other considerations may receive insufficient attention. Therefore, the use of ratios should be supplemented with other control measures. Organizations can hold managers accountable for market share, number of patents granted, sales of new products, human resources development, and other performance indicators.

CONTROL: THE HUMAN FACTOR

So far, you have learned about control from a mechanical viewpoint. But organizations are not mechanical; they are composed of people. Control systems are used to constrain people's behavior and make their future behavior predictable. But controlling human behavior is difficult and sometimes controversial, as the following example illustrates.

DRUG TESTING: A CONTROVERSIAL CONTROL SYSTEM

*E*mployee drug use is a serious problem. Possible consequences of employee drug use include injuries, illness, absenteeism, breakage, theft, and reduced productivity. It is estimated that in the United States the use of illegal drugs by employees costs industry $25 billion a year. The magnitude of the problem has challenged managers to find ways to discourage or prevent employee drug use. One common approach is to implement a drug-testing program.

Approximately three-fourths of all large companies have drug-testing programs. Companies test for cause (e.g., an accident or excessive absenteeism), randomly, on all employees, or on all applicants. The most common test is a urinalysis; the employee supplies a urine sample that is chemically tested for traces of drugs in his or her system.

Some people have strongly resisted drug testing. Many object to it on philosophical and constitutional grounds. They claim the tests intrude on their personal lives, particularly because the tests reveal drug use during personal time, the effects of which may have worn off. They also claim the tests violate the right to privacy and constitute unreasonable search and seizure. People also object because the urinalysis tests are not 100 percent accurate. "False positive" test results—which indicate illegal drugs when there are none in the person's system—can be triggered by some foods and legal over-the-counter drugs.

Employees have responded to this control system in ways beyond verbal protest. Many have challenged the programs by filing lawsuits. Others take the tests but try not to get caught with drugs in their systems. They change the timing or substance of their drug use, submit friends' urine samples as their own, or put substances in their own samples that will make the drugs less detectable. Also, clean urine samples can be purchased. When drug testing first became popular in the mid-1980s, people sold samples on the streets. Now they can even be purchased by mail order. Employers have responded by tightening the control system. A common technique is to have someone watch employees submit their samples to make sure no one cheats. Some companies use expensive and accurate chemical tests, and some even use undercover agents and drug-sniffing dogs. At least one company is now marketing an alternative approach: a video game that tests eye-hand coordination to assess fitness for work duty.

Source: J. Hamilton, "A Video Game That Tells if Employees Are Fit for Work," *Business Week,* June 3, 1991, p. 36; H. Hayghe, "Anti-Drug Programs in the Workplace: Are They Here to Stay?", *Monthly Labor Review* 114 (April 1991), pp. 26–29; M. Crant and T. Bateman, "Employee Responses to Drug-Testing Programs," *Employee Responsibilities and Rights Journal* (1989). ●

As you can see from the preceding example, people are not machines that automatically fall into line as the designers of control systems intend. In fact, control systems can lead to dysfunctional behavior. A control system cannot be effective without consideration of how people will react to it.

For effective control of employee behavior, managers should consider three types of potential responses to control: rigid bureaucratic behavior, tactical behavior, and resistance.[17]

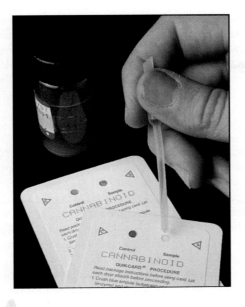

Many people favor employee drug testing as a control measure, but some change their minds when they are asked to personally submit a urine specimen.
(Charles Gupton/The Stock Market)

RIGID BUREAUCRATIC BEHAVIOR

Often people act in ways that will help them look good on the control system's measures. This tendency can be useful, because it causes people to focus on the behaviors management requires. But it can result in rigid, inflexible behavior geared toward doing *only* what the system requires.

Rigid bureaucratic behavior occurs when control systems prompt employees to stay out of trouble by following the rules. Unfortunately, such systems often lead to poor customer service and make the entire organization slow to act (recall the discussion of bureaucracy in Chapter 10). In one hospital, a patient with eye pains entered an emergency room at midnight. He was classified as a nonemergency case and referred to the hospital's eye clinic (which didn't open until the next morning). When he arrived at the clinic, the nurse asked for his referral slip, which the emergency room doctor had forgotten to give him. The patient returned to the emergency room, waited for another physician to screen him, and was referred back to the eye clinic and to a social worker to arrange payment. Then a third doctor looked in his eye and removed a small piece of metal—a 30-second procedure.[18] We all have been victimized by examples of rigid bureaucratic behavior.

TACTICAL BEHAVIOR

Control systems will be ineffective if employees engage in tactics aimed at "beating the system." The most common type of tactical behavior is to manipulate information or report false performance data.

People may produce two kinds of invalid data: about what *has* been done and about what *can* be done. False reporting about the past is less common, because it is easier to identify someone who misreports what happened than someone who gives an erroneous prediction or estimate of what might happen.[19] Still, managers sometimes change their accounting systems to "smooth out" the numbers. Also, people may intentionally feed false information into a management information system to cover up errors or poor performance.

More commonly, people falsify their predictions or requests for the future. When asked to give budgetary estimates, employees usually ask for larger amounts than they need. On the other hand, they sometimes submit unrealistically *low* estimates when they believe a low estimate will help them get a budget or a project approved. Budget-setting sessions can become tugs-of-war between subordinates trying to get slack in the budget and superiors attempting to minimize slack.

Similar tactics are exhibited when managers negotiate unrealistically low performance standards so that subordinates will have little trouble meeting them; when salespeople project low forecasts so they will look good by exceeding them; and when workers slow down the work pace when time-study analysts are setting work pace standards.[20] In these and other cases, people are concerned only with their own performance figures rather than with the overall performance of their departments or companies.

RESISTANCE TO CONTROL

Often people strongly resist control systems. This occurs for several reasons.[21] First, comprehensive control systems increase the accuracy of performance data and make employees more accountable for their actions. Control systems uncover mistakes, threaten people's job security and status, and decrease people's autonomy.

Second, control systems can change expertise and power structures. For example, management information systems can make the costing, purchasing, and production decisions previously made by managers. Thus, individuals fear a loss of expertise, power, and decision-making authority.

Third, control systems can change the social structure of the organization. They can create competition and disrupt social groups and friendships. People may end up competing against those with whom they formerly had comfortable, cooperative relationships. Because people's social needs are so important, they will resist control systems that reduce social need satisfaction.

DESIGNING EFFECTIVE CONTROL SYSTEMS

Effective control systems maximize the potential benefits and minimize dysfunctional behaviors. To achieve this, management needs to design control systems that (1) are based on valid performance standards; (2) communicate adequate information to employees; (3) are acceptable to employees; (4) use multiple approaches; and (5) recognize the relationship between empowerment and control.

ESTABLISH VALID PERFORMANCE STANDARDS

An effective control system must be based on valid performance standards. The most effective standards, as discussed earlier, are expressed in quantitative terms; they are objective rather than subjective. Also, the measures should not be capable of being easily sabotaged or faked.

Moreover, the system must incorporate all important aspects of performance. As you learned earlier, unmeasured behaviors are neglected. But management must also defend against another problem: too many measures that create overcontrol and employee resistance. To make many controls tolerable, managers can devote attention to a few key areas while setting "satisfactory" performance standards in others. Or they can establish simple priorities. The purchasing agent may have to meet targets in the following sequence: quality, availability, cost, inventory level. Finally, managers can set tolerance ranges. For example, in financial budgeting optimistic, expected, and minimum levels sometimes are specified.[22]

Many companies' budgets set cost targets only.[23] This causes managers to control spending, but also to neglect earnings. At Emerson Electric, profit rather than cost is the key measure. If an unanticipated opportunity to increase market share arises, managers can spend what they need to go after it. The phrase "it's not in the budget" is less likely to stifle people at Emerson than at most other companies.

This principle applies to nonfinancial aspects of performance as well. At Motorola, the recruiting department used to be measured by how much money it spent for each new hire. Now it is measured by how well its recruits subsequently perform.[24]

PROVIDE ADEQUATE INFORMATION

Management must adequately communicate to employees the importance and nature of the control system. Then people must receive feedback about their performance. Feedback motivates people and provides information that enables them to correct their own deviations from performance standards. Allowing people to initiate their own corrective action encourages self-control and reduces the need for outside supervision.

Speed

Information should be as accessible as possible, particularly when people must make decisions quickly and frequently. For example, a national food company with its own truck fleet had a difficult problem. The company wanted drivers to go through customer sales records every night, insert new prices from headquarters every morning, and still make their rounds—an impossible set of demands. To solve this control problem, the company installed microcomputers in more than 1,000 delivery trucks. Now drivers use their PCs for daily two-way communication with headquarters. Each night drivers send information about the stores, and each morning headquarters sends prices and recommended stock mixes.[25]

In general, a manager designing a control system should evaluate the information system in terms of the following questions:[26]

1. Does it provide people with data relevant to the decisions they need to make?
2. Does it provide the right amount of information to decision makers throughout the organization?
3. Does it provide enough information to each part of the organization about how other related parts of the organization are functioning?

ENSURE ACCEPTABILITY TO EMPLOYEES

Employees are less likely to resist a control system and exhibit dysunctional behaviors if they accept the system. They are more likely to accept systems that have useful performance standards but are not overcontrolling. One Food Lion (a supermarket chain) store manager said to a *Fortune* reporter about standards he considered unreasonable, "I put in more and more and more time—a hundred hours a week—but no matter . . . I could never satisfy the supervisors . . . They wanted 100 percent conditions, seven days a week, 24 hours a day. And there's no . . . way you could do it."[27] Employees will find systems more acceptable if they believe the standards are possible to achieve.

The control system should emphasize positive behavior rather than focus on controlling negative behavior alone. As noted earlier, companies like Emerson look at profits rather than costs. Jean-Marie Descarpentries of Franco-British CMB Packaging clearly prefers to highlight the positive: He has the heads of 94 profit centers project their best possible performance if everything goes perfectly. He wants his managers to "dream the impossible dream."[28] Then he avoids penalizing people who just miss their lofty goals by assessing them based on how they performed this year versus last year and against the performances of the best managers in the industry.

One of the best ways to establish reasonable standards and thus gain employee acceptance of the control system is to set standards participatively. As we discussed in Chapter 4, participation in decision making secures people's understanding and acceptance and results in better decisions. Allowing employees to participate in control system decisions that directly affect their jobs will help overcome resistance and foster acceptance of the system.

USE MULTIPLE APPROACHES

Multiple controls are necessary. For example, casinos exercise control over card dealers by (1) requiring them to have a card dealer's license before being hired; (2) using various forms of direct scrutiny, including up to three levels of direct supervision, closed-circuit cameras, and observation through one-way mirrors; and (3) requiring detailed paperwork to audit transfers of cash and cash equivalents.[29] As you learned earlier in this chapter, control systems generally should include both financial and nonfinancial performance targets and incorporate aspects of preliminary, concurrent, and feedback control.

Managers can apply three broad strategies for achieving organizational control: bureaucratic control, market control, and clan control.[30] **Bureaucratic control** is the use of rules, regulations, and authority to guide performance. **Market controls** are financial and economic, such as when CEOs of corporations are rewarded based on profit and loss. Performance is monitored and comparisons are made against other years, other divisions, or other companies.

MARKET CONTROLS FOR CEOs

*S*anford Weill, Chief Executive of The Travelers, received more than $45 million for doing his job in 1993. George Fisher, the new CEO of Eastman Kodak received $25.4 million; Time-Warner's Gerald Levin got $21.2 million. These huge payments, and scores of other multi-million-dollar paychecks to U.S. CEOs may seem excessive, but they are the result of a concept which most boards of directors believe to be eminently sensible: paying more for better performance. Since a big firm sells billions, invests millions, and employs thousands, it may indeed be right to pay its top managers to run it better.

Ironically, CEOs are usually seen as the ones controlling everyone else in the company, but the fact is that the CEO is accountable to the board of directors, and the board must devise ways to ensure that the CEO acts in their interest. Believe it or not, CEOs often do not want to accept the associated risk required to achieve higher profits for the owners, and consequently may act in ways that make them look good personally (such as making the company bigger or more diversified) but that don't translate into higher profits for the firm.

To attach some strings to the actions of CEOs, boards typically use at least two types of incentives on top of base salary: First, some type of bonus is tied to short-term profit targets such as return on equity. James Cayne, of Bear Stearns, received an $8.1 million bonus, buoyed by an excellent year on Wall Street. Charles Sanford of Bankers Trust New York Corp. also received a yearly bonus in excess of $8 million. In addition to short-term bonuses, boards also use some type of long-term incentives linked to the firm's share price, usually through stock options. Sanford Weill's hefty take in 1993 was composed mainly of the $41.3 million he received in long-term incentives and stock grants.

CEO Pay 1993 (in Thousands)					
CEO	Salary	Bonus	Other	Value of Long-Term Incentives and Stock Grants	Total
1. Sanford I. Weill, Travelers, Inc.	$1,019	$3,030	$ 245	$41,367	$45,660
2. George M.C. Fisher, Eastman Kodak	331	154	5,000	19,906	25,392
3. Gerasld M. Levin, Time Warner	1,050	4,000	244	15,870	21,164
4. James R. Mellor, General Dynamics	670	1,350	12,879	5,380	20,279
5. James E. Cayne, Bear Stearns	200	8,137	0	7,578	15,915
6. Louis V. Gerstner, International Business Machines	1,500	1,125	5,085	7,542	15,252
7. John S. Reed, Citicorp	1,150	3,000	69	8,906	13,125
8. Reuben Mark, Colgate-Palmolive	901	1,264	94	10,658	12,916
9. Harvey Golub, American Express	777	1,850	335	8,878	11,840
10. Alston D. Correll, Georgia-Pacific	817	550	667	9,625	11,659
11. Richard B. Fisher, Morgan Stanley Group	475	4,436	24	5,628	10,565
12. Richard K. Eamer, National Medical Enterprises	974	0	9,040	1,547	10,561
13. Daniel P. Tully, Merrill Lynch	500	6,200	161	3,605	10,466
14. Robert B. Palmer, Digital Equipment	738	0	9	9,473	10,220
15. Charles S. Sanford Jr., Bankers Trust New York Corp.	750	8,116	301	1,013	10,180

CEO	Salary	Bonus	Other	Value of Long-Term Incentives and Stock Grants	Total
16. John F. Welch Jr., General Electric	1,750	2,200	441	5,414	9,805
17. Donald B. Marron, Paine Webber Group	600	6,300	534	2,213	9,647
18. Charles F. Knight, Emerson Electric	900	1,100	45	7,593	9,538
19. Kenneth L. Lay, Enron	960	1,040	1,512	5,912	9,424
20. William J. Alley, American Brands	1,054	962	5,263	1,706	8,887
21. Rand V. Araskog, ITT	1,525	2,585	240	4,050	8,400
22. David W. Johnson, Campbell Soup	907	913	41	6,359	8,120
23. Dennis Weatherstone, J.P. Morgan & Co.	700	2,354	55	4,841	7,950
24. Charles Lazarus, Toys "R" Us	315	7,543	24	0	7,887
25. Eckhard Pfeiffer, Compaq Computer	1,000	1,500	0	5,111	7,611
26. William C. Steeve, Jr., Pfizer	1,100	900	64	5,114	7,078
27. Edward A. Brennan, Sears Roebuck	1,025	2,050	27	3,804	6,905
28. Robert J. Eaton, Chrysler	929	1,900	144	3,895	6,868
29. John H. Byran, Sara Lee	885	870	207	4,681	6,643
30. Bert C. Roberts, MCI Communications	800	900	497	4,369	6,566
31. Ray R. Irani, Occidental Petroleum	1,900	872	1,035	2,659	6,466
32. Maurice R. Greenberg, American International Group	1,232	1,100	3	3,836	6,171
33. John W. Teets, Dial	1,150	1,173	747	2,863	5,935
34. Lawrence A. Bossidy, Allied Signal	1,100	1,500	481	2,842	5,924
35. Alex Trotman, Ford Motor	717	1,000	136	3,648	5,501
36. Richard L. Gelb, Bristol-Myers Squibb	1,240	1,060	56	3,040	5,39
37. Daniel P. Amos, American Family Life	913	658	6	3,702	5,27
38. Drew Lewis, Union Pacific	850	1,994	240	2,265	5,258
39. Richard M. Rosenberg, BankAmerica	700	1,500	422	2,619	5,241
40. Randall L. Tobias, Eli Lily	503	419	813	3,469	5,204
41. Stanley C. Gault, Goodyear Tire & Rubber	935	1,019	36	3,185	5,175
42. Michael A. Miles, Philip Morris	1,000	345	160	3,564	5,069
43. John F. McGillicuddy, Chemical Banking Corp.	850	2,500	67	1,529	4,945
44. Michael H. Jordan, Westinghouse Electric	504	400	7	4,024	4,935
45. Robert E. Allen, American Telephone & Telegraph	1,032	1,357	246	2,195	4,830
46. Frank Shrontz, Boeing	797	624	678	3,306	4,795
47. Roberto C. Goizueta, Coca-Cola	1,454	2,200	139	996	4,788
48. Allen E. Murray, Mobil	1,325	1,100	339	1,970	4,734
49. Lee R. Raymond, Exxon	1,143	500	96	2,809	4,550
50. Gerald Grinstern, Burlington Northern	600	768	153	2,995	4,516

*May include the value of such items as insurance policies and club memberships; in some cases includes special departure compensation.

In addition to incentives to control what CEOs do on the job, market forces also influence what companies have to pay to hire a new CEO. George Fisher, for example, was paid a $5 million bonus to leave Motorola and take the top job at Kodak. When IBM hired Louis Gerstner away from RJR, $4.9 million of his $15.3 million package was a signing bonus. All of this suggests that boards of directors believe there are only a few individuals capable of running large, complex organizations, and they are willing to pay to get them. Once they do, they use market controls to make certain that CEOs work in their interests.

Sources: Brian Dumaine, "A Knockout Year for CEO Pay," *Fortune,* July 25, 1994, pp. 94–103; "Worthy of His Hire?" *The Economist,* February 1, 1992, pp. 19–22. ●

The third type of control, unlike the first two types, is a form of social control derived from other people. **Clan control** is based on the values, trust, and goals shared among group members. When members share goals and values and trust one another, formal controls are less necessary. Clan control is based on many of the interpersonal processes described in Chapter 14 on leadership, Chapter 16 on groups (e.g., group norms and cohesiveness), and Chapter 11 (corporate culture).

RECOGNIZE THE RELATIONSHIP BETWEEN EMPOWERMENT AND CONTROL

Although the concept of control has always been a central feature of organizations, the principles and philosophies underlying its use are changing. In the past, control has been almost exclusively focused on bureaucratic and market mechanisms. Generations of managers have been taught that they could maximize productivity by regulating what employees did on the job—through standard operating procedures, rules, regulations, and close supervision. To increase output on an assembly line, for example, managers in the past tried to identify the "one best way" to approach the work and then to monitor employee activities to make certain that they followed standard operating procedures. In short, they controlled work by dividing and simplifying tasks, a process we referred to in Chapter 2 as scientific management.

Increasingly, managers are discovering that control systems based solely on bureaucratic and market mechanisms are insufficient for directing today's workforce. There are several reasons for this. First, *employees' jobs have changed.* Employees working with computers, for example, have more variability in their jobs, and much of their work is intellectual, and therefore, invisible. Because of this, there is no one best way to perform a task, and programming or standardizing jobs becomes extremely difficult. Close supervision is also unrealistic since it is nearly impossible to supervise activities like reasoning and problem solving. Second, *the nature of management has changed.* It used to be the

TABLE 18.5

Management control in an empowered setting

1. *Put control where the operation is.* Layers of hierarchy, close supervision, and checks and balances are quickly disappearing and being replaced with self-guided teams. For centuries even the British Empire—as large as it was—never had more than six levels of management including the Queen.

2. *Use "real time" rather than after-the-fact controls.* Issues and problems must be solved at the source by the people doing the actual work. Managers become a resource to help out the team.

3. *Rebuild the assumptions underlying management control to build on trust rather than distrust.* Today's "high-flex" organizations are based on empowerment, not obedience. Information must facilitate decision making, not police it.

4. *Move to control based on peer norms.* Clan control is a powerful thing. Workers in Japan, for example, have been known to commit suicide rather than disappoint or lose face within their team. Although this is extreme, it underlines the power of peer influence. The Japanese have a far more homogeneous culture and set of values than we do. In North America, we must build peer norms systematically and put much less emphasis on managing by the numbers.

5. *Rebuild the incentive systems to reinforce responsiveness and teamwork.* The twin goals of adding value to the customer and team performance must become the dominant raison d'être of the measurement systems.

Source: Gerald H. B. Ross, "Revolution in Management Control," *Management Accounting,* November 1990, pp. 23–27.

case that managers knew more about the job than employees did. Today, it is typical for employees to know more about their jobs than anyone else. We refer to this as the shift from touch labor to knowledge workers.[31] When real expertise in organizations exists at the very lowest levels, hierarchical control becomes impractical. Third, *the social nature of work has changed.* It used to be that employees were most concerned about issues such as pay, job security, the hours of work, and the like. Today, however, more and more employees want to be more fully engaged in their work, taking part in decision making, deriving solutions to unique problems, and receiving assignments that are challenging and involving. They want to use their brains.

For these reasons, the concept of empowerment has not only become more and more popular in organizations, but become a necessary aspect of a manager's repertoire of control. With no "one best way" to approach a job, and no way to scrutinize what employees do every day, managers must empower employees to make decisions and trust that they will act in the best interests of the firm. But this does not mean giving up control. Instead it means that managers need to make better use of *clan control,* as opposed to authoritarian control.[32] Clan control involves creating relationships built on mutual respect, and encouraging each individual to take responsibility for his or her actions. Employees work within a guiding framework of values, and they are expected to use good judgment. At Nordstrom's, the retail company, for example, instead of a thick manual laying out company policies, employees are simply given a five-by-eight-inch card that reads: "Use your good judgment in all situations. There will be no additional rules."[33] The emphasis in an empowered organization is on satisfying customers, not on pleasing the boss. Mistakes are tolerated, even celebrated, as the unavoidable by-product of dealing with change and uncertainty, and viewed as opportunities to learn. And team members learn together. Table 18.5 provides a set of guidelines for managing in an empowered world.

KEY TERMS

activity-based costing, p. 471

assets, p. 473

balance sheet, p. 473

budgeting, p. 470

bureaucratic control, p. 479

clan control, p. 482

concurrent control, p. 467

control, p. 464

current ratio, p. 475

debt-equity ratio, p. 475

external audit, p. 469

feedback control, p. 467

internal audit, p. 469

liabilities, p. 473

management audits, p. 469

management myopia, p. 475

market controls, p. 480

operator control, p. 467

principle of exception, p. 466

profit and loss statement, p. 473

return on investment (ROI), p. 475

specialist control, p. 467

standard, p. 465

shareholders' equity, p. 473

SUMMARY OF LEARNING OBJECTIVES

Now that you have studied Chapter 18, you should know:

Why companies develop control systems for employees.

Left to their own devices, employees may act in ways that do not benefit the organization. Control systems are designed to eliminate idiosyncratic behavior and keep employees directed toward achieving the goals of the firm. Control systems are a steering mechanism for guiding resources, for helping each individual act in behalf of the organization.

How to design a basic control system.

The design of a basic control system involves four steps: (1) setting performance standards; (2) measuring performance; (3) comparing performance with the standards; and (4) eliminating unfavorable deviations by taking corrective action. Performance standards should be valid, and cover issues such as quantity, quality, time, and cost. Once performance is compared with the standards, the principle of exception suggests that the manager needs to direct attention to the exceptional cases that have significant deviations. Then the manager takes the action most likely to solve the problem.

The purposes for using budgets as a control device.

Budgets combine the benefits of feedforward, concurrent, and feedback control. They are used as an initial guide for allocating resources, a reference point for using funds, and a feedback mechanism for comparing actual levels of sales and expenses to their expected levels. Recently, companies have modified their budgeting processes to allocate costs over basic processes (such as customer service) rather than to functions or departments. By changing the way they prepare budgets, many companies have discovered ways to eliminate waste and improve business processes.

How to interpret financial ratios and other financial controls.

The basic financial statements are the balance sheet and the profit and loss statement. The balance sheet compares the value of company assets to the obligations it owes to owners and creditors. The profit and loss statement shows company income relative to costs incurred. In addition to these statements, companies look at liquidity ratios (whether the company can pay its short-term debts), leverage ratios (the extent to which the company is funding operations by going into debt), and profitability ratios (profit relative to investment). These ratios provide a goal for managers as well as a standard against which to evaluate performance.

The procedures for implementing effective control systems.

To maximize the effectiveness of controls, managers should (1) design control systems based on valid performance standards, (2) ensure that employees are provided with adequate information about their performance, (3) encourage employees to participate in the control system's design, (4) see that multiple approaches are used (such as bureaucratic, market, and clan control), and (5) recognize the relationship between empowerment and control.

How the process of control can be approached in an empowered organization.

Increasingly, it is not practical to approach control from a centralized, mechanistic viewpoint. In today's organizations, it is difficult to program "one best way" to approach work, and it is often difficult to monitor performance. To be responsive to customers, companies must harness the expertise of employees and give them the freedom to act on their own initiative. To maintain control while empowering employees, companies should (1) use self-guided teams, (2) allow decision making at the source of the problems, (3) build trust and mutual respect, (4) base control on a guiding framework of norms, (5) use incentive systems that encourage teamwork.

DISCUSSION QUESTIONS

1. Can you think of an instance where an organization did not use some form of control? What happened?
2. How are leadership and control different? How are planning and control different? How are structure and control different?
3. Of the four steps in the control process, which is the most important?
4. What are the pros and cons of bureaucratic controls such as rules, procedures, supervision, and the like?
5. How effective is organizational culture as a control mechanism? What are its strengths? Its limitations? When would a manager rely on clan control the most?
6. Does empowerment imply the loss of control? Why or why not?

CONCLUDING CASE

WHO NEEDS MANAGERS?

In March 1994, the Owens-Corning Insulation Division went on-line with FAST—the Field Automation Sales Team System—a sales force automation system that does away with bureaucracy and empowers salespeople to make more decisions on their own. The laptop computers cost $5,000 apiece, and training on the portable systems will cost over $300,000. But despite the cost, FAST promises to give salespeople information once available only to top managers, and at the same time provide managers with the ability to monitor sales force activities more closely than ever before.

FAST contains three types of software: (1) generic tools—word processing, fax transmission, and so on; (2) product information—customer specifications, pricing information; and (3) customer information—account information, buying history, products ordered, preferred payment terms. Updating will be almost automatic by hooking up to Owens-Corning central computers via modem.

On the manager's end of things, FAST provides up-to-date sales statistics and marketplace trends. Managers know which customers are buying what products, how well a promotion is doing as it's happening, and whether a salesperson is running into trouble in a territory. This information gives managers the ability to see things as they happen, and change tactics and strategies in "real time."

Clearly, information technology is changing both the salespeople's and their managers' jobs. By providing employees with comprehensive information, FAST empowers them to act on their own initiatives. At the same time, the technology also increases each manager's span of control because it enables him or her to monitor performance so much more effectively. The net effect is that Owens-Corning now has only half the managers that it did in 1986—having eliminated a whole layer of senior management—and it has steadily trimmed support staff as well. In preautomation days, these managers and support staff were the ones who dealt with customer complaints, watched for problem orders, and resolved irritating issues. Today, systems such as FAST empower people at the scene of the action to become "real managers of their own business and their own territories."

Owens-Corning's new automation system, nicknamed *FAST*, enables managers to monitor performance more closely than ever before while giving salespeople information once available to top managers only.
(Jon Riley/Tony Stone Images)

But is there a downside to sales force automation? Well, yes. Other companies such as PepsiCo, Johnson & Johnson, and Procter & Gamble have used similar systems—not always with unbridled enthusiasm on the part of employees. Electronic call reports, inherent in sales force automation systems, are viewed by some salespeople as creating needless "administrivia." Since the best employees spend a good deal of time with their customers, they learn a great deal about their preferences, interests, and buying demands. Much of this critical information they keep in their heads, so there's little benefit to constantly typing information into their laptops. Furthermore, many salespeople have become unhappy about what they refer to as "the sales force automation police"—managers who constantly monitor every activity they undertake and intimidate employees by "remote control." Effective field managers are often the ones who can create a climate of trust between themselves and their employees, but electronic monitoring threatens to destroy that trust, and jeopardize quality relationships in the process. The control freaks have gotten so out of hand, some say, that Senator Paul Simon has actually developed a workplace privacy bill that will regulate all aspects of business conduct. Will it include sales force automation systems?

QUESTIONS

1. What are the pros and cons of a system such as FAST for controlling salespeople?

2. As the automated system empowers salespeople, does it take away power from managers?

3. How would you judge control exerted via FAST as against control achieved through the company culture? Is there a conflict?

4. Do managers have a right to monitor detailed activities of the sales force?

Sources: Tony Seideman, "Who Needs Managers?" *Sales and Marketing Management* June 1994, pp. 14–17; Jack Falvey, "On Guard!" *Sales and Marketing Management,* January 1994, p. 41; "Groupware for the Virtual Office," *Network World,* August 29, 1994, p. 42.

VIDEO EXERCISE

ORGANIZATIONAL CONTROL

Managerial control is the process of measuring progress toward planned performance and, if necessary, taking corrective action. Typically, managerial control includes the use of financial controls, quality controls, and human resource controls. To ensure that planned activities occur in each of these critical areas, managers must set performance standards, measure performance, compare performance with the standard, and take corrective action if it's needed. Emphasizing the need for *measurable* goals, First National Bank of Chicago Senior Vice President Richard J. Gilgan said, "You can't manage what you don't understand, and you don't understand what you don't measure. So measurement is critical to understanding where our performance is improving or not improving, where we have problems, and we can then go back and identify the root causes of those problems."All managers are involved in controlling one or more of the three critical areas identified in the videotape: financial, quality, and human resources. Techniques and examples are discussed for each.

Financial Controls

Financial controls are implemented by a company so that it can measure and control activities that yield quantitative data such as sales (in dollars), inventory (in units), and productivity per worker. Budgeting is the most common type of financial control. Every company develops budgets that compare past, present, and anticipated future performance. Budgets allow managers to plan for and track the success of their business. Some of the work processes that are controlled through budgeting include sales and income forecasts; production budgets for input, output, and capacity of machinery; and cash budgets that measure anticipated receipts and expenses so a company can determine its working capital needs.

As an example of financial control through the use of budgets, consider the potato chip sales of Nalley Fine Foods. Sales of potato chips generate revenue for the company. All the materials that go into producing the chips are expenses or costs. Besides the cost of materials, there are other costs that must be accounted for, such as direct labor costs, machinery costs, and additional overhead such as management and administrative expenses, marketing costs, and distribution expenses. A simple budget for potato chip sales for Nalley Fine Foods might look something like the following:

$$\begin{array}{r} \text{Sales} \\ - \text{ Expenses} \\ \hline \text{Profit} \end{array}$$

A more detailed budget would provide a line item for each expense, and would probably include a line item by customer for sales. With such detail, Nalley managers could determine ways to reduce costs or improve sales. Even with the extra detail, however, in essence the budget is summarized by the simple equation:

$$\text{Sales} - \text{Expenses} = \text{Profit.}$$

Other types of financial controls that businesses typically use are the balance sheet, profit and loss statement, and financial ratios. These measures give managers a clear picture of how their business is performing from a financial perspective.

Quality Controls

The emphasis of the quality control function is to eliminate manufacturing defects, to improve customer service, and to institute procedures that emphasize doing things right the first time. Effective quality controls can often lead to cost reductions and higher rates of customer satisfaction. Motorola, for example, has made quality control a central piece of its overall operations. Their famous "Six Sigma" quality program strives to attain a defect rate of no more than 3.4 per million. To attain this remarkably low defect rate, Motorola has made statistical quality control techniques a part of every employee's job. Former Motorola CEO Robert Galvin, the man who brought the quality approach to the company, said, "Quality saves money, and makes products appealing and attractive. Anything that's wrong is costing you money. If you get the process exactly right, it's going to be cheaper and it's going to be better."

Quality management is a process that continually improves performance at every level of the organization. Management takes responsibility for the quality of what's produced, and develops cooperative systems with employees to create solutions to organizational problems. The complete changeover to a quality management approach may take time, but the benefits can be worth it. A successful quality management approach creates a work environment where all workers can achieve high performance and participate in all levels of decision making.

Human Resource Controls

The human resources of an organization are a vital key to its success. To effectively manage the use of human resources, management needs a control system that includes two basic components: valid and acceptable performance standards, and adequate information communicated between employees and management. Setting appropriate standards incorporates all important aspects of performance, and strikes a balance between too few controls and too many. Employee participation in decisions that directly affect their jobs is one way of ensuring reasonable, acceptable standards. Feedback from employees is necessary to accomplish this. The workforce also gains important information about accepted performance through feedback from management.

Listening to the staff enables empathy, trust, and esteem to grow within an organization. One way a manager can demonstrate listening skills is to get out on the floor and actively participate in the work that is being done. This has been called "management by walking around" or MBWA. As one hospital administrator put it, "If you want to improve service in an organization, you have to make the front-line people feel as if they're valued. And if they're well treated, they'll pass it on."

By establishing valid and acceptable standards, and by providing adequate information and feedback to employees, a company wide commitment is fostered. The primary goal of the managerial controlling function is to measure actual performance, and to implement corrective action, so that performance meets expected plans. This goal is achieved through the four steps of the control process:

- Setting standards.
- Measuring performance.
- Comparing performance with standards.
- Taking corrective action.

The understanding of managerial control gives management insight into questions like "What can be done to increase sales revenue?" or "What can be done to increase this organization's efficiency?" The answers to these questions are the starting points for feedback or corrective action processes in organizational control.

CRITICAL THINKING QUESTIONS

1. The videotape identified the three primary types of organizational control as financial, quality, and human resources. Describe instances in which controlling one of these areas may influence organizational performance in another. How should managers deal with this interaction?

2. Managerial control requires establishing clear performance standards. Why do you think it's necessary to have measurable standards? Can you think of some types of organizational performance that might be difficult to measure?

3. Quality control is becoming an increasingly important element of the overall performance of organizations. Even business schools are concerned about the quality of services they provide. Think of some quality control measures that a business school could use to determine its performance. Do you think your business school is performing at an optimal level on these measures? How could it improve?

EXPERIENTIAL EXERCISES

18.1 Safety Program

Objective

To understand some of the specific activities that fall under the management functions *planning, organizing, controlling and staffing,* and *directing.*

Instructions

After reading the following case, briefly describe the kinds of steps you would take as production manager in trying to solve your safety problem. Be sure to specifically relate your answer to the activities of *planning, organizing, controlling and staffing,* and *directing.*

MANAGING THE VAMP CO. SAFETY PROGRAM

If there are specific things that a manager does, how are they done? What does it "look like" when one manages? The following describes a typical situation in which a manager performs managerial functions:

As production manager of the Vamp Stamping Company, you've become quite concerned over the metal stamping shop's safety record. Accidents that resulted in operators' missing time on the job have increased quite rapidly in the past year. These more serious accidents have jumped from 3 percent of all accidents reported to a current level of 10 percent.

Since you're concerned about your workers' safety as well as the company's ability to meet its customers' orders, you want to reduce this downtime accident rate to its previous level or lower within the next six months.

You call the accident trend to the attention of your production supervisors, pointing out the seriousness of the sit-

uation and their continuing responsibility to enforce the gloves and safety goggles rules. Effective immediately, every supervisor will review his or her accident reports for the past year, file a report summarizing these accidents with you, and state their intended actions to correct recurring causes of the accidents. They will make out weekly safety reports as well as meet with you every Friday to discuss what is being done and any problems they are running into.

You request the union steward's cooperation in helping the safety supervisor set up a short program on shop safety practices.

Since the machine operators are having the accidents, you encourage your supervisors to talk to their workers and find out what they think can be done to reduce the downtime accident rate to its previous level.

While the program is going on, you review the weekly reports, looking for patterns that will tell you how effective the program is and where the trouble spots are. If a supervisor's operators are not decreasing their accident rate, you discuss the matter in considerable detail with the supervisor and his or her key workers.

Source: Reprinted with the permission of Simon & Schuster, Inc., from the Macmillan college text by Theodore T. Herbert, *The New Management: Study Guide,* 4th ed., p. 41. Copyright © 1988 by Macmillan College Publishing Company, Inc.

18.2 Preliminary, Concurrent, and Feedback Control

Objectives

1. To demonstrate the need for control procedures.
2. To gain experience in determining when to use preliminary, concurrent, and feedback controls.

Instructions

1. Read the text materials on preliminary, concurrent, and feedback control.
2. Read the Control Problem Situation and be prepared to resolve those control problems in a group setting.
3. Your instructor will divide the class into small groups. Each group completes the Preliminary, Concurrent, and Feedback Control Worksheet by achieving consensus on the types of control that should be applied in each situation. The group also develops responses to the discussion questions.
4. After the class reconvenes, group spokespersons present group findings.

Discussion Questions

1. For which control(s) was it easier to determine application? For which was it harder?
2. Would this exercise be better assigned to groups or to individuals?

CONTROL PROBLEM SITUATION

Your management consulting team has just been hired by Technocron International, a rapidly growing producer of electronic surveillance devices that are sold to commercial and government end users. Some sales are made through direct selling and some through industrial resellers. Direct-sale profits are being hurt by what seem to be exorbitant expenses paid to a few of the salespeople, especially those who fly all over the world in patterns that suggest little planning and control. There is trouble among the resellers because standard contracts have not been established and each reseller has an entirely different contractual relationship. Repayment schedules also vary widely from customer to customer. Also, profits are reduced by the need to specialize most orders, making mass production almost impossible. However, no effort has been made to create interchangeable components. There are also tremendous inventory problems. Some raw materials and parts are bought in such small quantities that new orders are being placed almost daily. Other orders are so large that there is hardly room to store everything. Many of these purchased components are later found to be defective and unusable, causing production delays. Engineering changes are made that make large numbers of old compo-

nents still in storage obsolete. Some delays result from designs that are very difficult to assemble, and assemblers complain that their corrective suggestions are ignored by engineering. To save money, untrained workers are hired and assigned to experienced "worker-buddies" who are expected to train them on the job. However, many of the new people are too poorly educated to understand their assignments, and their worker-buddies wind up doing a great deal of their work. This, along with the low pay and lack of consideration from engineering, is causing a great deal of worker unrest and talk of forming a union. Last week alone there were nine new worker grievances filed, and the U.S. Equal Employment Opportunity Commission has just announced intentions to investigate two charges of discrimination on the part of the company. There is also a serious cash flow problem, as a number of long-term debts are coming due at the same time. The cash flow problem could be relieved somewhat if some of the accounts payable could be collected.

The CEO manages corporate matters through five functional divisions: operations, engineering, marketing, finance, and human resources management and general administration.

PRELIMINARY, CONCURRENT, AND FEEDBACK CONTROL WORKSHEET

Technocron International is in need of a variety of controls. Complete the following matrix by noting the preliminary, concurrent, and feedback controls that are needed in each of the five functional divisions.

Divisions	Preliminary Controls	Concurrent Controls	Feedback Controls
HRM and general administration	_____	_____	_____
Operations	_____	_____	_____
Engineering	_____	_____	_____
Marketing	_____	_____	_____
Finance	_____	_____	_____

19

OPERATIONS MANAGEMENT

One machine can do the work of 50 ordinary men. No machine can
do the work of one extraordinary man.

Elbert Hubbard

LEARNING OBJECTIVES

After studying Chapter 19, you will know:

1. The new meaning of the word "customer."

2. The operations environments for manufacturing and services.

3. The important decisions in managing operations resources.

4. Today's most powerful tools for excellence in operations management.

LEVI'S® PERSONAL PAIR™ JEANS FOR WOMEN

*I*f you haven't seen this yet, you will soon: You walk into a store to buy a pair of jeans. The clerk takes a few measurements, enters them into a computer, and you purchase a pair of Levi's that fit you—perfectly. The first software to allow customers to do this, tested in Cincinnati in 1994, used four measurements to create 4,224 different sizings.

"This is revolutionary!" says a retail analyst. The approach will change the way people buy clothes. Previously, the most successful examples of mass-produced, customized products were specialty goods like greeting cards sold through computerized kiosks. Card buyers could choose a basic design and then personalize the greetings via a touch-screen computer. Levi Strauss represents the first mass-marketed clothing brand that can individually tailor its products.

A few other companies are also leaders in this new approach to manufacturing, called "mass customization." Motorola's customers can pick and choose a variety of manufacturing specifications, creating millions of customized pagers. Andersen Windows has computers in retail stores with which customers design almost an infinite number of factory-made windows. And now, Levi Strauss will allow you to design jeans that fit like a glove.

When you buy a pair of Levi's, the sales clerk will send your specifications to a computer that routes the order to a factory, where the denim is cut by a computer-driven cutting machine. The pieces are then sent through standard mass-production washing and sewing processes. Finally, scanning equipment will separate your jeans from the others, and then your jeans will be shipped to you directly by FedEx. The entire process now takes about two and a half weeks.

In the Cincinnati store where the computer service was first tested, sales increased 300 percent compared to the same period a year earlier, and returns dropped dramatically. At first, the company provided the service to women customers and not to men, for two reasons: (1) Research showed that women complained more about the poor fit of off-the-rack jeans, and (2) the company is already the clear leader in the men's market but far less strong in the women's market. If the women's line generates enough demand, the service will then be extended to men.

In the U.S. apparel industry, an estimated $25 billion worth of clothing goes unsold, or is sold only after severe price cuts. But with Levi's mass customization approach, the product isn't made until the sale is made.

■

For the woman whose jeans never fit "quite right," Levi Strauss & Co. now offers customized products. A fit is determined, measurements are entered on a computer, and three weeks later, the jeans are delivered to the customer's home.
(Courtesy Levi Strauss & Co.)

Sources: G. Rifkin, "Computerized Tailor Makes Levi's to Fit a Buyer's Curves," *The Wall Street Journal,* November 8, 1994; "Jeans that Really Fit No Longer Just a Dream," *The Columbus Dispatch,* December 27, 1994, p. 1D; B.Bradley, "Computers Fit the Levi's to the Lady," *The Commercial Appeal* (Memphis), December 11, 1994, final edition, p.1F; L. Jacobs, "At E Street, the Direction to Go Is Denim," *Chicago Tribune,* September 18, 1994, Lake final edition, Tempo Lake, p. 5. Zone L; R. Carter, "Chasing the Blues: Finding the Perfect Pair of Denims a Stretch for Shoppers," *The Cincinnati Enquirer,* September 6, 1994, p. C01.

*B*roadly defined, **operations management,** or OM, refers to the management of any activity in which inputs (resources) are transformed into outputs (goods or services). Traditionally, the manufacture of goods from inputs (materials and labor) has been viewed as the operations of business. Since the Industrial Revolution, managers have sought ways to make goods better, faster, and at lower cost. However, in recent years the service sector took on new prominence, and the applicability of operations management knowledge to service operations became vital.

North Americans undoubtedly learned more about operations in the past decade alone than they had throughout history. The impetus for this knowledge explosion was the heightened level of worldwide competition.[1] Several terms and concepts emerged to describe this phenomenon, including world-class manufacturing, world-class management, and world-class excellence. All stressed the theme that competition had become global. Moreover, all these concepts stressed the critical need to improve operations, strive for true excellence, and deliver the very best products possible.

The revitalization of manufacturing has restored U.S. competitiveness. Furthermore, the speed with which manufacturing has changed as new global players have emerged is a warning which service industries are taking note of. Service operations, like their manufacturing counterparts, are not immune to competitive pressure.

A broader view of OM has arrived. OM is no longer just about producing goods effectively and efficiently. OM today has a key mandate: perform business activities with the overriding objective of improving service to the customer.

A CUSTOMER FOCUS

Dr. Kenichi Ohmae points out that the formulation of the strategy for any business unit must take into account three key players: the *company* itself, the *competition,* and the *customer.* These components form what Ohmae refers to as the *strategic triangle,* as shown in Figure 19.1.[2]

Managers need to balance the strategic triangle. Successful operations ensure that the *company* uses its strengths to create value by matching *customer* requirements better than *competitors* do. It was not until the 1980s that successful operations managers finally addressed the last "corner" of Ohmae's triangle: They became more *customer* oriented.

One thing that prompted the new attention to customers was a different view of the word *customer* itself. Traditionally, the word referred to the *external* customer—someone in another company's purchasing department or some retail consumer. But during the

FIGURE 19.1

The strategic triangle

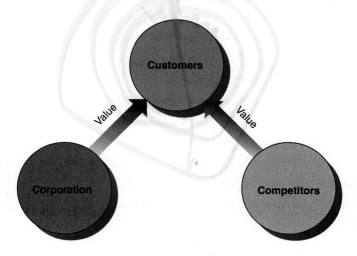

Source: Adapted from K. Ohmae, *The Mind of the Strategist* (New York: Penguin Books, 1982), p. 92.

1980s, due largely to a growing awareness in the United States of Dr. Kaoru Ishikawa's pioneering work in the quality management field, the word *customer* came to refer to the *next process,* or *wherever the work went next.*[3]

Thus, an *internal* customer concept was adopted, and for the first time all functions of the organization—not just marketing people—had to be concerned with customer satisfaction. All recipients of a person's work, whether co-worker, boss, subordinate, or external party, came to be viewed as the customer. Operations people could no longer ignore other departments in the world beyond the shop floor. Meeting a production schedule, for example, became less important, because schedules often reflect a department's own desire to utilize its efficiency goals more than they reflect customer needs for quality output.

As discussed throughout this book, customers want quality goods and service, low cost, innovative products, and speed. Traditional thinking considered these basic customer wants as a set of potential trade-offs. For instance, customers wanted high quality or low costs passed along in the form of low prices. But world-class companies today know that the "trade-off" mentality no longer applies. Customers want it *all,* and they are learning that somewhere a supplier exists that will provide it all.

But if all companies seek to satisfy customers, how can a company realize a competitive advantage? World-class companies have learned that any advantage ought to be considered temporary, for competitors will strive to catch up. Simply stated—though obviously not simply done—a company attains and retains competitive advantage by continuing to improve. This concept—*kaizen,* or continuous improvement—is an integral part of Japanese operations strategy. Motorola, a winner of the Malcolm Baldrige National Quality Award, operates with the philosophy that "the company that is satisfied with its progress will soon find that its customers are not."

PRINCIPLES OF OPERATIONS MANAGEMENT

As recently as the early 1980s, many U.S. companies regarded continuous improvement as an unreachable goal. But later in the decade, many companies surprised themselves and their competitors with continuing excellence in operations. They adopted practices founded on a set of 17 customer-serving principles. Those principles of operations management are listed in Table 19.1.

The principles are grounded in Ohmae's strategic triangle (Principle 1); they address continuous improvement (Principle 17); and they provide for basic customer wants (e.g., Principles 2 through 7). Also note that the principles work interdependently. For example, shorter throughput times (Principle 2) are more easily attained when search time is eliminated (Principle 9) and fewer components are used (Principle 6).

Notice also that the principles of operations management seek to improve conditions for employees in operations environments. Principle 10 stresses having a cross-trained workforce. Principles 11 and 12 address the operations advantage of letting the operator, or line employee, be the first to attack problems (armed with sufficient information). Principles 13 and 15 call for better care of existing resources (including people) and suggest that automation should be considered only when higher quality can be achieved in no other way.

OPERATIONS ENVIRONMENTS

Traditionally, the basic types of operations environments have included manufacturing and service operations. However, the differences between manufacturing and service organizations are decreasing rapidly, and many of the concepts discussed in this chapter can apply to both.

Manufacturing Operations

Historically, two factors have determined the operations environment or layout of organizations: volume and variety. Operations costs increase significantly as variety increases. Standardized components, and reduced setup and changeover times, help combat the high costs of variety.

TABLE 19.1

Principles of
operations
management

1. Get to know the customer and the competition.

2. Cut work in process (waiting lines), throughput times, flow distances, and space.

3. Cut setup and changeover times.

4. Produce and deliver at the customer's use rate (or a smoothed representation of it); decrease cycle interval and lot size.

5. Cut the number of suppliers to a few good ones.

6. Cut the number of components in a product or service.

7. Make it easy to make/provide goods and services without error—the *first* time.

8. Convert multipath flows to single-channel lanes; create cells and flow lines.

9. Arrange the workplace to eliminate search time.

10. Cross-train for mastery of multiple skills.

11. Record and retain output volume, quality, and problem data at the workplace.

12. Ensure that line people get first crack at problem-solving—before staff experts.

13. Maintain and improve present equipment and human work before thinking about new equipment.

14. Look for simple, cheap, movable equipment.

15. Automate incrementally, when process variability cannot otherwise be reduced.

16. Seek to have plural rather than singular workstations, machines, cells, and flow lines for each product, service, or customer.

17. Become dedicated to *continuous, rapid improvement.*

Source: R. J. Schonberger and E. M. Knod, Jr., *Operations Management: Improving Customer Service,* 4th ed. (Homewood, Ill.: Richard D. Irwin, 1991), ch. 1. Used with permission.

Today operations managers have to find a way to be effective producers of both high-volume and high-variety products at the same time. This high-volume/high-variety production activity is one of the operations manager's key challenges.

When goods or services are provided in very small volumes or batches, a company that does such work is called a **job shop.** An example is John Thomas, a specialty printer in Lansing, Michigan, that manufactures printed material for the florist and garden industry. A service example is the doctor's office, which provides a high variety of low-volume, customized services.

As volume increases, product variety usually decreases. Companies with higher volumes and lower varieties than a job shop are **batch manufacturers.** A short-run printer like Bookcrafters in Ann Arbor, Michigan, is an example of a batch manufacturer. **Repetitive production** produces higher volumes and lower variety. Examples of repetitive production are the auto assembly operations of General Motors and Ford Motor Company. At the very-high-volume end of the scale are companies that do **continuous production.** Examples are Domino Sugar and Standard Oil companies, where a very limited number of products are produced.

Product variety and the volume of each product generally dictate operations managers' choices regarding equipment, processes, and layout. For example, job shops usually require more general equipment, and repetitive manufacturers use specialty equipment.

Consider a company that manufactures custom-made picture frames (a job shop operation). The frames have a variety of sizes, shapes, and designs, but each order usually is for

Kaizen, or continuous improvement, is a concept that originated in Japan. It is part of the popular total quality movement.
(Charles Gupton/Tony Stone Images)

one or a few frames. This type of business might compete on the basis of quality, flexibility, and delivery time. The operations decisions must be consistent with those goals. The strategy might be to hire part-time help to staff up for peak demand (*delivery* as a competitive advantage); these part-time employees would not be used during periods of low demand. The company buys all its materials and assembles the product to order. For a small company, the process uses a cut-and-assemble activity with hand tools or simple multipurpose equipment (*flexibility* as a competitive advantage) with the capacity for a high level of accuracy and exactness (*quality* as a competitive advantage).

ROBOTICS IN THE OPERATIONS ENVIRONMENT

*R*obots have been called the industrial wave of the future. In some hospitals, robots lift patients, perform surgery, and move hazardous materials. But robots have fallen into disfavor in many manufacturing companies. At a GM plant, spray-painting robots sprayed each other instead of cars, and other robots installed parts into the wrong models, unable to tell the models apart. When breakdowns occurred, the line would stop and workers had to wait around until the robot contractor's technicians arrived.

GM learned from its experiences, however. It had simply grafted robots onto its old, inefficient system. People were confused by an army of different robots and complex software. GM was producing complicated products, but believed the technology could be implemented all at once and would work immediately and flawlessly.

On the other hand, robots *can* work well. In Volkswagen's Wolfsburg, Germany, plant, about 1,200 robots assemble 80 percent of each car. Instead of the traditional part-by-part assembly, the plant has a modular assembly system. A production line mechanically transports car bodies to 17 workstations. At each workstation, the body is stopped and positioned to within .01 millimeters.

Several parts, comprising preassembled modules, arrive via conveyor to each station, and robots pick them up and attach them to the body. For example, robots put together an engine, a gearbox, and a suspension into a "power block" module, which is then bolted into place in six seconds by 12 robot hands.

Because three large computers control the entire system, the robots can be reprogrammed to perform different tasks. The robots are also "responsible" for quality: They check all modules for defects before attaching them to bodies. They scan all bolts for proper length, width, and threads and check their torque after insertion.

One manual assembly line remains to guard against damage to the two automated lines and to avoid eliminating jobs too quickly. The plant employs several thousand workers, but fewer than a traditional plant would have. The workers are released from the manual labor to supervise overall quality, correct problem units, and concentrate on trim and customization—tasks robots cannot perform as well as people.

Even at Wolfsburg, for all its efficiency, robots are still not as flexible as the company would like. Flexibility remains the ultimate challenge.

Sources: M. Salter and W. Edesis, "Wolfsburg at the Center," *Harvard Business Review,* July–August 1991, p. 105; J. Griffiths, "Survey of Computers in Manufacturing," *Financial Times,* October 18, 1993; P. Ingrassia and J. White, *Comeback: The Fall and Rise of the American Automobile Industry* (New York: Simon & Schuster, 1994). ●

SERVICE OPERATIONS

Like manufacturing businesses, service organizations face volume and variety considerations. The product line at McDonald's has a high volume but a limited variety. The tax preparer provides a low-volume (usually one at a time) service with a higher variety of end products (completed returns). Likewise, the service operations manager makes decisions after top managers have considered volume and variety and the basis on which the organization will compete in the marketplace.

Activities in the service company fall into two broad categories: front end and back room. You are more familiar with the front-end (-room) activities of a service company because customer interaction generally occurs there. For example, you do your banking business in the front room of a bank at the teller's station, and you are served in the front room of a restaurant. For most of these services, the back room prepares the product (interest calculations or food).

Another consideration affecting the delivery of services is whether the company brings its service to the customer or the customer goes to the company to receive the service. In some cases, there is no choice. The plumber or house painter has to go to the work. Conversely, the customer has to go to the restaurant (usually), and the patient has to go to the hospital for the operation.

Some services have options. Either the TV repair person can go to the customer or the customer can deliver the TV to the back room (the repair shop). A service that traditionally has required the customer to come to its facility has a strategic advantage in changing that tradition. Suppose doctors began making house calls. That might be a strategic advantage for a doctor. The same might apply in a furniture repair business.

The operations manager makes important resource decisions, including:

- *Facilities.* Facilities choices for services include whether the client comes to the business or the business goes to the client. Facilities design also plays a large role in creating an appealing atmosphere or the right image for services like banks.
- *Capacity.* The capacity decision is the amount of input (e.g., customers) that can be processed or the amount of output that can be produced in a given time. In service firms, capacity often is controlled by scheduling appointments. Capacity may also need to be flexible to service fluctuating demand, such as in a restaurant.
- *Technology/process choice.* This decision focuses on details regarding how the customer will be served. Should the client interact with an employee (a human teller) or with a machine (an automated teller)? Also, a bank can have a uniline (where the teller handles all transactions) or multiple lines (for different types of transactions).

We will elaborate on these types of resource decisions below. They must be made in the context of manufacturing operations as well as services.

MANAGING
OPERATIONS
RESOURCES

Operations managers make decisions about, and actively manage, facilities, capacity, process technology, and planning and controlling in order to meet customer demand.

FACILITIES

The facility decision has two parts: the facility's location and its design.

Location

Facility location decisions are based on a number of quantitative and qualitative criteria identified by the operations manager. *Quantitative* factors focus on state and local taxes, local cost of living, and costs of insurance, transportation, local labor, utilities, construction, energy, and land.

Those costs are quantifiable, and the operations manager can usually make a decision among alternate sites by comparing their costs. If these costs were the only components, the operations manager's job would be easy. However, more *qualitative* issues often determine the outcome of the facility decision. Qualitative issues include: market proximity versus supplier proximity; climate; community attitudes; hospital and medical care; and many other factors.

Strategic advantage for the organization can be provided by the plant location decision. For example, some states have lower labor costs. A company can also pursue a strategic advantage by locating its facility close to suppliers or customers. For a manufacturing firm, choosing a location close to its suppliers may provide faster and less costly production. A major supplier of food products located a processing plant close to tomato fields. Therefore, the initial processing of tomatoes was done while they were freshest and had minimum shipping damage. The plant produced a paste, which was shipped to other processing plants throughout the United States that processed it into catsup and tomato soup. Overall the product quality improved, costs dropped, and the time from field to customer was reduced.

Design

Because Hewlett-Packard facilities have varying mixtures of R&D and production and those mixtures change regularly, the plants have three floors. The first and third floors are used for product development or production. The middle floor houses all the mechanical, heat, power, air conditioning, vacuum, exotic gases, and so on for plant operation. By feeding these services to the third or first floors, the mix of R&D and production can be changed to suit the current needs of that plant. Thus, facility design enhances the product design and technological flexibility.

Another type of facility is the **focused factory.** Wickham Skinner proposed that when factories grow too large, get too complex, and produce many different products, production becomes difficult to control.[4] As an alternative, he suggested that factories focus around a single product.

Focus means making a limited number of products, using a limited number of processes, and serving a limited number of customers.[5] This focus means that the factory does not compromise and satisfice across a wider variety of production elements as in the traditional general-purpose, do-everything plants that must work toward a variety of goals. Companies that have successfully used focused factories include Mead Corporation, The Foxboro Company, and Pratt & Whitney.

For companies that cannot or will not provide separate facilities for each product or product line, focusing is accomplished by a plant-within-a-plant strategy. For example, one area might focus on large, low-volume products for the commercial market, while another focuses on small, high-volume, standardized products for the residential market.

This focused factory concept dominated the late 1970s and still has many advocates today. But focused production does not serve well when companies must offer greater product variety to different customers.[6] For example, fast-food operation used to use a focus approach when hamburgers were their primary sandwich product. But Burger King, among others, struggled with this approach as they broadened their product offerings, and today all the fast-food companies have moved away from focused production to more complex operations. Later in the chapter you will learn about more complex operations.

CAPACITY

Tied to the facilities decision are the capacity decisions that operations managers make—how much to produce or how many clients to serve. Facility size is a capacity decision; so is the decision to add a new facility. Capacity decisions are usually based on an analysis of the future. However, the farther into the future the company forecasts, the less accurate the forecasts will be. Also, because many capacity decisions require a long lead time (the time to build a new facility is often one year or more), forecast accuracy problems arise and can affect capacity decisions.

Three basic types of capacity strategies are: lead, lag, and tracking.[7] In a **lead strategy,** the company adds capacity in anticipation of upswings in demand. When these upswings occur, the company is positioned to capture a larger market share with its increased capacity and manufacturing capability. This strategy is risky, because the added costs of extra capacity may be excessive if upturns in demand do not occur. This type of strategy has worked well for companies such as Steelcase, a manufacturer of office furniture. Steelcase steadily increased its market share to become the dominant firm in the market.

In a **lag strategy,** the company waits until demand increases and its operations are at full capacity before adding capacity. The advantage of this strategy is that it minimizes the risk of demand forecast error. However, because adding capacity often is slow, market opportunities may be missed.

With a **tracking strategy,** the company adds and takes away small amounts of capacity as changes in demand occur in the marketplace. The advantage of this strategy is that variations in demand can be followed with lower risk. The disadvantage is that changing small chunks is a more costly way to add and reduce capacity. Despite the problems with this strategy, most organizations still use it.

PROCESS/TECHNOLOGY CHOICE

Of all decisions the operations manager faces, the one with the greatest impact on the manufacturing operation's success is the *process/technology choice.* This decision addresses the questions "How will the product be made?" and "How will the service be provided?" The principles of operations management (Table 19.1) figure prominently into process decisions.

As you have already learned, the current and expected volume and variety of the company's products are important considerations in formulating operations strategy. With a limited variety of products, the technology is confined to highly specialized equipment that performs operations on the same product repetitively.

Organizations with a wide variety of products and low volumes choose multipurpose processes and equipment. The process must be capable of easy changeover to other setups, because products are constantly changing. During the life cycle of any product, as volumes and variety change, corresponding process changes become necessary. If product and process are not properly matched, the cost of manufacturing the product will be higher than it would be if the process were uniquely tuned to the volume and variety of the product offering.[8]

You will learn more about specific technologies and processes throughout the rest of the chapter.

MANUFACTURING PLANNING AND CONTROL SYSTEMS

Manufacturing planning and control (MPC) systems enable the company to move materials through the operation and schedule so that it satisfies customer needs at a minimal cost. The materials department handles the planning and control of production and inventories. Generally purchasing, production planning and control, and inventory planning and control are the core functions of the materials department. Other operations that usually report to materials are shipping, receiving, traffic, and warehousing.

Materials requirements planning (MRP) is a computerized manufacturing control system that has been around for a quarter of a century, and today is the most common production planning and control technique in the United States. **Manufacturing resource planning (MRP II)** is a more recent and comprehensive manufacturing planning and control system. MRP II is applied to the customer order-to-delivery cycle, and to integrated accounting and finance applications. Thus, MRP II cuts across *most* of any company's activities.

The organization's strategic and business plans drive the MRP II system. To plan and execute production effectively, a highly accurate database must be created. The information in the database includes current inventory status (raw materials, work in process, and finished goods), open order information (current customer orders that have not been produced), purchase order information (materials and components on order with suppliers), routing information (the steps necessary to make the product), and bill of material information (a listing of the components, parts, and assemblies that make up the product).

The planning system of MRP II answers the four basic questions of manufacturing:

1. What do you want to make? (What is the product, how many are needed, and when are they needed?)
2. How do you make it? (What components make up the product, and what are the steps in its manufacture?)
3. What do you have? (What is the current status of raw materials, work in process, and finished goods?)
4. What do you have to get? (What must you do to fill customer needs when you know the current status of all the above information?)

POWERFUL TOOLS FOR MODERN OPERATIONS

Although management of operations resources is critical, the effective operations manager gives first priority to satisfying customers. Customer needs are most likely to be met when operations managers implement their most powerful modern tools:

- Total quality management.
- Just-in-time operations.
- Lean manufacturing.
- Computer-integrated manufacturing.
- Flexible factories.
- Mass customization.
- Logistics.
- Time-based competition.
- Reengineering.

TOTAL QUALITY MANAGEMENT

Total quality management is a way of managing in which everyone is committed to continuous improvement of their part of the operation. In business, success depends on having quality products.

As described in Chapters 1 and 2 and throughout the book, TQM is a comprehensive approach to improving product quality and thereby customer satisfaction.[9] It is characterized by a strong orientation toward customers, the concept of internal customers described earlier in this chapter, quality as a competitive strategy, quality as an umbrella theme for organizing work, involvement of all people and all departments in improving quality in every aspect of the business, a problem-solving approach to continuous quality improvement, and a focus on information sharing and cooperation across business functions.

ISO 9000

The importance of quality has become even more acute with the emergence of ISO 9000 as a powerful force in business. **ISO 9000** is a series of quality standards developed by a committee working under the International Organization for Standardization.[10] The purpose of the standards is to improve total quality in all businesses for the benefit of producers and consumers alike. ISO 9000 was originally designed for manufacturing, and is currently having the greatest impact in that sector. However, most of the standards can also be readily applied to services operations.

U.S. companies first became interested in ISO 9000 because overseas customers, particularly the European Community (EC), embraced it. Companies that comply with the quality guidelines of ISO 9000 can apply for official certification; some countries and companies demand certification as an acknowledgment of compliance before they will do business. Now, some U.S. customers as well are making the same demand.[11]

Detailed discussion of the ISO 9000 standards are beyond the scope of this book. But you should be fully aware of their existence and their importance, and consider them yet another good reason to strive mightily for total quality.

Enhancing Total Quality

Organizations must first establish a "bias for quality," the notion that underlies all the techniques and tools of quality improvement. A bias for quality means that the company's managers are firmly committed to the priority of quality and will support it in every company function. When the entire organization is committed to improving the quality of its goods and services, it can progress from simple inspection of work, to investigation of problems, and then to the improvement of the entire operation.

An important element of TQM is the use of quantitative data. **Statistical process control** is the use of specific numerical data to monitor and control operations processes and

Companies like Ford emphasize the importance of quality.
(Courtesy Ford Motor Company)

BEFORE OUR DESIGNERS CREATE A CAR THEY TALK TO OUTSIDE *EXPERTS.*

BUCKLE UP—TOGETHER WE CAN SAVE LIVES.

SEVERAL times a year we invite people to come and brainstorm with Ford Motor Company designers and engineers. We talk about cars, sure. But often we talk about NON-CAR THINGS: computers, appliances, music, the environment, quality in very general terms. We know that to design cars and trucks with relevance and appeal, you have to LISTEN to your customers. It's part of the learning process that leads us to quality.

· FORD · FORD TRUCKS · *Ford* · LINCOLN · MERCURY ·

QUALITY IS JOB 1.

outputs. Products are sampled and assessed statistically in order to determine whether they meet standards, how consistently they meet standards, and which processes are causing problems. Computers, even on the shop floor, have greatly increased the use of SPC in all operations. Computers allow data to be collected in real time with minimal interruption of operations. The data are then used in ways discussed in Chapter 18 to identify deviations from targets, and take corrective action to improve processes and output.

The Baldrige Criteria and TQM in the United States

As you know, the Baldrige Award is the prestigious award given to U.S. companies that achieve quality excellence. The award is granted on the basis of the seven criteria highlighted below. Included are brief descriptions of one judge's assessment of the strengths, but also the still-needed improvements, in *very good* TQM companies that have applied for the Baldrige Award:[12]

1. *Leadership*—Senior managers in the very good TQM companies are committed to quality, have communicated quality values throughout their companies, and have instilled a strong customer orientation. But they still view their companies more on the basis of financial than operational measures.

2. *Information and analysis*—The very good TQM companies have excellent information systems, but the quality information is still not well organized to support quality management.

3. *Strategic quality planning*—The companies have written quality plans and quality goals (often stretch goals), but do not communicate to people how their areas' activities and objectives relate to the overall plans.

4. *Human resource development and management*—Many teams focus on quality improvement projects, all employees receive basic quality training, and plenty of resources are devoted to safety. But teams are often managed ineffectively, management does not truly empower as much as they believe they do, and the performance evaluation system is poorly aligned with the quality management system.

5. *Management of process quality*—Most companies use statistical process control, have quality programs in conjunction with their suppliers, have greatly improved the development of new goods and services, and have developed measures of the service production process. Areas for improvement include limited new-product development activity (particularly services), slow and inadequate feedback from customers, and the lack of quality systems audits.

6. *Quality and operational results*—The best companies demonstrate the quality of their products and their sustained year-to-year improvement with objective data, but even the award winners are not always the best in the *world.*

7. *Customer focus and satisfaction*—The better companies use surveys and focus groups to assess customer satisfaction, train their customer service representatives well, establish service standards, give more authority to service representatives to solve customer problems, and work hard to provide easy access and quick response times to customers. Nonetheless, customer needs and expectations are not clearly understood, customer data are not used adequately in new-product development, and companies pay too little attention to lost customers, new customers, and competitors' customers.

As you can see, total quality requires a thorough, extensive, integrated approach throughout the organization. Looking carefully at the strengths and improvement needs of good U.S. companies on the Baldrige criteria, you can see that quality comes from the issues and practices discussed throughout this course.

JUST-IN-TIME OPERATIONS

The logic of **just-in-time (JIT)** calls for subassemblies and components to be manufactured in very small lots and delivered to the next stage in the process precisely at the time needed, or "just in time." A customer order triggers a factory order and the production process. The supplying work centers do not produce the next lot of product until the consuming work center requires it. Even external suppliers deliver to the company just-in-time.

Just-in-time is a companywide philosophy oriented toward eliminating waste throughout all operations and improving materials throughout. In this way, excess inventory is eliminated and costs are reduced. The ultimate goal of JIT is to better serve the customer by providing higher levels of quality and service.[13]

JIT represents a number of key production concepts. The system, which originated in Japan's Toyota Motor Corporation, includes the following concepts:

- *Elimination of waste.* Eliminate all waste from the production process, including waste of time, people, machinery, space, and materials.

- *Perfect quality.* Produce perfect parts even when lot sizes are reduced, and produce the product exactly when it is needed in the exact quantities that are needed.

- *Reduced cycle times.* Accomplish the entire manufacturing process more rapidly. Reduce setup times for equipment, move parts only short distances (machinery is placed in closer proximity), and eliminate all delays. The goal is to reduce action to the time spent working on the parts. For most manufacturers today, the percentage of time parts are worked on is about 5 percent of the total production time. JIT seeks to eliminate the other 95 percent, that is, to reduce to zero the time spent not working on the parts.

- *Employee involvement.* In JIT, employee involvement is central to success. The workers are responsible for production decisions. Managers and supervisors are coaches. Top management pledges that there will never be layoffs due to improved productivity.

- *Value-added manufacturing.* Do only those things (actions, work, etc.) that add value to the finished product. If it doesn't add value, don't do it. For example, inspection does not add value to the finished product, so make the product correctly the first time and inspection will not be necessary.

- *Discovery of problems and prevention of recurrence.* Foolproofing, or failsafing, is a key component of JIT. To prevent problems from arising, their cause(s) must be known and acted on. Thus, in JIT operations, people try to find the "weak link in the chain" by forcing problem areas to the surface so that preventive measures may be determined and implemented.

Many believe that only a fraction of JIT's potential has been realized. JIT has been applied extensively to manufacturing, but not yet to other processes like service, distribution, and new-product development. Another potential benefit may come from applying JIT to information processes in offices.[14]

LEAN MANUFACTURING

Lean manufacturing means an operation that is both efficient and effective; it strives to achieve the highest possible productivity and total quality, cost effectively, by eliminating unnecessary steps in the production process and continually striving for improvement.[15] Rejects are unacceptable, and staff, overhead, and inventory are considered wasteful. In a lean operation, the emphasis is on quality, speed, and flexibility more than on cost, efficiency, and hierarchy. But with a well-managed lean production process—like the operations at Toyota and Chrysler—a company can develop, produce, and distribute products with half or less of the human effort, space, tools, time, and overall cost.

In recent years, many companies have tried to become more lean by cutting overhead costs, laying off operative-level workers, eliminating layers of management, and utilizing capital equipment more efficiently. But if the move to lean manufacturing is simply a harsh, haphazard cost-cutting approach, the result will be chaos, overworked people, and low morale.

For the lean approach to result in more effective operations, the following conditions must be met:[16] people are broadly trained rather than specialized; communication is informal and horizontal among line workers; equipment is general-purpose; work is organized in teams, or *cells,* that produce a group of similar products; supplier relationships are long-term and cooperative; and product development is concurrent, not sequential, and done by cross-functional teams.

COMPUTER-INTEGRATED MANUFACTURING

Since the availability of inexpensive computer power in the mid-1970s, process technologies have changed dramatically. Today **computer-integrated manufacturing (CIM)** encompasses a host of computerized production efforts. Two examples are computer-aided design and computer-aided manufacturing, which offer the ultimate in computerized process technologies. These process technologies must be chosen carefully and judiciously to provide and support a competitive advantage for the organization.

Group technology involves using multipurpose equipment for the manufacture of *part families* (parts grouped together because they have a similar physical shape or follow a similar process routing). When group technology is automated, the process approach is called a *flexible manufacturing system.* For example, a manufacturer's engineering network will contain a large variety of software used in both electronic and mechanical design. Scores of design team members can work on the network from remote sites, often their homes. These systems provide maximum process flexibility with lowest costs of production. They produce high-variety and high-volume products at the same time.

CIM potentially affords greater control and predictability of production processes, reduced waste, faster throughput times, and higher quality.[17] But a company cannot "buy" its way out of competitive trouble simply by investing in superior hardware (technology) alone. It must also ensure that it has strategic and "people" strengths, and a well-designed plan for implementing the technological changes.

FLEXIBLE FACTORIES

As the name implies, **flexible factories** provide more production options and a greater variety of products. They differ from traditional factories in three primary ways: lot size, flow patterns, and scheduling.[18]

First, the traditional factory has long production runs, generating high volumes of a standardized product. Flexible factories have much shorter production runs, with many different products. Second, traditional factories move parts down the line from one location in the production sequence to the next. Flexible factories are organized around products, in work cells or teams, so that people work closely together and parts move shorter distances with shorter or no delays. Third, traditional factories use centralized scheduling, which is time-consuming, inaccurate, and slow to adapt to changes. Flexible factories use local or decentralized scheduling, in which decisions are made on the shop floor by the people doing the work.

▌ FLEXIBLE MANUFACTURING AT MAZDA

*J*apanese competitors of Western automakers have cut costs and increased speed to market due in part to their innovative manufacturing techniques. *Flexible manufacturing* allows them to build up to eight different car models on a single assembly line. In the United States, most assembly lines and some entire plants are dedicated to a single model. If the model isn't selling, the line must shut down. GM says it likes flexible factories, but dedicated several new factories to building just one model each. When executives realized they needed to change, they couldn't do it without spending hundreds of millions of dollars to shut down and retool.

At Mazda's Ujina plant, different models and colors roll down the same assembly line. Welding, stamping, and components assembly operations are all done, computer-controlled, behind the scenes. Computer-controlled assembly allows last-minute changes. Mazda's production plans for a Monday are final on Friday afternoon.

Flexible manufacturing saves valuable time when the plant changes parts and tooling or reprograms computers for new model versions. Dies can be changed in minutes, whereas in U.S. plants changing dies took hours or even a full workday until recently. A changeover to a completely new car takes less than two months at Mazda, much less time than at U.S. auto plants.

Flexible manufacturing allows auto manufacturers to dramatically increase efficiency and profits per car and to deliver high-quality, customized cars quickly. With the advantages of speed, quality, and customized products, flexible manufacturing appears to be a mode of operations that auto companies must adopt for long-term survival.

Sources: M. Maynard, "Mazda Paves Road to Profit with Flexibility," *USA Today,* December 30, 1991, pp. 1B, 2B; D. P. Levin, "Hot Wheels," *New York Times Magazine,* September 30, 1990, pp. 32–78; P. Ingrassia and J. White, *Comeback: The Fall and Rise of the American Automobile Industry* (New York: Simon & Schuster, 1994). ●

MASS CUSTOMIZATION

We are now entering the next stage of operations. **Mass customization** is the production of varied, individually customized products at the low cost of standardized, mass-produced products.[19] Automobiles, clothes, computers, and other products will be manufactured to match each customer's taste, specifications, and budget. While this seemed like only a fantasy a few years ago, some experts now believe that mass customization will be the norm by the year 2000.

How will companies pull off that kind of customization at such low cost? They will organize around a dynamic network of relatively independent operating units.[20] Each unit will perform a module, a specific process or task like making a component, performing a credit check, or performing a particular welding method. Some of the module's tasks may be performed by outside suppliers or vendors. Different modules will join forces to make the good or provide a service. How and when the various modules interact with one another will be dictated by the unique requests of each customer.

As you read in Setting the Stage, Levi's has been testing mass customization in its women's line. Companies like Motorola, Bell Atlantic, and Hallmark are achieving great success with mass customization. Dow Jones, Amdahl, Mitsubishi, and Mazda are struggling with it, but expect positive results ultimately.

The manager's responsibility is to make it easier and less costly for modules to come together, complete their tasks, and then recombine to meet the next customer demand. The ultimate goal of mass customization is a never-ending campaign to expand the number of ways a company can satisfy customers.

LOGISTICS

Logistics, or distribution, is the movement of products from the organization to its customers.[21] The objective is to deliver the right goods in the right amount to the right place at the right time. Traditionally considered a routine and unglamorous business function, logistics today is often an important part of a company's strategic agenda and a potential source of competitive advantage.

Why is logistics so important? Compaq Computer lost up to $1 billion in sales in 1994 because its laptops and desktops were not available when and where they were needed. Compaq's chief financial officer stated, "We've changed the way we develop products, manufacturer, market, and advertise. The one piece of the puzzle we haven't addressed is logistics. It's the next source of competitive advantage. The possibilities are just astounding."[22]

Logistics is a great mass of parts, materials, and products moving via trucks, trains, planes, and ships. An average box of breakfast cereal spends 104 days getting from the

GM selected Ryder—the biggest logistics management firm in the United States—to perform most of its distribution for Saturn.

(Courtesy Ryder Systems, Inc.)

factory to the supermarket, moving through the warehouses of wholesalers, distributors, brokers, and others! If the grocery industry streamlined logistics, it could save an estimated $30 billion annually.[23] Depending on the product, the duplication and inefficiency in distribution can cost far more than making the product itself.

By contrast, Saturn's distribution system is world-class. GM selected Ryder—the biggest logistics management firm in the U.S.—to perform most of its distribution for Saturn. Suppliers, factories, and dealers are linked so tightly and efficiently that Saturn barely has any parts inventory.[24]

TIME-BASED COMPETITION

JIT production systems reduce the time it takes to manufacture products. Logistics speeds the delivery of products to customers. Both are essential steps toward bringing products to customers in the shortest time possible. In today's world, speed is essential.

Companies worldwide have devoted so much energy to improving product quality that high quality is now the standard attained by all top competitors. Competition has driven quality to such heights that quality products no longer are enough to distinguish one company from another. *Time* is emerging as the key competitive advantage that can separate market leaders from also-rans.[25]

Companies today must learn what the customer needs and meet those needs as quickly as possible. **Time-based competition (TBC)** refers to strategies aimed at reducing the total time it takes to deliver the product or service. TBC is a natural extension of JIT, which is a vital TBC component. But JIT concentrates on reducing time in only one function: manufacturing. TBC attempts to deliver speed in *all* functions—product development, manufacturing, logistics, and customer service. Customers will not be impressed if you manufacture quickly but it takes weeks for them to receive their products or get a problem solved.

Many companies are turning to **simultaneous engineering** as the cornerstone of TBC strategy implementation. Simultaneous engineering—also an important component of total quality management—is a major departure from the old development process in which tasks were assigned to various functions in sequence. When R&D completed its part of the project, the work was "passed over the wall" to engineering, which completed its task and passed it over the wall to manufacturing, and so on. This process was highly inefficient, and errors took a long time to correct.

In contrast, simultaneous engineering incorporates the issues and perspectives of all the functions—and customers and suppliers, as discussed in Chapter 18—from the beginning of the process. This team-based approach results in a higher-quality product that is designed for efficient manufacturing *and* customer needs. The team approach offers many advantages that speed up the process. The Impact, General Motors' new electric car, is a good example.

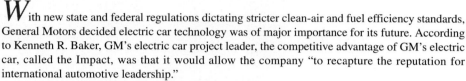

THE ELECTRIC CAR

*W*ith new state and federal regulations dictating stricter clean-air and fuel efficiency standards, General Motors decided electric car technology was of major importance for its future. According to Kenneth R. Baker, GM's electric car project leader, the competitive advantage of GM's electric car, called the Impact, was that it would allow the company "to recapture the reputation for international automotive leadership."

GM's traditional approach to producing a new-concept car was to use an inefficient army of engineers. Each functional group within the company, such as marketing and manufacturing, was involved in the development process sequentially throughout the project. GM's bureaucratic structure and protocol created delays and stifled potential.

To combat these problems in the development of the Impact, GM hand-picked 200 individuals from the functional areas and included production workers in the formation of the project team. The team worked together simultaneously to develop the car. The team's goal was to develop an electric car from scratch by breaking away from conventional thinking, imagining the impossible, and then forming a plan to make it happen.

Impact's design team successfully tackled every challenge from the ground up. The Impact had a 0–60 mph acceleration time of 7.9 seconds (beating a Nissan 300ZX sports car in a drag race); a 124-mile battery charge, which is acceptable for most commuting; exotic styling; and an assembly design that dramatically cut the number of total components to simplify manufacturing. Furthermore, the team approach accelerated the development process so that the Impact project had the very realistic goal of producing a production car from scratch in four years, versus the eight years it took to develop GM's Saturn.

GM has now backed off of the project, believing the product will not be profitable. But others in the United States are picking up the slack. Venture capitalists, the electric-utility industry, scientists, and environmentalists are working together to create the electric-car industry. And Robert Stempel, former GM Chairman, is pursuing his own electric car venture. He believes he has all the technology he needs to make the concept a marketable reality.

However these groups proceed, speed will be of the essence. It's not as if the Japanese and the Europeans are oblivious to the idea.

Sources: William J. Cook, "The Soul of a New Machine," *U.S. News and World Report,* September 2, 1991, pp. 80–82; D. Woodruff, "GM: All Charged Up over the Electric Car," *Business Week,* October 21, 1991, pp. 106–8; P. Frame, "Former GM Chief Throws the Switch on EV Project," *Raleigh News and Observer,* January 27, 1994, pp. 1D, 2D; and O. Suris, "Californians Collide with Folks in Detroit over the Electric Car," *The Wall Street Journal,* January 24, 1994, pp. A1, A5. ●

Some managers resist the idea of simultaneous engineering. Why should marketing, product planning and design, and R&D "allow" manufacturing to get involved in "their" work?[26] The answer is: because the decisions made during the early, product concept stage determine most of the manufacturing cost and quality. Furthermore, manufacturing can offer ideas about the product because of its experience with the prior generation of the product and with direct customer feedback. Also, the other functions must know early on what manufacturing can and cannot do. Finally, when manufacturing is in from the start, it is a full and true partner and will be more committed to decisions it helped make.

REENGINEERING

We introduced you to reengineering in Chapter 2. Now, because it is currently a very popular tool for operations management, we provide some additional detail.

Reengineering is also known as process innovation or core process redesign.[27] Its focus is on revolutionizing key operational processes like product development, order fulfillment, customer service, inventory management, billing, production, and so on. The basic approach behind reengineering is to start from scratch and then completely redesign the way work is done. That is, consider *every* task that has to be performed, and ask, "If we were a new organization, just starting out, what would be the best way to operate it?" Significantly, the question is answered from the customer's viewpoint: If you were the customer, how would you like us to operate? The answer to this question forms a vision for how the organization should run, and then decisions are made and actions are taken to make the organization operate like the vision.[28]

As you can see, reengineering is not about making minor changes here and there. It is about completely overhauling the operation, in revolutionary ways, in order to achieve the greatest possible results.[29] The goals of reengineering are truly ambitious: 70 percent decreases in cycle time, 40 percent decreases in costs; 40 percent increases in quality; 40 percent increases in customer satisfaction; 40 percent increases in revenue; and 25 percent growth in market share. Well-managed, reengineering is often said to deliver on these goals.[30]

For example: Procter & Gamble learned that the average family buying its products rather than private-label or low-priced brands pay an extra $725 per year. That figure, P&G realized, was far too high, and a signal that the company's high prices could drive the company to extinction.

Other data also signaled the need for P&G to change. Market shares of famous brands like Comet, Mr. Clean, and Ivory had been dropping for 25 years. P&G was making 55 price changes *daily* on about 80 brands, and inaccurate billings were common. Its plants were inefficient, and the company had the highest overhead in the business. It was clear that it had to cut prices, and to do that it had to cut costs.

In response, P&G reengineered. The company tore down and rebuilt nearly every activity that contributed to its high costs. It redesigned the way it develops, manufactures, distributes, prices, markets, and sells products. The reengineering was difficult, time-consuming, and expensive. But now, after the changes, price changes are rare, factories are far more efficient, inventory is way down, and sales and profits are up. And P&G brands are now priced comparably to store brands. P&G may have reinvented itself as a leader in the industry once again, and created for itself a long-term competitive advantage that others are scrambling to match.[31]

KEY TERMS

batch manufacturers, p. 494
computer-integrated manufacturing, p. 503
continuous production, p. 494
flexible factories, p. 503
focused factory, p. 497
group technology, p. 503
ISO 9000, p. 500
job shop, p. 494
just-in-time (JIT), p. 501
lag strategy, p. 498
lead strategy, p. 498
lean manufacturing, p. 502

logistics, p. 504
manufacturing planning and control systems (MPC), p. 498
manufacturing resource planning (MRP II), p. 499
materials requirement planning, p. 499
mass customization, p. 504
operations management, p. 492
repetitive production, p. 494
simultaneous engineering, p. 505
statistical process control, p. 500
time-based competition (TBC), p. 505
total quality management, p. 499
tracking strategy, p. 498

SUMMARY OF LEARNING OBJECTIVES

Now that you have studied Chapter 19, you should know:

The new meaning of the word "customer."

In the United States, operations managers are far more customer oriented now than they were just a few years ago. Customer satisfaction is now an overriding concern that drives many decisions. Moreover, "customer" now means more than the consumer who buys the product. People now view anyone inside the firm who receives their work as their internal customers. And the focus now needs to be on delivering it all to customers: quality goods, excellent service, low cost, speed, flexibility, and so on.

The operations environments for manufacturing and services.

Manufacturing is the traditional environment for operations. Since the Industrial Revolution, managers have sought to produce large quantities of goods, efficiently. Variety of outputs and volume of each type of output are the two key determinants of the operating environment. Projects and job shops exist for low-volume, high-variety companies. Batch manufacturers have higher volume and lower variety. Repetitive and continuous producers have still higher volume and lower variety. Today, operations managers have to find a way to be effective producers of both high-volume and high-variety products at the same time.

Service operations also revolve around issues of volume and variety. They also require consideration of front-end and back-room distinctions, and where and how the service is provided.

The important decisions in managing operations resources.

Both manufacturing and services operations require decisions about facilities, capacity, and process or technology. Capacity strategies may be lead, lag, or tracking. The choice of process/technology has the greatest impact on the manufacturing operation's success. That decision addresses the question of how the product will be made or the service provided. MPC, MRP, and MRP II are used for planning and control purposes.

Today's most powerful tools for excellence in operations management.

Change is the hallmark of OM. A wide variety of powerful tools is now available to help deliver quality products in ways that best meet customer demands. Total quality management, just-in-time, computer-integrated manufacturing, lean manufacturing, flexible factories, mass customization, improved logistics, time-based competition, and reengineering all provide great potential to help achieve and sustain competitive advantage.

DISCUSSION QUESTIONS

1. Discuss what operations management means in the context of your college or university.
2. When you think of "world-class excellence," what companies do you think of and why?
3. Why has it taken so long for so many companies to develop a strong customer focus? What are the implications of the older and newer perspectives on customers?
4. Consider the principles of operations management (Table 19.1) in the context of some company with which you are familiar. How does the company rate on those principles? Where and how could it improve?
5. Discuss the role of continuous improvement in securing competitive advantage.
6. Why is the "internal customer" concept important? Give examples.
7. Using examples of your own design, explain how the principles of operations are interdependent.
8. Generate examples of how product variety and production volume affect strategy decisions, in both manufacturing and service environments.
9. Identify some local businesses and discuss the advantages and disadvantages—to them, their customers, and their potential customers, not necessarily to you—of their locations.
10. Drawing from your own experience or from talking to other people, identify and describe specific manufacturing operations in terms of the concepts discussed in the chapter. How effective are those operations? What could be done to improve them?
11. Drawing from your own experience, identify and describe specific service operations. How effective are those operations? What could be done to improve them?

CONCLUDING CASE

DELIVERING QUALITY HEALTH CARE

Brazosport Memorial Hospital, a 165-bed community hospital in Lake Jackson, Texas, began facing serious competitive pressures as populations in neighboring communities declined and nearby Houston hospitals began attracting patients from the wider geographic area. Top management knew they had to establish and maintain a competitive advantage against local health care providers. Their strategy was to dramatically improve the quality of care Brazosport delivered to its patients.

Hospital administrators attended a seminar given by W. Edwards Deming and read extensively about his work. Deming was one of the founders of Japan's quality consciousness movement. He first went to Japan after World War II as one of a number of U.S. advisers. It is said that he became the most revered American after General Douglas MacArthur. But not until the 1980s did Deming become known in the United States.

America's post–World War II economic power bred widespread complacency. Deming's work in the United States was confined to a teaching position at New York University and a small consult-

Hospital administrators can use W. Edward Deming's 14 points to improve total quality in hospital operations.
(Reuters/Bettmann)

ing practice. Then, in 1980, he appeared on a television documentary titled "If Japan Can, Why Can't We?" Since then, his work has been embraced by major U.S. companies, including Ford Motor Company, AT&T, General Motors, and Procter & Gamble.

Deming advocates a "holistic" approach to management that demands intimate understanding of "the process"—the delicate interaction of materials, machines, and people that determines productivity, quality, and competitive advantage. Starting with a statistical analysis, which he likens to a surgeon's diagnosis before operating on a patient, the Deming approach expands into 14 management principles that revolve around casting the manager as a coordinator and coach, teamwork, relations with suppliers, and multidisciplinary problem solving.

Deming's famous "14 points" of quality are shown in the accompanying table. The administrators at Brazosport Memorial decided to use Deming's approach to improve total quality in all aspects of the hospital's operations.

The administrators targeted a number of operations for quality improvement: accuracy of patient billing, nursing retention, turnaround time in the emergency department, quality of

---

Deming's 14 points

1. *Create constancy of purpose.* Strive for long-term improvement more than short-term profits.

2. *Adopt the new philosophy.* Accept as gospel the need for total quality, with no tolerance for delays and mistakes.

3. *Cease dependence on mass inspection.* Build quality into the process, and identify and correct problems early rather than late.

4. *End the practice of awarding business on price tag alone.* Don't purchase from the cheapest supplier. Build long-term supplier relationships based on loyalty and trust.

5. *Improve constantly and forever the system of production and service.* At every stage of the process, strive to continually improve and satisfy internal as well as external customers.

6. *Institute training and retraining.* This includes continual updating and training in statistical methods and thinking.

7. *Institute leadership.* Remove barriers that prevent employees from performing effectively, and continually provide the resources needed for effectiveness.

8. *Drive out fear.* People must believe it is safe to report problems or mistakes or to ask for help.

9. *Break down barriers among departments.* Promote teamwork and communications across departments, and provide a common organizational vision.

10. *Eliminate slogans, exhortations, and arbitrary targets.* Supply methods, not just buzzwords.

11. *Eliminate numerical quotas.* Quotas place a limit on improvement and are contrary to the idea of *continuous* improvement.

12. *Remove barriers to pride in workmanship.* Allow autonomy and spontaneity. Regular performance reviews should be abandoned.

13. *Institute a vigorous program of education and retraining.* This is similar to Point 6, but is meant to highlight a philosophy that people are assets, not commodities.

14. *Take action to accomplish the transformation.* Provide access to top management, an organization structure, and information that allows the other 13 points to be adhered to on a daily basis.

dietary service, purchasing procedures, and promptness and completeness of medical record entries. They further decided to create teams of hospital employees as the primary mechanism for implementing operations improvements.

QUESTIONS

1. Propose a general plan for improving the total quality of hospital operations.

2. Choose two of the specific operations mentioned in the case, or other hospital operations with which you are familiar, and propose a specific quality improvement plan.

3. Do you agree with all of Deming's 14 points? Explain.

4. Why do you think U.S. companies were slow to embrace Deming's philosophies while the Japanese adopted them over 40 years ago?

5. Why do you think Deming's ideas have been applied more to manufacturing than to services?

Sources: R. F. Casalou, "Total Quality Management in Health Care," *Hospital and Health Services Administration,* Spring 1991, pp 134–47; M. L. Lynn, "Deming's Quality Principles: A Health Care Application," *Hospital and Health Services Administration,* Spring 1991, pp. 111–21; H. Rowen, "Bringing American Ideas Home from Japan," *Washington Post,* July 25, 1991, p. A17; and A. Gabor, "The Man Who Changed the World of Quality," *International Management,* March 1988, pp. 42–46.

VIDEO CASE

PRODUCTION AND OPERATIONS MANAGEMENT

Operations management refers to the range of techniques, skills, and tools used to produce products or services. An organization's *operations* are those functions that are needed to keep the company producing, referring to literally any function or series of functions enacted to carry out a strategic plan. Part of operations management is *production,* which refers to the direct processes by which a company produces a finished good. The basic principles of effective production can be applied across industrial boundaries. In manufacturing, production can be broken down into four general categories of processes: job shop, batch processing, assembly line, and continuous process. Operations managers must determine which process is appropriate for their organization by considering three main factors: product variety, equipment flexibility, and volume.

Product variety refers to how much the product changes from customer to customer. A steel manufacturer, for example, will normally produce a single product. A tool shop, on the other hand, produces each product based on the unique and specific needs of each customer.

The second determining factor is the flexibility of equipment used to produce the product. The steel manufacturer has rigid, highly integrated equipment needs, and each piece of equipment has a specific job that rarely changes. In the case of the tool shop, however, the project dictates what equipment will be required and how it will be configured. The equipment in the tool shop is flexible; it can be modified on a project-by-project basis.

The third factor that operations managers need to consider is the volume of product that needs to be produced. The steel plant, for example, produces in huge volumes, while tool shop will produce a comparatively small volume of custom tools depending on customer needs.

When a highly specialized product is needed in very low volumes, usually on a customer order basis, the production process generally used is called a *job shop.* A good example of this approach is a tool-and-die shop. In such a shop, precision metal workers manufacture durable, customized tools that are used to stamp out parts, forge steel, or act as a mold for liquefied metal or plastic. The equipment used in the production process can produce a wide variety of products in very low volumes. In the video example, a special stamping tool for the production of engine gaskets was ordered. The customer provided the tool-and-die shop with specifications. The part was then designed using computer-aided design (CAD) equipment. The CAD technology enables the operator to quickly design a wide variety of products in a short period of time, each product tailored to the needs of individual customers.

From the design stage, the product went to the machine shop where workers ground the metal into the required dimensions,

drilled and tapped holes, and locked the pieces in place. Finally, the product was tested by stamping out sample parts using the new tool. Inspectors using precise testing and measuring equipment ensured that the customer's specifications had been met. Note that in each step of the production process the equipment used could also have been used to manufacture a variety of other machine tools. Because every product is custom made, the equipment must be flexible enough to change with each new job.

When a higher (but still relatively low) volume of specialized products is needed, and the product designs are more standardized, a *batch* manufacturing process is normally used. A batch process uses what is called a "disconnected production line flow." In other words, batch products are normally produced in small lots or batches by plants that have been geared for that particular product. For example, Caterpillar company's agriculture and construction heavy equipment products are produced in a batch process. The company's production facility in Aurora, Illinois, uses flexible equipment to produce 24 different models of wheel loaders, compactors, excavators, and agricultural tractors, all in the same facility. Specifications for each vehicle vary, so most production equipment must be adjustable for multiple tasks. For example, the plant's machine center produces 58 different parts for Caterpillar drive trains. A variety of products produced at relatively low volume with flexible equipment are what characterize a batch manufacturing process.

When a narrow variety of highly standardized products needs to be produced in large volumes, an *assembly line* process is required. An assembly line typically utilizes a connected line flow production process that moves the product along, generally on a conveyor system, past a series of workstations. At each station parts are brought to the line to be added or assembled until the product is finished. A well-known example of the assembly line process is an automobile plant. The assembly line method in the production of automobiles allows a relatively large volume of cars to be produced. However, the process is very structured so that each line can produce only one model. A Ford assembly line design that produces the Taurus, for example, cannot easily switch production to a Mustang. Nonetheless, in the modern version of the assembly line there is enough flexibility at most workstations to offer a variety of options on the model being produced.

When a highly standardized product is needed in very large volumes a *continuous process* is the best production method to use. At the Nucor steel plant in Crawfordsville, Indiana, which produces 1 million tons of steel annually, the product is produced continuously. The Crawfordsville plant was designed for the specific purpose of producing a large volume of standardized goods in the most cost effective manner possible. Since the end product is very standardized, each piece of equipment performs a specific function and is rarely, if ever, modified for special needs. As the name "continuous process" implies, the product usually doesn't stop during the manufacturing process as it might at workstations on the assembly line. The Nucor plant uses a continuous process. In fact, as the plant is rolling thin slabs of steel at one end, more liquid steel is being prepared for casting at the other end.

The flexibility of the equipment, the variety of products produced, and the volume of products required are three factors that help determine the best method of manufacturing. The job shop process is used when a highly specialized product is needed. The batch process produces products in small lots or batches. The assembly line process is used for production of a limited variety of standardized products in large volumes. Finally, the continuous process is used for the manufacture of a relatively standardized product in large quantities.

These four manufacturing processes are really just four points on a product process continuum. Most manufacturing systems fall somewhere between the points; they aren't totally committed to a single approach to manufacturing. Many manufacturers use a mixture of these processes to achieve the cost advantages of the continuous process with the product variety of the job shop. Operations managers are responsible for determining the best method of production based on characteristics of their product and their customers. They are also responsible for putting these methods into action to produce quality products at the lowest possible cost. Accepting this challenge requires a working knowledge of the four manufacturing processes, and the three key factors that determine which one to use.

CRITICAL THINKING QUESTIONS

1. The video identified four different manufacturing processes. For each process, identify a company that uses such an approach, and determine whether it makes sense in light of their product variety, equipment flexibility, and volume. Identify a company or industry that needs to change its production processes. Explain why.

2. The automobile industry in America found itself in deep trouble in the late 1970s and early 1980s because of competition from abroad, most notably from Japan. Japanese cars had higher quality, and more options. How can operations management contribute to the improvement of quality, and to the introduction of more product options in American auto plants? Do you think the automobile industry is listening to its operations managers? Explain.

3. The videotape made the distinction between continuous-flow manufacturing and discontinuous-flow manufacturing. Identify a high-technology product that could be produced on a continuous-flow basis. Identify a high-technology product that can't use such a process. Describe the difference between the two products.

EXPERIENTIAL EXERCISES

19.1 Making Recommendations for Total Quality

Objectives

1. To focus on the ways a firm, in this case a fast-food restaurant, can compete through quality improvements.
2. To observe aspects of the operations and the service/product of a fast-food restaurant, and come up with real possibilities for improvement in one or more aspects that might increase competitiveness.

Instructions

Choose a fast-food restaurant chain such as McDonald's, Taco Bell, Boston Chicken, or Wendy's, and select an outlet to observe. Visit the outlet you selected. Focus your observations on the areas of interest listed in the left-hand column of the Total Quality Worksheet. Make note of the specific examples that illustrate your assessments. Rate each area on a scale of 1–10 and list implementable recommendations for improvement. Be prepared to discuss your findings and suggestions in class.

TOTAL QUALITY WORKSHEET

Name of outlet:_____

Area of Interest Recommendations	Examples	Rating (1–10)	Recommendations for Improvement
Quality of services	_____	_____	_____
	_____	_____	_____
	_____	_____	_____
Quality of good(s)	_____	_____	_____
	_____	_____	_____
	_____	_____	_____
Speed and efficiency	_____	_____	_____
	_____	_____	_____
	_____	_____	_____
Innovativeness	_____	_____	_____
	_____	_____	_____
	_____	_____	_____
Cost to consumer	_____	_____	_____
	_____	_____	_____
	_____	_____	_____

19.2 Fine Furniture, Inc.

Objectives

1. To envision ways to empower workers in a large manufacturing facility which has paid little attention to the quality of work life.
2. To explore the problem of employee disaffection and boredom in a highly specialized workplace, especially one in which the amount of automation is about to increase.

Instructions

1. Read the scenario below.
2. Individually or in small groups, design a QWL program for Fine Furniture.
3. In small groups or with the entire class, share the programs you have developed.

THE WORKFORCE OF FINE FURNITURE, INC.

Fine Furniture, Inc., manufactures Scandinavian-style, high-tech European-style, and Formica and lacquer contemporary bookcases and storage units. The company employs approximately 500 workers in its large manufacturing facility in the southeastern United States. Many of these employees pride themselves on being craftspeople in various aspects of furniture manufacturing. Currently the company emphasizes high specialization of work functions. The manufacturing process is divided into many discrete tasks, each performed by a separate individual. One worker, for example, may cut the backs of the bookcases; another may insert the shelf pegs into the frames; still another might attach the doors to the storage units. The plant is currently being automated.

Workers often complain that they are not really using their skills in furniture building, and describe their jobs as mechanical and boring. They also complain that they feel as if each is "a small cog in a very large machine." Retailers who distribute Fine Furniture's products have noticed an increase in the number of defective pieces they have received and that production slowdowns have delayed product delivery from three to six months.

Manufacturing employees receive an hourly wage that ranges between 10 and 20 dollars per hour, depending on their seniority and special skills. In peak production seasons, employees work overtime and can increase their earning by 25 to 50 percent. Employees are represented by a local of the International Teamsters Union, which has succeeded in negotiating a high-paying contract for its employees. Recently, however, employees have demonstrated some dissatisfaction with the union's lack of attention to ensuring job security. The introduction of automation to the manufacturing process has resulted in approximately 5 percent of the workforce receiving layoff notices in the past year.

Top management has informed both the union representatives and the manufacturing workforce that it intends to increase the amount of automation in the workplace, even introducing some new robotics successfully used to manufacture furniture abroad.

Discussion Questions

1. What elements do these programs have in common?
2. How will the programs address the problems at Fine Furniture?
3. What are the strengths and weaknesses of each program?
4. What should be the components of an effective QWL program?
5. What other options are available for improving the situation?

Source: J. Gordon, *A Diagnostic Approach to Organizational Behavior* (Englewood Cliffs, N.J.: Prentice-Hall, 1983), p. 669. Reprinted by permission of Prentice-Hall, Inc., Englewood Cliffs, N.J.

20

MANAGING TECHNOLOGY AND INNOVATION

A wise man will make more opportunities than he finds.

Francis Bacon

LEARNING OBJECTIVES

After studying Chapter 20, you will know:

1. The processes involved in the development of new technologies.

2. How technologies proceed through a life cycle.

3. How to manage technology for competitive advantage.

4. How to assess technology needs.

5. Where new technologies originate and the best strategies for acquiring them.

6. How people play a role in managing technology.

7. How to develop an innovative organization.

8. The key characteristics of successful development projects.

THE FUTURE IS NOW

*T*he rate of technological innovation is astounding, and is dramatically changing the face of business. Keeping up with all the developments in various industries is virtually impossible. Consider the following:

- TRW will soon install radar-activated cruise control on luxury cars to monitor speed and position of surrounding vehicles. If the car ahead of you slows down or speeds up, the cruise control adjusts the throttle automatically. In addition to smoothing traffic patterns and reducing accidents, the radar systems are being developed for blind spot detection.

- An international team of researchers is developing a titanium suit of armor with robotics technology at the arms and legs that when worn enhances a person's strength five times. Using technology similar to that now used with virtual-reality gloves, sensors and a built-in computer track the wearer's movements and instantly cause the robosuit to mimic those movements. The suits will be useful for rescue workers in, say, earthquake emergencies.

- Hanna Barbera Cartoons Inc. is using the latest biotechnology to prevent forgeries of Joseph Barbera's signature. Using a technique called polymerase chain reaction, the company can copy the DNA from a strand of Mr. Barbera's hair. The copied DNA is mixed into a special ink and used for Barbera's signature. A handheld scanner instantly reads the genetic ink, verifying the signature against a database of registered DNA cells.

- The U.S. Pentagon is installing a $70-million logistics-management system from Sayi Technology Inc. that will keep track of intermodal containers being sent around the world. The system is based on small two-way "radio tags" that are attached to shipping containers or to individual

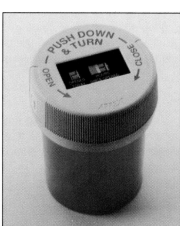

■
_____

With the escalation of technological innovation, people are witnessing changes in unforeseen areas. For example, Aprex Corporation builds the "smart" bottle cap pictured here. Complete with its own chip, alarm clock, and small display, the cap makes it almost impossible for people to forget to take their medication.

(Courtesy APREX Corporation)

cartons inside the containers. These tags are tracked by satellite to determine their location or to reset them for a new destination. A handheld "interrogator" reads a container's contents and address within a range of 300 feet, then triggers a beeper in the tag to help workers spot the specific unit.

- Aprex Corp., in Fremont, California, builds a "smart" bottle cap. The cap is equipped with its own chip, alarm clock, and a tiny display. The cap keeps track of how often the bottle is opened and, in the case of those forgetting to take medicine, can remind them with electronic beeps. The company has even added a modem that reads the cap's memory and automatically relays to Aprex the number of times the cap was removed that day. If the count isn't right, the patient gets a reminder call in the morning.

- Not all innovations are high-tech. Researchers at Penn State have found that an enzyme in common horseradish is remarkably effective for cleaning up industrial wastewater produced from steel and iron manufacturing, ore mining, paper bleaching, and other industrial operations. When minced horseradish and peroxide are added to water contaminated by phenols and other toxic pollutants, the contaminants harden and can be easily filtered out and disposed of. The treatment costs less than half that of conventional chemical and filtering technologies, and the horseradish can be reused as many as 30 times.

Sources: Alex Taylor III, "Cars That Beat Traffic," *Fortune,* February 20, 1995, pp. 65–72; Otis Port, "A Robosuit for Rescue Workers," *Business Week,* January 16, 1995, p. 80; Peter Coy, "Yabba Dabba Don't Swipe This Toon," *Business Week,* January 30, 1995, p. 75; Neil Gross, "Military Goods Get Digital Dog Tags," *Business Week,* February 6, 1995, p. 149; Otis Port, "These Bottles Nag You to Take Your Medicine," *Business Week,* February 13, 1995, p. 80; and Emily T. Smith, "This Condiment Also Goes with Wastewater," *Business Week,* February 20, 1995, p. 91.

*M*anaging technology in today's environment is complex, but it is vital for organizational success. Not long ago, new products took years to plan and develop, were standardized and mass produced, and were pushed onto the market through extensive selling and promotional campaigns. With sales lives for these products often measured in decades, production processes used equipment dedicated to making only those standardized products and achieved savings through economies of scale. But today's customers often demand products that have yet to be designed. Product development is now a race to become the first to introduce innovative products—products whose lives often are measured in months as they are quickly replaced by other, even more technologically sophisticated products.

Managing today's technology requires that managers understand how technologies emerge, develop, and affect the ways organizations compete and the ways people work. In this chapter, we discuss how technology can affect an organization's competitiveness and how to integrate technology into the organization's competitive strategy. Then we assess the technological needs of the organization and the means by which these needs can be met.

TECHNOLOGY AND INNOVATION

Broadly speaking, **technology** is the commercialization of science;[1] it is the systematic application of scientific knowledge to a new product, process, or service.[2] Technology is embedded in every product, service, and procedure used or produced.

If we find a better product, process, or procedure to accomplish our task, we have an innovation. **Innovation** is a change in technology—a departure from previous ways of doing things. Two fundamental types of innovation are product and process innovation.[3] *Process innovations* are changes that affect the methods of producing outputs. *Product innovations* are changes in the actual outputs (products and services) of the organization.[4]

There are definable and predictable patterns in the way technologies emerge, develop, and are replaced. Critical forces converge to create new technologies, which then follow well-defined life cycle patterns. Understanding the forces driving technological development and the patterns they follow can help a manager anticipate, monitor, and manage technologies more effectively.

First, there must be a *need,* or *demand,* for the technology. Without this need driving the process, there is no reason for technological innovation to occur. Second, meeting the need must be theoretically possible, and the *knowledge* to do so must be available from basic science. Third, we must be able to *convert* the scientific knowledge into practice, in both engineering and economic terms. If we can theoretically do something, but doing it is economically impractical, the technology cannot be expected to emerge. Fourth, the *funding, skilled labor, time, space,* and *other resources* needed to develop the technology must be available. Finally, *entrepreneurial initiative* is needed to identify and pull all the necessary elements together.

THE TECHNOLOGY LIFE CYCLE

Technological innovations typically follow a relatively predictable pattern called the **technology life cycle.** Figure 20.1 depicts the pattern. The cycle begins with the recognition of a need and a perception of a means by which the need can be satisfied through applied science or knowledge. The knowledge and ideas are brought together and developed, culminating in a new technological innovation. Early progress can be slow in these formative years as competitors experiment a great deal with product design and operational characteristics to meet consumer needs. Here is where the rate of product innovation tends to be highest. For example, during the early years of the auto industry, companies tried a wide range of machines including electric- and steam-driven cars to determine which product would be most effective. Eventually the internal combustion engine emerged as the dominant design, and the number of product innovations leveled off.

FIGURE 20.1

The technology life cycle

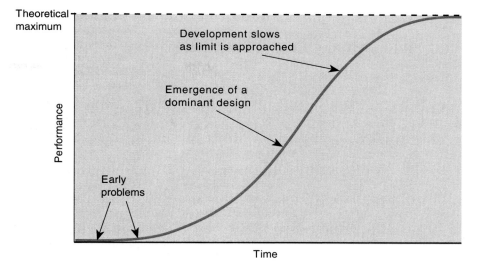

FIGURE 20.1

The technology life cycle

Once early problems are resolved and a dominant design emerges, improvements come more from process innovations to refine the technology.[5] It is at this point that companies can gain an advantage by pursuing process efficiencies and cost competitiveness. In the auto example, as companies settled on a product standard, they began leveraging the benefits of mass production and vertical integration to improve productivity. These process innovations were instrumental in lowering production costs, and bringing the price of automobiles in line with consumer budgets.

Eventually the new technology begins to reach the upper limits of both its performance capabilities and the spread of its usage. Development slows and becomes increasingly costly, and the market becomes saturated (i.e., there are few new customers). The technology can remain in this mature stage for some time—as in the case of autos—or be quickly replaced by another technology offering superior performance or economic advantage. As we shall see later in the chapter, U.S. auto companies are working right now on new aerospace technologies that will transform the automobile industry.

The evolution of life cycles can take decades or even centuries, as in the case of iron and steelmaking technologies. A dramatic example of a more rapidly evolving process is microprocessor technology, the core of today's personal computers.

INTEL INSIDE: LIFE CYCLES OF THE MICROPROCESSOR

*T*echnological innovations have been the driving force in the personal computer industry. In 1994 alone, Americans spent more collectively on PCs than they did on television sets, and annual industry sales now exceed $100 billion. The sophisticated brain that drives the PC is the microprocessor, and for some time the company that has set the standard for microprocessors has been Intel. Since its introduction, the Intel microprocessor has changed rapidly as the technology has evolved, and advanced microprocessors continue to replace one another with faster, more capable, and less-expensive machines.

In 1969, Intel developed one of the first microprocessors, the 4004, which was designed as a basis for electronic calculators and had a 4-bit internal register (the internal memory capacity for performing calculations). From this beginning, Intel developed the 8080 (in 1974), which doubled the 4004's computing capacity, and the 8086 (in 1978), which was 10 times more powerful than the 8080. In 1979, Intel introduced the 8088, which had about the same computing capacity as the 8080, but could use less-expensive support chips. Because this lowered the cost of producing a personal computer, it was the first chip used in the IBM PC.

In 1983, after five years of development work, Intel introduced the 80286, which increased memory addressing capability from 1MB to 16MB, had 130,000 transistors, and had an initial speed of 1 million instructions per second (MIPS). In 1986, Intel introduced the 80386 as the next phase of microprocessors. The 80386 was four years in development, had 275,000 transistors, and increased processing speed to 5 MIPS. The 80486, which came in 1990 after three years of development, had 1.2 million transistors, and quadrupled the speed of the 386 to 20 MIPS. Then in 1994, after three years of development, Intel introduced the Pentium chip, with 3.1 million transistors and a speed of 100 MIPS.

Intel does not plan to ride the wave of the Pentium chip for long, and has already developed the P6 microprocessor for introduction in 1996 and is working on the P7 for 1998 or 1999. The P6 has 5.5 million transistors and an estimated speed of 250 MIPS while the P7 is targeted for more than 10 million transistors and 500 MIPS. These figures highlight an interesting curve in the microprocessor industry. As the computer power of microprocessors is increasing exponentially, their life cycles are becoming much shorter. Not coincidentally, the cost of computing is also coming down as well. While in 1979, the cost for 1 MIPS was roughly $100,000, by 1994 that number had come down to only about $10.

While technology leadership has been a key to Intel's market dominance, it is not the only company achieving rapid innovation. Competitors such as Advanced Micro Devices, Cyrix, and NexGen are fighting for market share with Intel. At the same time, Apple Computer, IBM, and Motorola have been working on the PowerPC microprocessor designed to power both IBM and Macintosh machines. These types of developments are keeping Intel running.

Sources: Neil Gross, Peter Coy, and Otis Port, "The Technology Paradox," *Business Week,* March 6, 1995, pp. 76–84; "PowerPC Delivery Dates Set," *Computer World,* May 17, 1993, p. 8; Peter Burrows and Robert D. Hof, "Can This Chip Beat Pentium?" *Business Week,* August 20, 1994, pp. 83–86; B. R. Schlender, "The Future of the PC," *Fortune,* August 26, 1991, p. 40; L. Runyan, "40 Years on the Frontier," *Datamation,* March 15, 1991, p. 52; Brooke Crothers, "Smaller, Faster PowerPC Chip Rivals Pentium," *Infoworld,* April 4, 1994, p. 6; and Robert Hof, "Intel: Far Beyond the Pentium," *Business Week,* February 20, 1994, pp. 88–90. ●

As the Intel example shows, a technology life cycle typically is made up of many individual product life cycles. Each of these products is a relatively minor improvement over its predecessors. In this way, technological development involves significant innovations, often representing entirely new technologies, followed by a large number of small incremental innovations. Ongoing development of a technology increases the benefits gained through its use, makes the technology easier to use, and allows more applications. In the process, the use of the technology expands to new adopters.

DISSEMINATION OF A NEW TECHNOLOGY

The spread in the use of a new technology over time follows an S-shaped pattern (see Figure 20.2). This pattern, first observed in 1903, has been verified with many new tech-

The computer industry provides an especially compelling picture of the rapid rate of technological change. While Intel's Pentium chip was revolutionary when it was introduced in 1994, its more sophisticated replacements, to be released in 1996, 1998, and 1999, have already been developed.

(Courtesy Intel Corporation)

FIGURE 20.2

Technology
dissemination
pattern and
adopter categories

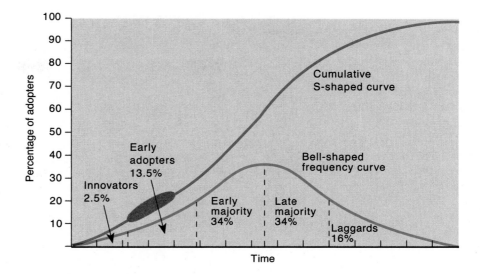

nologies and ideas in a wide variety of industries and settings.[6] The adopters of a new technology fall into five groups.

The first group, representing approximately 2.5 percent of adopters, are the *innovators*. Typically innovators are adventurous, but some might consider them headstrong or even extreme.

The next 13.5 percent of adopters are *early adopters*. This group is critical to the success of a new technology, because its members include well-respected opinion leaders. Early adopters often are the people or organizations others look to for leadership, ideas, and up-to-date technological information.

The next group, representing 34 percent of adopters, is the *early majority*. These adopters are more deliberate and take longer to decide to use something new. Often they are important members of a community or industry, but typically not the leaders.

Representing the next 34 percent are the *late majority*. Members of this group are more skeptical of technological change and approach innovation with great caution, often adopting only out of economic necessity or increasing social pressure.

The final 16 percent are *laggards*. Often isolated and highly conservative in their views, laggards are extremely suspicious of innovation and change.

Much of the speed with which an innovation spreads depends on five attributes.[7] An innovation will spread quickly if it (1) has a great advantage over its predecessor; (2) is compatible with existing systems, procedures, infrastructures, and ways of thinking; (3) has less rather than greater complexity; (4) can be easily tried or tested without significant cost or commitment; and (5) can be easily observed and copied. Designing products with these technological considerations in mind can make a critical difference in their success.

MANAGING TECHNOLOGY IN A COMPETITIVE ENVIRONMENT

A new technology can completely change the rules of competition within an industry.[8] Leading companies that respond ineffectively to the new technologies can falter while new companies seize on technological opportunities to emerge as the dominant firms. Industries are seldom transformed overnight, however. Typically, signals of the new technology's impact are visible well in advance, leaving time for companies and people to respond. Often the issue is not *whether* to adopt a new technology but *when* to adopt it and *how* to integrate the change with the organization's operating practices and strategies.

ADOPTION TIMING

The adage "timing is everything" is applied to many things, ranging from financial investments to telling jokes. It also applies to the development and adoption of new technologies.

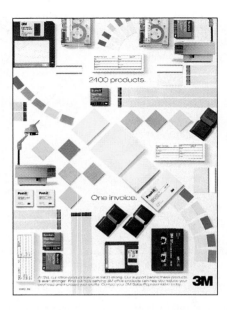

Maintaining the position of industrial leader is easier for companies that were first to market. For example, people take note of 3M products because the company established an early reputation for innovation.
(Courtesy 3M)

Industry leaders like Xerox, 3M, Hewlett-Packard, and Merck built and now maintain their competitive positions through early development and application of new technologies. However, early adoption also imposes costs and risks, and it is not the best timing for every organization (see Table 20.1).[9]

Advantages of Technology Leadership

What makes innovators and technology leadership attractive is the potential for high profits and first-mover advantages. Early adoption or being the first to market can provide significant competitive advantage. If technology leadership increases an organization's efficiency relative to competitors, it achieves a cost advantage. It can use the advantage to either reap greater profits than competitors or attract more customers by charging lower prices. Similarly, if a company is first to market with a new technology, it may be able to charge a premium price because it faces no competition. Higher prices and greater profits can defray the costs of developing new technologies.

This one-time advantage of being the technology leader can be turned into a sustainable advantage. Sustainability of a lead depends on competitors' ability to duplicate the technology and the organization's ability to keep building on the lead quickly enough to outpace competitors. It can do this in several ways. The reputation for being an innovator can create an ongoing advantage and even spill over to the company's other products. For example, 3M's reputation for innovation and quality differentiates some of its standard

TABLE 20.1

Advantages and disadvantages of technology leadership

Advantages	Disadvantages
First mover advantage	Greater risks
Little or no competition	Cost of technology development
Greater efficiency	Costs of market development and customer education
Higher profit margins	Infrastructure costs
Sustainable advantage	Costs of learning and eliminating defects
Reputation for innovation	Possible cannibalization of existing products
Establish entry barriers	
Occupy best market niches	
Opportunities to learn	

products like adhesive tape and allows the product to command a premium price. A competitor may be able to copy the product but not the reputation. Patents and other institutional barriers also can be used to block competitors and maintain leadership. Polaroid has successfully kept industry giant Kodak out of the instant-photography market for years through a series of patents. In 1991, Kodak agreed to pay Polaroid $925 million in compensation for patent infringement.[10]

The first mover can also preempt competitors by occupying the best market niches. If it can establish high switching costs (recall Chapter 3) for repeat customers, these positions can be difficult for competitors to capture. Apple Computer has dominated the school market for computers with its Apple II series despite its aging technology and assaults by IBM and other manufacturers. This is because of the large library of educational software that can be used only with Apple computers' unique hardware architecture. Although other companies can offer more advanced machines, their products are not as useful because they lack the extensive software support.

Technology leadership can provide a significant learning advantage. While competitors may be able to copy or adopt a new technology, ongoing learning by the technology leader can keep the company ahead by generating minor improvements that are difficult to imitate. Many Japanese manufacturers use several small incremental improvements generated with their *kaizen* programs (recall Chapter 19) to continuously upgrade the quality of their products and processes.[11] All these minor improvements cannot be easily copied by competitors, and collectively they can provide a significant advantage.

Disadvantages of Technology Leadership

However, being the first to adopt or develop a new technology does not always lead to immediate advantage and high profits. While such potential may exist, technology leadership imposes high costs and risks that followers are not required to bear. Being the leader thus can be more costly than being the follower. These costs include educating buyers unfamiliar with the new technology, building an infrastructure to support the technology, and developing complementary products to achieve the technology's full potential. Also, regulatory approval may be needed. For example, the cost of producing a new drug, including testing and the expense of obtaining FDA approval, is estimated at around $200 million.[12] While followers do not get the benefits of being first to market, they can copy the drug for a fraction of this cost once the original patents expire.

Being a pioneer carries other risks. If raw materials and equipment are new or have unique specifications, a ready supply at a reasonable cost may not be available. Or, the technology may not be fully developed and may have problems yet to be resolved. In addition, the unproved market for the technology creates uncertainty in demand. Finally, the new technology may have an adverse impact on existing structures or business. It may cannibalize current products or make existing investments obsolete.

TECHNOLOGY AND COMPETITIVE STRATEGY

Not all organizations are equally prepared to be technology leaders, nor would being a leader benefit each equally. Much of the difference in choosing to be a technology leader or follower depends on how a company positions itself to compete, the benefits gained through the use of a technology, and the characteristics of the organization.

Technology Leadership

In Chapter 5, we discussed two generic strategies a company can use to position itself in the market: low-cost leadership and product differentiation. With low-cost leadership, the company maintains an advantage because it has a lower cost than its competitors. With a differentiation strategy, the advantage comes from having a unique product or service for which customers are willing to pay a premium price.[13] Technology leadership can support either of these strategies. It can be used to gain cost advantage through pioneering lower-cost product designs and creating low-cost ways to perform needed operations. It can support differentiation by pioneering unique products or services that increase buyer value and thus command premium prices.

Technology Followership

Interestingly, technology *followership* also can be used to support both low-cost and differentiation strategies. If the follower learns from the leader's experience, it can avoid the costs and risks of technology leadership, thereby establishing a low-cost position. Manufacturers of IBM-compatible computers have been successful with this type of followership strategy. IBM's personal computer market share within the United States has been challenged largely because of low-cost technology followers such as Dell and Gateway. Followership can also support differentiation. By learning from the leader, the follower can adapt the products or delivery systems to more closely fit buyers' needs.

STRATEGIC USE OF TECHNOLOGY AT SAINSBURY'S

*S*ainsbury's is the United Kingdom's largest supermarket chain with sales in excess of £10 billion. Each week 8 million customers pass through its 350 stores, buying about 250 million products. What's interesting about Sainsbury's is that every stage of the business—from supplier to shelf to shopping cart—is monitored and controlled by computer.

During the past five years, Sainsbury's has spent more than £200 million on computers. Currently, the company employs 550 full-time information technology (IT) employees, with an additional 150 assigned to IT projects in other departments.

Running a supermarket chain is not complex in the sense of designing jet engines or plotting the weather, but the volume of data forced through the system day and night is enormous and reliability is crucial. At Sainsbury's, customers and purchasing agents generate some 1.5 million computer messages a day. For example, Sainsbury's automatic store reordering systems transmit details of what has been sold 10 times a day. This is consolidated centrally and triggers automatic orders to the 800 suppliers linked electronically to Sainsbury's, who then confirm receipt.

Interestingly, there are no manual backups to these systems, so to ensure technical reliability, Sainsbury's has two Amdahl mainframes positioned in duplicate computer centers on opposite sides of London. In the event of a crisis, each computer can take over the other's work and restore essential data. To ensure the relay system works, the company has a complete dry run every six months.

Other strategic uses of technology at Sainsbury's include using radio handsets in warehouses to communicate directly with forklift drivers so they can increase throughput without increasing the size of warehouses. In addition, software applications are being developed to optimize delivery truck routes, thereby cutting transportation costs and reducing environmental damage. Sainsbury's also has a substantial investment in forecasting programs that help predict consumer buying patterns. Unlike supermarkets in the United States, those in the U.K. do not have data on the lifestyles and buying patterns of their customers. The goal at Sainsbury's is to use the forecasts to help cut inventories, reduce waste, and provide fresher produce.

Despite Sainsbury's apparent leadership in the area of IT, Chris Montagnon, the company's director of information systems, insists that they do not want to be on the "bleeding edge" of computer innovation. Instead, Sainsbury's tries to be the first to put various elements of technology together in an innovative way that improves business processes. It is the strong focus on business drivers, rather than a passion for high technology, that has been one of the secrets of Sainsbury's success.

Source: "Looking After the Shop," *Management Today,* November 1993, pp. 78–82. ●

Strategic Needs and Capabilities

The most effective approach depends not only on the technology's potential to support the organization's strategic needs, but also on the organization's skills and capabilities to successfully exploit the technology. Every company has different capabilities to deal with new technology. As discussed previously, early adopters have characteristics different from late adopters. Early adopters of new technologies tend to be larger, more profitable, and more specialized.[14] Therefore, they are in an economic position to absorb the risks associated with early adoption while profiting more from its advantages. In addition, the people involved in early adoption are more highly educated, have a greater ability to deal with abstraction, can more effectively cope with uncertainty, and have strong problem-solving capabilities.[15] Thus, early adopters can more effectively manage the difficulties and uncertainty of a less fully developed technology.

Integrating the organization's strategic needs and technology skills with the capabilities of a new technology is a matter of timing. As discussed earlier, a technology does not emerge in its final state; rather, it undergoes *ongoing development* (see Figure 20.3). Development makes the technology easier to use and more adaptable to various strategies. At the same time, *complementary products and technologies* that make the technology more useful are being developed and introduced. For example, software technology and printer technology traditionally have lagged computer hardware technology, thereby limiting the usefulness of hardware technology breakthroughs.

These products and technologies combine with the *gradual diffusion* of the technology to form a shifting competitive impact from the technology.[16] The appropriate time for an organization to adopt is when the costs and risks of switching to the technology are outweighed by the benefits. This point differs among organizations and, as discussed earlier, depends largely on the company's characteristics and strategies. Thus, the organization's competitive strategy, the technical abilities of its personnel to deal with the new technology, the fit of the technology with the company's operations, and the company's ability to deal with the risks and ambiguities of adopting a new technology all must be timed to coincide with the dynamic forces of a developing technology. This does not always mean waiting for the technology to develop. Often it requires changing the capabilities and strategies of the organization to match the needs of the technology. This could include hiring new people, training existing employees, changing internal policies and procedures, and changing strategies.

ASSESSING TECHNOLOGY NEEDS

A decade ago, the major U.S. steel companies suffered from significant cost disadvantages relative to non-U.S. producers. These high costs were due largely to poor productivity resulting from aging plants and obsolete equipment. U.S. companies lagged their European and Japanese counterparts in adopting new, productivity-enhancing process technologies

FIGURE 20.3

Dynamic forces of a technology's competitive impact

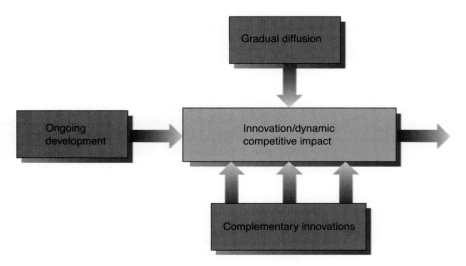

Source: D. M. Schroeder, "A Dynamic Perspective on the Impact of Process Innovation upon Competitive Strategies," *Strategic Management Journal,* January 1990, pp. 25–42.

such as the basic oxygen furnace and the continuous casting process.[17] Had the U.S. companies accurately assessed and adopted these technologies in a timely manner, the massive layoffs (about 60 percent) of the industry's work force could have been avoided.[18]

Assessing the technology needs of the organization involves measuring current technologies, benchmarking, and scanning.

MEASURING CURRENT TECHNOLOGIES

The most important dimension of a new technology is its competitive value. Arthur D. Little, Inc., has developed a technique for measuring competitive value that categorizes technologies as base, key, pacing, and emerging.[19]

- *Base* technologies are those that are commonplace in the industry; everyone must have them to be able to operate. Thus, they provide little competitive advantage.

- *Key* technologies have proven effective, but they also provide a strategic advantage because not everyone uses them. Knowledge and dissemination of these technologies are limited and they continue to provide some first-mover advantages.

- *Pacing* technologies have yet to prove their full value, but have the potential to alter the rules of competition by providing significant advantage.

- *Emerging* technologies are still under development and thus are unproved. They may, however, significantly alter the rules of competition in the more distant future.

Technologies can evolve rapidly through these categories. For example, electronic word processing was considered an emerging technology in the late 1970s. By the early 1980s, it could be considered pacing. While promising advantages, the technology's cost and capabilities restricted its usefulness to a limited number of applications. With continued improvements and more powerful computer chips, electronic word processing quickly became a key technology. Its costs dropped, its usage spread, and it demonstrated the capacity to enhance productivity. By the late 1980s, it was considered a base technology in most applications. Word processing technology is now so widely used that it is viewed as a routine activity in almost every office.

BENCHMARKING

As mentioned in Chapter 5, *benchmarking* is the process of comparing the organization's practices and technologies with those of other companies.

The ability to benchmark technologies against those of competitors can vary among industries. While competitors understandably are reluctant to share their secrets, information trading for benchmarking is not uncommon and can prove highly valuable. For example, Harley Davidson's recovery of its reputation for manufacturing quality motorcycles began only after company executives toured Honda's plant and witnessed firsthand the weaknesses of Harley's manufacturing technologies and the vast potential for improvement. In fact, Japanese companies often are willing to show U.S. competitors their operations because they believe the U.S. companies won't use the information!

It is important to benchmark against potential competitors in other nations. There may be key or pacing technologies in use that can easily be imported and offer significant advantage. Also, overseas firms may be more willing to share their knowledge if they are not direct competitors and if they are anxious to exchange information for the benefit of both companies.

SCANNING

Whereas benchmarking focuses on what is being done currently, scanning focuses on what can be done and what is being developed. In other words, benchmarking examines key and perhaps some pacing technologies, while scanning seeks out pacing and emerging technologies—those just being introduced and still in their development.

Scanning typically involves a number of tactics, many of them the same as those used in benchmarking. However, scanning places greater emphasis on identifying and monitoring the sources of new technologies for an industry. It may also dictate that executives read more cutting-edge research journals and attend research conferences and seminars. The extent to which scanning is done depends largely on how close to the cutting edge of technology the organization needs to operate.

SOURCING AND ACQUIRING NEW TECHNOLOGY

Developing new technology may conjure up visions of scientists and product developers working in R&D laboratories. In reality, new technology comes from many different sources, including suppliers, manufacturers, users, other industries, universities, the government, and overseas companies. While every source of innovation should be explored, each industry usually has specific sources for most of its new technologies. For example, because of the limited size of most farming operations, innovations in farming most often come from manufacturers, suppliers, and government extension services. Seed manufacturers develop and market new, superior hybrids, chemical producers improve pesticides and herbicides, and equipment manufacturers design improved farm equipment. Land grant universities develop new farming techniques, and extension agents spread their usage.

In many industries, however, the primary sources of new technology are the organizations that use the technology. For instance, over three-fourths of scientific innovations are developed by the users of the scientific instruments being improved and may subsequently be licensed or sold to manufacturers or suppliers.[20]

Essentially, the question of whether to acquire new technology is a **make-or-buy** decision. In other words, should the organization develop the technology itself or acquire it from an outside source? However, the decision is not that simple. There are many alternatives, and each has advantages and disadvantages. Some of the more common options are discussed in the following paragraphs.

Internal Development.   Developing a new technology within the company has the potential advantage of keeping the technology proprietary (exclusive to the organization). This provides an important advantage over competitors.

Purchase.   Most technology already is available in products or processes that can be openly purchased. For example, a bank that needs sophisticated information processing equipment need not develop the technology itself. It can simply purchase the technology from manufacturers or suppliers. In most situations, this is the simplest, easiest, and most cost-effective way to acquire new technology.

Contracted Development.   If the technology is not available and a company lacks the resources or time to develop it internally, it may choose to contract the development from outside sources. Possible contractors include other companies, independent research laboratories, and university and government institutions.

Licensing.   Certain technologies that are not easily purchased as part of a product can be licensed for a fee. Pioneers of the VHS format for videocassette recorders held the critical patents, but they freely licensed the technology and the right to use it to competing manufacturers of video equipment. This practice helped make VHS the dominant format (over Beta) by providing other manufacturers with easy access to the technology, thereby creating an industry standard.

Technology Trading.   Technology trading is another way to gain access to new technologies. Ironically, this tactic sometimes is used between rival companies. For example, U.S. steel producers that use the minimill concept freely trade a great deal of know-how among one another. In some cases, this activity extends to training without charge a competitor's employees on new process improvements.[21] While not all industries are amenable to technology sharing, trading is becoming increasingly common because of the high cost of developing advanced technologies independently.

Research Partnerships and Joint Ventures.   Research partnerships are arrangements designed to jointly pursue specific new-technology development. Typically, each member enters the partnership with different skills or resources needed for successful new-technology development. An effective combination is an established company and a start-up.[22] Joint ventures are similar in most respects to research partnerships, but they tend to have greater permanence and their outcomes result in entirely new companies.

BIG 3 AND WASHINGTON ARE TECHNOLOGY PARTNERS

*I*n February, 1993, President Clinton announced a partnership with Chrysler, General Motors, and Ford to use advanced aerospace technology to build more fuel-efficient vehicles. The goal of the partnership is to create a combined effort to build cars and light trucks that are three times more fuel efficient than today's vehicles. This partnership extends an earlier effort among the Big 3 automakers and the Electric Power Research Institute to develop batteries that allow electric vehicles to perform and be cost competitive with current gasoline-powered vehicles.

Under the new partnership, scientists and engineers from GM, Chrysler, and Ford will work with their counterparts at the Pentagon's research agencies and the Energy Department's weapons laboratories to use aerospace technologies to replace the internal combustion engine. The project will be managed by an interagency team composed of the Defense, Energy, Transportation, and Commerce Departments, the Environmental Protection Agency, NASA, and the National Science Foundation. Although each of the government agencies and all three auto companies are providing the funding for the research, the amounts that each party contributes varies from project to project. In general government funds are used for the riskier, longer-term projects, while industry funds are focused more on the near-term projects that have more immediate marketplace applications.

To date, the parties have developed coordinated lists of specific research and development projects, and have established a set of generic procedures to help Washington act quickly to support the R&D initiatives. Technology applications have been targeted in several areas:

- Virtual design and rapid prototyping from the Army Tank Command will be used to develop advanced manufacturing techniques, such as rapid computer-based design and testing systems for automation and control systems. In addition, advanced materials and composites will be developed from state-of-the-art weapons systems.

- Fuel cells developed at the Advanced Research Projects Agency (ARPA), and used for many years in the U.S. space program, will be utilized to convert hydrogen and oxygen into electricity. In addition, researchers are also examining gas turbines and improved internal combustion engines compatible with a variety of alternative fuels. These super-efficient motors, developed by ARPA, are complemented by other efficiency technologies, such as catalysts for reducing exhaust pollution.

- Ultra-capacitors, which store electricity, are being developed using technology from the Strategic Defense Initiative (AKA, Star Wars). Unlike a battery, ultra-capacitors release energy in quick bursts—ideal for starting or accelerating a car—or store energy quickly, which makes them ideal for capturing the energy dissipated when a car is braking.

The resource sharing that is created by this partnership is obviously impressive. And the consortium is proceeding at a fairly aggressive pace. In fact, their plans are to develop a concept vehicle within the next few years and to roll out a production prototype within 10 years.

Sources: James Krieger, "Development Efforts Target Advanced Electric Auto Batteries," *Chemical & Engineering News* 70, no. 46 (November 16, 1992), pp. 17–18; Paul Mann, "Clinton Policy Links Auto, Defense Technology," *Aviation Week & Space Technology,* October 4, 1993, p. 58; and Deborah L. Illman, "Automakers Move toward New Generation of 'Greener' Vehicles," *Chemical & Engineering News* 72, no. 31 (August 1, 1994), pp. 8–16. ●

Acquire an Owner of the Technology. If a company lacks the needed technology but wishes to acquire proprietary ownership of it, one option is to purchase the company that owns the technology. This transaction can take a number of forms, ranging from an outright purchase of the entire company to a minority interest sufficient to gain access to the technology. General Motors discovered that its need to modernize its information technologies was so extensive that it purchased EDS, a world leader in information services.

Choosing among these alternatives can be simplified by asking the following basic questions:

1. Is it important (and possible) in terms of competitive advantage that the technology remain proprietary?
2. Are the time, skills, and resources for internal development available?
3. Is the technology readily available outside the company?

TECHNOLOGY AND MANAGERIAL ROLES

As Figure 20.4 illustrates, the answers to these questions guide the manager to the most appropriate technology acquisition option. In organizations, technology traditionally has been the responsibility of vice presidents for research and development (R&D). These executives are directly responsible for corporate and divisional R&D laboratories. Typically their jobs have a functional orientation. But increasingly companies are creating the position of *chief technology officer (CTO)*. The CTO is a senior position at the corporate level with broad, integrative responsibilities.[23] CTOs coordinate the technological efforts of the various business units, act as a voice for technology in the top management team, supervise new-technology development, and assess the technological implications of major strategic initiatives such as acquisitions, new ventures, and strategic alliances.

CTOs also perform an important boundary role: They work directly with outside organizations. For example, they work with universities for funding research to stay abreast of technical developments and with regulatory agencies to ensure compliance with regulations, identify trends, and influence the regulatory process.

Other people play a variety of critical roles in developing new technology. Recall from Chapter 9 that it is the *entrepreneur* who, in an effort to exploit untried technologies, invents new products or finds new ways to produce old products. The entrepreneur opens up new possibilities that change the competitive structure of entire industries.[24] For example, Steven Jobs started Apple Computer in his garage and launched the multibillion-dollar personal computer industry.

FIGURE 20.4

Technology acquisition options

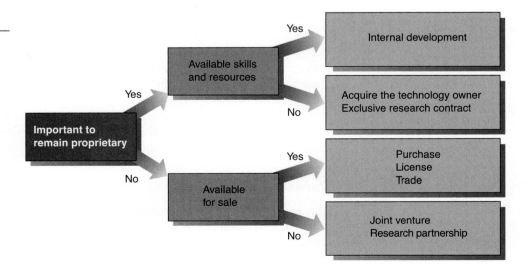

Key roles in acquiring and developing new technologies are the technical innovator, product champion, and executive champion.[25] The **technical innovator** develops the new technology or has the key skills needed to instill and operate the technology. This person possesses the requisite technical skills, but he or she may not have the managerial skills needed to push the idea forward and secure acceptance within the organization. This is where the **product champion** gets involved. Introducing new technology into an organization requires that someone promote the idea. The product champion—often at the risk of his or her position and prestige—promotes the idea throughout the organization, searching for support and acceptance. The champion can be a high-level manager, but often this is not the case. If the champion lacks the power and financial resources to make the required changes independently, she or he must convince people who have such authority to support the innovation. In other words, product champions must get sponsorship.

Sponsorship comes from the **executive champion,** who has the status, authority, and financial resources to support the project and protect the product champion. Without this support and protection, the product champion, and thus the new technology, could not succeed. Resources needed to develop the innovation would be unavailable, and without protection the champion would not be allowed to continue promoting the change.

ORGANIZING FOR INNOVATION

Organizing for innovation requires a balance between unleashing people's creative energies and capabilities and controlling the results to meet market needs in a timely manner.

UNLEASHING CREATIVITY

Innovation

3M derives about one-third of its revenues from new products.[26] 3M, along with other companies such as Merck, Hewlett-Packard, and Rubbermaid, have well-established histories of producing many successful new technologies and products. What sets these and other continuous innovators apart? The one thing these companies have in common is an organization culture that encourages innovation.

Consider the 3M legend from the early 1920s of inventor Francis G. Okie. Okie dreamed up the idea of using sandpaper instead of razor blades for shaving. The aim was to reduce the risk of nicks and avoid sharp instruments. The idea failed, but rather than being punished for the failure, Okie was encouraged to champion other ideas, which included 3M's first blockbuster success: waterproof sandpaper. A culture that permits failure is crucial for fostering the creative thinking and risk taking required for innovation.

As strange as it may seem, *celebrating* failure can be vital to the innovation process.[27] Failure is the essence of learning, growing, and succeeding. Innovative companies have many balls in the air at all times, with many people trying many new ideas. A majority of the ideas will fail—but it is only through this process that the few big "hits" will emerge that make a company an innovative star.

3M uses the simple set of rules listed in Table 20.2 to help foster innovation. These rules can be—and are—copied by other companies. But 3M has an advantage in that it has followed these rules since its inception and ingrained them in its culture. This culture is shared and passed on in part through stories. One such legend is about the 3M engineer who was fired because he refused to stop working on a project that his boss thought was wasting resources. Despite being fired, the engineer came to work as usual, finished the project, and demonstrated the value of his innovation. The engineer eventually was promoted to head a new division created to manufacture and market the innovation.

BUREAUCRACY BUSTING

Bureaucracy is an enemy of innovation. While bureaucracy is useful to maintain orderliness and gain efficiencies, it also can work directly against innovativeness. Developing radically different technologies requires a more fluid and flexible (organic) structure that does not restrict thought and action. However, such a structure can be chaotic and disruptive to

TABLE 20.2

3M's rules for an
innovative culture

- **Set goals for innovation.** By corporate decree, 25 to 30 percent of annual sales must come from new products that are five years old or less.
- **Commit to research and development.** 3M invests in R&D at almost double the rate of the average U.S. company. One R&D goal is to cut in half the time it takes to introduce new products.
- **Inspire intrapreneurship.** Champions are encouraged to run with new ideas, and they get a chance to manage their products as if they were running their own businesses. 3Mers are allowed to spend 15 percent of their time pursuing personal research interests unrelated to current company projects.
- **Facilitate, don't obstruct.** Divisions are kept small and allowed to operate with a great deal of independence, but have constant access to information and technical resources. Researchers with good ideas are awarded $50,000 Genesis grants to develop their brainstorms into new products.
- **Focus on the customer.** 3M's definition of quality is to demonstrate that the product can do what the *customer*—not some arbitrary standard—dictates.
- **Tolerate failure.** 3Mers know that if their ideas fail, they will still be encouraged to pursue other innovative ideas. Management knows that mistakes will be made, and that destructive criticism kills initiative.

Sources: Company reports; R. Mitchell, "Masters of Innovation: How 3M Keeps Its New Products Coming," *Business Week,* April 10, 1989, pp. 58–63; T. Katauskas, "Follow-Through: 3M's Formula for Success," *R&D,* November 1990; and Thomas J. Martin, "Ten Commandments for Managing Creative People," *Fortune,* January 16, 1995, pp. 135–36.

normal operations. Consequently, companies often establish special temporary project structures that are isolated from the rest of the organization and allowed to operate under different rules. These units go by many names, including "skunkworks" (recall Chapter 9), "greenhouses," and "reserves."

In Japan, *angura* is an "underground research" policy that allows scientists to spend up to 20 percent of their time pursuing projects that only the immediate supervisor knows about.[28] When Apple developed the Macintosh, Steve Jobs took a small group of young engineers and programmers and set up operations apart from the remainder of the plant. They started from scratch, trying to completely rethink the personal computer. A pirate's flag was flown over their operation to demonstrate that they were not part of the regular bureaucratic operating structure and defied conventional rules. The result was a very successful new product.

Other structural arrangements also facilitate innovation.[29] *Flat structures* reduce bureaucracy and allow flexibility and innovation. *Granting autonomy* to divisions, including giving them spending authority and other necessary resources, does the same. It is particularly important to break down differentiation based on functional area, as typified by the traditional, vertical hiearchy (Chapter 10). Instead, the organization should create a *horizontal orientation* in which communications flow across functions. The best way to do this is to establish *cross-functional teams.* The aim should be to destroy the traditional boundaries between design, engineering, manufacturing/operations, purchasing, marketing, and other functions.

IMPLEMENTING DEVELOPMENT PROJECTS

A powerful tool for managing technology and innovations is the **development project.**[30] A development project is a focused organizational effort to create a new product or process via technological advances. For example, in 1987 Eastman Kodak launched a development project to create the FunSaver Camera. The concept was simple: to package film in an inexpensive plastic camera body so that after the pictures were taken, the consumer could

Hewlett-Packard undertook a development project that resulted in the inkjet printer, a product that gave the company an unprecedented advantage in both cost and speed.
(Photo courtesy Hewlett-Packard Company)

simply drop the whole assembly with a photo finisher. While the Fun Saver utilized existing design knowledge, it was developed on a unique computer-aided design and manufacturing (CAD/CAM) system. Two years earlier, Hewlett-Packard had initiated a development project of its own to design a new class of low-cost computer printers based on ink-jet technology. HP's Deskjet Printer was one of the company's first attempts to integrate manufacturing, marketing, and R&D. The development project allowed the company to achieve an unprecedented advantage in both cost and speed.

In general, development projects fall into one of four categories: (1) *research or advanced development projects* designed to invent new science for application in a specific project; (2) *breakthrough development projects* designed to create the first generation of a product or process; (3) *platform development projects* that establish the basic architecture for a whole set of follow-on projects; and (4) *derivative development projects* that are narrower in scope and are designed to provide incremental improvements to an existing product or process.[31]

Development projects such as these typically feature a special cross-functional team that works together on an overall concept or idea. Like most cross-functional teams, their success depends on how well individuals work together to pursue a common vision. And in the case of development projects, teams must frequently interact with suppliers and customers—making the complexity of their task that much greater. Because of their urgency and strategic importance, most development projects are conducted under intense time and budget pressures, thus presenting a real-time test of the company's ability to innovate.

Managers should recognize that development projects have multiple benefits. Not only are they useful for creating new products and processes, but they frequently cultivate skills and knowledge that can be used for future endeavors. In other words, the capabilities that companies derive from a development project frequently can be turned into a source of competitive advantage. For example, in 1986 when Ford created a development project to design an air-conditioning compressor to outperform its Japanese rival, executives also discovered they had laid the foundation for new processes that Ford could use in future projects. Their new capability in integrated design and manufacturing helped Ford to reduce the costs and lead-times for other product developments. Thus, *organizational learning* had become an equally important criterion for evaluating the success of the project.

For development projects to achieve their fullest benefit, they should: build on core competencies (recall Chapters 5 and 11); have a guiding vision about what must be accomplished and why (Chapter 14); have a committed team (Chapters 14 and 16); instill a philosophy of continuous improvement (Chapter 19); and generate integrated, coordinated efforts across all units (Chapters 10, 11, and 19).

TECHNOLOGY, JOB DESIGN, AND HUMAN RESOURCES

Adopting a new technology typically requires changes in the way jobs are designed (Chapter 14). Often the way the task is redefined fits people to the demands of the technology to maximize the technology's operation. But this often fails to maximize total productivity, because it ignores the human part of the equation. The social relationships and human aspects of the task may suffer, lowering overall productivity.

The **sociotechnical systems** approach to work redesign specifically addresses this problem. This approach redesigns tasks in a manner that jointly optimizes the social and technical efficiency of work. Beginning with studies on the introduction of new coal-mining technologies in 1949, the sociotechnical systems approach to work design focused on small, self-regulating work groups.[32] Later it was found that such work arrangements could operate effectively only in an environment in which bureaucracy was limited. Today's trends in bureaucracy "bashing," lean and flat organizations, work teams and an empowered work force are logical extensions of the sociotechnical philosophy of work design. At the same time, the technologies of the information age—in which people at all organizational levels have access to vast amounts of information—make these leaner and less bureaucratic organizations possible.

Managers face several choices regarding how to apply a new technology. Technology can be used to limit the tasks and responsibilities of workers and "deskill" the workforce, thus turning workers into servants of the technology.

Alternatively, managers can select and train workers to master the technology, using it to achieve great accomplishments and improve the quality of their lives.[33] Chapter 15 provided an example of how computer numerically controlled (CNC) machine tools can enrich jobs. Technology, when managed effectively, can empower workers as it improves the competitiveness of organizations.

However, as managers make decisions about how to design jobs and manage employees, they also need to consider other human resource systems that complement the introduction of new technology. Table 20.3, for example, shows how compensation systems can be changed to facilitate the implementation of advanced manufacturing technology. In the

TABLE 20.3

Compensation practices in traditional and advanced manufacturing firms

Type of Compensation Practice	Traditional Factory	Integrated Manufacturing
Performance contingent	Focus on *individual incentives* reflects division of labor and separation of stages and functions.	Extensive use of *group incentives* to encourage teamwork, cooperation, and joint problem solving.
Job contingent	Use of *hourly wage* assumes that the differences in employee contribution are captured in job classifications and that performance is largely determined by the production system.	Use of *salary* assumes that employees' contributions transcend the job per se to substantially affect output. The distinctions between classes of employment are diminished.
Person contingent	*Seniority pay* rewards experience as a surrogate for knowledge and skill in a stable environment and rewards loyalty to reduce uncertainty within the system.	*Skill-based pay* rewards continuous learning and the value-added derived from increased flexibility in a dynamic environment.

Source: Scott A. Snell and James W. Dean, Jr., "Strategic Compensation for Integrated Manufacturing: The Moderating Effects of Jobs and Organizational Inertia," *Academy of Management Journal* 37, no. 5 (1994), pp. 1109–40.

contemporary setting, use of group incentives, salary, and skill-based pay systems helps reinforce collective effort (recall the use of cross-functional teams), professionalism, empowerment, and flexibility required for knowledge work. If a company's pay system is not aligned with the new technologies, it may not reward behavior that is needed to make the changes work. Worse yet, existing reward systems may actually reinforce old behaviors that run counter to what is needed for the new technology.

Taken as a whole, these ideas provide a set of guidelines for managing the strategic and organizational issues associated with technology and innovation. In Chapter 21, we expand this discussion to focus on how organizations can reshape themselves to adapt to a dynamic marketplace. Managing change and organizational learning are central elements of what it takes to become a world-class organization.

KEY TERMS

development project, p. 531
executive champion, p. 530
innovation, p. 518
make-or-buy decision, p. 527
product champion, p. 530

sociotechnical systems, p. 533
technical innovator, p. 530
technology, p. 518
technology life cycle, p. 518

SUMMARY OF LEARNING OBJECTIVES

Now that you have studied Chapter 20, you should know:

The processes involved in the development of new technologies.

Forces that compel the emergence of a new technology include (1) a need for the technology, (2) the requisite scientific knowledge, (3) technical convertibility of this knowledge, (4) the capital resources to fund development, and (5) the entrepreneurial insight and initiative to pull the components together.

How technologies proceed through a life cycle.

New technologies follow a predictable life cycle. First, a workable idea about how to meet a market need is developed into some product innovation. Early progress can be slow as competitors experiment with product designs. Eventually a dominant design emerges as the market accepts the technology, and further refinements to the technology occur from process innovations. As the technology begins to approach both the theoretical limits to its performance potential and market saturation, growth slows and the technology matures. At this point the technology can remain stable or be replaced by a new technology.

How to manage technology for competitive advantage.

Adopters of new technologies are categorized according to the timing of their adoption: innovators, early adopters, the early majority, the late majority, and laggards. Technology leadership has many first-mover advantages, but also poses significant disadvantages. The same may be said for followership. After that, technology that helps improve efficiency will support a low-cost strategy, while technologies that help make products more distinc-

tive or unique will support a differentiation strategy. Determining an appropriate technology strategy depends on the degree to which the technology supports the organization's competitive requirements and, if a technology leadership strategy is chosen, the company's ability, in terms of skills, resources, and commitment, to deal with the risks and uncertainties of leadership.

How to assess technology needs.

Assessing the technology needs of a company begins by benchmarking, or comparing, the technologies it employs with those of both competitors and noncompetitors. Benchmarking should be done on a global basis to understand practices used worldwide. Technology scanning helps identify emerging technologies and those still under development in an effort to project their eventual competitive impact.

Where new technologies originate and the best strategies for acquiring them.

New technologies can be acquired or developed. Options include internal development, purchase, contracted development, licensing, trading, research partnerships and joint ventures, and acquisition. The approach used depends on the existing availability of the technology, the skills, resources, and time available, and importance of keeping the technology proprietary.

How people play a role in managing technology.

People play many different roles in managing technology. For example, the chief technology officer (CTO) is the person with broad, integrative responsibility for technological innovation. In addition, the entrepreneur is the person who recognizes the competitive potential of the technology and finds new ways to exploit opportunities. The technical innovator has the key skills needed to develop or install and operate the technology. The product champion is the person who promotes the new idea(s) in order to gain support throughout the organization. The executive champion is the person with status and resources to support the project.

How to develop an innovative organization.

Organizing for innovation involves unleashing the creative energies of employees while directing their efforts toward meeting market needs in a timely manner. Culture, structure, development projects, and job design are critical for building an innovative organization.

The key characteristics of successful development projects.

For development projects to achieve their fullest benefit, they should: (1) build on core competencies; (2) have a guiding vision about what must be accomplished and why; (3) have a committed team; (4) instill a philosophy of continuous improvement; and (5) generate integrated, coordinated efforts across all teams and units.

 D I S C U S S I O N   Q U E S T I O N S

1. At the beginning of this chapter there is a quote by Francis Bacon that reads, "A wise man will make more opportunities than he finds." What does this have to do with technology and innovation? What does it have to do with competitive advantage?

2. What examples of technological innovation can you identify? What forces led to the commercialization of the science behind these technologies? Did the capability exist before the market demand, or was the demand there before the technology was available?

3. Thomas Edison once said that most innovations are 10 percent inspiration and 90 percent perspiration. How does this match with what you know about technology life cycles?

4. Why would a company choose to follow rather than lead technological innovations? Is the potential advantage of technological leadership greater when innovations are occurring rapidly, or is it better in this case to follow?

5. If you were in the grocery business, who would you benchmark for technological innovations? Would the companies be inside or outside your industry? Why?

6. How would you see the executive champion, the chief technology officer, and the product champion working together? Could the roles all be played by the same individual? Why or why not?

CONCLUDING CASE

MOTOROLA'S IRIDIUM PROJECT GETS OFF THE GROUND

Innovations are commonplace at Motorola: The company's six-sigma program has revolutionized total quality management, Motorola University has become the new standard for the delivery of company training programs, and Motorola's cellular phones and pagers have gained a commanding share of worldwide markets. So it's not surprising that a company this innovative has come up with another big idea. The latest brainstorm is called the IRIDIUM system—the creation of a network of low-level earth-orbiting satellites (LEOs) that provide wireless communications to *anyone, anytime, anywhere* in the world. Subscribers to IRIDIUM would use a pocket-sized handset similar to today's portable cellular phones, but be able to transmit voice, data, fax, and paging services to any location on the planet over a common technology platform.

While the idea of seamless global communications is appealing, the delivery system is enormously complex. Motorola named the project after the element Iridium, whose atomic number corresponded to the 77 satellites in the proposed network. Although refinements in the design of the IRIDIUM system have reduced the number of satellites to 66, the logistics are still staggering. The IRIDIUM network of satellites, each weighing about 1,500 lbs., will orbit the earth longitudinally, circling the planet from pole to pole at an altitude of 420 nautical miles. The LEO satellites will communicate with each other and connect up with established telephone networks via a collection of earth-based tracking dish antennas called gateways.

Although the original price for the handset could cost up to $3,000, with calls averaging $3 per minute, conservative estimates are that at least 2 million users will be on board by the year 2002. The most promising markets appear to be those in areas without existing telecommunications infrastructures, such as Russia, where only 10 million phones serve a population of 250 million people, or India, where thousands of villages have no telephone service at all.

Because of the global scope and cost ($3.37 billion) of the IRIDIUM system, Motorola needed a set of partners to help with design, implementation, and operation. To get an idea of the complexity of partner relationships, consider the following: Satellite buses made by Lockheed will be loaded with electronics made by Motorola and will be launched into space by Proton rockets made by Russia's Khrunichev Enterprise, as well as Delta 2 rockets made by McDonnell Douglas, and Long March IIc rockets from

■

Motorola's most recent technological innovation, the IRIDIUM system, consists of a network of low-level orbiting satellites that provide wireless communication to anyone, anytime, anywhere in the world.

[Courtesy Iridium, Inc.]

China's Great Wall Industry Corp. Once in orbit, the satellites will be controlled by General Electric software and will transfer calls to and from earth using technology from Scientific Atlanta and Canada's COM DEV. Raytheon Corp. is currently developing the satellite's main mission antennas. Other investors include BCE Mobile (Canada), Iridium Africa Corp. (Africa), Iridium Andes-Caribe (Venezuela), Iridium Middle East Corp. (Saudi Arabia), Nippon Iridium Corp. (Japan), Pacific Electric Wire & Cable (Taiwan), Sprint Corp. (USA), STET (Italy), and Thai Satellite Communications Corp. (Thailand).

To get the project off the ground, Motorola created a new strategic business unit called Satellite Communications Division (SATCOM), headed by Durrell Hillis, who provides the overall leadership and strategic vision for the project. From the beginning, Hillis and other executives were convinced that there was no way to manage the IRIDIUM system in a traditional manner, but that the organization should be a fluid structure of boundary-busting self-managed teams. Each of the teams is cross-functional and organized around work processes such as financing, regulatory, design, technical, and launch. This is not Motorola's first attempt to organize around processes or to use self-managing teams, but the IRIDIUM has been the first to span both organizational and geographic boundaries. Indeed, representatives from many of the project's suppliers sit on the various teams.

SATCOM has no organizational chart, and Hillis deliberately discourages formal structure and hierarchical titles because they destroy trust and empowerment among team members. Instead SATCOM can best be described as a network of interlocking rings. Each ring represents a team, and each team includes a team leader and team sponsor. The leadership roles shift as the work of the team progresses, and each team's sponsor (a member of SATCOM's executive team) provides resources and acts as an external facilitator. Teams form, disband, and reform around new tasks as needed. To date, the critical management tasks have been those associated with establishing integration between the teams—synchronizing a variety of efforts toward one shared goal. To make certain that everyone has up-to-date information and the ability to share knowledge, a software template has been developed to allow anyone in the business unit to enter a topic and, in return, receive a listing of the teams working in that area. In addition, to develop a common language, common tools, and shared guidelines, team members have gone through training together. To encourage "real-time" development, the training is delivered on a just-in-time basis, providing small work-bytes as needed.

Obviously, the IRIDIUM system represents a challenge, both technologically and organizationally. And Motorola is reinventing the way electronics and aerospace companies work together, and creating a new model for other large-scale innovation projects. Recently, other companies have tried to duplicate IRIDIUM's concept. Microsoft and McCaw Cellular (AT&T), for example, announced a $9 billion joint venture called Teledisc to create an 840-satellite network to compete with IRIDIUM. As aggressive as these and other technological innovations may be, most observers maintain that their chances for commercial success are still up in the air.

QUESTIONS

1. What are the advantages to Motorola of being the first to create a system such as IRIDIUM? Do you think they can sustain any advantage over competitors such as AT&T? How?

2. What are the reasons behind Motorola's seeking out partners for this project? Why did they choose the partners they did? Who else would have made a good partner? Why?

3. Why did the IRIDIUM system require a whole new organization structure? Why does Durrell Hillis discourage formalization and hierarchy?

4. What type of training and reward systems do you think would be most useful for the people working on IRIDIUM?

Sources: Theodore B. Kinni, "A Ma Bell for the Space Age," *Industry Week,* March 21, 1994, pp. 71–72; Theodore B. Kinni, "Boundary-Busting Teamwork," *Industry Week,* March 21, 1994, pp. 72–74; Charles F. Mason, "IRIDIUM Forges Ahead with Its Grand PCN Plan," *Telephony,* November 1, 1993; Michael Krantz, "Gates and McCaw Blast Off," *Mediaweek* 4, no. 13 (March 28, 1994), p. 12; Charles F. Mason, "Scientific-Atlanta Wins IRIDIUM Deal," *Telephony* 226, no. 6 (February 1994), p. 10; "IRIDIUM: A Closer Look," *Telecommunications* 27, no. 12 (December 1993), p. 27.

VIDEO CASE

MANAGING TECHNOLOGY AND INNOVATION AT NUCOR STEEL

During the first half of the 20th century, the United States built a manufacturing empire around the steel output of midwestern cities. However, over the last 25 years the steel industry in the U.S. has collapsed. Today, the midwestern region that had been the backbone of the steel industry is referred to as "the rust belt," because of all the shuttered factories. It's not that the global demand for steel has declined, quite the opposite. What has happened is the technology of steelmaking advanced beyond what was being used in American plants, and they were no longer competitive. During the 1970s and 1980s, the Japanese built their own steel manufacturing empire on the strength of their newer, more productive steel factories.

Today, one innovative American company is managing to reverse the trend toward Japanese steel with a bold new approach that is raising eyebrows throughout the steel industry. Nucor Steel, a division of Nucor Corporation, opened a new steel plant in 1989 in the rural town of Crawfordsville, Indiana. Nucor started a revolution in steel manufacturing in this unlikely setting with the world's most technologically advanced mill.

The idea behind the Crawfordsville plant was to construct the steel mill economically. Doing so allowed Nucor to reduce its labor requirements. Once the facility was built, the company also developed an internal culture that had not previously been a part of the American steel industry, eliminating much of the inefficient bureaucracy that had paralyzed American steel mills. The steelmaker has decentralized decision making so much that plant managers run almost every aspect of the business. And the company rewards its employees for performance. Steelworkers at the plant are eligible for productivity and quality bonuses that are typically 130 to 150 percent of base pay. That can give the non-unionized workers total pay of up to $50,000 per year.

The Nucor plant, which is relatively small by industry standards, is known as a "mini-mill." But it isn't small in terms of productivity. It was designed to produce 800,000 tons of finished strip steel each year from scrap metal. The plant accomplishes this feat through the aid of two major technological advantages: continuous casting equipment and computer integrated manufacturing. The mill is the first continuous thin slab cast, flat roll steelmaking facility in the world. It allows Nucor steel to transform molten metal into hot band in one uninterrupted operation.

This innovation dramatically shortens the traditional production process, saving valuable time, manpower, and resources. The other technological advantage is the unprecedented level of computer integrated manufacturing (CIM) and management which had only previously been applied in other industries and in small portions of other steel plants. The Nucor steel mill provided an opportunity to employ a CIM system from the start-up. Plant general manager Keith Busse remarked, "When you look at how productive a facility like this is, it's almost frightening. We're producing a hot rolled ton of steel in seven-tenths of a man-hour. And we produce a cold rolled ton of steel in 1.2 man-hours. When you compare that to the integrated industry, we're looking at enormous productivity differences." The industry average is over four worker-hours per ton.

Nucor's CIM system controls the plant at three levels: machine setup, process control, and business information. These levels are linked together, and data are transferred from computer to computer throughout the entire process beginning with the order entry. Information concerning the order goes to production scheduling, then to the hot mill, the cold mill, shipping, and finally invoicing. The CIM system tells employees throughout the plant how to handle each slab, strip, or coil of steel at each stage of the process. The Nucor process includes 11 interactive databases, 1,500 programs, and a million lines of COBOL code. The CIM system helps Nucor establish optimum production schedules. It also lets the company serve its customers better by being able to tell them where their order is at any stage of the production process.

Nucor's production process is known as a "pull system," since it produces steel only in response to specific customer orders. Each order "pulls" the steel through the production process. This approach eliminates the need to inventory finished steel in anticipation of customer orders. The production begins at the scrap yard, which maintains a computer-monitored inventory. The scrap yard crew reads the order on the computer monitor and begins the production by feeding high-quality scrap into one of two 150-ton electric furnaces. The electric charge melts the scrap into hot molten steel, the steel is then moved into a ladle, and into the continuous caster. The caster produces a hot slab two-inches thick by 52-inches wide. Next the slab moves to a computer-controlled, gas-fired soaking furnace where it is heated to 2,000 degrees, at which point it can be rolled. From there, the slab proceeds on to the finishing mill.

One mill operator in a pristine computer operating room known as "the pulpit" controls the entire mill from the time the scrap enters the furnace until the finished coils exit the plant on the other end. Finished coils of 10 to 24 tons are bar-coded for computer tracking when they leave the plant. About half of the plant's steel is sold as hot band coils directly from the hot mill. The rest is sent to a cold mill next door for further finishing, including pickling, tempering, cold rolling for thickness reduction, and annealing for stress reduction.

Each workstation in the cold mill has its own computer terminal that provides processing instructions. Determining the best production schedule is vital for peak efficiency and minimizing setup time. Even the overhead crane operators benefit from the CIM system. They have radio-frequency terminals that help them find coils and tell them where to move them. After they move the coils, they enter updated locations and schedules.

As a result of their success, the Crawfordsville plant was a model for a new plant in Hickman, Arkansas. At Hickman, Nucor has continued to decentralize decision making, giving its plant managers a high level of autonomy. Hickman plant manager Rodney B. Mott says that "Hickman operates like a separate company." Mott has a big say in his plant's expansion plans. In the spring of 1994, for example, he installed a second $50 million caster, which turns liquid metal into bands of steel, nearly doubling the Hickman plant's capacity, to 36,000 tons per week.

That doesn't mean that headquarters isn't paying attention. Frequent telephone conversations with the central office in Charlotte, North Carolina, are common. And almost every measurable aspect of each plant's performance is reported throughout the company. That, in turn, leads to plenty of competition among the plants. "There's a lot of little sibling rivalries going on," Mott acknowledged.

Because of the success of Nucor's new mini-mills, Mott and other plant managers have been sought by other American steel companies to help them turn around their operations. But Mott has steadfastly refused such offers, even when the positions paid more money. The reason? "I'd still be taking orders," he said. That would be quite a change from Nucor, where the usual advice Mott gets from his boss is "trust your gut." It's not always easy to do, but that's the way decisions are made at Nucor. And it's the combination of decentralized decision making and bold new technologies that has made Nucor a force to be reckoned with in the international steel industry.

CRITICAL THINKING QUESTIONS

1. Nucor Steel has become competitive in the international steel industry through technology and innovation. What do you think the company needs to do to maintain its momentum and continue to be competitive into the next century?

2. Nucor has effectively applied computer integrated manufacturing (CIM) to its production processes. What steps do you think the company had to take to ensure employees are able to make full use of the CIM system? What ongoing steps do you think the company should be taking to ensure that its workers use the system to full advantage?

3. A major issue in organizational control is whether decision making should be centralized or decentralized. Nucor uses a decentralized approach, devolving a significant amount of authority to plant managers. What are some of the advantages of this approach? What are some of the disadvantages?

Source: Wendy Zellner, Robert D. Hof, Richard Brandt, Robert Baker, and David Griesing, "Go-Go Goliaths," *Business Week,* February 13, 1995, pp. 64–70.

EXPERIENTIAL EXERCISES

20.1 Planning for Innovation

Objectives

1. To brainstorm innovative ideas for a company that has become stagnant.
2. To explore what are the elements of a good innovation plan.

Instructions

1. Read the Mason, Inc., scenario below.
2. Individually or in small groups, offer a plan for encouraging innovation at Mason, Inc. Discuss staffing, rewards, organizational structure, work design, and any other facets of organizational behavior that apply.
3. In small groups, or with the entire class, share the plans you developed.

MASON, INC., SCENARIO

Mason, Inc., is a *Fortune* 500 company that designs, develops, and manufactures personal grooming products. From 1950 to 1980 it was a leader in introducing new, profitable products into the marketplace. Its Research and Development Division grew from 20 to 150 professionals during that time. Since 1980, however, the company has relied on its past successes and has failed to introduce any significant innovative product into the marketplace. Top management wants to reestablish Mason's reputation as the number-one innovator in the industry.

Discussion Questions

1. What elements do these plans have in common?
2. How well do the plans follow the innovation process?
3. Do the plans incorporate provisions for fulfilling the various roles required for innovation?
4. What are the strengths and weaknesses of each plan?
5. What should be the components of an effective plan?

Source: J. Gordon, *A Diagnostic Approach to Organizational Behavior* (Englewood Cliffs, N.J.: Prentice-Hall, 1983), p. 654. Reprinted by permission of Prentice-Hall, Inc., Englewood Cliffs, N.J.

20.2   Innovation for the Future

Objective

To look ahead to the 21st century.

Instructions

Choose a partner. Together, develop an innovative product or service that will be popular in the year 2025. As you develop your product or service, ask yourselves the following questions:

1. What trends lead you to believe that this product or service will be successful?
2. What current technologies, services, or products will be replaced by your idea?

Present your idea to the class for discussion.

21

BECOMING WORLD CLASS

The world hates change, yet that is the only thing that has brought progress.

Charles Kettering

LEARNING OBJECTIVES

After studying Chapter 21, you will know:

1. What it takes to be world class.

2. How to manage change effectively.

3. How to best prepare for the future.

THE NEED TO CHANGE

- "Want a tough job? Try leading an organization through major change . . . Almost without exception, executives claim it's the hardest work they've ever done."—T. A. Stewart, *Fortune*.

- "You've got to be on the cutting edge of change. You can't simply maintain the status quo, because somebody's always coming from another country with another product, or consumer tastes change, or the cost structure does, or there's a technology breakthrough. If you're not fast and adaptable, you're vulnerable. This is true for every segment of every business in every country in the world."— Jack Welch, General Electric.

- "Even if your company's financials are terrific, you might want to . . . build support for improving your own performance before you're attacked. . . . We're starting almost from scratch in reshaping the way the whole enterprise runs."—Lawrence Bossidy, Allied Signal.

- "In terms of channeling the energies of all our people and unleashing our potential productivity, we're halfway home at best. And that's not bad. I know a lot of companies in the United States that may think they've come more than halfway, but I don't know very many that actually have come even that far."—Michael Walsh, Tenneco.

- "People always ask, 'Is the change over? Can we stop now?' You've got to tell them, 'No, it's just begun.'"—Jack Welch.

The CEOs pictured here, Larry Bossidy of Allied Signal, Bill Weiss of Ameritech, Mike Walsh of Tenneco, and Jack Welsh of GE, realize the importance of channeling their employees' energies in the direction of the cutting edge of change. *(John Abbott)*

Sources: T. A. Stewart, "How to Lead a Revolution," *Fortune*, November 28, 1994, pp. 48–61; and S. Sherman, "A Master Class in Radical Change," *Fortune*, December 13, 1993, pp. 82–90.

*T*he executives quoted above are all talking about the same things: the difficulties and challenges of changing organizations and the *need* to change—constantly—in order to achieve world-class excellence and competitive advantage for the future.

This chapter discusses managing change. Today's managers deal with and oversee far-reaching changes in their organizations as they respond to the pressures to become world class. We will examine why people resist change, and how the change process can best be managed. And we'll describe specific techniques for preparing for an uncertain future.

WORLD-CLASS EXCELLENCE

Managers today either *want,* or *should* want, their organizations to become world class.[1] To some people, striving for world-class excellence seems a lofty, impossible, unnecessary goal. But it is a goal that is essential to survival and success in today's intensely competitive business world.

Becoming world class does not mean merely improving. It means becoming one of the very best in the world at what you do. Some have estimated that for most companies, becoming world class requires increasing quality by 100 to 1,000 times, decreasing costs by 30 percent to 50 percent, increasing productivity by two to four times, decreasing order-to-delivery time by a factor of 5 to 10, and decreasing new-product development times by 30 percent to 60 percent. And even if your firm realizes these dramatic improvements, it still will have to keep on getting better![2]

What does it really take to achieve "being the very best"? World class means growing more rapidly than competitors (indicating that the market values your product more highly), hiring and keeping the best people, responding quickly and decisively to changing conditions, continually improving facilities, systems, and skills, and, for manufacturers, developing a top-notch engineering staff.[3]

World-class companies create high-value products and earn superior profits over the long run. They demolish the obsolete methods, systems, and cultures of the past that have impeded their competitive progress, and apply more effective competitive organizational strategies, structures, processes, and management of human resources. The result is an organization capable of competing successfully on a global basis.[4]

ACHIEVING WORLD-CLASS EXCELLENCE

To become world class, management must understand completely:[5] (1) the cost of its products, from its inputs from suppliers through the transformation processes performed by the firm, through the output to its global customers; (2) the complete quality picture, at every step of the process; and (3) total elapsed time for every step throughout the process. From there, it must also (4) be willing and able to innovate—that is, to change things for the better, with measurable results.

For example, providing world-class quality requires a *thorough* understanding of what quality really is.[6] Quality can be measured in terms of performance, additional features, reliability (failures or breakdowns), conformance to standards, durability, serviceability, and aesthetics. Only by moving beyond broad, generic concepts like "quality," to identifying the more specific elements of quality, can you identify problems, target needs, set performance standards more precisely, and deliver world-class value.

The same can be said about the other things that deliver value to customers. That is, they all can be broken down into subcomponents, each of which can be a problem and/or a source of added value. For example, cost to the consumer is not just the initial purchase price; it also includes operating costs and maintenance costs over the life of the product. Even delivery can be defined more broadly than just speedy arrival to the customer; it can include the condition of the product, ease of ordering, ease of return, accommodating special needs, and customer access to information about the status of the order.[7]

Customer service also can be broadly construed as multidimensional; there are many aspects to providing customers with world-class service.

ACHIEVING WORLD-CLASS SERVICE QUALITY

Quality

What can organizations do to achieve one of the most important dimensions of world-class excellence—great service quality?

- *Provide basic service:* Fundamentals are more important than fanciness. Performance is key, not empty promises. Automobile repair customers expect competence, respect, and explanations. Hotel customers want a clean and safe room, and want to be treated like guests. Insurance customers want their agents to keep them informed, be on their side, play fair, protect them, and deliver prompt results. These are not the extravagant, inflated, unreasonable expectations that some executives attribute to today's customers.

- *Be reliable.* Perform the promised service dependably and accurately. Hard Rock Cafe's philosophy is: Be careful and don't make a mistake in the first place—but if a mistake does occur, correct it before it reaches the customer.

- *Listen to customers:* Learn from customers the strengths and weaknesses of your company's services. Develop a complete service quality information system. It took them 15 years to learn it, but the downtown Chicago Marriott Hotel discovered that 66 percent of all guest calls to housekeeping were requests for irons and ironing boards. So they put irons and ironing boards in all guest rooms.

- *Listen to employees:* Learning what's on employees' minds is as important to good customer service as doing customer research. Employees often know what reduces service quality, because they see the service delivery system in action on a daily basis. They may even see early signs of a service breakdown before customers are exposed to it.

- *Solve problems:* When a problem arises, some service firms make things worse. The best service providers *encourage* customers to complain, respond quickly and personally, and have a system in place for solving problems.

- *Surprise customers:* Service providers must be reliable. Better yet is to surprise and even delight customers with special courtesy, competence, commitment, and actions. Don't meet customer expectations; exceed them, maybe even dramatically. They will never forget it, and they will tell their friends.

- *Be fair:* This is the essence underlying all customer expectations. Ask yourself: Is it fair to the customer? Does it look fair in his or her eyes? Customers won't return if they don't trust your company to deal with them fairly. A service guarantee sends the fairness message clearly. For example, Hampton Inn offers the night's stay for free to dissatisfied customers; almost nine out of ten guests who invoke the guarantee say that they will return.

Source: L. Berry, A. Parasuraman, and V. Zeithaml, "Improving Service Quality in America: Lessons Learned," *The Executive,* May 1994, pp. 32–45. ●

BUT DOESN'T EXCELLENCE REQUIRE TRADE-OFFS?

Quality

Cost

Historically, most American managers believed that production cost and product quality were "opposites"—that devoting time, effort, and money to improving quality would drive up the cost of production. But in his influential book *Quality Is Free,* Philip Crosby makes a convincing case that high quality improves sales and profits, and that making products right the first time is less costly than continuously correcting problems. Thus, quality more than pays for itself.

The relationship between quality and costs may not be quite that simple. An important study of automobile plants showed that in traditional plants, quality drove up costs. But in less-traditional plants, managed in the modern ways you have learned about in this course, costs were lower and quality was higher.[8]

Speed

Many managers also believe that focusing on speed will cause quality or cost to suffer. Again, the logic is that there is a fixed pie: gains in one thing presumably must be accompanied by losses in another. But, again, we are not necessarily playing a zero-sum game.[9] For example, JIT (Chapter 19) often improves both speed and quality. Faster processes often are simpler, and therefore cheaper and more flexible. Hewlett-Packard believes that doing things fast *forces* you to do them right the first time.[10]

Thus, potentially, the different capabilities are cumulative; compromises and trade-offs are not always necessary. Well-designed changes to improve organizational performance can reinforce one another and a variety of objectives, rather than improve one aspect at the expense of another.

Or, management can focus on improving one thing at a time, such that one change builds on the next in a cumulative improvement. For example, management might lay the groundwork for top quality, then work on speed, and then cost reduction.[11] One outcome is the immediate focus, but the others are maintained rather than forgotten.

Continuous Improvement: A Key to Excellence

Companies striving for world-class excellence must improve constantly. Continuous improvement, a concept introduced in Chapter 19 and made legendary by Toyota Motor Company, is a relentless drive to be better in every way: to find faster, more-efficient, low-cost methods to develop new, high-quality products. When Toyota became as successful as it has been at making low-cost, defect-free cars, it set the quality standard.[12]

For continuous improvement to really take hold, employees must be trained to solve problems. A well-known technique for really understanding problems, deep down, is to verify the evidence that a problem exists and then ask a single question—"Why?"—five times. With this approach, the problem is traced to its origins, and is more fully understood before people try to solve it.[13]

Another well-known method, often used with total quality programs but useful in a variety of contexts, is the Plan, Do, Check, Act cycle.[14] PDCA, also known as the Deming cycle, means implementing over and over again the general problem-solving approach discussed in Chapter 4 and the basic control process described in Chapter 18. Continuous improvement via the PDCA approach is illustrated in Figure 21.1.

FIGURE 21.1

Continuous improvement through the PDCA cycle

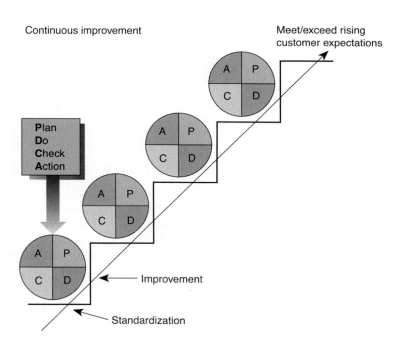

Source: M. Price and E. Chen, "Total Quality Management in a Small, High-Technology Company," *California Management Review,* Spring 1993, p. 99.

In an environment of continuous improvement, everyone makes sure that every process contributes to customer satisfaction by improving quality constantly. With this philosophy, and the appropriate approaches, you *can* have it all: low cost, high quality, flexibility, responsiveness, innovation, and speed.

MANAGING CHANGE

Achieving world-class excellence, total quality, and continuous improvement all imply *changing* the organization for the better. These and all important changes must be carefully *managed.* Successful change does not occur naturally; it results from taking inspired action on both problems and opportunities, motivating people to change, and taking a strategic approach to implementing change.

INSPIRATION FOR CHANGE: PROBLEMS AND OPPORTUNITIES

Change commonly occurs because the organization experiences some difficulty. Most change is driven by some sort of problem: legal difficulties, competitive inroads, obsolete technology, economic downturns. For example, in 1992, GM's car and truck business was on the brink of collapse.[15] What was wrong? Its cars were unappealing, its factories inefficient, and its costs were the highest in the industry. Cost cutting was one key to what now appears to have been the greatest turnaround in American corporate history. CEO Jack Smith closed plants and laid off workers, centralized the purchasing function and reduced materials costs, and simplified the product line. Another key was to abandon the traditional assembly lines, create a team-based production process, and improve dramatically the new-product development process.

Results were terrible at first, but after two years GM had gone from a $10.7 billion loss to a small profit. Two years later, profits were robust. By 1995, GM was well on the way back to global preeminence.

The Performance Gap

A performance gap is the usual precipitator of major change. A **performance gap** is the difference between the organization's actual performance and the performance it should have.[16] A gap typically implies poor performance; for example, sales, profits, stock price, or other financial indicators are down. This situation attracts management's attention, and management introduces changes to try to correct things.

Another, very important form of performance gap can exist. This type of gap can occur when performance is good but someone realizes that it could be better. Thus, the gap is between what is and what *could be.* This is where entrepreneurs seize opportunities and where companies that engage in strategic maneuvering gain a competitive edge. It is where innovators with ideas look for opportunities for application. Whereas many change efforts begin with the negative, it often is more valuable to identify strengths and potential and then develop new modes of operating from that positive perspective.[17]

As an impetus for change, a performance gap does not apply only to the organization as a whole; it also applies to departments, groups, and individuals. If a department or work group is not performing as well as others in the company, or if it sees an opportunity that it can exploit, that unit will be motivated to change. Similarly, an individual receives negative performance feedback or sees a personal opportunity on which to capitalize. Under these circumstances, the person will be more motivated to change than if no such gap existed.

Reactive and Proactive Change

Reactive change occurs when changes in the environment have already affected the firm's performance.[18] In other words, reactive changes are problem-driven. They tend to be incremental, imitative of others, and late in the game. They usually are minor in scope, minor in impact, and clearly indicate being a follower rather than a leader.

Proactive change is initiated by management before a problem has occurred.[19] Proactive changes often come from spotting or creating opportunities. They are often radical, inventive, and earlier than competitors'. They carry a higher risk of failure, but promise far greater rewards when they succeed. Proactive changes are particularly important in fast-changing industries.

Proactive changes are undertaken when there is no obvious and pressing need for change. In other words, the process does not occur from a sense of urgent necessity. Instead, management must *create* the discomfort and the motivation for change.[20] Benchmarking may reveal an inspiring model for improvement toward greatness; or management might conduct a small-scale experiment in-house that inspires the rest of the company to adopt the new idea.

MOTIVATING PEOPLE TO CHANGE

Individuals, teams, and organizations must be *motivated* to change. But if people perceive no performance gap, or if they consider the gap unimportant, they will not have this motivation. In fact, they may *resist* changes that management attempts to introduce.

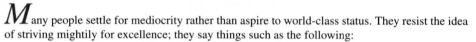

RESISTANCE TO BECOMING WORLD CLASS

*M*any people settle for mediocrity rather than aspire to world-class status. They resist the idea of striving mightily for excellence; they say things such as the following:

- "Those world-class performance numbers are ridiculous! I don't believe them, they are impossible! Maybe in some industries, some companies . . . but ours is unique . . ."

- "Sure, maybe some companies achieve those numbers, but there's no hurry . . . We're doing all right. Sales were up 5 percent this year, costs were down 2 percent. And we've got to keep cutting corners . . ."

- "We can't afford to be world class like those big global companies, we don't have the money or staff . . ."

- "Our workforce prevents us from being world class. You can't find anyone who is willing to work today. Our schools are doing a lousy job. Where's some old-fashioned street smarts, discipline, and work ethic?"

- "Yeah, we all know we have to change things around here. But who's going to tell our senior management? They're isolated in their headquarters, and only seem to care about short-term financial measures that satisfy Wall Street."

- "We don't believe this stuff about global markets and competitors. We don't need to expand internationally. One of our local competitors tried that a few years ago and lost its shirt."

- "It's not a level playing field . . . the others have unfair advantages . . ."

Excuses and rationalizations don't cut it. To survive and prosper today, organizations need to launch an assault on achieving world-class excellence.

Source: T. G. Gunn, *21st Century Manufacturing* (New York: HarperBusiness, 1992). ●

It is important to understand why people often resist change. Figure 21.2 shows the common reasons for resistance. Some reasons are general and arise in most change efforts. Other reasons for resistance relate to the specific nature of a change.

General Reasons for Resistance
Several reasons for resistance arise regardless of the actual content of the change.[21]

▪ **Inertia.** Usually people don't want to disturb the status quo. The old ways of doing things are comfortable and easy, so people don't want to shake things up and try

FIGURE 21.2

Reasons for
resistance to
change

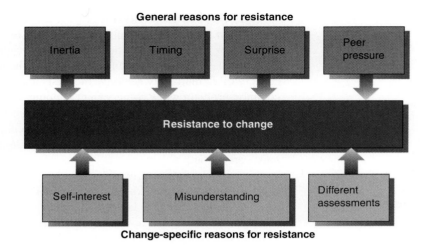

General reasons for resistance

| Inertia | Timing | Surprise | Peer pressure |

Resistance to change

| Self-interest | Misunderstanding | Different assessments |

Change-specific reasons for resistance

something new. For example, it is easier to stay in the same dorm, apartment, or house than to move to another.

▪ **Timing.** People often resist change because of poor timing. Maybe you would like to move to a different place to live, but do you want to move this week? Even if a place were available, you probably couldn't take the time. If managers or employees are unusually busy or under stress, or if relations between management and workers are strained, the timing is wrong for introducing new proposals. Where possible, managers should introduce change when people are receptive.

▪ **Surprise.** One key aspect of timing and receptivity is surprise. If the change is sudden, unexpected, or extreme, resistance may be the initial—almost reflexive—reaction. Suppose your university announced an increase in tuition, effective at the beginning of next term. Resistance would be high. At the very least, you would want to know about this change far enough in advance to give you time to prepare for it.

▪ **Peer pressure.** Sometimes work teams resist new ideas. Even if individual members do not strongly oppose a change suggested by management, the team may band together in opposition. If a group is highly cohesive and has antimanagement norms (recall Chapter 16), peer pressure will cause individuals to resist even reasonable changes.

Change-Specific Reasons for Resistance

Other causes of resistance arise from the specific nature of a proposed change. Change-specific reasons for resistance stem from what people perceive as the *personal consequences* of the change.[22]

▪ **Self-interest.** Most people care less about the organization's best interest than they do about their own best interests. They will resist a change if they think it will cause them to lose something of value.

What could people fear to lose? At worst, their jobs, if management is considering closing down a plant. A merger or reorganization, or technological change, could create the same fear. Despite assurances that no one will be laid off or fired, people might fear a cut in pay or loss of power and status under the new arrangement.

▪ **Misunderstanding.** Even when management proposes a change that will benefit everyone, people may resist because they don't fully understand its purpose. One company met resistance to the idea of introducing flexible working hours, a system in which workers have some say regarding the hours they work. This system can benefit employees, but a false rumor circulated among plant employees that people would have to work evenings, weekends, or whenever their supervisors wanted. The employees' union demanded that management drop the flexible-hours idea. The president was caught completely off guard by this unexpected resistance, and complied with the union's demand.

- **Different assessments.** Employees are exposed to different—and usually less—information than management receives. Even within top management ranks, some executives know more than others do. Such discrepancies cause people to develop different assessments of proposed changes. Some may be aware that the benefits outweigh the costs, while others may see only the costs and not perceive the advantages. This is a common problem when management announces a change, say, in work procedures and doesn't explain to employees why the change is to be implemented. Management expects advantages in terms of increased efficiency, but workers may see the change as another arbitrary, ill-informed management rule that causes headaches for those who must carry it out.

It is important to recognize that employees' assessments can be more accurate than management's; they may know a change won't work even if management doesn't. In this case, resistance to change is beneficial for the organization. Thus, even though management typically considers resistance a challenge to be overcome, it may actually represent an important signal that a proposed change requires further, more open-minded scrutiny.

A General Model for Managing Resistance

Figure 21.3 shows that motivating people to change often requires three basic stages: unfreezing, moving to institute the change, and refreezing.[23]

In the *unfreezing* stage, management realizes that its current practices are no longer appropriate and the company must break out of (unfreeze) its present mold. Unfreezing often results from an assessment of the company's adjustment to its present environment and its readiness for the future. The diagnosis should be thorough and unbiased. If management concludes that the fit between the company and its present or anticipated environment is poor, change is needed.

Particularly in turnaround situations, top management must take steps to unfreeze the old organization culture. People must come to recognize that some of the past ways of thinking, feeling, and doing things are obsolete.[24] Perhaps the most effective way to do this is to communicate to people the negative consequences of the old ways by comparing the organization's performance to its competitors'. However, care must be taken not to arouse people's defensiveness by pinning the blame directly and entirely on them.[25] As discussed in Chapter 17, management can share with employees data about costs, quality, and profits.[26]

Moving to institute the change begins with establishing a vision of where the company is heading. The vision can be realized through structural, cultural, and individual change. Changes in structure may involve moving to the divisional, matrix, or some other appropriate form (discussed in Chapters 10 and 11). Cultural changes (Chapter 11) are institutionalized through effective leadership (Chapters 14 through 17). Individuals will change as new personnel join the company (Chapters 12 and 13) and long-time staff adopt the leader's new vision for the future.

Finally, *refreezing* means strengthening the new behaviors that support the change. Cultural, structural, and strategic change must be diffused and stabilized throughout the company. Refreezing involves implementing control systems that support the change (Chapter 18), applying corrective action when necessary, and reinforcing performance (Chapter 15) that supports the agenda. Management should consistently support and reward all evidence of movement in the right direction.[27]

Figure 21.3

Implementing change

Specific Approaches to Enlist Cooperation

As discussed earlier, management must enlist the cooperation of its people to implement a change. But how can managers get people to cooperate? Specifically, how can they manage their employees' resistance to change?

Most managers underestimate the variety of ways they can influence people during a period of change.[28] Several effective approaches to managing resistance (see Table 21.1) and enlisting cooperation are:

1. **Education and communication.** Management should educate people about upcoming changes before they occur. It should communicate not only the *nature* of the change but its *logic*. This process can include one-on-one discussions, presentations to groups, or reports and memos. When Honeywell changed to a more participative management philosophy, it communicated the new approach through a variety of conferences, training tapes, brochures, and traveling road shows.[29]

2. **Participation and involvement.** It is important to listen to the people who are affected by the change. They should be involved in the change's design and implementation. When feasible, management should use their advice. Often it will be useful, and it may lead to consideration of important issues previously overlooked by management. When George Weyerhaeuser developed a general vision of what he thought the company should be like in 10 years, he asked his managers to develop their own specific visions of how their units would function within the broader picture. The managers met with their units and gained consensus about the changes they envisioned. They carried this process through lower levels and smaller units, right down to the shop floor.[30]

As you learned in Chapter 4, people who are involved in decisions understand them more fully and are more committed to them. People's understanding and commitment are

TABLE 21.1
_____

Methods for dealing with resistance to change

Approach	Commonly Used in Situations	Advantages	Drawbacks
Education and communication	Where there is a lack of information or inaccurate information and analysis.	Once persuaded, people will often help with the implementation of the change.	Can be very time-consuming if lots of people are involved.
Participation and involvement	Where the initiators do not have all the information they need to design the change, and where others have considerable power to resist.	People who participate will be committed to implementing change, and any relevant information they have will be integrated into the change plan.	Can be very time-consuming if participators design an inappropriate change.
Facilitation and support	Where people are resisting because of adjustment problems.	No other approach works as well with adjustment problems.	Can be time-consuming, expensive, and still fail.
Negotiation and agreement	Where someone or some group will clearly lose out in a change, and where that group has considerable power to resist.	Sometimes it is a relatively easy way to avoid major resistance.	Can be too expensive in many cases if it alerts others to negotiate for compliance.
Manipulation and cooptation	Where other tactics will not work, or are too expensive.	It can be a relatively quick and inexpensive solution to resistance problems.	Can lead to future problems if people feel manipulated.
Explicit and implicit coercion	Where speed is essential, and the change initiators possess considerable power.	It is speedy and can overcome any kind of resistance.	Can be risky if it leaves people angry at the initiators.

Source: Reprinted by permission of the *Harvard Business Review*. An exhibit from "Choosing Strategies for Change" by John P. Kotter and Leonard A. Schlesinger (March–April 1979). Copyright © 1979 by th President and Fellows of Harvard College; all rights reserved.

important ingredients in the successful implementation of a change. Participation also provides an excellent opportunity for education and communication.

3. **Facilitation and support.** Management should make the change as easy as possible for employees and be supportive of their efforts. Facilitation involves providing the training and other resources people need to carry out the change and perform their jobs under the new circumstances. This step often includes decentralizing authority and empowering people, that is, giving them the power to make the decisions and changes needed to improve their performance. For example, Weyerhaeuser gave each unit the authority to develop its own compensation system—one that it believed would reinforce the unit's vision and plan.

Offering support involves listening patiently to problems, being understanding if performance drops temporarily or the change is not perfected immediately, and generally being on the employees' side and showing consideration during a difficult period.

4. **Negotiation and rewards.** When necessary, management can offer concrete incentives for cooperation with the change. Perhaps job enrichment is acceptable only with a higher wage rate, or a work rule change is resisted until management agrees to a concession on some other rule (say, regarding taking breaks). Even among higher-level managers, one executive might agree to another's idea for a policy change only in return for support on some other issue of more personal importance. Rewards such as bonuses, wages and salaries, recognition, job assignments, and perks can be examined and perhaps restructured to reinforce the direction of the change.[31]

5. **Manipulation and cooptation.** Sometimes managers use more subtle, covert tactics to implement change. One form of manipulation is cooptation, which involves giving a resisting individual a desirable role in the change process. The leader of a resisting group often is coopted. For example, management might invite a union leader to be a member of an executive committee or ask a key member of an outside organization to join the company's board of directors. As a person becomes involved in the change, he or she may become less resistant to the actions of the coopting group or organization.

6. **Coercion.** Some managers apply punishment or the threat of punishment to those who resist change. With this approach, managers use force to make people comply with their wishes. For example, a boss insists that subordinates cooperate with the change and threatens them with job loss, denial of a promotion, or an unattractive work assignment.

Each approach to overcoming resistance has advantages and drawbacks, and, like many of the other situational or contingency management approaches described in the text, each is useful in different situations. Table 21.1 summarizes the advantages, drawbacks, and appropriate circumstances for these approaches to managing resistance to change. As the table implies, managers should not use just one or two general approaches, regardless of the circumstances. Effective change managers are familiar with the various approaches and know how to apply them according to the situation.

A STRATEGIC APPROACH TO MANAGING CHANGE

We will now integrate these ideas through a general strategy for implementing any kind of organizational change. This summary approach will alert you to a common management mistake: initiating a major change without a carefully constructed, coherent strategy for managing the overall process.[32]

The manager must have a clear understanding of how to manage change effectively. Organizational change is managed effectively when[33]

1. The organization is moved from its current state to some planned future state that will exist after the change.
2. The functioning of the organization in the future state meets expectations; that is, the change works as planned.
3. The transition is accomplished without excessive cost to the organization.
4. The transition is accomplished without excessive cost to individual organizational members.

FIGURE 21.4

Organizational change as a transition state

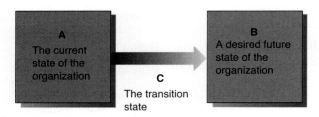

Source: D. A. Nadler, "Managing Organizational Change: An Integrative Approach," *Journal of Applied Behavioral Science* 17 (1981), pp. 191–211.

These standards are a useful framework for planning and implementing change. Next we describe how to implement change to achieve maximum effectiveness.

The Process of Implementing Change

Effective change management requires three steps, which are shown in Figure 21.4.[34] The first step is to *assess the current state* of the organization. Such an analysis identifies the current situation, problems, and the possible causes of those problems. By specifying the problems and the kinds of changes that are needed, this analysis performs the unfreezing function described earlier.[35]

The second step is to *design the future state* of the organization. This process involves determining the idealized, expected state of affairs after the change is implemented. Because confusion is common during a major organizational change, the clearest possible image of the future state must be developed and conveyed to everyone.[36] This image, or vision, will be a target or guideline that clarifies expectations, dispels rumors, and mobilizes people's energies. The portrait of the future also should communicate how the transition will occur, why the change is being implemented, and how people will be affected by the change.

GE offers a good example of the first two steps in the change process.

 WORLD-CLASS CHANGE MANAGEMENT AT GE

*W*hen Jack Welch took over at GE in 1981, the company was characterized by a strong balance sheet, a slow-moving bureaucracy, a nonglobal business, and modest technological expertise. Welch went on to identify GE's basic problems, which could be broken down into "hard" (quantifiable) and "soft" (nonquantifiable) problems.

The hard problems were average earnings growth, high capital expenditures, weak productivity growth, and low operating margins. GE's soft problems included slow decision making, internal conflict and politics, an inward focus (inadequate attention to the external environment), and a lack of innovation.

Welch faced several sources of resistance at GE. Bureaucratic traditions caused habit and inertia. Welch wanted to operate globally, but his managers feared the unknown because they were inexperienced in global operations. Welch was dissatisfied with the slow growth of once-powerful core businesses, and the leaders of those businesses saw their power threatened. And these same managers did not understand—they did not see things from Welch's more objective perspective—the competitive threats they were facing.

Figure 21.5 summaries Welch's vision for GE. As you can see, it entails a strategy, an organizational structure, and HRM practices for each of three key areas: technical, political, and cultural. Welch considered these areas the strands of the strategic rope: woven together, intertwined, they create strength.

Source: N. Tichy, "Revolutionize Your Company," *Fortune,* December 13, 1993, pp. 114–18. ●

FIGURE 21.5

Welch's 1990s
vision for GE

	Strategy	Organizational structure	Human resource management
Technical	• GE's businesses must be No. 1 or No. 2 in their markets. Otherwise, close, fix, or sell. • Aim for high-growth businesses.	• 13 businesses reporting into a central CEO leadership team. • Share best practices. • Boundaryless organization.	• Design pay systems designed to particular businesses. • Make training and development a continuous process.
Political	• Achieve synergy across many businesses—or what Welch calls "integrated diversity."	• No wedding cake hierarchy. • Demand cross-functional teamwork. • Empowerment decision making pushed to lower levels.	• Make rewards more flexible. • Have employee appraisals from below as well as above.
Cultural	• Speed, simplicity, and self-confidence. • Employees should act like entrepreneurs. • Institute "workout," a process for continuous revolution.	• Encourage cultural diversity but common values. • Common vision.	• Human resource systems designed to produce boundarylessness. • Screen employees for values.

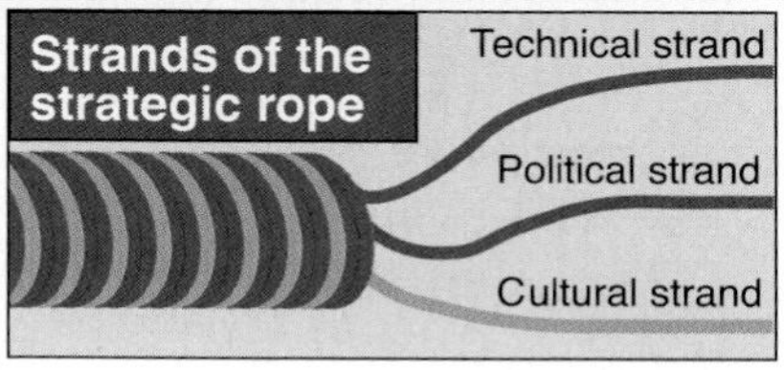

Strands of the strategic rope

Technical strand

Political strand

Cultural strand

Source: N. Tichy, "Revolutionize Your Company," *Fortune,* December 13, 1993, p. 115.

The third step in effective change management is the actual *implementation* of the change, or what Figure 21.4 refers to as managing the *transition state.* Certain organizational arrangements are useful for managing the transition. A *transition manager* can be appointed and given the power and authority to make the change. *Resources* like personnel, money, training, and consultation must be provided. A *transition plan* should be drawn up and should include goals, standards of performance, and responsibilities of key people. Perhaps special task forces, pilot projects, or other temporary structures are created.

Effective change management often requires resolving political difficulties during the change process. First, management should *acquire the support of key power groups.* Early in the process, the important groups or individuals who might oppose the change or whose support is necessary should be identified. Then management should develop and execute strategies to build these people's support or at least neutralize the opposition. One effective strategy is to implement a successful small-scale change to use as a model to follow for future changes or refer to a tangible example of how the change has worked in the past in other divisions, plants, or companies.[37]

Second, management should *use leadership skills to generate enthusiasm for the change.* Many of the leadership techniques described in Chapter 14—sharing visions and goals, acting as role models, expressing confidence in followers, showing consideration—

are useful during the change process. If many organizational leaders throw their energies into the change, the rest of the organization will be inspired to adopt it.

Third, management needs to *build in stability*. In the midst of change, turmoil, and uncertainty, people need anchors to latch onto. This means keeping some things constant and visible, such as key personnel, the organization's mission, office assignments, and announcements about which organizational components will not change. Such anchors will reduce anxiety and help overcome political resistance.

CONNECTING THE DOTS

Many people complain about their companies' "flavor-of-the-month" approach to change. That is, at any given time there is likely to be many different change efforts going on, and many of the changes are just the company's jumping on board the latest bandwagon or fad. The more these change fads come and go, the more cynical people become, and the more difficult it is to get them committed to making the change a success.[38]

A survey at a Harvard Business School conference found that the average attendee's company had five major change efforts going on at once.[39] The most common change programs were the things you have studied in this course: continuous improvement, TQM, time-based competition, and establishment of a learning organization, a team-based organization, a network organization, core competencies, and strategic alliances. The problem is, these efforts usually are simultaneous but not coordinated. The result for the people involved is confusion, frustration, low morale, and low motivation.

Management needs to "connect the dots"—that is, integrate the various efforts into a coherent picture that people can see, understand, and get behind.[40]

How do you connect the dots? You do it by understanding each change program and what its goals are, by identifying similarities among the programs and identifying their differences, and by dropping programs that don't meet priority goals with a clear results orientation. Most important, you do it by communicating to everyone concerned the common themes among the various programs: their common rationales, objectives, and methods. You show them how the various parts fit the strategic big picture, and how the changes will make things better for the company *and* its people. You must communicate these things thoroughly, honestly, and frequently.[41]

SHAPING THE FUTURE

Reactive change means responding to pressure, after the problem has arisen. It also means being a follower. Proactive change means anticipating and preparing for an uncertain future. It also means *creating* a future. On the road to the future, there are drivers, passengers, and road kill. It's best to be a driver.[42]

How do you become a driver? By exercising foresight, learning continuously, pursuing growth, seizing advantage, and creating futures.

EXERCISING FORESIGHT

If you think only about the present, or wallow in the uncertainties of the future, your survival is just a roll of the dice. It is far better to exercise foresight, set an agenda for the future, and pursue it with everything you've got.

So, contemplate the future.

ENVISIONING THE FUTURE

*N*issan's vision for its future is that it must provide the five *A*s: any volume, anytime, anybody, anywhere, anything.

Dow Jones' strategic goal is providing "business and financial news and information however, wherever, and whenever customers want to receive it."

And Motorola asks, "How do you use your Motorola pager?" Answers: "Anytime," "For anything," and "Anywhere I want."

These themes capture the new competitive reality. This reality is also exemplified by the Akihabara section of Tokyo. Akihabara is an eight-square-block retailing district that may be the most advanced consumer electronics shopping mall in the world. Walking through Akihabara, you will see an endless variety of products that are made available with incredible speed, and hear bargains being struck in every language of the world.

Your buying options at Akihabara are staggering. Vendors in tiny stalls sell computer chips by weight, just like fruits and vegetables. You can buy parts to assemble your own computer. You can choose from more than 250 varieties of Walkman, and you can buy ambidextrous refrigerators if you don't like opening yours with the same hand every time.

The place is always jumping. But few businesses actually make money. Only the very hottest new products survive. Because no one knows what customers will demand next, businesses don't know what they will be creating next. You cannot create a long-term strategy if you don't know what new market opportunities will appear.

If Akihabara is a metaphor for the coming business world, you'd better learn how to be flexible, responsive, agile, and quick—and to create market needs as well as fill them. You will have to offer a wider array of new products, in a wider variety of combinations to satisfy unique demands and small market niches, and be ready with newer products once again as your existing lines are made obsolete by competitors.

Innovation

Speed

Sources: J. Pine, B. Victor, and A. Boynton, "Making Mass Customization Work," *Harvard Business Review,* September–October 1993, pp. 108–22; J. Slocum, Jr., M. McGill, and D. Lei, "The New Learning Strategy: Anytime, Anything, Anywhere," *Organizational Dynamics,* Autumn 1994, pp. 33–47. ●

If you and your bosses think you know what you need to do to succeed in the future, you probably need a dose of humility—it is impossible to know the future with certainty. But this does not need to be a reactive, defeatist view. It can be highly proactive, in a subtle but vitally important way. Managers may acknowledge that they don't know exactly what customers will want in the future, and what products they will have to deliver. But they *can* know that they have, or can acquire, the *capabilities* to deliver.[43] Thus, the focus is on identifying and building core competencies, as discussed in Chapter 11, and on improving continuously in the activities that will enable your firm to succeed in the future.

The Akihabara section of Toyko, pictured here, is an eight-square-block retailing district that may be the most advanced shopping mall in the world. *(S. Vidler/SUPERSTOCK)*

LEARNING CONTINUOUSLY

Continuous learning is a vital route to renewable competitive advantage.[44] To learn continuously, your firm (and *you!*) need (1) a clear, strategic goal to learn new capabilities and (2) a real commitment to continuous experimentation.

Which set of capabilities will be most valuable to the company in the future? You can make a practice of adopting individual changes and practices not just to solve an immediate problem, but also to build new skills that open up new opportunities. For example, some companies choose between MRP and JIT systems (Chapter 19). One criterion for making the choice could be, what do we want our people to learn? What do they need to learn? JIT encourages skills in factory-floor problem solving, and fast response, whereas MRP fosters skills in using computers and database management. Identifying your learning needs can help you make important strategic decisions.

Experimentation means trying new things in the spirit of continuous improvement, investing in research and long-term development projects, encouraging risks, and tolerating failures. Companies like J&J, 3M, and Bally Engineering practice self-obsolescence. That is, they try to make their own products obsolete. Why? Because the products will become obsolete sooner or later, and it's better to replace them with their own new products than to have competitors beat them to it. Home Depot will even close a thriving store and open two smaller ones, in an effort to keep improving customers' shopping experiences.[45]

Similarly, Sony and Mitsubishi use "systematic abandonment" of their products.[46] When they introduce a new product, they establish a "sunset date" at which they will drop the product. Thus, they create a deadline for introducing a future product that will replace the brand new product, and begin those development efforts immediately. Their goal is to create three new products for every one they phase out: an incrementally improved product, a new product spin-off, and an entirely new innovation.

PURSUING GROWTH

Cutting costs can be vitally important, but can only get you so far. You must also grow. "You can't save your way to prosperity. That alone won't get you there," says Wayne Calloway, CEO of PepsiCo.[47]

In other words, you can raise profits by shrinking expenses (the denominator in financial ratios), and also by increasing revenues (the numerator).[48] Cutting costs is relatively easy. Higher revenues are more difficult to achieve than cutting costs. Unfortunately, the numerator has not received nearly the emphasis it deserves. States an influential management expert, "We've produced a generation of denominator managers in the U.S."[49]

Downsizing, reengineering, and other approaches to cost cutting sooner or later will reach their limits. You must also, then, be able to go for growth by increasing revenues. This requires focusing on things like technology, investment, product development, and creating new markets.

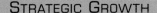

STRATEGIC GROWTH

- Union Carbide has a low-cost strategy, but it achieves low cost *and growth* through its competitive advantage in technology. Two decades ago it developed a low-cost process for making polyethylene, the most widely used basic plastic. And *it has constantly improved the process ever since* in order to increase its lead.

- Bausch & Lomb sold its weak businesses and used the money to modernize technology in its remaining businesses. It also scoured the globe asking consumers and health care professionals for expansion ideas. Its contact lenses and solutions grew into a general eye care business, and the company entered a number of other health-related growth businesses as well. Bausch & Lomb is now *entering emerging markets;* it *created* and dominates the Chinese contact lens market, and is expanding into India and Poland.

- CEO Harry Merlo of Louisiana-Pacific has devised new products to *substitute for old standards,* and is satisfying new customers and markets. He developed waferwood and took business away from plywood, and he developed a new board that is replacing Sheetrock because it is more soundproof, holds nails better, breaks less easily, and is produced more efficiently.

- Dell Computer and Price/Costco thrive via a strategy of *high quality bought easily and inexpensively.* Price/Costco is a chain of warehouse club stores. Its competitors offer some 50,000 items, whereas Price/Costco offers only 3,500 items. But it succeeds by *operational excellence* that customers love because it saves them hassle *and* money *and* offers an enjoyable shopping experience. Price/Costco rigorously evaluates and chooses and then sells only the best brand in each product category. This allows it to buy large quantities and negotiate better prices than competitors. Customers enjoy lower prices, and they don't have to spend time making decisions about which brand of coffee or appliance to buy. New items, a value-of-the-week atmosphere, and the smell of baking bread and pastries add to the pleasure of shopping.

- PepsiCo's growth is due in large part to its corporate culture. CEO Wayne Calloway wants managers to *look out on the competitive horizon* rather than on the trivial, the bureaucratic, and traditional markets. He believes growth keeps his people energized, vibrant, and ready for the future. He encourages risk taking, and wants his managers to *completely reconceive their businesses.* Calloway states, "It's that whole mindset that says, 'I don't have to keep on with what I'm doing. I can change the game.'" PepsiCo's sales have grown at an annual compound rate of 17 percent since 1984.

Sources: M. Magnet, "Let's Go for Growth," *Fortune,* March 7, 1994, pp. 60–72; M. Treacy and F. Wiersema, "How Market Leaders Keep Their Edge," *Fortune,* February 6, 1995, pp. 88–98. ●

The *Fortune* article from which the above examples are taken concludes, "Without doubt, it's easier to get a dollar of profit growth by cutting costs than by raising revenues. But investors, the final arbiters of value, well know that those two dollars are very unlike in terms of the future they presage."[50] In other words, cost cutting is not as essential to long-term great success as revenue growth and a proactive eye to the future.

SEIZING ADVANTAGE

Perhaps the ultimate form of proactive change is to create new markets or transform industries.[51] Competing for the future is creating and dominating emerging opportunities. Consider:

Instead of . . .	Why not . . . ?
- fitting the firm to the environment - preserving old advantages - locking in old markets - investing in fixed assets	- change the environment to fit the firm - create new advantages - create new markets - invest in evolving/emerging opportunities

Innovation

You need to create advantages. The challenge is not to maintain your position in the current competitive arena, but to create new competitive arenas, transform your industry, and imagine a future that others don't see. Creating advantage is better than playing catch-up through downsizing and reengineering. At best, such restructuring buys time; it cannot get you out ahead of the pack and buy world-class excellence.[52]

So, which should you and your firm do?

- Take the path of greatest familiarity, or the path of greatest opportunity, wherever that may lead?

- Be only a good benchmarker, or a pathbreaker?

Price/Costco is a chain of warehouse club stores that sells only the best brand in each product category. *(David Perry, Price/Costco)*

- Focus just on product time to market, or on time to global preeminence?
- Be a product leader, or also a core competence leader?
- Place priority on short-term financial returns, or on making a real, long-term impact?
- Look to the past, or live for the future?
- Do only what seems doable, or what is difficult and worthwhile?
- Change what is, or create what isn't?
- Solve problems, or create entirely new opportunities?

CREATING THE FUTURE

To get ahead of the pack, create the future.

CREATING FUTURES

- Apple Computer in the 1970s envisioned a world with "a computer for every man, woman, and child." And a few years later, with the help of Xerox, Apple engineers turned traditional thinking on its head by deciding to teach computers about people rather than forcing people to adapt to computers. This led to the Lisa, and then the Macintosh.

- Motorola sees a world in which telephone numbers will be assigned not to places but to people; small hand held devices allow communication between people no matter where they may be; and people send video images and data, not just voice signals. To realize this world, Motorola knows it must strengthen its competencies in digital compression, flat screen displays, and battery technology.

- General Magic, a consortium including Apple, Motorola, Philips, AT&T, and others, envisions a world in which people use hand held devices to visit a "virtual downtown" of travel agents, banks, libraries, and so on. "Information agents" in cyberspace make reservations, review financial data, or retrieve magazine articles. Has this world yet become a reality? Maybe not, but it never will, without the vision to create it. But vision and foresight, of course, must also be followed by creation.

- Dreamworks SKG is the new company created by Steven Spielberg, Jeffrey Katzenberg, and David Geffen. Spielberg directed *ET* and *Jurassic Park,* among other great films. Katzenberg was responsible for the great recent animated films from the Disney Co. Geffen is the music executive and producer associated with Nirvana, Guns N' Roses, the Eagles, Tom Cruise movies,

Fans and entertainment industry executives eagerly await the results of the partnership of the men pictured here—Steven Spielberg, Jeffrey Katzenberg, and David Geffen. These three entertainment giants have joined forces to create Dreamworks SKG, the "prototype plugged-in multimedia company of the new millennium."
(AP/Wide World Photos)

and *Cats.* Now they have joined forces to create what *Time* magazine calls the "prototype plugged-in multimedia company of the new millennium." Fans and industry executives the world over are anxious to see what kind of a future these leaders in their fields will create as a team.

How about a record store for the future? Envision this: At home, you call up on a screen any of thousands of pieces of music. You call up critical reviews of your selection, and listen to a sample. If you like it, you download it onto a digital recording device and get the bill later. Or, a "home juke box" allows you to listen for an evening to customized music, and you pay just for listening. What will happen to today's record stores? Would you rather own a traditional record store, or create the "store" of the future?

Sources: G. Hamel and C. K. Prahalad, *Competing for the Future* (Boston: Harvard Business School Press, 1994); R. Corliss, "Hey, Let's Put On a Show!" *Time,* March 27, 1995, pp. 54–60. ●

FIGURE 21.6

Vast opportunity

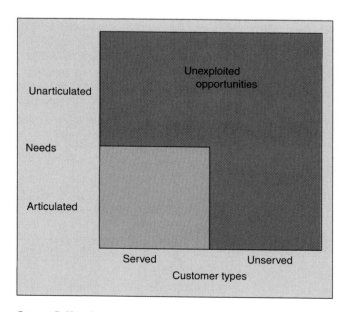

Source: G. Hamel and C. K. Prahalad, *Competing for the Future* (Boston: Harvard Business School Press, 1994).

Figure 21.6 illustrates the vast opportunity to create new markets. Articulated needs are those that customers acknowledge and try to satisfy. Unarticulated needs are those which customers have not yet experienced. Served customers are those to whom your company is now selling, and unserved customers are untapped markets.

Business-as-usual concentrates on the lower-left quadrant. The leaders who recreate the game are constantly trying to create new opportunities in the other three quadrants.[53]

Remember: industry leadership is not sustained automatically. It must be continually renewed and recreated.

KEY TERMS

performance gap, p. 547
proactive change, p. 547

reactive change, p. 547

SUMMARY OF LEARNING OBJECTIVES

Now that you have studied Chapter 21, you should know:

What it takes to be world class.

You *need* to strive for world-class excellence, which means becoming one of the very best in the world at what you do. To accomplish this, management must understand completely what goes on in the company and what customers want. The "bottom-line" concepts like quality, cost, and speed are all multidimensional, and it is important to strive for excellence on all dimensions. It helps to understand that trade-offs are not always necessary, and that continuous improvement is an essential philosophy and business practice.

How to manage change effectively.

Effective change management requires diagnosing the current state, designing the future state, and implementing the change. The entire process should involve unfreezing, moving, and refreezing stages. Implementing the change includes formulating a clear image of the desired future state and managing people's resistance to change.

People resist change for a variety of reasons, including inertia, poor timing, surprise, peer pressure, self-interest, misunderstanding, and different information about (and assessments of) the change. Many techniques, including education and communication, participation and involvement, facilitation and support, negotiation and rewards, manipulation and cooptation, and coercion, help implement change by managing people's resistance.

How to best prepare for the future.

Preparing for an uncertain future requires a proactive approach. Powerful proactive approaches include exercising foresight, being flexible, learning continuously, pursuing growth, implementing development projects, creating advantages, and creating the future. The process is never-ending.

DISCUSSION QUESTIONS

1. Review the quotes on page 548, in "Resistance to Becoming World Class." Why do some people resist the goal of becoming world class? What lies behind the quotes? How can this resistance be overcome?
2. Generate specific examples of the various elements of world-class service quality. Also generate examples of poor quality, for each of the elements. Why and how do some companies inspire world-class service, while others fail?
3. How can you make the concept of continuous improvement useful to you in your personal life and your career?
4. Generate and discuss examples of problems and opportunities that have inspired change, both in businesses and in you, personally.
5. Choose some specific types of changes you would like to see happen in groups or organizations with which you are

familiar. Imagine that you were to try to bring about these changes. What sources of resistance should you anticipate? How would you manage the resistance?
6. How would you "exercise foresight" with regard to your personal life and career?
7. Develop a specific plan for becoming a "continuous learner."
8. Consider a business with which you are familiar and discuss some ideas for how it should pursue a growth strategy. What are some pros and cons to your ideas? How might the best ideas be implemented?
9. In your own words, what does the idea of "creating the future" mean to you? How can you put this concept to good use? Again, generate some specific ideas that you can really use.

CONCLUDING CASE

BILL GATES AND MICROSOFT

In 1969, in eighth grade, Bill Gates and a friend built a clunky computer that played tic-tac-toe. His friend, Paul Allen, recalls Gates saying at the time, "Don't you think that some day everybody will have one of these things? And if they did, couldn't you deliver magazines and newspapers and stuff through them? I mean, I wonder if you could make money doing something like that?"

In 1996 Bill Gates was the wealthiest person in the United States. As founder and chairman of Microsoft, he dominated the PC industry.

Up to now, Gates has just been warming up. He wants much more. Despite its amazing success, and virtual monopoly power in the industry, Microsoft must transform itself.

Most people see the information highway as an entertainment vehicle. Gates sees that, too. But he also believes that most of the real traffic will be business. The highway will conduct on-line commerce—businesspeople will do real work on it, and spend real money on it. Gates envisions a giant digital shopping mall, as well as a vast arena for business-to-business transactions.

Gates is not just dreaming, he is taking action. He wants Microsoft code to be a part of everything on the network: consumer services, stock trading, credit card verification, and managing corporate databases, factories, and inventories. "This new electronic world of the information highway will generate a higher volume of transactions than anything has to date, and we're proposing that Windows be at the center, servicing all those transactions," says Gates.

As you can tell, Gates is not complacent. In fact, he is never satisfied. According to a good friend, "To Bill, life is school.

■

Bill Gates, Microsoft founder and chairman is the wealthiest person in the United States. Many wonder whether Microsoft can keep up with Gates' ambition. *(Reuters/Bettmann)*

There's always something more to learn." And his competitors are scared.

Many regard Gates as ruthless, rapacious, a robber baron. Some believe the industry is more like a controlled economy than a free market, with Microsoft attaining monopoly power. In fact, some competitors seem to think their best weapon against Microsoft is the Department of Justice.

Some wonder whether Microsoft can keep pace technologically with Gates' ambition. The company has a record of delivering products, behind schedule, that don't live up to expectations. Microsoft is, however, spending $600 million a year on R&D. Gates' attitude is: "I'm sure we'll have failures . . . But we can afford to make a few mistakes now, and we can't afford *not* to try . . . Everything's about big horizons at Microsoft now. But hey, we *can* tackle big horizons. We're *expected* to tackle big horizons. We *love* big horizons."

QUESTIONS

1. How would you describe Bill Gates and his actions in terms of the ideas in this chapter?

2. What obstacles do you see in Bill Gates' path?

3. Do you have to be a genius, or obsessed, to think like Bill Gates?

4. What are the implications of Gates' vision for you as a businessperson?

5. What ethical responsibilities does Bill Gates have as he tries to realize his vision?

Sources: B. Schlender, "What Bill Gates Really Wants," *Fortune,* January 16, 1995, pp. 34–63; B. Schendler, "What He Doesn't Want," *Fortune,* January 16, 1995, p. 40; B. Schendler and D. Kirkpatrick, "The Valley vs. Microsoft," *Fortune,* March 20, 1995, pp. 84–90.

VIDEO CASE

MANAGING ORGANIZATIONAL CHANGE AT ABTCO

Most modern observers of economic and social trends agree that the global economy has been experiencing an accelerating pace of change. New technologies, new competitive pressures, and new organizational structures have created an environment in which organizations are also changing rapidly. But change is disconcerting for most people, and it's even more disconcerting for employees when entire organizations are faced with change. There are five primary reasons for employee resistance to change: self-interest, habit, fear, peer pressure, and bureaucratic inertia. Fortunately, resistance to change can be overcome by using various techniques for managing change, such as employee empowerment, team building, and gainsharing. These techniques are all designed to give employees a stake in the outcomes of change.

Managing change requires that managers have a sense of the depth of the intervention they are making. Depth of intervention is defined as the degree of change that the intervention is intended to bring about. Team building and empowerment are examples of moderate depth intervention. The greater the depth of the intervention, the greater the amount of resistance.

The culture and structure of a company significantly affect the kinds of changes that can occur. To reshape the internal culture of a company, managers can adjust such elements as the internal reward system, educational and training opportunities, or the hiring and socialization processes. Through training and development, managers can encourage more interaction among employees, which helps them become more attuned to the culture and helps them feel a part of the change process. These important techniques for managing organizational change were effectively applied at Abitibi-Price Building Products Company.

Michigan-based Abitibi-Price, one of the largest building products and newsprint businesses in North America, found itself in serious financial trouble in the early 1990s. Sales were weak, especially in the newsprint division, and annual earnings had declined steadily from a high of $188.2 million in 1987 to a loss of $75.9 million in 1990. Employees were anxious over reports of weak sales and of the bleak outlook in their industry. Their company was for sale, and there were concerns about who the new employer would be, or whether anyone would buy the company to keep it afloat. The survival of their company was very much on the minds of the workers.

At the time Abitibi-Price was experiencing its problems, George Brophy, CEO of a Wisconsin-based building-products firm, was experiencing his own. He had been diagnosed with stomach cancer, and faced a struggle for his personal survival. Brophy successfully battled his cancer, and upon doing so sought a new challenge. He left his company in Wisconsin and joined forces with Kohlberg & Company, a leading merchant banking firm, to buy Abitibi-Price. This buyout rescued the company from certain doom.

Brophy and his partners instituted swift changes at the building products company. The first order of business was to put together a new management team. Drawing on the contacts he had made in his 27 years in the building-products industry, Brophy assembled a very experienced management team. Selecting a name for the new company was Brophy's next challenge. ABTCO (pronounced A-B-T-co) was selected because of its similarity to the well-known Abitibi. Stationery, signage, packaging, and advertising all had to be changed. But, more importantly, a new image had to be established.

When the new management team took over, ABTCO's product line included engineered wood for paneling and siding, and also plastic products for molding, architectural trim, and shutters. The new management team noted that, over the previous five years, the price of lumber had increased by over 20 percent for new home buyers. Therefore, the team decided to shift the company's focus to its plastic, simulated wood products. ABTCO's simulated wood products would enable builders to save $4,000 to $8,000 on an average home, while remodelers could save up to $2,000 on an average bathroom. Over the next two to three years ABTCO anticipated that 40 percent of its sales would be for new construction, which they expected to increase at about 10 percent per year. The rest of the business would come from repair and remodeling.

ABTCO's new management team was pleasantly surprised to discover little employee resistance to its change initiatives. This lack of resistance was primarily due to employee participation and empowerment's being a major part of the company's change process. According to Vice President of Marketing William J. Adams, "Our management style was one where a lower-level employee could pick up the telephone and call the vice president of his division. We interfaced with each other on a regular basis. We have teams that worked together on different projects just because we all happened to be involved. In the past, we had walls where marketing was over here, and manufacturing was over there, and the two were constantly doing battle. That never gets results, it only causes friction."

Under the change initiatives, managers began showing a new level of confidence in employees, giving them more discretion and flexibility in the workplace. This, in turn, gave managers the opportunity to focus more on customer needs and service, and increase the company's emphasis on quality. Top managers began meeting with customers, and customer response was overwhelmingly positive. CEO Brophy said, "It demonstrates that we are interested in the customer. Every top executive in this company has to visit at least 15 of our top customers each year."

Changes were also evident on the shop floor, both in terms of process and quality improvements. James P. Kinzler, operations manager, noting the improvement in the process of bringing new products to market, said, "What we've seen is we've been able to get new products to market very rapidly under the new ownership. We've been empowered at the plant level to make decisions here and keep things moving in the right direction." Tim Keeney, quality development manager, said, "I think the new ownership has taken a look at new markets. In the past we were tied to a do-ityourselfer or home-center type market. The new owners have helped expand that to where we are competing directly with wood, which is something we hadn't done before. The volumes with the wood market are much higher than what we had been restricted to previously so the possibility for growth coupled with the willingness to take some risks is a big change."

ABTCO's turnaround has been successful. Revenues are expected to increase 15 percent annually, and the company's stock price doubled in the first eight months of the new management's regime. ABTCO and CEO Brophy both came back from near disaster by managing and accepting change. Brophy summarized the change process at ABTCO by stating, "Everybody chipped in here. We had people giving concessions, we had people who were doing new jobs, we had new management that we brought in. It was a classic team effort."

CRITICAL THINKING QUESTIONS

1. ABTCO's new management team broke through resistance to change through employee participation and empowerment. Explain why this approach is effective in managing change.

2. Most of the measures of the effectiveness of the change intervention reported in this video concern sales, profits, and revenue projections. What are some other measures managers might use to determine the effectiveness of a major change initiative? Can you think of some nonquantitative measures?

3. Resistance to change is a very common phenomenon that managers experience. Discuss the five reasons for resisting change cited in the video. Do you think there are some other reasons people might resist change? How can these be overcome?

EXPERIENTIAL EXERCISES

21.1 A Force-Field Analysis

Objective

To introduce you to force-field analysis of organizations and challenges facing them.

Instructions

Read about force-field analysis below, and come up with an organizational problem of your own to analyze.

FORCE-FIELD ANALYSIS

A force-field analysis is one way to assess what is happening in an organization. This concept reflects the forces, driving and restraining, at work at a particular time. It helps to assess organizational strengths and to select forces to add or remove in order to create change. The theory of change suggested by Kurt Lewin, who developed the force-field analysis, is that while driving forces may be more easily affected, shifting them could increase opposition (tension and/or conflict) within the organization and add restraining forces. Therefore, it may be more effective to remove restraining forces to create change.

The use of the force-field analysis will demonstrate the range of forces pressing on an organization at a particular time. This analysis can increase the organization's optimism that it is possible to strategize and plan for change.

Example—Trying to increase student participation in student government.

Driving Forces	Restraining Forces
More money allocated for student government activities	High emphasis on grades—a need to study more.
Better publicity and public relations programs for student government.	Other activities—cultural, social, sports—divert interest.
Student government representatives go to classes and explain positive effects of student decisions.	Not much public relations work in the past.
Special career programs offered for student government participants.	Students do not see student government as effective or helping them get a job.

Present Balance Point

FORCE-FIELD ANALYSIS WORKSHEET

1. (10–15 min.) Complete the Problem Analysis section and fill in the model.
2. (20 min.) In groups of 3–4, discuss the driving and restraining forces in each person's problem.
3. (10 min.) Class discussion
   a. Why is it useful to break a problem situation up into driving and restraining forces?
   b. Would the model be used any differently whether applied to an individual or organizational problem?

Problem Analysis

1. Describe the problem in a few words.

_____

_____

_____

_____

_____

_____

_____

_____

2. A list of forces *driving* toward change would include:

    a. _____

    b. _____

    c. _____

    d. _____

    e. _____

    f. _____

3. A list of forces *restraining* change would include:

    a. _____

    b. _____

    c. _____

    d. _____

    e. _____

    f. _____

4. Put the driving and restraining forces of the problem on the force-field analysis below, according to their degree of impact on change.

Driving Forces	**Restraining Forces**
⟶	⟵
Low extreme—try to avoid	High

**Present Balance
Point**

Source: Dorothy Hai, "Force-Field Analysis" in *Organizational Behavior: Experiences and Cases* (St. Paul, Minn.: West, 1986), pp. 259–61. Reprinted by permission. Copyright © 1986 by West Publishing Company. All rights reserved.

21.2   Sears vs. Kmart

Objective

To analyze operations at two well-known retail firms, with a view to making recommendations for changes that will improve profitability, sales, and customer service.

Instructions

Your group, Fastalk Consultants, is known as the shrewdest, most insightful, and most overpaid management consulting firm in the country. You have been hired by the president of Sears to make recommendations for improving the motivation and performance of personnel in their operations. Let us assume that the key job activity in store operations is dealing with customers.

Recently, the president of Sears has come to suspect that his company's competitor, Kmart, is making heavy inroads into Sears' market. He has also hired a market research firm to investigate and compare the relative merits of products and prices in the two establishments, and has asked the market research firm to assess the advertising campaigns of the two organizations. Hence, you will not need to be concerned with marketing issues, except as they may have an impact on employee behavior. The president wants you to look into the organization of the two stores to determine the strengths and weaknesses of each.

The president has established an unusual contract with you. He wants you to make your recommendations based upon your observations *as a customer.* He does not want you to do a complete diagnosis with interviews, surveys, or behind-the-scenes observations. He wants your report in two parts.

SEARS VERSUS KMART WORKSHEET

1. Given his organization's goals of profitability, sales volume, and fast and courteous service, he wants an analysis that will compare and contrast Sears and Kmart in terms of the following concepts:

Organizational Goals

Conflict?_____

Clarity?_____

Environment

Stable/Changing? _____

Simple/Complex?_____

Certain/Uncertain?_____

Size

Large? _____

Medium?_____

Small? _____

Personnel

Knowledgeable?_____

Well Trained?_____

Jobs

Variety?_____

Wholeness?_____

Interaction? _____

Freedom? _____

Time of Work?

Location of Work? _____

Horizontal Division of Labor

Formalized Policies?_____

Departmentalization? _____

Standardization of Rules? _____

Vertical Division of Labor

Number of Levels? _____

Span of Control? _____

Centralization? _____

Communication?

Direction? _____

Openness? _____

Leadership Style

Task Oriented? _____

People Oriented? _____

Employee Motivation

Type? _____

Intrinsic/Extrinsic? _____

Rewards? _____

Support? _____

Coordination? _____

Decision Making? _____

How do Sears and Kmart differ in these aspects? Which company has the best approach?

_____

_____

2. Given the corporate goals listed under part 1, what specific changes might Sears' management make in the following areas to achieve these goals (profitability, sales volume, fast and courteous service)?

- Job design and work flow

  _____

  _____

- Organization structure (at the individual store level)

  _____

  _____

- Employee incentives

  _____

  _____

- Leadership

  _____

  _____

- Employee selection

  _____

  _____

3. Having completed your contract with the president of Sears, prepare a report for presentation to class. This should include specific recommendations you have considered in part 2 above.

Source: Excerpted from Lawrence R. Jauch, Arthur G. Bedeian, Sally A. Coltrin, and William F. Glueck, *The Managerial Experience: Cases, Exercises, and Readings,* 4th ed. Copyright © 1986 by The Dryden Press. Reprinted by permission of the publisher.

XEROX CORPORATION LOOKS TO THE FUTURE AND SEES ONLY QUALITY

Company Background

The organization now known as Xerox Corporation was incorporated on April 18, 1906, under the name Haloid Company. In 1958, the name was changed to Haloid Xerox Incorporated, and the present name was selected three years later.

Xerox is a multinational corporation divided into four segments. Document processing is the primary activity, but Xerox also provides insurance, third-party financing, and investment banking services. Xerox Corporation dominates the Western Hemisphere, while Rank Xerox, Ltd., operates and distributes in Europe, Africa, and most of Asia. Fuji Xerox, launched in 1962, covers the Pacific nations.

Originally, Xerox dominated the market for document processing. But by 1970, the Japanese were rapidly overtaking the industry with lower-cost products. Xerox was not worried: low cost meant low quality. All of American industry in the 1970s was reacting similarly to world competition—so assured were they of their superior quality and technology. They imagined they were untouchable.

American products were considered luxury, state of the art, and superior in quality to any foreign competitor's. The Japanese in particular posed no threat, because their products were seen as cheap, unreliable, and even laughable in quality.

After World War II, as Japan struggled to rise from the ashes, the label "Made in Japan" was a joke in the United States. But, with the help of Dr. William Edwards Deming (an American, ironically), Japan's production philosophies and quality turned around. By the 1970s, Japan was catching up. Costs were still low, but the product no longer was inconsequential in quality.

In 1970, Xerox all but monopolized the almost $2 billion copier industry. By 1977, although the industry market had quadrupled, Japanese market share had dramatically increased, IBM made a significant impact, and Xerox's share was drastically reduced. In 1974, the Japanese introduced the cheap and efficient plain paper copiers, while Xerox continued using coated paper. From 1975 to 1978, Japanese firms, such as Ricoh, Canon, and Konishiroku (not including Fuji Xerox), gained 25 percent of the world market for slow copiers.

Not only were competitors producing faster but the toner (liquid ink) that the Japanese were using was less expensive than Xerox's dry powder, and the parts used were less complex, mass produced, more reliable, and easier to fix. In addition, aggressive advertising and pricing by the Japanese allowed them to sell, rather than lease, their copiers, which released tied-up capital. Xerox was being outproduced and underpriced.

It was in 1979 that Xerox finally rallied and began to make the changes necessary for survival. Although Xerox stood at 36 in the Fortune 500 listings early in 1979, such managers as then-chairman and CEO C. Peter McColough had the foresight to see that they had to do better than simply relax to stay ahead of competitors.[1]

David Kearns, elected president and CEO in 1982, took the risk, bent the rules, and used creativity to make the necessary changes at Xerox. Kearns's total quality strategy gave Xerox employees the tools they needed to compete in the global market.

Xerox looks to Quality Improvement

When CEO David Kearns decided that Xerox was ready for significant changes, the corporate attitude concerning quality was the first thing to be scrutinized. As he had learned, "the better the quality, the lower the overall costs." This massive cultural change would be accomplished through extensive training. In 1983, Xerox implemented a "Quality through Leadership" program that had three objectives:

To improve profits as reflected in higher return on assets.

To improve customer satisfaction.

To improve market share.

Kearns at first believed all three of these goals to be equally important, and he did not want one to overshadow the others. Soon, however, conflicts became unavoidable. To increase the return on assets, employees would try to cut costs. These actions sometimes would be at the expense of customer satisfaction and, hence, market share would decline. At this time it was necessary to prioritize these goals: customer satisfaction became No. 1.

The "QTL" program cost an estimated $125 million and 4 million man-hours of work. It produced a 40 percent increase in customer satisfaction and a 60 percent decrease in complaints. It involved every level of the company from top to bottom. The orientation phase of the program took six months to complete. It took four years of training to reach the entire organization with the QTL message. Each supervisor learned from his supervisor, then trained and inspected his direct reports. Managers became coaches and a team approach was adopted.

After having promoted the "Leadership through Quality" campaign, employees came to the conclusion however, that promotions were not always based on criteria related to quality. The "Role Model Manager" concept was then created.[2] New criteria were developed to guide promotion decisions, based on leadership characteristics fundamental to the total quality concept.

By 1989, 75 percent of Xerox workers had participated in the drive for perfect quality, on more than 7,000 quality improvement teams. Spending for training was increased to 2.5 to 3.0 percent of annual revenues.[3]

TQC became the buzzword at Xerox—total quality control. This "has nothing to do with checking quality as your products roll off the assembly line," said Kearns. "It is empowering employees to take responsibility for quality."[4] Allowing the responsibility to be shifted to lower levels was of prime importance in reducing costs, especially for the largest supplier of cut-sheet paper in the world. In 1989, Xerox produced 600,000 tons of paper.

To attain quality in every area, role models were chosen: L.L. Bean for distribution, American Express for collection, and

American Hospital Supply Corporation on automated inventory control. These companies were selected as the most outstanding in these respective areas. Xerox investigated how these companies achieved their success and established goals for its employees as well as methods for achieving them. This process is known as competitive benchmarking, which is "the continuous process of measuring products, services, and practices against the company's toughest competitors or those companies renowned as industry leaders."[5] Benchmarking is the means by which practices required to achieve new goals are discovered. It forces continual focus on the environment. Xerox was one of the earliest U.S. proponents of benchmarking and institutionalized the practice in its organization.

Finally, Kearns realized that quality begins with suppliers. It is important to include suppliers in the quality program, and it is difficult to monitor 5,000 suppliers, so Xerox cut its base of vendors to 300 to gain more control over the quality of inputs and to reduce costs.

Quality Costs

Three different types of costs are involved in product production, and there are trade-offs within these types as methods vary. The goal of management is to reduce total costs, and it is most effective to do this by improving quality from the start.

1. *Prevention costs.* When defect-free products are demanded, prevention costs escalate. Each worker must be certain that each task is done perfectly the first time. The cost of this quality and perfection is prevention cost.
2. *Appraisal costs.* As the number of defects approaches zero, there becomes no necessity to inspect. The cost of inspectors and other ways of detecting defects drops to nothing.
3. *Internal and external failure costs.* Internal failure costs are experienced when defects are noted before shipping. External costs occur when flaws are not detected until after shipping. Both are reduced to zero when perfect quality is attained.

As the quality improves, prevention costs escalate, but the decline in appraisal costs and internal and external failure costs more than offset this increased expense. It is much cheaper to do it right the first time. As Dr. Deming had told the Japanese in 1946, and later told David Kearns, the closer a company comes to producing with zero defects the less money is necessary for quality control.

Production techniques were examined to determine ways to eliminate defects from the beginning, with the focus on producing products with no defects, as opposed to the earlier focus of simply catching all of the products below certain standards as they came off the assembly line. Suppliers were included in this drive. Xerox cut its supplier base to have more control over supply quality, and it became more demanding in terms of specifications.

The focus on producing no defects at each step in the production process reduces costs considerably. The cost to repair a mistake, or a defect, increases geometrically as the defective product moves away from the point of defect in the assembly or production process. For example, it may take only a few seconds of time and a few cents to correct a mistake while a product is in the production process. Once the defective product leaves the plant and gets into the hands of the final consumer, it may cost weeks of time and thousands of dollars to correct the same mistake.

If production operations are of perfect quality, there is no need for quality control, recalls, rejections, or repairs on machines necessitated by production faults. It is, therefore, very cost effective to use TQM as a philosophy for how to do business.

Through this focus on costs, manufacturing costs were reduced by more than 20 percent (despite inflation), the time needed to bring a new product to market was reduced by 60 percent, and quality improved. These improvements were possible without any factories being closed or any of the manufacturing being moved offshore.[6]

Hard Work Is Rewarded

The changes at Xerox implemented by Kearns were far-reaching. They included reorganizing the research and development staff and the marketing force, with the objective of viewing new products as systems. McColough was the first to describe Xerox as an information company, as opposed to a copier company. Xerox was on of the first companies to conclude that the "Industrial Age" is over and the "Information Age" has begun.

With this definition, "myopic marketing" was avoided, and Xerox began to develop its electronic "Office of the Future," with an office communications network and a new word processing system. The Ethernet network was similar to IBM's System Network architecture in that it connected many offices that were in one building, or in a group of buildings, but unlike IBM, Xerox's system did not need a mainframe. Working with Digital Equipment Corporation, a leader in the field, Xerox soon installed this high technology in the White House and Congress.

Although Xerox was still big in the upper end of the industry, management began to concentrate more on the lower end. Steps were taken to begin marketing in China and India, two of the biggest untapped plain paper copier markets. By working closely with Fuji Xerox, Xerox Corporation was able to learn more efficient and less costly ways of producing a more reliable product.[7]

By 1988, Xerox's management decided to undertake an extensive strategic review. The results of this endeavor led to savings of $60 million in the first year,[8] and winning the Malcolm Baldrige National Quality Award in 1989.

A decade after the implementation of these changes, the results are astounding. Customer satisfaction, the return on assets ratio, and market share are steadily rising. It took a while for the turnaround to take place—results were not immediate. Most of the key decisions were made in 1979, yet the upward swing did not become apparent until five years later. This was due partially to the sharp recession in the early 80s—the economy was at its worst in 1984.

The rise in customer satisfaction was due primarily to the increased involvement of employees, who now are directly responsible for keeping customers happy. As one executive says, "Employees are closest to the customer." so they would know best how to please the customer. Employees also are promised more job security. After the heavy layoffs in 1981 and 1982, Xerox agreed to abide by a no-layoff policy in 1983. Management stuck by this, even through the difficult years of 1983 and 1984.

Employees were included in more management decisions. Line workers and others, closer to the action, were invited to add their input concerning ways to improve production and service through quality improvement teams. By working with the unions instead of fighting them, union leadership was committed to the company's excellence. More money was spent on training employees.

With a smaller number of more closely monitored suppliers, the number of defect-free products rose to 99.95 percent; but, although they received the highest honor for a quality company, David Kearns was not happy—they had not yet reached 100 percent defect-free.

As you learned in Chapter 19, to qualify for the Malcolm Baldrige award, a company must be outstanding in these areas:

Leadership.
Information and analysis.
Planning.
Human resource utilization.
Quality assurance.
Quality results.
Customer satisfaction.

Leadership. In a company seeking a quality award, leadership must be exhibited not as an authoritarian style management but as a two-way system. Upper management must delegate much authority and decision making to line supervisors. Input from workers must be solicited. Leaders should be open to opinions and changes, keeping goals in sight but being flexible enough to adapt to environmental changes within or outside of the company. Public responsibility as exhibited by senior executives also plays a crucial role in determining the quality of leadership. (100 pts. in the Baldrige competition. See exhibit, "Examination Categories and Items.")

Information and analysis. This area examines the breadth and depth of the data collected and utilized by the corporation. Impressive benchmarks should have been set in terms of quality planning, evaluation, and improvement. Analysis techniques are scrutinized. (70 pts.)

Planning. To successfully compete in this area, a company must have mapped out, in some depth, both short-term and long-term management strategies. These plans must realize company goals, but they also must be flexible enough to change with unforeseen occurrences. (60 pts.)

Human resource utilization. Management must utilize the workforce to maximize its potential. Employees should feel involved in the company, and feel that they have contributed to making the company successful. All should be trained in quality production. Recognition and praise should be given often, on an equal basis. Morale should be maintained at a high level. (150 pts.)

Quality assurance. Tracing a product from its development through manufacturing, a company must be able to show how quality was assured in each stage. Each product should have been developed to meet key quality requirements, and it should have been constructed with the highest-quality materials from suppliers. Continual assessment and improvements must be made. (140 pts.)

Quality results. This category relies heavily on the activity of a firm's key competitors. Industry trends in quality improvement and levels must be assessed, along with the achievements of the industry's world leaders. After summarizing these trends and levels for business processes, operations, and support services, supplier quality must be discussed. For a product to be of superior quality, it must begin with superior materials. (180 pts.)

Customer satisfaction. Customer expectations are examined, as are corporate relationships with the customers. Information gained from these relationships, as well as complaints submitted, should be analyzed and utilized by management to improve quality. Customer satisfaction is compared with that of others in the industry. (300 pts.)

Examination Categories and Items— Malcolm Baldrige National Quality Award

1991 Examination Categories/Items		Maximum Points
1.0 Leadership:		
1.1 Senior executive leadership	40	
1.2 Quality values	15	
1.3 Management for quality	25	
1.4 Public responsibility	20	100
2.0 Information and analysis:		
2.1 Scope and management of quality data and information	20	
2.2 Competitive comparisons and benchmarks	30	
2.3 Analysis of quality data and information	20	70
3.0 Strategic quality planning:		
3.1 Strategic quality planning process	35	
3.2 Quality goals and plans	25	60
4.0 Human resource utilization:		
4.1 Human resource management	20	
4.2 Employee involvement	40	
4.3 Quality education and training	40	
4.4 Employee recognition and performance measurement	25	
4.5 Employee well-being and morale	25	150
5.0 Quality assurance of products and services:		
5.1 Design and introduction of quality products and services	35	
5.2 Process quality control	20	
5.3 Continuous improvement of processes	20	
5.4 Quality assessment	15	
5.5 Documentation	10	
5.6 Business process and support service quality	20	
5.7 Supplier quality	20	140
6.0 Quality results		
6.1 Product and service quality results	90	
6.2 Business process and support service quality	50	
6.3 Supplier quality results	40	180
7.0 Customer satisfaction		
7.1 Determining customer requirements and expectations	30	
7.2 Customer relationship management	50	
7.3 Customer service standards	20	
7.4 Commitment to customers	15	
7.5 Complaint resolution for quality improvement	25	
7.6 Determining customer satisfaction	20	
7.7 Customer satisfaction results	70	
7.8 Customer satisfaction comparison	70	300
Total points		1,000

As shown in the Exhibit, a perfect quality score would add up to 1,000 points.

In the words of Robert Mosbacher:

The winners of this award have made quality improvement a way of life. Quality is their bottom line, and that kind of can-do attitude makes for world-class products and services.

Source: This case was prepared by Neil H. Snyder, the Ralph A. Beeton Professor of Free Enterprise. University of Virginia; Katherine Lilley, McIntire School, University of Virginia; and Deborah Francis, University of South Carolina.

ROBOT REPERCUSSION

Victor Principal, vice president of industrial relations for General Manufacturing, Inc., sat in his office reviewing the list of benefits the company expected to realize from increasing its use of industrial robots. In a few minutes, he would walk down to the labor-management conference room for a meeting with Ralph McIntosh, president of the labor union local representing most of the company's industrial employees. The purpose of this meeting would be to informally exchange views and positions preliminary to the opening for formal contract negotiations later in the month, which would focus on the use of computer-integrated robotics systems and the resulting impact on employment, workers, and jobs.

Both Principal and McIntosh had access to similar information flows relevant to industrial robots, including the following. Unlike single-task machines, installed in earlier stages of automation, robots can be programmed to do one job and then reprogrammed to do another one. The pioneering generation of robots is mainly programmed to load machines, weld, forge, spray paint, handle materials, and inspect auto bodies. The latest generation of robots includes vision-controlled robots, which enable the machines to approximate the human ability to recognize and size up objects by using laser-beam patterns recorded by television cameras and transmitted to "smart" computers. The computer software interprets and manipulates the images relayed by the camera in a "smart" or artificially intelligent way.

Experts concluded that the impact of robot installation on employment would be profound, although the extent of the worker replacement was not clear. The inescapable conclusion was that robot usage had the capacity to increase manufacturing performance and to decrease manufacturing employment.

Principal walked down to the conference room. Finding McIntosh already there, Principal stated the company's position regarding installation of industrial robots: "The company needs the cooperation of the union and our workers. We don't wish to be perceived as callously exchanging human workers for robots." Then Principal listed the major advantages associated with robots: (1) improved quality of product as a result of the accuracy of robots; (2) reduced operating costs, as the per-hour operational cost of robots was about one-third of the per-hour cost of wages and benefits paid to an average employee; (3) reliability improvements, as robots work tirelessly and don't require behavioral support; and (4) greater manufacturing flexibility, because robots are readily reprogrammable for different jobs. Principal concluded that these advantages would make the company more competitive, which would allow it to grow and increase its workforce.

McIntosh's response was direct and strong: "We aren't Luddites racing around ruining machines. We know it's necessary to increase productivity and that robotic technology is here. But we can't give the company a blank check. We need safeguards and protection." McIntosh continued, "We intend to bargain for the following contract provisions:

1. Establishment of labor-management committees to negotiate *in advance* about the labor impact of robotics technology and, of equal importance, to have a voice in deciding how and whether it should be used.
2. Rights to advance notice about installation of new technology.
3. Retraining rights for workers displaced, to include retraining for new positions in the plant, the community, or other company plants.
4. Spread the work among workers by use of a four-day workweek or other acceptable plan as an alternative to reducing the workforce.

McIntosh's final sentence summed up the union's position: "We in the union believe the company is giving our jobs to robots to reduce the labor force."

Their meeting ended amiably, but Principal and McIntosh each knew that much hard bargaining lay ahead. As Principal returned to his office, the two opposing positions were obvious. On his yellow tablet, Principal listed the requirements as he saw them: (1) A clearly stated overall policy was needed to guide negotiation decisions and actions; (2) it was critical to decide on a company position regarding each of the union's announced demands and concerns; and (3) a plan must be developed.

As Principal considered these challenges, he idly contemplated a robot possessing artificial intelligence and vision capability that could help him in his work. Immediately a danger alarm sounded in his mind. A robot so constructed might be more than helpful and might take over this and other important aspects of his job. Slightly chagrined, Principal returned to his task. He needed help—but not from any "smart" robot.

Source: J. Champion and J. James, *Critical Incidents in Management: Decision and Policy Issues*, 6th ed. (Homewood, Ill.: Richard D. Irwin, 1989).

IMPLEMENTING STRATEGIC CHANGE

James Fulmer, chief executive officer of Allied Industries, reviewed three notes he had exchanged with Frank Curtis, director of fiscal affairs, now president of a company owned by Allied. The two executives were going to meet in a few minutes to discuss problems that had recently surfaced. During the past decade, Allied had aggressively pursued a growth objective based on a conglomerate strategy of acquiring companies in distress. CEO Fulmer's policy was to appoint a new chief operating officer for each acquisition with instructions to facilitate a turnaround. Fulmer reviewed two of the notes he had written to Curtis.

Date: January 15, 1992:
Memorandum

To: Frank Curtis, Director of Fiscal Affairs, Allied Industries

From: James Fulmer, Chairman, Allied Industries

Subject: Your Appointment as President, Lee Medical Supplies

You are aware that Allied Industries recently acquired Lee Medical Supplies. Mr. John Lee, founder and president of the company, has agreed to retire, and I am appointing you to replace him. Our acquisitions group will brief you on the company, but I want to warn you the Lee Medical Supplies has a history of mismanagement. As a distributor of medical items, the company's sales last year totaled approximately $300 million, with net earnings of only $12 million. Your job is to make company sales and profits compatible with Allied standards. You are reminded that it is my policy to call for an independent evaluation of company progress and your performance as president after 18 months.

Date: September 10, 1993:
Memorandum

To: Frank Curtis, President, Lee Medical Supplies

From: James Fulmer, Chairman, Allied Industries

Subject: Serious Problems at Lee Medical Supplies

In accord with corporate policy, consultants recently conducted an evaluation of Lee Medical Supplies. In a relatively short period of time, you have increased sales and profits to meet Allied's standards, but I am alarmed at other aspects of your performance. I am told that during the past 18 months, three of your nine vice presidents have resigned and that you have terminated four others. An opinion survey conducted by the consultants indicates that a low state of morale exists and that your managerial appointees are regarded by their subordinates as hard-nosed perfectionists obsessed with quotas and profits. Employees report that ruthless competition now exists between divisions, regions, and districts. They also note that the collegial, family-oriented atmosphere fostered by Mr. Lee has been replaced by a dog-eat-dog situation characterized by negative management attitudes toward employee feelings and needs. After you have studied the enclosed report from the consultants, we will meet to discuss their findings. I am particularly concerned with their final conclusion that "a form of corporate cancer seems to be spreading throughout Lee Medical Supplies."

As Fulmer prepared to read the third note, written by Frank Curtis, he reflected on his exit interview with the consultants. While Fulmer considered Curtis a financial expert and a turnaround specialist, his subordinates characterized Curtis as an autocrat and better suited to be a Marine boot camp commander.

Date: September 28, 1993:
Memorandum

To: James Fulmer

From: Frank Curtis

Subject: The So-Called "Serious Problems" at Lee Medical Supplies

I have received your memorandum dated September 10, 1992, and reviewed the consultants' report. When you appointed me to my present position I was instructed to take over an unprofitable company and make it profitable. I have done so in 18 months, although I inherited a family-owned business that by your own admission had been mismanaged for years. I found a group of managers and salespeople with an average company tenure of 22 years. Mr. Lee had centralized all personnel decisions so that only he could terminate an employee. He tolerated mediocre performance. All employees were paid on a straight salary basis, with seniority the sole criterion for advancement. Some emphasis was given to increasing sales each year, but none was given to reducing costs and increasing profits. Employees did indeed find the company a fun place to work, and the feeling of being a part of a family did permeate the company. Such attitudes were, however, accompanied by mediocrity, incompetence, and poor performance.

I found it necessary to implement immediate strategic changes in five areas: the organization's structure, employee rewards and incentives, management information systems, allocation of resources, and managerial leadership style. As a result, sales areas were reorganized into divisions, regions, and districts. Managers who I felt were incompetent and/or lacking in commitment to my objectives and methods were replaced. Unproductive and mediocre employees were encouraged to find jobs elsewhere. Authority for staffing and compensation decisions was decentralized to units at the division, region, and district levels. Managers of those units were informed that along with their authority went responsibility for reducing costs and for increasing sales and profits. Each unit was established as a profit center. A new department was established and charged with reviewing performance of those units. Improved accounting and control systems were implemented. A management by objectives program was developed to establish standards and monitor performance. Performance appraisals are now required for all employees. To encourage more aggressive action, bonuses and incentives are offered to managers of units showing increased profits. A commission plan based on measurable sales and profit performances has replaced straight salaries. Resources are allocated to units based on their performance.

My own leadership style has probably represented the most traumatic change for employees. Internal competition is a formally mandated policy throughout the company. It has been responsible for much of the progress achieved to date. Progress, however, is never made without costs, and I recognize that employees are not having as much fun as in the past. I was employed to achieve results and not to ensure that employees remain secure and happy in their work. Don't let a few crybabies unable to adjust to changes lead you to believe that problems take precedence over profits. Does it mean that I am not people oriented if I believe it is unlikely that a spirit of aggressiveness and competitiveness can coexist with an atmosphere of cooperativeness and family orientation? Do you feel that we are obligated to employees because of past practices? Frankly, I thought I had your support to do whatever was necessary to get this company turned around. In our meeting, tell me if you think my approaches have been wrong and, if so, tell me what I should have done differently.

Just as Fulmer finished reviewing the third memorandum, his secretary informed him that Curtis had arrived for their scheduled meeting. He realized he was undecided about how to communicate to Curtis his ideas and beliefs regarding how changes in an organization can best be implemented. One thing he did know: He didn't appreciate how Curtis had expressed his views in his memorandum, but he recognized that he probably should set aside emotions and respond to the questions Curtis posed.

Source: J. Champion and J. James, *Critical Incidents in Management: Decision and Policy Issues,* 6th ed. (Homewood, Ill.: Richard D. Irwin, 1989).

COMPANY DIRECTORY

A

ABB Flakt
(Subsidiary of Asea Brown Boveri, Inc.)
650 Ackerman Road
Columbus, OH 43202
(614) 261-2000
Sales: $200,000,000
Employees: 2,000

Advanced Micro Devices, Inc.
915 De Guigne Street
Box 3453
Sunnyvale, CA 94088
(408) 732-2400
Sales: $1,650,000,000
Employees: 11,250

Aetna Life & Casualty Co.
151 Farmington Avenue
Hartford, CT 06156
(203) 273-0123
Sales: $17,120,200,000
Employees: 42,631

Allied Signal, Inc.
101 Columbia Road
Morristown, NJ 07960
(201) 435-2000
Sales: $11,830,000,000
Employees: 86,400

Amdahl Corporation
1250 East Arques Avenue
Sunnyvale, CA 94088-3470
(408) 746-6000
Sales: $862,000,000
Employees: 7,000

American Airlines, Inc.
(Subsidiary of American Corporation)
P.O. Box 619616 DFW Arpt Street
Dallas, TX 65261-9616
(817) 355-1234
Sales: $14,400,000,000
Employees: 102,400

American Broadcasting Companies, Inc.
(Subsidiary of Capital Cities/ABC Inc.)

77 W. 66th Street
New York, NY 10023
(212) 456-7777
Sales: NA
Employees: NA

American Express Company
200 Vesey Street
American Express Tower
New York, NY 10285-4805
(212) 640-2000
Sales: $14,170,000,000
Employees: 100,188

American Motors Co.
(Subsidiary of Chrysler Corporation)
27777 Franklin Road
Southfield, MI 48034
(313) 827-1000
Sales: $4,030,000,000
Employees: 22,500

Ameritech
30 S. Wacker Drive
Chicago, IL 60606
(312) 750-5000
Sales: $11,710,000,000
Employees: 71,300

Amoco Corp.
200 East Randolph Drive
Chicago, IL 60601
(312) 856-6111
Sales: $28,900,000,000
Employees: 46,700

Ampex
65 E. 55th Street
New York, NY 10022
(212) 935-6144
Sales: $526,450,000
Employees: 3,000

Anheuser Busch Companies, Inc.
One Busch Place
St. Louis, MO 63118
(314) 577-2000
Sales: $11,500,000,000
Employees: 43,345

A&P Company, Inc.
2 Paragon Drive
Montvale, NJ 07645
(201) 930-4000
Sales: $557,157,000
Employees: 4,600

Apple Computers, Inc.
One Infinite Loop
Cupertino, CA 95014
(408) 996-1010
Sales: $8,000,000,000
Employees: 11,800

ARCO Pipe Line Co.
(Subsidiary of Atlantic Richfield Company)
5900 Cherry Avenue
Long Beach, CA 90805
(310) 428-9000
Sales: $48,000,000
Employees: 280

Argus Corporation Ltd.
(Subsidiary of Ravelston Corporation
Limited)
10 Toronto Street
Toronto, Canada M5C 2B7
(416) 363-8721
Sales: $20,560,000,000
Employees: 22,000

ASEA Brown Boveri
(Subsidiary of ABB ASEA Brown Boveri,
Ltd.)
900 Long Ridge Road
Stamford, CT 06902
(203) 329-8771
Sales: NA
Employees: NA

Ashland Oil
P.O. Box 391
Ashland, KY 41169
(606) 329-3333
Sales: $9,500,000,000
Employees: 33,000

Atlantic Richfield Co.
515 South Flower Street

Los Angeles, CA 47872
(213) 486-3511
Sales: $15,000,000,000
Employees: 31,300

AT&T Co.
550 Madison Avenue
New York, NY 10022
(212) 605-5500
Sales: $34,900,000,000
Employees: 365,000

Automatic Data Processing
One ADP Boulevard
Roseland, NJ 07068
(201) 994-5000
Sales: $2,220,000,000
Employees: 21,000

Avon Products, Inc.
9 W. 57th Street
New York, NY 10019
(212) 546-6015
Sales: $3,450,000,000
Employees: 34,500

B

Bally Engineered Structures
20 N. Front Street
Bally, PA 19503
(610) 845-2311
Sales: $25,000,000
Employees: 400

Banc One Corp.
100 E. Broad Street
Columbus, OH 43215
(614) 248-5944
Sales: $80,000,000,000
Employees: 42,800

Bankers Trust Company
(Subsidiary of Bankers Trust New York
Corp.)
P.O. Box 318 Church Street Station
New York, NY 10015
(212) 250-2500
Sales: NA
Employees: 12,500

**Bank of America National Trust and
Savings Association**
(Subsidiary of BankAmerica Corp.)
555 California Street
San Francisco, CA 94104
(415) 622-3456
Sales: NA
Employees: 78,500

Bausch & Lomb
One Chase Square Box 54
Rochester, NY 14601
(716) 338-6000
Sales: $1,870,000,000
Employees: 14,500

Baxter Healthcare Corp.
(Subsidiary of Baxter International, Inc.)
One Baxter Parkway
Deerfield, IL 60015
(708) 948-2000
Sales: $6,700,000,000
Employees: 40,900

Bayer AG
Bayerwerk
Leverkusen, West Germany 5090
0214-301
Sales: NA
Employees: 164,400

L. L. Bean, Inc.
Casco Street
Freeport, ME 04132
(207) 865-4761
Sales: $368,000,000
Employees: 1,920

The Bear Stearns Companies, Inc.
245 Park Avenue
New York, NY 10167
(212) 272-2000
Sales: $2,420,000,000
Employees: 7,454

Bechtel Group
50 Beale Street
San Francisco, CA 94105
(415) 768-1234
Sales: $7,000,000,000
Employees: 21,200

Bell Atlantic Corp.
1717 Arch Street
Philadelphia, PA 19103
(215) 963-6000
Sales: $13,000,000,000
Employees: 71,400

Bell & Howell
5215 Old Orchard Road
Skokie, IL 60077-1076
(708) 470-7100
Sales: $675,000,000
Employees: 5,718

BellSouth Corp.
1155 Peachtree Street N.E.
Atlanta, GA 30367
(404) 249-2000
Sales: $15,880,000,000
Employees: 95,100

Bertelsmann
(Subsidiary of Bertlesmann
Aktiengesellschaft)
1540 Broadway
New York, NY 10036
(212) 782-1000
Sales: $2,300,000,000
Employees: 5,100

Best Products Company, Inc.
P.O. Box 26303
Richmond, VA 23260
(804) 261-2000
Sales: $1,400,000,000
Employees: 18,500

Bethlehem Steel Corp.
1170 Eighth Avenue
Bethlehem, PA 18016
(610) 694-2424
Sales: $4,320,000,000
Employees: 20,500

BMW
Petuelring 130
Munich, West Germany 8000
089-3895-1
Sales: DM27,180,000,000
Employees: 70,950

The Boeing Co.
7755 East Marginal Way
Seattle, WA 98124
(206) 655-2121
Sales: $25,400,000,000
Employees: 123,000

Bombay Company, Inc.
550 Bailey Avenue
Fort Worth, TX 76107
(817) 347-8200
Sales: $231,740,000
Employees: 2,900

Borg-Warner Corp.
200 South Michigan Avenue
Chicago, IL 60604
(312) 322-8500
Sales: $3,330,000,000
Employees: 78,000

Brio Industries, Inc.
3728 N. Fraser Way
Burnaby, British Columbia
Canada V5J 5G1
(604) 436-5876
Sales: $1,850,000
Employees: 60

Bristol-Myers Squibb Co.
345 Park Avenue
New York, NY 10154

(212) 546-4000
Sales: $11,440,000,000
Employees: 49,500

British Petroleum Co.
One Finsbury Circle
Britannic House
Moor Lane
London, England EC242BU
44-71-496-4000
Sales: £40,280,000,000
Employees: 130,100

British Telecommunications
81 Newgate Street
London, England EC1A7 AJ
44-71-356-5000
Sales: $17,100,000,000
Employees: 156,000

Brooks Brothers
346 Madison Avenue
New York, NY 10017
(212) 682-8800
Sales: NA
Employees: 3,075

Browning Ferris
757 N. Eldridge
Houston, TX 77079
(713) 870-8100
Sales: $3,500,000,000
Employees: 29,400

Burger King Corp.
(Subsidiary of Grand Metropolitan plc)
17777 Old Cutler Road
Miami, FL 33157
(305) 378-7011
Sales: $6,100,000,000
Employees: 42,000

C

Canon Business Machines, Inc.
(Subsidiary of Canon, Inc.)
3191 Red Hill Avenue
Costa Mesa, CA 92626
(714) 556-4700
Sales: $50,000,000
Employees: 150

Carnival Corp.
3655 N.W. 87th Avenue
Miami, FL 33178
(305) 599-2600
Sales: $1,560,000,000
Employees: 1,400

Caterpillar, Inc.
100 Northeast Adams Street

Peoria, IL 61629
(309) 675-1000
Sales: $11,620,000,000
Employees: 51,200

CBS, Inc.
51 W. 52nd Street
New York, NY 10019
(212) 975-4321
Sales: $3,500,000,000
Employees: 6,000

Chase Manhattan Corp.
1 Chase Manhattan Plaza
New York, NY 10081
(212) 522-2222
Sales: $11,420,000,000
Employees: 31,100

Chevron Corp.
225 Bush Street
San Francisco, CA 94104
(415) 894-7700
Sales: $33,000,000,000
Employees: 55,123

Chiat/Day/Mojo Inc. Advertising
320 Hampton Drive
Venice, CA 90291
(310) 314-5000
Sales: NA
Employees: 300

Chiquita Brands International
(Subsidiary of American Fin Corp.)
250 E. 5th Street
Cincinnati, OH 45202
(513) 784-8000
Sales: $2,530,000,000
Employees: 45,000

Chrysler Corp.
12000 Chrysler Drive
Detroit, MI 48288-1919
(313) 956-5252
Sales: $43,600,000,000
Employees: 123,000

Citibank
(Subsidiary of Citicorp)
399 Park Avenue
New York, NY 10022
(212) 559-1000
Sales: NA
Employees: 81,000

Citicorp
399 Park Avenue
New York, NY 10022
(212) 559-1000
Sales: $32,200,000,000
Employees: 88,500

Coast Gas Industries, Inc.
885 Salinas Road
Watsonville, CA 95076
(408) 724-3200
Sales: $180,000,000
Employees: 275

The Coca-Cola Co.
One Coca-Cola Plaza N.W.
Atlanta, GA 30313
(404) 676-2121
Sales: $13,900,000,000
Employees: 31,312

Colgate-Palmolive
300 Park Avenue
New York, NY 10022
(212) 310-2000
Sales: $7,140,000,000
Employees: 29,000

COMPAQ Computer Corp.
555 SH 249
P.O. Box 69-2000
Houston, TX 77269
(713) 370-0670
Sales: $7,190,000,000
Employees: 9,500

Consolidated Natural Gas
CNG Tower
625 Liberty Avenue
Pittsburgh, PA 15222
(412) 227-1000
Sales: $3,180,000,000
Employees: 8,000

Control Data Corp.
8100 34th Avenue
Minneapolis, MN 55420
(612) 853-8100
Sales: $3,670,000,000
Employees: 38,800

Cooper Tire and Rubber Co.
Lima and Western Avenues
Findlay, OH 45840
(419) 423-1321
Sales: $1,190,000,000
Employees: 7,600

Adolph Coors Co.
NH470
Golden, CO 80401
(303) 279-6565
Sales: $1,580,000,000
Employees: 6,200

Corning Glass Works
Houghton Park
Corning, NY 14830
(607) 974-9000

Sales: $4,040,000,000
Employees: 39,000

Cowles Media Corp.
329 Portland Avenue
Minneapolis, MN 55415
(612) 375-7000
Sales: $256,000,000
Employees: 3,260

CSX
901 E. Cary Street
Richmond, VA 23219
(804) 782-1400
Sales: $8,940,000,000
Employees: 47,000

Cyrix Corp.
2703 N. Central Expressway
Richardson, TX 75080
(214) 894-8387
Sales: $125,100,000
Employees: 185

D

Dana Corp.
4500 Dorr Street
Toledo, OH 43697
(419) 535-4500
Sales: $5,400,000,000
Employees: 40,000

Data General Corp.
4400 Computer Drive
Westboro, MA 01580
(617) 366-8911
Sales: $1,230,000,000
Employees: 6,500

Days Inns of America, Inc.
(Subsidiary of Tollman-Hundley Lodging
Corp.)
100 Summit Lake Drive
Valhalla, NY 10595
(914) 747-3636
Sales: $117,800,000
Employees: 3,193

Dell Computer Co.
9505 Arboretum Boulevard
Austin, TX 78759
(512) 338-4400
Sales: $2,870,000,000
Employees: 5,000

Delta Air Lines, Inc.
Hartsfield International Airport
Atlanta, GA 30326
(404) 765-2600
Sales: $12,000,000,000
Employees: 73,533

Digital Equipment Corp.
146 Main Street
Maynard, MA 01754
(617) 897-5111
Sales: $14,370,000,000
Employees: 92,000

Domino's Pizza, Inc.
3001 Earhart Road
Ann Arbor, MI 48107
(313) 668-4000
Sales: $296,000,000
Employees: 51,300

Domino Sugar Corp.
1114 Avenue of the Americas
New York, NY 10036
(212) 789-9700
Sales: $1,300,000,000
Employees: 7,729

The Dow Chemical Co.
2030 Willard H. Dow Center
Midland, MI 48674
(517) 636-1000
Sales: $18,660,000,000
Employees: 62,000

Dow Corning Corp.
P.O. Box 994
Midland, MI 48686
(517) 496-4000
Sales: $1,760,000,000
Employees: 8,691

Dow Jones & Co., Inc.
200 Liberty Street
New York, NY 10281
(212) 416-2000
Sales: $1,930,000,000
Employees: 10,000

William Dudek Manufacturing Co.
4901 W. Armitage Avenue
Chicago, IL 60639
(312) 622-2727
Sales: $3,000,000
Employees: 50

Du Pont
1007 Market Street
Wilmington, DE 19509
(302) 774-1000
Sales: $37,100,000,000
Employees: 114,000

E

Eastern Airlines
(Sudsidiary of Continental Air Holdings,
Inc.)

Miami International Airport
Miami, FL 33148
(305) 873-2211
Sales: $1,500,000,000
Employees: 19,000

Eastman Kodak Co.
343 State Street
Rochester, NY 14650
(716) 724-4000
Sales: $16,360,000,000
Employees: 137,750

Eaton Corp.
1111 Superior Avenue N.E.
Cleveland, OH 44114
(216) 523-5000
Sales: $4,400,000,000
Employees: 50,000

Electro-Biology, Inc.
6 Upper Pond Road
Parsippany, NJ 07054
(201) 299-9022
Sales: $28,000,000
Employees: 350

Elizabeth Arden
1345 Avenue of the Americas
New York, NY 10105
(212) 261-1000
Sales: NA
Employees: 3,428

Emerson Electric Co.
8000 West Floussant Avenue
St. Louis, MO 63136
(314) 553-2000
Sales: $8,170,000,000
Employees: 71,600

Equitable Life Assurance Society
787 Seventh Avenue
New York, NY 10019
(212) 554-1234
Sales: $60,000,000,000
Employees: 20,000

Exxon Corp.
1251 Avenue of the Americas
New York, NY 10020-1198
(212) 333-1000
Sales: $74,400,000,000
Employees: 145,000

F

Federal Express Corp.
2007 Corporate Avenue
Memphis, TN 38132

(901) 369-3600
Sales: $7,800,000,000
Employees: 93,000

Federal National Mortgage Association
3900 Wisconsin Avenue N.W.
Washington, D.C. 20016
(202) 752-7000
Revenues: $16,050,000,000
Employees: 2,400

Firestone Tire & Rubber Co.
(Division of Bridgestone/Firestone, Inc.)
1200 Firestone Parkway
Akron, OH 44317
(216) 379-7000
Sales: NA
Employees: NA

First Boston Corp.
(Subsidiary of First Boston, Inc.)
Park Avenue Plaza
New York, NY 10055
(212) 909-2000
Sales: $1,300,000,000
Employees: 4,040

Fleet Financial Group, Inc.
50 Kennedy Plaza
Providence, RI 02903
(401) 278-5800
Sales: $4,680,000,000
Employees: 25,200

Food Lion, Inc.
P.O. Box 1330
Salisbury, NC 28145
(704) 633-8250
Sales: $7,600,000,000
Employees: 60,000

Ford Motor Co.
American Road
Dearborn, MI 48121
(313) 322-3000
Sales: $108,520,000,000
Employees: 332,700

The Foxboro Co.
(Subsidiary of Siebe plc)
33 Commercial Street
Foxboro, MA 02035
(508) 543-8750
Sales: $597,780,000
Employees: 4,700

Fox Television Stations, Inc.
5746 Sunset Boulevard
Los Angeles, CA 90028
(213) 856-1001
Sales: NA
Employees: 1,250

Funco, Inc.
10120 W. 76th Street
Eden Prairie, MN 55344
(612) 946-8883
Sales: $50,500,000
Employees: 380

G

Gateway Foods, Inc.
(Subsidiary of Scrivner, Inc.)
P.O. Box 1957
LaCrosse, WI 54602
(608) 785-1330
Sales: NA
Employees: 500

General Dynamics Corp.
3190 Fairview Park Drive
Falls Church, VA 22042
(703) 876-3000
Sales: $7,830,000,000
Employees: 107,000

General Electric Canada
2300 Meadowvale Boulevard
Mississauga, Ontario
Canada L5N 5P9
(416) 858-5100
Sales: $1,420,000
Employees: 4,248

General Electric Co.
3135 Easton Turnpike
Fairfield, CT 06432
(203) 373-2211
Sales: $60,600,000,000
Employees: 222,000

General Foods Corp.
(Subsidiary of Philip Morris Companies, Inc.)
250 North Street
White Plains, NY 10605
(914) 335-2500
Sales: NA
Employees: 55,000

General Mills, Inc.
One General Mills Boulevard
Minneapolis, MN 55426
(612) 549-2311
Sales: $8,130,000,000
Employees: 121,300

General Motors Corp.
3044 West Grand Boulevard
Detroit, MI 48202
(313) 556-5000
Sales: $130,220,000,000
Employees: 711,000

Glaxo Holdings
Clarges House
Berkeley Avenue
Greenford, Middlesex, England W1Y 8DH
44-71-493-4060
Sales: $1,500,000
Employees: 40,000

The Goodyear Tire & Rubber Co.
1144 East Market Street
Akron, OH 44316
(216) 796-2121
Sales: $11,640,000,000
Employees: 121,586

The Greyhound Corp.
Greyhound Tower
Phoenix, AZ 85077
(602) 248-4000
Sales: NA
Employees: 38,100

Grumman
1111 Stewart Avenue
Bethpage, NY 11714
(516) 575-0574
Revenues: $4,040,000,000
Employees: 28,900

Guinness
39 Portman Square
London, England W1H 9HB
44-71-486-0288
Sales: £4,660,000
Employees: 23,264

H

Hallmark Cards, Inc.
2501 McGee Trafficway
Kansas City, MO 64141
(816) 274-5111
Sales: $3,400,000,000
Employees: 22,000

John Hancock
John Hancock Plaza
Boston, MA 02117
(617) 572-6000
Assets: $36,220,000,000
Employees: 19,000

Hanna-Barbera, Inc.
(Subsidiary of Turner Broadcasting System, Inc.)
3400 Cahuenga Boulevard
Hollywood, CA 90068
(213) 851-5000
Sales: $59,700,000
Employees: 500

Harley-Davidson, Inc.
3700 W. Juneau Avenue
Box 653
Milwaukee, WI 53201
(414) 342-4680
Sales: $1,220,000,000
Employees: 5,600

Hasbro, Inc.
1027 Newport Avenue
Pawtucket, RI 02861
(401) 431-8697
Sales: $2,730,000,000
Employees: 10,000

Heineken
Postbus 28
Amsterdam, Netherlands
1000 AA
020-5239239
Sales: $9,500,000
Employees: 42

H. J. Heinz Co.
U.S. Steel Building
600 Grant Street SC
Pittsburgh, PA 15219
(412) 456-5700
Sales: $7,100,000,000
Employees: 37,700

Hewlett-Packard Co.
3000 Hanover Street
Palo Alto, CA 94304
(415) 857-1501
Sales: $20,320,000,000
Employees: 97,000

Hilton Hotels Corp.
9336 Civic Center Drive
Beverly Hills, CA 90210
(213) 278-4321
Sales: $1,390,000,000
Employees: 34,000

Honda
1-1 Minami-aoyama
Minato-ku
Tokyo, Japan 107
81-3-5412-1134
Sales: $37,450,000,000
Employees: 31,036

Honeywell, Inc.
Honeywell Plaza
Minneapolis, MN 55408
(612) 951-1000
Sales: $5,960,000,000
Employees: 52,300

I

Intel Corp.
3065 Bowers Avenue
Santa Clara, CA 95051
(408) 765-8080
Sales: $8,780,000,000
Employees: 24,600

International Business Machines (IBM)
Old Orchard Road
Armouk, NY 10504
(914) 765-1900
Sales: $62,720,000,000
Employees: 235,000

International Harvester Co.
(Stringers International Co.)
1000 Desoto Street
Clarksdale, MS 38614
(601) 624-4305
Sales: NA
Employees: 25

J

Johnson & Johnson
1 Johnson & Johnson Plaza
New Brunswick, NJ 08933
(210) 524-0400
Sales: $14,130,000,000
Employees: 81,600

Jostens, Inc.
5501 Norman Center Drive
Minneapolis, MN 55437
(612) 830-3300
Sales: $827,000,000
Employees: 8,000

K

Kellogg Co.
1 Kellogg Square
Battle Creek, MI 49016-3599
(616) 961-2000
Sales: $6,300,000,000
Employees: 16,500

Kentucky Fried Chicken
(Subsidiary of PepsiCo)
P.O. Box 32070
Louisville, KY 40232
(502) 456-8300
Sales: $3,000,000,000
Employees: 30,000

Kidder Peabody Group, Inc.
10 Hanover Square
New York, NY 10005
(212) 510-3000
Sales: $582,000,000
Employees: 5,700

Kindercare Learning Centers, Inc.
2400 Presidents Drive
Montgomery, AL 36116
(205) 277-5090
Sales: $437,200,000,000
Employees: 19,000

Kmart Corp.
3100 West Big Beaver Road
Troy, MI 48084
(313) 643-1000
Sales: $34,160,000,000
Employees: 320,000

Kollmorgen Corp.
1601 Trapelo Road
Waltham, MA 02154
(617) 890-5655
Sales: $185,540,000
Employees: 1,660

Kroger Co.
1014 Vine Street
Cincinnati, OH 45201
(513) 762-4000
Sales: $22,320,000,000
Employees: 170,000

L

Laidlaw Industries
(Subsidiary of Laidlaw, Inc.)
669 Airport Freeway
Suite 400
Hurst, TX 76053
(817) 282-7580
Sales: $942,000,000
Employees: 9,420

Lever Brothers Co.
(Subsidiary of Unilever United States, Inc.)
390 Park Avenue
New York, NY 10022
(212) 688-6000
Sales: $2,100,000,000
Employees: 4,900

Levi Strauss & Co.
(Subsidiary of Levi Strauss Assoc., Inc.)
1155 Battery Street
Levi's Plaza
San Francisco, CA 94111

(415) 544-6000
Sales: $5,900,000,000
Employees: 36,400

Lincoln Electric Co.
22801 St. Clair Avenue
Cleveland, OH 44117
(216) 481-8100
Sales: $846,000,000
Employees: 6,600

Arthur D. Little, Inc.
25 Acorn Park
Cambridge, MA 02140
(617) 864-5770
Sales: $341,000,000
Employees: 2,400

Lockheed Corp.
4500 Park Granada Boulevard
Calabasas, CA 90405
(818) 876-2000
Sales: $13,070,000,000
Employees: 71,000

Louisiana-Pacific Corp.
111 S.W. Fifth Avenue
Portland, OR 97204
(503) 221-0800
Sales: $2,500,000,000
Employees: 13,000

Louisville Gas & Electric
(Subsidiary of Louisville Gas & Electric
Energy Corp.)
220 W. Main Street
Louisville, KY 40232
(502) 627-2000
Sales: $775,130,000
Employees: 2,800

LTV Corp.
2001 Ross Avenue
Dallas, TX 75201
(214) 979-7711
Sales: $7,040,000,000
Employees: 54,800

M

R. H. Macy and Co., Inc.
151 West 34th Street
New York, NY 10001
(212) 695-4400
Sales: $6,970,000,000
Employees: 54,000

Marriott Corp.
Marriott Drive

Washington, D.C. 20058
(301) 897-9000
Sales: $4,240,000,000
Employees: 214,000

Martin Marietta Corp.
6801 Rockledge Drive
Bethesda, MD 20817
(301) 897-6000
Sales: $9,440,000,000
Employees: 92,786

Mary Kay Cosmetics
8787 Stemmons Freeway
Dallas, TX 75247
(214) 630-8787
Sales: $486,000,000
Employees: 100,000

Matsushita Electronic Co. of America
(Subsidiary of Matsushita Electric
Industrial Co., Ltd.)
1 Panasonic Way
Secaucus, NJ 07094
(201) 348-7000
Sales: NA
Employees: 7,000

Mattel, Inc.
333 Continental Boulevard
El Segundo, CA 90245
(213) 524-4600
Sales: $2,700,000,000
Employees: 17,500

Mazda Motor Manufacturing (USA) Corp.
(Subsidiary of Mazda Motor Corp.)
1 Mazda Drive
Flat Rock, MI 48134
(313) 782-7800
Sales: NA
Employees: 600

McCaw Cellular Communications, Inc.
(Subsidiary of AT&T Corp.)
5400 Carillon Point
Kirkland, WA 98033
(206) 827-4500
Sales: $2,190,000,000
Employees: 3,500

McDonald's Corp.
1 McDonald's Plaza
Oakbrook, IL 60521
(708) 575-3000
Sales: $14,400,000,000
Employees: 174,000

McDonnell Douglas Corp.
Lambert St. Louis Airport

St. Louis, MO 63166
(314) 232-0232
Sales: $14,490,000,000
Employees: 127,926

MCI Communications Corp.
1801 Pennsylvania Avenue
Washington, D.C. 20006
(202) 872-1600
Sales: $11,920,000,000
Employees: 34,000

The Mead Corp.
Courthouse Plaza, N.E.
Dayton, OH 45463
(513) 495-6323
Sales: $4,790,000,000
Employees: 21,600

Merck & Co., Inc.
One Merck Drive
Box 100
Whitehouse Station, NJ 08889
(908) 423-1000
Sales: $10,500,000,000
Employees: 47,100

Mervyn's
(Subsidiary of Dayton-Hudson Corp.)
25001 Industrial Boulevard
Hayward, CA 94545
(415) 785-8800
Sales: $2,862,300,000
Employees: 44,600

Metro-Goldwyn-Mayer, Inc.
7500 Broadway
Santa Monica, CA 90404
(310) 449-3000
Sales: $690,100,000,000
Employees: 830

Microsoft
One Microsoft Way
Redmond, WA 98052
(206) 882-8080
Sales: $4,650,000,000
Employees: 15,000

Miller Brewing Co.
(Subsidiary of Philip Morris Companies,
Inc.)
3939 West Highland Boulevard
Milwaukee, WI 53201
(414) 931-2000
Sales: $2,914,000,000
Employees: 1,618

Herman Miller, Inc.
55 E. Main Avenue
Zeeland, MI 49464

(616) 772-3300
Sales: $885,670,000
Employees: 5,400

Mirage Resorts, Inc.
3400 Las Vegas Boulevard South
Las Vegas, NV 89109
(702) 791-7111
Sales: $953,300,000
Employees: 12,000

Mitsubishi Motors
5-33-8 Shiba
Minato-ku
Tokyo, Japan 108
3-3456-1111
Sales: $19,850,000,000
Employees: 27,603

Mobil Corp.
3225 Gallows Road
Fairfax, VA 22037
(703) 846-3000
Sales: $63,470,000,000
Employees: 63,700

Monsanto Co.
800 North Lindbergh Boulevard
St. Louis, MO 63167
(314) 694-1000
Sales: $7,900,000,000
Employees: 33,797

J. P. Morgan & Co., Inc.
60 Wall Street
New York, NY 10260
(212) 483-2323
Sales: $1,590,000,000
Employees: 15,193

Morgan Stanley Group, Inc.
1251 Avenue of the Americas
New York, NY 10020
(212) 703-4000
Revenues: $11,160,000,000
Employees: 8,249

Motorola, Inc.
1303 East Algonquin Road
Schaumburg, IL 60196
(708) 397-5000
Sales: $16,960,000,000
Employees: 102,000

MTV Networks, Inc.
(Subsidiary of Viacom International)
1515 Broadway
New York, NY 10036
(212) 258-8000
Sales: $675,000,000
Employees: 1,700

N

NationsBank Corp.
101 N. Tryon Street
NationsBank Plaza
Charlotte, NC 28246
(704) 386-5000
Sales: $10,400,000,000
Employees: 760

NCR Corp.
1700 South Patterson Boulevard
Dayton, OH 45479
(513) 445-5000
Sales: $4,310,000,000
Employees: 62,000

Nestlé
800 N. Brand Drive
Glendale, CA 91203
(818) 549-6000
Sales: NA
Employees: 22,000

New Jersey Bell Telephone Co.
540 Broad Street
Newark, NJ 07102
(201) 649-9900
Sales: $2,500,000,000
Employees: 19,700

The News Corp., Ltd.
Two Holt Street
Sydney, NSW
Australia 2010
61-2-2883000
Sales: $7,400,000,000
Employees: 24,700

Nexagen, Inc.
2860 Wilderness Place
Boulder, CO 80301
(303) 444-5893
Sales: $1,890,000
Employees: 526

Nike, Inc.
One Bowerman Drive
Beaverton, OR 97005
(503) 641-6453
Sales: $3,790,000,000
Employees: 9,000

Nissan Motor Corp.
(Subsidiary of Nissan Motor Co., Ltd.,
Tokyo, Japan)
18501 South Figueroa Street
Carson, CA 90247
(213) 532-3111
Sales: $14,415,180,000
Employees: 3,000

Nordstrom, Inc.
1501 Fifth Avenue
Seattle, WA 98101-1603
(206) 628-2111
Sales: $3,590,000,000
Employees: 31,000

Northern Telecom, Inc.
(Subsidiary of Northern Telecom Ltd.)
200 Athens Way
Nashville, TN 37228
(615) 734-4000
Sales: NA
Employees: 20,000

Nucor Corp.
2100 Rexford Road
Charlotte, NC 28211
(704) 366-7000
Sales: $2,250,000,000
Employees: 5,900

O

Office Depot, Inc.
220 Old Germantown Road
Dehay Beach, FL 33445
(407) 278-4800
Sales: $2,580,000,000
Employees: 25,000

Olin Corp.
120 Long Ridge Road
Stamford, CT 06904
(203) 356-2000
Sales: $2,420,000,000
Employees: 12,400

Olsten Corp.
Merrick Avenue
Westbury, NY 11590
(516) 832-8200
Sales: $1,960,000,000
Employees: 1,200

Oryx
30 W. Century Road
Paramus, NJ 07652
(201) 261-0770
Sales: $3,000,000
Employees: NA

Owens-Corning Fiberglas Corp.
Fiberglas Tower
Toledo, OH 43659
(419) 248-8000
Sales: $2,940,000,000
Employees: 17,000

P

Pacific Gas & Electric
77 Beale Street
San Francisco, CA 94106
(415) 972-7000
Sales: $10,600,000,000
Employees: 23,000

J. C. Penney Co., Inc.
6501 Legacy Drive
Plano, TX 75024
(214) 431-1000
Sales: $19,580,000,000
Employees: 193,000

People's Bank
(Subsidiary of People's Mutual Holdings)
850 Main Street
Bridgeport, CT 06604
(203) 338-7171
Sales: $337,600,000
Employees: 2,500

PepsiCo, Inc.
Anderson Hill Road
Purchase, NY 10577
(914) 253-2000
Sales: $25,020,000,000
Employees: 423,000

Perkin-Elmer Corp.
761 Main Avenue
Norwalk, CT 06859
(203) 762-1000
Sales: $1,010,000,000
Employees: 6,000

Philips
(Subsidiary of Philips Industries, Inc.)
4801 Springfield Street
Dayton, OH 45431
(513) 253-7171
Sales: $945,000,000
Employees: 279

Pillsbury Co.
(Subsidiary of Gramet Holdings Corp.)
Pillsbury Center
200 South 6th Street
Minneapolis, MN 55402
(612) 330-4966
Sales: $6,120,000,000
Employees: 68,000

Pitney Bowles, Inc.
1 Elmcroft Road
Stamford, CT 06926-0790
(203) 356-5000
Sales: $3,540,000,000
Employees: 32,539

Pizza Hut, Inc.
(Subsidiary of PepsiCo)
9111 E. Douglas
Wichita, KS 67207
(316) 681-9000
Sales: $6,400,000,000
Employees: 151,000

Polaroid Corp.
549 Technology Square
Cambridge, MA 02139
(617) 577-2000
Sales: $2,250,000,000
Employees: 12,359

Polycast
(Subsidiary of the Jessup Group, Inc.)
402 S. Byrkit
Mishawaka, IN 46544
(219) 259-1259
Sales: $120,000,000
Employees: 733

Pratt & Whitney
(Subsidiary of United Technologies Corp.)
400 Main Street
Cumberland, RI 02864
(401) 333-6000
Sales: $3,500,000
Employees: 30

Price/Costco, Inc.
10809 120th Avenue N.E.
Kirkland, WA 98033
(206) 828-8100
Sales: $15,500,000,000
Employees: 18,100

The Procter & Gamble Co.
One Procter & Gamble Plaza
Cincinnati, OH 45202
(513) 983-1100
Sales: $30,430,000,000
Employees: 80,350

Prudential-Bache Properties, Inc.
One Seaport Plaza
New York, NY 10292
(212) 214-2178
Sales: NA
Employees: 11,000

Publix Stores, Inc.
1395 6th Street N.W.
Winter Haven, FL 33881
(813) 688-1188
Sales: $27,000,000
Employees: 279

R

Raychem Corp.
300 Constitution Drive
Menlo Park, CA 94025
(415) 361-3333
Sales: $1,500,000,000
Employees: 11,000

RCA Corp.
(Subsidiary of General Electric Co.)
30 Rockefeller Plaza
New York, NY 10020
(212) 621-6000
Sales: NA
Employees: 80,000

Reebok International, Ltd.
100 Technology Center Drive
Stoughton, MA 02072
(617) 341-5000
Sales: $2,890,000,000
Employees: 4,220

Reflexite Corp.
120 Darling Drive
Avon, CT 06001
(203) 676-7100
Sales: $40,000,000
Employees: 350

Reuters
410 11th Avenue South
Hopkins, MN 55343
(612) 935-6921
Sales: $26,300,000
Employees: 230

RJ Reynolds Tobacco Co.
(Subsidiary of RJR Nabisco, Inc.)
401 N. Main Street
Winston-Salem, NC 27101
(901) 741-5000
Sales: $8,100,000,000
Employees: 14,000

RJR Nabisco, Inc.
1100 Reynolds Boulevard
Winston-Salem, NC 27102
(919) 773-2000
Sales: $16,595,000,000
Employees: 130,000

Rockwell International Corp.
2201 Seal Beach Boulevard
Seal Beach, CA 90740
(310) 797-3311
Sales: $10,840,000,000
Employees: 77,028

Rohn and Haas Co.
100 Independence Mall West
Philadelphia, PA 19106
(215) 592-3000
Sales: $3,260,000,000
Employees: 13,000

Rubbermaid, Inc.
1147 Akron Road
Wooster, OH 44691
(216) 264-6464
Sales: $2,110,000,000
Employees: 12,371

Ryder System, Inc.
3600 N.W. 82nd Avenue
Miami, FL 33168
(305) 593-3726
Sales: $4,220,000,000
Employees: 40,000

S

Safeway, Inc.
201 Fourth Street
Oakland, CA 94660
(415) 891-3000
Sales: $15,210,000,000
Employees: 124,000

J. Sainsbury
Stamford House
Stamford Street
London, England SE1 9LL
071-921-6000
Sales: $11,220,000,000
Employees: 79,974

Saks Fifth Avenue
(Subsidiary of Investcorp.)
12 E. 49th Street
New York, NY 10017
(212) 753-4000
Sales: $1,400,000,000
Employees: 8,000

Savin Corporation
(Subsidiary of CDC Data Systems, Ltd.)
9 West Broad Street
Stamford, CT 06904-2270
(203) 967-5000
Sales: $198,000,000
Employees: 1,900

Scandinavian Airlines
138-02 Queens Boulevard
Jamaica, NY 11453
(718) 657-2575
Sales: $166,000,000
Employees: 610

Scott Paper
Scott Plaza
Philadelphia, PA 19113
(610) 522-5000
Sales: $4,750,000,000
Employees: 25,900

Seagram International
(Subsidiary of Seagold Vineyards Holding Corp.)
375 Park Avenue
New York, NY 10152
(212) 572-7000
Sales: $3,150,000,000
Employees: 10,200

Sears Roebuck & Co.
Sears Tower
Chicago, IL 60606
(312) 875-2500
Sales: $50,840,000,000
Employees: 363,000

Shaklee
(Subsidiary of Y-S Holding Corp.)
444 Market Street
San Francisco, CA 94111
(415) 954-3000
Sales: $480,000,000
Employees: 3,300

Shell Oil Co.
(Subsidiary of Shell Petroleum, Inc.)
One Shell Plaza
900 Louisiana
Houston, TX 77001
(713) 241-6161
Sales: $21,090,000,000
Employees: 22,212

Shenandoah Life Insurance Co.
2301 Brambleton Avenue S.W.
Roanoke, VA 24015
(703) 985-4400
Sales: $131,800,000
Employees: 212

Siemens Corp.
(Subsidiary of Siemens AG)
1301 Avenue of the Americas
New York, NY 10019
(212) 258-4000
Sales: $3,980,000,000
Employees: 376

Smith Barney
(Subsidiary of Travelers, Inc.)
1345 Avenue of the Americas
New York, NY 10105
(212) 399-6000
Sales: $950,000,000
Employees: 7,500

Solectron Corp.
777 Gilbraltar Drive
Milpitas, CA 95035
(408) 957-8500
Sales: $1,460,000,000
Employees: 6,000

Sony Corp. of America
(Subsidiary of Sony Corp.)
9 West 57th Street
New York, NY 10019
(212) 371-5800
Sales: $2,000,000,000
Employees: 6,900

Southwest Airlines Co.
Love Field
Box 37611
Dallas, TX 75235
(214) 902-4000
Sales: $2,300,000,000
Employees: 11,400

The Sperry Co., Inc.
9146 U.S. Highway 52
Brookville, IN 47012
(317) 647-4141
Sales: NA
Employees: 300

Spiegel, Inc.
3500 Lacey Road
Downers Grove, IL 60515
(708) 986-8800
Sales: $2,600,000,000
Employees: 12,000

Sprint Corp.
2330 Shawnee Mission Parkway
Westwood, KS 66205
(913) 624-3000
Sales: NA
Employees: NA

Square D
1415 S. Roselle Road
Palatine, IL 60067
(708) 397-2600
Sales: $1,720,000,000
Employees: 19,300

The Standard Oil Co.
(Subsidiary of British Petroleum Co. plc)
200 Public Square
Cleveland, OH 44114
(216) 586-4141
Sales: $14,780,000,000
Employees: 41,600

State Farm Mutual Auto Insurance Co.
One State Farm Plaza
Bloomington, IL 61701

(309) 766-2311
Sales: $22,000,000,000
Employees: 49,752

Sun Microsystems
2550 Gracia Avenue
Mountain View, CA 94043
(415) 960-1300
Sales: $4,310,000,000
Employees: 12,500

Sunoco
(Subsidiary of Sun Co., Inc.)
36 York Mills Road
Northyork, Ontario
Canada M2P 2C5
(416) 733-7300
Sales: $1,500,000,000
Employees: 4,115

T

Taco Bell
(Subsidiary of PepsiCo)
17901 Von Karmen Avenue
Irvine, CA 92714
(714) 863-4500
Sales: $1,470,000,000
Employees: 47,000

TCI International, Inc.
222 Caspien Drive
Sunnyville, CA 94089
(408) 747-6100
Sales: $28,260,000
Employees: 140

Teleflex Inc.
155 South Limerick Road
Royersford, PA 19468
(215) 948-5700
Sales: $175,000,000
Employees: 3,500

Tenneco, Inc.
1010 Milam
Houston, TX 77002
(713) 757-2131
Sales: $14,400,000,000
Employees: 90,000

Texaco, Inc.
2000 Westchester Avenue
White Plains, NY 10650
(914) 253-4000
Sales: $46,200,000,000
Employees: 54,400

Texas Instruments Inc.
13500 North Central Expressway
Dallas, TX 75265

(214) 995-2011
Sales: $4,920,000,000
Employees: 77,800

The Thermos Co.
300 N. Martingale Road
Schaumburg, IL 60173
(708) 240-3150
Sales: NA
Employees: 2,000

3M
3M Center
Minneapolis, MN 55144
(612) 733-1110
Sales: $8,600,000,000
Employees: 84,300

Time Warner, Inc.
1271 Avenue of the Americas
New York, NY 10020
(212) 484-8000
Sales: $14,500,000,000
Employees: 41,700

Toshiba International Corp.
(Subsidiary of Toshiba Corp.)
350 California Street
Suite 700
San Francisco, CA 94104
(415) 434-2340
Sales: $201,000,000
Employees: 506

Toyota Motor Sales USA, Inc.
(Subsidiary of Toyota Motor Corp.)
19001 South Western Avenue
Torrance, CA 90501
(213) 618-4000
Sales: $5,000,000,000
Employees: 2,200

Toys "Я" Us, Inc.
395 West Passaic Street
Rochelle Park, NJ 07662
(201) 845-5033
Sales: $2,444,903,000
Employees: 28,600

The Travelers Corp.
One Tower Square
Hartford, CT 06183-1050
(203) 277-0111
Sales: NA
Employees: 30,000

Triangle Industries, Inc.
900 Third Avenue
16th Floor
New York, NY 10022
(212) 230-3000
Sales: $1,640,000,000
Employees: 14,000

TRW, Inc.
1900 Richmond Road
Cleveland, OH 44124
(216) 291-7000
Sales: $5,490,000,000
Employees: 82,400

U

Ultra Pac, Inc.
22051 Industrial Boulevard
Rogers, MN 55374
(612) 428-8340
Sales: $11,590,000
Employees: 75

Unilever
(Subsidiary of Nederlandse Unilever
Bedrijuen)
390 Park Avenue
New York, NY 10022
(212) 885-1260
Sales: $8,110,000,000
Employees: 30,600

Union Carbide Corp.
Old Ridgebury Road
Section C-2
Danbury, CT 06817
(203) 794-0400
Sales: $9,000,000,000
Employees: 46,900

Union Pacific Corp.
Eighth and Eaton Avenues
Bethlehem, PA 18018
(610) 861-3200
Sales: $7,560,000,000
Employees: 233

Unisys Corp.
Unisys Place
Detroit, MI 48232
(313) 972-7000
Sales: $5,030,000,000
Employees: 100,000

United Airlines, Inc.
(Subsidiary of Allegis Corp.)
1200 Algonquin Road
Elk Grove Township, IL 60007
(708) 952-4000
Sales: $52,900,000,000
Employees: 54,300

United Parcel Service of America, Inc.
51 Weaver Street
Greenwich, CT 06830
(203) 622-6000
Sales: $8,610,000,000
Employees: 160,000

United Technologies Corp.
Main and Pearl Streets
Hartford, CT 06101
(203) 728-7000
Sales: $15,600,000,000
Employees: 193,000

US Air
2345 Crystal Drive
Arlington, VA 22227
(703) 418-7000
Sales: $6,260,000,000
Employees: 53,700

US Steel
(Subsidiary of USX Corp.)
600 Grant Street
Pittsburgh, PA 15219
(412) 433-1121
Sales: NA Employees: NA

USX Corp.
600 Grant Street
Pittsburgh, PA 15219
(412) 433-1121
Sales: $18,060,000,000
Employees: 45,592

V

Viacom, Inc.
(Subsidiary of National Amusements, Inc.)
1515 Broadway
New York, NY 10036
(212) 258-6000
Sales: $2,000,000,000
Employees: 4,900

Volkswagen
Wolfsburg, Germany
05-36190
Sales: $68,070,000,000
Employees: 267,038

W

Wal-Mart Stores
702 8th Street
Bentonville, AR 72712
(501) 273-4000
Sales: $11,900,000,000
Employees: 150,000

The Walt Disney Co.
500 South Buena Vista Street
Burbank, CA 91521
(818) 840-1000
Sales: $1,370,000,000
Employees: 30,000

Warner Communications
75 Rockefeller Plaza
New York, NY 10019
(212) 484-8000
Sales: $2,230,000,000
Employees: 8,000

Waste Management
3003 Butterfield Road
Hinsdale, IL 60521
(708) 572-8800
Sales: $4,480,000,000
Employees: 42,600

Westinghouse Electrical Corp.
Six Gateway Center
Pittsburgh, PA 15222
(412) 244-2000
Sales: $10,700,000,000
Employees: 133,000

Weyerhaeuser Co.
33663 32nd Drive S.E.
Federal Way, WA 98003
(206) 924-2345
Sales: $5,200,000,000
Employees: 41,700

Whirlpool
3000 M63 N.
Benton Harbor, MI 49022

(616) 926-5000
Sales: $6,290,000,000
Employees: 39,400

WHYCO Chromium Co.
Thomaston, CT 06787
(203) 283-5826
Sales: $14,000,000
Employees: 200

Woolworth Corp.
233 Broadway
Woolworth Building
New York, NY 10279
(212) 553-2000
Sales: $9,800,000,000
Employees: 73,000

X

Xerox Corp.
800 Long Ridge Road
Stamford, CT 06904
(203) 329-8700
Sales: $8,730,000,000
Employees: 98,500

Z

Zale Corp.
901 West Walnut Hill Lane
Irving, TX 75038-1003
(214) 580-4000
Sales: NA
Employees: 9,900

Zenith
1000 Milwaukee Avenue
Glenview, IL 60025
(708) 391-7000
Sales: $2,610,000,000
Employees: 32,000

GLOSSARY

A

ability People's beliefs about their own abilities to do their assigned jobs.

accounting audits Procedures used to verify accounting reports and statements.

accountability The expectation that employees perform a job, take corrective action when necessary, and report upward on the status and quality of their performance.

achievement-oriented leadership A path-goal leadership style where the leader is preoccupied with setting challenging goals for the work group.

acquisition A transaction in which a firm buys all or part of another business, and that is agreeable to all parties.

act utilitarianism An ethical system which seeks the greatest good for the greatest number.

activity-based costing A method of cost accounting designed to identify streams of activity, and then to allocate costs across particular business processes according to the amount of time employees devote to particular activities.

adhocracy A structure that consists of interacting project teams.

administrative management A classical management approach that attempted to identify major principles and functions that managers could use to achieve superior organizational performance.

adverse impact The discriminatory effect of a hiring practice.

advisory relationship A relationship created when units call on sources of expert knowledge to help solve problems.

advocacy advertising A technique organizations use to reach a general audience with messages about public policy issues.

affirmative action Attempts by an organization to match the number of its female and minority employees to the number of women and minorities available in the labor market.

allocation model A special-purpose linear programming algorithm developed to help decision makers minimize costs or maximize profits while working within specified organizational and environmental constraints. Also called *transportation method* or the *assignment method*.

arbitration The use of a neutral third party to resolve a labor dispute.

assessment center A managerial performance test in which candidates participate in a variety of exercises and situations.

assets The values of the various items the corporation owns.

audit relationship A relationship that exists when one group not directly in the chain of command evaluates the methods and performances of other groups.

authority The legitimate right to make decisions and to tell other people what to do.

authoritarianism The degree to which individuals respect, admire, and defer to authority.

authority levels The number of supervisory and managerial levels between the chairperson and the lowest-ranking employees in the organization.

autocratic leadership A form of leadership in which the leader makes decisions on his or her own and then announces those decisions to the group.

autonomy An employee's ability to make independent and discrete decisions.

avoidance A reaction to conflict that involves either ignoring the problem by doing nothing at all, or by de-emphasizing the disagreement.

B

balance The effort to spread risk among MNE subsidiaries. This approach attempts to equalize earnings for all plants, even if production levels vary from one country to another.

balance sheet A report that shows the financial picture of a company at a given time and itemizes assets, liabilities, and stockholders' equity.

balance sheet equation Assets = Liabilities + Stockholders' equity.

barriers to entry Conditions that prevent new companies from entering an industry.

base technology A technology that is basic in its industry and thus offers little competitive advantage for the organization.

batch manufacturer An operation with higher volumes and lower varieties than those characteristic of a job shop.

behavioral approach A leadership perspective that attempts to identify what good leaders do.

behavioral scales (BARS) Behaviorally anchored rating scales; performance measuring instruments that focus on specific, relevant behaviors.

benchmarking The process of comparing the organization's practices and technologies with those of other companies.

biosphere The natural environment, consisting of water, the atmosphere, soils, minerals, plants, animals, and energy provided by the sun.

bonus A payment plan in which employees receive a standard wage for productivity and then receive extra pay for additional productivity.

bootlegging Informal efforts by managers and workers to create new products and new processes.

boundary role An organizational role in which an employee spends considerable time outside the company, interacting with other people and organizations.

bounded rationality A less than perfect form of rationality suggesting that in the real world, decision makers are rarely able to conduct a complete, rational analysis because decisions are complex and complete information is unavailable.

brainstorming A process in which group members generate as many ideas about a problem as they can; criticism is withheld until all ideas have been proposed.

break-even point The point at which total income equals total expenditures and no loss exists.

budgeting The process of investigating what is being done and comparing the results with the corresponding budget data to verify accomplishments or remedy differences. Also called *budgetary controlling.*

budget period Period of time within which an enterprise's complete, normal activity takes place, and coinciding with other control devices such as balance sheets and statements of profit and loss.

bureaucracy A classical management approach emphasizing a structured, formal network of relationships among specialized positions in the organization.

bureaucratic control The use of rules, regulations, and authority to guide performance.

business incubator A protected environment for new, small businesses that offers low rent and shared costs.

business plan A formal planning step in starting a new business that focuses on the entire venture and describes all the elements involved in starting it.

business reengineering The process of starting all over, from scratch, rebuilding a company and overhauling its ways of doing business.

business strategy The major actions by which a business competes in a particular industry or market.

C

cafeteria Employee benefit programs in which employees choose from a menu of options to create a benefit package tailored to their needs.

career anchor Self-concepts that guide people's careers and provide meaningful personal standards for career success.

carrying capacity The ability of a finite resource to sustain a population.

centralized organization An organization in which high-level executives make most decisions and pass them down to lower levels for implementation.

certainty The state that exists when decision makers have accurate and comprehensive information.

charismatic leader A person who is dominant, self-confident, convinced of the moral righteousness of his or her beliefs, and able to arouse a sense of excitement and adventure in subordinates.

clan control Control based on the norms, values, shared goals, and trust among group members.

closed system A classical perspective of organizations that emphasized efficiency within the organization.

cluster organization A team-based design in which groups of employees from different disciplines work together on a semi-permanent basis.

coalition An informal network of allies who support and help implement ideas.

coalition building A strategy by which an organization attempts to find other organizations or groups of voters that share political interests on a particular legislative issue.

coercive power Control over punishments.

cohesiveness The degree to which a group is attractive to its members, members are motivated to remain in the group, and members influence one another.

command group A group responsible for performing on-going tasks, such as making or selling a product; includes a manager and her or his immediate subordinates.

communication The transmission of information and meaning from one party to another through the use of shared symbols.

comparable worth Principle of equal pay for different jobs of equal worth.

comparison person Another individual against whom a person compares his or her ratio of outcomes-to-inputs.

complex environment An environment in which many variables must be considered in decision making.

compliance-based ethics programs Company mechanisms typically designed by corporate counsel to prevent, detect, and punish legal violations.

computer-integrated manufacturing The use of computer-aided design and computer-aided manufacturing to sequence and optimize a number of production processes.

concentration A strategy employed for an organization that operates a single business and competes in a single industry.

concentric diversification A strategy used to add new businesses that produce related products or are involved in related markets and activities.

conceptual and decision skills Skills pertaining to a manager's ability to recognize complex and dynamic issues, examine the numerous and conflicting factors such issues involve, and resolve the problems for the benefit of the organization and its members.

concurrent control The control process used while plans are being carried out, including directing, monitoring, and fine-tuning activities as they are performed.

conflict Opposing pressures from different sources. Two levels of conflict are psychological conflict and conflict that arises among individuals or groups.

conglomerate diversification A strategy used to add new businesses that produce unrelated products or are involved in unrelated markets and activities.

conservation An environmental philosophy that seeks to avoid waste, promote the rational and efficient use of natural resources, and maximize long-term yields, especially of renewable resources.

consumerism A social trend characterized by increasing consumption of goods.

contingency perspective An approach to the study of management proposing that the managerial strategies, structures, and processes that result in high performance depend on the characteristics, or important contingencies, of the situation in which they are applied.

contingency plans Sophisticated planning processes that identify alternative courses of action to be implemented if key characteristics of the situation change.

continuous production A process that is highly automated and has a continuous production flow.

control The process of measuring progress toward planned performance and applying corrective measures to ensure that performance is in line with managers' objectives.

cooperative strategies Strategies used by two or more organizations working together to manage the external environment.

coordination The procedures that link the various parts of the organization for the purpose of achieving the organization's overall mission.

core competencies The specific skills or knowledge an organization possesses.

corporate constituency programs Programs that involve organizational efforts to identify, educate, and motivate to political action those individuals who may be influenced by public policies that affect the organization.

corporate legitimacy A motive for organizational involvement in the public policy process. The assumption is that organizations are legitimate to the extent that their goals, purposes, and methods are consistent with those of society.

corporate social responsibility A perspective stating that managers must consider the primary goals of society and the broad set of human needs in their decisions.

corporate social responsiveness A perspective stating that executives should look to laws and regulations as the ultimate arbiters of responsible corporate behavior.

corporate spin-off A new company started by innovators who are frustrated by the lack of support within a main organization.

corporate strategy The set of businesses, markets, or industries in which an organization competes and the distribution of resources among those entities.

cost competitiveness Pricing a product (good or service) so that it is attractive to consumers.

cross-functional teams Employees from different functional units that are organized into work groups with shared responsibilities and decision making.

culture shock The disorientation and stress associated with being in a foreign environment.

current ratio A liquidity ratio which indicates the extent to which short-term assets can decline and still be adequate to pay short-term liabilities.

customer departmentalization Subdividing an organization by distinctions between types of customers.

customer service The speed and dependability with which an organization can deliver what customers want.

custom-made solutions The combination of ideas into new, creative solutions.

D

debt-equity ratio A leverage ratio which indicates the company's ability to meet its long-term financial obligations.

decentralized organization An organization in which lower-level managers make important decisions.

decision support system (DSS) An interactive, computer-based system that helps decision makers solve ill-structured problems.

decision tree A graphic tool for analyzing all possible options for a decision under risk. Each decision is assigned a number of possible outcomes, and the probabilities of those outcomes are either known or estimated.

defenders Companies that stay within a stable product domain as a strategic maneuver.

delegation The assignment of new or additional responsibilities to a subordinate.

democratic leadership A form of leadership in which the leader solicits input from subordinates.

demographics Measures of various characteristics of the people who comprise groups or other social units.

departmentalization Subdividing an organization into smaller subunits.

development Teaching managers and professional employees broad skills needed for their present and future jobs.

development project A focused organizational effort to create a new product or process via technological advances.

devil's advocate A person who has the job of criticizing ideas to ensure that different viewpoints are fully explored.

diagnostic activities Activities for assessing the organization's current state with respect to its strengths and weaknesses, problems, employee attitudes, and other dimensions.

dialectic A structured debate between two conflicting courses of action.

dialogue A type of team discourse in which members explore complex issues from many viewpoints.

differentiation An aspect of the organization's internal environment created by job specialization and the division of labor.

differentiation strategy A strategy an organization uses to build competitive advantage by being unique in its industry or market segment along one or more dimensions.

direct foreign investment (DFI) The investment an organization makes to open a plant in another country.

directive leadership A path-goal leadership style with an emphasis on spelling out duties and responsibilities of an individual or group.

discount the future Weight short-term costs and benefits more heavily than longer-term costs and benefits.

discussion A type of team discourse in which each person attempts to win a debate by having his or her view accepted by the group.

diversity Individual differences in demographic and lifestyle characteristics, such as religion, age, disability status, military experience, sexual orientation, economic class, education, gender, race ethnicity, and nationality.

diversity training programs Programs that focus on identifying and reducing hidden biases against people with differences and developing the skills needed to effectively manage a diversified workforce.

division of labor The assignment of different tasks to different people or groups.

domain defense A form of defense involving activities intended to counter challenges to the organization's legitimacy.

downsizing The planned elimination of positions or jobs.

downward communication Information that flows from higher to lower levels in the organization's hierarchy.

dynamic environment An environment characterized by rapid changes.

dynamic style A communication style characterized by high energy and inspirational pleas; used to motivate workers and boost morale.

E

early adopters The second group of new technology adopters to whom others look for leadership, ideas, and up-to-date technological information.

early majority The third group of new technology adopters who are typically more deliberate and are often important community and industry members.

economic regulation Regulation originating in government agencies that controls entry, prices, and the quality of service within an industry.

economies of scale Reductions in the average cost of a unit of production as the total volume produced increases.

economies of scope Economies in which materials and processes employed in one product can be used to make other, related products.

effective manager An active leader who creates a positive work environment in which the organization and its employees have the opportunity and the incentive to achieve high performance.

effectiveness The degree to which the outputs of the organization correspond to the outputs that organizations and individuals in the external environment want.

efficiency The ratio of outputs to inputs.

egoism An ethical system which places self-interest first as long as others are not harmed.

emerging technology A technology that is still in its early stages and thus is unproved.

employment-at-will The concept that an employee can be dismissed arbitrarily.

empowerment The process of sharing power with employees, thereby enhancing their confidence in their ability to perform their jobs and their belief that they are influential contributors to the organization.

entrepreneurship The act of forming a new business.

environmental management Proactive strategies aimed at changing the environmental context in which the organization operates.

environmental movement An environmental philosophy postulating that the unintended negative effects of human economic activities on the environment are often greater than the benefits, and that nature should be preserved.

equalitarian style A communication style characterized by a two-way flow of shared information. Both parties express their ideas and opinions and understand and accept the other's viewpoints.

equifinality Principle that states there are many avenues to the same outcome, and not just one best way.

equity The degree to which employees believe they are being treated fairly, both internally and externally.

equity theory A theory stating that people assess how fairly they have been treated according to two key factors: outcomes and inputs.

ERG theory A human needs theory developed by Alderfer postulating that people have three basic sets of needs which can operate simultaneously.

ethical codes Codes that present an explicit set of guidelines for employees to follow in the workplace.

ethics The systematic inquiry into human conduct.

ethnocentric behavior Behavior that occurs when foreign subsidiaries depend on the parent company for competitive strength and the parent views them as extensions of itself.

executive champion An executive who supports a new technology and protects the product champion of the innovation.

expatriate A parent-company national who is sent to work at a foreign subsidiary.

expectancy Employees' perception of the likelihood that their efforts will enable them to attain their performance goals.

expectancy theory A theory proposing that people will behave based on their perceived likelihood that their behavior will lead to a certain outcome and on how highly they value that outcome.

expert power Possession of certain knowledge or expertise.

export A commodity sent from one country or region to another country or region.

external audit An evaluation conducted by one organization, such as a CPA firm, on another.

external environment All relevant forces outside a firm's boundaries, such as competitors, customers, the government, and the economy.

extinction   Withdrawing or failing to provide a reinforcing consequence.

extrinsic reward   A reinforcer a high-performing worker receives from a boss, company, or other person.

F

factors of production   The inputs into the production process, such as labor, energy, and raw materials.

failure rate   The number of expatriate managers of an overseas operation that come home early.

feedback   Information about job performance given to an employee.

feedback control   Control that focuses on the use of information about previous results to correct deviations from the acceptable standard.

feedforward control   The control process used before operations begin, including procedures, and rules designed to ensure that planned activities are carried out properly.

(Fiedler's) contingency model of leadership effectiveness   A situational approach to leadership postulating that effectiveness depends on the personal style of the leader and the degree to which the situation gives the leader power, control, and influence over the situation.

final customer   Those who purchased products in their finished form.

flexible benefit programs   Benefit programs in which employees are given credits to spend on benefits that fit their unique needs.

flexible factories   Manufacturing plants that have short production runs, are organized around products, and use decentralized scheduling.

focused factory   A factory designed to produce a single product.

foreign subsidiary   An overseas-based plant either wholly owned by the domestic organization or jointly owned by that organization and others.

formal communication   Official, organizationally sanctioned transmissions of information.

formal group   A group created by formal organizational authority to perform a particular job.

forming   A phase in group development in which members attempt to lay the ground rules for what types of behavior are acceptable.

framing effects   A psychological bias that refers to the way in which a problem or decision alternative is phrased or presented.

franchising   An arrangement whereby a company sells limited rights to use its brand name to a franchisee in return for a lump-sum payment and a share of the franchisee's profits.

functional departmentalization   Subdividing an organization by business functions such as accounting, marketing, human resources, etc.

functional strategies   Strategies implemented by each functional area of the organization to support the organization's business strategy.

functions of management   The four basic management processes consisting of planning, organizing, leading, and controlling.

G

Gantt chart   A chart containing information on a pair of activities and their planned completion dates; also includes projected start and duration times.

geocentric organization   An organization that maximizes total global return to a multinational enterprise and all its units.

geographical departmentalization   Subdividing an organization by geographical distinctions such as territories, regions, or countries.

glass ceiling   An invisible barrier that makes it difficult for certain groups, such as minorities and women, to move beyond a certain level in the organizational hierarchy.

global organization model   An organization model consisting of a company's overseas subsidiaries and characterized by centralized decision making and tight control by the parent company over most aspects of worldwide operations. Typically adopted by organizations that base their global competitive strategy on low cost.

global strategy   A strategy of global competition based on the assumption that no tangible differences exist among countries with regard to consumer tastes and preferences, competitive conditions, operating conditions, and political, legal, and social structures.

goal   A target or end that management desires to reach.

goal displacement   A condition that occurs when a decision-making group loses sight of its original goal and a new, possibly less important goal emerges.

goal-setting theory   A motivation theory that states people have conscious goals that energize them and direct their thoughts and behaviors toward one end.

grapevine   Informal communication network.

Grid Organization Development   A six-phase model of change involving the entire organization.

group   Two or more people who interact with and depend on one another and work toward some common goal or purpose.

group maintenance behaviors   Actions taken to ensure the satisfaction of group members, develop and maintain harmonious work relationships, and preserve the social stability of the group.

group maintenance specialist   An individual who develops and maintains harmony within a group.

group technology   A process that uses multipurpose equipment for the manufacture of parts.

groupthink   A phenomenon that occurs in decision making when group members avoid disagreement as they strive for consensus.

growth stage of the product life cycle   The stage at which a product has become well-defined and has gained market recognition; characterized by increased sales and substantial profits.

H

Hawthorne Effect   Workers' reactions to being observed or studied resulting in superficial rather than meaningful changes in behavior.

(Herzberg's) two-factor theory   An approach to job enrichment that distinguishes between two categories of factors—hygiene and motivators. Poor management of hygiene factors results in worker dissatisfaction, but good management of them will not lead to satisfaction. However, when motivators are present, workers should perceive jobs as satisfying and motivating.

hierarchy   The authority levels of the organizational pyramid.

high-involvement organization   A type of organization in which top management ensures that there is consensus about the direction in which the business is heading.

horizontal communication   Information shared among people in the same hierarchical level.

host-country nationals   Natives of the country where an overseas subsidiary is located.

human relations   A classical management approach that attempted to understand and explain how human psychological and social processes interact with the formal aspects of the work situation to influence performance.

human resources management (HRM)   Formal systems for the management of people within the organization. Divided into three major areas: staffing, rewarding, and designing work.

hygiene factors   Characteristics of the workplace, such as company policies, working conditions, pay, and supervision, that make a job more satisfying.

I

ill-structured problem   A problem that has no proven answer.

illusion of control   People's belief that they can influence events, even when they have no control over what will happen.

import   A commodity brought into one country or region from another country or region.

independent entrepreneur   An individual who establishes a new organization without the benefit of corporate experience.

independent entrepreneurship   The act of individually establishing a new organization without the benefit of corporate support.

independent strategies   Strategies that an organization acting on its own uses to change some aspect of its current environment.

informal communication   Unofficial, unsanctioned transmissions of information.

informal group   A group that evolves because of mutual attraction, common interests, or proximity of offices, desks, or workstations to one another.

informing   A team strategy that entails concentrating first on the internal team process to achieve a state of performance readiness, then informing outsiders of its intentions.

infrastructural variables   Variables that do not result in physical resources being put in place (*structural variables,* in contrast, focus on the organization's physical assets). Examples are quality systems, planning and control systems, organization structure, and human resources.

innovation   A change in technology; a departure from previous ways of doing things.

innovators   The earliest, most adventurous group of new technology adopters.

instrumentality   The perception that performance will be followed by a particular outcome.

integrating role   An organizational role that involves interaction and coordination with units outside a specific unit but within the organization.

integration   The degree to which differentiated work units work together and coordinate their efforts.

integrity-based ethics programs   Company mechanisms designed to instill in people a personal responsibility for ethical behavior.

integrity test   An employment test that assesses a candidate's honesty.

interdependencies   Linkages with individuals, groups, or organizations that have the power to affect an executive's job performance.

intergroup activities   Activities that deal with relationships among groups that sometimes work together.

intermediate consumer   Customers who purchase raw materials or wholesale before selling them to final customers.

internal audit   A periodic assessment of a company's own planning, organizing, leading, and controlling processes.

international organization model   An organization model that is composed of a company's overseas subsidiaries and characterized by greater control by the parent company over the research function and local product and marketing strategies than is the case in the multinational model.

interpersonal and communication skills   Human or people skills; the ability to lead, motivate, and communicate effectively with others.

intrapreneurs   New venture creators working in big corporations.

intrapreneurship   The act of creating new products and processes within an organization. The intrapreneur is a corporate entrepreneur.

intrinsic reward   A reinforcer a worker derives directly from performing the job itself.

introduction stage of the product life cycle   The stage characterized by innovative, distinctive, and focused products. The goal in this stage is market acceptance of the organization's new product.

ISO 9000   A series of quality standards developed by a committee working under the International Organization for Standardization to improve total quality in all businesses for the benefit of both producers and consumers.

J

job analysis A tool for determining what is done on a given job and what should be done on that job.

job enlargement Giving people additional tasks at the same time to alleviate boredom.

job enrichment The changing of a task to make it inherently more rewarding, motivating, and satisfying.

job maturity The level of the employee's skills and technical knowledge relative to the task being performed.

job rotation The changing from one routine task to another to alleviate boredom.

job shop An organization with a large variety of products, each produced in single quantities.

joint venture A subsidiary jointly owned by two or more companies, either overseas or domestic.

just-in-time (JIT) A system that calls for subassemblies and components to be manufactured in very small lots and delivered to the next stage of the production process just as they are needed.

K

key technology A technology that has proved its worth but has yet to come into widespread use. Such a technology provides a competitive advantage because its dissemination is limited.

L

labor relations The system of relations between workers and management.

laggards The last group of technology adopters who are often conservative, isolated, and suspicious of innovation and change.

lag strategy A strategy in which the organization waits until demand increases actually occur and its operations are at full capacity before adding capacity.

laissez-faire A leadership philosophy characterized by an absence of managerial decision making.

late majority The fourth group of new technology adopters who are skeptical of technological change, and adopt only out of economic necessity.

law of effect A theory formulated by Edward Thorndike in 1911 stating that behavior that is followed by positive consequences will likely be repeated.

leading The management function that involves the manager's efforts to stimulate high performance by employees.

lead strategy A strategy in which an organization adds capacity in anticipation of upswings in demand.

lean manufacturing An operation that strives to achieve the highest possible productivity and total quality, cost effectively, by eliminating unnecessary steps in the production process and continually strives for improvement.

learning organization An organization skilled at creating, acquiring, and transferring knowledge, and at modifying its behavior to reflect new knowledge and insights.

legitimate power The right or authority to tell subordinates what to do.

leveraged buyout (LBO) A type of acquisition in which a group buys the majority of stock in their own company from shareholders.

liabilities The amounts a corporation owes to various creditors.

liaison relationship A relationship that uses intermediaries among various groups.

licensing An arrangement in which a licensee in another country buys the rights to manufacture a company's product in its own country for a negotiated fee, such as royalty payments on number of units sold.

life-and career-planning activities Activities that help people identify their life and career objectives.

life-cycle analysis A process of evaluating all inputs and outputs to determine the total environmental impact of the production and use of a product.

line manager An employee responsible for activities that directly involve the organization's products or services, either in their creation or in getting them to customers.

liquidation and divestiture strategy A business strategy, implemented because of a weak competitive position or low industry growth, aimed at generating as much cash flow as possible while withdrawing from the business.

lobbying A strategy that involves efforts by political professionals or company executives to establish communication channels with regulatory bodies, legislators, and their staffs.

locus of control A concept, developed by Julian Rotter, that divides people into two groups—internals and externals—based on their perceived ability to control their lives or influence their fates.

logistics The movement of products from the right goods in the right amount to the right place at the right time.

low-cost strategy A strategy an organization uses to build competitive advantage by being efficient and offering a standard, no-frills product.

lower management The lowest level of management; includes office managers, sales managers, supervisors, and other first-line managers. Also called the *operational* level.

M

macroenvironment The most general environment; includes governments, economic conditions, and other fundamental factors that generally affect all organizations.

make-or-buy decision The question an organization asks itself about whether to acquire new technology from an outside source or develop it itself.

management The process of working with people and resources to accomplish organizational goals.

management audits　An evaluation of the effectiveness and efficiency of various systems within an organization.

management by objectives (MBO)　A process in which objectives set by a subordinate and supervisor must be reached within a given time period.

management information system (MIS)　A system in which information is collected, processed, and transmitted through an integrative, computer-based network.

management myopia　Focusing on short-term earnings and profits at the expense of longer-term strategic obligations.

managing diversity　Managing a culturally diverse workforce by recognizing the characteristics common to specific groups of employees while dealing with such employees as individuals and supporting, nurturing, and utilizing their differences to the organization's advantage.

manufacturing planning and control (MPC)　A system that enables an organization to move materials through the operation and schedule so that it meets customer needs at a minimal cost.

manufacturing resource planning (MRP II)　A comprehensive manufacturing planning and control system.

market control　Control based on the use of financial and economic information.

market focus strategy　A business strategy of concentrating on a specific market (sometimes called a *market niche*).

mass customization　The production of varied, individually customized products at the low cost of standardized, mass-produced products.

materials requirements planning (MRP)　A computerized manufacturing control system.

matrix organization　An organization composed of dual reporting relationships in which some managers report to two superiors, a functional manager, and a product manager.

maturity stage of the product life cycle　The stage in which the organization deals with a "commodity-type" product. Production is the main concern, and profit margins shrink.

maximax　A method of decision making in which the decision maker evaluates each decision row of the payoff table and selects the maximum return for each possible decision.

maximin　A conservative method of decision making in which the decision maker locates the minimum possible return associated with each decision row in the payoff table and then chooses the maximum of those returns.

maximize　A decision aimed at realizing the best possible outcome on one dimension, such as the decision to maximize profits.

mechanistic organization　A form of organization that seeks to maximize internal efficiency.

media richness　The degree to which a communication channel conveys information.

mentors　Higher level managers who help ensure that high-potential people are introduced to top management and socialized into the norms and values of the organization.

merger　The formation of one corporation from two companies by mutual agreement.

merit pay　A payment plan in which pay raises are distributed based on individual performance as assessed by subjective appraisals.

middle management　Second-level managers in charge of plants or departments and responsible for both the performance of their particular unit and how it relates to the rest of the organization.

mission　An organization's basic purpose and scope of operations.

monolithic organization　An organization that has a low degree of structural integration—employing few women, minorities, or other groups that differ from the majority—and thus has a highly homogeneous employee population.

motivation　Forces that energize, direct, and sustain a person's efforts.

motivators　Factors that make a job more motivating, such as additional job responsibilities, opportunities for personal growth and recognition, and feelings of achievement.

multicultural　The degree to which an organization values cultural diversity and is willing to utilize and encourage it.

multicultural organization　An organization that values cultural diversity and seeks to utilize and encourage it.

multidomestic strategy　A strategy of global competition based on the assumption that national markets differ widely with regard to consumer tastes and preferences, competitive conditions, operating conditions, and political, legal, and social structures.

multinational company　A business organization that competes in several countries. Also called a *multinational enterprise (MNE)*.

multinational organization model　An organization model that consists of the subsidiaries in each country in which a company does business, with ultimate control exercised by the parent company.

N

need for achievement　A need characterized by a strong orientation toward accomplishment and a high focus on success and goal attainment.

need for affiliation　A need characterized by a strong desire to be liked and accepted by other people.

need for power　A need characterized by a desire to influence or control other people.

need hierarchy　A human needs theory developed by Maslow organizing human needs into five major types, and postulating that people satisfy them one at a time from bottom to top.

needs assessment　An analysis identifying the jobs, people, and departments for which training is necessary.

negative reinforcement　Removing or withholding an undesirable consequence.

network organization　A collection of independent, mostly single-function firms.

niche strategy   A strategy that emphasizes specialization and focusing on a narrow segment of a market.

nonprogrammed decisions   New, novel, complex decisions having no proven answers.

nonrenewable resources   Resources, such as fossil fuels and minerals, that cannot be regenerated by natural processes.

norming   A phase in group development in which members agree on their shared goals, and norms and closer relationships develop.

norms   Shared beliefs about how group members should think and behave.

North American Free Trade Agreement (NAFTA)   An economic pact that combined the economies of the U.S., Canada, and Mexico into the world's largest trading block.

O

one-way communication   A process in which information flows in only one direction—from the sender to the receiver, with no feedback loop.

open-book management   Management practice of teaching line workers to understand revenues, costs, productivity, and strategic priorities.

open system   A perspective that expands the study of management to include the interaction between the organization and its environment.

operational manager   A lower-level manager who supervises one or more operations of the organization.

operational planning   The process of identifying the specific procedures and processes required at lower levels of the organization.

operational subsystem   The subsystem of the organization that performs the conversion of inputs into outputs. Also called the *technical core* of the organization.

operations management   A collective pattern of coordinated decisions for the formulation, reformulation, and deployment of operations resources.

operations strategy   A pattern of decisions that focus on resource configuration and deployment and provide a competitive advantage in support of the overall strategic initiative of the organization or strategic business unit.

operator control   A process used in computer-controlled production technology in which multiskilled operators rather than specialists can take corrective action.

opportunity analysis   A formal planning step in starting a new business that focuses on the opportunity, not the entire venture, and provides a basis for making a decision on whether to act.

optimize   To formulate a decision that cannot maximize on each of several outcomes but realizes the best possible array of outcomes.

orderly marketing arrangement (OMA)   An agreement between the United States and another country that limits the number of imports.

organic structure   An organizational form that emphasizes flexibility.

organization   A managed system designed and operated to achieve a specific set of objectives.

organization culture   The set of important assumptions about the organization and its goals and practices that members of the company share.

organizational behavior   A contemporary management approach that studies and identifies management activities that promote employee effectiveness by examining the complex and dynamic nature of individual, group, and organizational processes.

organizational behavior modification (OB Mod)   The application of reinforcement theory in organizational settings.

organizational development   A process of change that uses behavioral science knowledge and techniques to influence people's attitudes, beliefs, values, and behaviors on the job.

organizational technology   The process by which an organization produces final products or services.

organization chart   The reporting structure and division of labor in an organization.

organizing   The management function of assembling and coordinating of human, financial, physical, information and other resources needed to achieve goals.

outcome   Various things a person receives on the job, such as pay, recognition, benefits, etc.

outplacement   The process of helping people who have been dismissed from the company to regain employment.

P

pacing technology   A technology that has yet to prove its full value but has the potential to provide a significant competitive advantage.

parading   A team strategy that entails simultaneously emphasizing internal team building and achieving external visibility.

parallel ladder program   A program that gives career-oriented employees two different career paths along which they can progress.

parallel teams   Groups who operate separately from their regular work, and exist temporarily.

participation-in-decision-making   Dimension of the range of leadership behaviors—autocratic to democratic—that managers perform in involving their employees in making decisions.

participative leadership   A path-goal leadership style which emphasizes consulting with employees before making decisions.

path-goal theory   A theory that concerns how leaders influence subordinates' perceptions of their work goals and the paths they follow toward attainment of those goals.

payoff table   A procedure that arranges information to allow simultaneous examination of comparisons of all possible outcomes of a problem.

performance appraisal   Assessment of an employee's job performance.

performance gap   The difference between the organization's actual performance and the desired performance.

performing   A phase in group development in which the group channels its energies into performing its task.

piecework   A payment plan in which employees are paid a fixed amount of money for each unit of output produced.

planning   The management function of consciously and systematically making decisions about the goals and activities that an individual, a group, a work unit, or the overall organization will pursue in the future.

plans   The actions or means that managers intend to use to achieve organizational goals.

plural organization   An organization that has a relatively diverse employee population and makes an effort to involve employees from different gender, racial, or cultural backgrounds.

political action committee (PAC)   A political action group that represents an organization and makes donations to candidates for political office.

polycentric behavior   An approach to international operations that focuses on the differences among geographically segmented markets. Rather than having all decisions made by the parent company, there are several decision-making centers.

positive reinforcement   Applying valued consequences that increase the likelihood that a person will repeat the behavior that led to it.

post-heroic leadership   A new leadership perspective that de-emphasizes mythologizing one individual, and advocates spreading leadership abilities throughout the firm.

power   The ability to influence others.

preliminary control   The control process used before operations begin, including policies, procedures, and rules designed to ensure that planned activities will be carried out properly.

principle of exception   A managerial principle stating that control is enhanced by concentrating on the exceptions or significant deviations from the expected result or standard.

privatization   The sale of government-run enterprises to private owners.

proactive change   A response that is initiated before a performance gap has occurred.

probing   A team strategy that requires team members to interact frequently with outsiders, diagnose the needs of customers, and experiment with solutions.

process innovation   Changes that affect the methods of producing outputs.

product champion   A person who promotes a new technology throughout the organization in an effort to obtain acceptance and support for it.

product departmentalization   Subdividing an organization by a particular product or group of products.

product innovation   Changes in the outputs—products and/or services—of the organization.

profit and loss statement   An itemized financial statement of the income and expenses of a company's operations.

profit strategy   A business strategy designed to maximize return on the organization's existing resources and skills.

programmed decisions   Decisions encountered and made before, having objectively correct answers, and solvable by using simple rules, policies, or numerical computations.

project   A temporary program that uses human and technical resources from the organization's permanent units.

project and development teams   Groups who work on long-term projects over a period of years, but disband once the work is completed.

prospectors   Companies that continuously change the boundaries of their task environments by seeking new products and markets, diversifying and merging, or acquiring new enterprises.

psychological maturity   An employee's self-confidence and self-respect.

public affairs department   A department that monitors key events and trends in the organization's political and social environments, analyzes their effects on the organization, recommends organizational responses, and implements political strategies.

punishment   Administering an aversive consequence.

Q

quality   The excellence of a product, including such things as attractiveness, lack of defects, reliability, and long-term dependability.

quality circle (QC)   A group of employees who meet periodically to identify and solve work-related problems.

quality of work life (QWL)   Programs designed to create a workplace that enhances employee well-being.

quantitative management   A contemporary management approach that emphasizes the application of quantitative analysis to managerial decisions and problems.

R

ratio of current assets to current liabilities   The extent to which current assets can decline and still be sufficient to pay current liabilities. Also called the *current ratio* or *net working capital ratio.*

reactive change   A response that occurs when events in the environment have already affected the firm's performance; problem-driven change.

ready-made solutions   Ideas that have been seen or tried before, or follow the advice of others who have faced similar problems.

recruitment   The development of a pool of applicants for jobs in the organization.

referent power   Possession of personal characteristics that appeal to others.

reflection   A basic listening technique whereby a person attempts to repeat and clarify what he or she believes the other person is saying.

reinforcers   Positive consequences that motivate behavior.

relationship-motivated leadership   Leadership that places primary emphasis on maintaining good interpersonal relationships.

relationship-oriented behavior   Actions that emphasize maintaining good interpersonal relationships.

reliability   The consistency of test scores over time and across alternative measurements.

renewable resources   Resources, such as trees, that regenerate naturally despite use by people.

reorientation   A process that occurs when a company shifts its resources into more attractive markets and industries.

responsibility   The assignment of a task that an employee is supposed to carry out.

repetitive production   A form of production in which the company produces higher volume and lower variety, such as in an auto assembly plant.

return on investment (ROI)   A ratio of profit to capital used, or a rate of return from capital.

revitalization   A process an organization uses to give itself new life when its performance is mediocre or poor but survival is still possible.

reward power   Control of valued rewards.

rightsizing   A successful effort to achieve an appropriate size at which the company performs most effectively.

right to work   Legislation that allows employees to work without having to join a union.

risk   The state that exists when the probability of success is less than 100 percent.

roles   Different sets of expectations for how various individuals should behave.

rule utilitarianism   An ethical system which uses societal rules and customs to weigh the importance of conflicting values.

S

satisfice   To choose an option that is acceptable although not perfect.

scalar principle   A structure in which each person is part of one chain of command that extends from the top to the bottom of the organization.

scanning   A process that attempts to put the organization at the cutting edge of technology by identifying and monitoring sources of pacing and emerging technologies.

scenario   A narrative that describes a particular set of future conditions.

scientific management   A classical management approach that applied scientific methods to analyze and determine the "one best way" to complete production tasks.

self-actualization   A concept developed by Abraham Maslow implying that a person is self-motivated to develop multiple skills and use them to the fullest.

self-managed teams   Autonomous work groups in which workers are trained to do all or most of the jobs in a unit, have no immediate supervisor, and make decisions previously made by first-line supervisors.

sensitivity training   A process in which people share their feelings and perceptions about one another, helping them to learn more about themselves and improve their interpersonal relationships.

service relationships   Relationships that exist when top management centralizes an activity to which a large number of other units have access.

share-increasing strategy   A business strategy designed to achieve a significant and permanent increase in the organization's market share and requiring substantial investment.

simple environment   An environment in which only a few factors need be considered in decision making.

simultaneous engineering   A design approach in which all relevant functions cooperate jointly and continually in a maximum effort aimed at producing high-quality products that meet customers' needs.

situational analysis   A process planners use, within time and resource constraints, to gather, interpret, and summarize all information relevant to the planning issue under consideration.

situational approaches   Leadership perspectives proposing that universally important traits and behaviors do not exist, and that effective leadership behavior varies from situation to situation.

situational substitutes   Follower's task and/or organizational factors that provide the same influence on employees that leaders otherwise would have.

situational theory   A life cycle theory of leadership developed by Hersey and Blanchard postulating that a manager should consider an employee's psychological and job maturity before deciding whether task performance or maintenance behaviors are more important.

skills   Specific abilities resulting from knowledge, information, practice, and aptitude.

skill variety   A set of different job activities involving several skills and talents.

skunkworks   A project team consisting of 8 to 10 people designated to produce a new, innovative product.

Small Business Administration (SBA)   A federal government agency charged with promoting the growth of small business; provides financial, educational, and lobbying assistance.

socialization   The process by which an organization teaches new employees (or newly promoted managers) appropriate attitudes and behaviors.

social regulation   Regulation originating in agencies like the Occupational Safety and Health Administration and the Consumer Products Safety Commission that controls production processes and the quality of goods produced.

Social Security   An employee benefit that provides financial support to retirees and disabled employees.

sociotechnical systems approach   An approach to job design that attempts to redesign tasks to optimize operation of a new technology while preserving employees' interpersonal relationships and other human aspects of the work.

span of control   The number of subordinates who report directly to an executive or supervisor.

specialist control   A process used in computer-controlled production technology in which engineering experts take corrective actions.

specialization A process in which different individuals and units perform different tasks.

spin-off A new company started by innovators who are frustrated by the lack of support within the main organization.

stabilization relationship A relationship that involves auditing before the fact, that is, obtaining clearance from others before beginning or continuing an activity.

staff Employees who support the activities of line personnel and generally have more specialized or technical expertise.

stakeholders Groups and individuals who affect and are affected by the achievement of the organization's mission, goals, and strategies.

standard Expected performance for a given goal; a target that establishes a desired performance level, motivates performance, and serves as a benchmark against which actual performance is assessed.

standing committee A permanent task group that holds periodic meetings and will continue indefinitely because of its long-standing importance.

static environment An environment characterized by little or no change.

statistical process control The use of specific numerical data to monitor and control operations processes and outputs.

stereotyping Inaccurately perceiving and evaluating individuals' contributions, capabilities, aspirations and motivations based on one's own values, interests and experiences.

stockholders' equity The amount accruing to the corporation's owners.

stonewalling The use of public relations, legal action, and administrative processes to prevent or delay the introduction of legislation and regulation that may have an adverse impact on the organization.

storming A phase in group development in which hostilities and conflict arise, and people jockey for positions of power and status.

strategic alliance A formal relationship created with the purpose of joint pursuit of mutual goals.

strategic control system A system designed to support managers in evaluating the organization's progress regarding its strategy and, when discrepancies exist, taking corrective action.

strategic goals Major targets or end results relating to the organization's long-term survival, value, and growth.

strategic human resources planning A staffing activity with a strategic purpose derived from the organization's plans.

strategic management A process that involves managers from all parts of the organization in the formulation and implementation of strategic goals and strategies.

strategic managers Senior executives who are responsible for the organization's overall management.

strategic maneuvering The organization's conscious efforts to change the boundaries of its task environment.

strategic planning A set of procedures for making decisions about the organization's long-term goals and strategies.

strategic retreat A process that involves an organization's efforts to adapt its products and processes to changes in the political and social environments while minimizing the negative effects of those changes.

strategic subsystem The subsystem composed of the organization's senior executives that is concerned primarily with major interactions between the organization and the critical components of its environment.

strategic vision The long-term direction and strategic intent of a company.

strategy A pattern of actions and resource allocations designed to achieve the organization's goals.

subjectively expected utility (SEU) model A model in which individuals choose the option they subjectively believe will have the highest value or utility. In the simplest case, SEU is given by $V = \Sigma(p \times u)$.

substitutes for leadership Factors in the workplace that can exert the same influence on employees that leaders would provide.

subsystems Interdependent components of a system.

subunits Subdivisions of an organization.

supportive leadership A path-goal leadership style aimed at maintaining good interpersonal relationships.

survivor's syndrome Loss of productivity and morale in employees who remain after a downsizing.

sustainable growth Economic growth and development that meet the organization's present needs without harming the ability of future generations to meet their needs.

switching costs Fixed costs buyers face when they change suppliers.

synergy The sharing of benefits among the various operations within an MNE network.

system A set of interdependent parts that processes inputs into outputs.

systematic management A classical management approach that attempted to build into operations the specific procedures and processes that would ensure coordination of effort to achieve established goals and plans.

systems theory A theory stating that an organization is a set of interdependent elements, which in turn are interdependent with the external environment.

T

tableau A table containing all of the pertinent data in a structured format.

tactical managers Managers who are responsible for translating the general goals and plans developed by strategic managers into more specific objectives and activities.

tactical planning A set of procedures for translating broad strategic goals and plans into specific goals and plans that are relevant to a distinct portion of the organization, such as a functional area like marketing.

tactical subsystem   The subsystem consisting of middle managers and support services that facilitate and coordinate the work of the operational subsystem.

takeover   A type of acquisition in which a purchasing company makes a direct bid to the target company's stockholders because the target's management opposes the purchase.

task environment   The organization's environment that includes competitors, suppliers, customers, and other organizations with which the company interacts.

task group   A group composed of people assigned to work together on a particular problem or to complete a specific project.

task identity   A characteristic of job design that involves completing a whole, identifiable piece of work.

task-motivated leadership   Leadership that places primary emphasis on completing a task.

task-oriented behavior   Actions that emphasize completing a task.

task performance behaviors   Actions taken to ensure that the work group or organization reaches its goals.

task significance   The completion of a task that has an important, positive impact on the lives of others.

task specialist   An individual who has more advanced job-related skills and abilities than other group members possess.

team-based organization   An organic and responsive company that uses work teams as the basic building blocks.

team building   A process involving a number of activities designed to improve work group performance.

teams   A small number of people with complementary skills who are committed to a common purpose, set of performance goals, and approach for which they hold themselves mutually accountable.

technical innovator   A person who develops a new technology or has the key skills to install and operate the technology.

technical skill   The ability to perform a specialized task involving a particular method or process.

technology   The systematic application of scientific knowledge to a new product, process, or service.

technology life cycle   A predictable pattern followed by a technological innovation starting from its inception and development to market saturation and replacement.

termination interview   A discussion between a manager and an employee about the employee's dismissal.

third-country nationals   Natives of a country other than the home country or the host country of an overseas subsidiary.

time-based competition (TBC)   Strategies aimed at reducing the total time it takes to deliver a product or service.

top management   The strategic managers responsible for the entire organization; usually includes the CEO, president, and vice presidents.

total quality management   An integrative approach to management that supports the attainment of customer satisfaction through a wide variety of tools and techniques that result in high-quality goods and services.

tracking strategy   A plan to track capacity needs by adding and removing small amounts of capacity as changes in demand occur in the marketplace.

tragedy of the commons   A term describing the environmental destruction that results as individuals and businesses consume finite resources (i.e., the "commons") to serve their short-term interests without regard for the long-term consequences.

training   Teaching lower-level employees how to perform their present jobs.

trait approach   A leadership perspective that focuses on individual leaders and attempts to determine the personal characteristics that great leaders share.

trait scales   Performance measuring instruments that contain dimensions such as initiative, leadership, and attitude; raters are asked to indicate how much of a trait an employee possesses.

transformational leader   A leader who transforms things from what could be to what is and motivates people to transcend their personal interests for the good of the group.

transnational company   An organization that faces pressure for both global integration of manufacturing processes and local responsiveness to differences in consumer tastes and preferences.

transnational organization model   An organization model characterized by centralization of certain functions in locations that best achieve cost economies; basing of other functions in the company's national subsidiaries to facilitate greater local responsiveness; and fostering of communication among subsidiaries to permit transfer of technological expertise and skills.

turnaround   A situation in which a business has experienced serious losses and may fail to survive if it does not improve.

turnaround strategy   A business strategy designed to reverse a declining business as quickly as possible.

two-way communication   A process in which information flows in two directions—the receiver provides feedback and the sender is receptive to and responds to the feedback.

U

uncertainty   The state that exists when decision makers have insufficient information even if the available information is of high quality.

unemployment compensation   An employee benefit that provides financial support to employees who are laid off for reasons they cannot control.

union shop   An organization with a union and union security clause specifying that workers must join the union after a set period of time.

unit and small-batch production   A technology that involves manufacturing made-to-order products in small lot sizes.

unity of command   A structure in which each worker reports to one boss, who in turn reports to one boss.

upward communication   Information that flows from lower to higher levels in the organization's hierarchy.

utilitarianism   An ethical system which states that the greatest good for society should be the overriding concern of decision makers.

V

Valdez principles   A set of demands on business made by environmentalists, including reduction of wastes, prudent use of resources, marketing safe products, and taking responsibility for past damages to the environment.

valence   The value an outcome holds for the person contemplating it.

validity   The degree to which a selection test predicts or correlates with job performance.

vertical integration   The acquisition or development of new businesses that produce parts or components of the organization's product.

vertically integrated   A characteristic of a business that manufactures all the parts and components used in its product.

vigilance   A state that exists when a decision maker considers a wide range of alternatives; remembers the full range of objectives; weighs the costs and risks of each alternative; searches for useful new information; considers new information and advice, even if it does not support initial preferences; reexamines all alternatives and their possible consequences; and makes provisions for implementation, including contingency plans in the event things go wrong.

virtual office   Mobile work spaces in which employees are often equipped with laptop computers, pagers, and fax machines and work out of their homes, cars, or customer's offices.

vision   A mental image of a possible and desirable future state of the organization.

Vogel's approximation method (VAM)   A method for finding a low-cost, feasible solution that satisfies the given run requirements. Based on the differences between the lowest cost in each row of the tableau and the next lowest cost in the same row.

Vroom-Yetton-Jago model   A situational model of leadership that focuses on how leaders go about making decisions.

W

well-structured problem   A problem that has an objectively correct answer and can be solved by using simple rules or numerical computations.

wholly owned subsidiary   A corporation owned completely by another corporation (the parent company) which supervises its operations.

worker-oriented outcomes   Job analysis information regarding the knowledge, skills, and abilities (KSAs) needed to do a job.

workers' compensation   An employee benefit that provides financial support for employees suffering a work-related injury or illness.

work flow relationships   Relationships that develop as paperwork or other material passes from one department to another.

work-oriented outcomes   Job analysis information regarding the tasks, responsibilities, and functions performed by employees.

work teams   Groups who make or do things like manufacture, assemble, sell, or provide.

Z

zero defects   A goal of achieving no manufacturing flaws.

NOTES

Chapter 1

1. R. Henkoff, "Smartest and Dumbest Managerial Moves of 1994," *Fortune,* January 16, 1995, pp. 84–97.

2. Ibid.

3. T. Ehrenfeld, "The New and Improved American Small Business," *Inc.,* January 1995, pp. 34–45.

4. "Manufacturing Innovation," *Black Enterprise,* August 1991, p. 86.

5. M. Loeb, "How's Business?" *Fortune,* January 16, 1995, pp. 135–36.

6. L. R. Sayles, "Doing Things Right: A New Imperative for Middle Managers," *Organizational Dynamics,* Spring 1993, pp. 5–14.

7. A. Hadley, *The Straw Giant* (New York: Random House, 1986).

8. A. Farnham, "America's Most Admired Company," *Fortune,* February 7, 1994, pp. 50–54.

9. E. E. Lawler III, *The Ultimate Advantage* (San Francisco: Jossey-Bass, 1992).

10. Henkoff, "Smartest and Dumbest Managerial Moves of 1994."

11. Lawler, *The Ultimate Advantage.*

12. Henkoff, "Smartest and Dumbest Managerial Moves of 1994."

13. Ibid.

14. Lawler, *The Ultimate Advantage.*

15. Ehrenfeld, "The New and Improved American Small Business."

16. T. Ehrenfeld, "The Demise of Mom and Pop?" *Inc.,* January 1995, pp. 46–48.

17. Ibid.

18. T. Agins, "Fashion Knockoffs Hit Stores before Originals as Designers Seethe," *The Wall Street Journal,* August 8, 1994, pp. A1, A4.

19. Loeb, "How's Business?

20. R. Katz, "Skills of an Effective Administrator," *Harvard Business Review* 52 (September–October 1974), pp. 90–102.

21. H. Mintzberg, "The Manager's Job: Folklore and Fact," *Harvard Business Review* 53 (July–August 1975), pp. 49–61.

22. A. Deutschman, "The Trouble with MBAs," *Fortune,* July 29, 1991, pp. 67–79.

23. S. Lehrman, "Putting Management Potential to the Test," *Bryan–College Station Eagle,* December 8, 1985, p. 3F.

24. P. Sellers, "Does the CEO Really Matter?" *Fortune,* April 23, 1991, pp. 80–94.

25. W. Kiechel III, "A Manager's Career in the New Economy," *Fortune,* April 4, 1994, pp. 68–72.

26. Ibid.

27. T. Peters, *Liberation Management* (New York: Alfred A. Knopf, 1992).

Chapter 2

1. C. George, *The History of Management Thought* (Englewood Cliffs, N.J.: Prentice-Hall, 1972).

2. Ibid.

3. A. D. Chandler, *Scale and Scope: The Dynamic of Industrial Capitalism* (Cambridge, Mass.: Belknap Press of Harvard University Press, 1990).

4. Ibid.

5. J. Baughman, *The History of American Management* (Englewood Cliffs, N.J.: Prentice-Hall, 1969), chap. 1.

6. George, *The History of Management Thought,* chaps. 5–7; F. Taylor, *The Principles of Scientific Management* (New York: Harper & Row, 1911).

7. J. Case, "A Company of Businesspeople," *Inc.,* April 1993, pp. 79–93.

8. H. Fayol, *General and Industrial Management,* trans. C. Storrs (Marshfield, Mass.: Pitman Publishing, 1949).

9. George, *The History of Management Thought,* chap. 9; J. Massie, "Management Theory," in *Handbook of Organizations,* ed. J. March (Chicago: Rand McNally, 1965), pp. 387–422.

10. C. Barnard, *The Functions of the Executive* (Cambridge, Mass.: Harvard University Press, 1938).

11. George, *The History of Management Thought;* Massie, "Management Theory."

12. E. Mayo, *The Human Problems of Industrial Civilization* (New York: Macmillan, 1933); F. Roethlisberger and W. Dickson, *Management and the Worker* (Cambridge, Mass.: Harvard University Press, 1939).

13. A Maslow, "A Theory of Human Motivation," *Psychological Review* 50 (July 1943), pp. 370–96.

14. A. Carey, "The Hawthorne Studies: A Radical Criticism," *American Sociological Review* 32, no. 3 (1967), pp. 403–16.

15. M. Weber, *The Theory of Social and Economic Organizations,* trans. T. Parsons and A. Henderson (New York: Free Press, 1947).

16. George, *The History of Management Thought,* chap. 11.

17. D. McGregor, *The Human Side of Enterprise* (New York: McGraw-Hill, 1960).

18. C. Argyris, *Personality and Organization* (New York: Harper & Row, 1957).

19. R. Likert, *The Human Organization* (New York: McGraw-Hill, 1967).

20. L. von Bertalanffy, "The History and Status of General Systems Theory," *Academy of Management Journal* 15 (1972), pp. 407–26; D. Katz and R. Kahn, *The Social Psychology of Organizations,* 2nd ed. (New York: John Wiley & Sons, 1978).

21. C. Hofer and D. Schendel, *Strategy Formulation: Analytical Concepts* (St. Paul, Minn.: West, 1978), pp. 2–3.

22. J. Thompson, *Organizations in Action* (New York: McGraw-Hill, 1967); J. Galbraith, *Organization Design* (Reading, Mass.: Addison-Wesley, 1977); D. Miller and P. Friesen, *Organizations: A Quantum View* (Englewood Cliffs, N.J.: Prentice-Hall, 1984).

23. T. Peters, "Prometheus Barely Unbound," *The Executive,* November 1990, pp. 70–84.

24. W. J. Holstein, "The Stateless Corporation," *Business Week,* May 14, 1990, pp. 98–105.

25. R. Cole, P. Bacdayan, B.J. White, "Quality, Participation, and Competitiveness," *California Management Review* (1993), pp. 68–81.

26. J. Shea and D. Gobeli, "TQM: The Experiences of Ten Small Businesses," *Business Horizons,* January-February 1995, 71–77.

27. D. Bowen and E. E. Lawler III, "Total Quality-Oriented Human Resources Management," *Organizational Dynamics,* Spring 1992, pp. 29–41; R. Kreitner and A. Kinicki, *Organizational Behavior,* 3rd ed. (Burr Ridge: Richard D. Irwin, 1995).

28. T. Peters, *Liberation Management* (New York: Alfred A. Knopf, 1992).

29. P. Senge, *The Fifth Discipline* (New York: Doubleday, 1990); R. Hodgetts, F. Luthans, and S. Lee, "New Paradigm Organizations: From Total Quality to Learning to World-Class," *Organizational Dynamics,* Winter 1994, pp. 5–19.

30. M. Hammer and J. Champy, *Reengineering the Corporation: A Manifesto for Business Revolution* (New York: HarperCollins, 1993).

31. J. Hyatt, "Real-World Reengineering," *Inc.,* April 1995, 40–53.

32. T. A. Stewart, "Welcome to the Revolution," *Fortune,* December 13, 1993, pp. 66–80; S. Sherman, "A Brave New Darwinian Workplace," *Fortune,* January 25, 1993, pp. 50–56.

Chapter 3

1. M. Silva and B. Sjogren, *Europe 1992 and the New World Power Game* (New York: John Wiley & Sons, 1990).

2. J. Perez-Lopez, G. Schoepfle, and J. Yochelson, eds. *EC 1992: Implications for U.S. Workers* (Washington, D.C.: U.S. Department of Labor, 1990).

3. J. Yochelson and E. Lesser, "Overview of EC 92," in *EC 1992: Implications for U.S. Workers,* ed. J. Perez-Lopez, G. Schoepfle, and J. Yochelson (Washington, D.C.: U.S. Department of Labor, 1990).

4. "EU:MNCs Face New Challenges as Frontiers Merge," *Crossborder Monitor* 2, no. 10 (March 16, 1994), p. 1; Jane Sasseen, "EU Dateline," *International Management* 49, no 2. (March 1994), p. 5.

5. Perez-Lopez, Schoepfle, and Yochelson, *EC 1992.*

6. Kyohei Shibata, "Airline Privatization in Eastern Europe and Ex-USSR," *Logistics & Transportation Review* 30, no. 2 (June 1994), pp. 167–88.

7. T. Peters, "Prometheus Barely Unbound," *The Executive,* November 1990, pp. 70–84.

8. "The Opening of Asia," *Economist,* November 12, 1994, pp. 23–26; "It's Time to Open All of Asia's Markets," *Business Week,* November 14, 1994.

9. Rachel Kaplar, "Mexico, Here We Come," *International Management* 49, no. 5 (1994), pp. 44–46; Bran Christine, "NAFTA's Effect on the Mexican Economy," *Risk Management* 41, no. 6 (1994), p. 32; Richard L. Thomas, "NAFTA Changes the Game: A U.S. Perspective," *Bank Management* 70, no. 3 (May/June 1994), pp. 55–58; and Alan L. Rosas, Lawrence W. Whitehead, Maria T. Morandi, "The Nitty-Gritty of the Ratification Debate: NAFTA's Environmental Issues and Opportunities," *Business Mexico* 3, no. 9 (September 1993), pp. 42–45.

10. P. Belli, "Globalizing the Rest of the World," *Harvard Busines Review,* July-August 1991, pp. 50–55.

11. A. R. Dowd, "Protectionism in Disguise," *Fortune,* December 8, 1986, pp. 99–102.

12. T. May, "A Rebound with Zing," *Fortune,* July 15, 1991, pp. 60–63.

13. E. Weiner and S. Mufson, "All Roads Lead Out of South Africa," *Fortune,* November 3, 1986, pp. 24–25; L. Smith, "South Africa: Time to Stay—or Go?", *Fortune,* August 4, 1986, pp. 46–48.

14. T. Peters, *Thriving on Chaos* (New York: Alfred A. Knopf, 1987).

15. Ibid.

16. P. Lawrence and D. Dyer, *Renewing American Industry* (New York: Free Press, 1983).

17. T. Benson, "Robert Haas' Vision Scores 20/20," *Industry Week,* April 2, 1990, pp. 19–23.

18. P. Kotler, *Marketing Management* (Englewood Cliffs, N.J.: Prentice Hall, 1990).

19. J. Pfeffer, *Organizational Design* (Arlington Heights, Ill.: AHM Publishing, 1978).

20. J. Galbraith, *Organization Design* (Reading, Mass.: Addison-Wesley Publishing, 1977).

21. C. Zeithaml and V. Zeithaml, "Environmental Management: Revising the Marketing Perspetive," *Journal of Marketing* 48, (Spring 1984), pp. 46–53.

22. R. Miles and C. Snow, "Organizations: New Concepts for New Forms," *California Management Review* 28 (Spring 1986), pp. 62–73.

23. R. Miles and C. Snow, *Organizational Strategy, Structure, and Process* (New York: McGraw-Hill, 1978).

24. Zeithaml and Zeithaml, "Environmental Mangement."

25. Ibid.

Chapter 4

1. T. Peters, *Liberation Management* (New York: Alfred A. Knopf, 1992).

2. M. McCall and R. Kaplan, *Whatever It Takes: Decision Makers at Work* (Englewood Cliffs, N.J.: Prentice-Hall, 1985).

3. B. Bass, *Organizational Decision Making* (Homewood, Ill.: Richard D. Irwin, 1983).

4. J. March, "Bounded Rationality, Ambiguity, and the Engineering of Choice," *Bell Journal of Economics* 9 (1978), pp. 587–608.

5. McCall and Kaplan, *Whatever It Takes.*

6. K. MacCrimmon and R. Taylor, "Decision Making and Problem Solving," in *Handbook of Industrial and Organizational Psychology,* ed. M. D. Dunnette (Chicago: Rand McNally, 1976).

7. C. Gettys and S. Fisher, "Hypothesis Plausibility and Hypotheses Generation," *Organizational Behavior and Human Performance* 24 (1979), pp. 93–110.

8. E. R. Alexander, "The Design of Alternatives in Organizational Contexts: A Pilot Study," *Administrative Science Quarterly* 24 (1979), pp. 382–404.

9. P. Nayak and J. Ketteringham, *Breakthroughs* (New York: Rawson Associates, 1986).

10. R. Abelson and A. Levi, "Decision Making and Decision Theory," in *The Handbook of Social Psychology,* vol. 1, 3rd ed., ed. G. Lindzey and E. Aronson (New York: Random House, 1985).

11. J. O'Toole, *Vanguard Management: Redesigning the Corporate Future* (Garden City, N.Y.: Doubleday, 1985).

12. McCall and Kaplan, *Whatever It Takes.*

13. Ibid.

14. M. B. Stein, "Teaching Steelcase to Dance," *New York Times Magazine,* April 1, 1990, pp. 22ff.

15. D. Siebold, "Making Meetings More Successful," *Journal of Business Communication* 16 (Summer 1979), pp. 3–20.

16. I. Janis and L. Mann, *Decision Making* (New York: Free Press, 1977); Bass, *Organizational Decision Making.*

17. R. Nisbett and L. Ross, *Human Inference: Strategies and Shortcomings* (Englewood Cliffs, N.J.: Prentice-Hall, 1980).

18. T. Bateman and C. Zeithaml, "The Psychological Context of Strategic Decisions: A Model and Convergent Experimental Findings," *Strategic Management Journal* 10 (1989), pp. 59–74.

19. N. Adler, *International Dimensions of Organizational Behavior* (Boston: Kent, 1990).

20. K. M. Eisenhardt, "Speed and Strategic Choice: How Managers Accelerate Decision Making," *California Management Review* 32 (Spring 1990), pp. 39–54.

21. G. W. Hill, "Group versus Individual Performance: Are n + 1 Heads Better than 1?" *Psychological Bulletin* 91 (1982), pp. 517–39.

22. N. R. F. Maier, "Assets and Liabilities in Group Problem Solving: The Need for an Integrative Function," *Psychological Review* 74 (1967), pp. 239–49.

23. Ibid.

24. R. Cosier and C. Schwenk, "Agreement and Thinking Alike: Ingredients for Poor Decisions," *The Executive,* February 1990, pp. 69–74.

25. Ibid.

26. Cosier and Schwenk, "Agreement and Thinking Alike."

27. C. Knowlton, "How Disney Keeps the Magic Going," *Fortune,* December 4, 1989, pp. 115–32.

28. P. LaBerre, "The Creative Revolution," *Industry Week,* May 16, 1994, pp. 12–19.

29. J. V. Anderson, "Weirder than Fiction: The Reality and Myths of Creativity," *Academy of Management Executive,* November 1992, pp. 40–47.

30. A. Farnham, "How to Nurture Creative Sparks," *Fortune,* January 10, 1994, pp. 94–100; T. M. Amabile, "A Model of Creativity and Innovation in Organizations," in *Research and Organizational Behavior,* ed. B. Straw and L. Cummings, vol. 10 (1988), pp. 123–68.

31. J. E. Jackson and W. T. Schantz, "Crisis Management Lessons: When Push Shoved Nike," *Business Horizons,* January–February 1993, pp. 27–35.

32. C. M. Pearson and I. I. Mitroff, "From Crisis Prone to Crisis Prepared: A Framework for Crisis Management," The *Academy of Management Executive,* February 1993, pp. 48–59.

33. G. Meyers with J. Holusha, *When It Hits the Fan: Managing the Nine Crises of Business* (Boston: Houghton Mifflin, 1986).

34. McCall and Kaplan, *Whatever It Takes.*

Chapter 5

1. J. Bracker and J. Pearson, "Planning and Financial Performance of Small Mature Firms," *Strategic Management Journal* 7 (1986), pp. 503–22; Philip Waalewijn & Peter Segaar, "Strategic Management: The Key to Profitability in Small Companies," *Long Range Planning,* 26, no. 2 (April 1993): pp. 24–30.

2. F. Rice, "Profiting by Preseverance," *Fortune,* January 27, 1992, p. 84.

3. L. Therrien, "McRisky," *Business Week,* October 21, 1991, pp. 114–22.

4. F. Gluck, Strategic Management: An Overview," in *Handbook of Strategic Planning,* ed. J. Gardner, R. Rachlin, and A. Sweeny (New York: John Wiley & Sons, 1986), Chap. 1.

5. F. Gluck, S. Kaufman, and A. Walleck, "The Four Phases of Strategic Management," *The Journal of Business Strategy* 2, no. 3 (1982), pp. 9–21.

6. Arthur A. Thompson and A. J. Strickland III, *Strategic Management: Concepts and Cases,* Eighth Edition, Burr Ridge, Ill.: Irwin (1995): p. 23.

7. E. Freeman, "Strategic Management: A Stakeholder Approach," in *Advances in Strategic Management,* ed. R. Lamb (Greenwich, Conn.: JAI Press, 1983), pp. 31–60.

8. D. Georgoff and R. Murdick, "Manager's Guide to Forcasting," *Harvard Business Review* 64, no.1 (1986), pp. 110-20.

9. Bruce Nussbaum, "Hot Products—Smart Design is the Common Thread," *Business Week,* (June 7, 1993): pp.54–57. Julie Cohen Mason, "Strategic Alliances: Partnering for Success," 82, no. 5 (May 1993): pp. 10–11. Brad Burgess, Nasr Ullah, Peter Van Overen, and Deene Ogden, "The PowerPC 603 Microprocessor," *Communications of the ACM,* 37, no. 6 (June 1994): pp.34–42.

10. Arthur A. Thompson and A. J. Strickland III, *Strategic Management: Concepts and Cases,* Eighth Edition, Burr Ridge, Ill.: Irwin (1995). Jeremy Main, "How to Steal the Best Ideas Around," *Fortune,* (October 19, 1992): p. 106. Michael Hammer and James Champy, *Reengineering the Corporation* New York: Harper Collins (1993).

11. S. Gannes, "Merck Has Made Biotech Work," *Fortune,* January 19, 1987, pp. 58–64.

12. Mark Maremont, "Why Kodak's Dazzling Spin-Off Didn't Bedazzle," *Business Week,* (June 28, 1993): p. 34. Emily S. Plishner, "Eastman Chemical Spins Out of the Kodak Family Portrait," *Chemical Week,* 152, no. 24 (June 23, 1993): p. 7.

13. M. Porter, *Competitive Advantage* (New York: Free Press, 1985), pp. 11–14.

14. R. Neff, "Guess Who's Selling Barbies in Japan Now?", *Business Week,* December 9, 1991, pp. 72–76.

15. A. Fins, "Batten Down the Hatches and Rev Up the Jacuzzis," *Business Week,* August 19, 1991, pp. 88–89.

16. P. Lorange, M. Morton, And S. Ghoshal, *Strategic Control* (St. Paul, Minn.: West Publishing, 1986), p. 10.

17. Ibid., pp. 35, 53.

Chapter 6

1. R.E. Allinson, "A Call for Ethically Centered Management," *Academy of Management Executive,* February 1995, 73–76.

2. J. B. Ciulla, "Why Is Business Talking about Ethics? Reflections on Foreign Conversations," *California Management Review,* Fall 1991, pp. 67–80.

3. M. E. Guy, *Ethical Decision Making in Everyday Work Situations* (New York: Quorum Books, 1990).

4. Ibid.

5. J. Badarocco, Jr. and A. Webb, "Business Ethics: A View from the Trenches," *California Management Review,* Winter 1995, pp. 8–28.

6. G. Laczniak, M. Berkowitz, R. Brookes, and J. Hale, "The Business of Ethics: Improving or Deteriorating?" *Business Horizons,* January–February 1995, 39–47.

7. S. Brenner and E. Molander, "Is the Ethics of Business Changing?" in *Ethics in Practice: Managing the Moral Corporation,* ed. K. Andrews (Cambridge, Mass.: Harvard Business School Press, 1989).

8. R. A. Cooke, "Danger Signs of Unethical Behavior: How to Determine if Your Firm Is at Ethical Risk," *Journal of Business Ethics,* April 1991, pp. 249–53.

9. L. S. Paine, "Managing for Organizational Integrity," *Harvard Business Review,* March–April 1994, pp. 106–17.

10. F. Hall and E. Hall, "The ADA: Going beyond the Law," *The Academy of Management Executive,* February 1994, pp. 7–13; A. Farnham, "Brushing Up Your Vision Thing," *Fortune,* May 1, 1995, p. 129.

11. Paine, "Managing for Organizational Integrity."

12. Ciulla, "Why Is Business Talking about Ethics?"

13. A. Farnham, "State Your Values, Hold the Hot Air," *Fortune,* April 19, 1993, pp. 117–24.

14. Guy, *Ethical Decision Making;* D. Kirrane, "Managing Values: A Systematic Approach to Business Ethics," *Training and Development Journal,* November 1990, pp. 53–60.

15. R. P. Nielsen, "What Can Managers Do about Unethical Management?" *Journal of Business Ethics,* May 1987, pp. 309–20.

16. L. Preston and J. Post, eds., *Private Management and Public Policy* (Englewood Cliffs, N.J.: Prentice-Hall, 1975).

17. Ibid.

18. J. O'Toole, "Doing Well by Doing Good: The Business Enterprise Trust Awards," *California Management Review,* Spring 1991, pp. 9–24.

19. R. Ackerman and R. Bauer, *Corporate Social Responsiveness* (Reston, Va.: Reston, 1976).

20. J. Gale and R. A. Buchholz, "The Political Pursuit of Competitive Advantage: What Business Can Gain from Government," in *Business Strategy and Public Policy: Perspectives from Industry and Academia,* ed. A. A. Marcus, A. M. Kaufman, and D. R. Beam (Westport, Conn.: Greenwood Press, 1987), pp. 31–41.

21. T. Parsons and C. Perrow, *Complex Organizations,* 2nd ed. (Glenview, Ill.: Scott, Foresman, 1979).

22. B. Baysinger, "Domain Maintenance as an Objective of Business Political Activity," *Academy of Management Review* 9 (1984), pp. 248–58.

23. P. Andrews, "The Sticky Wicket of Evaluating Public Affairs: Thoughts about a Framework," *Public Affairs Review* 6 (1986), pp. 94–105.

24. S. Lusterman *The Organization and Staffing of Corporate Public Affairs* (New York: Conference Board, 1987).

25. C. Zeithaml, G. Keim, and B. Baysinger, "Toward an Integrated Strategic Management Process: An Empirical Review of Corporate Political Strategy," in *Strategic Management Frontiers,* ed. John H. Grant (Greenwich, Conn.: JAI Press, 1988), pp. 377–93.

26. G. Keim and C. Zeithaml, "Corporate Political Strategy and Legislative Decision Making, " *Academy of Management Review,* 1986, pp. 828–43.

Chapter 7

1. J. Post, "Managing as if the Earth Mattered," *Business Horizons,* July–August 1991, pp. 32–38.

2. C. J. Corbett and L. N. Van Wassenhove, "The Green Fee: Internationalizing and Operationalizing Environmental Issues," *California Management Review,* Fall 1993, pp. 116–33.

3. N. Walley and B. Whitehead, "It's Not Easy Being Green," *Harvard Business Review,* May–June 1994, pp. 46–51.

4. "The Challenge of Going Green," letters, *Harvard Business Review,* July–August 1994, pp. 37–50.

5. F. Rice, "Who Scores Best on the Environment," *Fortune,* July 26, 1993, pp. 114–22.

6. K. Dechant and B. Altman, "Environmental Leadership: From Compliance to Competitive Advantage," *The Academy of Management Executive,* August 1994, pp. 7–20.

7. R. Stavins, letter in "The Challenge of Going Green," *Harvard Business Review,* July–August 1994, 37–50.

8. Walley and Whitehead, "It's Not Easy Being Green"; Corbett and Van Wassenhove, "The Green Fee."

9. Walley and Whitehead, "It's Not Easy Being Green."

10. "The Challenge of Going Green."

11. Ibid.

12. F. B. Cross, "The Weaning of the Green: Environmentalism Comes of Age in the 1990s," *Business Horizons,* September–October 1990, pp. 40–46.

13. "The Challenge of Going Green."

14. E. Smith and V. Cahan, "The Greening of Corporate America," *Business Week,* April 23, 1990, pp. 96–103.

15. M. E. Porter, "America's Green Strategy," *Science,* April 1991, p. 168.

16. A. Kleiner, "What Does It Mean to Be Green?" *Harvard Business Review,* July–August 1991, pp. 38–47.

17. D. C. Kinlaw, *Competitive & Green: Sustainable Performance in the Environmental Age* (Amsterdam: Pfeiffer & Co., 1993).

18. Rice, "Who Scores Best on the Environment."

19. J. O'Toole, "Do Good, Do Well: The Business Enterprise Trust Awards," *California Management Review,* Spring 1991, pp. 9–24.

20. Rice, "Who Scores Best on the Environment?"

21. J. O'Toole, "Do Good, Do Well: The Business Enterprise Trust Awards," *California Management Review,* Spring 1991, pp. 9–24.

22. Post, "Managing as if the Earth Mattered."

23. D. C. Kinlaw, *Competitive and Green.*

24. G. Hardin, "The Tragedy of the Commons," *Science* 162 (1968), pp. 1243–48.

25. D. Kirkpatrick, "Environmentalism: The New Crusade," *Fortune,* February 12, 1990, pp. 44–55.

26. Ibid.

27. R. Carson, *The Silent Spring* (Boston: Houghton Mifflin, 1962); R. Paehlke, *Environmentalism and the Future of Progressive Politics* (New Haven: Yale University Press, 1989), pp. 13–41, 76–143; R. Nash, ed., *The American Environment* (Reading, Mass.: Addison-Wesley, 1968); R. Revelle and H. Landsberg, eds., *America's Changing Environment* (Boston: Beacon Press, 1970); L. Caldwell, *Environment: A Challenge to Modern Society* (Garden City, N.Y.: Anchor Books, 1971); J. M. Petulla, *Environmental Protection in the United States* (San Francisco: San Francisco Study Center, 1987).

28 P. Shrivastava, "Ecocentric Management for a Risk Society," *Academy of Management Review* 20 (1995), pp. 118–37.

29. B. Commoner, *Science and Survival* (New York: Viking Press, 1963); B. Commoner, *The Closing Circle: Nature, Man and Technology* (New York: Bantam Books, 1971).

30. Paehlke, *Environmentalism.*

31. Ibid.

32. Ibid.

33 P. Hawken, J. Ogilvy, and P. Schwartz, *Seven Tomorrows: Toward a Voluntary History* (New York: Bantam Books, 1982); Paehlke, *Environmentalism.*

34. Porter, "America's Green Strategy."

35. C. Morrison, *Managing Environmental Affairs: Corporate Practices in the U.S., Canada, and Europe* (New York: Conference Board, 1991).

36. Ibid.

37. Kleiner, "What Does It Mean to Be Green?"

38. K. Fischer and J. Schot, *Environmental Strategies for Industry* (Washington, D.C.: Island Press, 1993).

39. Rice, "Who Scores Best on the Environment?"

40. Dechant and Altman, "Environmental Leadership."

41. Ibid.

42. Ibid.

43. Ibid.

44. Ibid.

45. Smith and Cahan, "The Greening of Corporate America."

46. J. Elkington and T. Burke, *The Green Capitalists* (London: Victor Gullanez, 1989); M. Zetlin, "The Greening of Corporate America," *Management Review,* June 1990, pp. 10–17.

47. Smith and Cahan, "The Greening of Corporate America."

48. J. Stevens, "Assessing the Health Risks of Incinerating Garbage," *EURA Reporter,* October 1989, pp. 6–10.

49. L. Blumberg and R. Gottlieb, "The Resurrection of Incineration" and "The Economic Factors," in *War on Waste,* ed. L. Blumberg and R. Gottlieb (Washington, D.C.: Island Press, 1989).

50. L. Blumberg and R. Gottlieb, "Recycling's Unrealized Promise," in Blumberg and Gottlieb, *War on Waste,* pp. 191–226.

51. J. Elkington, "Towards the Sustainable Corporation: Win-Win-Win Business Strategies for Sustainable Development," *California Management Review,* Winter 1994, pp. 90–100.

52. Dechant and Altman, "Environmental Leadership."

53. Corbett and Van Wassenhove, "The Green Fee."

54. Ibid.

55. Ibid.

56. Ibid.

57. Elkington, "Towards the Sustainable Corporation."

58. F. S. Rowland, "Chlorofluorocarbons and the Depletion of Stratospheric Ozone," *American Scientist,* January–February 1989, pp. 36–45.

59. Elkington, "Towards the Sustainable Corporation."

60. Corbet and Van Wassenhove, "The Green Fee."

61. Elkington, "Towards the Sustainable Corporation."

Chapter 8

1. "If GATT Fails, MNCs Review Future of Worldwide Trade," *Crossborder Monitor,* November 17, 1993, p. 1

2. R. B. Reich, *The Work of Nations: Preparing Ourselves for 21st-Century Capitalism* (New York: Alfred A. Knopf, 1991), p. 113

3. R. A. Mosbacher, "Opening Export Doors for Smaller Firms," *Seattle Times,* July 24, 1991, p. A7.

4. *The Economist Book of Vital World Statistics* (New York: Random House, 1990).

5. "Foreign Investment and the Triad," *The Economist,* August 24, 1991, p . 57.

6. "Managing Your Oyster," *The Economist,* October 18, 1989, p. 78.

7. C. A. Bartlett and S. Ghoshal, *The Transnational Solution: Managing across Borders* (Boston: Harvard Business School Press, 1989).

8. T. Hout, M. E. Porter, and E. Rudden, "How Global Companies Win Out," *Harvard Business Review,* September–October 1982, pp. 98–108; T. Levitt, "The Globalization of Markets," *Harvard Business Review,* May–June 1983; S. Ghoshal, "Global Strategy: An Organizing Framework," *Strategic Management Journal* 8 (1987), pp. 425–40.

9. C. W. L. Hill, P. Hwang, and W. C. Kim, "An Eclectic Theory of the Choice of International Entry Mode," *Strategic Management Journal* 11 (1990), pp. 117–28.

10. Charlene Marmer Solomon, "Staff Selection Impacts Global Success," *Personnel Journal,* January 1994, pp. 88–101.

11. Nancy J. Adler and Susan Bartholomew, "Managing Globally Competent People," *Academy of Management Executive* 6, no. 3 (1992), pp. 52–65.

12. Cecil G. Howard, "Profile of the 21st-Century Expatriate Manager," *HRMagazine,* June 1992, pp. 93–100.

13. Donald C. Hambrick, James W. Fredrickson, Lester B. Korn, and Richard M. Ferry, "Reinventing the CEO," *21st Century Report* (Korn/Ferry and Columbia Graduate School of Business, 1989).

14. Gary W. Hogan and Jane R. Goodson, "The Key to Expatriate Success," *Training and Development Journal,* January 1990, pp. 50–52. See also, Allan Bird and Roger Dunbar, "Getting the Job Done Over There: Improving Expatriate Productivity," *National Productivity Review,* (Spring 1991), pp. 145–56.

15. Raymond J. Stone, "Expatriate Selection and Failure," *Human Resource Planning* 14, no. 1 (1991), pp. 9–18. See also, Rosalie L. Tung, "Selection and Training of Personnel for Overseas Assignments," *Columbia Journal of World Business* 16, no. 1 (Spring 1981), pp. 68–78; Rosalie L. Tung, *The New Expatriates: Managing Human Resources Abroad* (Cambridge, Mass.: Ballinger, 1988); Stewart J. Black and Hal B. Gregersen, "Antecedents to Cross-Cultural Adjustment for Expatriates in Pacific Rim Assignments," *Human Relations* 44, no. 5 (May 1991), pp. 497–515; Bruce W. Stening and Mitchell R. Hammer, "Cultural Baggage and the Adaptation of Expatriate American and Japanese Managers," *Management International Review* 32, no. 1 (1992), pp. 77–89.

16. Vern Terpstra and Kenneth David, *The Cultural Environment of International Business,* 3rd ed. (Cincinnati: South-Western, 1990).

17. Cecil G. Howard, "Profile of the 21st-Century Expatriate Manager."

18. Nancy J. Adler, "Women Managers in a Global Economy," *HRMagazine,* September 1993, pp. 52–55. See also, Nancy J. Adler, "Pacific Basin Managers: A Gaijin, Not a Woman," *Human Resource Management* 26, no. 2 (1987), pp. 169–91; Hilary Harris, "Women in International Management: Opportunity or Threat?" *Women in Management Review* 8, no. 5 (1993), pp. 9–14.

19. Sheila Rothwell, "Leadership Development and International HRM," *Manager Update* 4, no. 4 (Summer 1993), pg. 20–32. See also, Peter Blunt, "Recent Developments in Human Resource Management: The Good, the Bad and the Ugly," *International Journal of Human Resource Management* 1, no. 1 (June 1990), pp. 45–59.

20. Linda K. Trevino and Katherine A. Nelson, *Managing Business Ethics: Straight Talk about How to Do It Right* (New York: John Wiley and Sons, 1995).

Chapter 9

1. R. Hisrich and M. Peters, *Entrepreneurship: Starting, Developing, and Managing a New Enterprise* (Burr Ridge, Ill.: Richard D. Irwin, 1994).

2. J. A. Timmons, *New Venture Creation* (Burr Ridge, Ill.: Richard D. Irwin, 1994).

3. G. Pinchot, "How Intrapreneurs Innovate," *Management Today,* December 1985, pp. 54–61.

4. B. O'Reilly, "The New Face of Small Business," *Fortune,* May 2, 1994, pp. 82–88.

5. H. Aldrich, *Ethnic Entrepreneurs: Immigrant Business in Industrial Societies* (Newbury Park, Calif.: Sage, 1990).

6. A. E. Serwer, "Lessons from America's Fastest-Growing Companies," *Fortune,* August 8, 1994, pp. 42–60.

7. E. I. Altman, "Why Businesses Fail," *Journal of Business Strategy,* Winter 1983, pp. 15–35.

8. K. H. Vesper, *New Venture Mechanics* (Englewood Cliffs, N.J.: Prentice-Hall, 1993).

9. Ibid.

10. Ibid.

11. Ibid.

12. Timmons, *New Venture Creation.*

13. Hisrich and Peters, *Entrepreneurship.*

14. Ibid.

15. H. H. Stevenson, "A Perspective on Entrepreneurship," Harvard Business School Case No. 9-384-131.

16. S. McCartney, "Michael Dell—and His Company—Grow Up," *The Wall Street Journal,* January 31, 1995, pp. B1, B4.

17. A. F. Brattina, "The Diary of a Small-Company Owner," *Inc.*, May 1993, pp. 79–89, and June 1993, pp. 117–22.

18. *Nation's Business,* April 1991, pp. 46–48.

19. M. Porter, *Competitive Strategies* (New York: Free Press, 1980).

20. O'Reilly, "The New Face of Small Business."

21. C. Burck, "The Real World of the Entrepreneur," *Fortune,* April 5, 1993, pp. 62–81

22. G. Barsley and B. Kleiner, "Small Business Management: Ensuring Your Client's Success," *National Public Accountant,* February 1990, pp. 30–33.

23. Serwer, "Lessons From America's Fastest-Growing Companies," pp. 42–60.

24. R. Blunden, "A Framework for the Empirical Study of Venture Discontinuance," in *The Spirit of Entrepreneurship,* ed. R. G. Wycham et al. (Vancouver, B. C.: International Council of Small Business, 1987), p. 159.

25. P. F. Drucker, "How to Save the Family Business," *The Wall Street Journal,* August 19, 1994, p. A10.

26. R. M. Kanter et al., "Driving Corporate Entrepreneurship," *Management Review,* April 1987, pp. 14–16.

27. I. Chithelen, "Work in Progress," *Forbes,* November 12, 1990, pp. 226–27.

28. R. M. Kanter, *The Change Masters* (New York: Simon & Schuster, 1983).

29. D. Clark, "How a Woman's Passion and Persistence Made 'Bob'," *The Wall Street Journal,* January 10, 1995, pp. B1, B8

30. Kanter et al., "Driving Corporate Entrepreneurship."

31. Ibid.

32. J. Argenti, *Corporate Collapse: The Causes and Symptoms* (New York: John Wiley & Sons, 1979)

33. Kanter et al., "Driving Corporate Entrepreneurship."

Chapter 10

1. B. L. Thompson, *The New Manager's Handbook* (Burr Ridge, Ill.: Richard D. Irwin, 1995).

2. P. Lawrence and J. Lorsch, *Organization and Environment* (Homewood Ill.: Richard D. Irwin, 1969).

3. Ibid.

4. Ibid.

5. J. W. Lorsch, *Pawns or Potentates: The Reality of America's Corporate Boards* (Boston: Harvard Business School Press, 1989).

6. J. Bacon, *Corporate Boards and Corporate Governance* (New York: The Conference Board, 1993).

7. Ibid.

8. A. J. Michels, "Chief Executives as Idi Ahmin?" *Fortune,* July 1, 1991, p. 13.

9. P. Carillo and R. Kopelman, "Organization Structure and Productivity: Effects of Subunit Size, Vertical Complexity, and Administrative Intensity on Operating Efficiency," *Group and Organization Studies* 16 (1991), pp. 44–59.

10. H. Stieglitz, "What's Not on the Organization Chart," *The Conference Board Record,* November 1964, pp. 7–10.

11. D. Van Fleet and A. Bedeian, "A History of the Span of Management," *Academy of Management Review* 2 (1977), pp. 356–72.

12. Ibid.

13. S. Bushardt, D. Duhon, and A. R. Fowler, Jr., "Management Delegation Myths and the Paradox of Task Assignment," *Business Horizons* 34 (March–April 1991).

14. J. Lagges, "The Role of Delegation in Improving Productivity," *Personnel Journal,* November 1979, pp. 776–79.

15. G. Matthews, "Run Your Business or Build an Organization?" *Harvard Management Review,* March–April 1984, pp. 34–44.

16. T. Peters, "Letting Go of Controls," *Across the Board* 28 (June 1991), pp. 14–18.

17. R. Duncan, "What Is the Right Organization Structure?" *Organizational Dynamics* 7 (Winter 1979), pp. 59–80.

18. J. Galbraith, "The Business Unit of the Future," in J. Galbraith, E. E. Lawler III & Associates, *Organizing for the Future* (San Francisco: Jossey-Bass, 1993).

19. J. Galbraith, "The Business Unit of the Future."

20. R. Duncan, "What Is the Right Organization Structure?"

21. H. Kolodny, "Managing in a Matrix," *Business Horizons,* March–April 1981, pp. 17–24.

22. S. Davis and P. Lawrence, "Problems of Matrix Organizations," *Harvard Business Review,* May–June 1978, pp. 131–42.

23. C. Bartlett and S. Ghoshal, "Matrix Management: Not a Structure, a Frame of Mind," *Harvard Business Review* 68 (July–August 1990), pp. 138–45.

24. Davis and Lawrence, "Problems of Matrix Organizations."

25. E. E. Lawler III, "New Roles for the Staff Function: Strategic Support and Services," in Galbraith, Lawler & Associates, *Organizing for the Future.*

26. G. Strauss and L. Sayles, *Behavioral Strategies for Managers* (Englewood Cliffs, N.J.: Prentice-Hall, 1980).

27. M. Tushman and D. Nadler, "Implications of Political Models of Organization," in *Resourcebook in Macro Organizational Behavior,* ed. R. H. Miles (Santa Monica, Calif.: Goodyear, 1980).

Chapter 11

1. N. Nohria and J. Berkley, "An Action Perspective: The Crux of the New Management," *California Management Review,* Summer 1994, pp. 70–92.

2. Ibid.

3. T. Burns and G. Stalker, *The Management of Innovation* (London: Tavistock, 1961).

4. Ibid.

5. D. Nadler, J. Hackman and E. E. Lawler III, *Managing Organizational Behavior* (Boston: Little, Brown, 1979).

6. B. Dumaine, "The Bureaucracy Busters," *Fortune,* June 13, 1991, pp. 36–50.

7. B. Buell and R. Hof, "Hewlett-Packard Rethinks Itself," *Business Week,* April 1, 1991, pp. 76–79.

8. D. Robey, *Designing Organizations,* 3rd ed. (Homewood, Ill.: Richard D. Irwin, 1991).

9. Ibid.

10. "Why Big Might Remain Beautiful," *The Economist,* March 24, 1990, p. 79.

11. W. Zellner, "Go-Go Goliaths," *Business Week,* February 13, 1995, pp. 64–70.

12. R. Henkoff, "Keeping Motorola on a Roll," *Fortune,* April 18, 1994, pp. 67–78.

13. M. Selz, "Small Manufacturers Display the Nimbleness the Times Require," *The Wall Street Journal,* December 29, 1993, pp. A1, A2.

14. L. Berton, "Big Accounting Firms, Striving to Cut Costs, Irritate Small Clients," *The Wall Street Journal,* April 24, 1994, pp. A1, A8.

15. D. Kirkpatrick, "Gerstner's New Vision for IBM," *Fortune,* November 15, 1993, pp. 119–26; D. Depke, "IBM and Apple: Can Two Loners Learn to Say 'Teamwork'?" *Business Week,* July 22, 1981, p. 25.

16. R. Henkoff, "Keeping Motorola on a Roll."

17. J. Galbraith, "The Value-Adding Corporation: Matching Structure with Strategy," in J. Galbraith, E. E. Lawler III & Associates, *Organizing for the Future* (San Francisco: Jossey-Bass, 1993).

18. J. Galbraith, "Organization Design: An Information Processing View," *Interfaces* 4 (Fall 1974), pp. 28–36.

19. J. Galbraith, "Organization Design"; S. A. Mohrman, "Integrating Roles and Structure in the Lateral Organization," in J. Galbraith, E. E. Lawler III & Associates, *Organizing for the Future* (San Francisco: Jossey-Bass, 1993).

20. V. Sathe, *Culture and Related Corporate Realities* (Homewood, Ill.: Richard D. Irwin, 1985); A. Reichers and B. Schneider, "Climate and Culture: An Evolution of Constructs," in *Organization Climate and Culture,* ed. B. Schneider (San Francisco: Jossey-Bass, 1990).

21. J. B. Shaw, C. D. Fisher, and W. A. Randolph, "From Materialism to Accountability: The Changing Cultures of Ma Bell and Mother Russia," *The Executive* 5 (February 1991), pp. 7–20.

22. J. Collins and J. Porras, *Built to Last: Successful Habits of Visionary Companies* (New York: Harper Business, 1994); T. Deal and A. Kennedy, *Corporate Culture: The Rites and Rituals of Corporate Life* (Reading, Mass.: Addison-Wesley, 1982); T. Peters and R. Waterman, *In Search of Excellence* (New York: Harper & Row, 1982).

23. Peters and Waterman, *In Search of Excellence.*

24. B. Dumaine, "Creating a New Company Culture," *Fortune,* January 15, 1990, pp. 127–31.

25. Peters and Waterman, *In Search of Excellence.*

26. B. Uttal, "The Corporate Culture Vultures," *Fortune,* October 17, 1983, pp. 66–72.

27. E. Faltermayer, "The Deal Decade: Verdict on the Eighties," *Fortune,* August 26, 1991, pp. 58–70.

28. "Big Is Back in Style as Corporate America Deals, Buys, and Merges," *The Wall Street Journal,* August 4, 1994, pp. A1, A6.

29. J. Greenwald, "Come Together, Right Now," *Time,* August 15, 1994, pp. 28–30.

30. J. Cole, "Merger of Lockheed and Marietta Pushes Industry Trend," *The Wall Street Journal,* August 30, 1994, pp. A1, A5.

31. Greenwald, "Come Together, Right Now."

32. S. Moore and E. Tanouye, "Innovation Fails to Shield Glaxo in HMO World," *The Wall Street Journal,* January 25, 1995, pp. B1, B4.

33. "Big Is Back in Style."

34. R. Samuelson, "Megamergers—Now and Forever," *Newsweek,* September 26, 1994, p. 51.

35. E. Tanouye and G. Anders, "Drug Industry Takeovers Mean More Cost-Cutting, Less Research Spending," *The Wall Street Journal,* February 1, 1995, pp. B1, B4.

36. Samuelson, "Megamergers—Now and Forever."

37. A. F. Alkhafaji, *Restructuring American Corporations* (New York: Quorum Books, 1990).

38. J. R. Galbraith, "Structural Responses to Competitive Strategies," in *Making Organizations Competitive,* ed. R. Kilmann (San Francisco: Jossey-Bass, 1991).

39. P. Krugman, *The Age of Diminished Expectations* (Cambridge, Mass.: MIT Press, 1990).

40. Alkhafaji, *Restructuring American Corporations.*

41. Krugman, *The Age of Diminished Expectations.*

42. Ibid.

43. Faltermayer, "The Deal Decade."

44. Ibid.

45. Alkhafaji, *Restructuring American Corporations.*

46. W. Cascio, "Downsizing: What Do We Know? What Have We Learned?" *Academy of Management Executive,* February 1993, pp. 95–104.

47. Ibid.

48. M. Hitt, B. Keats, H. Harback, and R. Nixon, "Rightsizing: Building and Maintaining Strategic Leadership and Long-Term Competitiveness," *Organizational Dynamics,* Fall 1994, pp. 18–31.

49. Zellner, "Go-Go Goliaths," pp. 64–70.

50. Cascio, "Downsizing."

51. Hitt, Keats, Harback, and Nixon, "Rightsizing."

52. Ibid.

53. G. Hamel and C. K. Prahalad, "Competing for the Future," *Harvard Business Review,* July–August 1994, pp. 122–28.

54. G. Hamel and C. K. Prahalad, *Competing for the Future,* (Boston: Harvard Business School Press, 1994).

55. R. Miles and C. Snow, "Organizations: New Concepts for New Forms," *California Management Review* 28 (Spring 1986), pp. 62–73; Galbraith, "Structural Responses."

56. Miles and Snow, "Organizations."

57. S. Tully, "The Modular Corporation," *Fortune,* February 8, 1993, pp. 106–15.

58. D. Cravens, S. Shipp, and K. Cravens, "Reforming the Traditional Organization: The Mandate for Developing Networks," *Business Horizons,* July–August 1994, pp. 19–28.

59. Tully, "The Modular Corporation."

60. Ibid.

61. R. M. Kanter, "Becoming PALs: Pooling, Allying, and Linking across Companies," *Academy of Management Executives* 3 (August 1989), pp. 183–93.

62. B. A. Stertz, "In a U-Turn from Past Policy, Big Three of Detroit Speed into Era of Cooperation," *The Wall Street Journal*, June 28, 1991, pp. B1, B4.

63. R. Osborn and C. Baughn, "Forms of Interorganizational Governance for Multinational Alliances," *Academy of Management Journal* 33 (1990), pp. 503–19.

64. R. M. Kanter, "Collaborative Advantage: The Art of Alliances," *Harvard Business Review*, July–August 1994, pp. 96–108.

65. Ibid.

66. Ibid.

67. P. Senge, *The Fifth Discipline* (New York: Doubleday Currency, 1990).

68. D. A. Garvin, "Building a Learning Organization," *Harvard Business Review*, July–August 1993, pp. 78–91.

69. Ibid.

70. E. E. Lawler III, "Executives Behavior in High-Involvement Organizations," in *Making Organizations Competitive,* ed. R. Kilmann (San Francisco: Jossey-Bass, 1991).

71. Ibid.

72. E. E. Lawler III, "Total Quality Management and Employee Involvement: Are They Compatible?" *The Academy of Management Executive*, February 1994, pp. 68–76.

73. R. Wellins, W. Byham, and G. Dixon, *Inside Teams* (San Francisco: Jossey-Bass, 1994).

74. T. Peters, *Liberation Management* (New York: Alfred A. Knopf, 1992).

75. D. Q. Mills, *Rebirth of the Corporation* (New York: John Wiley & Sons, 1991).

76. Ibid.

77. T. Peters, *The Tom Peters Seminar* (New York: Vintage Books, 1994).

78. J. B. Quinn, "The Intelligent Enterprise: A New Paradigm," *The Academy of Management Executive,* November 1992, pp. 48–63.

Chapter 12

1. "Workplace: Working Out Personnel Puzzles of the 90s," *The Wall Street Journal,* July 6, 1990, pp. B1, B4; "Workplace Diversity," *HR Magazine,* April 1991.

2. W. B. Johnston, "Global Work Force 2000: The New World Labor Market," *Harvard Business Review* (March–April, 1991) pp. 115–27.

3. E. L. Levine, *Everything You Always Wanted to Know about Job Analysis: A Job Analysis Primer* (Tampa, Fla.: Mariner Publishing, 1983).

4. S. R. Burchett and K. P. DeMeuse, "Performance Appraisal and the Law," *Personnel,* July 1985, pp. 29–37.

5. R. D. Gatewood and H. S. Field, *Human Resource Selection* (Hinsdale, Ill.: Dryden Press, 1987); B. Schneider and N. Schmitt, *Staffing Organizations* (Glenview, Ill.: Scott, Foresman, 1986); R. D. Arvey and R. H Faley, *Fairness in Selecting Employees,* 2nd ed. (Reading, Mass.: Addison-Wesley Publishing, 1988).

6. P. G. Swaroff, L. A. Barclay, and A. R. Bass, "Recruiting Sources: Another Look," *Journal of Applied Psychology* 70 (1985), pp. 720–28.

7. V. R. Lindquist and F. S. Endicott, *Trends in the Employment of College and University Graduates in Business and Industry,* 40th annual report (Evanston, Ill.: Northwestern University Press, 1986).

8. R. A. Fear, *The Evaluation Interview* (New York: McGraw-Hill, 1984).

9. Bureau of National Affairs, *Employee Selection Procedures: ASPA-BNA Survey No. 45* (Washington, D.C.: U.S. Government Printing Office, 1983).

10. Ibid.

11. M. M. Harris and J. B. Dworkin, "Survey of Personnel Selection Procedure Practices," *EMA Journal 3* (Winter 1988), pp. 17–23; J. M. Crant and T. S. Bateman, "An Experimental Test of the Impact of Drug-Testing Programs on Potential Job Applicants' Attitudes and Intentions," *Journal of Applied Psychology* 75 (1990), pp. 127–31.

12. Bureau of National Affairs, *Employee Selection Procedures.*

13. Ibid.

14. Ibid.

15. P. R. Sackett, L. R. Burris, and C. Callahan, "Integrity Testing for Personnel Selection: An Update," *Personnel Psychology* 42 (1989), pp. 491–529; U.S. Office of Technology Assessment, *Use of Integrity Tests for Pre-employment Screening,* OTA-SET-442 (Washington, D.C.: U.S. Government Printing Office, 1990).

16. S. A. Youngblood and L. Bierman, "Due Process and Employment-at-Will: A Legal and Behavior Analysis," in *Research in Personnel and Human Resource Management,* Vol. 3, ed. K. Rowland and G. Ferris (Greenwich, Conn.: JAI Press, 1985), pp. 185–230; C. Schwoerer and B. Rosen, "Effects of Employment-at-Will Policies and Compensation Policies on Corporate Image and Job Pursuit Intentions," *Journal of Applied Psychology* 74 (1989), pp. 653–56.

17. J. R. Redecker, "Discipline, Part 1: Progressive Systems Work Only by Accident," *Personnel 62* (October 1985), pp. 8–12; A. W. Bryant, "Replacing Punitive Discipline Policy Capturing Approach," *Personnel Psychology* 43 (Spring 1990), pp. 117–34.

18. J. Jannotta, "Stroh's Outplacement Success," *Management Review,* January 1987, pp. 52-53.

19. L. Reibstein, "Survivors of Layoffs Help to Lift Morale and Instill Trust," *The Wall Street Journal,* March 13 1986, p. 13.

20. M. D. Levin-Epstein, *Primer of Equal Employment Opportunity,* 4th ed. (Washington, D.C.: Bureau of National Affairs, 1987).

21. R. A. Baysinger, "Disparate Treatment and Disparate Impact Theories of Discrimination: The Continuing Evolution of Title VII of the 1964 Civil Rights Act," in *Readings in Personnel and Human Resource Management,* ed. R. S. Schuler, S. A. Youngblood, and V. L. Huber (St. Paul, Minn.: West Publishing, 1987).

22. *A Professional and Legal Analysis of the Uniform Guidelines on Employee Selection Procedures* (Berea, Ohio: American Society for Personnel Administration, 1981).

23. Education, *The Wall Street Journal,* February 9, 1991, p. R5.

24. A. P. Carnevale, *America and the New Economy: How New Competitive Standards Are Radically Changing American Workplaces* (San Francisco: Jossey-Bass, 1991).

25. S. Overman, "Teamwork Boosts Quality at Wallace," *HR Magazine,* May 1991, pp. 31–34.

26. H. J. Bernardin and R. W. Beatty, *Performance Appraisal: Assessing Human Behavior at Work* (Boston: Kent Publishing, 1984).

27. R. S. Schuler, *Personnel and Human Resource Management* (St. Paul, Minn.: West Publishing, 1984).

28. W. A. Schiemann, "The Impact of Corporate Compensation and Benefit Policy on Employee Attitudes and Behavior and Corporate Profitability," *Journal of Business and Psychology* 2 (1987), pp. 8–26.

29. G. T. Milkovich and J. M. Newman, *Compensation* (Plano, Tex.: Business Publications, 1987).

30. J. Savage, "Incentive Programs at Nucor Corporation Boost Productivity," *Personnel Administrator,* August 1981, pp. 33–36.

31. D. W. Meyers, *Human Resource Management: Principles and Practice* (Chicago: Commerce Clearing House, 1986).

32. *Wage and Hour Manual, BNA Policy and Practice Series* (Washington, D.C.: Bureau of National Affairs, 1986).

33. E. A. Cooper and G. V. Barrett, "Equal Pay and Gender: Implications of Court Cases for Personnel Practices," *Academy of Management Review* (1984), pp. 84–94.

34. Milkovich and Newman, *Compensation.*

35. C. Trost, "In Minnesota, 'Pay Equity' Passes Test, but Foes See Trouble Ahead," *The Wall Street Journal,* May 10, 1984, p. 27.

36. T. Gup, "The Curse of Coal," *Time,* November 4, 1991, pp. 54–64.

37. A. Sloane and F. Witney, *Labor Relations* (Englewood Cliffs, N.J.: Prentice Hall, 1985).

38. S. Premack and J. E. Hunter, "Individual Unionization Decisions," *Psychological Bulletin* 103 (1988), pp. 223–34.

39. Ibid.

40. A. O. Hirschman, *Exit, Voice, and Loyalty: Responses to Decline in Firms, Organizations, and States* (Cambridge, Mass.: Harvard University Press, 1970).

41. A. A. Malinowski, "An Empirical Analysis of Discharge Cases and the Work History of Employees Reinstated by Labor Arbitrators," *Arbitration Journal* 36 (1981), pp. 31–46.

42. E. E. Lawler III and S. Mohrman, "Unions and the New Management," *Academy of Management Executive,* 1987, pp. 293–300.

43. J. H. Foegen, "Labor Unions—Don't Count Them Out Yet!" *Academy of Management Executives,* February 1989, pp. 67–69.

44. H. Love, A. L. Barrett, Jr., and L. Ozley, "The Transformation of National Steel Corporation," in *Corporate Transformation,* ed. R. Kilmann and T. J. Covin (San Francisco: Jossey-Bass, 1988).

Chapter 13

1. Charlene Marmer Solomon, "Managing Today's Immigrants," *Personnel Journal,* February 1993, pp. 57–65; Margaret L. Usdansky, "Minority Majorities in One in Six Cities," *USA Today,* June 9, 1993, p. 10A.

2. "Tomorrow's Jobs," *Occupational Outlook Handbook,* 1992–1993 ed. (Washington, D.C.: Bureau of Labor Statistics, May 1992), pp. 8–14. See also, Ronald E. Kutscher, "Outlook 1990–2005: Major Trends and Issues," *Occupational Outlook Quarterly,* Spring 1992, pp. 2–5.

3. "Four by Four," *Training and Development Journal,* February 1989, pp. 13–21.

4. "Tomorrow's Jobs," *Occupational Outlook Handbook;* Kutscher, "Outlook 1990–2005."

5. K. Kovach and J. Pearce, "HR Strategic Mandates for the 1990s," *Personnel,* April 1990, pp. 50–55.

6. *Opportunity 2000* (Indianapolis: Hudson Institute, 1988).

7. Kovach and Pearce, "HR Strategic Mandates."

8. T. O'Carolan, "Parenting Time: Whose Problem Is It?" *Personnel Administrator,* August 1987, pp. 58–65.

9. Kovach and Pearce, "HR Strategic Mandates."

10. Nancy Perry, "More Women Are Executive VPs," *Fortune,* July 12, 1993, p. 16.

11. Amanda Troy Segal and Wendy Zellner, "Corporate Women," *Business Week,* June 8, 1992, pp. 74–78.

12. "Tomorrow's Jobs," *Occupational Outlook Handbook.*

13. Kovach and Pearce, "HR Strategic Mandates"; Usdansky, "Minority Majorities."

14. "The Immigrants," *Business Week,* July 13, 1992, pp. 114–22; Jaclyn Fierman, "Is Immigration Hurting the U.S.?" *Fortune,* August 9, 1993, pp. 76–79.

15. Kovach and Pearce, "HR Strategic Mandates."

16. B. Dicken and R. Blomberg, "Immigrants—Can They Provide the Future Labor Force?" *Public Personnel Management,* Spring 1991, pp. 91–100; Usdansky, "Minority Majorities."

17. *Opportunity 2000,* p. 100.

18. S. Meisinger, "The Americans with Disabilities Act: Begin Preparing Now," Society for Human Resource Management, legal report, Winter 1991.

19. J. Peters, "How to Bridge the Hiring Gap," *Personnel Administrator,* October 1989, pp. 76–85.

20. "Tomorrow's Jobs," *Occupational Outlook Handbook.*

21. Ibid.

22. M. Finney, "The ASPA Labor Shortage Survey," *Personnel Administrator,* February 1988, pp. 35–42.

23. L. Copeland, "Learning to Manage a Multicultural Workforce," *Training,* May 1988, pp. 48–56.

24. N. Adler, *International Dimensions of Organizational Behavior,* 2nd ed. (Boston: PWS–Kent, 1991); T. Cox and S. Blake, "Managing Cultural Diversity: Implications for Organizational Competitiveness," *Academy of Management Executives* 5 (August 1991), pp. 45–56.

25. Ibid.

26. Adler, *International Dimensions.*

27. T. Cox, "The Multicultural Organization," *Academy of Management Executives* 5 (May 1991), pp. 34–47.

28. A. Livingston, "What Your Department Can Do," *Working Woman,* January 1991, pp. 59–60.

29. R. Zalman, "The Basics of In-House Skills Training," *Human Resource Magazine,* February 1991, pp. 74–78.

30. J. Oberle, "Teaching English as a Second Language," *Training,* April 1990, pp. 61–67.

31. L. Foxman and W. Polsky, "Cross-Cultural Understanding," *Personnel Journal,* November 1989, pp. 12–14.

32. Cox and Blake, "Managing Cultural Diversity."

33. B. Geber, "Managing Diversity," *Training,* July 1990, pp. 23–30.

34. N. Perry, "The Workers of the Future," *Fortune,* Spring–Summer 1991, pp. 68–72.

35. J. Dreyfus, "Get Ready for the New Work Force," *Fortune,* April 23, 1990, pp. 165–68.

36. *Opportunity 2000,* p. 133.

37. Cox and Blake, "Managing Cultural Diversity."

Part III Integrating Case

1. Gloria M. Curry, "Package Delivery Service: The Options Are Plentiful," *Office,* August 1989, pp. 60–62.

2. Charles Arthur "The War in the Air," *Business* [U.K.], November 1989, pp. 60–66.

3. Erik Guyot, "Air Courier Fight for Pacific Business," *Asian Finance* [Hong Kong], July 15, 1990, pp. 22–23.

4. James T. McKenna, "Airline Boosts International Cargo Services to Protect Market Shares," *Aviation Week & Space Technology,* November 20, 1989, pp. 124–25.

5. Dean Foust, "Mr. Smith Goes Global," *Business Week,* February 13, 1989, pp. 66–72.

6. Frederick W. Smith, "Empowering Employee," *Small Business Reports,* January 1991, pp. 15–20.

7. Perry A. Trunick, "Leadership and People Distinguish Federal Express," *Transportation & Distribution,* December 1989, pp. 18–22.

8. "Federal Express Spreads Its Wings," *Journal of Business Strategy,* July–August 1988, pp. 15–20.

9. Foust, "Mr. Smith Goes Global."

10. "Federal Express Spreads Its Wings." pp. 3–10.

11. Erik Calonius, "Federal express Battle Overseas," *Fortune,* 1989, December 3, 1990. pp. 137–40.

12. Foust, "Mr. Smith Goes Global."

13. James Ott, "Board Decision Muddle Rules on Union Role after Merger," *Aviation Week & Space Technology,* August 28, 1989, p. 68.

14. Foust, "Mr. Smith Goes Global."

Chapter 14

1. W. Bennis and B. Nanus, *Leaders* (New York: Harper & Row, 1985), p. 27.

2. Ibid.

3. Ibid., p. 144.

4. J. Kouzes and B. Posner, *The Leadership Challenge* (San Francisco: Jossey-Bass, 1987).

5. Ibid.

6. Ibid.

7. Ibid.

8. J. A. Conger, "The Dark Side of Leadership," *Organizational Dynamics* 19 (Autumn 1990), pp. 44–55.

9. J. P. Kotter, "What Leaders Really Do," *Harvard Business Review* 68 (May–June 1990), pp. 103–11.

10. A. Zaleznik, "The Leadership Gap," *The Executive* 4 (February 1990), pp. 7–22.

11. R. E. Kelly, "In Praise of Followers," *Harvard Business Review* 66 (November–December 1988), pp. 142–48.

12. Ibid.

13. J. R. P. French and B. Raven, "The Bases of Social Power," in *Studies in Social Power,* ed. D. Cartwright (Ann Arbor, Mich.: Institute for Social Research, 1959).

14. G. Yukl and C. Falbe, "Importance of Different Power Sources in Downward and Lateral Relations," *Journal of Applied Psychology* 76 (1991), pp. 416–23.

15. Ibid.

16. Ibid.

17. R. M. Stogdill, "Personal Factors Associated with Leadership: A Survey of the Literature," *Journal of Psychology* 25 (1948), pp. 35–71.

18. S. Kirkpatrick and E. Locke, "Leadership: Do Traits Matter?" *The Executive* 5 (May 1991), pp. 48–60.

19. G. A. Yukl, *Leadership in Organizations,* 2nd ed. (Englewood Cliffs, N.J.: Prentice-Hall, 1989).

20. J. P. Kotter, *The General Managers* (New York: Free Press, 1982).

21. S. Zaccaro, R. Foti, and D. Kenny, "Self-Monitoring and Trait-Based Variance in Leadership: An Investigation of Leader Flexibility across Multiple Group Situations," *Journal of Applied Psychology* 76 (1991), pp. 308–15.

22. J. Misumi and M. Peterson, "The Performance-Maintenance (PM) Theory of Leadership: Review of a Japanese Research Program," *Administrative Science Quarterly* 30 (June 1985), pp. 198–223.

23. Ibid.

24. J. Wagner III, "Participation's Effect on Performance and Satisfaction: A Reconsideration of Research," *Academy of Management Review,* April 1994, pp. 312–30.

25. R. White and R. Lippitt, *Autocracy and Democracy: An Experimental Inquiry* (New York: Harper & Brothers, 1960).

26. A. Tannenbaum and W. Schmidt, "How to Choose a Leadership Pattern," *Harvard Business Review* 36 (March–April 1958), pp. 95–101.

27. E. Fleishman and E. Harris, "Patterns of Leadership Behavior Related to Employee Grievances and Turnover," *Personnel Psychology* 15 (1962), pp. 43–56.

28. R. Likert, *The Human Organization: Its Management and Value* (New York: McGraw-Hill, 1967).

29. R. Blake and J. Mouton, *The Managerial Grid* (Houston: Gulf, 1964).

30. Misumi and Peterson, "The Performance-Maintenance (PM) Theory."

31. Tannenbaum and Schmidt, "How to Choose a Leadership Pattern."

32. R. J. House, "A Path Goal Theory of Leader Effectiveness," *Administrative Science Quarterly* 16 (1971), pp. 321–39.

33. J. Howell, D. Bowen, P. Dorfman, S. Kerr, and P. Podsakoff, "Substitutes for Leadership: Effective Alternatives to Ineffective Leadership," *Organizational Dynamics* 19 (Summer 1990), pp. 21–38.

34. B. M. Bass, *Leadership and Performance Beyond Expectations* (New York: Free Press, 1985).

35. R. J. House, "A 1976 Theory of Charismatic Leadership," in *Leadership: The Cutting Edge,* ed. J. G. Hunt and L. L. Larson (Carbondale, Ill.: Southern Illinois University Press, 1977).

36. M. Potts and P. Behr, *The Leading Edge* (New York: McGraw-Hill, 1987).

37. Ibid.

38. B. M. Bass, "Leadership: Good, Better, Best," *Organizational Dynamics,* Winter 1985, pp. 26–40.

39. Ibid.

40. Bennis and Nanus, *Leaders.*

41. B. Bass, B. Avolio, and L. Goodheim, "Biography and the Assessment of Transformational Leadership at the World-Class Level," *Journal of Management* 13 (1987), pp. 7–20.

42. K. Albrecht and R. Zemke, *Service America* (Homewood, Ill.: Dow Jones–Irwin, 1985).

43. J. Huey, "The New Post-Heroic Leadership," *Fortune,* February 21, 1994, pp. 42–50.

44. Ibid.

45. P. Block, *The Empowered Manager* (San Francisco: Jossey-Bass, 1991).

46. Ibid.

47. M. McCall, Jr., "Developing Leadership," in J. Galbraith and E. E. Lawler III, *Organizing for the Future* (San Francisco: Jossey-Bass, 1993).

48. F. E. Fiedler, *A Theory of Leadership Effectiveness* (New York: McGraw-Hill, 1967).

49. P. Hersey and K. Blanchard, *The Management of Organizational Behavior* (Englewood Cliffs, N.J.: Prentice-Hall, 1984).

50. Yukl, *Leadership in Organizations.*

51. V. Vroom and P. Yetton, *Leadership and Decision-Making* (Pittsburgh: University of Pittsburgh Press, 1973).

52. V. Vroom and A. Jago, *The New Leadership: Managing Participation in Organizations* (Englewood Cliffs, N.J.: Prentice-Hall, 1988).

53. Vroom and Jago, *The New Leadership;* R. Field and R. House, "A Test of the Vroom-Yetton Model Using Manager and Subordinate Reports," *Journal of Applied Psychology* 75 (1990), pp. 362–66.

Chapter 15

1. R. Kreitner and F. Luthans, "A Social Learning Approach to Behavioral Management: Radical Behaviorists 'Mellowing Out,'" *Organizational Dynamics,* Autumn 1984, pp. 47–65.

2. D. Katz and R. L. Kahn, *The Social Psychology of Organizations* (New York: John Wiley & Sons, 1966).

3. E. Locke, "Toward a Theory of Task Motivation and Incentives," *Organizational Behavior and Human Performance* 3 (1968), pp. 157–89.

4. R. H. Schaffer, "Demand Better Results—and Get Them," *Harvard Business Review* 69 (March–April 1991), pp. 142–49.

5. T. Mitchell and W. Silver, "Individual and Group Goals When Workers Are Interdependent: Effects on Task Strategies and Performance," *Journal of Applied Psychology* 75 (1990), pp. 185–93.

6. P. C. Early, T. Connolly, and G. Ekegren, "Goals, Strategy Development, and Task Performance: Some Limits on the Efficacy of Goal Setting," *Journal of Applied Psychology* 74 (1989), pp. 24–33; C. E. Shalley, "Effects of Productivity Goals, Creativity Goals, and Personal Discretion on Individual Creativity," *Journal of Applied Psychology* 76 (1991), pp. 179–85.

7. J. Main, "Is the Baldrige Overblown?" *Fortune*, July 1, 1991, pp. 62–65.

8. E. Thorndike, *Animal Intelligence* (New York: Macmillan, 1911).

9. S. C. Faludi, "At Nordstrom Stores, Service Comes First— but at a Big Price," *The Wall Street Journal*, February 20, 1990, pp. A1, A16.

10. S. Kerr, "On the Folly of Rewarding A, While Hoping for B," *Academy of Management Journal* 18 (1975), pp. 769–83.

11. J. Weber, "Farewell, Fast Track," *Business Week*, December 10, 1990, pp. 192–200.

12. A. Bennett, "When Money Is Tight, Bosses Scramble for Other Ways to Motivate the Troops," *The Wall Street Journal*, October 31, 1990, pp. B1, B5.

13. A. H. Maslow, "A Theory of Human Motivation," *Psychological Review*, July 1943, pp. 370–96.

14. M. Wahba and L. Birdwell, "Maslow Reconsidered: A Review of Research on the Need Hierarchy Theory," *Organizational Behavior and Human Performance* 15 (1976), pp. 212–40.

15. F. Rose, "A New Age for Business?" *Fortune*, October 8, 1990, pp. 156–64.

16. C. Bartlett and S. Ghoshal, "Changing the Role of Top Management: Beyond Strategy to Purpose," *Harvard Business Review*, November–December 1994, pp. 79–88.

17. Weber, "Farewell, Fast Track."

18. C. Alderfer, *Existence, Relatedness, and Growth: Human Needs in Organizational Settings* (Glencoe, Ill.: Free Press, 1972).

19. C. Pinder, *Work Motivation* (Glenview, Ill.: Scott, Foresman, 1984).

20. D. McClelland, *The Achieving Society* (New York: Van Nostrand Reinhold, 1961).

21. D. McClelland and R. Boyatzis, "Leadership Motive Pattern and Long-Term Success in Management," *Journal of Applied Psychology* 67 (1982), pp. 737–43.

22. N. Adler, *International Dimensions of Organizational Behavior*, 2nd ed. (Boston: Kent, 1991); G. Hofstede, *Cultures and Organizations* (London: McGraw-Hill, 1991).

23. M. Campion and G. Sanborn, "Job Design," in *Handbook of Industrial Engineering*, ed. G. Salvendy (New York: John Wiley & Sons, 1991).

24. B. G. Posner, "Role Changes," *Inc.*, February 1990, pp. 95–98.

25. M. Campion and D. McClelland, "Interdisciplinary Examination of the Costs and Benefits of Enlarged Jobs: A Job Design Quasi-Experiment," *Journal of Applied Psychology* 76 (1991), pp. 186–98.

26. F. Herzberg, *Work and the Nature of Men* (Cleveland: World, 1966).

27. J. R. Hackman, G. Oldham, R. Janson, and K. Purdy, "A New Strategy for Job Enrichment," *California Management Review* 16 (Fall 1975), pp. 57–71.

28. T. Ehrenfeld, "Cashing In," *Inc.*, July 1993, pp. 69–70.

29. D. Fenn, "Bottoms Up," *Inc.*, July 1993, pp. 58–60.

30. R. Rechheld, "Loyalty-Based Management," *Harvard Business Review*, March–April, 1993, pp. 64–73.

31. A. Bianchi, "True Believers," *Inc.*, July 1993, pp. 72–73.

32. Ibid.

33. J. Finegan, "People Power," *Inc.*, July 1993, pp. 62–63.

34. Ibid.

35. T. Peters and N. Austin, *A Passion for Excellence* (New York: Random House, 1985).

36. Ehrenfeld, "Cashing In."

37. Finegan, "People Power."

38. Campion and Sanborn, "Job Design."

39. Peters and Austin, *A Passion for Excellence*.

40. Price Waterhouse Change Integration Team, *Better Change* (Burr Ridge, Ill.: Richard D. Irwin, 1995).

41. Ibid.

42. J. Jasinowski and R. Hamrin, *Making It in America* (New York: Simon & Schuster, 1995).

43. V. H. Vroom, *Work and Motivation* (New York: John Wiley & Sons, 1964).

44. J. Adams, "Inequity in Social Exchange," in *Advances in Experimental Social Psychology*, ed. L. Berkowitz (New York: Academic Press, 1965).

45. D. Henne and E. Locke, "Job Dissatisfaction: What Are the Consequences?" *International Journal of Psychology* 20 (1985), pp. 221–40.

46. R. E. Walton, "Improving the Quality of Work Life," *Harvard Business Review*, May–June 1974, pp. 12, 16, 155.

47. E. E. Lawler III, "Strategies for Improving the Quality of Work Life," *American Psychologist* 37 (1982), pp. 486–93; J. L. Suttle, "Improving Life at Work: Problems and Prospects," in *Improving Life at Work*, ed. J. R. Hackman and J. L. Suttle (Santa Monica, Calif.: Goodyear, 1977).

Chapter 16

1. B. Dumaine, "Who Needs a Boss?" *Fortune*, May 7, 1990, pp. 52–60.

2. Ibid.

3. K. Wexley and S. Silverman, *Working Scared* (San Francisco: Jossey-Bass, 1993).

4. B. Dumaine, "The Trouble with Teams," *Fortune*, September 5, 1994, pp. 86–92.

5. Wexley and Silverman, *Working Scared*.

6. Dumaine, "The Trouble with Teams."

7. R. M. Kanter, "Championing Change: An Interview with Bell Atlantic's CEO Raymond Smith," *Harvard Business Review,* January–February 1991, pp. 188–37.

8. Dumaine, "Who Needs a Boss?"

9. J. Zenger and Associates, *Leading Teams* (Burr Ridge, Ill.: Business One Irwin, 1994).

10. D. Yeatts, M. Hipskind, and D. Barnes, "Lessons Learned from Self-Managed Work Teams," *Business Horizons,* July–August 1994, pp. 11–18.

11. J. Katzenback and D. Smith, "The Discipline of Teams," *Harvard Business Review,* March–April 1993, pp. 111–20.

12. S. Cohen, "New Approaches to Teams and Teamwork," in J. Galbraith, E. E. Lawler III, and Associates, *Organizing for the Future* (San Francisco: Jossey-Bass, 1993).

13. D. Nadler, J. R. Hackman, and E. E. Lawler III, *Managing Organizational Behavior* (Boston: Little, Brown, 1979).

14. B. W. Tuckman, "Developmental Sequence in Small Groups," *Psychological Bulletin* 63 (1965), pp. 384–99.

15. C. J. G. Gersick, "Time and Transition in Work Teams: Toward a New Model of Group Development," *Academy of Management Journal* 31 (1988), pp. 9–41.

16. J. R. Hackman, *Groups That Work (and Those That Don't)* (San Francisco: Jossey-Bass, 1990).

17. Zenger and Associates, *Leading Teams.*

18. Dumaine, "The Trouble with Teams."

19. J. Case, "What the Experts Forgot to Mention," *Inc.,* September 1993, pp. 66–78.

20. A. Nahavandi and E. Aranda, "Restructuring Teams for the Reengineered Organization," *Academy of Management Executive,* November 1994, pp. 58–68.

21. J. Katzenback and D. Smith, *The Wisdom of Teams* (Boston: Harvard Business School Press, 1993).

22. Nadler, Hackman, and Lawler, *Managing Organizational Behavior.*

23. P. Petty, "Behind the Brands at P&G: An Interview with John Smale," *Harvard Business Review,* November–December 1985, pp. 78–80.

24. T. Peters and N. Austin, *A Passion for Excellence* (New York: Random House, 1985).

25. T. Kidder, *The Soul of a New Machine* (Boston: Little, Brown, 1981).

26. Nadler, Hackman, and Lawler, *Managing Organizational Behavior.*

27. R. Wellins, R. Byham, and G. Dixon, *Inside Teams* (San Francisco: Jossey-Bass, 1994).

28. Katzenback and Smith, "The Discipline of Teams."

29. C. Meyer, "How the Right Measures Help Teams Excel," *Harvard Business Review,* May–June 1994, pp. 95–103.

30. Meyer, "How the Right Measures Help Teams Excel."

31. Katzenback and Smith, "The Discipline of Teams."

32. Ibid.

33. Wellins, Byham, and Dixon, *Inside Teams.*

34. Ibid.

35. Ibid.

36. J. O'Toole, *Vanguard Management: Redesigning the Corporate Future* (New York: Doubleday, 1985).

37. R. F. Bales, *Interaction Process Analysis: A Method for the Study of Small Groups* (Reading, Mass.: Addison-Wesley, 1950).

38. Katzenback and Smith, *The Wisdom of Teams.*

39. Wellins, Byham, and Dixon, *Inside Teams.*

40. C. Stoner and R. Hartman, "Team Building: Answering the Tough Questions," *Business Horizons,* September–October 1993, pp. 70–78.

41. S. E. Seashore, *Group Cohesiveness in the Industrial Work Group* (Ann Arbor, Mich.: University of Michigan Press, 1954).

42. Ibid.

43. B. Lott and A. Lott, "Group Cohesiveness as Interpersonal Attraction: A Review of Relationships with Antecedent and Consequent Variables," *Psychological Bulletin,* October 1965, pp. 259–309.

44. Hackman, *Groups That Work.*

45. Wellins, Byham, and Dixon, *Inside Teams.*

46. D. G. Ancona, "Outward Bound: Strategies for Team Survival in an Organization," *Academy of Management Journal* 33 (1990), pp. 334–65.

47. Ibid.

48. L. Sayles, *Leadership: What Effective Managers Really Do, and How They Do It* (New York: McGraw-Hill, 1979).

49. Ibid.

50. Stoner and Hartman, "Team Building."

51. D. Tjosvold, *Working Together to Get Things Done* (Lexington, Mass.: Lexington Books, 1986).

52. K. W. Thomas, "Conflict and Conflict Management," in *Handbook of Industrial and Organizational Psychology,* ed. M. D. Dunnette (Chicago: Rand McNally, 1976).

53. K. W. Thomas, "Toward Multi-Dimensional Values in Teaching: The Example of Conflict Behaviors," *Academy of Management Review* (1977), pp. 484–89.

Chapter 17

1. P. Senge, *The Fifth Discipline* (New York: Doubleday, 1990).

2. Ibid.

3. L. Penley, E. Alexander, I. E. Jernigan, and C. Henwood, "Communication Abilities of Managers: The Relationship to Performance," *Journal of Management* 17 (1991), pp. 57–76.

4. W. V. Haney, *Communication and Interpersonal Relations: Text and Cases* (Homewood, Ill.: Richard D. Irwin, 1986).

5. W. V. Haney, "A Comparative Study of Unilateral and Bilateral Communication," *Academy of Management Journal* 7 (1964), pp. 128–36.

6. T. W. Comstock, *Communicating in Business and Industry* (Albany, N.Y.: Delmar, 1985).

7. W. Ruch and M. Crawford, *Business Communication* (New York: Merrill, 1991).

8. J. Fulk and B. Boyd, "Emerging Theories of Communication in Organizations," *Journal of Management* 17 (1991), pp. 407–46.

9. R. Rice and D. Case, "Electronic Message Systems in the University: A Description of Use and Utility," *Journal of Communication* 33 (1983), pp. 131–52; C. Steinfield, "Dimensions of Electronic Mail Use in an Organizational Setting," Proceedings of the Academy of Management, San Diego, 1985.

10. J. Solomon, "As Electronic Mail Loosens Inhibitions, Impetuous Senders Feel Anything Goes," *The Wall Street Journal,* October 12, 1990, pp. B1, B8.

11. R. Lengel and R. Daft, "The Selection of Communication Media as an Executive Skill," *Academy of Management Executive* 2 (1988), pp. 225–32; L. Trevino, R. Daft, and R. Lengel, "Understanding Managers' Media Choices: A Symbolic Interactionist Perspective," in *Organizations and Communication Technology,* ed. J. Fulk and C. Steinfield (London: Sage, 1990).

12. Fulk and Boyd, "Emerging Theories of Communication."

13. P. G. Clampitt, *Communicating for Managerial Effectiveness* (London: Sage, 1991).

14. Ibid.

15. C. Argyris, "Good Communication That Blocks Learning," *Harvard Business Review,* July–August 1994, pp. 77–85.

16. Ibid.

17. Ibid.

18. C. Deutsch, "The Multimedia Benefits Kit," *The New York Times,* October 14, 1990, sec. 3, p. 25.

19. M. McCall, M. Lombardo, and A. Morrison, *The Lessons of Experience: How Successful Executives Develop on the Job* (Lexington, Mass.: Lexington, 1988).

20. C. M. Kelly, "Effective Communications—Beyond the Glitter and Flash," *Sloan Management Review,* Spring 1985, pp. 69–74.

21. K. Reardon, *Persuasion in Practice* (London: Sage, 1991).

22. H. K. Mintz, "Business Writing Styles for the 70's," *Business Horizons,* August 1972. Cited in *Readings in Interpersonal and Organizational Communication,* ed. R. C. Huseman, C. M. Logue, and D. L. Freshley (Boston: Allyn & Bacon, 1977).

23. M. Forbes, "Exorcising Demons from Important Business Letters," *Marketing Times,* March–April 1981, pp. 36–38.

24. W. Strunk Jr., and E. B. White, *The Elements of Style,* 3rd ed. (New York: Macmillan, 1979); H. R. Fowler, *The Little, Brown Handbook* (Boston: Little, Brown, 1986).

25. C. Chu, *The Asian Mind Game* (New York: Rawson Associates, 1991).

26. Comstock, *Communicating in Business and Industry.*

27. M. Korda, *Power: How to Get It, How to Use It* (New York: Random House, 1975).

28. A. Mehrabian, "Communication without Words," *Psychology Today,* September 1968, p. 52. Cited in M. B. McCaskey, "The Hidden Message Managers Send," *Harvard Business Review,* November–December 1979, pp. 135–48.

29. A. Athos and J. Gabarro, *Interpersonal Behavior* (Englewood Cliffs, N.J.: Prentice-Hall, 1978).

30. "Have You Heard about Sperry?" *Management Review* 69 (April 1980), p. 40.

31. G. Graham, J. Unruh, and P. Jennings, "The Impact of Nonverbal Communication in Organizations: A Survey of Perceptions," *Journal of Business Communications* 28 (1991), pp. 45–62.

32. N. Adler, *International Dimensions of Organizational Behavior,* 2nd ed. (Boston: Kent, 1991).

33. Chu, *The Asian Mind Game.*

34. W. C. Redding, *Communication within the Organization: An Interpretive Review of Theory and Research* (New York: Industrial Communication Council, 1972). Cited in F. M. Jablin, "Superior-Subordinate Communication: The State of the Art," *Psychological Bulletin* 86 (1979), pp. 1201–22.

35. Penley et al, "Communication Abilities of Managers."

36. J. W. Koehler, K. W. E. Anatol, and R. L. Applebaum, *Organizational Communication: Behavioral Perspectives* (Orlando, Fla.: Holt, Rinehart & Winston, 1981).

37. J. Case, "The Open-Book Managers," *Inc.,* September 1990, pp. 104–13.

38. J. Fierman, "Winning Ideas from Maverick Managers," *Fortune,* February 6, 1995, pp. 66–80.

39. Koehler, Anatol, and Applebaum, *Organizational Communication.*

40. W. V. Ruch, *Corporate Communications* (Westport, Conn.: Quorum, 1984).

41. Ibid.

42. Koehler, Anatol, and Applebaum, *Organizational Communication.*

43. D. K. Denton, "Open Communication," *Business Horizons,* September–October 1993, pp. 64–69.

44. R. L. Rosnow, "Rumor as Communication: A Contextual Approach," *Journal of Communication* 38 (1988), pp. 12–28.

45. K. Davis, "The Care and Cultivation of the Corporate Grapevine," *Dun's Review,* July 1973, pp. 44–47.

46. N. Difonzo, P. Bordia, and R. Rosnow, "Reining in Rumors," *Organizational Dynamics,* Summer 1994, pp. 47–62.

47. Ibid.

Chapter 18

1. James C. Collins, and Jerry I. Porras, *Built to Last: Successful Habits of Visionary Companies* (New York: HarperBusiness, 1994).

2. "Time Stealing," *Forbes,* December 20, 1982, p. 9

3. E. Flamholtz, "Behavioral Aspects of Accounting/Control Systems," in *Organizational Behavior,* ed. S. Kerr (Columbus, Ohio: Grid, 1979).

4. P. Drucker, "Permanent Cost Cutting," *The Wall Street Journal,* January 11, 1991, p. A10.

5. "Behind the UPS Mystique: Puritanism and Productivity," *Business Week,* June 6, 1990, pp. 66–73.

6. T. Wall, J. M. Corbett, R. Martin, C. Clegg, and P. Jackson, "Advanced Manufacturing Technology, Work Design, and Performance: A Change Study," *Journal of Applied Psychology* 75 (1990), pp. 691–97.

7. R. Henkoff, "Make Your Office More Productive," *Fortune,* February 25, 1990, p. 40–49.

8. R. C. Davis, *The Fundamentals of Top Management* (New York: Harper & Row, 1951); J. Donnelly, Jr., J. Gibson, and J. Ivancevich, *Fundamentals of Management* (Plano, Tex.: Business Publications, 1981).

9. F. Worthy, "Japan's Smart Secret Weapon," *Fortune,* August 12, 1991, pp. 72–75.

10. W. J. Bruns, Jr., and F. W. McFarlan, "Information Technology Puts Power in Control Systems," *Harvard Business Review,* September–October 1987, pp. 89–94.

11. F. Pomeranz, "Preemptive Auditing: Future Shock or Present Opportunity?" *Journal of Accounting, Auditing, and Finance,* Summer 1979, pp. 352–56.

12. R. Buchele, "How to Evaluate a Firm," *California Management Review,* Fall 1962, pp. 5–17.

13. R. Henkoff, "Cost Cutting: How to Do It Right," *Fortune,* April 9, 1990, pp. 40–49.

14. Ibid.

15. Terence P. Pare, "A New Tool for Managing Costs," *Fortune,* June 14, 1993, pp. 124–29; Robert Ochs and John Bicheno, "Activity-Based Cost Management Linked to Manufacturing Strategy," *IM,* January–February 1991, pp. 11–16.

16. K. Merchant, *Control in Business Organizations* (Boston: Pitman, 1985).

17. E. E. Lawler III and J. Rhode, *Information and Control in Organizations* (Pacific Palisades, Calif.: Goodyear, 1976).

18. J. Veiga and J. Yanouzas, *The Dynamics of Organization Theory,* 2nd ed. (St. Paul, Minn.: West, 1984).

19. Lawler and Rhode, *Information and Control in Organizations.*

20. Ibid; D. Robey, *Designing Organizations,* 3rd ed. (Homewood, Ill.: Richard D. Irwin, 1991).

21. Lawler and Rhode, *Information and Control in Organizations.*

22. W. H. Newman, *Constructive Control* (Englewood Cliffs, N.J.: Prentice-Hall, 1975).

23. T. A. Stewart, "Why Budgets Are Bad for Business," *Fortune,* June 4, 1990, pp. 179–90.

24. Henkoff, "Make Your Office More Productive."

25. Bruns and McFarlan, "Information Technology."

26. Lawler and Rhode, *Information and Control in Organizations.*

27. T. A. Stewart, "Do You Push Your People Too Hard?" *Fortune,* October 22, 1990, pp. 121–28.

28. S. Tully, "The CEO Who Sees Beyond Budgets," *Fortune,* October 22, 1990, pp. 121–28.

29. Merchant, *Control in Business Organizations.*

30. W. G. Ouchi, "Markets, Bureaucracies, and Clans," *Administrative Science Quarterly* 25 (1980), pp. 129–41.

31. S. A. Snell and J. W. Dean, Jr., "Strategic Compensation for Integrated Manufacturing: The Moderating Effects of Jobs and Organizational Inertia," *Academy of Management Journal* 37, no. 5 (1994), pp. 1109–40.

32. Michael Macoby, "Managers Must Unlearn the Psychology of Control," *Research Technology Management,* January–February 1993, pp. 49–51.

33. William C. Taylor, "Control in an Age of Chaos," *Harvard Business Review,* November–December 1994, pp. 64–76. See also Kevin Kelly, *Out of Control: The Rise of New-Biological Civilization* (Reading, Mass.: Addison-Wesley, 1994); James C. Collins and Jerry I. Porras, *Built to Last: Successful Habits of Visionary Companies* (New York: HarperBusiness, 1994); G. Pascal Zachary, *Showstopper! The Breakneck Race to Create Window NT and the Next Generation at Microsoft* (New York: Free Press, 1994).

Chapter 19

1. C. Giffi, A. V. Roth, and G. M. Seal, *Competing in World-Class Manufacturing: America's 21st Century Challenge* (Homewood, Ill.: Business One–Irwin, 1990).

2. K. Ohmae, *The Mind of the Strategist: Business Planning for Competitive Advantage* (New York: Penguin Books, 1983), Chap. 8.

3. K. Ishikawa, *What Is Total Quality Control? The Japanese Way,* trans. David J. Lu (Englewood Cliffs, N.J.: Prentice-Hall, 1985).

4. W. Skinner, "The Focused Factory," *Harvard Business Review,* May–June 1974, pp. 113–21.

5. R. Schroeder and M. Pesch, "Focusing the Factory: Eight Lessons," *Business Horizons,* September–October 1994, pp. 76–81.

6. Ibid.

7. R. H. Hayes and S. C. Wheelwright, "Link Manufacturing Process and Product Life Cycles," *Harvard Business Review,* January–February 1979, pp. 133–40.

8. Ibid.

9. Bureau of Business Practice, *ISO 9000: Handbook of Quality Standards and Compliance* (Needham Heights, Mass.: Allyn and Bacon, 1992).

10. Ibid.

11. M. Price and E. E. Chen, "Total Quality Management in a Small, High-Technology Company," *California Management Review,* Spring 1993, pp. 96–117.

12. G. Easton, "The 1993 State of U.S. Total Quality Management: A Baldrige Examiner's Perspective," *California Management Review,* Spring 1993, pp. 32–54.

13. M. Tucker and D. Davis, "Key Ingredients for Successful Implementation of Just-in-Time: A System for All Business Sizes," *Business Horizons,* May–June 1993, pp. 59–65.

14. G. Bassett, Operations Management for Service Industries (Westport, Conn.: Quorum Books, 1992).

15. J. Womack and D. Jones, "From Lean Production to the Lean Enterprise," *Harvard Business Review,* March–April 1994, pp. 93–103.

16. Ibid.

17. Schroeder and Pesch, "Focusing the Factory."

18. D. Upton, "The Management of Manufacturing Flexibility," *California Management Review,* Winter 1994, pp. 72–89.

19. O. Port, "Custom-Made, Direct from the Plant," *Business Week,* 1994 Special Issue, pp. 158–59.

20. B. J. Pine II, B. Victor, and A. Boynton, "Making Mass Customization Work," *Harvard Business Review,* September–October 1993, pp. 108–19.

21. R. Henkoff, "Delivering the Goods," *Fortune,* November 28, 1994, pp. 64–78.

22. Ibid.

23. Ibid.

24. Ibid.

25. J. D. Blackburn, *Time-Based Competition* (Homewood, Ill.: Richard D. Irwin, 1991).

26. D. Gerwin, "Integrating Manufacturing into the Strategic Phases of New Product Development," *California Management Review,* Summer 1993, pp. 123–36.

27. T. Stewart, "Reengineering: The Hot New Management Tool," *Fortune,* August 23, 1993, pp. 41–48.

28. Ibid.

29. M. Hammer and J. Champy, *Reengineering the Corporation* (New York: HarperCollins, 1992).

30. J. Champy, *Reengineering Management* (New York: HarperBusiness, 1995).

31. B. Saporito, "Behind the Tumult at P&G," *Fortune,* March 7, 1994, pp. 74–82.

Chapter 20

1. C. Snow and E. Ottensmeyer, "Managing Strategies and Technologies," in *Strategic Management in High Technology Firms,* ed. M. Lawless and L. Gomez-Mejia (Greenwich, Conn.: JAI Press, 1990).

2. H. Bahrami and S. Evans, "Stratocracy in High Technology Firms," *California Management Review* 30 (Fall 1987), pp. 51–66.

3. U. E. Gattiker, *Technology Management in Organizations* (Newbury Park, Calif.: Sage, 1990).

4. James M. Utterback, *Mastering the Dynamics of Innovation* (Boston: Harvard Business School Press, 1994).

5. Ibid.

6. E. M. Rogers, *Diffusion of Innovation,* 3rd ed. (New York: Free Press, 1983).

7. Ibid.

8. J. A. Schumpeter, *The Theory of Economic Development* (Boston: Harvard University Press, 1934).

9. G. Day and J. Freeman, "Burnout or Fadeout: The Risks of Early Entry into High Technology Markets," in Lawless and Gomez-Mejia, *Strategic Management in High Technology Firms;* Shaker A. Zahra, Sarah Nash, and Deborah J. Bickford, "Transforming Technological Pioneering in Competitive Advantage," *Academy of Management Executive* 9, no. 1 (1995), pp. 17–31.

10. "Kodak Settles with Polaroid," *New York Times,* July 16, 1991, p. D8.

11. M. Imai, *Kaizen: The Key to Japan's Competitive Success* (New York: Random House, 1986).

12. B. O'Reilly, "Drugmakers under Attack," *Fortune,* July 29, 1991, pp. 48–63.

13. M. E. Porter, *Competitive Strategy* (New York: Free Press, 1980); Joseph G. Monroe, "Technology and Competitive Advantage—The Role of General Management," *Research Technology Management,* March–April 1993, pp. 16–25.

14. Rogers, *Diffusion Of Innovation.*

15. Ibid.

16. D. M. Schroeder, "A Dynamic Perspective of the Impact of Process Innovation upon Competitive Strategies," *Strategic Management Journal* 11 (January 1990), pp. 25–42.

17. "Fool's Paradise," *The Economist,* February 3, 1990, p. 81.

18. Ibid.

19. Ibid.

20. E. von Hipple, *The Sources of Innovation* (New York: Oxford University Press, 1988).

21. Ibid.

22. T. Peters, "Get Innovative or Get Dead (Part 1)," *California Management Review,* Fall 1990, pp. 9–26.

23. P. Adler and K. Ferdows, "The Chief Technology Officer," *California Management Review,* Spring 1990, pp. 55–62; Joseph Maglitta, "Meet the New Boss," *Computerworld,* March 14, 1994, pp. 80–82.

24. Charles Burck, "The Real World of the Entrepreneur," *Fortune,* April 5, 1993, pp. 42–55; Leon Richardson, "The Successful Entrepreneur," *Asian Business,* July 1994, p. 71.

25. Clifford Siporin, "Want Speedy FDA Approval? Hire a 'Product Champion,' " *Medical Marketing & Media,* October 1993, pp. 22–28; Clifford Siporin, "How You Can Capitalize on Phase 3B," *Medical Marketing & Media,* October 1994, pp. 72–76.

26. Benjamin Schneider, Sarah K. Gunnarson, and Kathryn Niles-Jolly, "Creating the Climate and Culture of Success," *Organizational Dynamics* 23, no. 1 (Summer 1994), pp. 17–29; Thomas J. Martin, "Ten Commandments for Managing Creative People," *Fortune,* January 16, 1995, pp. 135–36.

27. Lisa K. Gundry, Jill R. Kickul, and Charles W. Prather, "Building the Creative Organization," *Organizational Dynamics* 22, no. 2 (Spring 1994), pp. 22–36; Thomas Kuczmarski, "Inspiring and Implementing the Innovation Mind-Set," *Planning Review,* September–October 1994, pp. 37–48.

28. R. Neff, "Toray May Have Found the Formula for Luck," *Business Week,* June 15, 1990, p. 110.

29. Peters, "Get Innovative (Part 2)," *California Management Review* 33, no. 2 (Winter 1991), pp. 9–23.

30. H. Kent Bowen, Kim B. Clark, Charles A. Holloway, and Steven C. Wheelwright, "Development Projects: The Engine of Renewal," *Harvard Business Review,* September–October 1994, pp. 110–20.

31. Steven C. Wheelwright and Kim B. Clark, *Revolutionizing Product Development* (New York: Free Press, 1992), pp. 49–50.

32. E. Trist, "The Evolution of Sociotechnical Systems as a Conceptual Framework and as an Action Research Program," in *Perspectives on Organizational Design and Behavior,* ed. A. Van de Ven and W. F. Joyce (New York: John Wiley & Sons, 1981), pp. 19–75.

33. S. Zuboff, *In the Age of the Smart Machine* (New York: Basic Books, 1988); Scott A. Snell and James W. Dean, Jr., "Strategic Compensation for Integrated Manufacturing: The Moderating Effects of Jobs and Organizational Inertia," *Academy of Management Journal* 37, no. 5 (1994), pp. 1109–40.

Chapter 21

1. C. Giffi, A. Roth, and G. Seal, *Competing in World-Class Manufacturing: America's 21st Century Challenge* (Homewood, Ill.: Business One Irwin, 1990).

2. T. G. Gunn, *21st Century Manufacturing* (New York: HarperBusiness, 1992).

3. Ibid.

4. Giffi, Roth, and Seal, *Competing in World-Class Manufacturing.*

5. Ibid.

6. D. A. Garvin, "Manufacturing Strategic Planning," *California Management Review,* Summer 1993, pp. 85–106.

7. Ibid.

8. J. Womack, D. Jones, and D. Ross, *The Machine That Changed the World* (New York: Rawson Associates, 1990).

9. C. Corbett and L. Van Wassenhove, "Trade-Offs? What Trade-Offs? Competence and Competitiveness in Manufacturing Strategy," *California Management Review,* Summer 1993, pp. 107–22.

10. Ibid.

11. Ibid.

12. B. J. Pine, B. Victor and A. Boynton, "Making Mass Customization Work," *Harvard Business Review,* September–October 1993, pp. 108–19.

13. M. Price and E. E. Chen, "Total Quality Management in a Small, High-Technology Company," *California Management Review,* Spring 1993, pp. 96–117.

14. Ibid.

15. A. Taylor III, "GM's $11 Billion Turnaround," *Fortune,* October 17, 1994, pp. 54–74.

16. D. Hellriegel and J. W. Slocum, Jr., *Management,* 4th ed. (Reading, Mass.: Addison-Wesley, 1986).

17. P. Harris, *New World, New Ways, New Management* (New York: American Management Association, 1983).

18. P. Strebel, "Choosing the Right Change Path," *California Management Review,* Winter 1994, pp. 29–51.

19. Ibid.

20. Ibid.

21. J. Stanislao and B. C. Stanislao, "Dealing with Resistance to Change," *Business Horizons,* July–August 1983, pp. 74–78.

22. J. P. Kotter and L. A. Schlesinger, "Choosing Strategies for Change," *Harvard Business Review,* March–April 1979, pp. 106–14.

23. G. Johnson, *Strategic Change and the Management Process* (New York: Basil Blackwell, 1987); K. Lewin, "Frontiers in Group Dynamics," *Human Relations* 1 (1947), pp. 5–41.

24. E. H. Schein, "Organizational Culture: What It Is and How to Change It," in *Human Resource Management in International Firms,* ed. P. Evans, Y. Doz, and A. Laurent (New York: St. Martin's Press, 1990).

25. E. E. Lawler III, "Transformation from Control to Involvement," in *Corporate Transformation,* ed. R. Kilmann and T. Covin (San Francisco: Jossey-Bass, 1988).

26. M. Beer, R. Eisenstat, and B. Spector, *The Critical Path to Corporate Renewal* (Cambridge, Mass.: Harvard Business School Press, 1990).

27. Schein, "Organizational Culture."

28. Kotter and Schlesinger, "Choosing Strategies for Change."

29. R. M. Kanter, *The Change Masters* (New York: Simon & Schuster, 1983).

30. Harris, *New World, New Ways, New Management.*

31. D. A. Nadler, "Managing Organizational Change: An Integrative Approach," *Journal of Applied Behavioral Science* 17 (1981), pp. 191–211.

32. Kotter and Schlesinger, "Choosing Strategies for Change."

33. Nadler, "Managing Organizational Change."

34. Ibid.

35. J. Kotter, "What Effective Managers Really Do," *Harvard Business Review,* November–December 1982, pp. 156–67.

36. R. Beckhard and R. Harris, *Organizational Transitions* (Reading, Mass.: Addison-Wesley, 1977).

37. Beer, Eisenstadt, and Spector, *The Critical Path to Corporate Renewal.*

38. N. Nohria and J. Berkley, "Whatever Happened to the Take-Charge Manager?" *Harvard Business Review,* January–February 1994, pp. 128–37.

39. The Price Waterhouse Change Integration Team, *Better Change: Best Practices for Transforming Your Organization* (Burr Ridge, Ill.: Irwin, 1995).

40. Ibid.

41. Ibid.

42. G. Hamel and C. K. Prahalad, *Competing for the Future* (Boston: Harvard Business School Press, 1994).

43. Pine, Victor, and Boynton, "Making Mass Customization Work."

44. J. W. Slocum, Jr., M. McGill, and D. Lei, "The New Learning Strategy: Anytime, Anything, Anywhere," *Organzational Dynamics,* Autumn 1994, pp. 33–47.

45. W. Zellner and D. Griesing, "Go-Go Goliaths," *Business Week,* February 13, 1995, pp. 64–70.

46. M. J. Kiernan, "The New Strategic Architecture: Learning to Compete in the Twenty-First Century," *The Academy of Management Executive,* February 1993, pp. 7–21.

47. M. Magnet, "Let's Go for Growth," *Fortune,* March 7, 1994, pp. 60–72.

48. Ibid.

49. Ibid.

50. Ibid.

51. Hamel and Prahalad, *Competing for the Future.*

52. Ibid.

53. Ibid.

Part V Integrating Case

1. Joseph F. McKenna, "The Great Expectations of David Kearns," *Industry Week,* June 17, 1991, p. 34.

2. G.M. Herrington, "The Catch-22 of Total Quality Management," *Across the Board,* September 1991.

3. M. Katherine Glover, "The Quest for Excellence," *Business America,* November 20, 1989, pp. 2–11.

4. David Kearns, "Quality in Copiers, Computers, and Floor Cleaning," *Management Review,* February 1989, pp. 61–63.

5. R.C. Camp, "Learning from the Best Leads to Superior Performance," *Journal of Business Strategy* 13, no. 3 (1992), pp. 3–6.

6. Paul Allaire, and Norman Rickard, "Quality and Participation at Xerox," *Journal for Quality and Participation,* March 1989, pp. 24–26.

7. Subrata N. Chakravarty, "Xerox—Back on the Road to Success," *Forbes,* July 7, 1980, pp. 40–42.

8. *1990 Moody's Industrial Manual,* pp. 4381–89.

NAME INDEX

SUBJECT INDEX

Delmar Plumbing, Heating & Air
    Conditioning, 216
Delta Airlines, 119
Demand (for employees) forcasts, 289
Deming cycle, 546
Democratic leaders, 359, 363
Demographics, as macroenvironment, 63–64
Denver International Airport, 15
Departmentalization, 249–253
    customer and geographical, 253
    functional departmentalization, 249–250
    future of, 250
    product departmentalization, 250–252
Development Dimensions International,
    414, 415
Development projects, 531–532
Development of work force, 297–301
Devil's advocate, 93
DHL, 345, 346
The dialectic, 93
Dialogue, discussion versus, 432
Differentiation
    in organizations, 240
    strategy, 125
Digital Equipment Corporation, 7, 219,
    302, 333, 480, 481, 570
Direct Data Link (DDL), 67–68
Directive leadership, 364
Disability Rights Education and Defense
    Fund, Inc., 325
Disabled workers, physically and mentally,
    325
Discount the future, 89
Discussion, dialogue versus, 432
Disney America, 151
Disney World, 463
Distribution (logistics), 504–505
Diversification
    concentric diversification, 123
    as strategic maneuvering, 70
Diversity, managing, 319–349
    affirmative action, 328–329
    brief history, 320
    challenges of diverse workforce,
        330–331
    competitive advantage and, 329–330
    cultivation of diverse workforce,
        332–339
    definition today, 320–321
    disabled, physically and mentally, 325
    future jobs and workforce qualifica-
        tions, 329
    gender issues, 322–324
    minorities and immigrants, 324–326
    monolithic organizations, 331
    multicultural organizations, 331–332
    older employees, 325–328
    plural organizations, 331
    size and diversity of workforce,
        321–322
Divestiture, as strategic maneuvering, 70

Division of labor, 240
Dogs, in BCG Matrix, 124
Dollar Auction Worksheet, 100
Domain defense, 146
Domain selection, as strategic maneuver-
    ing, 70
Domino's Pizza, 42
Domino Sugar, 494
Donna Karan Co., 234
Dorantes, Sergio, 60
Dow Chemical, 171, 174, 196, 254
Dow Corning, 254
Dow Europe, 174
Dow Jones, 504, 555
Downsizing, 273–274
    rightsizing, 273
    survivor's syndrome, 273–274
Downward communication, 442–444
Dreamworks SKG, 559–560
Drive, as leadership trait, 358
Drug testing, 476
Dudek manufacturing, 299
Du Pont, 171–173, 278, 389
Dynamic Organization (Follet), 36

E

Earth Day (1990), 172
Eastern Airlines, 435
Eastman Chemical, 125, 278, 415
Eastman Kodak, 46, 65–66, 161, 171, 184,
    188, 223, 250, 303, 327, 329, 480,
    523, 531
Eaton, 64
Ebony, 368
Economics and the environment, 167–168
Economies of scale, 30
Economies of scope, 266
Economy, as macroenvironment, 62
Ecotourism, 176
EDS, 218–219, 274
Education, to enlist cooperation, 551
Effectiveness, 42
Efficency, 42
Effluent securities, 179
Egoism, 138
Ego needs, 389
Electric Power Research Institute, 528
Electro-Biology, Inc., 219
Electronic media, as communications
    channel, 435
The Elements of Style (Strunk and White),
    438
Eli Lilly, 291
Elizabeth Arden, 115
E-mail, 435
Emerson Electric, 478–479, 481
Employee benefits, 305
Employee Retirement Income and Security
    Act (ERISA), 306

Empowerment, 394–395
    control and, 483–484
Enron, 481
Entrepreneur(s); *see also* Independent
    entrepreneur(s) *and* Intrapreneur(s)
    entrepreneur's creed, 218
    entrepreneurship, defined, 208
    myths about, 208
Entry modes to global expansion,
    191–195
    exporting, 191–192
    franchising, 192, 193–194
    joint ventures, 192–193
    licensing, 192
    wholly owned subsidiaries, 193
Environment; *see* External environment
    and Natural environment
Environmental analysis, 120–121
Environmental Defense Fund, 172
Environmental movement, 166
Environmental Protection Agency (EPA),
    61, 162, 164, 173, 327
Equal employment opportunity, 297–298
Equal Employment Opportunity
    Commission (EEOC), 61, 297, 448
Equal Pay Act (EPA; 1963), 305–306
Equifinality, 42
Equitable Life Assurance Society, 333
Equity theory, 397–398
ERG theory (Aldefer), 390
Ernst & Whinney, 266
Ernst & Young, 159, 250, 266
Esprit de Corp. (company), 334–235
Esquel group, 61
Ethics, 138–145; *see also* Business ethics
    defined, 138
    issues in international management,
        198–199
Ethics Resource Center, 142
Euro-Disneyland, 94, 99, 181–182
Eurofood, 186
European Union (EU), 182
Evolution of management, 28–53; *see also*
    Classical approaches to manage-
    ment; Contemporary approaches to
    management; *and* Future of man-
    agement
    early concepts and influences, 30–31
Exception, principle of, 466
Executive champion, 530
Existence needs, 390
Expatriate managers, 194
    failure rate of, 195
    skills required, 195–196, 197
Expectancy theory of performance,
    395–396
    managerial implications of, 396
Expert power, 358
Exporting, 191–192
External audit, 469